STARR ROLL 1894

(CHEROKEE PAYMENT ROLLS)

DISTRICTS: CANADIAN, COOWEESCOOWEE, AND DELAWARE

VOLUME ONE

TRANSCRIBED BY

JEFF BOWEN

NATIVE STUDY
Gallipolis, Ohio
USA

Copyright © 2014
by Jeff Bowen

ALL RIGHTS RESERVED
No part of this publication may be reproduced
or used in any form or manner whatsoever
without previous written permission from the
copyright holder or publisher.

Originally published:
Baltimore, Maryland
2014

Reprinted by:

Native Study LLC
Gallipolis, OH
www.nativestudy.com

Library of Congress Control Number: 2020914749

ISBN: 978-1-64968-021-1

Made in the United States of America.

This series is dedicated to my longtime friend and confidant, Kent Anderson.

Picture source: donated by Grant Foreman to the Smithsonian Institution Anthropological Archives. Treasurer E.E. Starr is seated at the center of the table. According to Foreman this photograph was taken shortly after distribution had begun for the Cherokee Strip payments. The picture is approximately 120 years old. Notice the armed guards, records and cash stacked on the table. Each eligible tribal member received $265.70.

Starr Family Tree

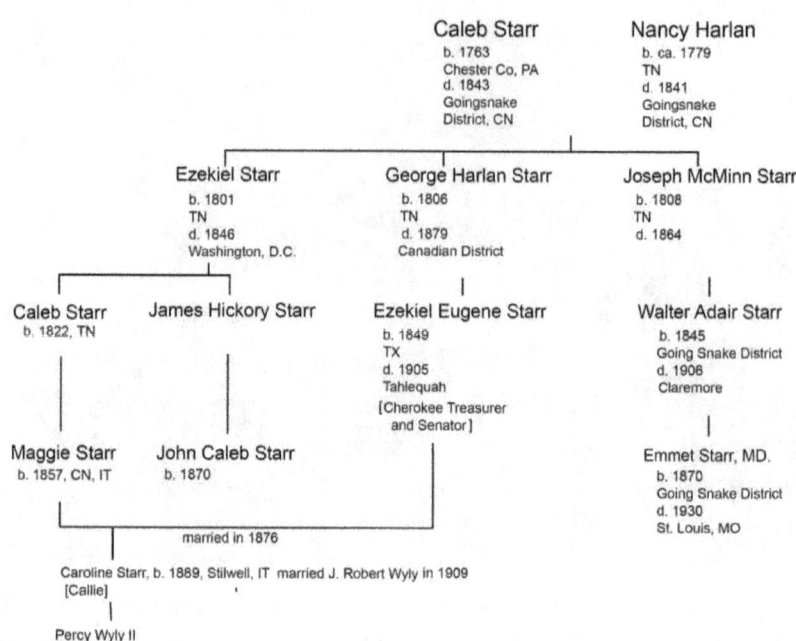

Table of Contents

	Introduction	ix
DISTRICTS		
	Canadian	1
	Cooweescoowee	90
	Delaware	272
INDEX		399

INTRODUCTION

The *Starr Roll (Cherokee Payment Rolls and Index 1894)*, is found in the National Archives film 7RA38, Rolls 1-5, under the heading Record Group 75. Many genealogists likely see the name Starr and think that these records were documented by the famous Cherokee genealogist Dr. Emmet Starr, (1870-1930), but discover that they were created by Ezekiel Eugene Starr, (1849-1905), who was elected a Cherokee Senator for the Flint District in 1883 and then Treasurer for the Western Cherokee Nation in 1891. Both Starr's were related but held different stations in life.

The background to the *Starr Roll* requires some telling. On March 3, 1893, Congress passed an act that authorized the sale of lands west of the Cherokee Nation known as the Cherokee Outlet, and later referred to as the 1894 Cherokee Strip Payment. The Cherokee Outlet, originally created by agreement with the Eastern Cherokee in 1835, occupied a strip of land 57 miles wide in present-day north/northwestern Oklahoma was intended as a "perpetual outlet west" for the Cherokee. After 1877, the Cherokee Nation leased the Outlet to the Cherokee Strip Livestock Association, who desired it for its rich grazing lands. Then in 1893, homesteaders were permitted to stake their claims to the land in the fourth and largest of Oklahoma's five land runs. In return for opening the Cherokee Outlet to white settlers, eligible members of the Cherokee Nation were paid a per-capita payment in the amount of $265.70.

E.E. Starr, then Cherokee treasurer, created the receipt roll for these payments and arranged it by each of the nine Cherokee Districts, and thereunder by each party's enrollment number. The contents of the receipt roll, transcribed for these volumes, includes the name of the head of household, names of other household members, name of person receiving the payment, as well as the name of a person that witnessed the transaction of record. The *Starr Roll* also includes an *Orphans Roll and Supplemental*, whose contents are self-explanatory within this transcription.

Jeff Bowen
Gallipolis, Ohio
NativeStudy.com

Canadian *(District)*

Starr Roll 1894

We, the undersigned citizens of the Cherokee Nation, by right of Cherokee blood, do hereby acknowledge to have received of E. E. Starr, National Treasurer of the Cherokee Nation, the sums set opposite our names respectively, in full of our shares in the per capita distribution authorized by an Act of the National Council, dated ___MAY 3 1894___ 1894.

Began paying on the 23rd day of July 1894.

	Names of Head, and Members of Families	Amount	To Whom Paid	Witness to Payment	Remarks
1	Alexander James				
2	" Aggie				
3	" Andy				
4	" John	1062.80	P J Scales	Henry Eiffert	*Check order*
5	Anderson James				
6	" Susan				
7	" George				
8	" Bettie				
9	Hendrick William	1328.50	H J Vann	Henry Eiffert	*Ck on order*
10	Ashes Jake	265.70	Johnson Barber	L B Bell	
11	Adington Annie				
12	" Trumon				
13	" Alice	797.00	John A Quintin	L B Bell	*order*
14	Amos Amand[sic] A.				
15	" William A.				
16	" James E.				
17	" Edwin R.				
18	" Ethel M.	1328.50	A A Amos	L B Bell	
19	Askins Lucinda		*D 2612*		
20	" Lucretia		*D 2622*		
21	" Alice	797.10	L A Mulkey	L B Bell	*on order*
22	Adington Liddia				
23	" Joel				
24	" William				
25	" Oscar	1062.80	John A Quintin	L B Bell	
26	Adkins Mary	265.70	Lafeyette[sic] Bros	Henry Eiffert	*Layfayette*[sic]
27	Agnew Walter S				
28	" Mary E.				
29	" Ella				
30	" John L.				
31	" Robert M.				

Starr Roll 1894

We, the undersigned citizens of the Cherokee Nation, by right of Cherokee blood, do hereby acknowledge to have received of E. E. Starr, National Treasurer of the Cherokee Nation, the sums set opposite our names respectively, in full of our shares in the per capita distribution authorized by an Act of the National Council, dated ___MAY 3 1894___ 1894.

	Names of Head, and Members of Families	Amount	To Whom Paid	Witness to Payment	Remarks
32	" Walter L.				
33	" Josephus	1859.90	H C Lowey	Henry Eiffert	
34	Allin Elliza	265.70	Eliza[sic] Allen	L B Bell	
35	Ashes John	256.70	John Ashes	L B Bell	
36	Abercrumbie Ruth	265.70	John Abercrumby[sic]	L B Bell	
37	Andrew Mary	265.70	(Illegible) Emery	L B Bell	
38	Alfred Maggie				
39	" Sue				
40	" Fannie	797.10	Moses W Lafayette	J C Starr	on order
41	Burk Fannie W				
42	" Florence L				
43	" Amy				
44	" Hellen E				
45	" Eva				
46	" Fannie	1594.20	Fannie M. Burk	Henry Eiffert	
47	Boles Jennie				
48	" Fred				
49	" Holland		*Claim to be Creek Indians. Jany 17, 1904. P.G.R.*		
50	" Perl		*Enrolled on Creek Card 3465*		
51	" Cherokee	1328.50	Frank Boles	L B Bell	
52	Blackstone Robert E				
53	" Jossie				
54	" Nip				
55	" Peachie				
56	" George				
57	" Katy	1594.20	R E Blackstone	Henry Eiffert	
58	Blackstone Edward				
59	" Mollie				
60	" Gypsie				
61	" Frank	1062.80	R E Blackstone	Henry Eiffert	Ck order

Starr Roll 1894

We, the undersigned citizens of the Cherokee Nation, by right of Cherokee blood, do hereby acknowledge to have received of E. E. Starr, National Treasurer of the Cherokee Nation, the sums set opposite our names respectively, in full of our shares in the per capita distribution authorized by an Act of the National Council, dated ___MAY 3 1894___ 1894.

	Names of Head, and Members of Families	Amount	To Whom Paid	Witness to Payment	Remarks
62	Blackman William	265.70	J.P. Carter	Robt B Ross	Paid Jan 8/96
63	Blackstone George W.	265.70	R E Blackstone	Henry Eiffert	C. E. Vann
64	Buchannan Bertha	265.70	J C Buchannon	Henry Eiffert	
65	Beaver Thomas				
66	" Martha				
67	" Charles				
68	" Lucy				
69	" Rabbit				
70	" Cherry				
71	" James				
72	" Mary	2125.60	Martha Beaver	L B Bell	
73	Blackstone Robert N.	265.70	R E Blackstone	Henry Eiffert	R Blackstone Ck
74	Barker Charlie				
75	" Susan				
76	" Kate				
77	" Joseph				
78	" Emma	1328.50	Jack Thompson		
79	Beaver Sarah M				
80	" Willie	531.40	R E Blackstone	Henry Eiffert	Ck
81	Bird Lillie				
82	" Marion				
83	" Charles	797.00	Lily Bird	L B Bell	
84	Barnes Alexander				
85	" Martha				
86	" Ancy Bell				
87	" Antonie W.	1062.80	Alexander Barnes	L B Bell	
88	Barker Ida L.	265.70	Ida L Ward family	Henry Eiffert	
89	Bright Nay	265.70	F.B. Severs	Henry Eiffert	Ck

Starr Roll 1894

We, the undersigned citizens of the Cherokee Nation, by right of Cherokee blood, do hereby acknowledge to have received of E. E. Starr, National Treasurer of the Cherokee Nation, the sums set opposite our names respectively, in full of our shares in the per capita distribution authorized by an Act of the National Council, dated ___MAY 3 1894___ 1894.

Names of Head, and Members of Families	Amount	To Whom Paid	Witness to Payment	Remarks

****

(The letters below were inserted in the logbook before the page containing Polly and Blue Boggs, #96-97.)

Cherokee Nation,
Cooweescoowee District.

    Personally comes before me Joe M. La Hay Clerk of the above named District, one,-- Patsy Roll*ings* of lawful age, and after being duly sworn, states that she is a citizen of the Cherokee Nation, and that she has been personally acquainted with Canzada Boggs, for the past six years, and I know that she is the mother of Blue Boggs; who is seven years old. She further states that the father of the said child is dead. She further states that she said Canzada Boggs is still supporting and caring for the said child. *She further states that the said Canzada Boggs is still supporting and caring for the said child.*

                       Her
                 Patsy Rollings x
                        mark

Subscribed and sworn to before me on this the 10th day of Sept., 1894.

                Joe M. Lahay
            Clerk of Cooweescoowee District, CN.

****

Cherokee Nation,
Cooweescoowee District.

    Personally comes before me Joe M. La Hay Clerk of the above named District, one, Jennie Writer, who being a citizen of the Cherokee Nation and of lawful age, and after being duly sworn, deposes and says, that she has been personally acquainted with ----- Canzada Boggs for the past six years, and know her to be the mother of Blue Boggs, who is now about seven years old, and whos[sic] father is dead, she further states that the said Canzada Boggs, has *(illegible ...)* that she has cared for him since the death of his father.

                     Her
              Jennie Writer x
                    mark

Subscribed and sworn to before me on this the 10th day of Sept., 1894.

                Joe M. Lahay
            Clerk of Cooweescoowee District, CN.

Starr Roll 1894

We, the undersigned citizens of the Cherokee Nation, by right of Cherokee blood, do hereby acknowledge to have received of E. E. Starr, National Treasurer of the Cherokee Nation, the sums set opposite our names respectively, in full of our shares in the per capita distribution authorized by an Act of the National Council, dated _____MAY 3 1894_____ 1894.

#	Names of Head, and Members of Families		Amount	To Whom Paid	Witness to Payment	Remarks
			************			
90	Barnes	Winona				
91	"	Hiram				
92	"	Charles				
93	"	Jane				
94	"	Cornelius				
95	"	Lelia	1594.20	Winona Barnes	L B Bell	
96	Boggs	Polly	265.70	Jennie Kettle	Henry Eiffert	minor Sep 11 94
97	"	Blue	265.70	Canzada Boggs	Henry Eiffert	Mother of child
98	Barber	Dutch	265.70	Dutch Barber	L B Bell	
99	Barber	Charlotte				Dead
100	"	Gropes				
101	"	Man				
102	Toney	Sequah[sic]				
103	"	Thomas				
104	Foster	Benjamin	1594.20	Charlotte Barber	L B Bell	
105	Bolin	Ross				
106	"	Kate				
107	"	John				
108	"	Annie				
109	"	Eliza				
110	"	Moza	1594.20	Moses W Lafeyette	J C Starr	on order
111	Barber	Johnston				
112	"	Jane	531.40	Johnson[sic] Barber	L B Bell	
113	Brimage	Frederick				Orphans no legal Guardian
114	"	Rachel				
115	"	Susan	797.10	Mary Rogers	L B Bell	
116	Bertholf	Richard				
117		Octavia				
118		Lelia				
119		Thomas				
120		William				
121		Minnie				

Starr Roll 1894

We, the undersigned citizens of the Cherokee Nation, by right of Cherokee blood, do hereby acknowledge to have received of E. E. Starr, National Treasurer of the Cherokee Nation, the sums set opposite our names respectively, in full of our shares in the per capita distribution authorized by an Act of the National Council, dated _____MAY 3 1894_____ 1894.

	Names of Head, and Members of Families	Amount	To Whom Paid	Witness to Payment	Remarks
122	Nonnie				
123	Grover				
124	Claud				
125	Richard	2657.00	Octavia Bertholf	L B Bell	
126	Bean Russel				
127	Susan				
128	Ellen				
129	Nannie	1062.80	Susan Bean	L B Bell	
130	Bearpaw Cynda	265.70	H.J. Vann	CA Thompson	H.J. Vann
131	Blythe, Jackson	265.70	Jackson Blythe	L B Bell	
132	" Eliza				
133	Roberts Joseph				
134	Bowls Thomas	797.10	Eliza Roberts	L B Bell	
135	Beargreese Nelly	265.70	Nelly Beargreese	L B Bell	
136	Bigby John	order			JR Pierce
137	" Betsy	531.40	JR Pierce	Henry Eiffert	
138	Barnett Ida	265.70	J N Barnett	L B Bell	
139	Burr Aaron	order 265.70	P J Scales	Henry Eiffert	
140	Beck Malinda				
141	Carroll	531.40	H B Beck	L B Bell	
142	Beck Thomas				
143	Eliza				
144	Henry G				
145	Cloud	1062.80	Thos Beck	L B Bell	
146	Baldridge James order	D 1385 265.70	E. S. Ellis	Henry Eiffert	Ellis
147	Brooks Mary W.				
148	Willis Claud M				
149	" Bessie E				
150	" Armer				
151	" Walter	1328.50	Mary W Brooks	L B Bell	

Starr Roll 1894

We, the undersigned citizens of the Cherokee Nation, by right of Cherokee blood, do hereby acknowledge to have received of E. E. Starr, National Treasurer of the Cherokee Nation, the sums set opposite our names respectively, in full of our shares in the per capita distribution authorized by an Act of the National Council, dated ___MAY 3 1894___ 1894.

	Names of Head, and Members of Families	Amount	To Whom Paid	Witness to Payment	Remarks
152	Bray George	265.70	Geo Bray	L B Bell	
153	Bumgarner John W.		~~D 2563~~		Enrolled as citizen of Choctaw Nat. Card No 4817
154	" Samuel	531.40	John W Bumgarner	Henry Eiffert	
155	Burr Frank	265.70	R.E. Blackstone	J C Starr	on order
156	Burr Eliza				
157	" Charles				
158	" Josie	797.10	R.E. Blackstone	J.C. Starr	on order
159	Blackmon Sarah	265.70	Sarah Blackmon	L B Bell	
160	Bertholf William H	out			
161	Amanda J				
162	Alice C	531.40	Isaac Bertholf	L B Bell	
163	Bertholf Emma H				On Creek Card No. 863 Enrollment Approved by Secy. of Interior March 13, 1902
164	" Myrtle M.	~~D 2564~~			
165	" Jessie M.				
166	" Dewit T.				
167	" Willie				
168	" Betty	1594.20	Isaac Bertholf	L B Bell	
169	Bertholf Isaac W.				
170	Thomas	531.40	Isaac Bertholf	L B Bell	
171	Bowls Richard	265.70	J R Pierce	Henry Eiffert	Pearce[sic]
172	Beck John W.				
173	" Cyntha				
174	Jessie B.	797.10	John W Beck	L B Bell	
175	Brice Georgia C.				
176	" Czrina[sic] V.				
177	" Charles M.				
178	" Annie L.				
179	" Alexina[sic] T.				
180	" Walter J.	1594.20	Walter Brice	L B Bell	
181	Backbone Calvin	265.70	J J Morgan	L B Bell	registered with J.J. Morgan family

Starr Roll 1894

We, the undersigned citizens of the Cherokee Nation, by right of Cherokee blood, do hereby acknowledge to have received of E. E. Starr, National Treasurer of the Cherokee Nation, the sums set opposite our names respectively, in full of our shares in the per capita distribution authorized by an Act of the National Council, dated ___MAY 3 1894___ 1894.

	Names of Head, and Members of Families	Amount	To Whom Paid	Witness to Payment	Remarks
182	Bridges Nannie J				
183	Augustus				
184	Thomas H				
185	Charles				
186	Owens Samuel	265.70	Joe Bridges	Henry Eiffert	*Guardian*
187	Autry Mary	1328.50	Joe Bridges	Henry Eiffert	
188	Brown Rachel				
189	Troy	531.40	Rachel Brown	L B Bell	
190	Bracken[sic] Cornelia				
191	" Hubbard				
192	" Harry				
193	" Alton				
194	" Bessie				
195	" Tracy P.	1594.20	Cornelia Bracket	L B Bell	
196	Bacon Sarah				
197	" Lucy B.				
198	" Bernice M.				
199	" Dana B.				
200	" John L.				
201	" Charles B.	1594.20	C H Bacon	L B Bell	
202	Bertholf John R.				
203	Electa	531.40	John R Bertholf	Henry Eiffert	
204	Bertholf Thomas E.	265.70	Thomas E Bertholf	Henry Eiffert	
205	Bertholf Percy E.	265.70	Thomas E Bertholf	Henry Eiffert	
206	Brown Quinn				
207	William				
208	Benjamin				
209	Gertie				
210	Docie				
211	Manchie	1594.20	George A Brown	L B Bell	
212	Bennett Simpson				
213	Emily	531.40	Simpson Bennett	L B Bell	

Starr Roll 1894

We, the undersigned citizens of the Cherokee Nation, by right of Cherokee blood, do hereby acknowledge to have received of E. E. Starr, National Treasurer of the Cherokee Nation, the sums set opposite our names respectively, in full of our shares in the per capita distribution authorized by an Act of the National Council, dated ___MAY 3 1894___ 1894.

	Names of Head, and Members of Families	Amount	To Whom Paid	Witness to Payment	Remarks
214	Beatty Emaline		1906		Emaline Beaty
215	Mamie	531.40	1982 Emeline Beatty	L B Bell	Legal Guardian
216	Barker William H				
217	Elvia C.				
218	Sallie B				
219	Whitington George				
220	" Lilla	1328.50	Wm H Barker	Henry Eiffert	
221	Bacon Irine				
222	Willie				
223	Harnage		R 705		
224	Jeanie		R 705		
225	Binia	1328.50	R 705 J.D. Bacon	L B Bell	
226	Beargreese Sarah				
227	Ellen				
228	Runaway	797.10	WN Morten	Henry Eiffert	Ck
229	Brown James	265.70	W.M. Gullager	S.W. Mayfield	
230	Beck W.M.	265.70	H C Lowery	Henry Eiffert	H C Lowry
231	Brown James				
232	Wade H	531.40	Jas Brown	L B Bell	
233	Blackstone Pleasant				
234	Jennie				
235	Louise				
236	Blackstone Robert				
237	Dewit				
238	Nannie	1594.20	P N Blackstone	Henry Eiffert	
239	Butler Samuel	265.70	(Name Illegible)	L B Bell	
240	" Ruth				
241	" Richard	531.40	Ruth McNutty	L B Bell	
242	Burrows James	265.70	Jas Burrows	L B Bell	
243	" Whit	265.70	Whit Burrows	L B Bell	
244	" Tobe	265.70	James Burrows	Henry Eiffert	

Starr Roll 1894

We, the undersigned citizens of the Cherokee Nation, by right of Cherokee blood, do hereby acknowledge to have received of E. E. Starr, National Treasurer of the Cherokee Nation, the sums set opposite our names respectively, in full of our shares in the per capita distribution authorized by an Act of the National Council, dated ____MAY 3 1894____ 1894.

Names of Head, and Members of Families	Amount	To Whom Paid	Witness to Payment	Remarks
245 Burrows Chas. C.				
246 Thomas C				
247 John H.				
248 Edward M.				
249 Christopher	1328.50	James Edward Burrows	L B Bell	Father of Children
250 Boggs, William T.				
251 " Purly	531.40	Wm. T. Boggs	L B Bell	
252 Bane B.F.				
253 Cordie				
254 Fanny				
255 Madge				
256 Leanord				
257 Josie				
258 Vina	Paid			
259 Duff	2125.60	John D Jordan	Henry Eiffert	order
260 Baily Malinda				
261 Benjamin L.				
262 Mary J				
263 Amanda W				
264 John C				
265 Francis	1594.20	John S Baily	L B Bell	
266 Barnes John	265.70	John Barnes	L B Bell	
267 Barnes Ellis				
268 " Elba				
269 " Alexander				
270 " Bashe	1062.80	John Barnes	L B Bell	
271 Bray William	265.70	William Bray	L B Bell	
272 " Richard	265.70	Richard Bray	L B Bell	
273 Beck Nannie				
274 Vianna				
275 William P.				
276 Leoger	1062.80	Nannie Beck	L B Bell	

Starr Roll 1894

We, the undersigned citizens of the Cherokee Nation, by right of Cherokee blood, do hereby acknowledge to have received of E. E. Starr, National Treasurer of the Cherokee Nation, the sums set opposite our names respectively, in full of our shares in the per capita distribution authorized by an Act of the National Council, dated ___MAY 3 1894___ 1894.

	Names of Head, and Members of Families	Amount	To Whom Paid	Witness to Payment	Remarks
277	Butler Bear				
278	Sokinna	531.40	Bear Butler	Henry Eiffert	
279	Butler Susie	265.70	James Girtz	L B Bell	
280	Barns Louiza	265.70	Willis McClanahan	Henry Eiffert	
281	Brewer Delila				
282	" Cherry				Orphan D Brewer
283	" Charles D	797.10	Delila Brewer	L B Bell	Guardian
284	Brewer Oliver P	265.70	Delila Brewer	L B Bell	
285	Blackhaw Sarah	265.70	Poly Lender	Henry Eiffert	Letter of Guardianship
286	Carlile Robert				
287	Charles				
288	Stephen Jr.				
289	Lena	1062.80	Stephen Carlisle	Henry Eiffert	
290	Crossland Richard				
291	Lizzie				
292	Lottie				
293	Cephas				
294	Kate	1328.50	Lizzie Crossland	L B Bell	
295	Coleman John				
296	" Nancy				
297	Griffin Olie	797.10	Nancy Coleman	L B Bell	
298	Colestone Taxie				
299	Clementine	531.40	H C Lowery	Henry Eiffert	HC Lowry
300	Campbell Alex C.				
301	Charlotte				
302	James A.				
303	May				
304	Minnie	1328.50	Charlotte Campbell	L B Bell	
305	Campbell Betty	265.70	R E Blackstone	Henry Eiffert	Check order R E Blackstone

Starr Roll 1894

We, the undersigned citizens of the Cherokee Nation, by right of Cherokee blood, do hereby acknowledge to have received of E. E. Starr, National Treasurer of the Cherokee Nation, the sums set opposite our names respectively, in full of our shares in the per capita distribution authorized by an Act of the National Council, dated ____MAY 3 1894____ 1894.

Names of Head, and Members of Families	Amount	To Whom Paid	Witness to Payment	Remarks
306 Clark Sophia				
307 " Hermon				
308 " Richard	797.10	Sophia Clark	L B Bell	
309 Crosland[sic] William				
310 " Ida				
311 " Richard Jr.				
312 " Willie				
313 Thomas Daily				
314 " Joseph Crossland	1594.20	William Crossland	Henry Eiffert	
315 Collins Mary J.				
316 William L				
317 Thomas E	797.10	JW Shoemake Guardian	L B Bell	
318 Shoemake Effie	*(No other information given.)*			
319 Crawler Dutch				
320 " Elsie	531.40	Elsey Crawler	L B Bell	
321 Cloud John	265.70	Martha Beaver	L B Bell	*order (illegible)*
322 Canary Anola				
323 Emma P				
324 Simon C	797.10	J D Canary	Henry Eiffert	
325 Coleman Newton	265.70	Newton Coleman	L B Bell	
326 " Samuel	265.70	W M Gibson	Henry Eiffert	*Ck Gibson*
327 Cramps Tildon	265.70	H J Vann	Henry Eiffert	*Ck*
328 Crane Bettie	*order*			*Lacy Crane*
329 " Francis				
330 " Nora				
331 " Ella	1062.80	Lacy Crane	L B Bell	
332 Coleman John	265.70	W M Gibson	Henry Eiffert	*Ck order*
333 Campbell Samuel				
334 " Lizzie				
335 " James				

Starr Roll 1894

We, the undersigned citizens of the Cherokee Nation, by right of Cherokee blood, do hereby acknowledge to have received of E. E. Starr, National Treasurer of the Cherokee Nation, the sums set opposite our names respectively, in full of our shares in the per capita distribution authorized by an Act of the National Council, dated ___MAY 3 1894___ 1894.

	Names of Head, and Members of Families	Amount	To Whom Paid	Witness to Payment	Remarks
336	Crane George	1062.80	Saml Campbell	L B Bell	
337	Campbell Bean	265.70	Saml Campbell	L B Bell	on order
338	Campbell John	265.70	John Campbell	L B Bell	
339	Chambers Robert	265.70	R E Blacksone[sic]	Henry Eiffert	Ck R E Blackstone
340	Crane Nannie				
341	" Dony	531.40	Nannie Crane	L B Bell	(illegible)
342	Cobbstill Martha J.				
343	" Mark	531.40	Jacob Cobbstill	L B Bell	
344	Chisholm Thomas	265.70	Thos Chisholm	L B Bell	
345	Chisholm George				
346	" Bettie				
347	" Jackson				
348	" Lena	1062.80	Thos Chisholm	L B Bell	
349	Chisholm James	~~D 1390~~	on Creek Card No. 1917 and enrollment approved by Sec. of Interior March 28, 1902		
350	" Ida	~~D 1392~~	on Creek Card No. 6029 and enrollment approved by Sec. of Interior March 28, 1902		
351	" Arley				
352	" Lizzie				
353	" Stanly				
354	" Kate	D 1396 DEAD.			
355	" Eliza				
356	Chisholm Emely	~~D 1399~~	on Creek field card No 747 Enrollment approved by Sec. of Interior March 13, 1902		
357	" Grover C.	2391.30	Jas Chisholm	L B Bell	
358	Checotah Aggy	~~D 1407~~	R 881		Sam Grayson
359	" Jeff	order			
360	" Martin	797.10	Samuel Grayson	Henry Eiffert	Ck
361	Crane Henry	265.70	Christian Gulager	Henry Eiffert	Ck Gulager

Starr Roll 1894

We, the undersigned citizens of the Cherokee Nation, by right of Cherokee blood, do hereby acknowledge to have received of E. E. Starr, National Treasurer of the Cherokee Nation, the sums set opposite our names respectively, in full of our shares in the per capita distribution authorized by an Act of the National Council, dated ____MAY 3 1894____ 1894.

	Names of Head, and Members of Families	Amount	To Whom Paid	Witness to Payment	Remarks
362	Collins Aurora				
363	" Wynonna				
364	" Roseol				
365	" Oerid				
366	" Emma				
367	" Cora	1594.20	Mose W Lafeyette	JC Starr	on order
368	Cannon Sterling P.	265.70	S P Cannon	L B Bell	
369	Clay, Columbus				Lafeyette Bros
370	" Minnie				
371	" Willie				
372	" Annie				
373	" Lula	1328.50	Lafeyette Bro	Henry Eiffert	Ck
374	Coughran, Eliza				
375	" Johnson				
376	" William				
377	" Franzell	1062.80	W B Beck	L B Bell	order
378	Cloud Josuah *order*	265.70	R E Blackstone	Henry Eiffert	Ck R Blackstone
379	Coughran Lyda				
380	" Mary				
381	" Jesse	797.10	Jasper Coughran	L B Bell	
382	Coody, Lewis				
383	" Myrtletopia				
384	" Daniel R.				
385	" Lewis W.	1062.80	Lewis Coody		
386	Cosstephens Nancy	256.70	William Cosstephens	L B Bell	
387	Cowand, Annie C.				
388	" Thomas W.	531.40	Annie C. Cowand	L B Bell	
389	Curry, Jay				
390	" Laura				
391	" Lenora				
392	" Jesse				

Starr Roll 1894

We, the undersigned citizens of the Cherokee Nation, by right of Cherokee blood, do hereby acknowledge to have received of E. E. Starr, National Treasurer of the Cherokee Nation, the sums set opposite our names respectively, in full of our shares in the per capita distribution authorized by an Act of the National Council, dated ____MAY 3 1894____ 1894.

	Names of Head, and Members of Families	Amount	To Whom Paid	Witness to Payment	Remarks
393	" Jennie O.	1328.50	H C Lowery	Henry Eiffert	
394	Cloud, Joseph	265.70	JW Beck Guardian	L B Bell	John W Beck Legal Guardian
395	Cline Ezeikiel[sic]				
396	" Benjamin				
397	" John				
398	" Eli				
399	" Ross				
400	" May	1594.20	Ezekiel Cline	Henry Eiffert	
401	Cornsilk Stephen	265.70	W.M. Gullager	S.W. Mayfield	Pd. on order May-25-95
402	Crittenden, Charles W				
403	" Katie				
404	" James				
405	" Mary J.	1062.80	Charles Crittenden	L B Bell	
406	Carpenter Claud	265.70	RE Blackstone	Henry Eiffert	
407	Crane Louisa				
408	" Bolivar				
409	" Maud	797.10	Louisa Crane	L B Bell	
410	Connally Emily J.				
411	Maggie M.	531.40	Jas Connally	L B Bell	
412	Compton, Clark				
413	" Larrance	531.40	Emma *(Illegible)*	Henry Eiffert	
414	Carver Lizzie				H C Lowry
415	" Walter *order*				
416	" Willie	797.10	H C Lowery	Henry Eiffert	Ck
417	Carver, Nannie				H C Lowry
418	" James *order*				
419	" Frank	797.10	H C Lowery	Henry Eiffert	Patterson Merctl Co Ck
420	Connally Bettie	265.70	Patterson Merctl Co	Henry Eiffert	Ck

Starr Roll 1894

We, the undersigned citizens of the Cherokee Nation, by right of Cherokee blood, do hereby acknowledge to have received of E. E. Starr, National Treasurer of the Cherokee Nation, the sums set opposite our names respectively, in full of our shares in the per capita distribution authorized by an Act of the National Council, dated ___MAY 3 1894___ 1894.

Names of Head, and Members of Families	Amount	To Whom Paid	Witness to Payment	Remarks
421 Cash, John A.				
422 " Samuel	531.40	John A Cash	L B Bell	
423 Cordry Thomas				
424 " Percy				
425 " Lula	1710			
426 " Hugh				WN Martin
427 " Bessie	1328.50	W.N. Martin	Henry Eiffert	Ck
428 Cordry, Wilson	265.70	R.L. Baugh	Henry Eiffert	Ck R.L. Baugh
429 Capps, Mary				
430 Keys, Nippy	531.40	Mary Capps	L B Bell	
431 Cordry, Andy				
432 " Mary				
433 " Annie J				
434 " Cornell	1062.80	Cale W Starr	L B Bell	
435 Cordry, Andy				
436 " John	531.40	Andy Cordry	L B Bell	
437 Cobb, Bent				
438 " Mary E.				
439 " Simpson				
440 " Susan				
441 " Bernie				
442 " Edos				
443 " Grover C.				
444 " Eula	2125.60	Bent Cobb	L B Bell	
445 Crittenden Andy	265.70	Walsh and Shutt	Henry Eiffert	W&S Ck
446 Crittenden George W.				
447 " Charles				
448 " James				
449 " Robert	1062.80	Ellen Crittenden	L B Bell	
450 Crittenden Thomas	265.70	John Kelly	L B Bell	Step Father

Starr Roll 1894

We, the undersigned citizens of the Cherokee Nation, by right of Cherokee blood, do hereby acknowledge to have received of E. E. Starr, National Treasurer of the Cherokee Nation, the sums set opposite our names respectively, in full of our shares in the per capita distribution authorized by an Act of the National Council, dated ___MAY 3 1894___ 1894.

Names of Head, and Members of Families	Amount	To Whom Paid	Witness to Payment	Remarks
451 Cowart Slater				
452 " Joanna				
453 " John				
454 " Alie	1062.80	Slater Cowart	L B Bell	
455 Cobb, James				
456 " Alice				
457 " Edward				
458 " Charles				
459 " Jack				
460 " William		K B Hutcheson		
461 " Susan	1859.90	Henry Eiffert	L B Bell	order
462 Compton, Thomas				
463 " Chillia				
464 " Ernest	797.10	Thomas Compton	L B Bell	
465 Crutchfield, Thomas	order			W&S
466 " Mary				
467 " Eli				
468 " Lewis				
469 " Sarah				
470 " John A.	1594.20	Walsh and Shutt	Henry Eiffert	Ck-
471 Davis Nancy	265.70	Nancy Davis	L B Bell	
472 Davis Minta	265.70	Minta Davis	L B Bell	
473 Davis Nanie[sic]	265.70	Nannie Davis	L B Bell	
474 Davis Jug				
475 " Bettie				
476 " Susie				
477 " Mollie	order			Robt Blackstone
478 " Leonie				
479 " Charles	1594.20	RE Blackstone	Henry Eiffert	Ck
480 Davis Ross				Scales
481 " Nancy	order			
482 " Lugy	797.10	PJ Scales	Henry Eiffert	

17

Starr Roll 1894

We, the undersigned citizens of the Cherokee Nation, by right of Cherokee blood, do hereby acknowledge to have received of E. E. Starr, National Treasurer of the Cherokee Nation, the sums set opposite our names respectively, in full of our shares in the per capita distribution authorized by an Act of the National Council, dated ___MAY 3 1894___ 1894.

Names of Head, and Members of Families	Amount	To Whom Paid	Witness to Payment	Remarks
~~Davis Henry~~	*This man claims to be forty years old & has sold to Pete Scales*			*Enrolled at the O. Asylum*
Davis Henry	265.70	Henry Davis	Henry Eiffert	
483 Daniel Joseph				
484 " Mary				
485 " John	797.10	Joseph Daniel	L B Bell	
486 Davis Jefferson	265.70	Jefferson Davis	Henry Eiffert	
487 Dunn Phebie	265.70	Pheby Dunn	L B Bell	
488 Downing David	265.70	Dave Downing	L B Bell	
489 Davis Thompson	*order* 265.70	P J Scales	Henry Eiffert	Pete Scales [Ck]
490 Davis Jack				
491 " Susan J				
492 " Joe D				
493 " Samuel L	1062.80	Jack Davis	Henry Eiffert	
494 Davis Loranza[sic] D				
495 " Betha				
496 " Earl				
497 " Ammon				
498 " Jeder	1328.50	Lonzo D Davis	Henry Eiffert	
499 Delona Charles	*order* 265.70	WE Gentry	Henry Eiffert	*Ck* WE Gentry
500 Doublehead Bird	*order* 265.70	*(Order withdrawn July 23, 94)*		~~W E Gentry~~
501 " Filie	265.70	Bird Doublehead	L B Bell	
502 Davis Jefferson				
503 " Ella				
~~" Stanu~~				*Enrolled in Isaac Groves fam*
504 " Pollie	797.10	Isaac Groves	Henry Eiffert	
505 Duncan Samuel				
506 " Elizabeth				
507 " Thomas				
508 " Nannie				

Starr Roll 1894

We, the undersigned citizens of the Cherokee Nation, by right of Cherokee blood, do hereby acknowledge to have received of E. E. Starr, National Treasurer of the Cherokee Nation, the sums set opposite our names respectively, in full of our shares in the per capita distribution authorized by an Act of the National Council, dated ___MAY 3 1894___ 1894.

	Names of Head, and Members of Families	Amount	To Whom Paid	Witness to Payment	Remarks
509	" James				
510	" Maggie				
511	" William				
512	" Ludlen	1594.20	Saml Duncan	L B Bell	
513	Downing George				
514	" Lucy				
515	" Jane				
516	" Samuel	1062.80	Geo Downing	L B Bell	
517	" Mariah				
518	" Jesse	531.40	Maria Downing	L B Bell	
519	Downing Thomas	265.70	WE Gentry	Henry Eiffert	WE Gentry
520	Davis Ciscera[sic]				
521	" Sydny				
522	" Rachael				
523	" Nannie				registered with this family
524	Foreman Jack	1328.50	Cicero Davis	L B Bell	
525	Davis Samuel L				
526	" Lucinda	531.40	Sam T. Davis	L B Bell	
527	Davis Jane S.	265.70	Sam T Davis	L B Bell	
528	Davis Rila[sic]				
529	" Daniel	531.40	Brilla Davis	Henry Eiffert	Nov 12/94
530	Dunagan Georgia				
531	" Summer C.				
532	" Mary A.				
533	" Lula				
534	" James B.	1328.50	Georgia Dunagan	L B Bell	
535	Downing Joseph				
536	" Kate				
537	" Nannie				
538	" Lucy				
539	" Edward				
540	" Lucie				

Starr Roll 1894

We, the undersigned citizens of the Cherokee Nation, by right of Cherokee blood, do hereby acknowledge to have received of E. E. Starr, National Treasurer of the Cherokee Nation, the sums set opposite our names respectively, in full of our shares in the per capita distribution authorized by an Act of the National Council, dated ___MAY 3 1894___ 1894.

#	Names of Head, and Members of Families	Amount	To Whom Paid	Witness to Payment	Remarks
541	" George				
542	" Mano	2125.60	Jo Downing	L B Bell	
543	Davis Robert L.				
544	" Ruth	531.40		L B Bell	
545	Davis Hanna				
546	" Letha N				
547	" Joel M.				
548	" Theadore				
549	" Ace				
550	" Isaac				
551	" John W.	1859.901	Asa Davis	L B Bell	
552	Dyer Eliza				
553	" Sarah	531.40	S W Gray	L B Bell	
554	Davis John				
555	" Lucy				
556	" Lizzie				
557	" Daisie				
558	" Jeff	1328.50	John Davis	Henry Eiffert	
559	Downing Benjamin	265.70	Christian Gulager	Henry Eiffert	(Illegible)
560	Davis James	265.70	*order* James Davis	L B Bell	
561	Daniel Ludie				*Minors No legal Father*
562	" Malcre	531.40	Richard Daniel	L B Bell (Illegible...)	*Guardian*
563	Downing Sarah				
564	Ravin Albert				
565	Martin Lizzie				
566	Hyson Thomas	1062.80	Johnson Riley	L B Bell	*on order*
567	Davis William *girl*	265.70	*or Wilson* Annie Ashbark	L B Bell	*mother of child Minor*
568	Duck Wolf	265.70	F.B. Severs	Henry Eiffert	*FB Severs*

Starr Roll 1894

We, the undersigned citizens of the Cherokee Nation, by right of Cherokee blood, do hereby acknowledge to have received of E. E. Starr, National Treasurer of the Cherokee Nation, the sums set opposite our names respectively, in full of our shares in the per capita distribution authorized by an Act of the National Council, dated ___MAY 3 1894___ 1894.

Names of Head, and Members of Families	Amount	To Whom Paid	Witness to Payment	Remarks
569 Duck Tahnie				
570 " Linda				
571 " Rachael				
572 " Jack	1062.80	WN Martin	Henry Eiffert	
573 Brown James				
574 Anderson Mandy	531.40	WN Martin	Henry Eiffert	
575 Dykes Ara Bella				WN Martin
576 " Nable H	order	order withdrawn by WN Martin		
577 " Nettie C				
578 " Bunk				
579 " Mary S.	1328.50	Arabella Dykes	L B Bell	
580 Earnest Ellen				
581 " Leroy				
582 " Albert	797.10	J.E. Earnest	L B Bell	
583 Eckert Louiza				
584 " Richard				
585 " Ammanda				
586 " Lizzie	order			R Blackstone
587 " Adie				
588 Horn Fannie				
589 " William	1859.90	R E Blackstone	Henry Eiffert	
590 Early Susan A.	265.70	SA Early	L B Bell	
591 Eckstein Melvira[sic]	265.70	Melvina Eckstein	L B Bell	
592 Eple Ella	order			CB McCaulley[sic]
593 " Annie				
594 " Besie[sic]	797.10	CB McCaully	Henry Eiffert	Ck
595 Eliott[sic] Robert	265.70	Robert Elliott	L B Bell	
596 Evans Alice				
597 " Walter	531.40	Ruler Evans	L B Bell	
598 Evans Catherine	265.70	William Evans	L B Bell	

Starr Roll 1894

We, the undersigned citizens of the Cherokee Nation, by right of Cherokee blood, do hereby acknowledge to have received of E. E. Starr, National Treasurer of the Cherokee Nation, the sums set opposite our names respectively, in full of our shares in the per capita distribution authorized by an Act of the National Council, dated ____MAY 3 1894____ 1894.

Names of Head, and Members of Families	Amount	To Whom Paid	Witness to Payment	Remarks
599 Eliott[sic] James				
600 " Jane	531.40	James Elliott	Henry Eiffert	
601 Evans Sue				
602 Jordan Belle				
603 " Mirtle				
604 " Alexander				
605 " Fannie				
606 Evans Minnie	1594.20	Sue Evans	Henry Eiffert	
607 Eiffert M A				
608 McClellen Margaret	531.40	M.A. Eiffert	L B Bell	
609 Edwards Kate				
610 " William				
611 " Bell				
612 " Mary				
613 " Rose	1328.50	Kate Evans	L B Bell	
614 Fry Lovely				Lovely Fry Ck
615 Burr Andy	531.40	E.S. Ellis	Henry Eiffert	guardian Ellis
616 Frazier Daniel				
617 " Lizzie				
618 " Emma				
619 " Undeen				
620 " Mary				
621 " Serena				Gibson
622 " Ella				
623 " Daniel Jr.				
624 " Robert				
625 " Walter	2657.00	WM Gibson	Henry Eiffert	
626 Frazier John Jr	265.70	WM Gibson	Henry Eiffert	
627 Frazier John Sen.				
628 " Bettie				
629 " Sallie				
630 " John Jr.				
631 " Lizzie				

Starr Roll 1894

We, the undersigned citizens of the Cherokee Nation, by right of Cherokee blood, do hereby acknowledge to have received of E. E. Starr, National Treasurer of the Cherokee Nation, the sums set opposite our names respectively, in full of our shares in the per capita distribution authorized by an Act of the National Council, dated ___MAY 3 1894___ 1894.

	Names of Head, and Members of Families	Amount	To Whom Paid	Witness to Payment	Remarks
632	" Ivie				
633	" Lewis				
634	Crapo Chales[sic]	2125.60	John Frazier	Henry Eiffert	
635	Filmo Millard	*order*			
636	" Emma				R Blackstone
637	" Hattie				
638	" Neppie				
639	" George	1328.50	R E Blackstone	Henry Eiffert	
640	Filmo Cherry	*order*			Children
641	" Ella			R Blackstone	of Millard Filmo
642	" Della	797.10	R E Blackstone	Henry Eiffert	Emma "
643	Foreman Emma				
644	" Ina	531.40	Emma Foreman	L B Bell	
645	Fields Squirl[sic]				
646	" Betsy				
647	" Bettie	797.10	Betsy Fields	L B Bell	
648	Fool Jack	*order*			2
649	" John T.	531.40	H J Vann	Henry Eiffert	
	Fool Thomas				
	" Celey	*See 2104*			
	" William				
650	Folley Adelina				
651	" Kate				
652	" Mary				
653	" Margaret				
654	" Laura				
655	" Clarance				
656	" Lizzie				
657	" Sarah				
658	" Nellie				
659	" Lawrance	2657.00	Patrick Folley	Henry Eiffert	

Starr Roll 1894

We, the undersigned citizens of the Cherokee Nation, by right of Cherokee blood, do hereby acknowledge to have received of E. E. Starr, National Treasurer of the Cherokee Nation, the sums set opposite our names respectively, in full of our shares in the per capita distribution authorized by an Act of the National Council, dated ____MAY 3 1894____ 1894.

	Names of Head, and Members of Families	Amount	To Whom Paid	Witness to Payment	Remarks
660	Foreman Samuel				
661	" Victory				
662	" William J.	797.10	Y J Mackey	L B Bell	
663	Farmer Belle				
664	" Alice				
665	" Lewis				
666	" Gracie				
667	" Leaty				
668	" May	1594.20	Isabella Farmer	L B Bell	
669	Fields Thomas F				
670	" Sarah				
671	" Coreline[sic] B				
672	" Bushyhead				
673	" Mary W.				
674	" William S				
675	" Calie L.				
676	" Ella				
677	" Rachael E	2391.30	Thos F Fields	L B Bell	
678	Foreman Johnson				
679	" Nancy E.				
680	" William J.				
681	" Charles H.				
682	" Jesse E.	1328.50	Johnson Foreman		
683	Foreman John T.	265.70	John T Foreman	Henry Eiffert	
684	Fields Kate	265.70	Jack Thompson	Henry Eiffert	
685	Fisk Menerva				
686	" Harry				
687	" Cora	797.10	*(Illegible)* Fisk	L B Bell	
688	Foreman William	265.70	Wm Foreman	L B Bell	
689	Fields Walter G.				
690	" Louvenia				
691	" Joseph A.	797.10	Walter G. Fields	Henry Eiffert	

Starr Roll 1894

We, the undersigned citizens of the Cherokee Nation, by right of Cherokee blood, do hereby acknowledge to have received of E. E. Starr, National Treasurer of the Cherokee Nation, the sums set opposite our names respectively, in full of our shares in the per capita distribution authorized by an Act of the National Council, dated ___MAY 3 1894___ 1894.

	Names of Head, and Members of Families	Amount	To Whom Paid	Witness to Payment	Remarks
692	Fooy Samuel W.	265.70	Geo Kirk	L B Bell	
693	Flowers Minty *Dead*	265.70	Minty Flowers	L B Bell	
694	Flying Jones P.				
695	" Crawford				
696	" Nepie				
697	" Leonard	1062.80	J P Flying	L B Bell	
698	Falling Henry				
699	" Maggie	531.40	Henry Falling	J.C. Starr	
700	Foreman Susan	265.70	Henry Eiffert	J.C. Starr	*Check on order*
701	Fisher Lucy B.				
702	" Carrie				
703	" Ollie				
704	" Elouisa	1062.80	Henry Fisher	L B Bell	
705	Fields Vicie				
706	" Frank				
707	" Frederick *order*				
708	" Alexander				
709	" Abie				
710	Roberson John	1594.20	H J Vann	Henry Eiffert	*Ck Vann*
711	Foster Jefferson				
712	" Lucy				
713	" Bluford				
714	" Sarah	1062.80	Jefferson Foster	Henry Eiffert	
715	Fletcher Rachael M.				*Mother adopted*
716	" Mary A.	531.40	J.L. Fletcher	L B Bell	*white*
717	Fields Richard				
718	" Texanna				
719	" Claud				
720	" Charles				
721	" Wert				
722	" Jesse				
723	" Joel M.	1859.90	Richard Fields	L B Bell	*Grayson*

Starr Roll 1894

We, the undersigned citizens of the Cherokee Nation, by right of Cherokee blood, do hereby acknowledge to have received of E. E. Starr, National Treasurer of the Cherokee Nation, the sums set opposite our names respectively, in full of our shares in the per capita distribution authorized by an Act of the National Council, dated ___MAY 3 1894___ 1894.

Names of Head, and Members of Families	Amount	To Whom Paid	Witness to Payment	Remarks
724 Fisher William	order D 1406			
725 " George	531.40	SW Grayson	Henry Eiffert	Ck
726 Fields Mollie	265.70	Kate McClure	L B Bell	
727 Freeney John E.				
728 " Susie	531.70	Charlotte Freeney	L B Bell	
729 Fields Charlott	265.70	Charlott Fields	Henry Eiffert	
730 Fields John	265.70	Charlott Fields	Henry Eiffert	
731 Fields James	265.70	Charlott Fields	Henry Eiffert	
732 Freeney Martha				
733 " Mary				
734 " Ella				
735 " Robert				
736 " Walter	1328.50	R. C. Freeney	J.C. Starr	Sept 20, 1894.
737 Graves Thomas				
738 " Bettie				
739 Butler Susie	797.10	Thomas Graves	Henry Eiffert	
740 Gibson James E.				
741 " William M.				
742 " Mary N.W.				
743 " Minnie L.				
744 " Nettie	1328.50	Wm Gibson	L B Bell	
745 Girty Daniel				
746 " Oscar				
747 " Daniel Jr	797.10	Dan'l Girty	J.C. Starr	
748 Grason[sic] Watt	265.70	Minta Davis	L B Bell	on order
749 Girty Susie	265.70	Susie Girty	L B Bell	
750 Girty Ester				
751 " Peggie	order			
752 " Mary				

Starr Roll 1894

We, the undersigned citizens of the Cherokee Nation, by right of Cherokee blood, do hereby acknowledge to have received of E. E. Starr, National Treasurer of the Cherokee Nation, the sums set opposite our names respectively, in full of our shares in the per capita distribution authorized by an Act of the National Council, dated ___MAY 3 1894___ 1894.

Names of Head, and Members of Families	Amount	To Whom Paid	Witness to Payment	Remarks
753 " Alexander				R Blackstone
754 Davis Jennie				
755 Crapo James				
756 " Collins	1859.90	R E Blackstone	Henry Eiffert	
757 Girty James	265.70	James Girty	L B Bell	
758 Girty Thomas	265.70	Thomas Girty	L B Bell	of age
759 Girty Mary	265.70	James Girty	L B Bell	mother unknown
760 Grove[sic] Bettie	265.70	Bettie Groves	L B Bell	
761 Girty Snake				
762 " Uh-k hu-ster				
763 " Martha				
764 " Jennie				
765 " Ned	1328.50	Snake Girty	Henry Eiffert	
766 Groves Annie	265.70	Annie Groves	L B Bell	
767 Glass George				
768 " Mattie				
769 " Lizzie				
770 " Cornelius				
771 Lee Annie	1328.50	George Glass	Henry Eiffert	
772 Girty Wilson				
773 " Ester	531.40	Wilson Girty	Henry Eiffert	
774 Gritts Franklin				
775 " Dora	531.40	Franklin Gritts	L B Bell	
776 Gripenkerl Mary	*order* 265.70	Sam Grayson	Henry Eiffert	Sam Grayson
777 Garvin Laura				J Burdett
778 " Henry	*order*			
779 " Earnest	797.10	J Burdett	Henry Eiffert	
780 Goard Lizzie				
781 " Jessie				
782 " Franklin	797.10	James Goard	Henry Eiffert	

Starr Roll 1894

We, the undersigned citizens of the Cherokee Nation, by right of Cherokee blood, do hereby acknowledge to have received of E. E. Starr, National Treasurer of the Cherokee Nation, the sums set opposite our names respectively, in full of our shares in the per capita distribution authorized by an Act of the National Council, dated _____MAY 3 1894_____ 1894.

#	Names of Head, and Members of Families	Amount	To Whom Paid	Witness to Payment	Remarks
783	Groves Isaac				
784	" Eliza				
785	" Chas E.				
786	" Eveen				
787	" James				
788	" Susan				
789	" Eward[sic]				
790	" Fannie				
791	" Poram	2391.40	Isaac Groves	Henry Eiffert	
	~~" Johnson~~				*Isaac Groves*
	~~Davis Ella~~	} On O. Asylum Roll			*Guardian*
	~~" Stand~~				
792	Griffin James Sen.				
793	" Mary				
794	" Joseph				
795	" Kate	*order*			*W N Martin*
796	" James Jr.				
797	" Nannie				
798	" Addie	1859.90	W N Martin	Henry Eiffert	*Ck*
799	Grove Suiate	265.70	Isaac Groves	Henry Eiffert	
800	Graham Elcy[sic]				
801	" Nancy				
802	" Sarah	797.10	Alsey Graham	L B Bell	
803	Gray S.W.				
804	" Electa V				
805	" Emmit E				
806	" Desota				
807	" Nancy M.	1328.50	SW Gray	Henry Eiffert	
808	Gibson Nannie	265.70	S A Early	L B Bell	*order*
809	Griffin George				
810	" Bettie				
811	" Enoch	797.10	Walsh and Shutt	Henry Eiffert	
812	Graham Moissouri[sic]	*10750* ~~D1124~~			
813	" Florance P	265.70	Charles Branham	L B Bell	

Starr Roll 1894

We, the undersigned citizens of the Cherokee Nation, by right of Cherokee blood, do hereby acknowledge to have received of E. E. Starr, National Treasurer of the Cherokee Nation, the sums set opposite our names respectively, in full of our shares in the per capita distribution authorized by an Act of the National Council, dated ___MAY 3 1894___ 1894.

#	Names of Head, and Members of Families	Amount	To Whom Paid	Witness to Payment	Remarks
814	" Joseph W	~~D1127~~ 10753			
815	" Eddie	~~D1125~~ 10751			
816	" John F.	~~D1126~~ 10752			
817	" Temp V.				
818	" Robert L.	1594.20	J W Graham	L B Bell	
819	Graham James	~~D1128~~ 10754			
820	" Marion	531.40	~~James~~ Graham	L B Bell	
821	Griffin Looney				order drawn
822	" Mary	order			WN Martin
823	" Luggie	797.10	Looney Griffin	L B Bell	
824	Griffin Comodole				Martin
825	" Carolina	order			
826	" Ned	797.10	WN Martin	Henry Eiffert	
827	Garland Tookah	~~D1408~~	On Creek Card No. 5097 Enrollment approved by Sec. of Interior March 28, 1902		
828	" Lewis	~~D1409~~	On Creek Card No. 5098 Enrollment approved by Sec. of Interior		
829	" Lizzie				
831	" Libbie				
831	" David	1328.50	Sim Garland	L B Bell	
832	Garland John	265.70	HC Lowery	Henry Eiffert	
833	Guster[sic] Henry				minor
834	" Elizabeth				mother of
835	" Charles E				the children
836	" Melvina	1062.80	Melvina Gustine	L B Bell	
837	Gritts Susie				At Flint Court House
838	Hopper Jennie	531.40	Susie Gritts	L B Bell	Aug 2, 94
839	Glass Charles	265.70	Charles Glass	L B Bell	
840	Griggs Patty	R 100 ENROLLMENT REFUSED.			
841	" Mary E				
842	" Charles	ENROLLMENT REFUSED			
843	" Abert	1062.80	W H Griggs R 100	L B Bell	check

Starr Roll 1894

We, the undersigned citizens of the Cherokee Nation, by right of Cherokee blood, do hereby acknowledge to have received of E. E. Starr, National Treasurer of the Cherokee Nation, the sums set opposite our names respectively, in full of our shares in the per capita distribution authorized by an Act of the National Council, dated ___MAY 3 1894___ 1894.

Names of Head, and Members of Families	Amount	To Whom Paid	Witness to Payment	Remarks
844 Griggs Henry				
845 " Volie				
846 " Elizabeth	797.10	WH Griggs	L B Bell	
847 Girty Mary	*order*			W & S
848 " William	531.40	Walsh and Shutt	Henry Eiffert	Ck
849 Gilmore Cherokee	*order*			Sam Severs
850 " Cyrus M.				
851 " Harry W.	797.10	Sam Severs	Henry Eiffert	Ck
852 Grayson Nancy	265.70	SW Gray	L B Bell	
853 Griffin Kate	265.70	Commodoe[sic] Griffin	Henry Eiffert	Dead
854 Hood James	*order*			
855 " William	531.40	Walsh & Shutt	Henry Eiffert	W&S
856 Hanks Calvin				
857 " Ora M.	*order*			
858 " Otto	797.10	R E Blackstone	Henry Eiffert	Robt Blackston
859 Handles Sallie	265.70	Walsh and Shutt	Henry Eiffert	W&S
860 " Frona		O L Hayes	Henry Eiffert	Hayes
861 " Susie				W&S
862 " John	531.40	Walsh and Shutt	Henry Eiffert	W&S
863 Hilderbrand George				
864 " Jessie				
865 " Sallie				
866 " Mose	1062.80	George Hildebrand	Henry Eiffert	
867 Hicks Joseph	265.70	Irvin Vore	Henry Eiffert	
868 Harlas Eliza	*order* 265.70	RE Blackstone	Henry Eiffert	Ck R Blackston

Starr Roll 1894

We, the undersigned citizens of the Cherokee Nation, by right of Cherokee blood, do hereby acknowledge to have received of E. E. Starr, National Treasurer of the Cherokee Nation, the sums set opposite our names respectively, in full of our shares in the per capita distribution authorized by an Act of the National Council, dated ___MAY 3 1894___ 1894.

Names of Head, and Members of Families	Amount	To Whom Paid	Witness to Payment	Remarks
869 Harmon Cyntha				
870 " Elizabeth				
871 " McGilbrie				
872 " Benjamin				
873 " Lena	1328.50	Daniel Harmon	L B Bell	
874 Harmon Henryeta	265.70	Henrietta Harmon	Henry Eiffert	
875 Harmon Laura	265.70	Laura Harmon	Henry Eiffert	
876 Hughs George DEAD				Scales
877 " Jane	531.40	P J Scales	Henry Eiffert	Ck.
878 Hanks Emma Sr.				
879 " Daisie				
880 " Emma Jr				
881 " Calvin J	1062.80	Emma Hanks	Henry Eiffert	
882 Hood Maud	265.70	Nora Hood	L B Bell	mother of child minor
883 Hood John				
884 " Mary				
885 " Charles				
886 " Lizzie				Pete Scales
887 " Jane	1328.50	Pete Scales	Henry Eiffert	
888 Hheaton[sic] Ester				
889 " Charles				
890 " David				
891 " Benjamin DEAD.				
892 Wicket Jessie	1328.50	Ester Heaton	Henry Eiffert	
893 Hayes Vicie				
894 " Pearl				
895 " Cora				
896 " Estela	1062.80	Brannan & Hayes	Henry Eiffert	

Starr Roll 1894

We, the undersigned citizens of the Cherokee Nation, by right of Cherokee blood, do hereby acknowledge to have received of E. E. Starr, National Treasurer of the Cherokee Nation, the sums set opposite our names respectively, in full of our shares in the per capita distribution authorized by an Act of the National Council, dated ___MAY 3 1894___ 1894.

Names of Head, and Members of Families	Amount	To Whom Paid	Witness to Payment	Remarks
897 Hayes Richard				
898 " Eliza				
899 " Emma	797.10	Ric^d Hayes	L B Bell	
900 Hilderbrand Stephen				
901 " Nannie				
902 " Peggie				
903 " Mary	1062.80	Stephen Hilderbrand	L B Bell	
904 Holder Amanda	265.70	J H Holder	L B Bell	
905 Harris Thomas	2285 265.70	H J Vann	Henry Eiffert	Vann
906 " William	265.70	PJ Scales	Henry Eiffert	P.J. Scales
907 " David				Vann
908 " Claud	531.40	H J Vann	Henry Eiffert	V
909 Hunton Julia A				
910 " Lovena	531.40	W A Hunton	L B Bell	
911 Howard Russell	265.70	*(Illegible)* Robbs	Henry Eiffert	
912 Harmon Charles				
913 " James	531.40	Charles Harmon	L B Bell	
914 Harmon Nanie	265.70	J W *(Illegible)*	Henry Eiffert	
915 Hooping John Cely	265.70	Sam Grayson	Henry Eiffert	
916 Helvenston Addie				
917 " Mary E				
918 " Charles				
919 " Ruth				
920 " Claud	1328.50	John Helvenston	L B Bell	
921 Hilterbrand[sic] Minnie	265.70	Minnie Hilderbrand	L B Bell	
922 Headricks William	265.70	Christian Gulager	Henry Eiffert	CK Gulager

Starr Roll 1894

We, the undersigned citizens of the Cherokee Nation, by right of Cherokee blood, do hereby acknowledge to have received of E. E. Starr, National Treasurer of the Cherokee Nation, the sums set opposite our names respectively, in full of our shares in the per capita distribution authorized by an Act of the National Council, dated ____MAY 3 1894____ 1894.

#	Names of Head, and Members of Families	Amount	To Whom Paid	Witness to Payment	Remarks
923	Howell Becky				
924	" Emmit L.	531.40	Isaac Howell	L B Bell	
925	Harmon John				
926	" Mary	531.40	John Harmon	Henry Eiffert	
927	Hicks Mary	265.70	Aaron Hicks	L B Bell	on order
928	Meeks Charles	265.70	Joe Downey	Henry Eiffert	Letter Guardian for
929	Hicks Aaron	265.70	Aaron Hicks	L B Bell	
930	Hicks George	265.70	Geo Hicks	L B Bell	
931	Harris Charles				
932	" Janett				
933	" Bettie				Lafeyette Bros
934	" Marlin				
935	" Lucy	1328.50	Lafeyette Bros	Henry Eiffert	Ck
936	Hood David	265.70	WM Gibson	Henry Eiffert	Ck Gibson
937	" Sallie				c/o Lafeyette Bros
938	" Daisie	531.50	Lafeyette Bros		
939	Hood Sterling				
940	" Henry				
941	" Jackson	797.10	WM Gibson	Henry Eiffert	Wm Gibson
942	Halfbreed Lucinda	265.70	Thos Leader	L B Bell	
943	Hutchens Lydia	265.70	JR Pierce	Henry Eiffert	JR Pierce
944	Hulsey Sarah M.				
945	" Earl	R 542!			
946	" Rosalee				
947	" Laurinda				
948	" Charles				
949	" Roscoe	1594.20	Susan Hulsey	L B Bell	
950	Hulsey Ella V	265.70	SW Gray	Henry Eiffert	SW Gray

Starr Roll 1894

We, the undersigned citizens of the Cherokee Nation, by right of Cherokee blood, do hereby acknowledge to have received of E. E. Starr, National Treasurer of the Cherokee Nation, the sums set opposite our names respectively, in full of our shares in the per capita distribution authorized by an Act of the National Council, dated ___MAY 3 1894___ 1894.

Names of Head, and Members of Families	Amount	To Whom Paid	Witness to Payment	Remarks
951 Hulsey Honzo	265.70	SW Gray	Henry Eiffert	SW Gray
952 Horn George W				
953 " James A.				
954 Severe Jack	797.10	Geo W Horn	L B Bell	
955 Harpper[sic] Emma	265.70	Lafeyette Bros	Henry Eiffert	Lafeyette Bros
956 Hereford Sabra				
957 " Joseph L.				
958 " Lennie B.				
959 " James Jr				
960 " Robert				
961 " Jess				
962 " Burk	1859.90	Sabra Hereford	L B Bell	
963 Howland Suanna[sic]				
964 " William				
965 " Susan	797.10	Susanna Howland	L B Bell	
966 Howland John	265.70	Susan Howland	L B Bell	
967 Howland Mary	265.70	Susanna Howland	L B Bell	
968 Hedrick Rebecca	265.70	Rebecca Headrick	Henry Eiffert	
969 Hayes Elvira				
970 McClain Thomas	531.40	William Hayes	L B Bell	
971 Harris Effie				
972 " Thomas				minors
973 " Denis V.	797.10	Martha Harris	L B Bell	
974 Hoyt Emma	265.70	WN Martin	Eiffert Henry	WN Martin

Starr Roll 1894

We, the undersigned citizens of the Cherokee Nation, by right of Cherokee blood, do hereby acknowledge to have received of E. E. Starr, National Treasurer of the Cherokee Nation, the sums set opposite our names respectively, in full of our shares in the per capita distribution authorized by an Act of the National Council, dated ____MAY 3 1894____ 1894.

#	Names of Head, and Members of Families	Amount	To Whom Paid	Witness to Payment	Remarks
975	Hoyt Hemnan[sic] L.				paid check
976	" Susan				No 68521
977	" Florance				on order
978	" Susan	1062.80	R.E. Blackstone	J.C. Starr	
979	Hoyt Milo A *Dead*	265.70	Milo A Hoyt	L B Bell	Dead
980	Harnage William W.				
981	" Jennie				R L Baugh
982	" Richard				
983	" Charles D.	1062.80	R L Baugh	Henry Eiffert	
984	Hommer[sic] Peggie				
985	" Jennie				
986	Downing William	797.10	Peggy Hamner	L B Bell	
987	Harris Joe B.	265.70	Jas S Harris	L B Bell	
988	Heath Olive	265.70	Ruler Evans	L B Bell	
989	Hendrix Caroline				
990	" Haretta				
991	" Milo D				
992	" Theodosia	1062.80	SW Gray	Henry Eiffert	
993	Hibbs Mary M.				
994	" John A.				
995	" Mary E				
996	" David A.				
997	" Emma M.				
998	" Carl C.	1594.20	Sylvester Hibbs	L B Bell	
999	Henchoz Jennie				
1000	" Luellen	531.40	Jennie Henchoz	L B Bell	
1001	Hammer Looney	1922			
1002	" Jennie	1922			
1003	" Josephine	797.10	Looney Hammer	L B Bell	

Starr Roll 1894

We, the undersigned citizens of the Cherokee Nation, by right of Cherokee blood, do hereby acknowledge to have received of E. E. Starr, National Treasurer of the Cherokee Nation, the sums set opposite our names respectively, in full of our shares in the per capita distribution authorized by an Act of the National Council, dated ___MAY 3 1894___ 1894.

Names of Head, and Members of Families	Amount	To Whom Paid	Witness to Payment	Remarks
1004 Hardyshell Clint	265.70	Janine Harris	Henry Eiffert	*(illegible)* minor
1005 Hosmer John	265.70	John Hosmer	L B Bell	
1006 Harris Hanna[sic]				
1007 " Thomas	531.40	Hannah Harris	L B Bell	
1008 Harris Joseph	265.70	Joseph Harris	L B Bell	
1009 Harris John	265.70	Hannah Harris	L B Bell	
1010 Hughes Martha E.	265.70	W.L. Willis	L B Bell	
1011 Hefermon[sic] Joanna				
1012 " Annie				
1013 " Pearl	797.10	Joanna Hefferman	L B Bell	
1014 Harris Christopher				
1015 " Lucy				
1016 " Chester				
1017 " Sallie				
1018 " Willie				
1019 " Beacher	1594.20	C.B. Harris	L B Bell	
1020 Hendrix Manerva[sic]				
1021 " Chancy	531.40	Minerva Hendrix	L B Bell	
1022 Hilderbrand Joseph				
1023 " Elmira J.				
1024 " Tookah	797.10	Thomas McDaniel	Henry Eiffert	
1025 Harris James S.	265.70	James S Harris	L B Bell	
1026 Harris Parker C.				
1027 " Robert				
1028 " Colonel P.				
1029 " Emily				

Starr Roll 1894

We, the undersigned citizens of the Cherokee Nation, by right of Cherokee blood, do hereby acknowledge to have received of E. E. Starr, National Treasurer of the Cherokee Nation, the sums set opposite our names respectively, in full of our shares in the per capita distribution authorized by an Act of the National Council, dated ___MAY 3 1894___ 1894.

Names of Head, and Members of Families	Amount	To Whom Paid	Witness to Payment	Remarks
1030 " Suella				
1031 " James				
1032 " John				
1033 " Mary S	2125.60	Parker Harris	L B Bell	
1034 Howell Mose	265.70	John E Whisenhunt	Henry Eiffert	
1035 Harris Bird	7649	Creek allottee - Does not apply		(illegible)
1036 " Ellen	531.40	Patterson Meritl Co	Henry Eiffert	Mercte Co
1037 Harris Cheasquah	265.70	Patterson Mert Co	Henry Eiffert	Ck
~~Harris John P~~				Enrolled in Tah Ds
Harris William R.				Enrolled in Tah Ds
~~" Cal J~~				
~~" Ellen~~				
~~" Thomas~~				
1038 Hendricks Joseph	265.70	Joseph Hendricks	L B Bell	
1039 Hosmer Solomon P	265.70	Solomon Hosmer	Henry Eiffert	
1040 Howard Charles				minors
1041 " Hellen	531.40	Mary Robbs	Henry Eiffert	
1042 Headricks[sic] Samuel	265.70	Saml Hedrick[sic]	L B Bell	
1043 " William				
1044 " Mary J.	531.40	Saml Headrick guardian	L B Bell	
1045 Hair Martha				
1046 " Nellie				J R Pierce
1047 " Joseph				
1048 Skimmerhorn James	1062.80	J.R. Pierce	Henry Eiffert	Ck
1049 Headrick John	265.70	John Headrick	Henry Eiffert	

Starr Roll 1894

We, the undersigned citizens of the Cherokee Nation, by right of Cherokee blood, do hereby acknowledge to have received of E. E. Starr, National Treasurer of the Cherokee Nation, the sums set opposite our names respectively, in full of our shares in the per capita distribution authorized by an Act of the National Council, dated ___MAY 3 1894___ 1894.

Names of Head, and Members of Families	Amount	To Whom Paid	Witness to Payment	Remarks
1050 Harris Charles	265.70	Hannah Harris	L B Bell	
1051 Harris Filo	265.70	Philo Harris	L B Bell	
1052 Hervey Agnes	265.70	Mary Capps	L B Bell	
1053 Iseral[sic] Peggie				
1054 " Walter	531.40	Susie Isreal[sic]	L B Bell	
1055 Ivey Della				minor
1056 " Ada	531.40	Belle Ivey	L B Bell	mother
1057 Jordan Perry				minor
1058 " Kate	531.40	WM Gibson	Henry Eiffert	WM Gibson
1059 Jennings George Sr				
1060 " Lizzie				
1061 " Sallie				
1062 " Nellie				
1063 " George Jr				
1064 Swimmer Nannie	1594.20	George Jennings Sr	J.C. Starr	
1065 Jones Oscar				
1066 " Coowie				minors
1067 " Jess				
1068 Jones Charles				
1069 " Mary				
1070 " Rufus				
1071 " Pierce				
1072 " Margaret	1328.50	Charles Jones	L B Bell	
1073 Jackson Mary				
1074 " Honnar				
1075 " Lular	order			R Blackstone
1076 " Cuffs				
1077 " Carnelius[sic]	1594.20	R E Blackstone	Henry Eiffert	

38

Starr Roll 1894

We, the undersigned citizens of the Cherokee Nation, by right of Cherokee blood, do hereby acknowledge to have received of E. E. Starr, National Treasurer of the Cherokee Nation, the sums set opposite our names respectively, in full of our shares in the per capita distribution authorized by an Act of the National Council, dated ___MAY 3 1894___ 1894.

Names of Head, and Members of Families	Amount	To Whom Paid	Witness to Payment	Remarks
1078 Julian Robert W.	265.70	R W Julian	L B Bell	
1079 Jackson Lucy A.	265.70	R E Blackstone	Henry Eiffert	
1080 Julian Susan J.				
1081 " Evan				
1082 " Etta P.	797.10	Susan Julian	L B Bell	
1083 Julian William B.	265.70	Susan Julian	L B Bell	
1084 Julian Ed. C.	265.70	Ed P Julian	L B Bell	
1085 John Cydney				
1086 " Thomas L				*Layfeyette*[sic] *Bro*
1087 " Effie	797.10	Lafeyette Bros.	Henry Eiffert	*Ck*
1088 Jordan Joseph M				
1089 " Sarah E.				
1090 " Frost				
1091 " J. L.	1062.80	Jos. M Jordan	Henry Eiffert	
1092 Jordan John C.				
1093 " Mason	531.40	Louisa Crane	L B Bell	*on order*
1094 Jones Ella				
1095 " Cleavland	531.40	Ella Jones	Henry Eiffert	
1096 Jordan John D.				
1097 " James A				
1098 " Joseph H				
1099 " John V				
1100 " William S	D 2574			*John D Jordan*
1101 Oakley William T.	1594.20	John D Jordan	Henry Eiffert	*Guardian*
1102 Johnson Annie	265.70	Annie Johnson	L B Bell	

Starr Roll 1894

We, the undersigned citizens of the Cherokee Nation, by right of Cherokee blood, do hereby acknowledge to have received of E. E. Starr, National Treasurer of the Cherokee Nation, the sums set opposite our names respectively, in full of our shares in the per capita distribution authorized by an Act of the National Council, dated ___MAY 3 1894___ 1894.

Names of Head, and Members of Families	Amount	To Whom Paid	Witness to Payment	Remarks
1103 Jordan Alex				
1104 " Irene	531.40	Alex Jordan	Henry Eiffert	
1105 Jordan Robert				R.L. Baugh
1106 " Charles	531.40	R L Baugh	Henry Eiffert	
1107 Jordan Alix[sic] V. Jr	265.70	Alex V Jordan	Henry Eiffert	
1108 Johnson Alexander				
1109 " Bettie				
1110 " Martin				J R Pierce
1111 " Maggie	1062.80	JR Pierce	Henry Eiffert	
1112 Jackson Josephine	265.70	O Blackmon	Henry Eiffert	order
1113 Jackson Henryetta				
1114 " Willie				
1115 " Annie				
1116 " Susan				
1117 Scott Jeff				
1118 " Alfort				
1119 " Annetta				
1120 " William A	2125.80	Jeff Scott	L B Bell	
1121 Kyle Adda				
1122 " James				
1123 " Maggie				
1124 " Charles				
1125 " Daisie				
1126 " Pollie				
1127 " Robert	1859.90	Adda Kyle	L B Bell	
1128 Keith Freeman				
1129 " Albert	531.40	Freeman Keith	L B Bell	
1130 Kettle Nacy				O. L. Hayes Ck
1131 Grass Josie	531.40	OL Hayes	Henry Eiffert	OL Hayes

Starr Roll 1894

We, the undersigned citizens of the Cherokee Nation, by right of Cherokee blood, do hereby acknowledge to have received of E. E. Starr, National Treasurer of the Cherokee Nation, the sums set opposite our names respectively, in full of our shares in the per capita distribution authorized by an Act of the National Council, dated ___MAY 3 1894___ 1894.

	Names of Head, and Members of Families	Amount	To Whom Paid	Witness to Payment	Remarks
1132	Kettle John	order			R E Blackstone
1133	" Jane	531.40	R E Blackstone	Henry Eiffert	Ck order
1134	Keys Samuel	265.70	S.W. Gray	L B Bell	order
1135	Keys Ed	265.70	SW Gray	L B Bell	
1136	Keys Richard				
1137	" James				
1138	" Willie				
1139	" Leroy				
1140	" Ellen				
1141	" Addie	1594.20	SW Gray	L B Bell	
1142	Keys Samuel Jr				
	" Jess	531.40	SW Gray	L B Bell	
1143	Kerr Frederick A.	order			
1144	" Jessie				
1145	" Ida				
1146	" John				
1147	" Adda				
1148	" Blancha				
1149	" Sarelda	1859.90	WN Martin	Henry Eiffert	
1150	Kerr Neville C.	order			Sam Grayson
1151	" Lucindy				
1152	" John L				
1153	" William W.				
1154	" Nannie				
1155	" Albert				
1156	" George	1859.90	~~WN Martin~~ Sam Grayson	Henry Eiffert	Ck
1157	Kindred Ellen				
1158	" William A.	order			
1159	" Mary	797.10	Lafeyette Bros	Henry Eiffert	Layfayette[sic] Bros
1160	Keith Matthew[sic]	265.70	Mathew Keith	L B Bell	

Starr Roll 1894

We, the undersigned citizens of the Cherokee Nation, by right of Cherokee blood, do hereby acknowledge to have received of E. E. Starr, National Treasurer of the Cherokee Nation, the sums set opposite our names respectively, in full of our shares in the per capita distribution authorized by an Act of the National Council, dated ___MAY 3 1894___ 1894.

Names of Head, and Members of Families	Amount	To Whom Paid	Witness to Payment	Remarks
1161 Keith Gordan	265.70	J N Keith	L B Bell	
1162 Keith Mirtice				*minors*
1163 " Hampton	531.40	J.R. Keith	L B Bell	
1164 Kelly John				
1165 " Dee B.				
1166 Criddenton[sic] John	797.10	John Kelly	L B Bell	
1167 Kirk Amanda	DEAD			
1168 " Francis M				
1169 " Viola				
1170 " Cyrus R.				
1171 " Samantha E.				
1172 " George J.				
1173 " Walter F				
1174 " Quinn D				
1175 Reynolds William A.	2391.30	Geo Kirk	L B Bell	Geo Kirk legal Guardian
1176 Kelley[sic] Elijah				
1177 " Riddle A				
1178 " Willie				
1179 " Jack				
1180 " Ellen	1328.50	Elijah Kelly	Henry Eiffert	
1181 Kash Ella				
1182 " Perry				
1183 " James M.				
1184 West John				*of age*
1185 " Richard	1328.50	J A Kash	Henry Eiffert	
1186 Keys William				
1187 " George	*order* 531.40	WN Martin	Henry Eiffert	WN Martin
1188 Kell Bud T.	265.70	R L Baugh ~~D1226~~ 9338	Henry Eiffert	R L Baugh

Starr Roll 1894

We, the undersigned citizens of the Cherokee Nation, by right of Cherokee blood, do hereby acknowledge to have received of E. E. Starr, National Treasurer of the Cherokee Nation, the sums set opposite our names respectively, in full of our shares in the per capita distribution authorized by an Act of the National Council, dated ____MAY 3 1894____ 1894.

#	Names of Head, and Members of Families		Amount	To Whom Paid	Witness to Payment	Remarks
1189	Koehler	Mary E	Order			R L Baugh
1190	"	Charles				
1191	"	Annie				
1192	"	Margrett				
1193	"	Lizzie				
1194	"	George				
1195	"	Alice				
1196	"	William B.	2125.60	R L Baugh	Henry Eiffert	Ck
1197	Koehler	John	265.70	R L Baugh	Henry Eiffert	ck Baugh
1198	Lynch	Susan T.				
1199	"	Joseph				
1200	"	Clausene				
1201	"	Lizza				
1202	"	Nellie				
1203	"	Getter				
1204	"	Jack	~~D234~~ 9537 1859.90	Susan Lynch	Henry Eiffert	
1205	Lephew	Henry	order 265.70	J A Buchannan	Henry Eiffert	Wm McLain has letters of Guardianship for those Heirs
1206	Bradshaw	Lizzie	(Illegible)	of McLain guardian Father of the children		
1207	Bradshaw	James	531.40	AC Bradshaw	L B Bell	
1208	Latta	Felix				
1209	"	Cintha				
1210	"	Henry				
1211	"	Mary	1062.80	Felix Latta	Henry Eiffert	
1212	Lewis	Silba				
1213	"	Dena				
1214	"	Ida	797.10	Silba Lewis	L B Bell	
1215	Rome	Andrew				
1216	"	Thomas				minor mother of these children
1217	"	James	797.10	Jane Prater	L B Bell	

Starr Roll 1894

We, the undersigned citizens of the Cherokee Nation, by right of Cherokee blood, do hereby acknowledge to have received of E. E. Starr, National Treasurer of the Cherokee Nation, the sums set opposite our names respectively, in full of our shares in the per capita distribution authorized by an Act of the National Council, dated ___MAY 3 1894___ 1894.

Names of Head, and Members of Families	Amount	To Whom Paid	Witness to Payment	Remarks
1218 Lawry Ellen	265.70	Ellen Lawry	C.C. Starr	
1219 Allen Minnie W.	265.70	J C West	L B Bell	
1220 Lowry Alice				
1221 Starr Cooie				
1222 " Tucksie				
1223 " Caleb	1062.80	Alice Lowry	L B Bell	
1224 Lawry Pickens				
1225 " Laura				
1226 " Omma				
1227 " Geter B.	1062.80	Laura Lowry[sic]	L B Bell	
1228 Lowry Return	265.70	Return Lowry	L B Bell	
1229 Lewis Jane		*Creek Card #1918*		*Grayson*
1230 " Francis	531.50	Sara ~~Creek~~ Grayson	~~Henry Eiffert~~	Ck
1231 Lasley James				*Sam Grayson*
1232 " Robert				
1233 " Minnie	797.10	Sam Grayson	Henry Eiffert	Ck
1234 Lindsey Ida				
1235 " Mary				
1236 " William				
1237 " Edward				
1238 " Lewis				
1239 " Francis				
1240 " Douglas				
1241 " Grady				
1242 " Robert	2391.30	Ida Lindsey	L B Bell	
1243 Leach Mima				
1244 " Burton				*Gibson*
1245 " Franklin				
1246 " Kate	1062.80	Wm N Gibson	Henry Eiffert	Ck

Starr Roll 1894

We, the undersigned citizens of the Cherokee Nation, by right of Cherokee blood, do hereby acknowledge to have received of E. E. Starr, National Treasurer of the Cherokee Nation, the sums set opposite our names respectively, in full of our shares in the per capita distribution authorized by an Act of the National Council, dated ___MAY 3 1894___ 1894.

	Names of Head, and Members of Families	Amount	To Whom Paid	Witness to Payment	Remarks
1247	Lacey Jane				
1248	" James				
1249	" Henry				
1250	" Susan	1062.80	Jane Lacy	L B Bell	
1251	Lacy Lizzie	265.70	Lizzy Lacy	L B Bell	D1293
1252	Lowerry[sic] Ellis				
1253	" Johnson				
1254	" Kate	797.10	WN Martin	Henry Eiffert	W Martin
1255	Lowerry John Sr				
1256	" William				
1257	" Jefferson				
1258	" Murtle				
1259	" Kate				
1260	" Annie				
1261	" John Jr	1859.90	John Lowery	Henry Eiffert	
1262	Lowerry[sic] Henry C.				
1263	" Elsie				
1264	Clay Lizzie	797.10	H C Lowery	Henry Eiffert	
1265	Looney William	265.70	Queen Lane	L B Bell	on order
1266	Lynch Lucy				
1267	Tiger Robert	Enrolled on Creek Card Field #(2241)			
1268	" Mary	797.10	Lucy Lynch #(2242)	L B Bell	
1269	Langley James				
1270	" Sallie				
1271	" Susie				
1272	Cobb James				
1273	" Jeff	1328.50	James Langly[sic]	L B Bell	

Starr Roll 1894

We, the undersigned citizens of the Cherokee Nation, by right of Cherokee blood, do hereby acknowledge to have received of E. E. Starr, National Treasurer of the Cherokee Nation, the sums set opposite our names respectively, in full of our shares in the per capita distribution authorized by an Act of the National Council, dated _____ MAY 3 1894 _____ 1894.

Names of Head, and Members of Families	Amount	To Whom Paid	Witness to Payment	Remarks
1274 Lawry[sic] James				
1275 " Clarinda				
1276 " Mary				
1277 " George				
1278 " Ellis				
1279 " Emma				
1280 " Henry				
1281 " Earrie[sic]				
1282 " Mose				
1283 " John	2657.00	James Lowry	L B Bell	
1284 Lawry[sic] James M Sr				
1285 " Susan Sr				
1286 " Raphael				
1287 " Anderson				
1288 " Elliza				
1289 " Mary				
1290 " James Jr				
1291 " Minnie				
1292 " Susan Jr				
1293 " Jennie	2657.00	N C Lowery	H Eiffert	
1294 Latty Luvenna[sic]				
1295 " Mary				
1296 " Rachael				
1297 " Maud	1062.80	Levena Latta	Henry Eiffert	
1298 Lee John				
1299 " Rachael				
1300 " Robert				
1301 " John Jr.				
1302 " Walter				
1303 " Lizzie				
1304 " Lafaett[sic]	1859.90	John Lee	Henry Eiffert	
1305 Brimage Thomas	265.70	Thomas Corline on Apr 30th 1902		*unpaid*
1306 Leek Betsie	265.70	James Neal	L B Bell	*on order*

Starr Roll 1894

We, the undersigned citizens of the Cherokee Nation, by right of Cherokee blood, do hereby acknowledge to have received of E. E. Starr, National Treasurer of the Cherokee Nation, the sums set opposite our names respectively, in full of our shares in the per capita distribution authorized by an Act of the National Council, dated ___MAY 3 1894___ 1894.

Names of Head, and Members of Families	Amount	To Whom Paid	Witness to Payment	Remarks
1307 Spaniard Lucy	265.70	James Neal	L B Bell	*on order*
1308 Lattie Emily	265.70	Felix Latta	Henry Eiffert	
1309 Lindsey Bettie J	265.70	Bettie Lindsey	L B Bell	
1310 Leader Thomas F.	265.70	Thos F Leader	L B Bell	
1311 Lee Walter Sr				*Henry Bacon*
1312 " Walter Jr				
1313 " Lilly	797.10	Henry Bacon	L B Bell	
1314 Leader Duncan				
1315 " Pollie				
1316 " Ruth				
1317 " Reaner				
1318 " Ellen				
1319 " Eward[sic]				
1320 " Peggie				
1321 " Andrew				
1322 " Charles	2125.60	Duncan Leader	L B Bell	
1323 Leader James	265.70	Duncan Leader	L B Bell	
1324 LeBarge[sic] Jane	DEAD.			
1325 " Martha				
1326 " Juliette				
1327 " Ida				
1328 " Maud	1328.50	Daniel La Barge	Henry Eiffert	
1329 Lawry William	265.70	Johnson Riley	L B Bell	
1330 Lane Queen				
1331 Lucy Sevorrover	531.40	Queen Lane	L B Bell	

Starr Roll 1894

We, the undersigned citizens of the Cherokee Nation, by right of Cherokee blood, do hereby acknowledge to have received of E. E. Starr, National Treasurer of the Cherokee Nation, the sums set opposite our names respectively, in full of our shares in the per capita distribution authorized by an Act of the National Council, dated ___MAY 3 1894___ 1894.

	Names of Head, and Members of Families	Amount	To Whom Paid	Witness to Payment	Remarks
1332	McDaniel Robert				
1333	" Cinderella				
1334	" Ida				
1335	" Johnson				
1336	" Lewie	1328.50	Robt McDaniel	Henry Eiffert	
1337	McEachin Maggie *order*	265.70	JE Long	Henry Eiffert	Ck JE Long
1338	Mayfield John				dead
1339	" Ella				
1340	" Nora				
1341	" Roy	1062.80	Annie Mayfield	L B Bell	mother
1342	Musrat Mary				
1343	" Beckey				Hayes
1344	" Thomas	797.10	OL Hayes	Henry Eiffert	Ck
1345	Musrat James				Stephen McDaniel
1346	" Annie				
1347	" Lewis				
1348	" Arch				
1349	" Nicy	1328.50	Stephen McDaniel	Henry Eiffert	Ck
1350	Musrat Wilson				
1351	" Sallie				
1352	" Malinda				
1353	" Katie				
1354	" Lyda	1328.50	Wilson Musrat	Henry Eiffert	
1355	Griffin Jack	265.70 ⌀488	OL Hayes	Henry Eiffert	OL Hayes
1356	Milligan Susie				
1357	" Caleb				
1358	" Gracie				
1359	" Frank	1062.80	Susie Mulligan	L B Bell	

Starr Roll 1894

We, the undersigned citizens of the Cherokee Nation, by right of Cherokee blood, do hereby acknowledge to have received of E. E. Starr, National Treasurer of the Cherokee Nation, the sums set opposite our names respectively, in full of our shares in the per capita distribution authorized by an Act of the National Council, dated ___MAY 3 1894___ 1894.

#	Names of Head, and Members of Families	Amount	To Whom Paid	Witness to Payment	Remarks
1360	Markham[sic] John				
1361	" Cissaro				
1362	" Allen				
1363	" Burk	1062.80	Sallie Marcum	L B Bell	
1364	McClain[sic] William				
1365	" Jess				
1366	" Kalley				
1367	" Lelila				
1368	" Josie				
1369	" William F.	1594.20	Wm McLain	L B Bell	
1370	McCorkle David W.	265.70	D W McCorkle	L B Bell	
1371	McCorkle Emma				
1372	Roberson Mary				
1373	" Milton				
1374	" Emma	1062.80	Emma McCorkle	L B Bell	
1375	Mackey Laura DEAD.				
1376	Jennings Artemer DEAD.				R E Blackstone
1377	" Eloise	797.10 (order)	R E Blackstone	Henry Eiffert	
1378	McDaniel Estella	265.70	Fanny McDaniel	L B Bell	minor Martin
1379	McIngtush Thomas	265.70	SW Gray	L B Bell	
1380	Murphy James				
1381	" Emma				
1382	" Bettie				
1383	" Pearlla A				
1384	" Minnie M				
1385	" Edney	1594.20	James Murhly[sic] 1714	Henry Eiffert	
1386	Miller Jess T				R Blackstone minor
1387	" John H				mother
1388	" Lenora				S.M. White

Starr Roll 1894

We, the undersigned citizens of the Cherokee Nation, by right of Cherokee blood, do hereby acknowledge to have received of E. E. Starr, National Treasurer of the Cherokee Nation, the sums set opposite our names respectively, in full of our shares in the per capita distribution authorized by an Act of the National Council, dated _____ MAY 3 1894 _____ 1894.

#	Names of Head, and Members of Families	Amount	To Whom Paid	Witness to Payment	Remarks
1389	" Caladonia	1062.80	R.E. Blackstone	J.C. Starr	check on order
1390	Miller James J.				
1391	" Charles				
1392	" Mattie DEAD	797.10	James J Miller	Henry Eiffert	
1393	Miller George	265.70	George Miller	L B Bell	
1394	Miller Henry	order			Gibson
1395	" Francis E.				
1396	" Etha	797.10	W.M. Gibson	J.C. Starr	Check on order
1397	McDaniel Eliza				
1398	Muskrat Jack	531.40	Stephen McDaniel	L B Bell	
					HJ Vann
1399	Muskrat Calhoun	order			
1400	" Eliza	531.40	H.J. Vann	JC Starr	check on order
1401	McClure James	265.70	James McClure	L B Bell	
1402	McGlomor[sic] Rosa				
1403	" Felix	531.40	Rosa McGlamor	L B Bell	
1404	Marshall Matte J				
1405	" William B.				
1406	" Ether				
1407	" Paul	order			
1408	" Fannie				R Blackstone
1409	" Mirtle	194.20	R E Blackstone	Henry Eiffert	ck
1410	McClure Robert	265.70	Brannan & Hayes	Henry Eiffert	
1411	McClure Henry				
1412	" Mattie				
1413	" James				
1414	" Kate				
1415	" Thomas				
1416	" Lucy	1594.20	Henry McClure	Henry Eiffert	

Starr Roll 1894

We, the undersigned citizens of the Cherokee Nation, by right of Cherokee blood, do hereby acknowledge to have received of E. E. Starr, National Treasurer of the Cherokee Nation, the sums set opposite our names respectively, in full of our shares in the per capita distribution authorized by an Act of the National Council, dated ___ MAY 3 1894 ___ 1894.

Names of Head, and Members of Families	Amount	To Whom Paid	Witness to Payment	Remarks
1417 Muskrat Joseph	order 265.70	O.L. Hayes	Henry Eiffert	Hayes
1418 Mabry Sallie				
1419 " John				
1420 " Ethel M				
1421 " Clarance				
1422 Foreman Mary	1328.50	Sallie Mabry	L B Bell	
1423 Mulkey William R.				
1424 " Richard J				
1425 " John R	797.10	W R Mulkey	L B Bell	
1426 McClure Charles				
1427 " Edwin				
1428 " Francis				
1429 " Dellie				
1430 " Hattie	1328.50	Charles McClure	L B Bell	
1431 Muskrat Susan	265.70	Susan Muskrat	L B Bell	(#)
1432 Martin Cora				John minors Martin white
1433 " John A.				
1434 " George D.	797.10	John A Martin	L B Bell	
1435 McLaughlin David C.				G.W. Eaton
1436 " Francis	order			
1437 " Leo B	797.10	G.W. Eaton	Henry Eiffert	Ck
1438 Miller George	order			JA Martin
1439 " John	531.40	J.A. Martin	Henry Eiffert	
1440 Martin Annie				
1441 " James	531.40	Annie Martin	L B Bell	
1442 Miller Mary	265.70	Mary Miller	L B Bell	
1443 Martin James	265.70	James Martin	Henry Eiffert	

Starr Roll 1894

We, the undersigned citizens of the Cherokee Nation, by right of Cherokee blood, do hereby acknowledge to have received of E. E. Starr, National Treasurer of the Cherokee Nation, the sums set opposite our names respectively, in full of our shares in the per capita distribution authorized by an Act of the National Council, dated ____MAY 3 1894____ 1894.

	Names of Head, and Members of Families		Amount	To Whom Paid	Witness to Payment	Remarks
1444	"	Sallie	265.70	Sallie Martin	L B Bell	
1445	"	Jane				
1446	"	Bunch	531.40	James Martin	Henry Eiffert	
1447	McClure	William				
1448	"	John	531.40	Wm McClure	L B Bell	
1449	McNulty	Jeff				
1450	"	Cherokee				
1451	"	Lena				
1452	"	George W.				
1453	"	Maud A				
1454	"	Annie				
1455	"	Leona E				
1456	"	Thomas	2125.60	Jeff McNulty	L B Bell	
1457	Miller	Eliza M.				
1458	"	Leo W.				
1459	"	Mamie	797.10	Eliza Miller	L B Bell	
1460	Mulkey	Lewis A.				
1461	"	Julia				withdrawn by EH Lawrence
1462	"	James J	order			
1463	"	Vida				
1464	"	Jack A.	1328.50	LA Mulkey	L B Bell	
1465	Mulkey	James	2222			W&S
1466	"	James E Jr	2222			
1467	"	Earnest	2222			
1468	"	Watt	1062.80	Walsh & Shutt	Henry Eiffert	
1469	McDaniel	Rose				W&S
1470	"	John	531.40	Walsh & Shutt	Henry Eiffert	W&S
1471	Murry[sic]	Nannie				
1472	"	James				HC Lowery
1473	"	Mary E				

Starr Roll 1894

We, the undersigned citizens of the Cherokee Nation, by right of Cherokee blood, do hereby acknowledge to have received of E. E. Starr, National Treasurer of the Cherokee Nation, the sums set opposite our names respectively, in full of our shares in the per capita distribution authorized by an Act of the National Council, dated ___MAY 3 1894___ 1894.

	Names of Head, and Members of Families		Amount	To Whom Paid	Witness to Payment	Remarks
1474	"	Malcolm	1062.80	HC Lowery	Henry Eiffert	
1475	Mulkey	James D.				
1476	"	Charles A				
1477	"	Lewis W.				
1478	"	Johnathan D.				
1479	"	Eliza J				
1480	"	Rose E C	1594.20	Elizabeth Mulkey	L B Bell	on order
1481	"	Warren O. {order	265.70	Walsh & Shutt	J.C. Starr	No 1465
1482	Mulkey	Honzo S.	265.70	Elizabeth Mulkey	L B Bell	
1483	Mulkey	Wyly A	265.70	E S Ellis	Henry Eiffert	Ck Ellis
1484	Measles	Emily B.	4484 265.70	Emily Measels[sic]	L B Bell	
1485	Measles	Vannie				
1486	"	Minner				
1487	"	Ellis				
1488	"	Algie				
1489	"	Barnie	1328.50	Jeff Measels[sic]	L B Bell	husband
1490	Meher	Elvira				
1491	"	William				
1492	"	Henry				
1493	"	David				
1494	"	Jess				
1495	"	Frank				
1496	"	Charles	1859.90	HC Lowery	Henry Eiffert	
1497	Morris	Ella				
1498	"	Lydia				
1499	Morris	Stand W				
1500	"	Harry				
1501	"	Carry	1328.50	Charles Morris	L B Bell	

Starr Roll 1894

We, the undersigned citizens of the Cherokee Nation, by right of Cherokee blood, do hereby acknowledge to have received of E. E. Starr, National Treasurer of the Cherokee Nation, the sums set opposite our names respectively, in full of our shares in the per capita distribution authorized by an Act of the National Council, dated ____MAY 3 1894____ 1894.

	Names of Head, and Members of Families	Amount	To Whom Paid	Witness to Payment	Remarks
1502	Morgan Mark				WN Martin
1503	" Sophrona	*order*			
1504	" Lizzie				
1505	Taylor Looney				
1506	Griffin Lucinda	1328.50	WN Martin 1955	Henry Eiffert	ck
1507	Morgan Lone				
1508	" Josephine				
1509	" Hannah E				
1510	" Eli				
1511	" Bettie				
1512	" Florance				
1513	" Martha J	1859.90	Lone Morgan	Henry Eiffert	
1514	Murphy Jessie C.				
1515	" Augustine				
1516	" Iris				
1517	" Bunnie				
1518	" Leila				
1519	" Oliver				
1520	" Wyche	1859.90	H C Lowery	Henry Eiffert	
1521	Miller Noah	265.70	WN Martin	Henry Eiffert	WN Martin
1522	Miller Janetta				
1523	" Mattie				WN Martin
1524	" Mary E	797.10	WN Martin	Henry Eiffert	ck
1525	Markus Mattie	D995 265.70	H C Lowery	Henry Eiffert	ck HC Lowery
1526	McDonold[sic] George	*order*			
1527	" Emmily[sic]	531.40	WN Gibson	Henry Eiffert	Gibson
1528	" Texas A	265.70	Walter A Ashley	L B Bell	
1529	" William C.				
1530	" Ora B.				Gibson
1531	" Narcenah				
1532	" Edward	1062.80	WN Gibson	Henry Eiffert	

Starr Roll 1894

We, the undersigned citizens of the Cherokee Nation, by right of Cherokee blood, do hereby acknowledge to have received of E. E. Starr, National Treasurer of the Cherokee Nation, the sums set opposite our names respectively, in full of our shares in the per capita distribution authorized by an Act of the National Council, dated ___MAY 3 1894___ 1894.

Names of Head, and Members of Families	Amount	To Whom Paid	Witness to Payment	Remarks
1533 Murphy Sarah	265.70	Corny Murphy	L B Bell	
1534 McNeal Elizabeth	265.70	R.B. Hutchins	Henry Eiffert	Hutchins
1535 Madden Lelitia	265.70	John Bertholf	Henry Eiffert	order
1536 McMakins Savana				
1537 " Jennie				
1538 " Kennie	order			RB Hutchins
1539 " Parker				
1540 " Andrew				
1541 " Charles	1594.20	RB Hutchins	Henry Eiffert	ck
1542 Marrow[sic] Nancy				
1543 Watkins Kate				
1544 " Della	797.10	JT Morrow	L B Bell	
1545 Monks Peggie	265.70	R.E. Blackstone	Henry Eiffert	Ck R Blackstone
1546 Morris Mary				
1547 " Nancy J.				
1548 " Sarah C.				
1549 " John W.				
1550 " Charles				
1551 " Della	1594.20	Mary Morris	L B Bell	
1552 Markham Doc	265.70	Wm M. Gulager on (Power of Attorney) Robt B Ross		pd/Dec 3/96
1553 Miller John L				
1554 " Jesse V				
1555 " Annie	797.10	Jno L. Miller	L B Bell	
1556 McIngtush[sic] Chesie				
1557 " Freland				
1558 " Vann A.				
1559 " Daniel N.				
1560 " Woldo E.	1328.50	Cheesie McIntosh	L B Bell	

Starr Roll 1894

We, the undersigned citizens of the Cherokee Nation, by right of Cherokee blood, do hereby acknowledge to have received of E. E. Starr, National Treasurer of the Cherokee Nation, the sums set opposite our names respectively, in full of our shares in the per capita distribution authorized by an Act of the National Council, dated ___MAY 3 1894___ 1894.

Names of Head, and Members of Families	Amount	To Whom Paid	Witness to Payment	Remarks
1561 Minks Nelly				
1562 Green Sallie	531.40	Jng[sic] Davis	J.C. Starr	
1563 McPhearson Jack	265.70	J.R. Pierce	Henry Eiffert	JR Pierce
1564 McPhearson Harriet	265.70	Harriett McPherson	L B Bell	
1565 Mitchell Nancy W				
1566 " Isaac G	531.40	R M Mitchell	Henry Eiffert	
1567 Miller Nancy				
1568 " Caroline	531.40	Nancy Miller	L B Bell	
1569 Morgan J. J.				
1570 " Malinda J				
1571 " Maud M.				
1572 " Malinda J. Jr	1062.80	J J Morgan	L B Bell	
1573 Marshall Cornelia	265.70	Charly Marshall	L B Bell	
1574 Monroe Dora				Mrs Fisk Legal Guardian
1575 " Nannie				
1576 " Mirtle	797.10	Wm Fisk	L B Bell	
1577 Miller Toney	265.70	Wm Gibson	Henry Eiffert	
1578 McElmeel William H				
1579 " Elizabeth	~~265.70~~	~~R B Hutchinson~~	~~L B Bell~~	~~on order~~
1580 " Ora				
1581 " Peter	1062.80	W H M^c *(Illegible)*	L B Bell	
1582 Motte William				
1583 " Emily				H C Lowery
1584 " Joseph	797.10	H C Lowery	Henry Eiffert	
1585 Mayfield Sarah	265.70	Mrs W H Barker	L B Bell	

Starr Roll 1894

We, the undersigned citizens of the Cherokee Nation, by right of Cherokee blood, do hereby acknowledge to have received of E. E. Starr, National Treasurer of the Cherokee Nation, the sums set opposite our names respectively, in full of our shares in the per capita distribution authorized by an Act of the National Council, dated ___MAY 3 1894___ 1894.

Names of Head, and Members of Families	Amount	To Whom Paid	Witness to Payment	Remarks
1586 McDaniel Nancy				
1587 " George				
1588 Barber Dannie	797.10	Thomas McDaniel	Henry Eiffert	
1589 McLain James	265.70	E.S. Ellis	Henry Eiffert	Ellis
1590 Neff William				
1591 " Mattie				
1592 " Hooly				
1593 " Ezra	1062.80	William Neff	Henry Eiffert	
1594 Neal James				
1595 " Pollie				
1596 " Samuel				
1597 " Nannie	1062.80	James Neal	L B Bell	
1598 Narcomie Farney	265.70	Sam Grayson	Henry Eiffert	ck Sam Grayson
1599 Neal Richard Sr				
1600 " James	531.40	James Neal *order with Crane by Ellis*	L B Bell	
1601 " Richard Jr.	265.70	Martha Neal	L B Bell	
1602 Nivens Floyd	265.70	Julia Nivens *D2572*	L B Bell	
1603 Nivens Jeff C.	265.70	Julia Nivens	L B Bell	
1604 Nelson Effie				
1605 " Jess W	531.40	Effie Nelson	L B Bell	
1606 Nitts Ice				Vann
1607 " Nagy	531.40	H.J. Vann	Henry Eiffert	Ck
1608 Nicholson Henry F				
1609 " Lizzie	531.40	Mary H Nicholson	L B Bell	
1610 Nivens Delila	265.70	Sim Garland	L B Bell	order

Starr Roll 1894

We, the undersigned citizens of the Cherokee Nation, by right of Cherokee blood, do hereby acknowledge to have received of E. E. Starr, National Treasurer of the Cherokee Nation, the sums set opposite our names respectively, in full of our shares in the per capita distribution authorized by an Act of the National Council, dated ___MAY 3 1894___ 1894.

Names of Head, and Members of Families	Amount	To Whom Paid	Witness to Payment	Remarks
1611 Nivens Josephine	~~D1440~~		On Creek Card Roll No 5810 Enrollment
1612 " William	D2573		approved by Secy of Interior March 28 1902
1613 " Jessie	797.10	Sim Garland D6573 4526	L B Bell	order
1614 Owens Henry	265.70	Henry Owens	L B Bell	
1615 Owens Martin	265.70	P J Scales	Henry Eiffert	Scales
1616 Porter Mary J	265.70	Mary J Porter	Henry Eiffert	
1617 Pheasant Jane	265.70	Jane Pheasant	L B Bell	
1618 Phillips Harvey	265.70	Harvey Phillips	L B Bell	
1619 Phillips Walter	265.70	Walter Phillips	L B Bell	
1620 Pettyjohn Alice				dead
1621 " Georgie A				
1622 " Thomas A	797.10	Geo Pettyjohn	L B Bell	
1623 Miller Samuel	265.70	Jake Miller	L B Bell	
1624 Phillips Henry P. Sr				
1625 " Elma				
1626 " Roxie				
1627 " Henry Jr.	1062.80	H P Phillips Sr	L B Bell	
1628 Pheasant George	265.70	Geo Pheasant	L B Bell	
1629 Pettit Timothy	265.70	SW Gray	Henry Eiffert	SW Gray
1630 " Aggy	265.70	Tim Pettit	L B Bell	Ck
1631 Phillips Frank				
1632 " Elizabeth				
1633 " Fannie				
1634 " Jess				
1635 " Nancy				
1636 " Ida				
1637 " Laura				

Starr Roll 1894

We, the undersigned citizens of the Cherokee Nation, by right of Cherokee blood, do hereby acknowledge to have received of E. E. Starr, National Treasurer of the Cherokee Nation, the sums set opposite our names respectively, in full of our shares in the per capita distribution authorized by an Act of the National Council, dated ___MAY 3 1894___ 1894.

	Names of Head, and Members of Families	Amount	To Whom Paid	Witness to Payment	Remarks
1638	McDaniel Mary				
1639	" Ella	2391.30	Frank Phillips	L B Bell	
1640	Phillips William M.	DEAD.			
1641	" Mary				
1642	" Andrew				
1643	" Caroline	1662.80	W M Phillips	L B Bell	
1644	Phillips Henry	265.70	W M Phillips	L B Bell	
1645	Pickard Mary E				
1646	" William				
1647	" Narcis J.	797.10	Louisa Crane	L B Bell	
1648	Parker Lizzie				
1649	" Jess	531.40	W.N. Martin	CA Thompson	minors
1650	Petty John T.	265.70	John T Petty	Henry Eiffert	
1651	Parris Andrew				
1652	" Charles				
1653	" Annie				
1654	" Mose				
1655	" John				
1656	" Fannie	1594.20	AR Wilson & Bro	Henry Eiffert	order
1657	Pugh Mary J	265.70	Bent Cobb	L B Bell	
1658	Price Addie				
1659	" Jane				
1660	" Leonard	797.10	Thomas Price	L B Bell	
1661	Parnoskey Sarah	265.70	Melvina Exstein	L B Bell	
1662	Porter William A.				
1663	" Pleasant S.				
1664	" Mamy				

Starr Roll 1894

We, the undersigned citizens of the Cherokee Nation, by right of Cherokee blood, do hereby acknowledge to have received of E. E. Starr, National Treasurer of the Cherokee Nation, the sums set opposite our names respectively, in full of our shares in the per capita distribution authorized by an Act of the National Council, dated _____MAY 3 1894_____ 1894.

Names of Head, and Members of Families	Amount	To Whom Paid	Witness to Payment	Remarks
1665 " Lenora	1062.80	P N Blackstone	Henry Eiffert	*order*
1666 Pope James Sr				
1667 " Benjamin	DEAD.			
1668 " James Jr.				
1669 " Sarah E.				
1670 " Sydney				
1671 " Charles				
1672 " Jennie				
1673 " Andy	2125.60	James Pope	Henry Eiffert	
1674 Preston Dora	265.70	Walsh and Shutt	Henry Eiffert	Ck
1675 Puyor[sic] Florida	DEAD.			
1676 " Francis M.				
1677 " Hamilton Z.	797.10	Florida Puryear	L B Bell	
1678 Poorwolf Charlotte	265.70	Wilson Gertz	Henry Eiffert	
1679 Patrick John A.				
1680 " Cleavland N.	531.40	Walsh and Shutt	Henry Eiffert	W&S Ck
1681 Quinton John				
1682 " Roxie				
1683 " Ethel				
1684 " Isaac				
1685 " Nancy				
1686 Barnett Joel	1594.20	John Quinton	L B Bell	
1687 Reeves Arlie				
1688 " Nettie				
1689 " Bertha	797.10	Arlie Reeves	L B Bell	
1690 Raymond Jess	265.70	Susan Lynch	Henry Eiffert	
1691 Ray Acy				
1692 " Pearl	531.40	Acy Ray	Henry Eiffert	

Starr Roll 1894

We, the undersigned citizens of the Cherokee Nation, by right of Cherokee blood, do hereby acknowledge to have received of E. E. Starr, National Treasurer of the Cherokee Nation, the sums set opposite our names respectively, in full of our shares in the per capita distribution authorized by an Act of the National Council, dated ___MAY 3 1894___ 1894.

Names of Head, and Members of Families	Amount	To Whom Paid	Witness to Payment	Remarks
1693 Rogers Mary	265.70	Mary Rogers	L B Bell	
1694 Ross William				
1695 " Lizzie				
1696 " Ozy				
1697 " Johnson	1062.80	P J Scales	Henry Eiffert	PJ Scales
1698 Ratley Rider				
1699 " Lizzie	order	See Protest		
1700 " Levina		D2578		Vann
1701 " Lydia	1062.80	H J Vann	Henry Eiffert	Ck
1702 Ray [Bell] Sallie	265.70	Charles Jones	L B Bell	
1703 Ross Robert F.				
1704 " Arra				
1705 " Robert Jr.				
1706 " Charles F.				
1707 " Pearl E.	1328.50	Robt F Ross	L B Bell	
1708 Rogers Emma	265.70	Ried[sic] Rogers	L B Bell	
1709 Ross Jess T.				
1710 " Cora				
1711 " Carry				
1712 " Nora				
1713 " Lora L.				
1714 " Tim	1594.20	Jesse T Ross	Henry Eiffert	
1715 Hargrove Magnora				
1716 " Andrusha	531.40	G.S. Hargrove	by Permssn of Guardian Jess Ross Henry Eiffert	
1717 Ross Wasker[sic] L.	265.70	Waska L Ross	Henry Eiffert	
1718 Redding Eliza C.				
1719 " Lula M.				
1720 " Samuel				
1721 " Amanda L.				

Starr Roll 1894

We, the undersigned citizens of the Cherokee Nation, by right of Cherokee blood, do hereby acknowledge to have received of E. E. Starr, National Treasurer of the Cherokee Nation, the sums set opposite our names respectively, in full of our shares in the per capita distribution authorized by an Act of the National Council, dated ___MAY 3 1894___ 1894.

	Names of Head, and Members of Families	Amount	To Whom Paid	Witness to Payment	Remarks
1722	" Jessie M.				
1723	" Isaacesco	1594.20	Eliza C. Redding	L B Bell	
1724	Russell Robert L.				
1725	" Maud M.				R Blackstone
1726	" Gus	797.10	R E Blackstone	Henry Eiffert	Ck
					order
1727	Russell Walter R.				
1728	" Fannie	531.40	W R Russell	L B Bell	
1729	Robinson John C.	265.70	Ella Robinson	Henry Eiffert	
1730	Robins Benjamin				
1731	" Henry				
1732	" Charles				
1733	" Claud				
1734	" James	1328.50	Benj Robins	Henry Eiffert	
1735	Roberson Nancy	265.70	Nancy Roberson	L B Bell	
1736	" Lucy	265.70	R.E. Blackstone	JC Starr	on order
1737	" Charles	265.70	Nancy Roberson	L B Bell	
1738	" Lizzie	265.70	Nancy Roberson	L B Bell	
1739	" Maggie	265.70	Nancy Roberson	L B Bell	
1740	" John Jr	265.70	Nancy Roberson	L B Bell	
1741	Roberson Samuel	265.70	R E Blackstone	Henry Eiffert	R Blackstone
1742	Roberson Albert				
1743	" William	531.40	Albert Roberson	L B Bell	
1744	Russell William H.				minor
1745	" Edward	531.40	Wm H Russell	Henry Eiffert	
1746	Robbs Mary				
1747	" Mina	531.40	Mary Robbs	Henry Eiffert	
1748	Robbins[sic] Mahala	265.70	Mahala Robins	L B Bell	

Starr Roll 1894

We, the undersigned citizens of the Cherokee Nation, by right of Cherokee blood, do hereby acknowledge to have received of E. E. Starr, National Treasurer of the Cherokee Nation, the sums set opposite our names respectively, in full of our shares in the per capita distribution authorized by an Act of the National Council, dated ___MAY 3 1894___ 1894.

Names of Head, and Members of Families	Amount	To Whom Paid	Witness to Payment	Remarks
1749 Richey Mary	265.70	Mary A Richey	H Lindsy	
1750 Roberts Nancy				
1751 " Mury[sic]				
1752 " Leroy				
1753 " Commodore				
1754 " Maurice				
1755 " Arthur				
1756 " Vennie	1859.90	William Roberts	Henry Eiffert	
1757 Robinson Ella				
1758 " Mary E.	531.40	Ella Robinson	Henry Eiffert	
1759 Rock John				
1760 " Jane				
1761 " Daniel				
1762 " Lee	1062.80	John Rock	L B Bell	
1763 Runnels William				
1764 " Ella				
1765 " Jess				
1766 " Minnie				
1767 " George	1328.50	W E Gentry &Co	Henry Eiffert	
1768 Riddle James H. (age 10)	265.70	Wm Riddle	L B Bell	father no legal guardian
1769 Roland Emily	265.70	Emily Roland	L B Bell	
1770 Reeves Angerona				
1771 " Nannie				
1772 " Ollietta				
1773 " Bailey				
1774 Harris Susan				
1775 Reeves Lettie	1594.20	Angerona Reeves		

Starr Roll 1894

We, the undersigned citizens of the Cherokee Nation, by right of Cherokee blood, do hereby acknowledge to have received of E. E. Starr, National Treasurer of the Cherokee Nation, the sums set opposite our names respectively, in full of our shares in the per capita distribution authorized by an Act of the National Council, dated ___MAY 3 1894___ 1894.

	Names of Head, and Members of Families	Amount	To Whom Paid	Witness to Payment	Remarks
1776	Russell Martha A				
1777	" Connie				
1778	" Carlisle				
1779	" Christopher	1062.80	Campbell Russell	L B Bell	
1780	Rogers Dave	265.70	Dave Rogers	L B Bell	
1781	Rain Nannie				
1782	" Artie M.	531.40	Nannie Rain	L B Bell	
1783	Reese Charles				
1784	" Nellie				
1785	" Tukie				
1786	" Nancy				
1787	" Rachael				CW Turner
1788	" Felix				
1789	" Cleaveland	1869.90	CW Turner	Henry Eiffert	Ck
1790	Reid Josephine				
1791	" Alice				
1792	" Francis R.				
1793	" Clarance A.				
1794	" Leola				
1795	" Earnest				
1796	" Bertha				
1797	" Gracie				
1798	" Mary R.	2391.30	Josephine Reid	Henry Eiffert	
1799	Ross Joshua	36			
1800	" Susan				
1801	" Joshua Jr.				
1802	" John Y.				
1803	" Jennie P.	1328.50	Susan Ross	L B Bell	
1804	Raven Willie	265.70	Willie Raven	L B Bell	

(order)

Starr Roll 1894

We, the undersigned citizens of the Cherokee Nation, by right of Cherokee blood, do hereby acknowledge to have received of E. E. Starr, National Treasurer of the Cherokee Nation, the sums set opposite our names respectively, in full of our shares in the per capita distribution authorized by an Act of the National Council, dated ___MAY 3 1894___ 1894.

Names of Head, and Members of Families	Amount	To Whom Paid	Witness to Payment	Remarks
1805 Rogers Lavega	*Claimed to be a Choctaw*			
1806 " George				
1807 " Coone	797.10	La Vega Rogers	L B Bell	
1808 Ratliff Jefferson				
1809 " Lorence	531.40	Jeff Ratly[sic]	L B Bell	
1810 Ross James	*order*			Martin
1811 " Daniel		D2581		
1812 " Nannie				
1813 " Jennie	1062.80	WN Martin	Henry Eiffert	
1814 Reaves John	265.70	Mollie Reaves	Henry Eiffert	
1815 Reaves Charles	265.70	~~DW~~ C.D. Reaves	L B Bell	
1816 Reaves Willie T.	265.70	Wm T Reaves	Henry Eiffert	
1817 " Mollie E.	265.70	Mollie Reaves	Henry Eiffert	
1818 " Effie M.	265.70	C D Reaves	L B Bell	
1819 Reaves Dimor W	265.70	D W Reaves	L B Bell	
1820 Rider Nannie	265.70	Fred Mayes	L B Bell	
1821 Ragsdale Thomas	265.70	Thos Ragsdale	L B Bell	
1822 Rhomer May				
1823 " Nora				
1824 " May F.				
1825 " Maggie B	1062.80	May Rhomer	J.C. Starr	
1826 Rider Josephine				See order
1827 Vann David	531.40	Wm P Ross	Henry Eiffert	Reynolds
1828 Ratlingoard[sic] John	265.70	John Rattlingoard	Henry Eiffert	
1829 Riley Johnson				
1830 Earbob Lily	531.40	Johnson Riley	L B Bell	

Starr Roll 1894

We, the undersigned citizens of the Cherokee Nation, by right of Cherokee blood, do hereby acknowledge to have received of E. E. Starr, National Treasurer of the Cherokee Nation, the sums set opposite our names respectively, in full of our shares in the per capita distribution authorized by an Act of the National Council, dated ____MAY 3 1894____ 1894.

Names of Head, and Members of Families	Amount	To Whom Paid	Witness to Payment	Remarks
1831 Roberson Laura				
1832 " Richard				
1833 " Lizzie	797.10	H C Lowery	Henry Eiffert	
1834 Sevier James J.				
1835 " Callie				
1836 " Anna E				
1837 " Jerry				
1838 " James C. Jr				
1839 " Alice				
1840 " Charlie F.				
1841 " Leo	2125.60	J J Sevier	L B Bell	
1842 Shoemake William Sr				
1843 " Gergie[sic]				Hayes
1844 " William H. Jr	797.10	OL Hayes	Henry Eiffert	Ck
1845 Shepard[sic] Boon				
1846 " Gus				
1847 " Charles Jr				
1848 " Edward				
1849 " Watie	1328.50	Boon Shepherd	L B Bell	
1850 Smith Carty				
1851 " Martha				
1852 " Kiahna	*order*			
1853 " Lizzie				Blackstone
1854 " Famous	1328.50	R.E. Blackstone	Henry Eiffert	Ck
1855 Sanders Nancy	*order*			
1856 Davis Maud	531.40	R E Blackstone	Henry Eiffert	R Blackstone
1857 Sevier Susan				in J.A. Sevier
1858 " Jess	531.40	John Sevier	Henry Eiffert	family

Starr Roll 1894

We, the undersigned citizens of the Cherokee Nation, by right of Cherokee blood, do hereby acknowledge to have received of E. E. Starr, National Treasurer of the Cherokee Nation, the sums set opposite our names respectively, in full of our shares in the per capita distribution authorized by an Act of the National Council, dated ___MAY 3 1894___ 1894.

Names of Head, and Members of Families	Amount	To Whom Paid	Witness to Payment	Remarks
1859 Smith McCoy				
1860 " Jennie				
1861 " Edward				
1862 " Walter				
1863 " Juletta				
1864 " Wilson				
1865 " Mammie				
1866 " May				
1867 " Junie	2391.30	McCoy(Juni)Smith	L B Bell	
1868 Scott Sanford	265.70	Sanford Scott	Henry Eiffert	
1869 Sanders Nealy				
1870 " Maud				
1871 " Clyde	797.10	Nealy Sanders	L B Bell	
1872 Sykes Alex				
1873 " Marion	531.40	Alex Sykes	L B Bell	
1874 Smith Edward				
1875 " Lulitin				
1876 " Willie	797.10	Edward Smith	J.C. Starr	
1877 Smart Henry				
1878 " Hellin	531.40	Henry Smart	L B Bell	
1879 Shepard Charles	265.70	W.M. Gulager	Henry Eiffert	WM Gulager
1880 Sevier Joe				
1881 " George	531.40	James Sevier	L B Bell	with James Sevier
1882 Shoemake William H				
1883 " Thomas H				
1884 " Rody				
1885 " Lula B.				
1886 " Mary E	1328.50	W.H. Shoemake	L B Bell	

Starr Roll 1894

We, the undersigned citizens of the Cherokee Nation, by right of Cherokee blood, do hereby acknowledge to have received of E. E. Starr, National Treasurer of the Cherokee Nation, the sums set opposite our names respectively, in full of our shares in the per capita distribution authorized by an Act of the National Council, dated ___ MAY 3 1894 ___ 1894.

	Names of Head, and Members of Families	Amount	To Whom Paid	Witness to Payment	Remarks
1887	Shoemake Hugh	265.70	Hugh Shoemake	L B Bell	
1888	Shoemake[sic] Charles F.	265.70	Charles Shumake	L B Bell	
1889	Shoemake[sic] John W.				
1890	" Mattie B.				
1891	" Minnie N				
1892	" Calvin B.				
1893	" Lula G.				
1894	" Claud				
1895	" Maud				
1896	" Maggie M.	2125.60	J H Shumake	L B Bell	
1897	Shepard Richard	265.70	Rick Sheppard	L B Bell	
1898	Sims[sic] Tennessee	1095			
1899	" Jess C.				
1900	Hinds Franklin	1106			
1901	" Henry				
1902	" Ida				
1903	" Claud	1594.20	H L Simms	L B Bell	
1904	Scales J.A.	order 265.70	JA Scales		Bell
1905	" A.P.	265.70	Amanda Scales		
1906	" Callie	265.70	Callie Scales		
1907	Sunday Thomas				
1908	" Lena				
1909	" Peggie	DEAD.			
1910	" George				
1911	" James	order			
1912	" Izra				
1913	" Avy				
1914	Cramp Sallie	2125.60	H.J. Vann	Henry Eiffert	check
1915	Smallwood Samuel	265.70	Martha Beaver	L B Bell	minor

Starr Roll 1894

We, the undersigned citizens of the Cherokee Nation, by right of Cherokee blood, do hereby acknowledge to have received of E. E. Starr, National Treasurer of the Cherokee Nation, the sums set opposite our names respectively, in full of our shares in the per capita distribution authorized by an Act of the National Council, dated ____MAY 3 1894____ 1894.

	Names of Head, and Members of Families	Amount	To Whom Paid	Witness to Payment	Remarks
1916	Shoemake Harmon				
1917	" Rose A.				
1918	" James W.				
1919	" Harmon	1062.80	Harmon A Shumake	L B Bell	
1920	Sevier John A.				
1921	" May				
1922	" John C.				
1923	Simons Benty	1062.80	John A Sevier	L B Bell	
1924	Sheriff John	265.70 *order*	C.P. Clark	Henry Eiffert	*Guardian*
1925	Smedly Richard				
1926	" Jackson	531.40	Wm Smedly	L B Bell	
1927	Smedly William	265.70	Wm Smedly	L B Bell	
1928	Smedly John L	265.70	J L Smedly	L B Bell	
1929	Simmons Alexander				
1930	" Sarah *order*				W&S
1931	" Maggie				
1932	" Columbus	1062.80	Walsh and Shutt	Henry Eiffert	*Ck*
1933	Starr Tuxie				
1934	" Sis				
1935	" Susan				
1936	" Milo				
1937	" Mollie				
1938	" Richard	1594.20	Tuxie Starr	L B Bell	
1939	Starr Thomas				
1940	" Sqirrel[sic] *Fredrick*				
1941	" Ruth	797.10	Thos Starr	L B Bell	

Starr Roll 1894

We, the undersigned citizens of the Cherokee Nation, by right of Cherokee blood, do hereby acknowledge to have received of E. E. Starr, National Treasurer of the Cherokee Nation, the sums set opposite our names respectively, in full of our shares in the per capita distribution authorized by an Act of the National Council, dated ___MAY 3 1894___ 1894.

Names of Head, and Members of Families	Amount	To Whom Paid	Witness to Payment	Remarks
1942 Starr Eliza				
1943 " Samuel				
1944 " Moss				
1945 " Kate	1062.80	Eliza Starr	L B Bell	
1946 Starr William	265.70	William Starr	Henry Eiffert	
1947 Soap Thomas	*order* 265.70	H J Vann	Henry Eiffert	
1948 Starr Thomas				
1949 " Samuel				
1950 " Henry				
1951 " Nelly				
1952 " Kate				
1953 " James	1594.20	Thos Starr	L B Bell	
1954 Starr Lucy				
1955 " Sophia	531.40	Thos Starr	L B Bell	
1956 Smith Simmy				
1957 " Delia				
1958 " John				
1959 " Minnie	1062.80	Simmy Smith	Henry Eiffert	
1960 Starr Frost				
1961 " Fannie				
1962 " Lucy				
1963 " Spihechee[sic]				
1964 " Bunch				
1965 " Cherokee	1594.20	Fannie Starr	L B Bell	
1966 Starr Leesie	265.70	Teesa Starr	808 on Census Roll L B Bell	
1967 Starr Ellis	265.70	Ellis Starr	L B Bell	

Starr Roll 1894

We, the undersigned citizens of the Cherokee Nation, by right of Cherokee blood, do hereby acknowledge to have received of E. E. Starr, National Treasurer of the Cherokee Nation, the sums set opposite our names respectively, in full of our shares in the per capita distribution authorized by an Act of the National Council, dated __MAY 3 1894__ 1894.

#	Names of Head, and Members of Families	Amount	To Whom Paid	Witness to Payment	Remarks
1968	Splitnose Thomas	265.70	E S Ellis	Henry Eiffert	Ellis
1969	" Charles				
1970	Wilson George	531.40	Walsh & Shutt	Henry Eiffert	W & S
1971	Stewart William H				WN Martin
1972	" Annie	531.40	WN Martin	Henry Eiffert	
1973	Starr William				
1974	" John				
1975	" Bean	797.10	William Starr	Henry Eiffert	
1976	Scott Annie	265.70	Lafayette Bros *not applied for Creek allottee*	Henry Eiffert	Lafayette Bros
1977	Scudder Lewis B.				
1978	" Narcisus J.				
1979	" Cherokee G.				
1980	" Alford B.				
1981	" Bessie	1328.50	L B Scudder	L B Bell	
1982	Scuder Jacob M	265.70	J M Scuder	L B Bell	
1983	Sanders Dora				minors
1984	" Leler				
1985	" Sallie	797.10	Dora Sanders	L B Bell	
1986	Scoonover Annie				
1987	" Henry F.				
1988	" Rebecca A.				
1989	" Mary A.				
1990	" Thomas J.				
1991	" Stonewall W.				
1992	" Grover C.	1859.90	Henry Scoonover	L B Bell	
1993	Simpson Eliza				
1994	Nelson Mary	531.40	R E Blackstone	Henry Eiffert	R Blackstone
1995	Shinn Jane E.				dead
1996	" Joseph	DEAD. D2582 DEAD.			
1997	" Alexander	797.10	Campbell Russell	L B Bell	

Starr Roll 1894

We, the undersigned citizens of the Cherokee Nation, by right of Cherokee blood, do hereby acknowledge to have received of E. E. Starr, National Treasurer of the Cherokee Nation, the sums set opposite our names respectively, in full of our shares in the per capita distribution authorized by an Act of the National Council, dated ___MAY 3 1894___ 1894.

	Names of Head, and Members of Families	Amount	To Whom Paid	Witness to Payment	Remarks
1998	Shinn Columbus	265.70	Campbell Russell	L B Bell	
1999	Shinn John	265.70	Campbell Russell	L B Bell	
2000	Shoemake Jess S.				
2001	" Oscar				
2002	" Maud				
2003	" Hugh	1062.80	J.S. Shumake	L B Bell	
2004	Sanders John	7609			
2005	Hilderbrand Jack				
2006	" Mary	797.10	R E Blackstone	Henry Eiffert	
2007	Smith Lutie				
2008	" Louiza				
2009	" Florance				
2010	" Mittie	1062.80	R E Blackstone	Henry Eiffert	
2011	Summerfield James	265.70	James Summerfield	L B Bell	
2012	Scales Peter J.				
2013	" Sophie				
2014	" Rose	797.10	Pete J Scales	Henry Eiffert	
2015	Smith Maud				
2016	" Famous				
2017	" Joseph				
2018	" Eliza				
2019	" Nannie				
2020	" Frank				
2021	" David				
2022	" Cherry				
2023	" Susie	2391.30	Maud Smith	L B Bell	
2024	Severs Samuel B. Sr.		Cd #19		
2025	" Florance E.				
2026	" Bessie M.		19		

Starr Roll 1894

We, the undersigned citizens of the Cherokee Nation, by right of Cherokee blood, do hereby acknowledge to have received of E. E. Starr, National Treasurer of the Cherokee Nation, the sums set opposite our names respectively, in full of our shares in the per capita distribution authorized by an Act of the National Council, dated ___MAY 3 1894___ 1894.

	Names of Head, and Members of Families	Amount	To Whom Paid	Witness to Payment	Remarks
2027	" Ellen	19			
2028	" Charles J.	19			
2029	" Samuel B. Jr.	19			
2030	" Emma M.	19			
2031	" Barton	2125.60	Samuel B Severs	Henry Eiffert	
2032	Smith Frank				
2033	" Sallie				
2034	" Juliaetta T.				
2035	" Thomas				
2036	" Nancy				
2037	" Susie				
2038	" Samuel				
2039	" Roach				
2040	" Emma	2391.30	Frank Smith	Henry Eiffert	
2041	Starks Lucy				
2042	" Mattie	531.40	Charles Starks	L B Bell	
2043	Scott Ida L				
2044	" Lee				
2045	" Vivian				
2046	" Chester				
2047	" Corinne				
2048	" Patterson				
2049	" Lucy A.	1859.90	George Scott	L B Bell	
2050	Shuetz Susana	265.70	Phillip Shuetz	Henry Eiffert	minor age 4
2051	Scott Dave				
2052	" Kiah				
2053	" Gurtrude	797.10	S W Gray	L B Bell	
2054	Scott James				
2055	" Buck	531.40	W E Gentry	Henry Eiffert	W E Gentry minor & orphan
2056	Starr Mary	265.70	Mary Starr	L B Bell	

Starr Roll 1894

We, the undersigned citizens of the Cherokee Nation, by right of Cherokee blood, do hereby acknowledge to have received of E. E. Starr, National Treasurer of the Cherokee Nation, the sums set opposite our names respectively, in full of our shares in the per capita distribution authorized by an Act of the National Council, dated _____ MAY 3 1894 _____ 1894.

Names of Head, and Members of Families	Amount	To Whom Paid	Witness to Payment	Remarks
2057 Splitnose Nannie	265.70	Nannie Splitnose	S.W. Mayfield	by order of WM Gulager
2058 Shepard Eliza	265.70	Eliza Sheppard	Henry Eiffert	
2059 Starr Calvin	265.70	Calvin Starr	L B Bell	
2060 Shoemake Richard W.				
2061 " Ada	531.40	RW Shumake	L B Bell	
2062 Splitnose Betsey	265.70	Wilson Girtz	Henry Eiffert	
2063 Smith Samuel	265.70	Wm Gibson	Henry Eiffert	Wm Gibson
2064 Shoemake James H.				
2065 " John W.	797.10	J H Shumake	L B Bell	
2066 Sheperd[sic] Mollie				
2067 " Elizabeth	531.40	Mollie Shepard	L B Bell	
2068 Still Clarance				
2069 " Beula				
2070 " William H	797.10	J F Hollingsworth	L B Bell	
2071 Stephenson Samantha	D~~1756~~ 1322			
2072 " James	D1451			
2073 " Thomas				
2074 " Alice	1062.80	Samantha Stephens	L B Bell	
2075 Shoemake Frederick M	265.70	James Shoemake	L B Bell	father
2076 Steele RV.	$265.70	R.V. Steele	Robt B Ross	
2077 Tyner Lydia				
2078 " Maggie				
2079 " Lydia Jr				
2080 " Mary	1062.80	R J Tyner	Henry Eiffert	

Starr Roll 1894

We, the undersigned citizens of the Cherokee Nation, by right of Cherokee blood, do hereby acknowledge to have received of E. E. Starr, National Treasurer of the Cherokee Nation, the sums set opposite our names respectively, in full of our shares in the per capita distribution authorized by an Act of the National Council, dated _____MAY 3 1894_____ 1894.

#	Names of Head, and Members of Families	Amount	To Whom Paid	Witness to Payment	Remarks
2081	Thompson Charles				
2082	" Jennie	531.40	Charles Thompson	L B Bell	
2083	Toney John				
2084	" Jennie				
2085	" Nancy				
2086	" Mary				
2087	" George	1328.50	John Toney	L B Bell	
2088	Taylor Juletta	265.70	R E Blackstone	Henry Eiffert	R Blackstone
2089	Turnover Margaret	1632			
2090	Hood John	1632			
2091	" Lena	1632			
2092	" Vanda	1632			Gibson
2093	" Hannah	~~1328.50~~ 1632	W M Gibson	Henry Eiffert	Ck
2094	Turquett Nannie	265.70	Jasper Turquett	Henry Eiffert	
2095	Tittle Lizzie	6030			
2096	" Gola	6030			
2097	" Clyda L.	~~797.10~~ 6030	Lizzie Tittle	L B Bell	
2098	Taylor Icum	265.70	OL Hayes D245	Henry Eiffert	O.L. Hayes
2099	Thompson Jack				
2100	" Narcisa				
2101	" William				
2102	" Gracie				
2103	" Kate	1328.50	Jack Thompson	Henry Eiffert	
2104	Fool Thomas	order			Ck The name of this
2105	" Ceily	531.40	H J Vann	Henry Eiffert	family may be "Fool"
2106	Trott William L.	265.70	Wm L. Trott	Henry Eiffert	

Starr Roll 1894

We, the undersigned citizens of the Cherokee Nation, by right of Cherokee blood, do hereby acknowledge to have received of E. E. Starr, National Treasurer of the Cherokee Nation, the sums set opposite our names respectively, in full of our shares in the per capita distribution authorized by an Act of the National Council, dated ___MAY 3 1894___ 1894.

#	Names of Head, and Members of Families	Amount	To Whom Paid	Witness to Payment	Remarks
2107	Toney Levi				
2108	" Susan				
2109	" Calvin				
2110	" Looney				
2111	" Betty	1328.50	Levi Toney	L B Bell	
2112	Thornberry Annie				
2113	" John	order	D2585		Gibson
2114	" Lena		D2585	Listed for enrollment Creek Nation Case No. 180	
2115	" Rachel		D2585		
2116	" Willie	1328.50	Wm Gibson (D2585)	CA Thompson	
2117	Tully John D.	265.70	John Tully	L B Bell	
2118	Taylor John	265.70	John Taylor	L B Bell	
2119	Fool William	order 265.70	H J Vann	Henry Eiffert	or "Fool" Ck
2120	Terrell Albert				
2121	" Willie E.				
2122	" Lula M.				
2123	" Oliver C.				
2124	" Una				
2125	" Pearl				
2126	" May				
2127	" Ed M.	2125.60	Albert Terrell	L B Bell	
2128	Triplet[sic] Edward	265.70	Ed Triplett	L B Bell	
2129	Tally Bettie	265.70	Bettie Tally	L B Bell	
2130	Tally Andrew	265.70	Andrew Tally	L B Bell	
2131	Tally Sirbert[sic]	265.70	Sibert Tally	L B Bell	

Starr Roll 1894

We, the undersigned citizens of the Cherokee Nation, by right of Cherokee blood, do hereby acknowledge to have received of E. E. Starr, National Treasurer of the Cherokee Nation, the sums set opposite our names respectively, in full of our shares in the per capita distribution authorized by an Act of the National Council, dated ____MAY 3 1894____ 1894.

	Names of Head, and Members of Families	Amount	To Whom Paid	Witness to Payment	Remarks
2132	Thompson Malinda L.				
2133	" Nora B.				
2134	" Nellie F.				
2135	" Florance E	1062.80	Malinda Thompson	L B Bell	
2136	Trent Edward A.	265.70	ES Ellis	CA Thompson	Ellis
2137	Trent Ella	265.70	ES Ellis	CA Thompson	Ellis
2138	Triplet Mary A.	265.70	M A Triplett	L B Bell	
2139	Teehee Kate				
2140	Griffin Nannie	531.40	Kate McClure	L B Bell	
2141	Tolbert Rufus	265.70	Emily Measels	L B Bell	
2142	Timpson John	265.70 1725	Walsh & Shutt	CA Thompson	W&S
2143	Timberlake John A	265.70	GW Williams	L B Bell	Order
2144	Timberlake William	265.70	Walsh & Shutt	CA Thompson	W&S
2145	Vore Frank				
2146	" Charles F.				
2147	" Frank Jr.				
2148	" Hellen	1062.80	Frank Vore	J.C. Starr	
2149	Vann William				
2150	" Ellen				
2151	" Georgia A.				
2152	" Lular				
2153	" William Jr.	1328.50	William Vann	J.C. Starr	
2154	Vann David				
2155	" Lular	431.40	David Vann	Henry Eiffert	
2156	Vann James W.	265.70	Mary Rogers	L B Bell	

Starr Roll 1894

We, the undersigned citizens of the Cherokee Nation, by right of Cherokee blood, do hereby acknowledge to have received of E. E. Starr, National Treasurer of the Cherokee Nation, the sums set opposite our names respectively, in full of our shares in the per capita distribution authorized by an Act of the National Council, dated ___MAY 3 1894___ 1894.

Names of Head, and Members of Families	Amount	To Whom Paid	Witness to Payment	Remarks
2157 Vaught Lucinda				
2158 " Jennie				
2159 " Joanna				
2160 " General				
2161 " Joseph				
2162 " John				
2163 McDaniel Thomas	1859.90	R.E. Blackstone	J.C. Starr	on order
2164 Vaught Lucy	order 265.70	R.E. Blackstone	CA Thompson	R Blackston
2165 Vann James W.	265.70	William Vann	J.C. Starr	minor
2166 Vann Frederix				minor
2167 Swain Nancy	531.40	WN Gibson	Henry Eiffert	order
2168 Vann Elizabeth	265.70	CE Vann	Henry Eiffert	
2169 Vann Robert Sr				
2170 " Cooie				
2171 " Ninnie				
2172 " Joseph				
2173 " Frank				
2174 " Mittie				
2175 " Edward				
2176 " Robert Jr.				
2177 " Lizzie	2391.30	Cooie Vann	L B Bell	
2178 Vann Charles E.				
2179 " Ada				
2180 " John S.	797.10	C.E. Vann	Henry Eiffert	
2181 Vann George				
2182 " Maud				
2183 " Perry				
2184 " Holmes	1062.80	George Vann	Henry Eiffert	

Starr Roll 1894

We, the undersigned citizens of the Cherokee Nation, by right of Cherokee blood, do hereby acknowledge to have received of E. E. Starr, National Treasurer of the Cherokee Nation, the sums set opposite our names respectively, in full of our shares in the per capita distribution authorized by an Act of the National Council, dated ___MAY 3 1894___ 1894.

Names of Head, and Members of Families	Amount	To Whom Paid	Witness to Payment	Remarks
2185 Vickery John				
2186 " Bettie				
2187 " Henry				
2188 " Nancy				
2189 " Timsey				
2190 " Samuel				
2191 " Charles				
2192 " Susan				
2193 " Andrew	2391.30	John Vickery	L B Bell	
2194 Vore Irving				
2195 Backman William	531.40	Irvin Vore	Henry Eiffert	
2196 Shepherd William E				
2197 " Bessie	531.40	Mattie Long	Henry Eiffert	mother of these children
2198 Vann Herman J.				
2199 " Lizzie				
2200 " Hampton				
2201 " Clem				
2202 " Joseph				
2203 " William				
2204 " Sophia				
2205 " Lola				
2206 " Elnora	2391.30	Herman J. Vann	J.C. Starr	
2207 Vann Nancy	265.70	WE Gentry & Co	Henry Eiffert	
2208 Wicket Lem				
2209 " Ruth				
2210 " Alpha				
2211 Smith Vernon				
2212 " Floid	1328.50	Ruth Wickett	L B Bell	
2213 West John				
2214 " Margaret				
2215 " Laura				
2216 " Luellen				

Starr Roll 1894

We, the undersigned citizens of the Cherokee Nation, by right of Cherokee blood, do hereby acknowledge to have received of E. E. Starr, National Treasurer of the Cherokee Nation, the sums set opposite our names respectively, in full of our shares in the per capita distribution authorized by an Act of the National Council, dated ___MAY 3 1894___ 1894.

	Names of Head, and Members of Families	Amount	To Whom Paid	Witness to Payment	Remarks
2217	" Frank				
2218	" Mary				
2219	" Nannie	1859.90	John West	Henry Eiffert	
2220	West John H. Jr	265.70	John West	Henry Eiffert	
2221	West Ellis	265.70	Ellis West	L B Bell	
2222	West Richard	265.70	Rich West	L B Bell	
2223	Weaver Alice				
2224	" Felix				order
2225	" Nancy	797.10	~~H J Vann~~ P.J. Scales	CA Thompson	
2226	Weaver Florance D.				
2227	" Hermon				
2228	" Laura B.				
2229	" Fannie				
2230	" Maud	1328.50	Florence D Weaver	L B Bell	
2231	West Thomas C.	265.70	T C West	L B Bell	
2232	Wilkerson Sarah				
2233	" Lizzie				
2234	" Ruth				
2235	" Mattie				
2236	" Ellen	1328.50	Sarah Wilkerson	L B Bell	
2237	Wilkerson Eli				
2238	" Eliza				
2239	" Susan				
2240	" Nancy				
2241	" Arley				
2242	Davis Mary	1594.20	Eli Wilkerson	L B Bell	

Starr Roll 1894

We, the undersigned citizens of the Cherokee Nation, by right of Cherokee blood, do hereby acknowledge to have received of E. E. Starr, National Treasurer of the Cherokee Nation, the sums set opposite our names respectively, in full of our shares in the per capita distribution authorized by an Act of the National Council, dated ___MAY 3 1894___ 1894.

Names of Head, and Members of Families	Amount	To Whom Paid	Witness to Payment	Remarks
2243 Whitzenhunt[sic] Nancy				
2244 " Andrew B.				
2245 " Robert L				
2246 " Young E.				
2247 " Fred	1328.50	Noah Whisenhunt	L B Bell	
2248 Whitzenhunt John E.				
2249 " Henryetta	531.40	John E Whitzenhunt	Henry Eiffert	
2250 Watts Thomas				
2251 " Lavenia				
2252 " Henryetta	~~D1463~~	On Creek Card No. 2340 Enrollment approved by Secy. of Interior March 28, 1902		
2253 " John				
2254 M°Ingtush Luellen	1328.50	Thomas Watts	L B Bell	
2255 Watts William	265.70	Thomas Watts	L B Bell	
2256 West Robert E.				
2257 " William C.	531.40	Robt. E West	Henry Eiffert	
2258 Whitzenhunt[sic] Joanna				
2259 " Mary A				
2260 " Jane H				
2261 " Charles E				
2262 " Wyly				
2263 " Noah	1594.20	William Whisenhunt	L B Bell	
2264 Wilson Melvina				
2265 " Ada L	order 531.40	J R Pierce	CA Thompson	JR Pierce
2266 Warspeaker Lavena	265.70	(Illegible) 7659	L B Bell	minor
2267 Warwick Jacob M				
2268 " George F.				
2269 " Albert S				
2270 " William L				
2271 " Alice C				

Starr Roll 1894

We, the undersigned citizens of the Cherokee Nation, by right of Cherokee blood, do hereby acknowledge to have received of E. E. Starr, National Treasurer of the Cherokee Nation, the sums set opposite our names respectively, in full of our shares in the per capita distribution authorized by an Act of the National Council, dated _____ MAY 3 1894 _____ 1894.

Names of Head, and Members of Families	Amount	To Whom Paid	Witness to Payment	Remarks
2272 " Francis M.	1594.20	J M Warwick	L B Bell	
2273 West James K. P.				
2274 " Calvin				
2275 " Jane				
2276 " William				
2277 " John				
2278 " Jeff	1594.20	M E West	L B Bell	
2279 Woodard William	265.70	William Woodard	L B Bell	
2280 Whitzenhunt Ruth	265.70	Jas Whisenhunt	L B Bell	
2281 Whitfield William	265.70	*(illegible)*	L B Bell	
2282 Wells Mary				
2283 " Lutilia				
2284 " Joseph J.				
2285 " Besey				
2286 " Elizabeth M	1328.50	L C Wells	L B Bell	
2287 Whitzenhunt Jeff W				
2288 " Mattie				
2289 " Lily O.	797.10	Jeff Whisenhunt	L B Bell	
2290 Woodall Thomas F.				
2291 " Emma V.				
2292 " Nannie				
2293 " Susie	1062.80	Emma Woodall	L B Bell	
2294 Wyche Robert D	265.70	Robt D Wyche	Henry Eiffert	Aug 31 94
2295 Whitfield Mary	265.70	Mary Whitfield	L B Bell	
2296 Wicket John				
2297 " Vaden				
2298 " Alice				

Starr Roll 1894

We, the undersigned citizens of the Cherokee Nation, by right of Cherokee blood, do hereby acknowledge to have received of E. E. Starr, National Treasurer of the Cherokee Nation, the sums set opposite our names respectively, in full of our shares in the per capita distribution authorized by an Act of the National Council, dated ____MAY 3 1894____ 1894.

	Names of Head, and Members of Families	Amount	To Whom Paid	Witness to Payment	Remarks
2299	" Jessie				
2300	" John Jr.				
2301	" Nannie	1594.20	John Wicket	Henry Eiffert	
2302	Wicket Abert[sic]	265.70	W.N. Martin	CA Thompson	Martin
2303	Wilkerson James	265.70	James Gertz	Henry Eiffert	Guarden[sic]
2304	Woods Henry	265.70	Henry Woods	L B Bell	minor no Guardian
2305	Wallace Lilly				
2306	" Clora				
2307	" Cid				
2308	" Jennie				
2309	" Nannie				
2310	" John T	1594.20	Lindsey Wallace	Henry Eiffert	
2311	Whitewater Lizzie				
2312	" David				
2313	" Sallie				W.N. Martin
2314	" Tobin				
2315	" Thomas				
2316	" Arch	1594.20	W N Martin	CA Thompson	
2317	Wicket Mammie		Pd by check		
2318	Carey Walker	531.40	Chas Jones–administration Mch 23/96	JC Dannenberg	
2319	Wicket Bettie M.	265.70	W.N. Martin	CA Thompson	WN Martin
2320	Watson Ellen				
2321	" Robert		D-2939		
2322	" George		D-2940		Layfayette Bro
2323	" John		D-2589		
2324	" Nellie		D-2589		
2325	" Luda		D-2589		
2326	" Annie	1869.90	Layfayette Bro	CA Thompson	

Starr Roll 1894

We, the undersigned citizens of the Cherokee Nation, by right of Cherokee blood, do hereby acknowledge to have received of E. E. Starr, National Treasurer of the Cherokee Nation, the sums set opposite our names respectively, in full of our shares in the per capita distribution authorized by an Act of the National Council, dated MAY 3 1894   1894.

Names of Head, and Members of Families	Amount	To Whom Paid	Witness to Payment	Remarks
2327 Warwick Lena	265.70	Jacob N Warwick	L B Bell	
2328 " Thomas A.	265.70	Jack Warwick	L B Bell	order
2329 Willis Prestly E	265.70	P.E. Willis	L B Bell	

****

(The information below was inserted in the logbook before the page containing Watuck, #2330 - 2336)

Letters of Guardianship.

CHEREOKEE NATION.
Canadian **District.**

OFFICE DISTRICT JUDGE.
Canadian   District.

To Whom It May Concern:

KNOW YE, That I   *H. J. Vann*   Judge of the District Court of the District and Nation aforesaid, do, by virtue of authority in me vested by law, this day make, constitue and appoint in the name and by the authority of the CHEROKEE NATION *Alcy Watuck* as Guardian of *Ice, Polly, Fannie, Lunie, and Liley Watuck* minor child*ren* of *John & Alcy Watuck* of *Canadian* District Cherokee Nation, the said *Alcy Watuck* having complied with and performed all duties required by law of *her* precedent to the appointment.

In testimony whereof I hereunto set my hand on this the *23* day of *June* 18*93*

Seal.

H. J. Vann
Judge District Court.

Attest: *C.E. Vann*
Clerk *Canadian* District

****

Starr Roll 1894

We, the undersigned citizens of the Cherokee Nation, by right of Cherokee blood, do hereby acknowledge to have received of E. E. Starr, National Treasurer of the Cherokee Nation, the sums set opposite our names respectively, in full of our shares in the per capita distribution authorized by an Act of the National Council, dated ___MAY 3 1894___ 1894.

Names of Head, and Members of Families	Amount	To Whom Paid	Witness to Payment	Remarks

(The Protest Notice below was originally handwritten.)

Protest Notice

Webbers Falls I.T. July 21st 1894

To Hon. E. E. Starr
    Treasurer Cherokee Nation

Dear Sir:

    This is to certify that I am separated from my husband John Watuck (Banty) and have been for more than a year last past. That he has wholly neglected to contribute to the support of myself or our 5 children. That I am obliged to care for and support said children and am the head of the family and duly appointed legal guardian of said child, and am alone entitled to draw the per capita strip money due myself and children, and you are hereby notified not to pay the same to anyone but myself or my order and I further protest against the payment of said money or any part thereof to any other person than E. S. Ellis to whom I have given an order to draw said money for me. The following are the names of my 5 children - Ice (or Cornelius) Polly (or Dora), Fannie, Lunie (or Luna) and Lily (or Lila) - Watuck - our english[sic] name is Banty - and I am known both as "Alice" and "Alsy".

    Witness my hand this 21st day of July 1894.

                                    her
                              Alice x Banty (or Watuck)
                                mark

Edward Kennedy ⎫
                     ⎬ Witness
Albertus Parker ⎭

****

Starr Roll 1894

We, the undersigned citizens of the Cherokee Nation, by right of Cherokee blood, do hereby acknowledge to have received of E. E. Starr, National Treasurer of the Cherokee Nation, the sums set opposite our names respectively, in full of our shares in the per capita distribution authorized by an Act of the National Council, dated ____MAY 3 1894____ 1894.

	Names of Head, and Members of Families	Amount	To Whom Paid	Witness to Payment	Remarks
2330	Watuck John W	265.70	HJ Vann	CA Thompson	Vann
2331	" Alsie				
2332	" Ice				
2333	" Pollie				EC Ellis
2334	" Fannie				
2335	" Cornelius				
2336	" Lilly	1594.20	E S Ellis	CA Thompson	
2337	Wilkerson Katie				
2338	" Walter				
2339	" John	797.10	Katie Wilkerson	L B Bell	
2340	Wilkerson Frost	265.70 *order*	PJ Scales	Henry Eiffert	PJ Scales
2341	Wartuck[sic] Nancy	265.70	Nancy Watuck	L B Bell	
2342	Wilkerson Ace DEAD.	265.70	PJ Scales	CA Thompson	Scales
2343	Wilkerson Whilby				
2344	" Ellen				
2345	" Estellar				
2346	" Lona DEAD.				
2347	" Daniel				
2348	" Mary DEAD.				
2349	" Osa				
2350	Winpigle Bessie	2125.60	Whilby Wilkerson	L B Bell	
2351	Wilson Finny				
2352	" Ella				
2353	" William	797.10	Finny Wilson	L B Bell	
2354	Wilkerson Ace				
2355	" Margaret				
2356	" Cordelia	*order (for 9)*			
2357	" Robert				
2358	" Spencer				R Blackstone
2359	" Daniel				

Starr Roll 1894

We, the undersigned citizens of the Cherokee Nation, by right of Cherokee blood, do hereby acknowledge to have received of E. E. Starr, National Treasurer of the Cherokee Nation, the sums set opposite our names respectively, in full of our shares in the per capita distribution authorized by an Act of the National Council, dated ___MAY 3 1894___ 1894.

#	Names of Head, and Members of Families	Amount	To Whom Paid	Witness to Payment	Remarks
2360	" Luster				
2361	" Carnelius DEAD				
2362	" Margaret Jr	~~2391.30~~			
2363	" John H. DEAD				
2364	" Annie DEAD	2922.70	R E Blackstone	CA Thompson	
2365	Woodard George				
2366	" Martha				
2367	" Sarah				
2368	" Nannie				
2369	" John				R E Blackstone
2370	" Annie				
2371	" Arlie				
2372	" Mary				
2373	" Lizzie	2391.30	R E Blackstone	CA Thompson	
2374	Wyly Josaphine[sic]				
2375	Phillips Henry				
2376	" Julias				
2377	" Charles				
2378	" Alice				
2379	" Willie	1594.20	Josephine Wyley	L B Bell	
2380	Woodard Susan	265.70	O Blackman	Henry Eiffert	
2381	Woods Mattie				
2382	" John				
2383	" Laura	797.10	John West	Henry Eiffert	
2384	Watson Adda C.				
2385	" Adda Jr.				
2386	" Lucy				
2387	" Drucilla				W N Martin
2388	" Nathaniel				
2389	Lester Lular P.	1594.20	W N Martin	CA Thompson	
2390	Williams Nancy D	265.70	G W Williams	L B Bell	

Starr Roll 1894

We, the undersigned citizens of the Cherokee Nation, by right of Cherokee blood, do hereby acknowledge to have received of E. E. Starr, National Treasurer of the Cherokee Nation, the sums set opposite our names respectively, in full of our shares in the per capita distribution authorized by an Act of the National Council, dated _____MAY 3 1894_____ 1894.

	Names of Head, and Members of Families	Amount	To Whom Paid	Witness to Payment	Remarks
2391	Watkins John	#1			B F Fite
2392	" Lucy	#1			
2393	" Joel M.	797.10 #1	Bartow Fite	CA Thompson	
2394	Wicket Newt	265.70	Newt Wicket	L B Bell	
2395	Watts Jacob				
2396	" Nannie				W.N. Martin
2397	" Mary				
2398	" John	1062.80	W N Martin	CA Thompson	
2399	Wicket Ophelia	265.70	Ophelia Wicket	L B Bell	
2400	Wyche John W.	265.70	~~Ophelia Wicket~~ H C Lowery	~~L B Bell~~ Henry Eiffert	
2401	Wells James M.				J.F. McClellan
2402	" Charles H.	531.40 order		CA Thompson	
2403	Yount Mary				
2404	" Sarah	531.40 order	N S Drake	CA Thompson	N S Drake
2405	Zufall Maggie Sr				
2406	" George Jr				
2407	" Pearl				
2408	" Otto				
2409	" Maggie Jr.				
2410	" Benjamin				
2411	" Grace				
2412	" Herbert	2125.60	Maggie Zufall Sr	L B Bell	
2413	Zufall Lewis	265.70	Maggie Zufall	L B Bell	
2414	Zufall Nannie				
2415	" Roy				
2416	" John				
2417	" Irenna				
2418	" Mattie	1328.50	John Bertholf	Henry Eiffert	

Starr Roll 1894

Tahlequah, Ind. Ter., *June 1st,* 189 4.

I, C. J. Harris, Principal Chief, and I, E. E. Starr, Treasurer, of the Cherokee Nation, Do hereby certify that the foregoing enrollment of Cherokees by blood, resident in Canadian District, is a correct transcript from the original census authorized by the Act of the National Council, approved May 15th, 1893, and that the number ascertained to participate in the pre-capita distribution provided for by the Act of the National Council, approved May 3rd, 1894, is 2418.

Attest.
Seal of the Cherokee Nation.

C. J. Harris
Principal Chief.

E. E. Starr
Treasurer.

****

Cooweescoowee *(District)*

Starr Roll 1894

We, the undersigned citizens of the Cherokee Nation, by right of Cherokee blood, do hereby acknowledge to have received of E. E. Starr, National Treasurer of the Cherokee Nation, the sums set opposite our names respectively, in full of our shares in the per capita distribution authorized by an Act of the National Council, dated ___MAY 3 1894___ 1894.

Names of Head, and Members of Families	Amount	To Whom Paid	Witness to Payment	Remarks
27 Audd Flora				
28 " Coody	*(Any other information given is covered*			
29 " Clare	*by an extra piece of paper.)*			
30 " Mary				
31 " Clyde				
32 Adair Wm P.				J.C.H.
33 " Maggie	order			
34 " David J.	797.10	J C Hogan	Henry Eiffert	Check
35 Archer Mary F.				
36 " Charlotte	531.40	F.W. Mayes	G W Benge	
37 Allison John				
38 " Willie				
39 " Elmer R				
40 " James	order			
41 " John				
42 " Mary				
43 " Una	1859.90	J C Hogan	Henry Eiffert	
44 Adair Walter T.				
45 " Fannie				
46 " Joseph F				
47 " Lola D.				
48 " Walter T. (Jr)	1328.50	J.F. Adair	G W Benge	
49 Anderson Nannie E.				J.C.H.
50 " Austin				
51 " Nellie				
52 " Rena	1062.80	J C Hogan	Henry Eiffert	Check
53 Allen Susan				
54 " William	531.40	Noah Allen	G W Benge	

Starr Roll 1894

We, the undersigned citizens of the Cherokee Nation, by right of Cherokee blood, do hereby acknowledge to have received of E. E. Starr, National Treasurer of the Cherokee Nation, the sums set opposite our names respectively, in full of our shares in the per capita distribution authorized by an Act of the National Council, dated ___MAY 3 1894___ 1894.

Names of Head, and Members of Families	Amount	To Whom Paid	Witness to Payment	Remarks
55 Adair Edward A.				
56 " Donnie				
57 " Patton A.	797.10	E.A. Adair	G W Benge	
58 Adair Virgil H.				
59 " Viola	531.40	V.H. Adair	G W Benge	
~~Arnold Jennie O.~~				Enrolled with Ivsie Carr Mother
60 Alloway Delilah				
61 " Katie				
62 " William				
63 " Salina				
64 " Belle				
65 " Leroy	1594.20	C C Alloway	L B Bell	
66 Ahshutz Mary	265.70	Mary Anshutz	G W Benge	
67 Atkins Martha	265.70	Martha J Atkins	L B Bell	
68 Alberty Geo. W.	265.70	Wm Alberty Adm	L B Bell	
69 " Emma				
70 " David				
71 " Elnora				
72 " Frank	1328.50	Wm Alberty	J.C. Starr	
73 " Mary	~~1594.20~~	William Alberty Admin	L B Bell	
74 Arledge Sarah				
75 " Addie				
76 " Maggie				
77 " John				
78 " Maud				
79 " Clarie	1594.20	Sarah Arledge	J.C. Starr	
80 Alberty William	265.70	Wm Alberty	L B Bell	
81 Alberty Eli	265.70	Eli Alberty	J.C. Starr	

Starr Roll 1894

We, the undersigned citizens of the Cherokee Nation, by right of Cherokee blood, do hereby acknowledge to have received of E. E. Starr, National Treasurer of the Cherokee Nation, the sums set opposite our names respectively, in full of our shares in the per capita distribution authorized by an Act of the National Council, dated ___MAY 3 1894___ 1894.

	Names of Head, and Members of Families	Amount	To Whom Paid	Witness to Payment	Remarks
82	Arnold Victoria				
83	" Myrtle				
84	" Cecil				
85	" Georgia				
86	" Mary				
87	" Herbert				
88	" Halbert				
89	" Joseph	2125.60	C. W. Pool	G W Benge	
90	Adams Carrie F.				
91	" Leo D.	order			CM London & Co
92	" Wm H.	797.10	CM London & Co	Henry Eiffert	(Illegible)
	~~Armstrong Frank~~				Enrolled in Nancy
	~~" Albert~~				Duglass[sic] family
93	Adair Robt L.				
94	" Minnie	531.40	R.S. Adair	G W Benge	

****

(The letter below was inserted in between the log book pages. Originally handwritten and typed as given.)

                                Vinita IT
                                July 20-94

To The Hon E E Starr Treasurer

                    Dear Sir

This is to certify that I gave my order to J S Thomason to draw my shear in the per capita payment (Strip Money) and he is the only man I traided with on order my money

                              Respt
                       Joe Hilderbrand

****

Starr Roll 1894

We, the undersigned citizens of the Cherokee Nation, by right of Cherokee blood, do hereby acknowledge to have received of E. E. Starr, National Treasurer of the Cherokee Nation, the sums set opposite our names respectively, in full of our shares in the per capita distribution authorized by an Act of the National Council, dated ___MAY 3 1894___ 1894.

	Names of Head, and Members of Families	Amount	To Whom Paid	Witness to Payment	Remarks
95	Adair Rollan K.				
96	" Rachel T.				
97	" Charles B.				
98	" Robert N.				
99	" David W.				
100	" Susan T.				
101	" Sadie K.				R.K. Adair guardian
102	Crutchfield Jimmie				
103	" Alice	2391.30	R.K. Adair	G W Benge	
104	Akin Fannie C.				
105	" Reuby L.				
106	" Willie M.				
107	" Vinita J.				
108	" Walter S.				
109	" Ulrich R.	1594.20	J.H. Akins	G W Benge	
110	Armor Annie				
111	" Daisy				
112	" Norma				
113	" Myrtle				
114	" George	1328.50	Annie Armor	G W Benge	
115	Armstrong Frank	7025 265.70	J. S. Thomason	G W Benge	on order
116	Andrews Callie D.	order			
117	" Mary E.	531.40	L B Bell	G W Benge	on order
118	Anderson Mabel W.				
119	" Gladys				
120	" Rebecca	797.10	J.C. Anderson	G W Benge	
121	Ar-loo-lee John				
122	" Eliza				
123	" Susie	797.10	John Ar loo lee	G W Benge	
	~~Ashbrook Sadie~~				Registered with
	~~" Clarence~~				Sarah P. Nelso

Starr Roll 1894

We, the undersigned citizens of the Cherokee Nation, by right of Cherokee blood, do hereby acknowledge to have received of E. E. Starr, National Treasurer of the Cherokee Nation, the sums set opposite our names respectively, in full of our shares in the per capita distribution authorized by an Act of the National Council, dated ___MAY 3 1894___ 1894.

#	Names of Head, and Members of Families	Amount	To Whom Paid	Witness to Payment	Remarks
124	Allen Mary				
125	" Myrah	531.40	D.N. Allen	G W Benge	
126	Allen Joe C.	265.70	D.N. Allen	G W Benge	
127	Anderson Addie				
128	" Rachel C.	531.40	Addie Anderson	G W Benge	
129	Alberty Cynthia	D1522			
130	" George				
131	" Lizzie				
132	Musgrove Ellen	D1523			
133	" Willie	D1524 1328.50	Jas T Musgrove	L B Bell	
134	Allen Susan E.				
135	" Henry				
136	" Rebecca				
137	" John				
138	" Jennie	1328.50	Susan E Allen	L B Bell	
139	Allen Lula	265.70 ~~4972~~	Lula Allen	L B Bell	
140	Allton Susie				
141	" David C.				
142	" Eliza B.				
143	" Percy	1062.80	Joseph Allton	L B Bell	
144	Adair Dora S	order 265.70 ~~D1470~~	C W Turner	~~L G Starr~~	On order Creek Card No 2188. Enrollment approved by Secy of Interior March 13 1907 copy on file
	~~Archer Florence~~				Allottee
	~~" Mattie~~				"
145	" John E.	265.70	Florence Archer	L B Bell	ok
146	Adair Robt E.	order			First N. B
147	" Ida L.	531.40	1s National Bank Vinita	Henry Eiffert	Check
148	Anderson W^m	265.70	Wm Anderson	G W Benge	

Starr Roll 1894

We, the undersigned citizens of the Cherokee Nation, by right of Cherokee blood, do hereby acknowledge to have received of E. E. Starr, National Treasurer of the Cherokee Nation, the sums set opposite our names respectively, in full of our shares in the per capita distribution authorized by an Act of the National Council, dated ___MAY 3 1894___ 1894.

Names of Head, and Members of Families	Amount	To Whom Paid	Witness to Payment	Remarks
149 Atkins Lizzie	~~10733~~ ~~D584~~			
150 " Authur	~~D584~~ 10733 531.40	W^m V Carey	G W Benge	
151 Alston Sarah C				
152 " William	531.40	G.W. Cleland	G W Benge	
153 Bird Emily				
154 Eddie Watts[sic]				
155 Lucy Watts[sic]				
156 Pearl Bird[sic]	1062.80	Emily Bird	L B Bell	
157 Bryan Ella P.				
158 " Roy V.	531.40	S.A. Bryan	G W Benge	
159 Brown Walter P.				
160 " Nannie				
161 " Carrie				
162 " Bill				
163 " John G.				
164 " Emmet V ⎫ Twins				
165 " Kiowa ⎭	1859.90	Nannie Brown	G W Benge	
166 Buffington Coo-ie				
167 " Nannie				
168 " Carrie R.	797.10	Cooie Buffington	G W Benge	
169 Booth Alice				
170 " Liddie				
171 " Grover G.	797.10	F.M. Booth	G W Benge	
172 Bendura Eddie	order 265.70	W.T. Whitaker	JC Starr	Whitaker order Sarah Livingston
173 Barney Felix	order 265.70	C.W. Pool	G W Benge	on order C W Pool
174 Bendura John	order 265.70	Mills	Henry Eiffert	WR Mills check
175 Beck Samuel	order 265.70	J.S. Thomason	L B Bell Aug 28,94	No 68621 Check

Starr Roll 1894

We, the undersigned citizens of the Cherokee Nation, by right of Cherokee blood, do hereby acknowledge to have received of E. E. Starr, National Treasurer of the Cherokee Nation, the sums set opposite our names respectively, in full of our shares in the per capita distribution authorized by an Act of the National Council, dated ____MAY 3 1894____ 1894.

	Names of Head, and Members of Families	Amount	To Whom Paid	Witness to Payment	Remarks
176	Bradshaw Ellen				
177	" Charley				
178	" Sophia	797.10	JW Bradshaw	G W Benge	
179	Ballard James				
180	" Henry T.	531.40	James Ballard	G W Benge	
	~~Baugh Joel L.~~		On Lottee Roll		
181	Baugh Dollie				
182	" Lotta				
183	" Joel L. (Jr.)	797.10	Joel L Baugh	G W Benge	
184	Bledsoe Belle				
185	" Henry W				
186	" Sallie M.	797.10	Bell Bledsoe	G W Benge	
187	Ballard Henry C.				
188	" Alma M.	531.40	H.C. Ballard	G W Benge	
189	Bryant Joseph V.				
190	" James A.				
191	" Vinnie				
192	" Leonidas				
193	" Jessie	1328.50	J.V. Bryant	G W Benge	
194	Butler Robt E.				
195	" Carrie L.	531.40 ~~2213~~	Carrie L Butler	G W Benge	
196	Brown Thomas	order			Hogan
197	" Luther	531.40	J.C. Hogan	L B Bell	
198	Butler ~~Mary~~ Mannie G.				
199	" Lizzie D.				
200	" Fount G.	797.10	M.G. Butler	G W Benge	
201	Bard Daniel	265.70	Daniel Bard	G W Benge	

Starr Roll 1894

We, the undersigned citizens of the Cherokee Nation, by right of Cherokee blood, do hereby acknowledge to have received of E. E. Starr, National Treasurer of the Cherokee Nation, the sums set opposite our names respectively, in full of our shares in the per capita distribution authorized by an Act of the National Council, dated ___MAY 3 1894___ 1894.

#	Names of Head, and Members of Families	Amount	To Whom Paid	Witness to Payment	Remarks
202	Barnwell Elizabeth C				
203	" Steven				
204	" Middleton				
205	" Carlton	1062.80	E.C. Barnwell	G W Benge	
206	Baker Maggie				J.C.H.
207	" Polly J.				
208	" John O.	*order*			
209	" Joseph F.	1062.80	J C Hogan	Henry Eiffert	check
210	Brown Annie	265.70	Annie Brown	L B Bell	
211	" Martha A.	265.70	Henry Eiffert	S.W. Mayfield	pd on order Aug 21-95
212	Blake Georgia				
213	" Jennie A.				
214	" Nita E.	797.10	Samuel C. Blake	J.C. Starr	
215	Battles Addie				W.T.W or J.C.H.
216	" Foster				J.C.H.
217	" Stephen		D 2631		
218	" Bruce	*order*	D 2632		
219	" Daisy				
220	" William		D 2633		
221	" Fox	1859.90	Addie Battles	G W Benge	
222	Battles Fannie				
223	" Addie				
224	" Zedie	797.10	Addie Battles	G W Benge	
225	Baugh Robt L.				
226	" Monna J.	531.40	R.L. Baugh	G W Benge	
227	Boudinot Samson	*order*			Neilson
228	" Susan				
229	" Nannie				
230	" Sallie	1062.80	F.A. Neilson	J.C. Starr	Check on order

Starr Roll 1894

We, the undersigned citizens of the Cherokee Nation, by right of Cherokee blood, do hereby acknowledge to have received of E. E. Starr, National Treasurer of the Cherokee Nation, the sums set opposite our names respectively, in full of our shares in the per capita distribution authorized by an Act of the National Council, dated _____MAY 3 1894_____ 1894.

#	Names of Head, and Members of Families	Amount	To Whom Paid	Witness to Payment	Remarks
231	Burr Blanche				J.C.H.
232	" James W.				
233	" John W.				
234	" Jessie E.	*order*			
235	" Etta				
236	" Alice				
237	" Harris				
238	" Samuel	2125.60	J C Hogan	Henry Eiffert	*check*
239	Brown Susan L.				
240	" Margaret C.				
241	" Florence R.				
242	" James M.	1062.80	S.L. Brown	G W Benge	
243	Bean Watt	265.70 [269]	J C Hogan	Henry Eiffert	J.C.H. *check*
244	Brown John B.				
245	" Susan F.	*order*	D2627		
246	" Ebbin		D2628		
247	" Nathie		D2627		
248	" Amos		D2627		
249	" Ada	1594.20	C.W. Pool	G W Benge	*on order*
250	Barnett Dora S	*order*			H. Langley
251	" Mary B.				
252	" Annie F.	797.10	H. Langley	J.C. Starr	
253	Barthell Mollie				
254	" Annie				
255	" Frank	797.10	Frank Barthell	G W Benge	
256	Brown Celia	265.70	Wm Brown	G W Benge	
257	Blythe James	265.70	James Blythe	G W Benge	

Starr Roll 1894

We, the undersigned citizens of the Cherokee Nation, by right of Cherokee blood, do hereby acknowledge to have received of E. E. Starr, National Treasurer of the Cherokee Nation, the sums set opposite our names respectively, in full of our shares in the per capita distribution authorized by an Act of the National Council, dated ___MAY 3 1894___ 1894.

	Names of Head, and Members of Families	Amount	To Whom Paid	Witness to Payment	Remarks
258	Bachtel Mary				
259	" Daniel				
260	" Odus				
261	" Elzy				
262	Habich Lula	1328.50	Mary Bachtel	G W Benge	
263	Ballinger Julia A.				
264	" Ethel				
265	" Thos B.	797.10	Bird B Ballinger	G W Benge	
266	Blair John	~~265~~.70 order	J.S. Thomason	G W Benge	on order
267	Beaver George	265.70	Geo Beaver	Ed D Hicks	Order to F.A. Nei~~EWB~~
	Boggs (Illegible)				Registered in Canada
268	Blackwell Rosa				
269	" King David				
270	" Soloman				
271	Campbell Delora	1062.80	Rosa Blackwell	G W Benge	
272	Brown Sallie E.				
273	" Patsey M.				
274	" Mollie V.				
275	" James M.				
276	" Edner M.				
277	" Hiram C.	1594.20	Sallie E. Brown	G W Benge	
278	Brown Nancy L				
279	" Albert B.				
280	" Effie M.				
281	" Nora H.	1062.80	N L Brown	L B Bell	
282	Brown Ellis P.				
283	" Frances E.				
284	" Mary E.				
285	" Beatrice	1062.80	F.E. Brown	G W Benge	

Starr Roll 1894

We, the undersigned citizens of the Cherokee Nation, by right of Cherokee blood, do hereby acknowledge to have received of E. E. Starr, National Treasurer of the Cherokee Nation, the sums set opposite our names respectively, in full of our shares in the per capita distribution authorized by an Act of the National Council, dated _____MAY 3 1894_____ 1894.

#	Names of Head, and Members of Families	Amount	To Whom Paid	Witness to Payment	Remarks
286	Bussey Dottie	order			F.A. Neilson
287	" Dava				
288	" Frankie				
289	" Freddie	1062.80	F.A. Neilson	J.C. Starr	check on order
290	Bussey Maud F	order			Neilson
291	" Johnnie				
292	" Emma	797.10	F.A. Neilson	J.C. Starr	Check on order
293	Bonny Samuel	265.70	WE Halwell	Henry Eiffert	WE Halwell
294	Blackbird Lizzie	265.70	F.A. Neilson	J.C. Starr	check order
295	Boyd Jane				
296	" S Samuel E.	531.40	Jane Boyd	L B Bell	
297	Burgess Jack	5236			
298	" Cora				
299	" Alena	order			J M Hall
300	" Daniel	1062.80	J M Hall	Henry Eiffert	
301	Burgess W^m	5233			
302	" Coo-wa				
303	" Benjamin				
304	" Mart	1062.80	Wm Burgess	G W Benge	
305	Burgess John	order			F.A. Neilson
306	" Hettie		D2629		
307	" Mattie		D2629		
308	Sunday Nancy		F A Neilson	Henry Eiffert	Nancy Sunday drew money in Creek Nation
309	Bougher Florence		order withdrawn by P.		W.C. Patton
310	" Charles	order			
311	" William R.	797.10	Florence Bougher	G.W. Benge	
312	Blackbird Katie	order 265.70	F.A. Neilson	J.C. Starr	Check Neilson on order

Starr Roll 1894

We, the undersigned citizens of the Cherokee Nation, by right of Cherokee blood, do hereby acknowledge to have received of E. E. Starr, National Treasurer of the Cherokee Nation, the sums set opposite our names respectively, in full of our shares in the per capita distribution authorized by an Act of the National Council, dated ___MAY 3 1894___ 1894.

Names of Head, and Members of Families	Amount	To Whom Paid	Witness to Payment	Remarks
313 Brown Tillie	order			Neilson
314 " Minnie L.				
315 " Josephine				
316 " Thos W.	1062.80	F.A. Neilson	J.C. Starr	Check on order
317 Brown Lydia				
318 " Louisa	531.40	Lydia Brown	L B Bell	
319 Buchannan Mary				
320 Lenard, James	531.40	Wm Buchanan	G W Benge	
321 Blythe Elijah				
322 " Ninna	531.40	Elijah Blythe	G W Benge	
323 Brown Rufus				
324 " Lillie	order			W C Rogers
325 " Bessie May	797.10	W C Rogers	L B Bell	
326 Bivins David T.				
327 " Walter M.	4247			
328 " Catherine G.	797.10	Waliam[sic] Taylor by WE Sunday	L B Bell	
329 Brady Geo W.	5268			
330 " Mary	5268			
331 " Frank	5268			
332 " Lizzie	5268 / 1062.80	Edeth[sic] Brady	G W Benge	
333 Byrd Jane				
334 " Henry				
335 " Daisy	797.10	Edward Byrd	G W Benge	
336 Baker Elizabeth				
337 " Susan E.				
338 " Sarah A.				
339 " Webster C.	1062.80	Jno H Baker	G W Benge	

Starr Roll 1894

We, the undersigned citizens of the Cherokee Nation, by right of Cherokee blood, do hereby acknowledge to have received of E. E. Starr, National Treasurer of the Cherokee Nation, the sums set opposite our names respectively, in full of our shares in the per capita distribution authorized by an Act of the National Council, dated ___MAY 3 1894___ 1894.

Names of Head, and Members of Families	Amount	To Whom Paid	Witness to Payment	Remarks
340 Blair Emma				
341 " Min				
342 " Maude				
343 Harlan Jessie	1062.80	Emma Blair	L B Bell	
344 Brown Rebecca				
345 " Robt L.	531.40	Rebecca Brown	L B Bell	
346 Bennett Joseph				
347 " Roxie				
348 " Mary E.				
349 " Glenn				
350 " Marion	1328.50	J H Bennett	G W Benge	
351 Bibles Margaret				
352 " Sallie				
353 " Wiley				
354 " Henry				
355 " Edward				
356 " James	1594.20	C.W. Pool	G W Benge	on order
357 Bozeman Lizzie	265.70	W E Bozeman	G W Benge	
358 Bard Laura M.				
359 " Thos D.				
360 " Emily L.				
361 " Robt B Ross.	1062.80	L.M. Bard	G W Benge	
362 Bard Elizabeth H	265.70	E.H. Bard	G W Benge	
363 Bard Sarah B.	265.70	S.B. Bard	G W Benge	
364 Bard Laura M.	265.70	L.M. Bard	G W Benge	
365 Bard James R.	265.70	L.M. Bard	G W Benge	

Starr Roll 1894

We, the undersigned citizens of the Cherokee Nation, by right of Cherokee blood, do hereby acknowledge to have received of E. E. Starr, National Treasurer of the Cherokee Nation, the sums set opposite our names respectively, in full of our shares in the per capita distribution authorized by an Act of the National Council, dated ___MAY 3 1894___ 1894.

	Names of Head, and Members of Families	Amount	To Whom Paid	Witness to Payment	Remarks
366	Bankhead John L.				
367	" Frank G.				
368	" Elizabeth				
369	" Unise A.				
370	" Joel T.				
371	" Jno H	1594.20	John Bankhead	G W Benge	
372	Bankhead Geo W.				
373	" Frader				
374	" Mary				
375	" John				
376	" Charles				
377	" Susie				
378	" Lottie				
379	" John H. *Eva*	2125.60	G W Bankhead	G W Benge	*See* (illegible)
380	Brink Lidia				
381	" Georgia				
382	" Mary				
383	" Charles				
384	" Albert	1328.50	M.J. Brink	G W Benge	
385	Bell John M.				
386	" Nannie C.				
387	" Emma W.				
388	" Ida L.				
389	" Andrew L.				
390	" Etta	1594.20	John M. Bell	G W Benge	
391	Bray John	265.70	J S Thomason	Henry Eiffert	
392	Bibles Jess	} order	*Walsh & Shutt on order of Nixon*		*C.T. Nixon*
392 1/2	" Lewis	531.40	C.T. Nixon	G W Benge	*on order*

103

Starr Roll 1894

We, the undersigned citizens of the Cherokee Nation, by right of Cherokee blood, do hereby acknowledge to have received of E. E. Starr, National Treasurer of the Cherokee Nation, the sums set opposite our names respectively, in full of our shares in the per capita distribution authorized by an Act of the National Council, dated ___MAY 3 1894___ 1894.

	Names of Head, and Members of Families	Amount	To Whom Paid	Witness to Payment	Remarks
393	Bibles Lewis				
394	" James P.				
395	" Cora B.				
396	" Lewis A.				
397	" Cris R.				
398	" Wm G.	1594.20	Lewis Bibles	L B Bell	
399	Bibles Arthur	265.70	Arthur Bibles	G W Benge	
400	Breedon Martha				
401	" Sarah	531.40	Martha Breedon	L B Bell	
402	Bean Eveline				
403	" Annie				
404	" Estah				
405	" Deverre				
406	" Ward				
407	" Henry				
408	" Lucy				
409	" Mamie	2125.60	Eveline Bean	G W Benge	
410	Beck David				
411	" Ellis				
412	" Ausborn				
413	" Wesley				
414	" Dave (Jr)				
415	" Martha				
416	" Walter				
417	" George	2125.60	David Beck	G W Benge	
418	Byrd Elizabeth				
419	" Henry A				
420	" Randolph S.				
421	" Mary E.				
422	" Leroy A.				
423	" Prince E.	1594.20	Elizabeth Byrd	G W Benge	

Starr Roll 1894

We, the undersigned citizens of the Cherokee Nation, by right of Cherokee blood, do hereby acknowledge to have received of E. E. Starr, National Treasurer of the Cherokee Nation, the sums set opposite our names respectively, in full of our shares in the per capita distribution authorized by an Act of the National Council, dated ___MAY 3 1894___ 1894.

Names of Head, and Members of Families	Amount	To Whom Paid	Witness to Payment	Remarks
424 Branson Emma	order			J.C.H.
424 1/2 " Attie	531.40	J C Hogan	Henry Eiffert	check
425 Boynton Nancy E	~~order~~ 265.70	F.A. Neilson	J.C. Starr	Check on order Neilson
426 Ballard Wm R.	265.70	J E Campbell	L B Bell	
427 Ball Missouri A.				
428 " Alfred C.				
429 " Julia C.				
430 " John C.				
431 " James T.				
432 " Rachel A.				
433 " Lydia J.				
434 " Mary J.				
435 " Wm E.	2391.30	J.S. Ball	G W Benge	
436 Beck John H.				C.M.B.
437 " Harvey M.	order			
438 " Gertrude B.				
439 " Walter Ray				
440 " William A.	1328.50	C M Ball	Henry Eiffert	check
441 Brown Geo Hammer				
442 " Pearl H.				
443 " Anna H.				
444 " Ethel H.	1062.80	Geo H. Brown	G W Benge	
445 Brown Lizzie H.				
446 Roberson Arthur				
447 " Freddie				
448 " Nora				
449 " George				
450 " Lulu Lola	1594.20	Lizzie H Brown	L B Bell	

Starr Roll 1894

We, the undersigned citizens of the Cherokee Nation, by right of Cherokee blood, do hereby acknowledge to have received of E. E. Starr, National Treasurer of the Cherokee Nation, the sums set opposite our names respectively, in full of our shares in the per capita distribution authorized by an Act of the National Council, dated ___MAY 3 1894___ 1894.

Names of Head, and Members of Families	Amount	To Whom Paid	Witness to Payment	Remarks
451 Brown Rachel H.				
452 Nave Francis				
453 Roberson Dora	797.10	G.W. Linington	G W Benge	
454 Brown Mary H	order			
455 Little George				J J Barndollar
456 " Martha Ella				
457 " Lulu Belle	1062.80	J J Barndollar	Henry Eiffert	
458 Brown Sila H.	order			
459 " William				J J Barndollar
460 " George	797.10	J J Barndollar	Henry Eiffert	
461 Brown Sarah Ellen	265.70	Sarah E. Brown	G W Benge	
462 " Joana	265.70	Lizie[sic] Hall	G W Benge	
463 Ziegler Mary	265.70	Sarah E Brown	G W Benge	
464 Blythe Mary				
465 Madden Ora	~~D642~~	9780		
466 " Minnie	797.10	Mary Blythe	G W Benge	
467 Burns[sic] Bernie D.	265.70	Sam Burnes	G W Benge	
468 Brown Ruth E.				Wm Martin
469 Bigelow Wm	order	Ruth E Brown		
470 " Emma	797.10	~~Wm Martin~~	J.C. Starr	Check on order
471 Bone Ida				
472 " Ruth Jane	265.70	Ida Bone	G W Benge	
473 Bibles Geo B.	265.70	J E Campbell	L B Bell	
474 Bibles John	order			Geo Bibles
475 " Rebecca	531.40	John Bibles	Henry Eiffert	

Starr Roll 1894

We, the undersigned citizens of the Cherokee Nation, by right of Cherokee blood, do hereby acknowledge to have received of E. E. Starr, National Treasurer of the Cherokee Nation, the sums set opposite our names respectively, in full of our shares in the per capita distribution authorized by an Act of the National Council, dated ____MAY 3 1894____ 1894.

Names of Head, and Members of Families	Amount	To Whom Paid	Witness to Payment	Remarks
476 Bibles Wm C.				
477 " Delila				
478 " Clem				
479 " Bessie Ann	1062.80	W^m C Bibles	L B Bell	
480 Bibles James T.				
481 " Mary				
482 " Eva M.				
483 " George B.				
484 " Josephine	1328.50	J.T. Bibles	L B Bell	
485 Bibles Wm H.				
486 " Jno A.	4416			
487 " Wm T.	4415			
488 " Lizzie J.	1062.80	W^m H Bibles	L B Bell	
489 Bushyhead Delila	265.70	Delila Bushyhead	G W Benge	
490 Bushyhead Nancy	265.70	Nancy Bushyhead	G W Benge	
X= W E Quit here				
491 Bushyhead Wilson				
492 " Martha				
493 " Emma				
494 " Sarah				
495 " Ellen	1328.50	Wilson Bushyhead	L B Bell	
496 Bushyhead W^m				
497 " Charlotte				
498 " Isaac	797.10	Wilson Bushyhead	L B Bell	
499 Baker Eliza				
500 " Earl	531.40	M L Baker		
501 Baker Sallie E.				
502 " Minnie M.				
503 " Millie E.	797.10	W^m R Baker	L B Bell	

Starr Roll 1894

We, the undersigned citizens of the Cherokee Nation, by right of Cherokee blood, do hereby acknowledge to have received of E. E. Starr, National Treasurer of the Cherokee Nation, the sums set opposite our names respectively, in full of our shares in the per capita distribution authorized by an Act of the National Council, dated ___MAY 3 1894___ 1894.

Names of Head, and Members of Families	Amount	To Whom Paid	Witness to Payment	Remarks
504 Benge Charles O.	265.70	A.F. McCobb	J.C. Starr	
505 Bean Ton-yah	265.70 ~~Order~~	W E Sanders	Henry Eiffert	W.E. Sanders
506 Bushyhead Charley	265.70 ~~Order~~	F.A. Neilson	J.C. Starr	check Neilson
507 Bell Mattie M.				
508 " Dannel H.				
509 Stone Lelia				
510 " Foster	1062.80	Mattie Bell	L B Bell	
511 Beams Susan F.	265.780	Susan F Beams	L B Bell	
512 Bradshaw Emma F.	order			W.T.
513 " Ethel T.				
514 " Susan S.				
515 " Oscar				
516 " Eva L.				
517 " Jessie P.				
518 " Albert H.	1859.90	W T Whitaker	Henry Eiffert	Ck
519 Berry Fannie L.				
520 " Annie Marie	531.40	J B Cobb Jr.	G W Benge	
521 Brown Zenie	order			Neilson
522 " Ollie Belle				
523 " Patrie Ellen	797.10	F.A. Neilson	J.C. Starr	Check on order
524 Brady Ed	order			J M B
525 " Hettie	531.40	J.M. Boling	G W Benge	Check on order
526 Bigheart Alice	265.70	Keeler and Johnson	Henry Eiffert	check
527 Bigwood James				
528 " Arlena				
529 " Myrtle	797.10	James Bigwood	G W Benge	
530 Bigwood Lidy Jane	265.70	L.J. Bigwood	G W Benge	

Starr Roll 1894

We, the undersigned citizens of the Cherokee Nation, by right of Cherokee blood, do hereby acknowledge to have received of E. E. Starr, National Treasurer of the Cherokee Nation, the sums set opposite our names respectively, in full of our shares in the per capita distribution authorized by an Act of the National Council, dated ___MAY 3 1894___ 1894.

Names of Head, and Members of Families	Amount	To Whom Paid	Witness to Payment	Remarks
531 Bigwood James H.	265.70	J.H. Bigwood	G W Benge	
532 Bigwood Laura	265.70	Laura Bigwood	G W Benge	
~~Brooks Samuel~~				*Enrolled with Katur[sic] Wolf*
533 Badgett Mamie				
534 " Ross				
535 " Mary	797.10	W.R. Badgett	G W Benge	
536 Bivin[sic] Sophronia	265.70	S Bivins	G W Benge	
537 Bond Francis L.				
538 Brown James H.				
539 Bond Ed S.				
540 Bond Wm P.	1062.80	S.W. Bond	G W Benge	
541 Bennett Mary	265.70	Mary Bennett	G W Benge	
542 Blythe Jemima S.	265.70	J.S. Blythe	G W Benge	
543 Blosser Joseph D.	265.70	Eliza Lang	G W Benge	
544 Burns Etta H.				
545 " Lillie D.	531.40	Sam Burnes	G W Benge	
546 Browning Mary J.				
547 " Fannie M.				
548 " Robert E.	797.10	M.J. Browning	G W Benge	
549 Brown W^m	*order*			
550 " Richard				
551 " Eddie				
552 " Herman				
553 " Emily	1328.50	J.S. Thomason	L B Bell	

Starr Roll 1894

We, the undersigned citizens of the Cherokee Nation, by right of Cherokee blood, do hereby acknowledge to have received of E. E. Starr, National Treasurer of the Cherokee Nation, the sums set opposite our names respectively, in full of our shares in the per capita distribution authorized by an Act of the National Council, dated ____MAY 3 1894____ 1894.

#	Names of Head, and Members of Families	Amount	To Whom Paid	Witness to Payment	Remarks
554	Boot William	265.70	Nellie Boot	G W Benge	wife
555	Beck Rachel				
556	Daugherty Dave *(Dora)*	531.40	Rachel Beck	G W Benge	
557	Buzzard Betsey	265.70	Betsy Buzzard	G W Benge	
558	Billingslea Jennette	265.70	Frank Billingslea	G W Benge	
559	" Mack	265.70	Mack Billingslea *1020.9*	G W Benge	
560	" Frank				
561	" Helen				
562	" Willie				
563	" Joe	1062.80	Frank Billingslea	G W Benge	
564	Butler Mattie				
565	" Frank	531.40	Mattie Butler	G W Benge	
566	Brock Ollie				
567	" Lewis C.	531.40	P.G. Brock	G W Benge	
568	Barrett Sophronia				
569	" Bessie	531.40	John Barrett	Henry Eiffert	
570	Barrett Lee	265.70	John Barrett	Henry Eiffert	
571	Barrett John	265.70	John Barrett	Henry Eiffert	
572	Barnes Flora L.				
573	Mandy L Barnes	531.40	Flora L. Barnes	G W Benge	
574	Beck Thos	*order*			J.S. Thomason
575	" Sarah	531.40	J.S. Thomason	G W Benge	on order
576	Brackett Margaret				
577	" Bessie S.	531.40	Henry Eiffert	G W Benge	
578	Bacon Harvey	*order* 265.70	Harvey Bacon	G W Benge	

110

Starr Roll 1894

We, the undersigned citizens of the Cherokee Nation, by right of Cherokee blood, do hereby acknowledge to have received of E. E. Starr, National Treasurer of the Cherokee Nation, the sums set opposite our names respectively, in full of our shares in the per capita distribution authorized by an Act of the National Council, dated ___MAY 3 1894___ 1894.

	Names of Head, and Members of Families	Amount	To Whom Paid	Witness to Payment	Remarks
579	Bread Samuel	265.70	J.S. Thomason	G W Benge	on order
580	Blaylock John				
581	" Susan	531.40	J.S. Thomason	G W Benge	on order E Ellis
582	Blaylock Charles	265.70	E.S. Ellis	G W Benge	on order
583	Brewer William	265.70	William Brewer	G W Benge	
584	Brown Wm P.	265.70	W.P. Brown	G W Benge	
585	Brown Thos	265.70	W H Brown	G W Benge	children of Wm H. Brown
586	" Ida	265.70	Ida Brown	G W Benge	
587	" Ada				
588	" Sarah				
589	" Frank				
590	" Mary				
591	" Nannie	1328.50	W.H. Brown	G W Benge	
592	Brown Larkin				
593	" Martha A.	531.40	Larkin Brown	G W Benge	
594	Barker Mary A.				
595	" Josie G.				
596	" Ethel G.				
597	" Eva				
598	" Sequoyah				
599	" Artemus B.	1594.20	M.A. Barker	G W Benge	
600	Bean Edward				
601	" Laura				
602	" Eliza				
603	" Laura				
604	" Dot				
605	" Tot	1594.20	Edward Bean	G W Benge	

Starr Roll 1894

We, the undersigned citizens of the Cherokee Nation, by right of Cherokee blood, do hereby acknowledge to have received of E. E. Starr, National Treasurer of the Cherokee Nation, the sums set opposite our names respectively, in full of our shares in the per capita distribution authorized by an Act of the National Council, dated ____MAY 3 1894____ 1894.

Names of Head, and Members of Families	Amount	To Whom Paid	Witness to Payment	Remarks
606 Beard John M.				
607 " Annie				
608 " Henry				
609 " Beulah	1062.80	John M. Beard	G W Benge	
610 Boling Julia M.	265.70	J M Boling	L B Bell	
611 Bear Wm D.	265.70	W.D. Bear	G W Benge	
612 Buster William				
613 " Ellen				
614 " Charles	797.10	Wm Buster	J.C. Starr	
615 Burgess Benjamin	order 265.70	F.A. Neilson	J.C. Starr	Check on order Neilson
616 Brown Johnnie A.	order			Neilson
617 " Sarnia E.				
618 " Laura E.				
619 " John L.	1062.80	F.A. Neilson	J.C. Starr	Check on order
620 Burgess Bean	4671 265.70	Bean Burgess	J.C. Starr	
621 Buster James	265.70	James Buster	L B Bell	
622 Buster John				
623 " Watie				
624 " John (Jr)	797.10	John Buster	J.C. Starr	
625 Bryan Rachel M	265.70	Rachel M Bryan	J.C. Starr	
626 Buffing[sic] Susie	265.70	Susie Buffington	L B Bell	
627 Bradshaw Nora				
628 " Rose E.	531.40	J.B. Bradshaw	G W Benge	
629 Bushyhead Smith	265.70	Smith Bushyhead	G W Benge	
630 Bean Joe	order 265.70	Johnson and Keeler	Henry Eiffert	check

Starr Roll 1894

We, the undersigned citizens of the Cherokee Nation, by right of Cherokee blood, do hereby acknowledge to have received of E. E. Starr, National Treasurer of the Cherokee Nation, the sums set opposite our names respectively, in full of our shares in the per capita distribution authorized by an Act of the National Council, dated ___MAY 3 1894___ 1894.

	Names of Head, and Members of Families	Amount	To Whom Paid	Witness to Payment	Remarks
631	Brown Charles				Whitiker[sic]
632	" Lou	*order*			
633	" Lizzie				
634	" George	1062.80	W.T. Whitaker	Henry Eiffert	
635	Brassfield John	6415 265.70	L B Bell	G W Benge	*on order*
636	Beeson Perry	265.70	Mariah Flemming	G W Benge	
637	Beck Chas	~~265.70~~ *order*	C.W. Poole	L B Bell	*H.C. Coehn*
638	Brown Loui[sic] F	*order* 265.70	Lee Barrett	L B Bell	
639	Buckmaster Lillie				
640	" Mary L.	531.40	Lillie Buckmaster	L B Bell	
641	Beck Emma J	265.70	E J Beck	L B Bell	
642	Childers Levi	265.70	Levi Childers	G W Benge	
643	Carman[sic] Katie				
644	" Hugh	531.40	Joshua Carmen	L B Bell	
645	Cobb Joel B	265.70	J B Cobb	G W Benge	
646	Cobb Sam'l S.	265.70	S.S. Cobb	G W Benge	
647	Coats John	265.70	John Coats	G W Benge	
	~~Chaney Ida B.~~		*On Tahlequah Rolls*		
	~~" Florence E.~~		*(Nos 420 + 421 respectively)*		
648	Cleland Geo W.	265.70	G W Benge	G W Benge	
649	Cleland Geo W. Jr				
650	" Amelia	531.40	Geo W Cleland	G W Benge	

Starr Roll 1894

We, the undersigned citizens of the Cherokee Nation, by right of Cherokee blood, do hereby acknowledge to have received of E. E. Starr, National Treasurer of the Cherokee Nation, the sums set opposite our names respectively, in full of our shares in the per capita distribution authorized by an Act of the National Council, dated ___MAY 3 1894___ 1894.

Names of Head, and Members of Families	Amount	To Whom Paid	Witness to Payment	Remarks
651 Cleland Jas B.	265.70	J.B. Cleland	G W Benge	
652 Cowan Alex C.				
653 " Stella				
654 " Cherrie				
655 " Terry	1062.80	A.C. Cowan	G W Benge	
656 Crow Lucinda				
657 " Claude				
658 " Johnson	797.10	H.C. Crow	G W Benge	
659 Cobb Evaline	265.70	J B Cobb	G W Benge	
660 Cobb Belle	265.70	Belle Cobb	L B Bell	
661 Clarke Mattie	265.70	J B Cobb	G W Benge	
662 Cobb Alex C.				
663 " Albert B.				
664 " Mary J.	797.10	A.C. Cobb	G W Benge	
665 Clingan Wm D.				
666 " Mary J.				
667 " Mattie E.				
668 " Therman A.				
669 " Cora M.				
670 " Samuel D.	1594.20	W. D. Clingan	G W Benge	
671 Cole Laura R.				
672 Rogers John M.				
673 Cole Bonney M	797.10	L B Cole	G W Benge	
674 Cartwright Essie	DEAD.			
675 " John H.				
676 " Letitia				
677 " Wm Thos	1062.80	J.H. Cartwright	G W Benge	

Starr Roll 1894

We, the undersigned citizens of the Cherokee Nation, by right of Cherokee blood, do hereby acknowledge to have received of E. E. Starr, National Treasurer of the Cherokee Nation, the sums set opposite our names respectively, in full of our shares in the per capita distribution authorized by an Act of the National Council, dated ___MAY 3 1894___ 1894.

Names of Head, and Members of Families	Amount	To Whom Paid	Witness to Payment	Remarks
678 Cleland Emmet S.				
679 " Emmet S. Jr	531.40	E.S. Cleland	G W Benge	
680 Calvert Cynthia				
681 " Maude				
682 " Charles	797.10	William Calvert	G W Benge	
683 Carrington Annie D.				
684 " Wyly V.	531.40	RE. Carrington	G W Benge	
685 Cates Emma				
686 " Levena				
687 " Edmond	797.10	T.A. Cates	G W Benge	
688 Choate Wᵐ S.	265.70	W.S. Choate	G W Benge	
689 Coody Sarah J	D148			
690 " Eula				
691 " Minnie				
692 " Amanda	1062.80	M. J. Butler	G W Benge	
693 Coody Wᵐ S.	265.70	M J Butler	G W Benge	
694 Coats Charles				
695 " Ellen L.				
696 " Clara H.				
697 " William				
698 " Charles J				
699 Coats John	1394.20	Charles Coats	G W Benge	
700 Carter Deloria				
701 " Candis J.	531.40	Deloria Carter	G W Benge	

Starr Roll 1894

We, the undersigned citizens of the Cherokee Nation, by right of Cherokee blood, do hereby acknowledge to have received of E. E. Starr, National Treasurer of the Cherokee Nation, the sums set opposite our names respectively, in full of our shares in the per capita distribution authorized by an Act of the National Council, dated ___MAY 3 1894___ 1894.

#	Names of Head, and Members of Families	Amount	To Whom Paid	Witness to Payment	Remarks
702	Cole Mary				W.T.W.
703	" Mary A.				
704	" Jennie E.				
705	" Maude				
706	" Effie	1328.50	W T Whitaker	Henry Eiffert	
707	Choate John B.				
708	" Robt M.	531.40	J.B. Choate	G W Benge	
709	Collier Lettie				
710	" Mack	Contested			
711	" Flora	" by S M Collier			
712	" Katie	"			
713	" James		S M Collier &		
714	" Charlotte	1594.20	Lettie Collier	L B Bell	
715	Cole Lucy				
716	Riley Minnie V.				
717	" Rebecca H.	797.10	Lucy Cole	G W Benge	
718	Cole Bertie				
719	" Mart E.				
720	" Jack H.	797.10	Lucy Cole	G W Benge	
721	Cole Dora				
722	" Sissie				
723	" John				
724	" Vinnie				
725	" Clem				
726	" Felix				
727	" Drewsy	1859.90	Boon Cole	G W Benge	
728	Curtsinger[sic] Fannie L				
729	" Fred				
730	" Etta	797.10	F.L. Cartsinger	G W Benge	
731	Collins Eliza				
732	" Annie	531.40	Henry Eiffert	Henry Eiffert	

Starr Roll 1894

We, the undersigned citizens of the Cherokee Nation, by right of Cherokee blood, do hereby acknowledge to have received of E. E. Starr, National Treasurer of the Cherokee Nation, the sums set opposite our names respectively, in full of our shares in the per capita distribution authorized by an Act of the National Council, dated ___MAY 3 1894___ 1894.

	Names of Head, and Members of Families	Amount	To Whom Paid	Witness to Payment	Remarks
733	Clark Wm A.				
734	" Josie	531.40	W^m A Clark	G W Benge	
735	Crittenden Watt S.	265.70	W.S. Crittenden	G W Benge	
736	Chesnut[sic] Mary				J.C.H.
737	" Alex	*order*			
738	" Hallie	797.10	J.C. Hogan	Henry Eiffert	check
739	Chesnut Amanda	265.70	J C Hogan	Henry Eiffert	check
740	Coats James				
741	" Jennie B.	531.40	James M Coats	L B Bell	
742	Cromwell Margaret	*order*			
743	" Campbell	531.40	W T Whitaker	Henry Eiffert	
744	Cumiford Pleasant				J.C.H.
745	" Rosie A.				
746	" Robt	*order*			
747	" Henry S.				
748	" Julia A.				
749	" Bennie F.				
750	" Julia	1859.90	J C Hogan	Henry Eiffert	check
751	Colbard Gudger				Registered in family of
752	" Myrtle				W. T. Whitaker
753	" Odin				
754	" Annie	1062.80	W.T. Whitaker	G W Benge	
755	Chapman Cynthia				
756	" Mary E.				
757	" Don L.	797.10	Cynthia Chapman	G W Benge	
758	Conklin Annie				
759	" Bertha	531.40	Annie Conklin	G W Benge	

unpaid (noted beside 744–746)

Starr Roll 1894

We, the undersigned citizens of the Cherokee Nation, by right of Cherokee blood, do hereby acknowledge to have received of E. E. Starr, National Treasurer of the Cherokee Nation, the sums set opposite our names respectively, in full of our shares in the per capita distribution authorized by an Act of the National Council, dated ___MAY 3 1894___ 1894.

	Names of Head, and Members of Families	Amount	To Whom Paid	Witness to Payment	Remarks
760	Cummins Flora B.		contest		by D.S.C
761	" Maggie E.	531.40		G W Benge	
762	Coats Samuel				
763	" Ethel N.	531.40	Samuel Coats	G W Benge	
764	Clark Geo W.				
765	" Lydia A.				
766	" Susie				
767	" Geo W. Jr				
768	" Ross				
769	" Effie M.				
770	Clark Henry				
771	Clark Lizzie M.				
772	Clark Lydia	2391.30	G W Clark	G W Benge	
773	Clark Wm C.	265.70	W.C. Clark	G W Benge	
774	Caldwell Callie				Dead.
775	" John L.				
776	" Fannie				
777	" Ben M.				
778	" Mary				
779	" Lula	1594.20	J.J. Caldwell	G W Benge	
780	Chamberlin Ed W.				
781	" Laura H.				
782	" Edward R.				
783	" John R.	1062.80	E.W. Chamberlin	G W Benge	
784	Coyne Maggie				
785	" Mary Ellen	531.40	Maggie Coyne	G W Benge	

Starr Roll 1894

We, the undersigned citizens of the Cherokee Nation, by right of Cherokee blood, do hereby acknowledge to have received of E. E. Starr, National Treasurer of the Cherokee Nation, the sums set opposite our names respectively, in full of our shares in the per capita distribution authorized by an Act of the National Council, dated ___MAY 3 1894___ 1894.

#	Names of Head, and Members of Families	Amount	To Whom Paid	Witness to Payment	Remarks
786	Cass Josie E.				
787	" Alonzo B.				
788	Arnold Jennie	797.10	E.H. Miller	G W Benge	
789	Chambers Henry C.				
790	" Mary				
791	" James				
792	" Johnny				
793	" Clementine	1328.50	Henry C Chambers	J.C. Starr	
794	Crutchfield Dolphus				
795	" Jennie	531.40	Jenny Crutchfield	L B Bell	
796	Chisolm Lucy	265.70 (10383)	*(Illegible)* Chisolm	G W Benge	
797	Crowder Rosa	265.70 *order*	F.A. Neilson	J C Starr	Check on order Neilson
798	Carlile Henrietta	265.70	GW Eaton	Henry Eiffert	GW Eaton Check
799	Cummings Cora				Dead
800	" Penny				Alex McDaniel Guardian
801	" Grace				
802	" David				
803	" Edna				
804	" Ruby				
805	" Mary	1859.90	Alex L McDaniel	J.C. Starr	
806	Candy George	265.70	A H Norwood	L B Bell	Julia Walls mother A H Norwood
807	Cochran George				
808	" Julia	*order*			WEH
809	" Victoria	797.10	WE Halsell	Henry Eiffert	
810	Cromwell Annie P.	*order*			W.C. Patton
811	" Zeddie R.	531.40	WC Patton	G W Benge	on order
812	Colston Lewis R.	265.70	W.C. Colston	G W Benge	

Starr Roll 1894

We, the undersigned citizens of the Cherokee Nation, by right of Cherokee blood, do hereby acknowledge to have received of E. E. Starr, National Treasurer of the Cherokee Nation, the sums set opposite our names respectively, in full of our shares in the per capita distribution authorized by an Act of the National Council, dated ___MAY 3 1894___ 1894.

#	Names of Head, and Members of Families	Amount	To Whom Paid	Witness to Payment	Remarks
813	Cleghorn Rosa				
814	Shoemake Jennie				A H N
815	" James	order			A H Norwood
816	Cleghorn Fannie				on order of Rosa Cleghorn
817	" Thomas	1328.50	A H Norwood	L B Bell	
818	Corban Sarah	265.70	Frank Corban	L B Bell	
819	Crutchfield Claude				
820	" Mary				J.K. Crutchfield Guardian
821	" Roy				
822	" Grady	1062.80	J.K. Crutchfield	G W Benge	
823	Charley Samuel				
824	" Lillie				
825	" Ross	order			JM Hull
826	" Lelia	1062.80	JM Hull	Henry Eiffert	
827	Charley Frank	order			
828	" Sarah J	531.40	JM Hull	Henry Eiffert	J.M. Hull
829	Charley Mary	265.70 order	JM Hull	Henry Eiffert	J M Hull
830	Crittendon Andrew F.	265.70	Bell Quinton	G W Benge	Minor child Wesley Tiblow Guardian
831	Carr Sarah A.				
832	" Frank N.				
833	" Sarah L.				
834	" Josie M.				
835	" Beulah M.	1328.50	N.F Carr	G W Benge	
836	Cobb Mack	265.70	Mack Cobb	J.C. Starr	
837	Cobb John	265.70	John Cobb	J.C. Starr	
838	Carter John R.				
839	" Sarah	531.40	Sarah Carter	J.C. Starr	

Starr Roll 1894

We, the undersigned citizens of the Cherokee Nation, by right of Cherokee blood, do hereby acknowledge to have received of E. E. Starr, National Treasurer of the Cherokee Nation, the sums set opposite our names respectively, in full of our shares in the per capita distribution authorized by an Act of the National Council, dated ___MAY 3 1894___ 1894.

Names of Head, and Members of Families	Amount	To Whom Paid	Witness to Payment	Remarks
840 Crowder Sarah A.				
841 Peirson Mary				
842 Crowder Geo A.				
843 " Jerry M.				
844 " Ethel Lee	1328.50	Sarah Crowder	L B Bell	
845 Carter Annie				
846 " Walter	531.40	G.B. Keeler	G W Benge	
847 Colston Charles	order 265.70	Johnson and Keeler	Henry Eiffert	Check
848 Carr Wm A.	order 265.70	Johnson and Keeler	Henry Eiffert	Check
849 Clingan Judge K.				
850 " Claude	531.40	J. K. Clingan	G W Benge	
851 Cavender Sarah F.	265.70	S.F. Cavender	G W Benge	
852 Couch Victoria E.				
853 " Mae				
854 " Clara				
855 " Cherokee				
856 " Marion W.				
857 " James C.				
858 " William	1859.90	M.W. Couch	G W Benge	
859 " Nannie E.	265.70	W.A. Miller	G W Benge	
860 Couch Jno F.	265.70	Jno F. Couch	G W Benge	
861 Couch Jessie F.	265.70	M.W. Couch	G W Benge	
862 Couch Robt L.	265.70	M.W. Couch	G W Benge	
863 Carmicle Mary				
864 " Lewis				
865 " William C.				
866 " Ora J.				
867 " Clarence				

Starr Roll 1894

We, the undersigned citizens of the Cherokee Nation, by right of Cherokee blood, do hereby acknowledge to have received of E. E. Starr, National Treasurer of the Cherokee Nation, the sums set opposite our names respectively, in full of our shares in the per capita distribution authorized by an Act of the National Council, dated ___MAY 3 1894___ 1894.

#	Names of Head, and Members of Families	Amount	To Whom Paid	Witness to Payment	Remarks
868	" Annie B				
869	" Walter				
870	" Thomas				
871	" Mary E.	2391.30	Mary Carmicle	G W Benge	
872	Campbell Rope				
873	" Betsy	531.40	A Foyil	L B Bell	
874	Carr Waller W.	265.70	1" Nat͟a͟s͟ Bank	Henry Eiffert	Check Fst.N.B.
875	Chisolm Ingue	265.70 (D̶1̶2̶8̶1̶ / 10382)	Ingue C͟h͟i͟s͟o͟l͟m [sic]	G W Benge	
876	Crutchfield Thos				
877	" Kate				
878	" Susie	79.10	Kate Crutchfield	G W Benge	
879	Cochran Jessie				
880	" Susie				
881	" Clinton				
882	" John				
883	" Clarence	1328.50	Jessie Cochran	L B Bell	
884	Cochran Jessie (Jr)	265.70	Jesse Cochran Jr	G W Benge	
885	Coker Josie	265.70	Elizabeth Coker	G W Benge	
886	Cloud Henry				
887	" Samuel B.	531.40 order	C.M. Ball	G W Benge	C M Ball on order
888	Coker David N.				
889	" Ora				
890	" Mary	797.10 order	F.A. Neilson	J.C. Starr	Neilson Check on order
891	Chambers Tee-sey				
892	" Minnie				
893	" Nancy J.				
894	" Joseph				

Starr Roll 1894

We, the undersigned citizens of the Cherokee Nation, by right of Cherokee blood, do hereby acknowledge to have received of E. E. Starr, National Treasurer of the Cherokee Nation, the sums set opposite our names respectively, in full of our shares in the per capita distribution authorized by an Act of the National Council, dated ___MAY 3 1894___ 1894.

	Names of Head, and Members of Families	Amount	To Whom Paid	Witness to Payment	Remarks
895	" Evans				
896	" Claude	1394.20	Tee-see Chambers	G W Benge	
897	Cochran Alex				
898	" Annie				
899	" Return				
900	" Nellie				
901	" Ruthie				
902	" Lettie				
903	" Zeddie	1859.90	Annie Cochran	L B Bell	
904	Cochran Jennie	265.70	Jenny Cochran	L B Bell	
905	Campbell Wm R.				
906	" Carrie				
907	" Flora	797.10	W^m R Campbell	G W Benge	
	~~Crutchfield Jennie M.~~				R.K. Adair Guardia
	~~" Alice~~				
908	Carey Wm V.				
909	" Lelia M.	531.40	Wm V. Carey	G W Benge	Wife a Delawar
910	Carey Gabriel	265.70	Gabriel Carey	J.C. Starr	
911	Coker Lewis				W.V.C.
912	" Mattie T.				
913	" Calvin F.	*order*			
914	" Arthur L.				
915	" Mary L.				
916	" Benjamin F.				
917	" Joseph C.				
918	" Miller	2125.60	Wm V. Carey	G W Benge	on order
919	Coker Wm W.	265.70	Lewis Coker	G W Benge	

Starr Roll 1894

We, the undersigned citizens of the Cherokee Nation, by right of Cherokee blood, do hereby acknowledge to have received of E. E. Starr, National Treasurer of the Cherokee Nation, the sums set opposite our names respectively, in full of our shares in the per capita distribution authorized by an Act of the National Council, dated ___MAY 3 1894___ 1894.

Names of Head, and Members of Families	Amount	To Whom Paid	Witness to Payment	Remarks
920 Cessna Sallie				
921 Vinita Johnny				
922 " Albert				
923 " Dora				
924 " Da-ro-ta-ro	1328.50	Sallie Cessna	L B Bell	
925 Coody John H.				
926 " Mary A.				
927 " Richard H.				
928 " William E.	1062.60	Mary A. Coody	J.C. Starr	
929 Coker Calvin				
930 " Eliza J.				
931 " Myers Willie				
932 Coker John R.				
933 " Ida Mary				
934 " William P.				
935 " Franklin R.				
936 " Calvin E.				
937 " Joseph C.				
938 " Lizzie	2657.00	Calvin Coker	G W Benge	
939 Couch Mitchell M.				
940 " Cynthia				
941 " Nannie	797.10	M. M. Couch	G W Benge	
942 Chaney Julia				
943 " Susan				
944 " Sadie				
945 " Eliza				
946 " Mamie				
947 " Della				
948 " Ethel				
949 " Louella	2125.60	J M Chaney	G W Benge	
950 Chaney Chas P.	265.70	J M Chaney	G W Benge	

Starr Roll 1894

We, the undersigned citizens of the Cherokee Nation, by right of Cherokee blood, do hereby acknowledge to have received of E. E. Starr, National Treasurer of the Cherokee Nation, the sums set opposite our names respectively, in full of our shares in the per capita distribution authorized by an Act of the National Council, dated MAY 3 1894 1894.

Names of Head, and Members of Families	Amount	To Whom Paid	Witness to Payment	Remarks
951 Coker Charley				J.E.C.
952 " Mary E.				
953 " Lillie C.	order 797.10	J E Campbell	G W Benge	on order
954 Daniel Joseph M	265.70	J.E. Campbell	J.C. Starr	
955 Curry Margaret E.				
956 " Charles J.				
957 " Susie Lee				
958 " Anna May				
959 " Sabrina L.				
960 " Mamie Viola	1594.20	M.E. Curry	G W Benge	
961 Coody Belinda	265.70	Belinda Coody	J.C. Starr	
962 Comwell James	265.70	James *(Illegible)*	G W Benge	
963 Clark Sequoyah D.	265.70	Geo Eaton	Henry Eiffert	Check
964 Countryman Hoolie				
965 " Sabra				
966 " George				
967 " Eva				
968 " Riley				
969 " Nora	1594.20	Hoolie Countryman	G W Benge	
970 Clark Emily L.				
971 " Mary E.				
972 " Sarah E. R.				
973 " Lucy C.				
974 " Addie C.				
975 " Emily Lee (Jr)	1594.20	Emily L Clark	L B Bell	Check
976 Canada Fannie E.				
977 " Henry Lee				
978 " Ida	797.10	Fannie E Canada	L B Bell	
979 Codry William	order 265.70	Walsh and Shutt	Henry Eiffert	W&S Check

Paid in two checks at Flint Court House Aug 4, 1894

Starr Roll 1894

We, the undersigned citizens of the Cherokee Nation, by right of Cherokee blood, do hereby acknowledge to have received of E. E. Starr, National Treasurer of the Cherokee Nation, the sums set opposite our names respectively, in full of our shares in the per capita distribution authorized by an Act of the National Council, dated ___MAY 3 1894___ 1894.

Names of Head, and Members of Families	Amount	To Whom Paid	Witness to Payment	Remarks
980 Crutchfield Ida				
981 " Leroy A.				
982 " Cuba				
983 " Maggie O.	1062.80	Ida Crutchfield	G W Benge	
984 Crutchfield John K.				
985 " Leroy C.				
986 " Ewing H.	797.10	J.K. Crutchfield	G W Benge	
987 Cook Henry A.	265.70	Susan Sanders	G W Benge	
988 Cook Wm D.	265.70	Susan Sanders	G W Benge	
989 Cook Isabelle	265.70	Susan Sanders	G W Benge	
990 Collins Annie				
991 " Mary F.				
992 " Albert H.	797.10	Annie Collins	J.C. Starr	
993 Charlie Jennie				
994 " Ruth	531.40	Jennie Charley	J.C. Starr	
995 Chambers Geo S.	265.70	Geo S Chambers	J P Carter	Nov 17th 1894
996 Carroll[sic] Mary C.				
997 " Myrtle J.	531.40	J.M. Carrell	G W Benge	
998 Carr John	265.70	John Carr	G W Benge	
999 Chambers Jefferson P.				
1000 " Manda B.	531.40	J.P. Chambers	G W Benge	
1001 Choate Rufus Mark				
1002 " William P.	531.40	E.L. Choate	G W Benge	
1003 Campbell Minnie Rosa	265.70	Minnie Rosa Campbell	J.P. Carter	

Starr Roll 1894

We, the undersigned citizens of the Cherokee Nation, by right of Cherokee blood, do hereby acknowledge to have received of E. E. Starr, National Treasurer of the Cherokee Nation, the sums set opposite our names respectively, in full of our shares in the per capita distribution authorized by an Act of the National Council, dated ___MAY 3 1894___ 1894.

	Names of Head, and Members of Families	Amount	To Whom Paid	Witness to Payment	Remarks
1004	Coney Eliza J.				
1005	" George	531.40	E.J. Coney	G W Benge	
1006	Colston Wilson				
1007	" Lizzie				
1008	" Bettie				
1009	" Kynes				
1010	" Cynthia	1328.50	Lizzie Colston	G W Benge	
1011	Cowan Felix	265.70	Felix Cowan	G W Benge	
1012	Crutchfield Leroy T				
1013	" Sabrina J.				
1014	" John H.	797.10	L.L. Crutchfield	G W Benge	
1015	Craig Granville		Gravil[sic] Craig	G W Benge	
1016	" George				
1017	Craig Carl	797.10	Granvil Craig	G W Benge	
1018	Coats James E	265.70	J.E. Coats	G W Benge	
1019	Coats Louisa J.				
1020	" John W.				
1021	" Annie L.				
1022	Coats Charles F.	1062.80	L.J. Coats	G W Benge	
1023	Carter Indianola M.				
1024	" Flossie E.				
1025	" May M.				
1026	" William S.				
1027	" Alma A.	1328.50	J.H. Akin	G W Benge	*on order*
1028	Chamberlain Eunice	265.70	A.F. Chamberlin	G W Benge	
1029	Chamberlain Abbie E.	265.70	A.F. Chamberlin	G W Benge	

Starr Roll 1894

We, the undersigned citizens of the Cherokee Nation, by right of Cherokee blood, do hereby acknowledge to have received of E. E. Starr, National Treasurer of the Cherokee Nation, the sums set opposite our names respectively, in full of our shares in the per capita distribution authorized by an Act of the National Council, dated ___MAY 3 1894___ 1894.

	Names of Head, and Members of Families	Amount	To Whom Paid	Witness to Payment	Remarks
1030	Chamberlain Arthur F.				
1031	" Dollie E.				
1032	" Catharine D.	797.10	A F Chamberlin	G W Benge	
1033	Chamberlain Wm C.				
1034	" Flora H.				
1035	" Clara E.				
1036	" Winfred C				
1037	" Maggie L.	1328.50	A.F. Chamberlin	G W Benge	
1038	Cooper Laura				
1039	" Onida				
1040	" Alice				
1041	" Glen	1062.80	Henry Eiffert	G W Benge	
1042	Chamberlain Nelson B				
1043	" Emma G.				
1044	" Eunice				
1045	" William N.				
1046	" Abbie O.				
1047	" Evastus D.				
1048	" Mary	1859.90	N.B. Chamberlin	G W Benge	
1049	Crutchfield Taylor F.	265.70	J.M. Taylor	G W Benge	on order Executor of will
1050	Calvert Sarah E.				
1051	" Amanda A.				
1052	" Charles E.	797.10	S.E. Calvert	G W Benge	
1053	Clinkscales Annie E.				
1054	" Louis D.				
1055	" Lucille	797.10	A.M. Clinkscales	G W Benge	
1056	Casey Arch	order 265.70	J.S. Thomason	G W Benge	J.S. Thomason on order

Starr Roll 1894

We, the undersigned citizens of the Cherokee Nation, by right of Cherokee blood, do hereby acknowledge to have received of E. E. Starr, National Treasurer of the Cherokee Nation, the sums set opposite our names respectively, in full of our shares in the per capita distribution authorized by an Act of the National Council, dated ___MAY 3 1894___ 1894.

Names of Head, and Members of Families	Amount	To Whom Paid	Witness to Payment	Remarks
1057 Chamberlain Robt L.	3659			
1058 " Pearl L.				
1059 " Amery P.	797.10	Robt L Chamberlin	G W Benge	
1060 Craig Wm L.	265.70	W L. Craig	G W Benge	
1061 Childers Lucre Kia N.				
1062 " Thomas B.	531.40	Mary Allice Jones	G W Benge	
1063 Crittenden Sam	265.70	John H Crittenden	J.C. Starr	
1064 Craig Frank W.				
1065 " Robt W.				
1066 " Edna E.				
1067 " Eva S.				
1068 " Elgy C.				
1069 " Laura	1594.20	Katie Craig	G W Benge	
1070 Crittendon John H.				
1071 " Killie				
1072 " Barbara	797.10	John H Crittenden	J.C. Starr	
1073 Chambers White	265.70	F A Neilson	Henry Eiffert	
1074 Cunningham Alf	265.70	Charles Starr	G W Benge	
1075 Chambers Vann				
1075 1/2 " Jennie				
1076 " Lizzie		W.H. Mayes for this family of (Illegible) this payment		
1077 " Lewis				
1078 " Sanders				
1079 " Clara				
1080 " Cora	1859.90	Vann Chambers	J.C. Starr	
1081 Chambers Juliette	265.70	F.A. Neilson	J.C. Starr	Cherkeitssorde

Starr Roll 1894

We, the undersigned citizens of the Cherokee Nation, by right of Cherokee blood, do hereby acknowledge to have received of E. E. Starr, National Treasurer of the Cherokee Nation, the sums set opposite our names respectively, in full of our shares in the per capita distribution authorized by an Act of the National Council, dated ___MAY 3 1894___ 1894.

	Names of Head, and Members of Families	Amount	To Whom Paid	Witness to Payment	Remarks
1082	Chisolm Nancy L	~~1280~~ 10381			
1083	" Rose	10384			
1084	" Ezekiel	~~1280~~ 10381			
1085	" Lizzie	~~1280~~ 10386			
1086	" Arle	~~1280~~ 10381 1328.50	Nancy L Chisolm	G W Benge	
1087	Chisolm Tuxie	~~1280~~ 10381			
1088	" Oo-li-chey	~~1280~~ 10381			
1089	" Jackson	Dead 797.10	Nancy S Chisolm	G W Benge	
1090	Candy Sam	265.70	Sam Candy	G W Benge	
1091	Creech Rebecca	order			Neilson
1092	" Ruth				
1093	" Alice				
1094	" Lulu				
1095	" Willie	1328.50	F.A. Neilson	J.C. Starr	Check on order
1096	Chambers James				
1097	" Katie	531.40	James Chambers	L B Bell	
1098	Chambers Joseph				
1099	" Nancy J.	531.40	Joseph Chambers	J.C. Starr	
1100	Carter Minnie	265.70	Minnie carter	J.C. Starr	
1101	Chambers Pickens	265.70	Pickens Chambers	L B Bell	
1102	Coffee George	order 265.70	Walsh and Shutt	Henry Eiffert	W & S ~~Check~~
1103	Crittendon[sic] Abraham				
1104	" Riley				
1105	" Cordia				
1106	" Ira	1062.80	Abraham Crittenden	J.C. Starr	
1107	Chambers David	265.70	David Chambers	L B Bell	

Starr Roll 1894

We, the undersigned citizens of the Cherokee Nation, by right of Cherokee blood, do hereby acknowledge to have received of E. E. Starr, National Treasurer of the Cherokee Nation, the sums set opposite our names respectively, in full of our shares in the per capita distribution authorized by an Act of the National Council, dated ____MAY 3 1894____ 1894.

	Names of Head, and Members of Families	Amount	To Whom Paid	Witness to Payment	Remarks
1108	Chambers Wm W.				
1109	" William D.				
1110	" Eliza D				
1111	" Jessie S.				
1112	" Leo				
1113	" Joe H.				
1114	Chambers Ezekiel	1859.90	W^m W Chambers	G W Benge	
1115	Chambers Willie E.				
1116	" Nannie E.				
1117	" Joseph W.				
1118	" Tuxie				
1119	" Pearl I				
1120	Carey Jessie	1594.20	Nannie E Chambers	J.C. Starr	
1121	Cochran Jessie	265.70	Jessie Cochran	G W Benge	
1122	Cochran Clue	265.70	W.M. Gulager	Robt B Ross	P^d July 20/96
1123	Chambers Robt.	265.70	Robt Chambers	G W Benge	
1124	Crutchfield James				
1125	" Vinita	531.40	J.M. Taylor	G W Benge	Executor of Will
1126	Crow Laura E.	265.70	L.E. Crow	G W Benge	
1127	Chambers W^m A				
1128	" William L.	531.40	W^m A Chambers	G W Benge	
1129	Creech Jefferson		order		F.A. Neilson
1130	" Nettie	531.40	F.A. Neilson	G W Benge	on order
1131	Collins Ida M.	265.70	Ida M. Collins	J.C. Starr	From Del. roll
1132	Collins George	265.70	George Collins	J.C. Starr	

Starr Roll 1894

We, the undersigned citizens of the Cherokee Nation, by right of Cherokee blood, do hereby acknowledge to have received of E. E. Starr, National Treasurer of the Cherokee Nation, the sums set opposite our names respectively, in full of our shares in the per capita distribution authorized by an Act of the National Council, dated ___MAY 3 1894___ 1894.

	Names of Head, and Members of Families	Amount	To Whom Paid	Witness to Payment	Remarks
1133	Claywell Kate				
1134	Taylor Kate	531.40	Kate Claywell	G W Benge	
1135	Chandler Susie	265.70	James Kell	G W Benge	
1136	Coon Ellen	265.70	Ellen Coon	L B Bell	
1137	Carr Minnie				
1138	" Clidy				
1139	" Tessie				
1140	" Edward	1062.80	Quinn Carr	G W Benge	
1141	Collier Chas A	265.70	Chas A Collier	G W Benge	
1142	Crane Susie	order 265.70	F.A. Neilson	J.C. Starr	Check~~kids~~ order
1143	Coker John	order 265.70	W.L. Moore	G W Benge	on order
1144	Creek Mary	order			GM Eaten
1145	" Belle M.	531.40	G.M. Eatin	Henry Eiffert	Check
1146	Chambers Maxwell	265.70	M Chambers	G W Benge	
1147	Dryden Mary E				
1148	" Mattie B.				
1149	" Lucy A.				
1150	" Laura				
1151	" Rose E.				
1152	" William				
1153	" Flora	1859.90	H.R. Dryden	G W Benge	
1154	Dial Nathaniel H.				
1155	" Hugh H.				
1156	" Nola M.				
1157	" Bettie E.				
1158	" Lelia A.				
1159	" Daniel F.	1594.20	N.H. Dial	G W Benge	

Starr Roll 1894

We, the undersigned citizens of the Cherokee Nation, by right of Cherokee blood, do hereby acknowledge to have received of E. E. Starr, National Treasurer of the Cherokee Nation, the sums set opposite our names respectively, in full of our shares in the per capita distribution authorized by an Act of the National Council, dated ___MAY 3 1894___ 1894.

	Names of Head, and Members of Families	Amount	To Whom Paid	Witness to Payment	Remarks
1160	Dannenberg Nath B.				
1161	" Elizabeth				
1162	" Truxie				
1163	" Oby				
1164	" Alice				
1165	" Grady		First Natl Bank		
1166	" N.W.	1859.90	~~J.C. Starr~~ Vinita	J.C. Starr	Sept 22, 1894
1167	Duncan John C.				W & Shutt
1168	" Joana C.	531.40 (order)	Walsh and Shutt	Henry Eiffert	Check
1169	Daugherty Ett				C H
1170	" Clem H.	531.40 (order)	C. Haden	G W Benge	on order
1171	Drew George	265.70	George Drew	G W Benge	
1172	Daugherty Charles	265.70	Charles Daugherty	G W Benge	
1173	Dial Nancy	265.70	H.A. Loflin	G W Benge	
1174	Davis John	265.70 (order)	JC Hogan	Henry Eiffert	J.C.H.
1175	Dege Laura				
1176	" Laura A.				
1177	" Walter T.				
1178	" Mary E.				
1179	" Phillip				
1180	" William	1594.20	Laura Dege	G W Benge	
1181	Dege James T.	265.70	J.J. Dupree	G W Benge	
1182	Dege Charles F.	265.70	C.F. Dege	G W Benge	
1183	Dege John J.	265.70	J.J. Dupree	G W Benge	

Starr Roll 1894

We, the undersigned citizens of the Cherokee Nation, by right of Cherokee blood, do hereby acknowledge to have received of E. E. Starr, National Treasurer of the Cherokee Nation, the sums set opposite our names respectively, in full of our shares in the per capita distribution authorized by an Act of the National Council, dated ____MAY 3 1894____ 1894.

#	Names of Head, and Members of Families	Amount	To Whom Paid	Witness to Payment	Remarks
1184	Dooly Margaret J.	5351			
1185	" Mirth	5351			
1186	" Earth	5351 797.10	N. Dooly	J.C. Starr	(Hayden)
1187	Delozier Georgie V.				
1188	" Fontain G.				
1189	" Manford V.				
1190	" John E.	1062.80	E.A. Adair	G W Benge	
1191	Dial Mary E.				
1192	" Mary T.	531.40	M.E. Dial	G W Benge	
1193	Downing Felix				
1194	" Lizzie				
1195	" Nancy	797.10	Lizzie Downing	G W Benge	
1196	Duncan Nettie M.	265.70	N.M. Duncan	G W Benge	
1197	Dick Lorenzo				
1198	" Christie				
1199	" Walter				
1200	" George				
1201	" Myrtle	1328.50	Lorenzo Dick	G W Benge	
~~1202~~					
1203	Duck John	265.70	WC Patton	Henry Eiffert	claimed by check W C Patten
1204	Daugherty John	265.70	John Daugherty	G W Benge	
	~~Duck Richard~~		On Lottee Roll		Allottee
1205	Duck Emaline				
1206	Writer Annie				
1207	" Jennie		order Emaline Duck	L B Bell order	will order
1208	Duck George	1062.80	~~W C Patton~~	~~G W Benge~~	~~on order~~

Starr Roll 1894

We, the undersigned citizens of the Cherokee Nation, by right of Cherokee blood, do hereby acknowledge to have received of E. E. Starr, National Treasurer of the Cherokee Nation, the sums set opposite our names respectively, in full of our shares in the per capita distribution authorized by an Act of the National Council, dated ____MAY 3 1894____ 1894.

	Names of Head, and Members of Families	Amount	To Whom Paid	Witness to Payment	Remarks
1209	Davis John				W.C. Patton
1210	" Nellie	*order*			
1211	" Ella	797.10	W.C. Patton		on order
					Neilson
1212	Davis Thomas				
1213	" William				
1214	" Bird	*order*			Neilson
1215	" Kim				
1216	" Lulu	1328.50	F.A. Neilson	J.C. Starr	Check on order
1217	Davis Napoleon C				
1218	Chambers Mack				Neilson
1219	" Halla	~~2747~~ 797.10	F.A. ~~10264~~ Neilson	J.C. Starr	Check on order
1220	Denbo ~~Nettie~~ Lettie V				
1221	" Jno L.				
1222	" Minnie M.	265.70	M. M. Denboo[sic]	G W Benge	
1223	" Robt. L.				
1224	" Oce				
1225	" Belle	1328.50	N.V. Denbo	G W Benge	
1226	Dimond James	$265.70	W.M. Gulager	JC Dannenberg	March 2/9(?)
1227	Dimond Polly	$265.70	W.M. Gulager	JC Dannenberg	" " "
1228	Davis John D	797.10	W.H. Gullager	S.W. Mayfield	
1229	" Jennie	"	" " "	" "	
1230	" Susie	"	" " "	" "	
					WC Rogers
1231	Denver George	*order* 265.70	Johnson and Keeler	L B Bell	
1232	Davis Charles	*order*			
1233	" Barney	531.40	Johnson and Keeler	Henry Eiffert	Check

Starr Roll 1894

We, the undersigned citizens of the Cherokee Nation, by right of Cherokee blood, do hereby acknowledge to have received of E. E. Starr, National Treasurer of the Cherokee Nation, the sums set opposite our names respectively, in full of our shares in the per capita distribution authorized by an Act of the National Council, dated ___MAY 3 1894___ 1894.

	Names of Head, and Members of Families	Amount	To Whom Paid	Witness to Payment	Remarks
1234	Daniels George				
1235	" Richards	order			
1236	" Lucinda				
1237	" Thomas	1062.80	Johnson & Keeler	Henry Eiffert	Check
1238	Daniels Annie	order 265.70	Keeler & Johnson	L B Bell	Johnson & Keeler
1239	Daniels Osa	order 265.70	Johnson&Keeler	Henry Eiffert	check Johnson&Keeler
1240	Davis Newton	order 265.70	Johnson&Keeler	Henry Eiffert	Check
1241	Downing Sarah				
1242	" Enorley	order			
1243	" David				
1244	" Sallie	1062.80	Johnson&Keeler	Henry Eiffert	Check
1245	Daniels Gar-ker-les-top				
1246	" Kay-hor-key				Johnson&Keeler
1247	" Susie	order			
1248	" Eddie	1062.80	Johnson&Keeler	Henry Eiffert	Check
1249	Dick Jacob				
1250	" Joseph				
1251	" Alsie	order			
1252	" Cassie				
1253	" Ellen	1328.50	Johnson&Keeler	Henry Eiffert	Check
1254	Davis Alice V.				
1255	" John B.				
1256	" Lyta	order			
1257	" Arthur				
1258	" Mable	1328.50	BD Pennyton	Henry Eiffert	Check
1259	Downing Mary				
1260	Smoke Sallie				
1261	Toney Isaac	797.10	Mary Downing	L B Bell	

Starr Roll 1894

We, the undersigned citizens of the Cherokee Nation, by right of Cherokee blood, do hereby acknowledge to have received of E. E. Starr, National Treasurer of the Cherokee Nation, the sums set opposite our names respectively, in full of our shares in the per capita distribution authorized by an Act of the National Council, dated ____MAY 3 1894____ 1894.

	Names of Head, and Members of Families	Amount	To Whom Paid	Witness to Payment	Remarks
1262	Davis Edna E.				
1263	" Olivia	531.40	Patrick Henry	G W Benge	
1264	Drake Emily J.				O.B
1265	" Mary B.				
1266	" Bessie W.	*order*			
1267	" John E				
1268	" Emma L.				
1269	" Nannie E.	1594.20	J.P. Drake	G W Benge	
1270	Downing Jacob				
1271	" Nellie	*order*			
1272	" James				
1273	" Ellis	*7527*			
1274	" Benjamin	1328.50	L.B. Bell	G W Benge	*on order*
1275	Downing George	265.70	E S Ellis	Henry Eiffert	*Check on order*
1276	Dickson Cynthia				
1277	" Claude				
1278	" Serena	797.10	G.B. Dickson	G W Benge	
1279	Derrick Jossie				
1280	" Nellie				
1281	" Jennie A.				
1282	" Katie				
1283	" Henrietta				
1284	" Eddie	1594.20	Josie Derrick	G W Benge	
1285	Downing Wooster	265.70	A. Foyil	L B Bell	
1286	Davis Loyd				P.H.
1287	" Ella				
1288	" Dawson	*order*			
1289	" Cora				
1290	" Claude	1328.50	Patrick Henry	G W Benge	

Starr Roll 1894

We, the undersigned citizens of the Cherokee Nation, by right of Cherokee blood, do hereby acknowledge to have received of E. E. Starr, National Treasurer of the Cherokee Nation, the sums set opposite our names respectively, in full of our shares in the per capita distribution authorized by an Act of the National Council, dated _____MAY 3 1894_____ 1894.

#	Names of Head, and Members of Families	Amount	To Whom Paid	Witness to Payment	Remarks
1291	Dick Washington				
1292	" Bertha				
1293	" Arthur	797.10	Sarah Dick	G W Benge	on order
1294	Deal Mack	265.70	Mack Deal	L B Bell	
1295	Deal William	265.70	Wm Deal	G W Benge	
1296	Douglas Nancy				
1297	" Ella				
1298	" Walter C.				
1299	" John A.				
1300	Armstrong Frank				
1301	" Albert	1594.20	J.E. Campbell (order)	J.C. Starr	
1302	Dawson Laura	order			Neilson
1303	" James	531.40	F.A. Neilson	J.C. Starr	Check on order
1304	Dale James	265.70	J E Campbell	G W Benge	
1305	Downing Richard	order			J.S. Thomason
1306	" Leroy	531.40	J.S. Thomason	G W Benge	on order
1307	Dannels Rebecca A	265.70	W^m. V. Carey	G W Benge	
1308	Duncan Henry	265.70	Lizzie Duncan	J.C. Starr	
1309	Davidson William				
1310	" Mary M.	531.40	William Davidson	G W Benge	
1311	Dawson Elbert				
1312	" Ella				
1313	" Burton	order D608			
1314	" Dick W.	1062.80	L B Bell D617	G W Benge	on order
1315	Dawson Frank	265.70	G R Broadwell	Henry Eiffert	child
1316	Dawson Wm C.	265.70	Allice Dawson D604	G W Benge	
1317	Dawson John	265.70	John Dawson D589	G W Benge	

Starr Roll 1894

We, the undersigned citizens of the Cherokee Nation, by right of Cherokee blood, do hereby acknowledge to have received of E. E. Starr, National Treasurer of the Cherokee Nation, the sums set opposite our names respectively, in full of our shares in the per capita distribution authorized by an Act of the National Council, dated ___MAY 3 1894___ 1894.

	Names of Head, and Members of Families	Amount	To Whom Paid	Witness to Payment	Remarks
1318	Dameron Luella				
1319	" Samuel D.	531.40	Luella Dameron	G W Benge	
1320	Davis Susan	265.70	Susan Davis	G W Benge	30 yrs old
1321	Denton Randolph	or 265.70	Geo Eaton D. 2638	Henry Eiffert	Geo Eaton
1322	Daugherty Jennie				
1323	" John				
1324	" Ethel				
1325	" Agnes	1062.80	F.A. Neilson Guardian	J.C. Starr	
1326	Dick Ellis				
1327	" Mary				
1328	" Thomas				
1329	" Rosie				
1330	" Cherokee	1328.50	Mary Dick	G W Benge	
1331	Dick George	265.70	Mary Dick	G W Benge	
1332	Daniels Marmaduke				
1333	" Jesse J.				
1334	" William D.				
1335	" Stafford	1062.80	M. Daniel	G W Benge	
1336	Dupree Charlotte B.	265.70	C.B. Dupree 3328	G W Benge	
1337	Dupree Maud E	265.70	M.E. Dupree	G W Benge	
1338	Dupree Wm E.				
1339	" Elmer				
1340	" Herbert				
1341	" Emma				
1342	" Wright				
1343	" Bessie	1594.20	W.E. Dupree	G W Benge	

Starr Roll 1894

We, the undersigned citizens of the Cherokee Nation, by right of Cherokee blood, do hereby acknowledge to have received of E. E. Starr, National Treasurer of the Cherokee Nation, the sums set opposite our names respectively, in full of our shares in the per capita distribution authorized by an Act of the National Council, dated ___MAY 3 1894___ 1894.

#	Names of Head, and Members of Families	Amount	To Whom Paid	Witness to Payment	Remarks
1344	Donnelly Emma J.				
1345	" Willie				
1346	" Thomas				
1347	" Emma				
1348	" Paul				
1349	" Ada	1594.20	Henry Donnelly	G W Benge	
1350	Donnelly James	265.70	James Donnelly	G W Benge	
1351	Donnelly Mattie	265.70	M. Daniels	J.C. Starr	pd on order
1352	Deems Johny				
1353	" Edna	531.40	W P Henderson	G W Benge	
1354	Drew Wm H				
1355	" Ellen E.				
1356	" Pearl				
1357	" Willie R.				
1358	" Nana				
1359	" Ruby				
1360	" Jennie				
1361	Drew Jessie B.	2125.60	Jessie B. Drew	G W Benge	by order from Father
1362	Duncan Walter T.				
1363	" Ethel	531.40	W.T. Duncan	G W Benge	
1364	Dobkins Ben				(Illegible...) father L B Bell
1365	" Ida				
1366	" Nora	order			
1367	" Hugh	1062.80	L.B. Bell	G.W. Benge	
	~~Dick Oce C.~~		(Delaware Dist. Page 383 No. 889 as Oce Dick)		see Delaware Roll #3386
1368	Downing Peggie	265.70	Peggy Downing	L B Bell	

Starr Roll 1894

We, the undersigned citizens of the Cherokee Nation, by right of Cherokee blood, do hereby acknowledge to have received of E. E. Starr, National Treasurer of the Cherokee Nation, the sums set opposite our names respectively, in full of our shares in the per capita distribution authorized by an Act of the National Council, dated ___MAY 3 1894___ 1894.

	Names of Head, and Members of Families	Amount	To Whom Paid	Witness to Payment	Remarks
1369	Davis John	~~D696~~ 9901			
1370	" Susie				
1371	" Mary	~~D696~~ 9901			
1372	" Rachel				
1373	" Burwell	~~D696~~ 9901 1328.50	John Davis	G W Benge	
1374	Denton Rufus	order			
1375	" Hettie				
1376	" Frank				
1377	" Susie				
1378	" Mattie				
1379	" Unce	1594.20	Wᵐ L Moore	J.C. Starr	
1380	Dodson Nancy	265.70	W.J. Dodson	J.C. Starr	
1381	Dick Belle	order			
1382	" Willie				order
1383	Chambers Bettie	797.10	F A Neilson	Henry Eiffert	Dead
1384	Davis Frog	265.70	A H Norwood	Henry Eiffert	This man is in prison and don't want his money paid to any one order Sept 23 9
1385	Dowell Lee J.				G.W.E.
1386	" Morgan	order			
1387	" Claude				
1388	" Virdia A.				
1389	" William E.	1328.50	G W Eaton	Henry Eiffert	check
1390	Davis Monroe D.				
1391	" Neppie				
1392	" John				W E Halsell
1393	" Mack	order			
1394	" Hattie	5346			
1395	" Kim	1594.20	WE Halsell	Henry Eiffert	
1396	Danderson Lizzie				
1397	Enloe Willie				
1398	Danderson John Otis	797.10	Lizzie Danderson	G W Benge	

141

Starr Roll 1894

We, the undersigned citizens of the Cherokee Nation, by right of Cherokee blood, do hereby acknowledge to have received of E. E. Starr, National Treasurer of the Cherokee Nation, the sums set opposite our names respectively, in full of our shares in the per capita distribution authorized by an Act of the National Council, dated ___MAY 3 1894___ 1894.

#	Names of Head, and Members of Families	Amount	To Whom Paid	Witness to Payment	Remarks
1399	Davenport GuAlma[sic]				
1400	" Willard	531.40	J.S. Davenport	G W Benge	
~~1401~~					
1402	Downing Walter	order 265.70	J.S. Thomason	G W Benge	on order
1403	Dawson Robert	D605 265.70	Robert Dawson	L B Bell	
1404	Eaton Taylor	order 265.70	Chas Hayden	Henry Eiffert	C.H. Check
1405	Elliott George	DEAD.			W.S. Nelson
1406	" James				
1407	" Elizabeth				
1408	" Sarah	order			
1409	" Maude				
1410	" Georgie	1594.20	L.B. Bell	G W Benge	
1411	Elliott Lizzie				H. & W.T.W.
1412	" Wm T.				
1413	" Riley A.	order 797.10	W.T. Whitaker	Henry Eiffert	
1414	Elliott Annie E.				
1415	" Mamie	531.40	A.E. Elliott	G W Benge	
1416	Elliott Wm H.	265.70	W.H. Elliott	G W Benge	
1417	Etter Bertie	5275 265.70	E.A. Etter	G W Benge	
1418	Ellis Thomas				
1419	" Daby				
1420	" Webster	D564			
1421	" Rosey	order			JM Hall
1422	" Isaac M.				
1423	" William	1594.20	JM Hall	Henry Eiffert	
1424	Edwards Susan				
1425	Philips Myrtle				
1426	" Ettie	797.10	WS Edwards	G W Benge	

Starr Roll 1894

We, the undersigned citizens of the Cherokee Nation, by right of Cherokee blood, do hereby acknowledge to have received of E. E. Starr, National Treasurer of the Cherokee Nation, the sums set opposite our names respectively, in full of our shares in the per capita distribution authorized by an Act of the National Council, dated ___MAY 3 1894___ 1894.

	Names of Head, and Members of Families	Amount	To Whom Paid	Witness to Payment	Remarks
1427	Ellis Eli				
1428	" Nancy				
1429	" Annie	order			JM Hall
1430	" Robert				
1431	" July	1328.50	J M Hall	Henry Eiffert	Check
1432	Ezell Ola		10165		
1433	" Eva	order 531.40	C W Pool 10165	Henry Eiffert	Check
1434	Edmons Susie	D367	10180		
1435	" William	order 531.40	C W Pool	Henry Eiffert	Check
1436	England John				
1437	" Belle				
1438	" Lucy				
1439	" Joseph				
1440	" Frances				
1441	" Elvie				
1442	" Beulah				
1443	" Benjamin	2125.60	John England	G W Benge	
1444	Essex Addie				
1445	" Cale C.	531.40	C B Essex	G W Benge	
1446	Emerson Emma		~~D683~~ R690		George Emerson
1447	" Georgia	531.40	Their people are all out of the Nation Geo Emerson ~~D683~~ guard.	L B Bell R690	Children Sept 25 1894
1448	Elliott Jack	265.70	W E Halsell	L B Bell	E C (Illegible)
1449	Evans Eliza	DEAD.			
1450	" James P.				
1451	" Robt. H.				
1452	" Effie				
1453	Morgan Lou E.				
1454	" Minnie	472			
1455	Sixkiller Cora				
1456	" Samuel				

Starr Roll 1894

We, the undersigned citizens of the Cherokee Nation, by right of Cherokee blood, do hereby acknowledge to have received of E. E. Starr, National Treasurer of the Cherokee Nation, the sums set opposite our names respectively, in full of our shares in the per capita distribution authorized by an Act of the National Council, dated ___MAY 3 1894___ 1894.

	Names of Head, and Members of Families	Amount	To Whom Paid	Witness to Payment	Remarks
1457	" Fannie				
1458	Evans Walter N. Jr	2657.00	Eliza Evans	L B Bell	
1459	Erwin Charles	265.70	W.J. Kuhn	G W Benge	
1460	Emerson George	265.70	James M Keys	Henry Eiffert	Check
1461	Ellison Charlotte E.				
1462	" Robert S.	531.40	C E Ellison	G W Benge	
1463	Ellis Ollie				
1464	" Otto				
1465	" Mary (May)	797.10	J.T. Gunter	G W Benge	
1466	Elliott Mary				
1467	" Watt				
1468	" Archie				
1469	" Delia				
1470	" Jessie				
1471	Rogers Charles	1594.20	Mary Elliott	G W Benge	
1472	Eaton Ellis M.				
1473	" Mollie				
1474	" Lelia				
1475	" Richard				Neilson
1476	" Willie	order 1328.50	F.A. Neilson	J.C. Starr	on order
1477	Eaton Nancy				
1478	" Mattie				
1479	" Merritt	797.10	G.W. Eaton		
1480	Eaton Callie	265.70	Geo Eaton	L B Bell	
1481	Eaton Calvin	265.70	Calvin Eaton	J.C. Starr	
1482	Eaton Walter	order 265.70	F A Neilson	Henry Eiffert	Neilson

Starr Roll 1894

We, the undersigned citizens of the Cherokee Nation, by right of Cherokee blood, do hereby acknowledge to have received of E. E. Starr, National Treasurer of the Cherokee Nation, the sums set opposite our names respectively, in full of our shares in the per capita distribution authorized by an Act of the National Council, dated ___MAY 3 1894___ 1894.

	Names of Head, and Members of Families	Amount	To Whom Paid	Witness to Payment	Remarks
1483	Eaton Elizabeth	order 265.70	F A Neilson	Henry Eiffert	Neilson
1484	Eater Field				Dead
1485	" " Nancy	order			
1486	Melton Carrie				Step children
1487	" Lee				Field Eater
1488	" James				
1489	Hartgrove William	1594.20	JE Campbell	Henry Eiffert	Check
1490	Fay Linne A.				
1491	" Alfred J.	531.40	M.A Spriggs	G W Benge	
1492	Fisher Ben				
1493	" Eliza				
1494	" Jake				
1495	" Betsey				
1496	" Sarah				
1497	" Annie				
1498	" Josie	1859.90	Ben Fisher	G W Benge	
1499	" Lucy	265.70	Lucy Fisher	G W Benge	
1500	" Jessie	265.70	Ben Fisher	G W Benge	
1501	Fair Rena				
1502	" Ross				
1503	" Bettie	797.10	Rena Fair	G W Benge	
1504	Fair Ella	2623			
1505	" Dora	531.40	Ella Fair	G W Benge	
1506	Fields James	265.70	James Fields	G W Benge	
1507	Fisher Rufus				
1508	" Charlotte				
1509	" Maggie				
1510	" Aggie	1062.80	Rufus Fisher	G W Benge	
1511	Fisher Johnson	265.70	Johnson Fisher	G W Benge	

Starr Roll 1894

We, the undersigned citizens of the Cherokee Nation, by right of Cherokee blood, do hereby acknowledge to have received of E. E. Starr, National Treasurer of the Cherokee Nation, the sums set opposite our names respectively, in full of our shares in the per capita distribution authorized by an Act of the National Council, dated ___MAY 3 1894___ 1894.

Names of Head, and Members of Families	Amount	To Whom Paid	Witness to Payment	Remarks
1512 Fisher Moses	*Paid See opposite page*			
1513 Fisher Sarah				
1514 " Ella				
1515 " Isaac				
1516 " Susie				
1517 " Richard	1594.20	Sarah Fisher	G W Benge	
1518 Fields William L.				
1519 " Henry F.				
1520 " Elizabeth J.				
1521 " Carrie R.	1062.80	Amanda J Fields	G W Benge	
1522 Fite Julia P.				
1523 " William P.				
1524 " Frances	797.10	F.B. Fite	G W Benge	
1525 Fortner Annie W.				
1526 " Frank B.				
1527 " Samuel H.				
1528 " Ralph H.	1062.80	W.R. Fortner	G W Benge	
1529 Fields Levi O.				
1530 " Lucy O.	531.40	Levi O Field	G W Benge	*These names should have been written O'Fields*
1531 Fields Dick O.	265.70	Levi O Field	G W Benge	
1532 Foreman Andy	265.70	Andy Foreman	G W Benge	
1533 French Thomas	265.70	L B Bell	Henry Eiffert	*Check*
1534 Franks Josephine				
1535 " Ida				
1536 " William				
1537 " Caraal[sic]				
1538 " Lillie				
1539 " Mary				

Starr Roll 1894

We, the undersigned citizens of the Cherokee Nation, by right of Cherokee blood, do hereby acknowledge to have received of E. E. Starr, National Treasurer of the Cherokee Nation, the sums set opposite our names respectively, in full of our shares in the per capita distribution authorized by an Act of the National Council, dated ___MAY 3 1894___ 1894.

	Names of Head, and Members of Families	Amount	To Whom Paid	Witness to Payment	Remarks
1540	" Lulu				
1541	" Edgar				
1542	" Joel				
1543	" Myrtle	2657.00	Josephine Franks	L B Bell	
1544	Fallen Jess				
1545	" Lucinda				
1546	" John	*order*			*Neilson*
1547	" Charles	1062.80	F.A. Neilson	J.C. Starr	*on order*
1548	Fields Linnie	*4463*			
1549	" Jeffie				
1550	" George				
1551	" Lewis				
1552	" Joseph				
1553	" Pearl				
1554	" Cyrintha				
1555	Fields Lafayette				
1556	Fields Charlie	2391.30	Jeff J. Fields	G W Benge	
1557	Fields Jeff J.				
1558	" Cora				
1559	" Fannie				
1560	" May	1062.80	Jeff J. Fields	G W Benge	
1561	Flournoy Annie				
1562	" Rolly				
1563	" Walter				
1564	" Clara	1062.80	D H Flournoy	G W Benge	
1565	Flournoy Lilla	265.70	Lilla Flournoy	G W Benge	

Starr Roll 1894

We, the undersigned citizens of the Cherokee Nation, by right of Cherokee blood, do hereby acknowledge to have received of E. E. Starr, National Treasurer of the Cherokee Nation, the sums set opposite our names respectively, in full of our shares in the per capita distribution authorized by an Act of the National Council, dated ___MAY 3 1894___ 1894.

	Names of Head, and Members of Families	Amount	To Whom Paid	Witness to Payment	Remarks
1566	Foreman Everett G.				
1567	" Isabell				
1568	" Maggie B.				
1569	" Jeremiah				
1570	" Sarah C.				
1571	" Amelia G.	1594.20	E.G. Foreman	G W Benge	
1572	Forsythe Jane				
1573	" Sarah E.				
1574	" Lulu L.	797.10	J.E. Campbell	G W Benge	
1575	Foreman Nelson	order			J E C
1576	" Nannie				
1577	" Doss				
1578	" Essie				
1579	" Laura				
1580	" Ellis				
1581	" James L.	1859.90	JE Campbell	Henry Eiffert	check
1582	Francis Nancy				
1583	Jackson Jules L.				
1584	Francis Carrie E.	797.10	Nancy Francis	G W Benge	
1585	Foreman James				
1586	" Nellie				
1587	" Maude	order			
1588	" Dock				
1589	" Joseph				
1590	" Henry				
1591	" Charles	1859.90	A Foyil	Henry Eiffert	Check
1592	Fryer Wm H.				
1593	" Paul W.				
1594	" Edward B.	797.10	Wm H. Frye	J.C. Starr	
1595	Fallen Sarah J.				
1596	" Ida	531.40	S.J. Fallen	J.C. Starr	

Starr Roll 1894

We, the undersigned citizens of the Cherokee Nation, by right of Cherokee blood, do hereby acknowledge to have received of E. E. Starr, National Treasurer of the Cherokee Nation, the sums set opposite our names respectively, in full of our shares in the per capita distribution authorized by an Act of the National Council, dated ___MAY 3 1894___ 1894.

	Names of Head, and Members of Families	Amount	To Whom Paid	Witness to Payment	Remarks
1597	Frazier Lelia				
1598	" Ethel	531.40	M.C. Frazier	J.C. Starr	
1599	Flannagan Mary				
1600	" Jessie B.				
1601	" William W.				
1602	" Charlie A.				
1603	" Frank J.				
1604	" Mary E.				
1605	" Mike				
1606	" Truda H.	2125.60	Pat *(Illegible)*	L B Bell	
1607	Fields[sic] Emaline				
1608	Fields Charley	531.40	Emaline Field	G.W. Benge	
1609	Flint Victoria				
1610	" Caroline W.				
1611	" Amos V.	797.10	L.D. Flint	G W Benge	
1612	Fitzsimmons Ida J.				
1613	" John A.				
1614	" Susan J.	797.10	Ida J Fitzsimmons	G W Benge	
1615	Fitzsimmons Mary E.				
1616	" Mary J.				
1617	Don Carlos Lewis A				
1618	" Susan M.				
1619	" Frank L.				
1620	" Annie B	1594.20	M.E. Fitzsimmons	G W Benge	
1621	Foster Belle				
1622	" Dora				
1623	" Jane	797.10	Belle Foster	L B Bell	

Starr Roll 1894

We, the undersigned citizens of the Cherokee Nation, by right of Cherokee blood, do hereby acknowledge to have received of E. E. Starr, National Treasurer of the Cherokee Nation, the sums set opposite our names respectively, in full of our shares in the per capita distribution authorized by an Act of the National Council, dated ___MAY 3 1894___ 1894.

	Names of Head, and Members of Families	Amount	To Whom Paid	Witness to Payment	Remarks
1624	Foust Rosie E.				F.M.C.
1625	" Thos J.	order			
1626	" Bertha	797.10	J.W. Foust	G.W. Benge	
1627	Foreman Herman L.				
1628	" David W.	531.40	H.L. Foreman	L B Bell	
1629	Floyd Carrie				
1630	" Annie L.				
1631	" James D.				
1632	" Donie May				
1633	" Miller B.				
1634	" George R.	1594.20	Carrie Floyd	L B Bell	
1635	Fitzgerald Catherine				
1636	" Mamie				
1637	" Catherine				
1638	" Elnora				
1639	" Polly				
1640	" William R.	1594.20	E.H. Fizgerald[sic]	G W Benge	
1641	Foster Artemus				
1642	" Baby	$531.40	W.M. Gullager	S W Mayfield	
1643	Fields Thomas R.				
1644	" Walter L.	531.40	Artemim Foster	L B Bell	
1645	Fields Susan E.	797.10	T.R. Fields	G W Benge	
1646	Fletcher Thomas	265.70 [272.9]	Walsh and Shutt	Henry Eiffert	Check
1647	Fritz Edward				
1648	" Fannie	order			
1649	" Elizabeth				
1650	" Frances				on order of J S Thomason
1651	" Katie	1328.50	L B Bell	L B Bell	

Starr Roll 1894

We, the undersigned citizens of the Cherokee Nation, by right of Cherokee blood, do hereby acknowledge to have received of E. E. Starr, National Treasurer of the Cherokee Nation, the sums set opposite our names respectively, in full of our shares in the per capita distribution authorized by an Act of the National Council, dated ____MAY 3 1894____ 1894.

#	Names of Head, and Members of Families	Amount	To Whom Paid	Witness to Payment	Remarks
1652	Fields William				
1653	" Mollie				
1654	" Jessie				
1655	" Bird				
1656	" Dora				
1657	" Roy	1594.20	Wm Fields	G W Benge	
1658	Fortner Lucy J.				
1659	" Grace				
1660	" Lucille	797.10	B.F. Fortner	G W Benge	
1661	Foreman A.W.				
1662	" Emma E.				
1663	" Flora E.				
1664	" Eminta				
1665	Galagher Birdie	1328.50 #3807	A.W. Foreman	G W Benge	
1666	Flemings Maria[sic]				
1667	Beeson Edward	531.40	Mariah Flemings	G W Benge	
1668	Fields William				
1669	" Della	531.40	William Fields	G W Benge	
1670	Fitzgerald Martha J.				
1671	" Nora	531.40	Richard Fitzgerald	G W Benge	
1672	Fields Thomas				
1673	" Ethel	531.40	Thomas Fields	G W Benge	
1674	Smith Zella	265.70	J.H. *(Illegible)*	Henry Eiffert	
1675	Forster Lulu	265.70	Lulu Forster	J.C. Starr	
1676	Fields[sic] Lou				*Nellie Field (Mother)*
1677	" Edward	531.40	Ella Fields	G.W. Benge	
1678	Farnar Salcie	*order*			*W L M*
1679	" Leo V.	531.40	WL Moore	Henry Eiffert	*Check*

Starr Roll 1894

We, the undersigned citizens of the Cherokee Nation, by right of Cherokee blood, do hereby acknowledge to have received of E. E. Starr, National Treasurer of the Cherokee Nation, the sums set opposite our names respectively, in full of our shares in the per capita distribution authorized by an Act of the National Council, dated ___MAY 3 1894___ 1894.

	Names of Head, and Members of Families	Amount	To Whom Paid	Witness to Payment	Remarks
1680	Forster John				
1681	" Susie	order			WEH
1682	" Jane	797.10	Halsell W E	Henry Eiffert	Check
1683	Flint Sabra				
1684	" Florence				
1685	" Willie				
1686	" Essie				
1687	" Eva				
1688	" James E.	1594.20	M.T. Flint	J.C. Starr	
1689	Frye Mack	265.70	Mack Frye	J.C. Starr	
1690	" Katie [Kittie]				
1691	" Jennie				
1692	" Culla				
1693	" Annie				
1694	" Amelia	1328.50	William Frye	L B Bell	
1695	Fagan Joseph	265.70	F.A. Neilson Guardian	J.C. Starr	
1696	Foreman Lulu S.				
1697	" Jennie M.				
1698	" Ada L.				
1699	" Victoria E.				
1700	" Taylor W.				
1701	" Perry A.	1594.20	Ada Foreman	L B Bell	
1702	Foreman Jno A.				
1703	" Johny F.H.L.				
1704	" Leonard W.	797.10	Amanda Foreman	L B Bell	
1705	Foreman Jno E.	265.70	Jno. E. Foreman	G W Benge	
1706	Foreman Josie G.	265.70	J.G. Foreman	G W Benge	
1707	Foyil Charlott				
1708	" Milo	531.50	A Foil[sic]	G W Benge	

Starr Roll 1894

We, the undersigned citizens of the Cherokee Nation, by right of Cherokee blood, do hereby acknowledge to have received of E. E. Starr, National Treasurer of the Cherokee Nation, the sums set opposite our names respectively, in full of our shares in the per capita distribution authorized by an Act of the National Council, dated ___MAY 3 1894___ 1894.

Names of Head, and Members of Families	Amount	To Whom Paid	Witness to Payment	Remarks
1709 France Sallie	265.70	Sallie France	G W Benge	
1710 Foster Samuel				
1711 " Mattie				
1712 " Sylva E.	797.10	Martha Foster	G W Benge	
1713 Gaylor Bettie				
1714 " Lena				
1715 " Thomas				
1716 " Hogan				
1717 " Grover				
1718 " Perry	1594.20	Thomas Gaylor	G W Benge	
1719 Gear Rosa				
1720 " Sam	531.40	Rosa Gear	L B Bell	
1721 Gray Annie L.				J.C.H.
1722 Larry Willis				
1723 " Martha A.				
1724 " Billy	order			
1725 " Nellie				
1726 " Cora	1594.20	JC Hogan	Henry Eiffert	Check
~~Galkiller Wilson~~				Enrolled with Dave Tadpole fam
1727 Gray Mary A	265.70	M Gray	G W Benge	
1728 Griggs Colonel				
1729 " Frank	531.40	W.J. Griggs	G W Benge	
1730 Goss Wash				
1731 " Alice				
1732 " Ben F.	797.10	Wash Goss	G.W. Benge	On Orphan Roll
~~Mayes Sallie~~				

Starr Roll 1894

We, the undersigned citizens of the Cherokee Nation, by right of Cherokee blood, do hereby acknowledge to have received of E. E. Starr, National Treasurer of the Cherokee Nation, the sums set opposite our names respectively, in full of our shares in the per capita distribution authorized by an Act of the National Council, dated ___MAY 3 1894___ 1894.

	Names of Head, and Members of Families	Amount	To Whom Paid	Witness to Payment	Remarks
1733	Gass Lucy A				
1734	" Louisa				
1735	" Martha	797.10	F.A. Neilson	J.C. Starr	on order
1736	Gwartney Susan	order			J.C.H.
1737	" Carrie J.				
1738	" Mary A.				
1739	" Dollie				
1740	" Stella E.	1328.50	JC Hogan	Henry Eiffert	Check
1741	Glass George	265.70	CW Poole	L B Bell	
1742	" Mary or (Nellie)	265.70	Mary Boot	G W Benge	
1743	" Louis				
1744	" Oma	531.40	CW Poole	L B Bell	
1745	Gillis Ellen	265.70	Ellen Gillis	L B Bell	
1746	Gravitt Columbus F.				
1747	" Luther O.				
1748	" Ora B.				
1749	" Lillie P.				
1750	" Alice				
1751	" Addie				
1752	" Earl				
1753	" Ular	2125.60	C.F. Gravitt	G W Benge	
1754	Gravitt James M.	265.70	James Gravit[sic]	L B Bell	
1755	Gravitt Jefferson M.	265.70	J.M. Gravett[sic]	J.C. Starr	
1756	Gassoway Mary E.	order			J.C.H.
1757	" Henry W.				
1758	" May				
1759	" Noma				
1760	" Lulu B.	1328.50	JC Hogan	Henry Eiffert	Check
1761	Gunter Henry	265.70	Henry Gunter	L B Bell	

Starr Roll 1894

We, the undersigned citizens of the Cherokee Nation, by right of Cherokee blood, do hereby acknowledge to have received of E. E. Starr, National Treasurer of the Cherokee Nation, the sums set opposite our names respectively, in full of our shares in the per capita distribution authorized by an Act of the National Council, dated ___MAY 3 1894___ 1894.

	Names of Head, and Members of Families	Amount	To Whom Paid	Witness to Payment	Remarks
1762	Gillstrap Demsey	265.70	Demsey Gillstrap	J.C. Starr	
1763	Green Emeline	265.70	Emeline Green	G W Benge	
1764	Gillstrap Jennie M.	265.70	F.A. Neilson	J.C. Starr	on order
1765	Glass John				
1766	" Jennie				
1767	" Annie				
1768	" Ellen				
1769	" Mollie				
1770	" Buck	1594.20	CW Poole	L B Bell	
1771	Garlin Sallie	265.70 *order*	S.L. Garlin	E W Buffington	
1772	Gearheart Rachel				
1773	Glass Geo W.				
1774	" James				
1775	" Eliza				
1776	" Betsey				
1777	" Johnson	1594.20	Rachel Gearheart	G W Benge	
1778	Greer Eugenia O.				
1779	" Kirmie L.	531.40	E O Greer	G W Benge	
1780	Greenway Alonzo G.	265.70	J E Campbell	Henry Eiffert	J.E.C. Check
1781	Goddard Katie L.				
1782	" Lidia Thomas	531.40	K.L. Goddard	G W Benge	
1783	Gibbs Eliza				
1784	" Charlotte				Dead
1785	" Charles	797.10	J L Gibbs Jr	G W Benge	
1786	Gilbert George				
1787	" Kiamitia C.				
1788	" Dennis	797.10	Allen Gilbert	G W Benge	

Starr Roll 1894

We, the undersigned citizens of the Cherokee Nation, by right of Cherokee blood, do hereby acknowledge to have received of E. E. Starr, National Treasurer of the Cherokee Nation, the sums set opposite our names respectively, in full of our shares in the per capita distribution authorized by an Act of the National Council, dated ___MAY 3 1894___ 1894.

	Names of Head, and Members of Families	Amount	To Whom Paid	Witness to Payment	Remarks
1789	Gott Susan				
1790	Harris Lucinda	531.40	Ale Gott	G W Benge	
1791	Goodman Catherine B.				
1792	" Eddie J.				
1793	" Ora M.				
1794	" Albert A.				
1795	" Susan				
1796	" Robert F.				
1797	" Joseph W.	1859.90	W.S. Goodman	G W Benge	
1798	Goddard W^m	265.70	Wm Goddard	G W Benge	
1799	Guess George	265.70 order	F.M. Crowell	G W Benge	F.M.C. order
1800	Griggs Jno R.	ENROLLMENT REFUSED. R101			
1801	" Jessie	ENROLLMENT REFUSED. R101			
1802	" Alice	ENROLLMENT REFUSED. R101			
1803	" Johnny	1063.80	J.R. Griggs	G W Benge	
1804	Grayson Kate R.				
1805	" Della E.				
1806	" Claude R.				
1807	" Jennie M.				
1808	" Vinie				
1809	" Myrtle	1594.20	Sam Grayson	G W Benge	
1810	GoodyKoontz[sic] Amanda				
1811	" Frank A.				
1812	" Ethel P.	797.10	Amanda GoobyKoontz	G W Benge	
1813	Gunter Jno T.				
1814	" Mabel	531.40	J.T. Gunter	G W Benge	

Starr Roll 1894

We, the undersigned citizens of the Cherokee Nation, by right of Cherokee blood, do hereby acknowledge to have received of E. E. Starr, National Treasurer of the Cherokee Nation, the sums set opposite our names respectively, in full of our shares in the per capita distribution authorized by an Act of the National Council, dated _____MAY 3 1894_____ 1894.

	Names of Head, and Members of Families	Amount	To Whom Paid	Witness to Payment	Remarks
1815	Green Maggie				
1816	" Ernest				
1817	" Ethel				
1818	" Herbert Lee	1062.80	Maggie Green	G W Benge	
1819	Gray Mary E.	265.70	J.C. Gray	G W Benge	
1820	Gray Walter				
1821	" Frances E.	531.40	Walter Gray	G W Benge	
1822	Whipple Andrew	265.70	L B Bell	H Eiffert	
1823	Goddard Henry	265.70	Henry Goddard	G W Benge	
1824	Goodwin W^m	265.70	W.E. Sanders *order*	G W Benge	*W.E.S. on order*
1825	Gant Katie	*order*			*Neilson*
1826	" Maggie				
1827	" William				
1828	" Mattie				
1829	" John	1328.50	F.A. Neilson	J.C. Starr	*on order*
1830	Gourd Looney R.				
1831	" Sarah R.				
1832	" Tecumseh R.				
1833	" Jeeter R.				
1834	" Augusta	1328.50	Dorothee R Gourd	L B Bell	
1835	Gourd James R	~~265.70~~	W^m L Moore	Henry Eiffert	*W.L.M. Check*
1836	Gourd Henry R.	~~265.70~~ *order*	GW Eaton	Henry Eiffert	*Check - G.E.*
1837	Goodall Lila	*order*			*Neilson*
1838	" Caroline				
1839	" Ida				
1840	" Lee				
1841	" Elizabeth				
1842	" William E.	1594.20	F.A. Neilson	J.C. Starr	*on order*

Starr Roll 1894

We, the undersigned citizens of the Cherokee Nation, by right of Cherokee blood, do hereby acknowledge to have received of E. E. Starr, National Treasurer of the Cherokee Nation, the sums set opposite our names respectively, in full of our shares in the per capita distribution authorized by an Act of the National Council, dated ___MAY 3 1894___ 1894.

	Names of Head, and Members of Families	Amount	To Whom Paid	Witness to Payment	Remarks
1843	Grass Benjamin	order			Neilson
1844	" Vinil				
1845	" Minnie	797.10	F.A. Neilson	J.C. Starr	on order
1846	Gourd Thos R.				
1847	" Paralee				
1848	" Dan				
1849	" Edward				
1850	" Taylor				
1851	" Jack				
1852	" George				
1853	" Calvin	2125.60	Paralee R Gourd	J.C. Starr	
1854	Gunter John E.				W E H
1855	" Sammie E.				
1856	Taylor Georgie L.	797.10	J.E. Gunter	G W Benge	
1857	Galcatcher Lee				
1858	" Ellen				Geo W Eaton
1859	" Henry	order			
1860	" Mattie				
1861	" Joseph				
1862	Burgess Sarah				
1863	McCoy Mary E.	1859.90	Geo Eaton	Henry Eiffert	Check
1864	Galcatcher Nancy	order			Bowling
1865	" Thomas				
1866	Cochran George	797.10	JM Boling	Henry Eiffert	Check
1867	Galcatcher Mary	order 265.70	JM Boling	Henry Eiffert	Boling Child
1868	Galcatcher Lou	order 265.70	F.A. Neilson	J.C. Starr	on order

Starr Roll 1894

We, the undersigned citizens of the Cherokee Nation, by right of Cherokee blood, do hereby acknowledge to have received of E. E. Starr, National Treasurer of the Cherokee Nation, the sums set opposite our names respectively, in full of our shares in the per capita distribution authorized by an Act of the National Council, dated ____MAY 3 1894____ 1894.

Names of Head, and Members of Families	Amount	To Whom Paid	Witness to Payment	Remarks
1869 Gourd John R.				
1870 " Artemissie R.				
1871 " Charles R.				
1872 " Nora R.				
1873 " Gertie R.	1328.50	A.R. Gourd	G W Benge	
1874 Gourd Alex R.				
1875 " Artemus				
1876 " Susie	797.10	A.R. Gourd	J.C. Starr	
1877 Gourd Grass R.	order 265.70	GW Eaton	Henry Eiffert	check GWEaton
1878 Goodhue Jennie	order 265.70	Johnson&Keeler	Henry Eiffert	check
1879 Gulager Wm M.	265.70	W^m M Gulager	G W Benge	
1880 Green Melvina	265.70	J.R. Green	J.C. Starr	
1881 Gilstrap Levi	order 265.70	JM Hall	Henry Eiffert	JM Hall minor
1882 Goss Amy	R460 ENROLLMENT REFUSED.			
1883 " Lelia	R460 531.40	Amy Goss R460	G W Benge	
1884 Gray Birt	4198 265.70	Laura A Rogers	G W Benge	
1885 Grace Alcie C.	265.70	AC. D281 Grace	G.W. Benge	Book 1, Page 2
1886 Galloway Dollie E.	265.70	Frank Billingslie	G W Benge	Book 4 Page 13
1887 Garland Elizabeth				Admitted Sep 7'8
1888 " Florie				
1889 " Dollie				
1890 " Agnis				
1891 " Francis				
1892 " Lillie				
1893 " John				
1894 " Dorie	2125.60	Boxta Garland	J.C. Starr	

Starr Roll 1894

We, the undersigned citizens of the Cherokee Nation, by right of Cherokee blood, do hereby acknowledge to have received of E. E. Starr, National Treasurer of the Cherokee Nation, the sums set opposite our names respectively, in full of our shares in the per capita distribution authorized by an Act of the National Council, dated ___MAY 3 1894___ 1894.

	Names of Head, and Members of Families	Amount	To Whom Paid	Witness to Payment	Remarks
1895	Hughes Ella				
1896	" Margaret				
1897	" George	797.10	Ella Hughes	G W Benge	
1898	Harrison Dolly M.	~~D1122~~ R662			Creek Field Card 2037
1899	" Floyd	Elects to take allotment in Creek Nation			P.G.R.
1900	" Irene	" " " " " " "			Jany 30, 1901
1901	" Clifford	1062.80	L.M. Harrison	G W Benge	
1902	Hammer Ned				
1903	" Annie	531.40	Ned Hammer	G W Benge	
1904	Hughes W^m				
1905	" Eliza				
1906	Downing Polly	797.10	Wm Hughes	G W Benge	
1907	Holt Sabra R.				
1908	" Nora				
1909	" John W.				
1910	" Charles W.				
1911	" Sarah	1328.50	Cooie Buffington	G W Benge	
1912	Hightman Mollie				
1913	" Bee				
1914	" Maude				
1915	" Henry	1062.80	Mollie Hightman	G W Benge	
1916	Hatchet Thomas				
1917	" Nancy				
1918	White Rosie	797.10	Thomas Hatchet	G W Benge	
1919	Hayden Clara / Carrie				
1920	" Charley				Dead
1921	" Minnie				
1922	" Clarence				
1923	" Ida M.				
1924	" Lona				

Starr Roll 1894

We, the undersigned citizens of the Cherokee Nation, by right of Cherokee blood, do hereby acknowledge to have received of E. E. Starr, National Treasurer of the Cherokee Nation, the sums set opposite our names respectively, in full of our shares in the per capita distribution authorized by an Act of the National Council, dated ___MAY 3 1894___ 1894.

	Names of Head, and Members of Families	Amount	To Whom Paid	Witness to Payment	Remarks
1925	" Lela				
1926	" Essie	2125.60	Clem Hayden	G W Benge	
1927	Holleman Martha				
1928	" Beulah				
1929	" Charley				
1930	" Harvey				
1931	" Henry				
1932	" Fred	1594.20	J.J. Holleman	G W Benge	
1933	Holt Victoria				J.C.H.
1934	" Walter L.	order			
1935	" Melvia	797.10	JC Hogan	Henry Eiffert	Check
1936	Horn Margaret		~~R271~~ R653		W.T.W.
1937	" Wᵐ G.C.	order	order R152 ENROLLMENT REFUSED.		
1938	" Robt L.	order			W.T.W.
1939	" Florence	1062.80	~~R277~~ R654 ~~W.T. Whitaker~~	Henry Eiffert	W.T.W.
1940	Horn Charles W.		ENR~~O133~~MENT REFUSED.		W.T.W.
1941	" Thomas L.				
1942	" William J.	order			
1943	" Cynthia	1062.80 order	W T Whitaker	Henry Eiffert	W.T.W.
1944	Henry John	265.70	W E Halsell[sic]	Henry Eiffert	W E Halsell
1945	Helterbrand Dennis	265.70	Benjamin Helterbrand	G W Benge	
1946	" John W.	265.70 order	A H Norwood 1946	Henry Eiffert	A.H. Norwood
1947	" Thomas A.				
1948	" Joseph J.				
1949	" Annie J.				
1950	" James F.				
1951	" John T.	1328.50	Dennis Helterbrand	J.C. Starr	
					J.C.H.

Starr Roll 1894

We, the undersigned citizens of the Cherokee Nation, by right of Cherokee blood, do hereby acknowledge to have received of E. E. Starr, National Treasurer of the Cherokee Nation, the sums set opposite our names respectively, in full of our shares in the per capita distribution authorized by an Act of the National Council, dated ____MAY 3 1894____ 1894.

#	Names of Head, and Members of Families	Amount	To Whom Paid	Witness to Payment	Remarks
1952	Henry Josiah				
1953	" Alice	order			
1954	" William				
1955	" Rose				
1956	" Rachel				
1957	" Ben				
1958	" Addie	1859.90	JC Hogan	Henry Eiffert	Check
1959	Henry Jessie	265.70	Josiah Henry	J.C. Starr	
1960	Hogan Margaret M				
1961	" John Z.				
1962	" Graham				
1963	" Mable	1062.80	JC Hogan	G W Benge	
1964	Horn Jno W.		D379		
1965	" Pearl		D379		
1966	" Ruby	797.10	Jno W Horn	G W Benge	
1967	Hilderbrand Joseph	265.70	Johnson & Keeler D1505	Henry Eiffert	
1968	Harmon Flora A.				
1969	" Lillie				
1970	" Claude	797.10	F.A. Harmon	G W Benge	
1971	Howie Mary	265.70	Thomas Howie	G W Benge	
1972	Curby Charles	265.70	Chas Curby	G W Benge	
1973	Habich George E.	265.70	Mary Bachtel	G W Benge	
1974	Hampton Andy				
1975	" Clara				
1976	" Lulu				
1977	" Dora	1062.80	Andy Hampton	G W Benge	

Starr Roll 1894

We, the undersigned citizens of the Cherokee Nation, by right of Cherokee blood, do hereby acknowledge to have received of E. E. Starr, National Treasurer of the Cherokee Nation, the sums set opposite our names respectively, in full of our shares in the per capita distribution authorized by an Act of the National Council, dated ____MAY 3 1894____ 1894.

	Names of Head, and Members of Families	Amount	To Whom Paid	Witness to Payment	Remarks
1978	Hood Susan				
1979	" Radford				order withdrawn
1980	" Harrison				
1981	" Nettie	1062.80	Susan Hood	G W Benge	
1982	Harrison Mary A				
1983	" Nevada				
1984	" Nathan	797.10	DW Harrison	G W Benge	
1985	Harrison Andrew P.	265.70	A.P. Harrison	G W Benge	
1986	Harris Ida J.				
1987	" Flora M.				
1988	" Gertie N.				
1989	" Ula-lah S.				
1990	Roy C.	1328.50	I. J. Harris	G W Benge	
1991	Hampton W^m				J.S.T.
1992	" Floretta M.	531.40 order	J.S. Thomason	G W Benge	on order
1993	Hampton Elizabeth	265.70	Elizabeth Hampton	G W Benge	
1994	Hefflefinger Elizabeth				
1995	" Erasmus				
1996	" Fannie B.	797.10	Elizabeth Hefflefinger	L B Bell	
1997	Henson Andrew	265.70	W E Halsell	G W Benge	on order
1998	" Martha	265.70 order	W E Halsell	Henry Eiffert	W E Halsell
1999	" Chilla	265.70	W E Halsell	G W Benge	on order
2000	" Luvena	265.70 order	WE Halsell	Henry Eiffert	W E Halsell
2001	Whitewater Lee	265.70 order 5139	W E Halsell	Henry Eiffert	W E Halsell
2002	Hair Lillie	265.70 order	A H Norwood	L B Bell	Julia Wales AH Norwood Mother
2003	Holly Ada				See Tah Rolls W.C. Patton
2004	" Ethel A.	531.40 order	W C Patton	G W Benge	on order

Starr Roll 1894

We, the undersigned citizens of the Cherokee Nation, by right of Cherokee blood, do hereby acknowledge to have received of E. E. Starr, National Treasurer of the Cherokee Nation, the sums set opposite our names respectively, in full of our shares in the per capita distribution authorized by an Act of the National Council, dated ___MAY 3 1894___ 1894.

	Names of Head, and Members of Families	Amount	To Whom Paid	Witness to Payment	Remarks
2005	Harlin Levi				
2006	" Zeke	531.40	Nancy Sage	L B Bell	
2007	Harlow Alabama				
2008	" Laura				
2009	" Nellie				
2010	" Bessie				
2011	" John				
2012	" William				
2013	" Samuel	1859.90	Alabama Harlow	G W Benge	
2014	Hall Eugene				
2015	" May E.	531.40	10174 Eugene Hall	G W Benge	
2016	Hayes Jennie	265.70	A H Norwood	L B Bell	on order of Rosa Cleghorn A H Norwood
2017	Hutton Thomas	265.70	Wm Howell[sic] 7175	G W Benge	
2018	Henly Clarie	order			Neilson
2019	" Edward				
2020	" Walter				
2021	" Lillie M.	1062.80	F.A. Neilson	J.C. Starr	on order
2022	Helterbrand Joseph	order 265.70	J.S. Thomason	G W Benge	on order
2023	Hair William M.	order 265.70	JS Davenport	Henry Eiffert	order Check J.S.D.
2024	Henry Patric[sic]				
2025	" Marie				
2026	" Bessie L.				
2027	" Clarence	1062.80	Patric Henry	G W Benge	
2028	Henry Gibbs				
2029	" Myrtle				
2030	" Dewitt	797.10	Patrick Henry	G W Benge	
2031	Henry Albert G.	order 265.70	Patrick Henry	G W Benge	on order

Starr Roll 1894

We, the undersigned citizens of the Cherokee Nation, by right of Cherokee blood, do hereby acknowledge to have received of E. E. Starr, National Treasurer of the Cherokee Nation, the sums set opposite our names respectively, in full of our shares in the per capita distribution authorized by an Act of the National Council, dated ____MAY 3 1894____ 1894.

	Names of Head, and Members of Families	Amount	To Whom Paid	Witness to Payment	Remarks
2032	Henry Patric				
2033	" Odney				
2034	" Archie Lee	797.10	Patrick Henry	G W Benge	
2035	Henderson [Hudson] Lewis B.				
2036	" Samuel				
2037	" Lena				
2038	" Maud	1062.80	L.B. Hudson	G W Benge	
2039	~~Henderson~~ [Hudson] Harrison A	265.70	L.B. Hudson	G W Benge	
2040	Harnage Ezekiel	265.70	Ezekiel Harnage	G W Benge	
2041	House Martha	265.70	Martha House	L B Bell	
2042	Hall Martha				
2043	" Catherine		*D2775*		
2044	" Ibbie				
2045	" Rhoda				
2046	" Benjamin	1328.50	W.H. Hall	G W Benge	
2047	Hall Frank	265.70	Frank Hall	G W Benge	
2048	Hall Frederick	265.70	F. Hall	G W Benge	
2049	Hawkins Rutha				
2050	" Glendyn E.				
2051	" Mary L				
2052	" Katie E.	1062.80	CH Hawkins	G W Benge	
2053	Condry Mary A.	*controlled by H T Landrum*			
2054	" Sterling H.	431.40	C.H. Hawkins	G W Benge	
2055	Hindselman Sarah E.				
2056	" Ada E.	531.40	S.E. Hindselman	G W Benge	

Starr Roll 1894

We, the undersigned citizens of the Cherokee Nation, by right of Cherokee blood, do hereby acknowledge to have received of E. E. Starr, National Treasurer of the Cherokee Nation, the sums set opposite our names respectively, in full of our shares in the per capita distribution authorized by an Act of the National Council, dated ___MAY 3 1894___ 1894.

	Names of Head, and Members of Families	Amount	To Whom Paid	Witness to Payment	Remarks
2057	Harris Lottie				
2058	" Baxter				
2059	" Mack	797.10	Lottie Harris	L B Bell	
2060	Hicks Andrew				
2061	" Eddie				
2062	" Lona				
2063	" Frank				
2064	" Amelia				
2065	" Annie				
2066	" Elvia				
2067	" Willie	2125.60	Andrew Hicks	L B Bell	
2068	Henry Jerry				
2069	" Murriel				
2070	" Walter	797.10	Jerry Henry	G.W. Benge	
2071	Heaps Sarena[sic]				
2072	" Walter	531.40	Serena Heaps	L B Bell	
2073	Herberger Polly	order			Neilson
2074	" Annie				
2075	" William M.	797.10	F.A. Neilson	J.C. Starr	on order
2076	Hosley Mary				
2077	Goodin[sic] John	531.40	Mary Hosley	G W Benge	
2078	Hogan Georgian[sic]				
2079	" Tynie	531.40	Georgan Hogan	G W Benge	
2080	Hoffman Ruth				
2081	" James				
2082	" Allen				
2083	" Minnie	1062.80	Ruth Hoffman	L B Bell	

Starr Roll 1894

We, the undersigned citizens of the Cherokee Nation, by right of Cherokee blood, do hereby acknowledge to have received of E. E. Starr, National Treasurer of the Cherokee Nation, the sums set opposite our names respectively, in full of our shares in the per capita distribution authorized by an Act of the National Council, dated ____MAY 3 1894____ 1894.

	Names of Head, and Members of Families	Amount	To Whom Paid	Witness to Payment	Remarks
2084	Harris Emma				or[sic]
2085	" Janey				
2086	" Sue T.				
2087	" Fred W.				
2088	" Minnie	order			
2089	" Charles J.	1594.20	HW Reed	L B Bell	HW Reed
2090	Hefner Lula M.				
2091	" Roy	531.40	L.M. Hefner	G W Benge	
2092	Harris Martha				
2093	" Charles				
2094	" Katie L.				
2095	" Johana				
2096	" Robert P.	1328.50	Martha Harris	L B Bell	
2097	Hewitt Susan R.	265.70	R.M. Swain	G W Benge	
2098	Hammer Lizzie	265.70	Lizzie Hammer	G W Benge	
2099	Hendrix White	order 265.70	JW Reed	Henry Eiffert	J.W. Reed check
2100	Hendrix Willis	265.70	F.A. Neilson Admin	J.C. Starr	
2101	" Robert				
2102	" Willis (Jr)	531.40	F.A. Neilson	Henry Eiffert	Dead
2103	Hogan Ellen	265.70	Ellen Hogan	L B Bell	
2104	Hurd George	order 265.70	JJ Barndollar	Henry Eiffert	JJ Barndollar
2105	Henry W.A.				
2106	" Amelia D.				
2107	" Archie B.		D 2649		
2108	" Eva May				
2109	" Ada A.				
2110	" Elsie				
2111	" Mabel				

Starr Roll 1894

We, the undersigned citizens of the Cherokee Nation, by right of Cherokee blood, do hereby acknowledge to have received of E. E. Starr, National Treasurer of the Cherokee Nation, the sums set opposite our names respectively, in full of our shares in the per capita distribution authorized by an Act of the National Council, dated ___MAY 3 1894___ 1894.

	Names of Head, and Members of Families	Amount	To Whom Paid	Witness to Payment	Remarks
2112	" Mark				
2113	" Agnes	2391.30	Amelia D Henry	G W Benge	
2114	Hall Wm O.				
2115	" Jesse Swan	531.40	Joseph Ann Hall	G W Benge	
2116	Ellis Edward	*order*			
2117	" Colbert				Hall
2118	" Lizzie				
2119	" Nellie				
2120	" Minnie				*check on order*
2121	" Jessie	1594.20	J.M. Hall	J.C. Starr	
2122	Sallie Sarah B.				
2123	Thornton Josie M.	531.40	S B Salley	L B Bell	
2124	Hause Che-nah-sah	265.70	Che nah sah Hause	L B Bell	
2125	Henry Joseph J.	265.70	Patric Henry	G.W. Benge	
2126	Henry Polly	265.70	Polly Henry	L B Bell	
2127	Hunter Maude	*order* 265.70	F.A. Neilson	J C Hogan	*Neilson on order*
2128	Hancock Viola S.	265.70	W.A. Hancock	G W Benge	
2129	Herod Ely	*order* 265.70	Ely Herod	*order with drawn* G W Benge	T.J.M.
2130	Hawk John				
2131	" Mary				
2132	" Wily				
2133	" Peter	1062.80	Ben Helderbrand	G W Benge	
2134	Helterbrand[sic] Benj.				
2135	" Sampson				
2136	" Lucinda				
2137	" Eliza^Ezra				
2138	" Rosie				
2139	" Separa				

Starr Roll 1894

We, the undersigned citizens of the Cherokee Nation, by right of Cherokee blood, do hereby acknowledge to have received of E. E. Starr, National Treasurer of the Cherokee Nation, the sums set opposite our names respectively, in full of our shares in the per capita distribution authorized by an Act of the National Council, dated ___MAY 3 1894___ 1894.

	Names of Head, and Members of Families	Amount	To Whom Paid	Witness to Payment	Remarks
2140	Helterbrand Laura	1859.90	Laura Helterbrand	G W Benge (wife of Benj.)	
2141	Hall Sewel W				
2142	" Bessie	order 531.40	L.B. Bell	G W Benge	on order
2143	Hall Ed	order 265.70	J.S. Thomason	G W Benge	J S Thomason on order
2144	Harlan George				
2145	" Minnie B.				
2146	" James	797.10	George Harlan	G W Benge	
2147	Harlan Wm L.	265.70	W.L. Harlan	G W Benge	
2148	Harnage Custus L.	265.70	C.L. Harnage	J.C. Starr	
2149	Highsmith Mary F				
2150	" Myrtle A.				
2151	" Roy B. L.				
2152	" Cora E.	1062.80	M.F. Highsmith	G W Benge	
2153	Hall Mary E.				
2154	Hall Ludy S.				
2155	Hall Janie P.				
2156	Hall David C.	1062.80	M.E. Hall	G W Benge	
2157	Hall Joseph Ann	265.70	Eugen[sic] Hall (10174)	G W Benge	
2158	Hall Blanche	265.70	JosephAnn Hall	G W Benge	
2159	Highland Nettie				
2160	" Maggie		9748		
2161	" James				
2162	" Patrick				
2163	" Sarah				
2164	" William	1594.20	Nettie Highland	G W Benge	

Starr Roll 1894

We, the undersigned citizens of the Cherokee Nation, by right of Cherokee blood, do hereby acknowledge to have received of E. E. Starr, National Treasurer of the Cherokee Nation, the sums set opposite our names respectively, in full of our shares in the per capita distribution authorized by an Act of the National Council, dated ___MAY 3 1894___ 1894.

#	Names of Head, and Members of Families	Amount	To Whom Paid	Witness to Payment	Remarks
2165	Halsell Pauline	265.70	E.L. Halsell	G W Benge	
2166	Horsefly James	order			E.N.R.
2167	" Arey				
2168	" Nannie				
2169	" Willie	1062.80	E.N. Ratcliff	G W Benge	on order
2170	Humphry John	265.70	J.T. Gunter	G W Benge	
2171	Galagher Tom	265.70	Ella Hoffman	G W Benge	
2172	Hoffman Ella	265.70	Ella Hoffman	G W Benge	
2173	Halsell Alice				Dead
2174	" Ewing				
2175	" Eva				
2176	" Clarence				
2177	" Mary	1328.50	Henry Eiffert	G W Benge	
2178	Harlow Jno H.				
2179	" Clifford L.				
2180	" Ola	797.10	F.B. Harlan	G W Benge	
2181	Heddy Ella M.				
2182	" Ethel	531.40	Ella M. Heddy	G W Benge	
2183	Harlan Nathan L.	265.70	N.L. Harlan	G W Benge	
2184	Helterbrand[sic] John	order	D1509		
2185	" Richard				
2186	" Samuel				
2187	" Susan		John Helderbrand	G W Benge	
2188	Hilderbrand[sic] David	1328.50	John Helderbrand D1507	G W Benge	
2189	Hilderbrand Joe	265.70	Johnson Lyman	G W Benge	
2190	Hill Rachel	265.70	Davis Hill	G W Benge	

Starr Roll 1894

We, the undersigned citizens of the Cherokee Nation, by right of Cherokee blood, do hereby acknowledge to have received of E. E. Starr, National Treasurer of the Cherokee Nation, the sums set opposite our names respectively, in full of our shares in the per capita distribution authorized by an Act of the National Council, dated ____MAY 3 1894_____ 1894.

	Names of Head, and Members of Families	Amount	To Whom Paid	Witness to Payment	Remarks
2191	Hill Davis				
2192	" Fannie E.				
2193	" George R.				
2194	" James J.	1062.80	Davis Hill	G.W. Benge	
2195	Housely Elizabeth				J.S.T & S.W.B.
2196	" Mary E.	*order*			
2197	" Louisa R.	797.10	J.S. Thomason	G W Benge	*on order*
2198	Hunt Ruth				
2199	" Charles				
2200	" Janey				
2201	" Nathaniel				
2202	" Joseph Jr.				
2203	" Nancy				
2204	" Lucille	1859.90	Ruth Hunt	G W Benge	
2205	Hunt Fannie	265.70	Ruth Hunt	G W Benge	
2206	Henry Ione	*See # 1231 Deleware[sic] Dist (Same person)*			
2207	Hunter Charles	*order* 265.70	L.W. Buffington	G W Benge	
2208	Hall William	4164			
2209	" John	4164			
2210	" Dora	4164 797.10	Henry Sanders	G W Benge	
2211	High Sarah				
2212	" Eddie				
2213	" William J.	797.10	Albert High	G W Benge	
2214	Hall Mary J.				
2215	" Josephine				
2216	" Annie				
2217	" John R.				
2218	" Maude	1328.50	S.R. Hall	G W Benge	

Starr Roll 1894

We, the undersigned citizens of the Cherokee Nation, by right of Cherokee blood, do hereby acknowledge to have received of E. E. Starr, National Treasurer of the Cherokee Nation, the sums set opposite our names respectively, in full of our shares in the per capita distribution authorized by an Act of the National Council, dated ____MAY 3 1894____ 1894.

Names of Head, and Members of Families	Amount	To Whom Paid	Witness to Payment	Remarks
2219 Hurst Sylvester R.				
2220 " Walter E.				
2221 " John W.				
2222 " Annie M.				
2223 " Maggie E.				
2224 " Gracie A.	1594.20	S.R. Hurst	G W Benge	
2225 Holderman Bertie J.	265.70 *order*	J.S. Davenport	G W Benge	*on order*
2226 Holderman Curtis E.	265.70	C.E. Holderman	G W Benge	
2227 Holderman Henry C.	265.70	Mary Holderman	L B Bell	*Check*
2228 Harris Amelia	265.70	Amelia Harris	G W Benge	
2229 Hick[sic] Robt L.	265.70	Ida Hicks	J.C. Starr	
2230 Hill Robt L.	265.70	Rob't L. Hill	J.C. Starr	
2231 Hendrix Robert				
2232 " Cassie				
2233 " Tee-sey	797.10	Rob't Hendricks	J.C. Starr	
2234 Hendrix[sic] Mack	265.70	Mack Hendricks	J.C. Starr	
2235 Hicks John R.				
2236 " Ross		J.R. Hicks		
2237 Hicks Henry	797.10	J.R. Hicks	G W Benge	
2238 Haddock Rettie				
2239 " Charles	531.40	John Haddock	G W Benge	
2240 Harris Susan				
2241 " Mary J.				
2242 " Nancy D.				*Neilson*
2243 " Cora B.	*order*			

Starr Roll 1894

We, the undersigned citizens of the Cherokee Nation, by right of Cherokee blood, do hereby acknowledge to have received of E. E. Starr, National Treasurer of the Cherokee Nation, the sums set opposite our names respectively, in full of our shares in the per capita distribution authorized by an Act of the National Council, dated ___MAY 3 1894___ 1894.

Names of Head, and Members of Families	Amount	To Whom Paid	Witness to Payment	Remarks
2244 " James H.	1328.50	F.A. Neilson	J.C. Starr	on order
2245 Morris Frances	265.70	Francis Hocket	G W Benge	
2246 Henson Lorena	265.70	Lorena Henson	G W Benge	
2247 Henson Joseph	order 265.70	F.A. Neilson	J.C. Starr	on order
2248 Henry Levi J.	265.70 order	Wm L. Moore	G W Benge	on order W.L.M.
2249 Henson Richard	order			Neilson
2250 " Alice				
2251 " Maggie	797.10	D1221 F.A. Neilson	J.C. Starr	on order
2252 Hendrix Willis	Do Not Pay See No 2100	Paid down twice	Each (Illegible)	
2253 " Willis Jr	" " 2102	See No 2100	Duplicate of 2100 & 2102	
2254 Hendrix Robt.	order 265.70	Cale W Starr	G W Benge	(Illegible)
2255 Hardge[sic] Sarah				
2256 Gunter George				
2257 " Luman				
2258 Morris Mertie				
2259 " Jumbo		1328.50	Sarah Hodges	name on roll spelled wrong
2260 Hause Daniel M.				
2261 " Lillie V.				
2262 " George W.				
2263 " Sarah				
2264 " Joseph				
2265 " Caleb				
2266 " Ruth E	1859.90	D.M. Hause	G W Benge	
2267 Hurst John	4773			
2268 " Christopher C.	4773			
2269 " Ella	5228			
2270 " Rachel	4773			
2271 " Albert J.	4773 1328.50	John Hurst	G W Benge	

Starr Roll 1894

We, the undersigned citizens of the Cherokee Nation, by right of Cherokee blood, do hereby acknowledge to have received of E. E. Starr, National Treasurer of the Cherokee Nation, the sums set opposite our names respectively, in full of our shares in the per capita distribution authorized by an Act of the National Council, dated ___MAY 3 1894___ 1894.

	Names of Head, and Members of Families	Amount	To Whom Paid	Witness to Payment	Remarks
2272	Harlow Peggie A.				
2273	" Bertha				
2274	" Walter				
2275	" Alice				
2276	" James				
2277	" Joseph				
2278	" Alexander				
2279	Riley Richard	2125.60	P.A. Harlow	G W Benge	
2280	Hulsey Josephine	265.70	Josephine Hulsey	G W Benge	
2281	Hutchins Nettie	order			Neilson
2282	" Low W.				
2283	" Bluford R.	797.10	F.A. Neilson	J.C. Starr	on order
2284	Hanes Delilah				
2285	" Henny C.				
2286	" Nathaniel				
2287	" Gertrude				
2288	" Thomas				
2289	" Charles E.				
2290	" Ama V.				
2291	" Sonore				
2292	" Lee R.	2391.30	Delilah Hanes	G W Benge	
2293	Haworth[sic] Ida				
2294	" Lucille S.				
2295	" Pearsie E.	797.10	O.H. Hayworth	G W Benge	
2296	Hair Jane				
2297	" Sarah				
2298	" Eddie	797.10	Jane Hair	L B Bell	
2299	Hair Annie	265.70	Jane Hair	L B Bell	
2300	Hunter Lucretia				
2301	" Willie	531.40	W.W. Breedlove Guardian	J.C. Starr	No 27 1894

Starr Roll 1894

We, the undersigned citizens of the Cherokee Nation, by right of Cherokee blood, do hereby acknowledge to have received of E. E. Starr, National Treasurer of the Cherokee Nation, the sums set opposite our names respectively, in full of our shares in the per capita distribution authorized by an Act of the National Council, dated _____MAY 3 1894_____ 1894.

	Names of Head, and Members of Families	Amount	To Whom Paid	Witness to Payment	Remarks
2302	Hilderbrand Cherokee	265.70	Janus Hilderbrand	G W Benge	
2303	Hicks Cora	265.70	Elizabeth *(Illegible)*	L B Bell	
2304	Jackson Andrew	265.70	Andrew Jackson	G W Benge	
2305	Jackson Martha E	265.70	Wm Jackson	G W Benge	
2306	Jackson Minnie	265.70	Wm Jackson	G W Benge	
2307	Jackson Sarah				
2308	" Lydia				
2309	" Maggie	797.10	J.A. Jackson	G.W. Benge	
2310	Jackson Jno A.	*order* 265.70	Walsh and Shutt	Henry Eiffert	W. & S.
2311	Jones Mary				J.C.H.
2312	" John E.				
2313	" Oliver	*order*			
2314	" Perry				
2315	" Jennie				
2316	Hair Eliza	1594.20	JC Hogan	Henry Eiffert	Check
2317	Jackson Lidie	265.70	Sarah Jackson	L B Bell	
2318	" Hugh E.	265.70	R L Prather	Henry Eiffert	*order* Paid Oct 2 94
2319	Jones Ada				
2320	" Vera				
2321	" Ara				
2322	" Jeans	1062.80	D.V. Jones	G.W. Benge	
2323	Johnson Ella				
2324	" Claude	531.40	Ella Johnson	G W Benge	
2325	Jones Levi	265.70	Levi Jones	G.W. Benge	

Starr Roll 1894

We, the undersigned citizens of the Cherokee Nation, by right of Cherokee blood, do hereby acknowledge to have received of E. E. Starr, National Treasurer of the Cherokee Nation, the sums set opposite our names respectively, in full of our shares in the per capita distribution authorized by an Act of the National Council, dated ___MAY 3 1894___ 1894.

	Names of Head, and Members of Families	Amount	To Whom Paid	Witness to Payment	Remarks
2326	Johnson Sarah				Neilson
2327	" Willie	order			
2328	" Joe				
2329	" Ella				
2330	" Jessie				
2331	" Eddie	1594.20	F.A. Neilson	J.C. Starr	on order
2332	Johnson Charles	order 265.70	Walsh and Shutt	Henry Eiffert	W. & S. check
2333	Jackson Mack	order			
2334	" Eliza				
2335	" Caroline	797.10	Johnson and Keeler	Henry Eiffert	Check
2336	Johnson Josephine B.				
2337	" Fredrick W.O.				
2338	" Lillyetta				
2339	" Flonnce E.				
2340	" Claude M.				
2341	" Ada L.				
2342	" Howard B.	1859.90	W C Rogers	L B Bell	
2343	Johnson Jennie				
2344	" Frank	531.40	N.F. Carr	G W Benge	
2345	Jackson Mary O.	265.70	Mary E Jackson	L B Bell	
2346	Jackson Bryant B.	265.70	Nancy Francis	G W Benge	
2347	Johnson Mina M.				
2348	" Morris S.				
2349	" John W.				
2350	" Robert H.				
2351	" Mary E.				
2352	" Arthur T.	1594.20	A.F. Johnson	G W Benge	
2353	Jolly Lucy D.	order			Wm V. Curry
2354	Dale Joseph	531.40	W.V. Curry	Henry Eiffert	check

Starr Roll 1894

We, the undersigned citizens of the Cherokee Nation, by right of Cherokee blood, do hereby acknowledge to have received of E. E. Starr, National Treasurer of the Cherokee Nation, the sums set opposite our names respectively, in full of our shares in the per capita distribution authorized by an Act of the National Council, dated _____MAY 3 1894_____ 1894.

Names of Head, and Members of Families	Amount	To Whom Paid	Witness to Payment	Remarks
2355 Journeycake Eliza A.				
2356 " Robert J.				
2357 " Jessie B.				
2358 " Okie	1062.80	Eliza A Journeycake	L B Bell	
2359 Jordon[sic] Nancy E.				
2360 " Victoria M				
2361 " Lucy				
2362 " Daisey	1062.80	N.E. Jordan	G.W. Benge	
2363 Johnson John	265.70	John Johnson	G W Benge	
~~Jones Agnes~~				On Orphan Rol
~~" Carrie~~				" " "
2364 Jones Chaney	265.70	M.J. Hulsey	J.C. Starr	Guardian
2365 Jones Nancy A.	265.70	Nancy A Jones	G W Benge	
2366 Jones Theodore	265.70	Theodore Jones	G W Benge	
2367 Jackson Susan				
2368 Chaney Willie	order			H & WTW
2369 " Addie (Ada)	797.10	WT Whitaker	Henry Eiffert	
2370 Jenkins Henry W.				
2371 " Mandy M.	531.40	H.M. Jenkins	G W Benge	
2372 Jenkins Amanda				
2373 " Walter L.				
2374 " Fannie	797.10	Amanda Jenkins	G W Benge	
2375 " Maude M.	265.70	Annie Jenkins	Henry Eiffert	
2376 " Jno H.				
2377 " Elias H.	531.40	Amanda Jenkins	G W Benge	
2378 Jackson Jennie	265.70	E.A. Jackson	G W Benge	

Starr Roll 1894

We, the undersigned citizens of the Cherokee Nation, by right of Cherokee blood, do hereby acknowledge to have received of E. E. Starr, National Treasurer of the Cherokee Nation, the sums set opposite our names respectively, in full of our shares in the per capita distribution authorized by an Act of the National Council, dated ___MAY 3 1894___ 1894.

Names of Head, and Members of Families	Amount	To Whom Paid	Witness to Payment	Remarks
2379 Jones Carrie				
2380 Ross Ola F.	531.40	Carrie Jones	L B Bell	
2381 Jones Magnola[sic]	265.70	Magnolia Jones	G W Benge	
2382 Johnston [Johnson] Mamie L	265.70	Dora Johnson	L B Bell	pd to mother (Minor child)
2383 Keyes[sic] James M.				
2384 " Nan J.				
2385 " Dennis				
2386 " Blue				
2387 " Lizzie	1328.50	J.M. Keys	G W Benge	
2388 Keyes Jessie				
2389 " Nellie				
2390 " Myrtle	797.10	Mattie Keys	L B Bell	mother
2391 Keeler Josephine				
2392 " Willard				
2393 " Frank				
2394 " Albert				
2395 " Frederick				
2396 " Maude				
2397 " Lillie				
2398 " Pearl				
2399 " Minnie				
2400 Dintpot Conner				
2401 " Nellie				
2402 Keeler Chas R.	3188.40	G.B. Keeler	G W Benge	
2403 Keyes Leroy				
2404 " Albert L.				
2405 " Pearl	797.10	G.B. Keeler	G W Benge	
2406 Kell James	265.70	James Kell	G W Benge	

Starr Roll 1894

We, the undersigned citizens of the Cherokee Nation, by right of Cherokee blood, do hereby acknowledge to have received of E. E. Starr, National Treasurer of the Cherokee Nation, the sums set opposite our names respectively, in full of our shares in the per capita distribution authorized by an Act of the National Council, dated ___MAY 3 1894___ 1894.

Names of Head, and Members of Families	Amount	To Whom Paid	Witness to Payment	Remarks
2407 Keyes Shellie				
2408 " Bettie	*order*			
2409 " Campbell				
2410 " Katie	1062.80	J T *(Illegible)*	Henry Eiffert	J.T. *(Illegible)*
2411 Keyes Victoria				
2412 " Lulu	*order*			
2413 " Nellie				
2414 " Lizzie				
2415 " Lillie	1328.50	A Foyil	Henry Eiffert	check
2416 Keyes Nettie				
2417 " Minnie				
2418 " Carrie				
2419 Spencer Lillie				
2420 " Allen	1328.50	Nettie Keyes	J.C. Starr	
2421 Keyes Samuel H.	265.70	S.H. Keys	L B Bell	
2422 Kelley Sabrina E.	265.70	A.A. Kelley	G.W. Benge	
2423 Keyes Monroe	265.70	A.F. Chamberlin	G W Benge	
2424 Keyes Lucy L.	265.70	L.L. Keys	G W Benge	
2425 Keyes Lydia E.	265.70	L.E. Keys	G W Benge	
2426 Keyes Lizie				
2427 Keyes Lucy	531.40	L.L. Keys	G W Benge	
2428 Kelley Lulu N.				
2429 " Pauline G.				
2430 " Fred L. (Jr)	797.10	Fred L Kelley	G W Benge	

Starr Roll 1894

We, the undersigned citizens of the Cherokee Nation, by right of Cherokee blood, do hereby acknowledge to have received of E. E. Starr, National Treasurer of the Cherokee Nation, the sums set opposite our names respectively, in full of our shares in the per capita distribution authorized by an Act of the National Council, dated ___MAY 3 1894___ 1894.

	Names of Head, and Members of Families	Amount	To Whom Paid	Witness to Payment	Remarks
2431	Klaus Alice A.				
2432	" Robt (Jr)				
2433	" Annie M.	797.10	Robt Klaus	G W Benge	
2434	Klaus Wm H.	265.70	Rot[sic] Klaus	G W Benge	
2435	Kinnison[sic] Austraphine				
2436	" Addie R.	265.70	Addie R Kinnisson	G W Benge	
2437	" Oma E.				
2438	" Lenora A.				
2439	" Joseph D.				
2440	" Lizzie V.				
2441	" John A.				
2442	" Paschal B.	1859.90	P.B. Kinnisson	G W Benge	
2443	Kay Angie				
2444	" Ora L.				
2445	" William E.				
2446	Cox Freddie				
2447	" Annie	1328.50	J.B. Kay	L B Bell	
2448	Kepheart Ruth E.	265.70	R E Kepheart	L B Bell	
2449	Kirk John				
2450	Amanda	531.40	John Kirk	G.W. Benge	
2451	King Jennie				
2452	" Carrie				
2453	" Etta				
2454	" Joel B.	1062.80	Jesse King	G W Benge	
2455	Knightkiller Zeke	265.70	Zeke Knightkiller	G W Benge	
2456	Alley	265.70	Alley Knightkiller	G.W. Benge	
2457	Keener Thomas				
2458	" Aggie	531.40	Aggie Keener	G W Benge	

Starr Roll 1894

We, the undersigned citizens of the Cherokee Nation, by right of Cherokee blood, do hereby acknowledge to have received of E. E. Starr, National Treasurer of the Cherokee Nation, the sums set opposite our names respectively, in full of our shares in the per capita distribution authorized by an Act of the National Council, dated ___MAY 3 1894___ 1894.

	Names of Head, and Members of Families	Amount	To Whom Paid	Witness to Payment	Remarks
2459	Kelly William				
2460	Fannie	531.40	William Kelley	G W Benge	
2461	Keyes Osie				JC Hogan
2462	Tishie				
2463	Leroy	*order*			
2464	Lillie				
2465	John L.				
2466	Jane E.	1594.20	JC Hogan	Henry Eiffert	
2467	Kendell Frankie				(Minor children)
2468	Frostie	531.40	Lula Morris	G W Benge	
2469	Keyes Richard	265.70	Richard Keys	L B Bell	
2470	Keys Susan F.	*order*			E.B.B.
2471	Thomas L				
2472	James N.	797.10	E B Bender	Henry Eiffert	paid order
2473	Kuhn Jane	265.70	Jane Kuhn	G.W. Benge	
2474	Kingkiller[sic] Betsy	265.70	Betsy Knightkiller	G.W. Benge	
2475	Kimbrough John	265.70	J.F. McCobb	J.C. Starr	order
2476	Livingston Sarah				W.T.W.
2477	" Alfred	*order*			
2478	Bendura Charley				
2479	Livingston Loonie				
2480	" Robert	1328.50	W T Whitaker	Henry Eiffert	
2481	Lowters Lee				W.L. Moore
2482	" Watson B.				
2483	" Jessie	*order*			
2484	" Katie L.				
2485	" Mathew				
2486	" Millard F.	1594.20	W L Moore	Henry Eiffert	Check

Starr Roll 1894

We, the undersigned citizens of the Cherokee Nation, by right of Cherokee blood, do hereby acknowledge to have received of E. E. Starr, National Treasurer of the Cherokee Nation, the sums set opposite our names respectively, in full of our shares in the per capita distribution authorized by an Act of the National Council, dated ___MAY 3 1894___ 1894.

#	Names of Head, and Members of Families	Amount	To Whom Paid	Witness to Payment	Remarks
2487	Lewis Caroline E.				
2488	" Geo W.	531.40	C.E. Lewis	G W Benge	
2489	Lindsay Maria				
2490	" Flora				
2491	" Goodon				
2492	" Virgie Lee				
2493	" Clyde				
2494	Lindsay Annie R.	1594.30	W.R. Lindsey	G W Benge	
2495	Lindsay Wm D.	265.70	W^m D Lindsey	G W Benge	
2496	Lindsay Hattie	265.70	Hattie Lindsey	G W Benge	
2497	Lindsay North	265.70	W.R. Lindsey	G W Benge	
2498	Lindsay[sic] Joseph	265.70	W.R. Lindsey	G W Benge	
2499	Lindsay[sic] Carrie R.				
2500	" Edna				
2501	" Riley D.	797.10	Clem Hayden	G W Benge	
2502	Landrum Thomas				J.C.H.
2503	" Nannie	order	D2659		
2504	" Mony		D2659		
2505	" Lulu		D2659		
2506	" Lewis	1328.50	JC Hogan D2659	Henry Eiffert	Check
2507	Loflin Rebecca J.				
2508	" Stella				
2509	" Addie A.				
2510	" Vaul D.				
2511	" Chester C.				
2512	" Harris A.				
2513	" Clarence R.				
2514	Loflin Chas M.	$2125.60	H A Loflin	G.W. Benge	

Starr Roll 1894

We, the undersigned citizens of the Cherokee Nation, by right of Cherokee blood, do hereby acknowledge to have received of E. E. Starr, National Treasurer of the Cherokee Nation, the sums set opposite our names respectively, in full of our shares in the per capita distribution authorized by an Act of the National Council, dated ___MAY 3 1894___ 1894.

	Names of Head, and Members of Families	Amount	To Whom Paid	Witness to Payment	Remarks
2515	Landrum Ed.	265.70	H.T. Landrum	G W Benge	Dead
2516	Lessenbee Jack	265.70	S.S. Cobb	G W Benge	
2517	Lamb Jesse B.				
2518	" Lawrence E.				
2519	" Mary J.	797.10	Jessie B. Lamb	G W Benge	
2520	Lenoir Annie C.	265.70	M.O. Lenoir	G W Benge	
2521	Lenoir Mary O.	265.70	M.O. Lenoir	G W Benge	
2522	Leforce Sallie	265.70	Sallie Leforce	G W Benge	
2523	Looking Arch	265.70	Lorena Henson	Henry Eiffert	
2524	" Maggie	~~order~~ 265.70	*(Illegible)*	L B Bell	
2525	Lewis Joseph	~~P1166~~ 10379			
2526	" Sallie	~~P1166~~ R897			
2527	" Nannie	~~P1166~~ 10379			
2528	" Jeff	~~P1166~~ 10379			J M Hall
2529	" Runabout	~~P1166~~ 10379			order
2530	" David	~~P1166~~ 10379			
2531	" William D	DEAD.			
2532	" Bird	~~P1166~~ 10379			
2533	" Lydia D	DEAD 2391.30	J M Hall	Henry Eiffert	Check
2534	Lewis Che-go-neler				
2535	" Jennie	~~P1167~~ 10380			
2536	" John	~~P1167~~ 10380			
2537	" Che-wan	~~P1167~~ 1063.80	~~10380~~ Che go nelen[sic]	G W Benge	
2538	Lewis Charles D	265.70	W C Rogers	L B Bell	
2539	Lasley Joseph				
2540	" Nancy				
2541	" Samuel		D2660		

Starr Roll 1894

We, the undersigned citizens of the Cherokee Nation, by right of Cherokee blood, do hereby acknowledge to have received of E. E. Starr, National Treasurer of the Cherokee Nation, the sums set opposite our names respectively, in full of our shares in the per capita distribution authorized by an Act of the National Council, dated ___MAY 3 1894___ 1894.

	Names of Head, and Members of Families	Amount	To Whom Paid	Witness to Payment	Remarks
2542	" George				
2543	" Joseph	1328.50	Joseph Lasly[sic]	L B Bell	
2544	Lamar Jessie				
2545	" Ursula				
2546	" Paden	797.10	Jessie Lamar	G W Benge	
2547	Lynch Rachel	265.70	Rachel Lynch	L B Bell	
2548	Lane Maude				
2549	" Estelle	531.40	C.V. Rogers	G W Benge	
2550	Lacy John D.	D340			
2551	" Myrtle	D340			
2552	" William D.	D340 *order*			
2553	" Shellie M.	D340			
2554	" Miles L.	D340 / 1328.50	C W Poole	L B Bell	
2555	Luton Rebecca	*order*			*Neilson*
2556	" Lewis				
2557	" Willie				
2558	" Samuel				
2559	" Dempsey				
2560	" Ruthie				
2561	" Joseph M.	1859.90	F.A. Neilson	J.C. Starr	*on order*
2562	Langley Fannie				
2563	" Alexandria	5318			
2564	" Johnnie	4664 *order*			W.E.H.
2565	" Margarite L	5318			
2566	" Bathanie	1328.50	WE Halsell	Henry Eiffert	
2567	Lowery Henry	*order* 265.70	W^m L Moore	Henry Eiffert	D.L.S.

184

Starr Roll 1894

We, the undersigned citizens of the Cherokee Nation, by right of Cherokee blood, do hereby acknowledge to have received of E. E. Starr, National Treasurer of the Cherokee Nation, the sums set opposite our names respectively, in full of our shares in the per capita distribution authorized by an Act of the National Council, dated ___MAY 3 1894___ 1894.

Names of Head, and Members of Families	Amount	To Whom Paid	Witness to Payment	Remarks
2568 Lipsey Lizzie	265.70 *order*	(Illegible)	J.C. Starr	D.L.S.
2569 " Stella				
2570 Fields Pat				
2571 " Mike	797.10	E.B. Bender	J.C. Starr	pd on order
2572 Lynam Mary	265.70	Mary Lynam	G W Benge	
2573 Locker Nellie	265.70	Nellie Locker	L B Bell	
2574 Locker Richard M.	265.70 *order*	JE Campbell	Henry Eiffert	J.E.C. Check
2575 Lindsay William	*order* 265.70	Walsh and Shutt	Henry Eiffert	Check W&S
2576 Lipe Clark C.				
2577 " Maggie E.				
2578 " Herman V.				
2579 " Caspar				
2580 " Clinton				
2581 " Beulah				
2582 " Jake (Jr)				
2583 " Clarence	2125.60	C.C. Lipe	L B Bell	
2584 Langley Noah	265.70	Lucinda Lagley[sic]	J.C. Starr	
2585 Langley Thomas	265.70	Paid Walsh *Paid to W.H. Mayes the balance paid to Langley*		#61438 W & S
2586 " Maggie				
2587 Trent Jeff	*order*			
2588 Patton Duckie				
2589 " Earl	1328.50	Walsh and Shutt	Henry Eiffert	Check
2590 Lovett John	*order* 265.70	Annie Martin	L B Bell	~~F.A. Neilson~~
2591 Lyman Johnson				
2592 " Evaline				
2593 " James				
2594 " Joseph				
2595 " Martha				

Starr Roll 1894

We, the undersigned citizens of the Cherokee Nation, by right of Cherokee blood, do hereby acknowledge to have received of E. E. Starr, National Treasurer of the Cherokee Nation, the sums set opposite our names respectively, in full of our shares in the per capita distribution authorized by an Act of the National Council, dated ___MAY 3 1894___ 1894.

	Names of Head, and Members of Families	Amount	To Whom Paid	Witness to Payment	Remarks
2596	" Callie	1594.20	Johnson Lyman	G W Benge	
2597	Long Eliza	265.70	Eliza Long	G W Benge	
2598	Leforce Fannie M.				
2599	" Flossie M.	531.40	F.M. Leforce	G W Benge	
2600	Little Frank	265.70	Frank Little	G W Benge	
2601	" William				
2602	" Joseph C.				
2603	" Elizabeth				
2604	" Claude J.				
2605	Little Mary L.	1328.50	Boog Little	G W Benge	
2606	Lucky Martin				
2607	" Myrtle	531.40	G W Lucky	G W Benge	
2608	Lucky Sarah F.	265.70	Sarah F Lucky	G W Benge	
2609	Lucky Sabrina	265.70	Sabrina Lucky	G W Benge	
2610	Land Joseph C.				
2611	" De Loyd				
2612	" Annie A.				
2613	" Houston E.				
2614	" William H.				
2615	" Susan E.				
2616	" Roxie M.				
2617	" Joseph G.	2125.60	J.C. Land	G W Benge	
2618	Lafon[sic] Sarah				
2619	" Claude				
2620	" Amos				
2621	" Flossie				
2622	" Essie	1328.50	Sarah Lofan	G W Benge	

Starr Roll 1894

We, the undersigned citizens of the Cherokee Nation, by right of Cherokee blood, do hereby acknowledge to have received of E. E. Starr, National Treasurer of the Cherokee Nation, the sums set opposite our names respectively, in full of our shares in the per capita distribution authorized by an Act of the National Council, dated _____MAY 3 1894_____ 1894.

	Names of Head, and Members of Families	Amount	To Whom Paid	Witness to Payment	Remarks
2623	Lloid Rachel				
2624	" Clarence				
2625	" Thomas				
2626	" Laura	1063.80	Rachel Lloid	G W Benge	
2627	Lloid Jennie				
2628	" Albert L.				
2629	" Robt L.				
2630	" William				
2631	" Maggie E.				
2632	" Nannie R.	1594.20	G.C. Lloid	G W Benge	
2633	Lipe D. W.				
2634	" Mary E				
2635	" Lola	797.10	D W Lipe	L B Bell	
2636	Lipe Nannie E.	265.70	D W Lipe	L B Bell	
2637	Lipe Victoria S.	265.70	D W Lipe	L B Bell	
2638	Lipe Jno G.	265.70	J G Lipe	G W Benge	
2639	Lahay[sic] Joseph M.				
2640	" John F.				
2641	" Maggie	797.10	J M Lahoy	L B Bell	
2642	Lawther Josie				Buffington
2643	" Madenia				& Woodson
2644	" Grover C.				
2645	" Willie A.	1062.80	M.D. Woodson	J.C. Starr	on order
2646	Langley Lucinda				DL Denny
2647	" Charles	order 4754 531.40	DL Denny	G.W. Benge	GW Eaton on order
2648	Langley Lock	order 5326 265.70	DL Denny	Henry Eiffert	D L Denny
2649	Louther Eugene	order 265.70	F.A. Neilson	J.C. Starr	on order Neilson

Starr Roll 1894

We, the undersigned citizens of the Cherokee Nation, by right of Cherokee blood, do hereby acknowledge to have received of E. E. Starr, National Treasurer of the Cherokee Nation, the sums set opposite our names respectively, in full of our shares in the per capita distribution authorized by an Act of the National Council, dated ___MAY 3 1894___ 1894.

#	Names of Head, and Members of Families	Amount	To Whom Paid	Witness to Payment	Remarks
2650	Lewis Alice	~~D1168~~			
2651	Chism Jim	~~D1168~~			
2652	" Teder	(Harry) ~~D1168~~			
2653	" Dannel	1062.80	Alice Lewis	G W Benge	
2654	Landrum Benjamin M^c	265.70	Ben Mc Landrum	L B Bell	
2655	Leach John W.				
2656	" George C.				
2657	" Annie E.	797.10	J.W. Leach	G W Benge	
2658	Lenox Fanny L.				
2659	" Birtie				
2660	" Mirtle	797.10	F.L. Lenox	G W Benge	
2661	Lewis Samuel	265.70	Samuel Lewis	Henry Eiffert	
2662	Litton Nellie W.	~~D569~~ R684			
2663	" Jamitu				
2664	" Cecil	797.10	A P Litton	L B Bell	
2665	La Boytaux Mollie				
2666	" Willis	531.40	Wm Howel	Geo W Benge	
2667	Lowther Jane	order 265.70	WL Moore	Henry Eiffert	Check W.L. Moore
2668	Larry James	order 265.70	James Larry ~~WT Whitaker~~	Henry Eiffert	J.D. Boyd & W.T.W.
2669	Miller Eva M.				
2670	Miller Mattie				
2671	Miller Will B.				
2672	" Critt				
2673	" John H.	1328.50	Mary E. Miller	G W Benge	
2674	Marsh Fred W.	265.70	S.A. Bryan	G W Benge	

Starr Roll 1894

We, the undersigned citizens of the Cherokee Nation, by right of Cherokee blood, do hereby acknowledge to have received of E. E. Starr, National Treasurer of the Cherokee Nation, the sums set opposite our names respectively, in full of our shares in the per capita distribution authorized by an Act of the National Council, dated _____MAY 3 1894_____ 1894.

	Names of Head, and Members of Families	Amount	To Whom Paid	Witness to Payment	Remarks
2675	McKenzy Simon				
2676	" Frances				
2677	" John S.	797.10	Simon McKenzy	G W Benge	
2678	Miller Annie	265.70	Clem Hayden	L B Bell	
2679	McCracken Dora				
2680	" Joe	531.40	*(Illegible)*	G W Benge	
2681	Markham Sallie	265.70	Charlotte Wilder	G W Benge	
2682	McKenzie Jefferson				
2683	" Nancy				
2684	McKenzie Mary	797.10	Jefferson McKenzy	G W Benge	
2685	Mauck Emily				
2686	" Nora				
2687	" Jacob				
2687 1/2	" Ora				Dead
2688	" Maggie	1328.50	WP Mauck	L B Bell	
2689	McCoy Frank				
2690	" Charley	531.40	Frank McCoy	L B Bell	
2691	Manuel Wilson	265.70	Wilson Manuel	G W Benge	
2692	Manuel Elgie				
2693	Downing Cornelia				
2694	" Alex				
2695	" Clem				
2696	" Nancy	1328.50	Elizie Manuel	G W Benge	
2697	Moon William	2652			
2698	" Susie	2652			
2699	" John	2652 797.10	Wm Moon	G W Benge	

Starr Roll 1894

We, the undersigned citizens of the Cherokee Nation, by right of Cherokee blood, do hereby acknowledge to have received of E. E. Starr, National Treasurer of the Cherokee Nation, the sums set opposite our names respectively, in full of our shares in the per capita distribution authorized by an Act of the National Council, dated ___MAY 3 1894___ 1894.

	Names of Head, and Members of Families	Amount	To Whom Paid	Witness to Payment	Remarks
2700	Moore Addie	ord 265.70	JL Baugh & C.D.Markum	Henry Eiffert	J.L.B. Check
2701	McCay Alfred				
2702	" Rebecca				
2703	" James J.				
2704	" John B.				
2705	" Elbrina D.				
2706	" William (Jr.)	1594.20	Alfred McCoy	G W Benge	
2707	Morris Nancy J.	265.70	R774 10377 N.J. Morris	G W Benge	
2708	McBain Thomas	265.70	J F Merren	Henry Eiffert	(Illegible)
2709	Mayes Tip C.				
2710	" Mary	531.50	Mary Mayes	G W Benge	
2711	Mills Wm R.				
2712	" James E.				
2713	" Annie L.	797.10	M.W. Mills	G W Benge	
2714	Milton David				
2715	" Elizabeth J.				
2716	" William H.				
2717	" Mary H.				
2718	" Annie				
2719	" Julia	1594.20	David Milton	G W Benge	
2720	Mayes Wm H.				
2721	" Susan				
2722	" Mary				
2723	" Joel B. (Jr.)	1062.80	Chas W. Storn	G W Benge	
2724	Myers Orlena[sic] F.	~~D242~~			
2725	" Deely				
2726	" John S.				
2727	" Marion A.	~~D242~~	ENROLLMENT REFUSED.		
2728	" Walter P.	~~D242~~	ENROLLMENT REFUSED.		

Starr Roll 1894

We, the undersigned citizens of the Cherokee Nation, by right of Cherokee blood, do hereby acknowledge to have received of E. E. Starr, National Treasurer of the Cherokee Nation, the sums set opposite our names respectively, in full of our shares in the per capita distribution authorized by an Act of the National Council, dated ___MAY 3 1894___ 1894.

	Names of Head, and Members of Families	Amount	To Whom Paid	Witness to Payment	Remarks
2729	" Hiram	~~D292~~	ENROLLMENT ~~REFUSED~~.	R844	
2730	" Eunice	~~D292~~ 1869.90	Olena F Myers	R844 G W Benge	
2731	Mayes Geo. W.				
2732	" Susie				
2733	" Pixie				
2734	" Edwin				
2735	" Richard				
2736	" George	1594.20	G.W. Mayes	G W Benge	
2737	Martin Ruth E.				
2738	" Robert C.				
2739	" Martha T.				
2740	" Thomas A.				
2741	Martin Wm J.				
2742	Martin Mary C.				
2743	Martin Geo W.	1859.90	Ruth E. Martin	G W Benge	
2744	Mayes[sic] Thomas	265.70	Thomas Mays	G W Benge	
2745	McKnight Louisa Z.				
2746	" Martha E.				
2747	" Addie L.				
2748	" Ruth	1062.80	L.Z. McKnight	G W Benge	
2749	McIntosh Lou				
2750	" Lucille				
2751	Rowe Nita	797.10	G.W. Mayes	G W Benge	
2752	Mayes Watt A.				
2753	" Nannie R.				
2754	" Hall				
2755	" Wash (Jr)	1062.90	W.A. Mayes	G W Benge	

Starr Roll 1894

We, the undersigned citizens of the Cherokee Nation, by right of Cherokee blood, do hereby acknowledge to have received of E. E. Starr, National Treasurer of the Cherokee Nation, the sums set opposite our names respectively, in full of our shares in the per capita distribution authorized by an Act of the National Council, dated ___MAY 3 1894___ 1894.

	Names of Head, and Members of Families	Amount	To Whom Paid	Witness to Payment	Remarks
2756	Mayes Jno T.	order	DEAD.		
2757					
2758	" Jessie	797.10	1st Nat Bank Vinita	Henry Eiffert	
2759	Mayes Wiley B.				
2760	" Mina V.				
2761	" Simon				
2762	" Lilia	1062.80	S H Mayes	G W Benge	
2763	Mayes Sam H.				
2764	" Martha E.				
2765	" Joseph F.				
2766	" Carrie M.				
2767	McNair Henrietta				
2768	Mayes Wm L.	1594.20	S H Mayes	G W Benge	
2769	Mayor Paralee				J.C.H.
2770	" William	order			
2771	" Ida				
2772	" Lee				
2773	" Fred	1328.50	JC Hogan	Henry Eiffert	Check
2774	McNair Kinney				
2775	" Oscar				
2776	" Clem	797.10	Kinney McNair	G W Benge	
2777	McLain Martha				
2778	" Loyd	531.40	R.L. McCain	G W Benge	
2779	Mayes Mary D.	265.70	S H Mays	L B Bell	
2780	Mills James L.	order 265.70	(Illegible) Ward	EWBuffington	on order C.W.
2781	McPhearson[sic] Ben F.				
2782	" Veneere				
2783	" Lewis	797.10	Ben F. McPherson	G W Benge	

Starr Roll 1894

We, the undersigned citizens of the Cherokee Nation, by right of Cherokee blood, do hereby acknowledge to have received of E. E. Starr, National Treasurer of the Cherokee Nation, the sums set opposite our names respectively, in full of our shares in the per capita distribution authorized by an Act of the National Council, dated ___MAY 3 1894___ 1894.

	Names of Head, and Members of Families	Amount	To Whom Paid	Witness to Payment	Remarks
2784	Martin Arcena				
2785	" Willie V.	531.40	J.R. Rogers	G.W. Benge	
2786	Moore Josephine				
2787	Carmon Spencer W.				
2788	" Geo L.				
2789	" Robt L.				
2790	" Annie B.				
2791	" Addie N.				
2792	Moore Jessie J.				
2793	" Frank P.				
2794	" Fannie L.	2391.30	Josephine Moore	G W Benge	
2795	McDonald Virgil T.	265.70	V.T. McDonald	G.W. Benge	
2796	Marker Laura				
2797	" William R.	531.40	Laura Marker	G W Benge	
2798	Morse Ida H.				
2799	Ewers Chas E.				
2800	" John Y.				
2801	" Eloise M.				
2802	" William A.	1328.50	Ida H. Morse	G.W. Benge	
2803	Moore Ellis	order			J S Thomason
2804	" Noah				
2805	" Lizzie	797.10	J S Thomason	L B Bell	
2806	Meroney Jno L.	order			W^m V Carey
2807	" Lou				
2808	" Dillard				
2809	" Mabel	1062.80	W V Carey	Henry Eiffert	Check
2810	McCoy Chester F.	265.70	C.F. McCoy	G W Benge	

Starr Roll 1894

We, the undersigned citizens of the Cherokee Nation, by right of Cherokee blood, do hereby acknowledge to have received of E. E. Starr, National Treasurer of the Cherokee Nation, the sums set opposite our names respectively, in full of our shares in the per capita distribution authorized by an Act of the National Council, dated ____MAY 3 1894____ 1894.

	Names of Head, and Members of Families	Amount	To Whom Paid	Witness to Payment	Remarks
2811	Mickels[sic] Mollie				
2812	Martin Augusta				
2813	Martin Sarah				
2814	Martin Cora	1062.80	Mollie Michels	G.W. Benge	
2815	Martin Amanda				
2816	" Susan				
2817	" Polly	797.10	Amanda Martin	G.W. Benge	
2818	Morrell James				
2819	" Rachel				
2820	" Minerva				
2821	" Senora				
2822	" Delila				
2823	" William P.				
2824	" Mary				
2825	" Lillie	2125.60	Rachel Morrell	L B Bell	
2826	McNair Robert L	265.70	R.L. McNair	J.C. Starr	
2827	McCaleb[sic] Addison F.				
2828	" Lulu				
2829	" Flossie	797.10	Addison F. McCobb	J.C. Starr	
2830	Morrison Susan K.				
2831	" Mollie M.				J.S.
2832	" Maggie V.				
2833	" Robert T.				
2834	Hogan Emma				
2835	Morrison Delia L.				
2836	" Ellen				
2837	" Claude	2125.60	John *(Illegible)*	Henry Eiffert	Check
2838	Manahan Susan				
2839	" Henry A.				
2840	" Samuel C.				
2841	" Emma				

Starr Roll 1894

We, the undersigned citizens of the Cherokee Nation, by right of Cherokee blood, do hereby acknowledge to have received of E. E. Starr, National Treasurer of the Cherokee Nation, the sums set opposite our names respectively, in full of our shares in the per capita distribution authorized by an Act of the National Council, dated ____MAY 3 1894____ 1894.

	Names of Head, and Members of Families	Amount	To Whom Paid	Witness to Payment	Remarks
2842	" Mary E.				
2843	" Frank (Jr.)	1594.20	Frank Manahan	G W Benge	
2844	Martin Wm P.	265.70	W^m P Martin	G.W. Benge	
2845	Martin James A.	order			G.A.M.
2846	" Annie L				
2847	" Tom				
2848	" Ola				
2849	" Lelia E.				
2850	" William H.				
2851	" Josie J.				
2852	" Flora L.				
2853	Martin Joseph K.	~~D618~~	order R734		G.A.M.
2854	" Pearl	2657.00	GA Martin	Henry Eiffert	Check
2855	Martin John M.	265.70	J.M. Martin	G.W. Benge	
2856	Martin Geo A.	265.70	G.A. Martin	G.W. Benge	
2857	Martin Frank B.	~~D633~~	R762		
2858	" Avis R.	~~D633~~	R762		
2859	" Robt L.	~~D633~~	R762		
2860	" Clara	~~D633~~	R762		
2861	" George M	~~D633~~ 1328.50	R76[sic] GA Martin	Henry Eiffert	Check
2862	Martin Sarah				
2863	" Joel				
2864	" Robert				
2865	" Mandy				
2866	" William P.				
2867	" Carrie				
2868	Martin Geo W.	1859.90	Wm Martin	G W Benge	
2869	Martin Geo W.				
2870	" James	531.40	G W Martin	G.W. Benge	

Starr Roll 1894

We, the undersigned citizens of the Cherokee Nation, by right of Cherokee blood, do hereby acknowledge to have received of E. E. Starr, National Treasurer of the Cherokee Nation, the sums set opposite our names respectively, in full of our shares in the per capita distribution authorized by an Act of the National Council, dated ___MAY 3 1894___ 1894.

#	Names of Head, and Members of Families	Amount	To Whom Paid	Witness to Payment	Remarks
2871	McDaniel Jno M.				
2872	" Jessie R.				
2873	" Charles R.				
2874	" John A.				
2875	" Claude I.	1328.50	Jno M McDaniel	J C Starr	
2876	McConnell Lizzie	797.10	J.E. Campbell	L B Bell	
2877	" W.F.				
2878	Cromwell Cornelius				
2879	Mayfield Frances M				
2880	" John T.				
2881	" Elizabeth				
2882	" Frederick				
2883	" Julia	1328.50	I M Mayfield	L B Bell	
2884	Moon Daniel				
2885	" Eliza				
2886	" Lulu				
2887	" Donnie				
2888	" Nora	1329.50	Daniel Moon	L B Bell	
2889	Mayfield Elijah	265.70	Elijah Mayfield Jr	G W Benge	paid adm ~~Dead~~
2890	Maroney Bailey B.	order			Wm V.C.
2891	" William H.				
2892	" Elizabeth W.	797.10	~~C W Pool~~ W^m V Carey Henry Eiffert		Check
2893	Martin Annie	order			Neilson
2894	Lovett Louisa	531.40	F.A. Neilson	J.C. Starr	on order
	~~Mabry (Illegible)~~	10769 ~~D974~~	Stricken from the rolls by direction of an Act approved May 5th 1894		
	" ~~Robert~~				
	" ~~Charley~~				
2895	Merrell Josie C.	265.70	J.C. Merrell	G.W. Benge	

Starr Roll 1894

We, the undersigned citizens of the Cherokee Nation, by right of Cherokee blood, do hereby acknowledge to have received of E. E. Starr, National Treasurer of the Cherokee Nation, the sums set opposite our names respectively, in full of our shares in the per capita distribution authorized by an Act of the National Council, dated ___MAY 3 1894___ 1894.

Names of Head, and Members of Families	Amount	To Whom Paid	Witness to Payment	Remarks
2896 Meeks Lillie				
2897 " Myrtle				
2898 Jones Pearl	797.10	Lillie Meeks	G W Benge	
2899 Meeks James B.	*order* 265.70	L B Bell	Henry Eiffert	Check LBB
2900 Meeks Annie B.				
2901 " William A.				
2902 " Sabina E.	797.10	Abrum Meeks	G W Benge	
2903 McDonald Isaac N.				
2904 " Roy				
2905 " Ray	797.10	I.N. McDonald	G W Benge	
2906 McDonald John O.	D533			
2907 " Velma E.	D533			
2908 " Newton O.	797.10 D533	J.O. McDonald	G W Benge	
2909 Martin Charlotte				
2910 " Rudolph				
2911 " Viola				
2912 " Claude D.	1062.80	Charlotte Martin	G W Benge	
2913 Martin Susie				
2914 " Lizzie				
2915 Martin Jennie	797.10	David Martin	G W Benge	
2916 McClure Fannie				
2917 " Slater				
2918 " Roy				
2919 " William				
2920 " Hugh				
2921 " Margaret	1594.20	Jennie Williams	G W Benge	
2922 McKay W^m				
2923 " Mary J.	531.40	W^m McKay	G W Benge	

Starr Roll 1894

We, the undersigned citizens of the Cherokee Nation, by right of Cherokee blood, do hereby acknowledge to have received of E. E. Starr, National Treasurer of the Cherokee Nation, the sums set opposite our names respectively, in full of our shares in the per capita distribution authorized by an Act of the National Council, dated _____ MAY 3 1894 _____ 1894.

	Names of Head, and Members of Families	Amount	To Whom Paid	Witness to Payment	Remarks
2924	McKay Jno S.	or 265.70 *der*	Wm McKay	G W Benge	Check W Moore
2925	McCrary Napoleon P.				
2926	" William C.				
2927	" Sterling P.				
2928	" Mary E.				
2929	McCrary ~~Jno~~ *James* R.	1328.50	N.P. McCrary	G W Benge	
2930	Marks Fannie				
2931	" Albert B.				
2932	" Walter R.				
2933	" Marjore M.	1062.80	Fannie Marks	G W Benge	
2934	Moore Charlotte				
2935	Stubbs Jno S.	531.40	Charlotte Moore	G W Benge	
2936	Martin Nancy				
2937	" Jno W.	531.40	Nancy Martin	G W Benge	
2938	Martin Eunice	265.70	~~D410~~ R683	G W Benge	
~~2939~~					
2940	Martin Harvey	~~531.40~~	D2667		~~G M Ball~~
2941	" Jno E.	265.70	J S Thomason	Henry Eiffert	J.S.T. Check
2942	Miller Mary				J.S.T.
2943	" Guy	*order*			
2944	" Pearl				
2945	" Mattie	1062.80	J S Thomason	Henry Eiffert	Check
2946	Miller Ellen H				
2947	" Ray				
2948	" Etta R.	797.10	E.H. Miller	G W Benge	
2949	Morris Albert				
2950	" Bessie	531.40	Albert Morris	G W Benge	On Del Roll

Starr Roll 1894

We, the undersigned citizens of the Cherokee Nation, by right of Cherokee blood, do hereby acknowledge to have received of E. E. Starr, National Treasurer of the Cherokee Nation, the sums set opposite our names respectively, in full of our shares in the per capita distribution authorized by an Act of the National Council, dated ___MAY 3 1894___ 1894.

	Names of Head, and Members of Families	Amount	To Whom Paid	Witness to Payment	Remarks
2951	Morris Jordon	265.70	Albert Morris	G W Benge	
2952	Morris Jno H.				
2953	" William O.				
2954	" Rosie	797.10	Jno H Morris	G W Benge	
2955	McGee Albert				
2956	" Nellie J.				
2957	" Sarah A.	797.10	Albert McGhee	G.W. Benge	
2958	Milliner William	265.70	Mary Milliner	L B Bell	
2959	Martin Lucy	265.70	M.H. Martin	G W Benge	
2960	Mayfield Lena E.				
2961	" Logan				
2962	" Alena				
2963	" Luther				
2964	" Clarence	1328.50	Lena E Mayfield	G W Benge	
2965	Meek[sic] Mary J.				
2966	" Walter G.A.				
2967	" Lizzie t.				
2968	" Mary F.	1062.80	M.J. Meeks	G W Benge	
2969	McGhee Jno H.				
2970	" Ambrose H.				
2971	" Mary A.				
2972	" Elizabeth				
2973	" Joseph H.				
2974	" Berley	1394.20	Rhodee McGhee	G W Benge	
2975	McElhaney[sic] Mary	265.70	Mary McElhany	J.C. Starr	
2976	Milliner[sic] Mary				
2977	" Florence				
2978	" John				

Starr Roll 1894

We, the undersigned citizens of the Cherokee Nation, by right of Cherokee blood, do hereby acknowledge to have received of E. E. Starr, National Treasurer of the Cherokee Nation, the sums set opposite our names respectively, in full of our shares in the per capita distribution authorized by an Act of the National Council, dated ____MAY 3 1894____ 1894.

	Names of Head, and Members of Families	Amount	To Whom Paid	Witness to Payment	Remarks
2979	" Josephine	1062.80	Mary Millner	L B Bell	
	~~Musgrove Ellen~~				*Enrolled with*
	~~" Willie~~				*Cynthia Alberty*
2980	McCoy Margarette				
2981	" Jno. A.	531.40	Margaret McCoy	J.C. Starr	
2982	McClain Martha	~~order~~ 265.70	Martha McLain guardian		*Neilson*
	~~Eldridge Jeff~~				*On Orphan A Roll.*
2983	McClain Maria	*order* 265.70	Martha McLain	L B Bell	*Neilson*
2984	McClain Annie	*order*			*Neilson*
2985	" Minnie	531.40	Martha McLain	L B Bell	
2986	Martin Susie J.	*order*			*Neilson*
2987	" Amanda				
2988	" Levi T.				
2989	" George N.				
2990	" David E.				
2991	" Mabel E.	1594.20	F.A. Neilson	J.C. Starr	*on order*
2992	Mitchell W^m D	265.70	WD Mitchell	L B Bell	
2993	McCoy Mary A.	265.70	Mary A McCoy	J.C. Starr	
2994	McCoy Hoolie	265.70	Margaret McCoy	J.C. Starr	
2995	Miles Rosie L.				
2996	" Louisa	531.40	Rosie L. Miles	J.C. Starr	
2997	Mitchell Franklin	*order*			*Neilson*
2998	" Bertine				
2999	" Bruce	797.10	F.A. Neilson	E.W. Buffington	
3000	Miller Joseph	265.70	Joseph Miller	L B Bell	

Starr Roll 1894

We, the undersigned citizens of the Cherokee Nation, by right of Cherokee blood, do hereby acknowledge to have received of E. E. Starr, National Treasurer of the Cherokee Nation, the sums set opposite our names respectively, in full of our shares in the per capita distribution authorized by an Act of the National Council, dated ___MAY 3 1894___ 1894.

Names of Head, and Members of Families	Amount	To Whom Paid	Witness to Payment	Remarks
3001 Miller Jane	265.70	Joseph Miller	L B Bell	
3002 Miller William				
3003 " Charles W.				
3004 " Henry Mayes				
3005 " Joseph G.				
3006 " David A.	1328.50	William Miller	L B Bell	
3007 McIntosh Ellen	*order*			*Neilson*
3008 Rogers Chicken	531.40	F A Neilson	Henry Eiffert	
3009 McDaniel Alex L.				
3010 " Susie				
3011 " Mamie				
3012 " Robert				
3013 " Katie	1328.50	A.L. McDaniel	J.C. Starr	
3014 Murphy Annie	*order* 265.70	F.A. Neilson	E W Buffington	*Neilson*
3015 Millhollan[sic] Sarah F.				
3016 " Daisey B.				
3017 " John D.	797.10	J.T. Millhulland	G W Benge	
3018 Moore Thomas	*order* 265.70	F.A. Neilson	E.W. Buffington	*Charles Hutchins Guard*
3019 Miller Cornna				
3020 " Willis				
3021 " Nannie				
3022 " Lou O.	1062.80	Cornna Miller	G W Benge	
3023 Musgrove Frank M.				
3024 " Clara E.				
3025 " Maggie M.				
3026 " Cora A.				
3027 " Clem R.				
3028 " Frank F.				
3029 " Andrew L.	1859.90	F M Musgrove	L B Bell	

Starr Roll 1894

We, the undersigned citizens of the Cherokee Nation, by right of Cherokee blood, do hereby acknowledge to have received of E. E. Starr, National Treasurer of the Cherokee Nation, the sums set opposite our names respectively, in full of our shares in the per capita distribution authorized by an Act of the National Council, dated ___MAY 3 1894___ 1894.

	Names of Head, and Members of Families	Amount	To Whom Paid	Witness to Payment	Remarks
3030	Musgrove Willie A.	265.70	F M Musgrove	L B Bell	
3031	Musgrove Jas T.	265.70	Jas T Musgrove	L B Bell	
3032	Mills George	order			F.J.A.
3033	" Lewis				
3034	" Looney	797.10	F J Archer	Henry Eiffert	Check
3035	Murray Susie				Dead Neilson
3036	" Frank	order			Dead
3037	" Elmo				Dead
3038	" Mark				
3039	" Robt L.				
3040	" Ross				
3041	" Jack	1859.90	F.A. Neilson	J C Starr	on order
~~3042~~					
3043	McClain William	order 265.70	WE Halsell	Henry Eiffert	W E Halsell
~~3044~~					
3045	McKenzie James	order			Neilson
3046	" Liddie	order			
3047	Foster Joseph	order 797.10	F A Neilson	Henry Eiffert	on order
3048	Mannan Wooster				
3049	" Peggie	order			J M Hall
3050	" Lucy				
3051	" Johnson	1062.80	JM Hall	Henry Eiffert	
3052	McCracken James				
3053	" Katie				
3054	" Willie				
3055	" Russell				
3056	" James T.	1328.50	Jno McCracken	L B Bell	
3057	Maxfield Steven	265.70	Steven Maxfield	G W Benge	
3058	McDanniel Martin	order			Neilson
3059	" Willie	531.40	F.A. Neilson	J.C. Starr	on order

Starr Roll 1894

We, the undersigned citizens of the Cherokee Nation, by right of Cherokee blood, do hereby acknowledge to have received of E. E. Starr, National Treasurer of the Cherokee Nation, the sums set opposite our names respectively, in full of our shares in the per capita distribution authorized by an Act of the National Council, dated ___MAY 3 1894___ 1894.

	Names of Head, and Members of Families	Amount	To Whom Paid	Witness to Payment	Remarks
3060	Morgan Katie	265.70	Wm Alberty Admin	J.C. Starr	
3061	Maddison Nannie				
3062	" Virgie	531.40	DM Maddison	J.C. Starr	
3063	Miller Neppa				
3064	" Mormie				
3065	" Homer				
3066	" Nellie				
3067	" Thomas				
3068	" Berl				
3069	" Rosa	1859.90	Neppie Miller	J.C. Starr	
3070	McCracken John W.	order 265.70	J.W. McCracken	G W Benge	order withdrawn by W.V.C.
3071	McFall Lizzie M.				
3072	" John V.				
3073	" Edward L.				
3074	" Louisa M.	1062.80	John McFall	G W Benge	
3075	McSpadden Sallie				
3076	" Clem				
3077	" May				
3078	" Herbert T.	1062.80	C.V. Rogers	G.W. Benge	
3079	McSpadden Serena				
3080	" Zoe				
3081	" Floyd				
3082	" Roscoe C.	1062.80	C.V. Rogers	G W Benge	
3083	McIntush[sic] Jno R.				
3084	" Maria L.				
3085	" Beatrice	797.10	J.R. McIntosh	G W Benge	
3086	McIntush John				
3087	" Belle				
3088	" Myrtle	797.10	CW Pool	Henry Eiffert	Check

Starr Roll 1894

We, the undersigned citizens of the Cherokee Nation, by right of Cherokee blood, do hereby acknowledge to have received of E. E. Starr, National Treasurer of the Cherokee Nation, the sums set opposite our names respectively, in full of our shares in the per capita distribution authorized by an Act of the National Council, dated ___MAY 3 1894___ 1894.

Names of Head, and Members of Families	Amount	To Whom Paid	Witness to Payment	Remarks
3089 Miller Warren H.	265.70	W.A. Miller	G.W. Benge	
3090 Munson Henry	265.70	Josie Derrick (order)	J.C. Starr	
3091 Mehlin Elizabeth	265.70	J.G. Mehlin	G W Benge	
3092 Mehlin Chas H.	265.70	J.G. Mehlin	G W Benge	

****

(The information below was inserted between the pages of the logbook.)

Letters of Guardianship.

CHEROKEE NATION, I.T.
    DELAWARE DISTRICT.

    OFFICE DISTRICT JUDGE.
    DELAWARE DISTRICT.

To Whom it May Concern:

KNOW YE, That I *E.M. Landrum* Judge of the District Court of the District and Nation aforesaid, do by virtue of authority in me vested by law, this day make, constitute and appoint in the name and by the authority of the CHEROKEE NATION *Polly Ann Scott* as guardian of *Mantie Downing*

....
....minor chil - of *William Downing* deceased late of *Delaware* District, Cherokee Nation, the said *Polly Ann Scott* having complied with and performed all the duties required by law of *her* precedent to the appointment.

Starr Roll 1894

We, the undersigned citizens of the Cherokee Nation, by right of Cherokee blood, do hereby acknowledge to have received of E. E. Starr, National Treasurer of the Cherokee Nation, the sums set opposite our names respectively, in full of our shares in the per capita distribution authorized by an Act of the National Council, dated ___MAY 3 1894___ 1894.

Names of Head, and Members of Families	Amount	To Whom Paid	Witness to Payment	Remarks

In testimony whereof I hereunto set my hand on this the **16th** day of **May** A.D. 189**4**

E. M. Landrum
Judge District Court.
of **Delaware** District, C.N.

[Seal.]

Attest: J Duncan   Clerk District aforesaid.

****

No.	Name	Amount	To Whom Paid	Witness	Remarks
3093	McSpadden Florence E				
3094	" Thomas B.				
3095	" Ella B.				
3096	" Lizzie P.				
3097	" Maude				
3098	" Forest K.				
3099	" Theodore R.				
3100	" Oscar L.	2125.60	C.V. Rogers	G W Benge	
3101	McCarter Frances				
3102	" Frank				
3103	" Fred				
3104	" Liddie				
3105	" Ruby				
3106	" Moses				
3107	" John				
3108	" Nannie				
3109	McCarter Thomas	2391.30	J H McCarter	G.W. Benge	
3110	Milan Sarah				
3111	" Jennie				
3112	" Jessie				
3113	" Alice				
3114	" Nula				
3115	" Viola				
3116	" Charles	1859.90	Sarah Milan	G.W. Benge	

Starr Roll 1894

We, the undersigned citizens of the Cherokee Nation, by right of Cherokee blood, do hereby acknowledge to have received of E. E. Starr, National Treasurer of the Cherokee Nation, the sums set opposite our names respectively, in full of our shares in the per capita distribution authorized by an Act of the National Council, dated ___MAY 3 1894___ 1894.

#	Names of Head, and Members of Families	Amount	To Whom Paid	Witness to Payment	Remarks
3117	McComie Isabella C.	~~D620~~ ~~R687~~ 10786 order	10786		G.A.M.
3118	" Bonnie C	531.40	G A Martin ~~D620~~ ~~R687~~	Henry Eiffert	Check
3119	Mizer Susie				
3120	" Lillie				
3121	" John W.				
3122	" Carsalowie	1062.80	Susie Mizer	G W Benge	
3123	Matthews[sic] Ada	~~R310~~ 10094	ENROLLMENT REFUSED.		Also see doubtful card #697
3124	" Mary L.	~~R310~~ 10094	ENROLLMENT REFUSED.		
3125	" William L. L.	~~R310~~ 10094 797.10	ENROLLMENT REFUSED. Ada Mathews	G W Benge	
3126	Morris Thad	order			Neilson
3127	" Dee				
3128	" Lila	797.10	F.A. Neilson	J.C. Starr	on order
3129	McCoy Arch				
3130	" Augustine B.				
3131	" Arch C.	797.10	Augustine B. McCoy	J.C. Starr	
3132	Morris Henry	265.70	Henry Morris	L B Bell	
3133	Markham Nancy	265.70	EC Alberty administrator	L B Bell	
3134	Mortz Clara S	~~265.70~~	W.T. Whitaker	Henry Eiffert	WTW
3135	Martin Patsy M				
3136	" Tom				
3137	Browning May	797.10	GA Martin	Henry Eiffert	Check
3138	Miles Eliza	265.70	WE Miles	G W Benge	
3139	Mayfield Sarah	265.70	Sarah Mayfield	L B Bell	
3140	McDonald C.C.				see 2nd page Book 1
3141	French Maud	531.40	C.C. McDonald	G W Benge	

Starr Roll 1894

We, the undersigned citizens of the Cherokee Nation, by right of Cherokee blood, do hereby acknowledge to have received of E. E. Starr, National Treasurer of the Cherokee Nation, the sums set opposite our names respectively, in full of our shares in the per capita distribution authorized by an Act of the National Council, dated _____MAY 3 1894_____ 1894.

	Names of Head, and Members of Families	Amount	To Whom Paid	Witness to Payment	Remarks
3142	Norman Martha J.				
3143	Norman Albert C.				
3144	Norman Cynes W.	797.10	M.J. Norman	G.W. Benge	
3145	Norman James A.				
3146	" Clyde C.	531.40	J.A. Norman	G W Benge	
3147	Nickles Josephine				
3148	" Frank	531.40	John Nickles	G.W. Benge	
3149	Nash Lewis R.				
3150	" Fairy F.				
3151	" Edgar R	797.10	E.B. Nash	G.W. Benge	
3152	Nelms John				
3153	" Abbie				
3154	" John Jr.				
3155	" Luke	*order*			
3156	" James				
3157	" Victoria				
3158	" Allen	1859.90	A Foyil	Henry Eiffert	Che<
3159	Nelms Arch	265.70	John Nelms *guardian*	L B Bell	
3160	Nichols Octava	265.70	C J Harris	Emmet Starr	By ord
3161	Nicholson Ed V.	265.70	E.V. Nicholson	G W Benge	
3162	Nicholson Eva M.				
3163	" Ora C				
3164	" James P.	797.10	*(Illegible)* Nicholson		
3165	Nelms Felix				
3166	" Mary	531.40	B D Pennyton	Henry Eiffert	C

Starr Roll 1894

We, the undersigned citizens of the Cherokee Nation, by right of Cherokee blood, do hereby acknowledge to have received of E. E. Starr, National Treasurer of the Cherokee Nation, the sums set opposite our names respectively, in full of our shares in the per capita distribution authorized by an Act of the National Council, dated ___MAY 3 1894___ 1894.

Names of Head, and Members of Families	Amount	To Whom Paid	Witness to Payment	Remarks
3167 Nicholson Richard H.	265.70	R.H. Nicholson	G W Benge	
3168 Nicholson Thos K.	265.70	T.K. Nicholson	G W Benge	
3169 Nicholson Richard R.	265.70	R R Nicholson	G W Benge	
3170 Nicholson James E.	265.70	J.E. Nicholson	G W Benge	
3171 Nelson Ella				
3172 " Baby Ann				
3173 " Polly A.				
3174 " Effie	1062.80	J.C. Nelson	G W Benge	
3175 Nicholson Richard E.				
3176 " Daniel G.				
3177 " Henry				
3178 " Lettie M.				
3179 " Sim	1328.50	George Bibb *guardian*	L B Bell	*Check*
3180 Nickols Taylor O.	265.70	T.O. Nichols	G W Benge	
3181 Nichols Augustus B.				
3182 " Lucy				
3183 " Willie				
3184 " Claude				
3185 " Clifford				
3186 " Maude	1594.20	A.B. Nichols	G W Benge	
~~Nelms Sarah P.~~				
3187 Nobles Ellen				
3188 " Cleveland				
3189 " Roscoe				
3190 " Joel M.	1063.80	Ellen Noble	G W Benge	

Starr Roll 1894

We, the undersigned citizens of the Cherokee Nation, by right of Cherokee blood, do hereby acknowledge to have received of E. E. Starr, National Treasurer of the Cherokee Nation, the sums set opposite our names respectively, in full of our shares in the per capita distribution authorized by an Act of the National Council, dated ___MAY 3 1894___ 1894.

	Names of Head, and Members of Families	Amount	To Whom Paid	Witness to Payment	Remarks
3191	Nave Joseph	order			Wm L. M
3192	" Alice				
3193	" Lila				
3194	" Ida				
3195	" Joseph (Jr)	1328.50	W L Moore	Henry Eiffert	Check
3196	Nelms Sarah P.				
3197	Ashbrook Sadie				
3198	Clarence	797.10	Sarah P Nelms	G W Benge	
3199	Nippers Alice T				
3200	" Robert				
3201	Walkley Sallie				
3202	" Maggie	1062.80	Aallice[sic] Nippers	G W Benge	
3203	Nolen Saphronia				
3204	" Clara N.				
3205	" Janus				
3206	" Newton				
3207	Rogers Lewis				
3208	Manes Olif V.	1594.20	J.A. Nolen	G W Benge	
3209	Nare Walter	265.70	F A Neilson	E W Buffington	on Nea
3210	Owen Cherokee I.				
3211	" Cora S.	531.40	C.C. McDonald	G W Benge	
3212	Odell Margaret				
3213	" Mary				
3214	" Martha				
3215	Wing Victoria				
3216	" Vick				
3217	" Dora				
3218	" Otis	1859.90	Margeret[sic] Odell	L B Bell	
3219	Oneal Lou	order 265.70	CW Pool	Henry Eiffert	Check

Starr Roll 1894

We, the undersigned citizens of the Cherokee Nation, by right of Cherokee blood, do hereby acknowledge to have received of E. E. Starr, National Treasurer of the Cherokee Nation, the sums set opposite our names respectively, in full of our shares in the per capita distribution authorized by an Act of the National Council, dated ___MAY 3 1894___ 1894.

#	Names of Head, and Members of Families	Amount	To Whom Paid	Witness to Payment	Remarks
3220	Fields William				
3221	" Fannie				
3222	" Chick	797.10	Wm O. Fields	G W Benge	
3223	Owen Alice D826	~~265.70~~	William Owen	Henry Eiffert	Wm Owen
3224	" Alice (Jr) D826	265.70	William Owen	Henry Eiffert	
3225	Owen Janey D826	order 265.70	William Owen	Henry Eiffert	Wm Owen
3226	Owen William	265.70	William Owen	G W Benge	
3227	Owen Charles	order 265.70	William Owen D651	Henry Eiffert	Wm Owen
3228	Owen Owen[sic]	order 265.70	William Owen D651	Henry Eiffert	Wm Owen
3229	Owen Robt L.	order 265.70	Wm Owen 5599	Henry Eiffert	Sept 11 '94 order
3230	" William O.C.	265.70	Wm Owen	Henry Eiffert	
3231	Owen Narcissa	5601 265.70	Narcissa Owen	G.W. Benge	
3232	Owen William O.	order 5600 265.70	Wm Owen	Henry Eiffert	
3233	Oskison John				
3234	" Richard	531.40	John Oskison	G W Benge	
3235	Owen Robt O.				
3236	" William Otway	531.40	Wm Owen	Henry Eiffert	
3237	Oliver Sarah				
3238	" James M.				
3239	" William F.				
3240	" Jamie				
3241	" Maude				
3242	" Rexie	1594.20	Savanah Oliver Condry	G W Benge	

Starr Roll 1894

We, the undersigned citizens of the Cherokee Nation, by right of Cherokee blood, do hereby acknowledge to have received of E. E. Starr, National Treasurer of the Cherokee Nation, the sums set opposite our names respectively, in full of our shares in the per capita distribution authorized by an Act of the National Council, dated ____MAY 3 1894____ 1894.

	Names of Head, and Members of Families	Amount	To Whom Paid	Witness to Payment	Remarks
3243	Oskeeson Wm	265.70	John Oskison	G.W. Benge	
3244	Pruett Mary A.	order 265.70	Walsh & Shutt	G W Benge	W & on ord
3245	Parkinson Addie M.				
3246	" Rachel M.				
3247	" Ruth	797.10	Addie M Parkinson	G W Benge	
3248	Parks Robt C.				
3249	" Robt C. Jr.				
3250	" Jno R.B.				
3251	" Bernie				
3252	" Milton B.				
3253	" Alexander B.				
3254	" Mary E.				
3255	" Susan A.	2125.60	Robt G. Parks	L B Bell	
3256	Pumpkin George				
3257	" Peggy	531.40	George Pumpkin	G W Benge	
3258	Putnam Josie	265.70	Josie Putnam	G W Benge	
3259	Pevehouse Sonora				
3260	" Arthur W.				
3261	Pyatt Fannie C.				
3262	" Bessie L.				
3263	" Marchie				
3264	Pevehouse Sarah E.	1594.20	W.F. Pevehouse	G W Benge	
3265	Pharris John				
3266	" Alena	531.40	John Pharris	G W Benge	
3267	Peek Dollie M.	order			W T W
3268	" Henry H.				
3269	" Gracie O.	797.10	WT Whitaker	Henry Eiffert	
3270	Potts Susan	order			W & S
3271	" Henry				

Starr Roll 1894

We, the undersigned citizens of the Cherokee Nation, by right of Cherokee blood, do hereby acknowledge to have received of E. E. Starr, National Treasurer of the Cherokee Nation, the sums set opposite our names respectively, in full of our shares in the per capita distribution authorized by an Act of the National Council, dated ___MAY 3 1894___ 1894.

#	Names of Head, and Members of Families	Amount	To Whom Paid	Witness to Payment	Remarks
3272	" Mary B.	797.10	Walsh and Shutt	Henry Eiffert	Check
3273	Pharriss Pleasant H.				
3274	" Minnie	531.40	P.H. Pharriss	G W Benge	
3275	Pharriss Jackson L.	265.70	J.L. Pharris[sic]	G W Benge	
3276	Pharriss Farley W.	D789			
3277	" Allen	D789 531.40	john Pharris	G W Benge	
3278	Pharriss Agnes	D789 265.70	John Pharris	L B Bell	
3279	Prater Watt				JC Hogan
3280	" Geo D.				
3281	" William	order			
3282	" Hattie	1062.80	J.C. Hogan	J.C. Starr	Paid on order
3283	Propp Mary E.	265.70	Mary E. Propp	G.W. Benge	
3284	Perry Silas A.	Dead R124	ENROLLMENT REFUSED.		
3285	" Marion S.				
3286	" Earnest	D1120 R124	ENROLLMENT REFUSED.		Feb 21-1901
3287	" Amanda	R124	ENROLLMENT REFUSED.		"
3288	" Mary G.	1328.50	S A Perry D1120	G W Benge	
3289	Pinner Elizabeth				
3290	" John				
3291	" Pearley	797.10 order	Elizabeth Pinner	G W Benge	on order W.C.
3292	Potato Edward	265.70	W C Patton	G W Benge	Patton
3293	Price James	order 265.70	F.A. Neilson	E.W. Buffington	on order Neilson
3294	Palone Wilson	order 265.70	F A Neilson	E.W. Buffington	on order Neilson
3295	Puckett Peche				
3296	" Fannie				
3297	" Ellen				WE Halsell

Starr Roll 1894

We, the undersigned citizens of the Cherokee Nation, by right of Cherokee blood, do hereby acknowledge to have received of E. E. Starr, National Treasurer of the Cherokee Nation, the sums set opposite our names respectively, in full of our shares in the per capita distribution authorized by an Act of the National Council, dated ____MAY 3 1894____ 1894.

	Names of Head, and Members of Families	Amount	To Whom Paid	Witness to Payment	Remarks
3298	Poorboy George	1062.80	WE Halsell	Henry Eiffert	
3299	Pierce Augustus				Dead
3300	" Hazel M.				
3301	" Raymond O.	797.10	M.T. Pierce	G W Benge	
3302	Pathkiller Charles	order 265.70	Johnson&Keeler	Henry Eiffert	Chec
3303	Parks Annie	265.70	Annie Parks	G W Benge	
3304	Poole Chas W.				
3305	" Walton				
3306	" Claude	797.10	C.W. Poole	G W Benge	
3307	Pace Minnie				
3308	" Lora				
3309	" Nellie	797.10	Minnie Pace	L B Bell	
3310	Parris Levi				
3311	" Annie E.				
3312	" Frank				
3313	" John				
3314	" Delbert C.				
3315	" Marion				
3316	Hornstine Samuel		Levi Parris	G W Benge	
3317	Parks Sterling				H Lan
3318	" Robert	order			
3319	" Ada				
3320	" Rosie				
3321	" Maude				Pai
3322	" Richard	1594.20	Howard Langly	J.C. Starr	on
3323	Palmore Chas F.				
3324	" Ina				
3325	" Acie				
3326	" Newton D.				

Starr Roll 1894

We, the undersigned citizens of the Cherokee Nation, by right of Cherokee blood, do hereby acknowledge to have received of E. E. Starr, National Treasurer of the Cherokee Nation, the sums set opposite our names respectively, in full of our shares in the per capita distribution authorized by an Act of the National Council, dated ___MAY 3 1894___ 1894.

#	Names of Head, and Members of Families	Amount	To Whom Paid	Witness to Payment	Remarks
3327	" Paul A.	1328.50	C F Palmore	G W Benge	
3328	Palmore James A.	265.70	J.A. Palmour	G W Benge	
3329	Parris Frank W.				
3330	" Cora				
3331	" Mattie				
3332	" Katie	1062.80	F. W. Parris	G W Benge	
3333	Pigeon Looney				
3334	" William	order 531.40	CW Pool	Henry Eiffert	Check
3335	Parris Lemuel				
3336	" Mattie				
3337	" Susie				
3338	" Arch	1062.80	Lemuel Parris	G W Benge	
3339	Payne Wm P.				
3340	" Henry				
3341	" George A.				
3342	" Wesley				
3343	" Claude	1328.50	J.J. Payne	G W Benge	
3344	Palmore Evaline[sic]	265.70	Eveline Palmore	G W Benge	
3345	Powell Arthur	order 265.70	C.W. Pool	Henry Eiffert	Check
3346	Parsley Nannie				
3347	" Pauline	531.40	Nannie Parsley	G W Benge	
3348	Parris Henry	order 265.70	Henry Parris	L B Bell	E C Thompson
3349	Parham Emma	265.70	F A Neilson (order)	G W Benge	F.A.N. oh order
3350	Parrish Alvin H.	order 265.70	WV Carey	Henry Eiffert	Wm V. Carey check
3351	Porter Florence	order			W.V.C.

Starr Roll 1894

We, the undersigned citizens of the Cherokee Nation, by right of Cherokee blood, do hereby acknowledge to have received of E. E. Starr, National Treasurer of the Cherokee Nation, the sums set opposite our names respectively, in full of our shares in the per capita distribution authorized by an Act of the National Council, dated ___MAY 3 1894___ 1894.

	Names of Head, and Members of Families	Amount	To Whom Paid	Witness to Payment	Remarks
3352	" James D W				
3353	" Iris	797.10 *order*	W.V. Carey	Henry Eiffert	Check
3354	Patton Chas H.	265.70	J E Campbell	Henry Eiffert	J.E.C. Ck
3355	Parrish Walter S.				
3356	" Bertha				
3357	" William T.				
3358	" Joseph D.				
3359	" George Lee				
3360	" John M.				
3361	" James L.	1859.90	J E Campbell	L B Bell	
3362	Parsons Henry F.				
3363	" William O.				
3364	" Rosetha A.				
3365	" Cora I.	1062.80	E.W. Parsons	G W Benge	
3366	Parker Laura				
3367	" Josephine	*Taken off The Delaware roll*			
3368	" Edna	797.10	Johnson&Keeler	L B Bell	by Mr Joh
3369	" Emma	265.70	Job Parker	Henry Eiffert	
3370	Price Dan C.				
3371	" Annie Bell	531.40	Don C. Price	J.C. Starr	
3372	Price Joseph M^c D	265.70	J.M. Donald	L B Bell	
3373	Price Looney	265.70	Looney Price	L B Bell	
3374	Price Monte[sic]	265.70	Monti Price	L B Bell	
3375	Palmour Jno D.				
3376	" Mollie				
3377	" Alaska				
3378	" Keziah	1062.80	J.D. Palmour	G.W. Benge	

Starr Roll 1894

We, the undersigned citizens of the Cherokee Nation, by right of Cherokee blood, do hereby acknowledge to have received of E. E. Starr, National Treasurer of the Cherokee Nation, the sums set opposite our names respectively, in full of our shares in the per capita distribution authorized by an Act of the National Council, dated ___MAY 3 1894___ 1894.

#	Names of Head, and Members of Families	Amount	To Whom Paid	Witness to Payment	Remarks
3379	Palmour David S.				
3380	" Emma L.		D2671		
3381	" Roxie M.				
3382	" Fronie B.K.				
3383	" John R.				
3384	" Fannie A.				
3385	" Emily E.	1859.90	D.S. Palmour	G W Benge	
3386	Palmour Ben F.	~~D888~~	~~R704~~ 10387		
3387	" Virginia	D889			
3388	" John D Jr	~~D888~~	~~R704~~ 10387		
3389	" Bessie	~~D888~~	~~R704~~ 10387		
3390	" Robert	~~D888~~	~~R704~~ 10387		
3391	" Mary	~~D888~~	~~R704~~ 10387		
3392	" Sallie	~~D888~~	~~R704~~ 10387		
3393	" Hugh	~~D888~~ 2125.60	~~R704~~ 10387 B.F. Palmour	G.W. Benge	
	~~Palmour Emma G.~~				Registered as Lelia
	~~" Lila~~				Amy Goss
3394	Panther Eliza		D2672		
3395	" Collins	order	D2673		
3396	" Lillie	797.10	~~JM Hall~~ P2672	Henry Eiffert	JM Hall
3397	Peppin Mary	order 265.70	Johnson and Keeler	Henry Eiffert	check
3398	Phillips Frank	265.70	Frank Phillips	G W Benge	
3399	Payne John				RD Knight
3400	" Laura	order 531.40	R D Knight	Henry Eiffert	
3401	Payne Amsey M.				
3402	" Lewis L.				
3403	" Joseph Earl	797.10	A.M. Payne	G W Benge	

Starr Roll 1894

We, the undersigned citizens of the Cherokee Nation, by right of Cherokee blood, do hereby acknowledge to have received of E. E. Starr, National Treasurer of the Cherokee Nation, the sums set opposite our names respectively, in full of our shares in the per capita distribution authorized by an Act of the National Council, dated ___MAY 3 1894___ 1894.

Names of Head, and Members of Families	Amount	To Whom Paid	Witness to Payment	Remarks
3404 Patton Jane				
3405 Patton Eva	531.40	E.L. Halsell	G W Benge	
3406 Petee[sic] Myrtle	Non Citz – Does not apply –			
3407 " Hiram	R190 Enrollment Refused			
3408 " Eddie	R190 797.10	Myrtle Pettee	G W Benge	
3409 Parris William	order 265.70	J.S. Thomason	J.C. Starr	Paid J.S.T.
3410 Pate Albert N.				
3411 Pate Laura R.	531.40	Albert N Pate	G W Benge	
3412 Pate Althea	order 265.70	J.H. Akin	G W Benge	on order
3413 Pate Joseph B.				
3414 " Mary A.				
3415 " Althea F.	797.10	J.B. Pate	G W Benge	
3416 Prather Cherokee E.	order			
3417 Payne Andrew L.				Neilson
3418 Prather Eddie				
3419 " George E.				
3420 " Lizzie		F A Neilson	E W Buffington	
3421 " Josie M.	1594.20	JC Hogan	Henry Eiffert	
3422 Payne Chas H.	265.70	W.M. Gullager	S.W. Mayfield	
3423 Pevihouse Lizzie	order 265.70	F A Neilson	Henry Eiffert	order Neilson
3424 Payne Rosie E.				
3425 " Winona				
3426 " Floyd B.				
3427 " Ruth A.	1062.80	Rosie E. Payne	L B Bell	
3428 Pickaman Martha	order			Neilson
3429 " Clara				
3430 " Clarence				

Starr Roll 1894

We, the undersigned citizens of the Cherokee Nation, by right of Cherokee blood, do hereby acknowledge to have received of E. E. Starr, National Treasurer of the Cherokee Nation, the sums set opposite our names respectively, in full of our shares in the per capita distribution authorized by an Act of the National Council, dated ___MAY 3 1894___ 1894.

	Names of Head, and Members of Families	Amount	To Whom Paid	Witness to Payment	Remarks
3431	" Jennie				
3432	" Augustus	1328.50	F A Neilson	E.W. Buffington	on order
3433	Price Charles	265.70	Charles Price	L B Bell	
3434	Parris Rachel				
3435	" Anna				
3436	" Willie	797.10	Alex Cochran	L B Bell	on order Rachel Parris
3437	Pfamekuch Agnes				
3427 1/2	" Charles	531.40	A Pfamekuch	G W Benge	
3438	Patton Arminty				J.E.C.
3439	" William W.				
3440	" Elizabeth M.				
3441	" John H.				
3442	" Emmie	1328.50	JE Campbell	Henry Eiffert	check
3443	Price George	265.70	JT Wettack	Henry Eiffert	W̶e̶t̶t̶a̶c̶k̶ check
3444	Queen George	order 265.70	LW Buffington	Henry Eiffert	L.W.B. Check
3445	Quinton Nellie	order			GW Eaton Check
3446	Fletcher Mattie	531.40	GW Eaton	Henry Eiffert	
3447	Quinton Felix	2̶6̶5̶.̶7̶0̶	WE Halsell	Henry Eiffert	WE Halsell check
3448	Quinton Jack	order 7427			W&S check
3449	" Jess	531.40	Walsh and Shutt	Henry Eiffert	
3450	Rogers Ed				
3451	" Frank W.				
3452	" Nora M.	797.10	Ed Rogers	G.W. Benge	
3453	Robison[sic] Henrietta				
3454	" Josie				
3455	" Jessie				
3456	" Effie	1068.80	P P Robinson	G.W. Benge	

Starr Roll 1894

We, the undersigned citizens of the Cherokee Nation, by right of Cherokee blood, do hereby acknowledge to have received of E. E. Starr, National Treasurer of the Cherokee Nation, the sums set opposite our names respectively, in full of our shares in the per capita distribution authorized by an Act of the National Council, dated ___ MAY 3 1894 ___ 1894.

	Names of Head, and Members of Families	Amount	To Whom Paid	Witness to Payment	Remarks
3457	Raper Jno A.	order 265.70	W T Whitaker	Henry Eiffert	W.T.
3458	Raper Henry M.	order 265.70	W T Whitaker	Henry Eiffert	W.T.
3459	Roberts Callie	265.70	Callie Roberts	G.W. Benge	
3460	Raper William P.	order 5237			W.T.
3461	" Claude				
3462	" Alvin	797.10 5237	W T Whitaker	Henry Eiffert	
3463	Raper Jack				
3464	" Elizabeth				
3465	" Louis	797.10	Nancy Raper	G W Benge	
3466	Rabbit Andy				
3467	" Sallie				
3468	" Mattie				
3469	" Ida				
3470	" Alsie				
3471	" Ross	1594.20	Andy Rabbit	G W Benge	
3472	Rogers Sallie				
3473	" Pearl				
3474	" Frank	797.10	John Rogers	J.C. Starr	
3475	Rucker Dora				
3476	" Ola Ave				
3477	" Ernest				
3478	" Mabel	1062.80	F.M. Rucker	J.C. Starr	
3479	Riley John M.				
3480	" Nannie E.				
3481	" Richard				
3482	" Mattie				
3483	" Cora				
3484	" Nannie				
3485	" Lucy				
3486	" Wilder				

Starr Roll 1894

We, the undersigned citizens of the Cherokee Nation, by right of Cherokee blood, do hereby acknowledge to have received of E. E. Starr, National Treasurer of the Cherokee Nation, the sums set opposite our names respectively, in full of our shares in the per capita distribution authorized by an Act of the National Council, dated ____MAY 3 1894____ 1894.

	Names of Head, and Members of Families	Amount	To Whom Paid	Witness to Payment	Remarks
3487	" Owens				
3488	" Grover C.	2657.00	John M. Riley	G W Benge	
3489	Ross George				
3490	" Comodore	531.40	George Ross	G.W. Benge	
	~~Rogers Paul~~	(Illinois Dist. Page 817 No 1503)			Illinois
3491	Rogers Joseph				W.T.W.
3491	" Eva	*order*			
3493	" Sarah	797.10	WT Whitaker	Henry Eiffert	
3494	Rogers Mary E.	265.70	M.E. Rogers	G W Benge	
3495	Rogers David M.	265.70	David M Rogers	G W Benge	
3496	" Cora L.	265.70	Cora L Rogers	G W Benge	
3497	Rogers Lena M	265.70	L.M. Rogers	G W Benge	
3498	Rogers Love	265.70	David M Rogers	G W Benge	
3499	Rogers Joseph R.				
3500	" Vickie R.				
3501	" Oscar L.				
3502	" Robt R.				
3503	" Martin G.				
3504	" Guy R.	1594.20	J.R. Rogers	G.W. Benge	
3505	Rogers Claude[sic]				
3506	" Nancy E.				
3507	" Catherine				
3508	" Knox	1062.80	Claud Rogers	G W Benge	
3509	Rogers Laura A.				
3510	Gray Frank E.	531.40	Laura A Rogers	G W Benge	

Starr Roll 1894

We, the undersigned citizens of the Cherokee Nation, by right of Cherokee blood, do hereby acknowledge to have received of E. E. Starr, National Treasurer of the Cherokee Nation, the sums set opposite our names respectively, in full of our shares in the per capita distribution authorized by an Act of the National Council, dated ____MAY 3 1894____ 1894.

	Names of Head, and Members of Families	Amount	To Whom Paid	Witness to Payment	Remarks
3511	Rogers Jennie[sic] H.				
3512	Martin Willie A.				
3513	" Cunnie A.	797.10	Jinnie H Rogers	G.W. Benge	
3514	Rogers Mary E.				
3515	" Arthur L.				Paid on order c
3516	" Thomas L.				Cyntha Alberty
3617	" Granville	1062.80	J.T. Musgrove	JC Starr	Guardian
3518	Rogers Jno M.	265.70	Jas.T.Musgrove	J.C. Starr	Paid on order Cynthia Alberty Guard
3519	Rider Thomas	265.70	W.H.Clark D2676	G W Benge	on orde WH Clark
3520	Roberts Annie				
3521	" Annie				
3522	" Lena				
3523	" Marion				
3524	" Jno H.				
3525	" Earl L.				
3526	" Arthur				
3527	" Mary	2125.60	Annie Roberts	G W Benge	
3528	Rice James A.	order			Neilson
3529	" Annie				
3530	" James A (Jr)				
3531	" Ida				
3532	" Ruby				
3533	" Violet E.	1594.20	F A Neilson	Henry Eiffert	order
3534	Rollings Pastey[sic]	order			Neilson
3535	Payne Alice	531.40	F A Neilson	Henry Eiffert	on order
3536	Reddington Isabel	order 265.79	WC Patton	G W Benge	on order WC Patton
3537	Ruddle Norris	265.70	Jene Ruddle Guardian	L B Bell	
3538	Rease Richard	265.70	W.M. Gulager	S.W. Mayfield	Pd. on or June 21, 1

Starr Roll 1894

We, the undersigned citizens of the Cherokee Nation, by right of Cherokee blood, do hereby acknowledge to have received of E. E. Starr, National Treasurer of the Cherokee Nation, the sums set opposite our names respectively, in full of our shares in the per capita distribution authorized by an Act of the National Council, dated ___MAY 3 1894___ 1894.

Names of Head, and Members of Families	Amount	To Whom Paid	Witness to Payment	Remarks
3539 Rogers Mary K	265.70	M. K. Rogers	G W Benge	
3540 Runyan Katie				
3541 " Elma				
3542 " Sammie				
3543 Tyner Frayzer				
3544 " Ella				
3545 " Lulu	1594.20	C.C. Runyan	L B Bell	
3546 Rogers Willington[sic]				
3547 " Susie				
3548 " Julia	797.10	Wellington Rogers	L B Bell	
3549 " Ida	265.70 order	WC Rogers	Henry Eiffert	check to W.C. Rogers
3550 Rogers William C.	265.70	William C Rogers	J.C. Starr	
3551 Reed Andy				
3552 " Lenora	order			
3553 " Nancy	797.10	Johnson & Keeler	Henry Eiffert	check
3554 Rogers William G.				
3555 " Lulu N.	order			
3556 " William E.	797.10	Johnson & Keeler	Henry Eiffert	check
3557 Rogers William H.	265.70	H C Rogers	G W Benge	on order
3558 Rogers Henry C.	265.70	W.R. Rogers	G W Benge	
3559 Rogers Louisa P.	265.70	L P Rogers	G W Benge	
3560 Redmond Malinda	order 265.70	CW Poole	Henry Eiffert	check
3561 Rogers Jackson				
3562 " Sarah	531.40	Jackson Rogers	G W Benge	
3563 Wofford Laura	265.70	Laura Wofford	G.W. Benge	
3564 Rogers Ridge W.	265.70	R W Rogers	G W Benge	

Starr Roll 1894

We, the undersigned citizens of the Cherokee Nation, by right of Cherokee blood, do hereby acknowledge to have received of E. E. Starr, National Treasurer of the Cherokee Nation, the sums set opposite our names respectively, in full of our shares in the per capita distribution authorized by an Act of the National Council, dated ____MAY 3 1894____ 1894.

Names of Head, and Members of Families	Amount	To Whom Paid	Witness to Payment	Remarks
3565 Roberson Sarah F.				
3566 " William H.				
3567 " Sarah F.	797.10	Sarah F. Roberson	J.C. Starr (cwp)	
3568 Roberts Mary E.				
3569 " James T.				
3570 " William E.				
3571 " Charles A.	1062.80	M.E. Roberts	G W Benge	
3572 Rippetoe Rebecca				
3573 " Arthur B.				
3574 " Cora E.				
3575 " Bessie M.	1062.80	Isaac Rippetoe	G W Benge	
3576 Riggs Laura				
3577 " Frank				
3578 " Nadia	797.10	H.O. Riggs	G.W. Benge	
3579 Robison Minerva				
3580 " Rosie E.				
3581 " Mary E.				
3582 " Minnie E.				
3583 " Samuel L.				
3584 " Chas W.	1594.20	Minerva Robison	L B Bell	
3585 Robison Esta				
3586 " Katie				
3587 " Joseph C.				
3588 " De Witt				
3589 " Clara	1328.50	Jack Roberson	G W Benge	
3590 Riley Geo W.	*order* 265.70	JE Campbell	Henry Eiffert	J.E.C.
3591 Rolston James D.	265.70	J.D. Rolston	G.W. Benge	
3592 Robins Josie V. *1 mo.*	265.70	W.L. Robins	G W Benge	

Starr Roll 1894

We, the undersigned citizens of the Cherokee Nation, by right of Cherokee blood, do hereby acknowledge to have received of E. E. Starr, National Treasurer of the Cherokee Nation, the sums set opposite our names respectively, in full of our shares in the per capita distribution authorized by an Act of the National Council, dated ___MAY 3 1894___ 1894.

	Names of Head, and Members of Families	Amount	To Whom Paid	Witness to Payment	Remarks
3593	Rider Bluford W.				
3594	" Liddie				
3595	" Maude				
3596	" May				
3597	" Sam				
3598	" Percivall	1594.20	B W Rider	G W Benge	
3599	Rider Austin				
3600	" James				
3601	Rider John	797.10	B.W. Rider	G W Benge	
3602	Rogers Ruth				
3603	" Maude	531.40	Ruth Rogers	J.C. Starr	
3604	Rosenthal Elizabeth				
3605	" Nancy H.	531.40	E Rosenthal	G W Benge	
3606	Rowden Luvada				
3607	" Amona	531.40	Luvada Rowden	G W Benge	
3608	Riley Samuel R	265.70	S.R. Riley	G W Benge	
3609	Riley Rufus R.	265.70	R.R. Riley	G W Benge	
3610	" Allwood	265.70	Bettie Riley	G W Benge	
3611	Reinhardt Kinney				
3612	Lambert Jno E.				
3613	Reinhardt Sarah	797.10	Chas Reinhardt	G.W. Benge	
3614	Reinhardt Cassie				
3615	" Henry H.				
3616	" Ada				
3617	" Walter	1062.80	Nancy Reinhardt	L B Bell	
3618	Rider William P.	order 265.70	W E Halsell	Henry Eiffert	WEH check

Starr Roll 1894

We, the undersigned citizens of the Cherokee Nation, by right of Cherokee blood, do hereby acknowledge to have received of E. E. Starr, National Treasurer of the Cherokee Nation, the sums set opposite our names respectively, in full of our shares in the per capita distribution authorized by an Act of the National Council, dated ___MAY 3 1894___ 1894.

	Names of Head, and Members of Families	Amount	To Whom Paid	Witness to Payment	Remarks
3619	Raley Nancy J.	order			W^m V C
3620	" William L.				
3621	" Bertha Pearl	797.10	WV Carey	Henry Eiffert	ch
3622	Riley Minnie	order			E B Bend
3622 1/2	" Elizabeth	531.40	EB Bender	Henry Eiffert	check
3623	Rogers Thos L.	order 265.70	JC Hogan	Henry Eiffert	J.C.H.
3624	Riley James S.	265.70	J.S. Riley	G W Benge	
3625	Reynolds Wm G.	order			J.E.C.
3626	" Bessie	531.40	JE Campbell	Henry Eiffert	ck
3627	Ross Susan E.				
3628	" Walter Lee				
3629	" Clarence S.				
3630	" Charles R.				
3631	" Mary E.	1328.50	Susan E Ross	L B Bell	
3632	Ross Perry				
3633	" Jessie				
3634	" Minnie	797.10	Susan E Ross	L B Bell	
3635	Riley Lewis				
3636	" John W.				
3637	" Clnora				
3638	" Cora	1062.80	Lewis Riley	L B Bell	
3639	" Sallie L.	265.70	Sallie L Riley	G W Benge	
3640	Reed Almira				
3641	" Lucy	531.40	J J Barndollar Scott nee Reed letter as regards this payment Mch 4/96 Coffeyville Kans	Henry Eiffert	JE Campb
3642	Roberson Hank	265.70	Mary Guen guardian	L B Bell	
3643	Roberson Cyntha E.				
3643 1/2	" Mary J.	531.40	Cynthia Roberson	L B Bell	

Starr Roll 1894

We, the undersigned citizens of the Cherokee Nation, by right of Cherokee blood, do hereby acknowledge to have received of E. E. Starr, National Treasurer of the Cherokee Nation, the sums set opposite our names respectively, in full of our shares in the per capita distribution authorized by an Act of the National Council, dated ____MAY 3 1894____ 1894.

#	Names of Head, and Members of Families	Amount	To Whom Paid	Witness to Payment	Remarks
3644	Rogers Clem V.				
3645	" Mary				
3646	" Willie P.	797.10	CV Rogers	L B Bell	
3647	Rogers Jack				
3648	" George	~~D1326~~ D770			
3649	" Jackie				
3650	" Rosie	1062.80	W.C. Rogers	Henry Eiffert	
3651	Ringo Lucy A.				
3652	" Charles				
3653	" George G.				
3654	" Nona F.				
3655	" William P.				
3656	" Libbie	1594.20	L.A. Ringo	G W Benge	
3657	Rogers Robt L.	order 265.70	J S Thomason	Henry Eiffert	J.S. Thomason
3658	Ruddles Jessie				
3659	" Jessie (Jr)				
3660	" Clara				
3661	" Charles	1062.80	Jessie Ruddles	L B Bell	
3662	Richards Eliza	265.70	J G Schrimsher	G.W. Benge	J.G. Schrimsher Guardian
3663	Risman Martha				
3664	" John				
3665	" Dannie	797.10	Martha Risman	G.W. Benge	
3666	Riddle Fannie J.				
3667	" Ida J.				
3668	" Fred F.	797.10	F.J. Riddle D2675 pd Oct 9th 96	G W Benge	
3669	Rogers Robt	265.70	Wm Gulager	JC Dannenberg	
3670	Ralston Robt D.	ENROLLMENT REFUSED. R179			
3671	" Eva R.				
3672	" Lillie D.	DEAD.			

Starr Roll 1894

We, the undersigned citizens of the Cherokee Nation, by right of Cherokee blood, do hereby acknowledge to have received of E. E. Starr, National Treasurer of the Cherokee Nation, the sums set opposite our names respectively, in full of our shares in the per capita distribution authorized by an Act of the National Council, dated ___MAY 3 1894___ 1894.

#	Names of Head, and Members of Families	Amount	To Whom Paid	Witness to Payment	Remarks
3673	" Mary C.	DEAD.			
3674	" Robt L.		~~D437~~ R658		
3675	" Violet		~~D437~~ R658		
3676	" Ruby DEAD.	1859.90	R.D. Ralston	G W Benge	
3677	Rogers Athelstan				
3678	" Roy				
3679	" Homer				
3680	" Edgar	1062.80	Josie Rogers	G W Benge	
3681	Ryne John	order 265.70	James Thompson	Henry Eiffert	Jim Thom
3682	Rogers Henry	265.70	Henry Rogers	G W Benge	
3683	Rame Fred	265.70	Martha Risman	G.W. Benge	
3684	Ratlingourd Liddie				
3685	Pigeon John	531.40	L.R. Gourd	G W Benge	
3686	Ratcliff Eva E.				
3687	" Fred F.				
3688	" James W.				
3689	" Finnis R.				
3690	" Eva M.				
3691	" Norville	1594.20	E.N. Ratcliff	G W Benge	
3692	Raymond Amanda	265.70	Amanda Raymond	G.W. Benge	
3693	Rogers Thomas J.				
3694	" Alva M.				
3695	" Lewis	797.10	T.J. Rogers	G W Benge	
3696	Riddle Louisa	265.70	Louisa Riddle	G W Benge	
3697	Ross Leonard				
3698	Raper Ella				
3699	" Charles				

Starr Roll 1894

We, the undersigned citizens of the Cherokee Nation, by right of Cherokee blood, do hereby acknowledge to have received of E. E. Starr, National Treasurer of the Cherokee Nation, the sums set opposite our names respectively, in full of our shares in the per capita distribution authorized by an Act of the National Council, dated ___MAY 3 1894___ 1894.

#	Names of Head, and Members of Families	Amount	To Whom Paid	Witness to Payment	Remarks
3700	" Thomas	1062.80	Leonard Ross	L B Bell	4884
3701	Rogers Jane				
3702	" Allie B. *Pelila*	order			GW Eaton
3703	" Charles H.	797.10	Jane Rogers	L B Bell	Eaton withdrew this order
3704	Riggs Rosie E.				
3705	" Joseph	531.40	Rosie E. Riggs	J.C. Starr	Geo Eaton
3706	Railey Martha				
3707	" George *W.*	order			GW Eaton
3708	" Oliver				
3709	" Oscar C.				
3710	" William H.	1328.50	GW Eaton	Henry Eiffert	check
3711	Rollins Mina				
3712	" Cora	531.40	Mina Rollins	L B Bell	
3713	Ross Jack	265.70	Jack Ross	L B Bell	
3714	Ross Melissa	order			Neilson
3715	" Eddie	531.40	F A Neilson	Henry Eiffert	order
3716	Ross Geo S.				
3717	" Nellie				
3718	" Wayne M^{c}V.				
3719	" Roy V.	1062.80	Geo S Ross	J.C. Starr	
3720	Rogers Sue M.	order 265.70 *Elect to enroll as a Creek* CW Turner		Henry Eiffert	D1301 C W T Ck
3721	Riley Belle	265.70	J M Keys	G.W. Benge	
3722	Rider Charles R.	order 265.70	WL Moore	Henry Eiffert	W.L.M.
3723	Riley John	265.70	John Riley	G W Benge	

Starr Roll 1894

We, the undersigned citizens of the Cherokee Nation, by right of Cherokee blood, do hereby acknowledge to have received of E. E. Starr, National Treasurer of the Cherokee Nation, the sums set opposite our names respectively, in full of our shares in the per capita distribution authorized by an Act of the National Council, dated ___MAY 3 1894___ 1894.

	Names of Head, and Members of Families	Amount	To Whom Paid	Witness to Payment	Remarks
3724	Reed Cyntha A.		4882		
3725	" Thomas L.				
3726	" Claude	797.10	Cyntha A Reed	G W Benge	
3727	Ridge John	265.70	John Ridge	G W Benge	
3728	Riggs Eliza				
3729	" Josie				
3730	Downing William	797.10	Eliza Riggs	G.W. Benge	
3731	Spriggs Mary A.	265.70	M.A. Spriggs	G W Benge	
3732	Stout Mary A.				
3733	" Nancy E.				
3734	" Annie B.				
3735	" Louisa				
3736	" Ellen				
3737	" Susan				
3738	" Jaeb				
3739	" James	2125.60	Abram Stout	L B Bell	
3740	Sequoyah Maude				
3741	Sanders Berry	531.40	Maud Sequoyah	G W Benge	
3742	Sequoyah Dick		D1533		
3743	" Lucy				
3744	" Dave				Dead
3745	Johns Frances	1062.80	Dick Sequoyah	G W Benge	
3746	Sloan Ellic G.				
3747	" Robert				
3748	" Nora				
3749	" Lizzie				
3750	" Cora	1328.50	Ellec G Sloan	G W Benge	
3751	Sloan Thomas A.	265.70	T A Sloan	G W Benge	

Starr Roll 1894

We, the undersigned citizens of the Cherokee Nation, by right of Cherokee blood, do hereby acknowledge to have received of E. E. Starr, National Treasurer of the Cherokee Nation, the sums set opposite our names respectively, in full of our shares in the per capita distribution authorized by an Act of the National Council, dated ___MAY 3 1894___ 1894.

#	Names of Head, and Members of Families	Amount	To Whom Paid	Witness to Payment	Remarks
3752	Sloan Hattie	265.70	Hattie Sloan	G W Benge	
3753	Still Samuel	265.70	Samuel Still	G W Benge	
3754	Sixkiller Martin	*order*			C D Markham
3755	" Hooley				
3756	" Maude				
3757	" Lola				
3758	" Rachel				
3759	" Mary	1594.20	C.D. Markham	G W Benge	
3760	Stroup Clara	*order*	4822		Neilson
3761	" Royal		4822		
3762	" Earl		4822		
3763	" Pearl		4822		
3764	" Jessie	1328.50	F A Neilson	Henry Eiffert	*order*
3765	Spriggs Alexander				
3766	" John B.				
3767	" Annie B				
3768	" Marnie P				
3769	" Henry A.	1328.50	Alexander Spriggs	G W Benge	
3770	Sanders Rat				
3771	" Annie				
3772	" Nellie	797.10	Joseph Sanders	J.C. Starr	*on order*
3773	Sanders Joseph				
3774	" Frances				
3775	" Jesse	797.10	Joseph Sanders	J.C. Starr	
3776	Shackleford Cora				
3777	" Charlotta	531.40	W.R. Shackleford	G W Benge	
3778	Swimmer John	265.70	John Swimmer	G W Benge	
3779	Steens Susan				
3780	" Sarah				

Starr Roll 1894

We, the undersigned citizens of the Cherokee Nation, by right of Cherokee blood, do hereby acknowledge to have received of E. E. Starr, National Treasurer of the Cherokee Nation, the sums set opposite our names respectively, in full of our shares in the per capita distribution authorized by an Act of the National Council, dated _____MAY 3 1894_____ 1894.

	Names of Head, and Members of Families	Amount	To Whom Paid	Witness to Payment	Remarks
3781	" Annie	797.10	*(Illegible)*	L B Bell	
3782	Steeler Lydia	265.70	Lydia Steeler	G W Benge	
3783	Starr Blue W				
3784	" Charley C.				
3785	" Orange W.				
3786	" Glenn				
3787	" Jess M.	1328.50	Bluford Starr	L B Bell	
3788	Sears Charlotte				
3789	" Ida				
3790	" Mary				
3791	" Steven				
3792	" Sam				
3793	" David				
3794	" Joel	1859.90	Charlott Sears		
3795	Sunday Emily				
3796	" Susie				
3797	" Betsey	797.10	Emily Sunday	L B Bell	
3798	Sixkiller Eliza	265.70	Eliza Sixkiller	G W Benge	
3799	Sunday Ezekiel	*order* 265.70	Walsh and Shutt	Henry Eiffert	W&S C
3800	Stalley James				W.T.W.
3801	" Nannie	*order*			
3802	" Noley				
3803	" Jessie	1062.80	W T Whitaker	Henry Eiffert	
3804	Summers Joseph	265.70	Joseph Summers	G W Benge	
3805	Stiles Lizzie	*order* 265.70	JC Hogan	Henry Eiffert	Or J.C.H.
3806	Scroggins Lucy	*order*			J C Hog
3807	" Maude				

Starr Roll 1894

We, the undersigned citizens of the Cherokee Nation, by right of Cherokee blood, do hereby acknowledge to have received of E. E. Starr, National Treasurer of the Cherokee Nation, the sums set opposite our names respectively, in full of our shares in the per capita distribution authorized by an Act of the National Council, dated ___MAY 3 1894___ 1894.

#	Names of Head, and Members of Families	Amount	To Whom Paid	Witness to Payment	Remarks
3808	" Effie				
3809	" Oma				
3810	" Lola				
3811	" Jess E.	1594.20	J.C. Hogan	Henry Eiffert	Ck
3812	Sullivan James	order			F.A. Neilson
3813	" Nancy				order Neilson
3814	" Frank	order 797.10	F A Neilson	Henry Eiffert	order withdrawn
3815	Sixkiller Joseph	order 265.70	Joseph Sixkiller	G W Benge	H.&B.
3816	Shutt Jno W.	265.70	J.W. Shutt	G W Benge	
3817	Shutt Clem W.	265./70	C W Shutt	G W Benge	
3818	Shutt Bessie	265.70	Bessie Shutt	G W Benge	
3819	Sanders Nicholas				
3820	" Irene				
3821	Fields Elmer	797.10	Nicholas Sanders	G.W. Benge	
3822	Sanders James	order			J.C. Hogan
3823	" Oce	531.40	JC Hogan	Henry Eiffert	Ck
3824	Skinner Lucy C.				
3825	" Rosie L.				
3826	" Willie				
3827	" Tom F.				
3828	" Morgan D.				
3829	" Gallagher				
3830	" Betsey A.				
3831	" James W. Jr				
3832	" Mary	2391.30	L.C. Skinner	G.W. Benge	
3833	Sterling Ella	D249			
3834	" Lillie E.	531.ᴅ249	Ella Sterling	G W Benge	

Starr Roll 1894

We, the undersigned citizens of the Cherokee Nation, by right of Cherokee blood, do hereby acknowledge to have received of E. E. Starr, National Treasurer of the Cherokee Nation, the sums set opposite our names respectively, in full of our shares in the per capita distribution authorized by an Act of the National Council, dated ___MAY 3 1894___ 1894.

	Names of Head, and Members of Families	Amount	To Whom Paid	Witness to Payment	Remarks
3835	South Kate				
3836	" Ellen				
3837	" Charles C.				
3838	" Wilson C.				
3839	" Kate	1528.50	J.C. South	G W Benge	
3840	Shanahan Charlotte				
3841	" Mary				
3842	" Kittie				
3843	" Winnie	1062.80	P Shanahan	G W Benge	
3844	Shanahan Ella				
3845	" William	531.40	Pat Shanahan	G.W. Benge	
3846	Smart Dasy P.				
3847	" Susie P.				
3848	" Athalie	797.10	L.R. Smart	G W Benge	
3849	Schrimsher Laura				
3850	" Eddie	531.40	Laura Schrimsher	G W Benge	
3851	Smith Kittie J.				
3852	" Martha M.	531.40	O.J. Smith	G.W. Benge	
3853	Sweatman Mattie	265.70	Mattie Sweatman	G.W. Benge	
3854	Smith Joseph	265.70	Mary Chambers (Guardian)	JC Dannenberg	
3855	Sunday William				
3856	" Annason ⎤		D2677		
3857	" Alex ⎬ Creek		D2677		RN Bynum
3858	" Ellen ⎦	order 1062.80	R.N. Bynum ~~D2670~~ D267	J.C. Starr	Paid on an order
3859	Ska-lane William	265.70	F A Neilson ~~D2670~~ 9893	Henry Eiffert	Neilson
3860	Johnson Ellie	265.70	Ellsee Johnson	G W Benge	
3861	Starr Peggie	265.70	Peggy Starr	L B Bell	

Starr Roll 1894

We, the undersigned citizens of the Cherokee Nation, by right of Cherokee blood, do hereby acknowledge to have received of E. E. Starr, National Treasurer of the Cherokee Nation, the sums set opposite our names respectively, in full of our shares in the per capita distribution authorized by an Act of the National Council, dated ___MAY 3 1894___ 1894.

Names of Head, and Members of Families	Amount	To Whom Paid	Witness to Payment	Remarks
3862 Sage Nancy	265.70	Nancy Sage	G.W. Benge	
3863 Settle Martha				
3864 " Randolph				
3865 " Lore Ann				
3866 " Eugene				
3867 " Martha				
3868 " Arthur		Martha Settle		
3869 Settle Lee	1859.90	Martha Settle	G W Benge	
3870 Sweeten Rebecca				
3871 " Emoria				
3872 " Cora				
3873 " Clein				
3874 " Samuel	1328.50	Rebecca Sweeten	L B Bell	
3875 Sweeten Philip	265.70	Phillip Sweeten	G W Benge	
3876 Sweeten Eva	265.70	Eva Sweeten	L B Bell	
3877 Stokes Georgia A.				
3878 " Floyd M.				
3879 " Oliver M.				
3880 " Greta	1062.80		Henry Eiffert	ck
3881 Steeler George				Dead
3882 " Nancy				
3883 " Johnson				
3884 " Willie	1062.80	Johnson & Keeler	Henry Eiffert	Ck
3885 Ska-lane Aggie	order 265.70	Johnson & Keeler	Henry Eiffert	Ck
3886 Ska-lane John				
3887 " Jennie				
3888 " Bear				
3889 " James				

Starr Roll 1894

We, the undersigned citizens of the Cherokee Nation, by right of Cherokee blood, do hereby acknowledge to have received of E. E. Starr, National Treasurer of the Cherokee Nation, the sums set opposite our names respectively, in full of our shares in the per capita distribution authorized by an Act of the National Council, dated ___MAY 3 1894___ 1894.

	Names of Head, and Members of Families	Amount	To Whom Paid	Witness to Payment	Remarks
3890	" Mary				
3891	" William				
3892	" Dick	2125.60	Johnson & Keeler	Henry Eiffert	Ck
3893	Ska-lane Danniel				
3894	" Lizzie	order			Thomason
3895	" Joseph	797.10	J.S. Thomason	J.C. Starr	Paid on o
3896	Scudder Wm H.				
3897	" Mary E.	265.70	M E Scudder	G.W. Benge	
3898	" Gordon H.				
3899	" Newton G.				
3900	" Maggie L.				
3901	" Nellie V.				
3902	" Aimie C.				
3903	" William H.				
3904	" Julia I.				
3905	Camp Ora M.				
3906	" James M.	2657.00	W^m H Scudder	G W Benge	
3907	Scudder Ida J.	265.70	Ida J Scudder	G.W. Benge	
3908	Scudder Laura K.	265.70	L.K. Scudder	G W Benge	
3909	Simon Sarah	265.70	Sarah Simon	G W Benge	
3910	Samuel Myra	265.70	Myra Samuel	G W Benge	
3911	Strange Mary R.	265.70	M.R. Strange	G W Benge	
3912	Smith Georgia A.				
3913	" Clarence				
3914	" Maude A.				
3915	" Freeman	1062.80	W.M. Smith	G W Benge	
3916	Sequitchie Martha	order 265.70	WT Whitaker	Henry Eiffert	W.T.W.

Starr Roll 1894

We, the undersigned citizens of the Cherokee Nation, by right of Cherokee blood, do hereby acknowledge to have received of E. E. Starr, National Treasurer of the Cherokee Nation, the sums set opposite our names respectively, in full of our shares in the per capita distribution authorized by an Act of the National Council, dated ____MAY 3 1894____ 1894.

	Names of Head, and Members of Families	Amount	To Whom Paid	Witness to Payment	Remarks
3917	Sequitchie Archie	order 265.70	WT Whitaker	Henry Eiffert	W.T.W.
3918	Swan Susie				
3919	" Paul	531.40	WT Whitaker	Henry Eiffert	
3920	Swarm[sic] Nellie	order 265.70	WT Whitaker	Henry Eiffert	W.T.W.
3921	Stokes Mary				
3922	" Ewing				
3923	" Hershel				
3924	" William				
3925	" Maude				
3926	" Robert	1594.20	Mary Stokes	L B Bell	
3927	Smith Alice	265.70	Allice Smith	G W Benge	
3928	Smith Susie	265.70	Susan Smith	G W Benge	
3929	Snyder Annie				
3930	" Thomas B.				
3931	" Perry E.	797.10	Annie Snyder	G W Benge	
3932	Swan Boudinot	order 265.70	CW Poole	Henry Eiffert	Ck
3933	Swim Mary E.				
3934	" John				
3935	" Sarah E.	797.10	R.W. Swim	G W Benge	
3936	Snow Mary A.	265.70	Mary A Snow	L B Bell	
3937	Snow Rachel	265.70	Mary A Snow	L B Bell	
3938	Stephens Spencer A.	265.70	S.A. Stephens	Geo W Benge	
3939	Stucker Minerva	order 265.70	F A Neilson	Henry Eiffert	Neilson

Starr Roll 1894

We, the undersigned citizens of the Cherokee Nation, by right of Cherokee blood, do hereby acknowledge to have received of E. E. Starr, National Treasurer of the Cherokee Nation, the sums set opposite our names respectively, in full of our shares in the per capita distribution authorized by an Act of the National Council, dated ___MAY 3 1894___ 1894.

	Names of Head, and Members of Families	Amount	To Whom Paid	Witness to Payment	Remarks
3940	Stucker Myrtle	order			Neilson
3941	" Pearl				
3942	" Lewis	797.10	F A Neilson	Henry Eiffert	order
3943	Sanders Edward				
3944	" Gunter				
3945	" Etta J.	797.10	Edward Sanders	G W Benge	
3946	Sullivan William	order			Neilson
3947	" Georgia				
3948	" Mary				
3949	" Annie	Paid over to Neilson			
3950	Sullivan Jno L.		Order		
3951	" Eliza				
3952	" George	1859.90	F A Neilson	Henry Eiffert	order
3953	Sudderth[sic] Linnie Louise				
3954	" Hallie B.	531.40	J.P. Suddeth	G W Benge	
3955	Spencer Samuel F	265.70	F A Neilson	Henry Eiffert	order
3956	Sharp Nancy A.				
3957	" Mary E.				
3958	Sharp Wm C.	797.10	N A Sharp	G.W. Benge	
3959	Smith Kittie E.				
3960	" Hiram R.				
3961	" Beulah	797.10	Frank Smith	G.W. Benge	
3962	Starr Henry	265.70	Mary E Walker	L B Bell	
3963	Sutherlin[sic] Pollie				
3964	" Allie B.				
3965	" Sam A.				
3966	" Leroy				
3967	" Herbert F.	1328.50	Pollie Southerland	G W Benge	

Starr Roll 1894

We, the undersigned citizens of the Cherokee Nation, by right of Cherokee blood, do hereby acknowledge to have received of E. E. Starr, National Treasurer of the Cherokee Nation, the sums set opposite our names respectively, in full of our shares in the per capita distribution authorized by an Act of the National Council, dated ___MAY 3 1894___ 1894.

#	Names of Head, and Members of Families	Amount	To Whom Paid	Witness to Payment	Remarks
3968	Sullivan Willie S.				
3969	" Conrad D.				
3970	" Oral[sic] Lee				
3971	" Wm H.	1062.80	W. S. Sullivan	L B Bell	
3972	Sullivan Jeff D.	order			Neilson
3973	" George T.				
3974	" Arthur I.				
3975	" Maude E.	1068.80	F A Neilson	Henry Eiffert	order
3976	Smith James O.	order 265.70	James O. Smith	J.C. Starr	W&S
3977	Sarver[sic] Winona				
3978	" Ivan E.	531.40	Winona Sower	L B Bell	
3979	Sanders Geo M.				
3980	Elaridge[sic] Jesse	531.40	A H Norwood guardian	L B Bell	A H Norwood Guardian
3981	Stovall Susie				
3982	" Lucille	531.40	Susie Stoval	L B Bell	
3983	Skidmore Annie F.				
3984	" Eugene O.				
3985	" Ottis T.				
3986	" Annie E				
3987	" Clarence H.				
3988	" Letitia F.				
3989	" Ben F.	1859.90	A F Skidmore	L B Bell	
3990	Steward Mina				
3991	" John J.	531.40	W.C. Steward	G.W. Benge	Paid on order JM Bowling
3992	Sixkiller Joel H.	order 265.70	J.M. Bowling	J.C. Starr	
3993	Smith Mike	order 265.70	GW Eaton	Henry Eiffert	GWE Ck
3994	Smith Mary J	order			Neilson
3995	" Jno H.				

Starr Roll 1894

We, the undersigned citizens of the Cherokee Nation, by right of Cherokee blood, do hereby acknowledge to have received of E. E. Starr, National Treasurer of the Cherokee Nation, the sums set opposite our names respectively, in full of our shares in the per capita distribution authorized by an Act of the National Council, dated ___MAY 3 1894___ 1894.

	Names of Head, and Members of Families	Amount	To Whom Paid	Witness to Payment	Remarks
3996	" Elizabeth R.	797.10	F A Neilson	Henry Eiffert	order
3997	Sunday Edward				
3998	" Jane				
3999	" William				
4000	" Lou				
4001	" Edward Jr				
4002	" Ellen	1594.20	Edward Sunday	L B Bell	
4003	Sanders Clem				
4004	" Frank	531.40	Maggie Sunday	G W Benge	
4005	Smith Tressie	265.70	C.C. Lipe Guardian	J.C. Starr	C.C. Lipe Gua
4006	Shimp[sic] Louisa				
4007	" Thos Roy	531.40	John Shimp	L B Bell	
4008	Smith Sallie A				
4009	" Mabel				
4010	" Robt E.				
4011	" Winnie	1062.80	Sallie A Smith	G W Benge	
4012	Strickland Sarah C.				
4013	" Katie C.				
4014	" Elizabeth L.				
4015	" Roger	1062.80	S.C. Strickland	G W Benge	
4016	Sears Calvin	order 265.70	Charlott Sears	G W Benge	Illegal ord
4017	Sampson Austin	order 265.70	Austin Sampson	L B Bell	
4018	Smith Betsey	265.70	Betsey Smith	G.W. Benge	
4019	Smith Elizabeth	265.70	Elizabeth Smith	G W Benge	
4020	Smith Sylvester S.				
4021	" Logan				
4022	" Harrison	797.10	S.S. Smith	G.W. Benge	

Starr Roll 1894

We, the undersigned citizens of the Cherokee Nation, by right of Cherokee blood, do hereby acknowledge to have received of E. E. Starr, National Treasurer of the Cherokee Nation, the sums set opposite our names respectively, in full of our shares in the per capita distribution authorized by an Act of the National Council, dated ___MAY 3 1894___ 1894.

	Names of Head, and Members of Families	Amount	To Whom Paid	Witness to Payment	Remarks	
4023	Scott Lulu	265.70	Lulu Scott	G.W. Benge		
4024	Smith James	order 265.70	J S Thomason	Henry Eiffert	J.S.T.	Ck
4025	Southerland Arabella	265.70	A Southerland	G W Benge		
4026	Shanahan Jennie					
4027	" Maggie	531.40	Jennie Shanahan	G W Benge		
4028	Smith Elizabeth					
4029	Viola					
4030	Eliza	797.10	Elizabeth Smith	G.W. Benge		
4031	Smith Eliza					
4032	William					
4033	Laura					
4034	Newton	1062.80	Eliza Smith	G W Benge		
4035	Skinner Louie					
4036	" Johnie					
4037	" Ray	797.10	Nat Skinner	G.W. Benge		
4038	Scott Lena L.					
4039	" Chas. D.	531.40	L.L. Scott	G W Benge		
4040	Skillman Sarah					
4041	" Bessie	531.40	Sarah Skillman	G.W. Benge		
4042	Sheehan Annie	265.70	Annie Sheehan	G.W. Benge		
4043	Spurlock Hannah					
4044	Hardin H					
4045	Lone B.	797.10	Hannah Spurlock	G.W. Benge		
4046	Salsberry Catharine					
4047	Coon Bernard L.	531.40	Catharine Salsberry	G.W. Benge		

Starr Roll 1894

We, the undersigned citizens of the Cherokee Nation, by right of Cherokee blood, do hereby acknowledge to have received of E. E. Starr, National Treasurer of the Cherokee Nation, the sums set opposite our names respectively, in full of our shares in the per capita distribution authorized by an Act of the National Council, dated ___MAY 3 1894___ 1894.

	Names of Head, and Members of Families	Amount	To Whom Paid	Witness to Payment	Remarks
4048	Stinger Louisa				
4049	" Noble D.				
4050	" Albert				
4051	" Cora	1062.80	Louisa Stinger	G W Benge	
4052	Sanders Martha J.				
4053	" Katie				
4054	" Martha				
4055	" Eva	1062.80	Mary J Bachtel	G W Benge	
	~~Silk Alice~~				Enrolled on Orp Supplmt Rol
4056	Starr Watt				
4057	" George C.				
4058	" Mary B.				
4059	" Lettie B.				
4060	" Joseph	1328.50	Watt Starr	L B Bell	
4061	Starr Ella	265.70	Watt Starr	L B Bell	
4062	Chambers John				
4063	" Torchee chu				
4064	" Mattie	797.10	Louisa J. Wilkinson *Guardian*	J.C. Starr	
4065	Starr Emmit	265.70	Emmit Starr	G.W. Benge	
4066	Sanders John				
4067	" Clara				
4068	" Frank				
4069	" Etta				
4070	" Charles	1328.50	John Sanders	G.W. Benge	
4071	Sanders John				
4072	" Katie	531.40	Katie Sanders	L B Bell	
4073	Silk Levi	*order*			F.A. Neilse
4074	" Melvina				
4075	" Nancy J				
4076	" William	1062.80	F A Neilson	Henry Eiffert	Ck

Starr Roll 1894

We, the undersigned citizens of the Cherokee Nation, by right of Cherokee blood, do hereby acknowledge to have received of E. E. Starr, National Treasurer of the Cherokee Nation, the sums set opposite our names respectively, in full of our shares in the per capita distribution authorized by an Act of the National Council, dated ___MAY 3 1894___ 1894.

	Names of Head, and Members of Families	Amount	To Whom Paid	Witness to Payment	Remarks
4077	Sullivan Geo L.	order			Neilson
4078	Jefferson D				
4079	John W.	797.10	F A Neilson	Henry Eiffert	order
4080	Sixkiller Emma T.	265.70	Eliza Evans	L B Bell	
4081	Sixkiller James	265.70	Jas Sixkiller	L B Bell	
4082	Stupp Laura	order			Neilson
4083	" George C.	531.40	F A Neilson	Henry Eiffert	order
4084	Starr Ida	265.70	Geo. W. Eaton	J.C. Starr	Check on order
4085	Scrimpsher[sic] John G				
4086	Juliette				
4087	Juliette Jr	797.10	John G Schrimsher	J.C. Starr	
4088	Scrimpsher Bessie B.	265.70	Bessie Schrimsher	L B Bell	
4089	Scrimpsher Earnest	265.70	John G Scrimsher[sic]	J.C. Starr	
4090	Stealer Lewis	order			F.A. Neilson
4091	" Sarah				
4092	" Thomas				
4093	" Jennie				
4094	" Mariah				
4095	" David	1594.20	F A Neilson	Henry Eiffert	order
4096	Sequitchie Joe	order 265.70	J S Thomason	Henry Eiffert	CK LWB
4097	Scott Sue	265.70	D.L. Scott	L B Bell	
4098	Smith Nancy J	~~265.70~~	F A Neilson	Henry Eiffert	order Neilson
4099	Smith W. L.	265.70	Wm Gulager	JC Dannenberg	P^d Feby 20th 1896
4100	Samson Jim	order 265.70	WC Patton	G W Benge	on order W C Patton

242

Starr Roll 1894

We, the undersigned citizens of the Cherokee Nation, by right of Cherokee blood, do hereby acknowledge to have received of E. E. Starr, National Treasurer of the Cherokee Nation, the sums set opposite our names respectively, in full of our shares in the per capita distribution authorized by an Act of the National Council, dated ___MAY 3 1894___ 1894.

	Names of Head, and Members of Families	Amount	To Whom Paid	Witness to Payment	Remarks
4101	Sanders Susan				
4102	Cook Florence				
4103	" Thomas M	797.10	Susan Sanders	G.W. Benge	
4104	Sounegooyah[sic]				
4105	" Lizzie	531.40	Sonegooyah	J.C. Starr	
4106	Skinner Dora	265.70	Dora Skinner	G.W. Benge	
4107	Samson[sic] Austin	265.70	Austin Sampson	Henry Eiffert	
4108	Shoemaker Atta M.	order 265.70	J.S. Thomason	J.C. Starr	Paid on JST
4109	Sanford Lacy Nellie	265.70	WP Henderson	G W Benge	
4110	" Minnie Lacy				
4111	" Mattie Lacy	5531.40	WP Henderson	G W Benge	
4112	Halley John	265.70	Josiah Henry	Henry Eiffert	order Nov
4113	Thompson Hooley D.				
4114	" John M				
4115	" Ethel May				
4116	" George L.	1062.80	H.D. Thompson	G.W. Benge	
4117	Thompson William D				
4118	Thompson Exa				
4119	" Hicks E.				
4120	" Eula L.	1062.80	W.D. Thompson	G W Benge	
4121	Thompson Thos. F.	D428 265.70	T.F Thompson	G W Benge	
4122	Thornborough Hortensia	265.70	Hortensia Thornborough	G W Benge	
4123	Taylor Andrew J.		C.H. Taylor	G W Benge	
4124	Taylor Campbell				
4125	" Stacy B.				
4126	" C. H. (Jr)	1062.80	C H Taylor	G W Benge	

Starr Roll 1894

We, the undersigned citizens of the Cherokee Nation, by right of Cherokee blood, do hereby acknowledge to have received of E. E. Starr, National Treasurer of the Cherokee Nation, the sums set opposite our names respectively, in full of our shares in the per capita distribution authorized by an Act of the National Council, dated ___MAY 3 1894___ 1894.

#	Names of Head, and Members of Families	Amount	To Whom Paid	Witness to Payment	Remarks
4127	Taylor Wm T.	order			Halsell
4128	" Adda	531.40	W.E. Halsell	J.C. Starr	paid on order
4129	Trainor Thomas J.	265.70	T J Trainor	G W Benge	
	~~Tokun Mary~~ (These names cannot be found on the original)		These names are entered as Mary Mokum & John V. Mokum		
	~~" John V.~~				
4130	Turner Racheal[sic]				
4131	" Stella				
4132	" Tennessee				
4133	" John W.				
4134	" Edith	1328.50	Rachel Turner	G W Benge	
4135	Taylor Caldonia C.				
4136	" Henry				
4137	" Gussie B.				
4138	" Annie				
4139	" Delta L				order
4140	" Jackson				
4141	" Mattie	1859.90	C.C. Taylor	G W Benge	
4142	Thompson Mary E				
4143	" Lettie				
4144	" Mary	797.10	Milton Thompson	G.W. Benge	
4145	Tassell[sic] Whitewater	265.70	WhiteWater Tassle	G W Benge	
4146	Trap Joe	265.70	~~order~~ W.E. Halsell	Henry Eiffert	W.E.H. Ck
4147	Terley Alsie	order 265.70	WC Rogers	Henry Eiffert	W C Rogers
4148	Thornton James	order 265.70	S.R. Walkingstick	G.W. Benge	S.R.W. on order

Starr Roll 1894

We, the undersigned citizens of the Cherokee Nation, by right of Cherokee blood, do hereby acknowledge to have received of E. E. Starr, National Treasurer of the Cherokee Nation, the sums set opposite our names respectively, in full of our shares in the per capita distribution authorized by an Act of the National Council, dated ___MAY 3 1894___ 1894.

	Names of Head, and Members of Families	Amount	To Whom Paid	Witness to Payment	Remarks
4149	Tyner Carter				
4150	" Thomas J.				
4151	" Lydia J.	797.10	Carter Tyner	J.C. Starr	Jas T Musg*
4152	Thornton Marion	265.70	Mary Horsley	Henry Eiffert	Letts Admi* Dead Eat*
4153	" Lizzie				Orphans
4154	" Smith				"
4155	" Mary				"
4156	" Henry J.	1062.80	Mary Horsly Guardian	L B Bell	"
4157	Tyner Lewis				
4158	" Bushyhead				
4159	" John				
4160	" Racheal	order			JM Hall
4161	" Davis	1328.50	JM Hall	Henry Eiffert	
4162	Tyner Lewis C.				
4163	" Susie				
4164	" Redbird	797.10	Susie Tyner	L B Bell	
4165	Tyner James				J.C.H.
4166	" Quatie				
4167	" Fannie	order			
4168	" Delila				
4169	" Aaron				
4170	" James (Jr)				
4171	" Ralph	1859.90	James Tyner	J.C. Starr	
4172	Tucker Andrew				
4173	" May				
4174	" Calvin	order			
4175	" Thomas				
4176	" Wesly				
4177	" Nellie				
4178	" Munroe				
4179	" Viola	2125.60	Johnson & Keeler	Henry Eiffert	Ck

Starr Roll 1894

We, the undersigned citizens of the Cherokee Nation, by right of Cherokee blood, do hereby acknowledge to have received of E. E. Starr, National Treasurer of the Cherokee Nation, the sums set opposite our names respectively, in full of our shares in the per capita distribution authorized by an Act of the National Council, dated ___MAY 3 1894___ 1894.

	Names of Head, and Members of Families	Amount	To Whom Paid	Witness to Payment	Remarks
4180	Tucker John				
4181	" Guy				
4182	" Eva	797.10	John Tucker	L B Bell	
4183	Tucker Annie				
4184	" Florence	order 531.40	JM Hall	Henry Eiffert	JM Hall
4185	Tyner Rubin R.				
4186	Emma				
4187	May				
4188	Lenard				
4189	Wever[sic]				
4190	Laura				
4191	Maud				
4192	Lou W.	2125.60	R R Taylor[sic]	L B Bell	
4193	Tyner Emitt	265.70	R R Tyner	L B Bell	
4194	Tyner George				
4195	Clinton				
4196	Cleve				
4197	John				
4198	Austin				
4199	Fannie A.	1594.20	George Tyner	G W Benge	
4200	Tyner John A.	265.70	John A Tyner	Henry Eiffert	
4201	Thompson Jessie				Dead
4202	" Lizzie				
4203	" Daniel	order			
4204	" Jennie				
4205	" Newton	1328.50	Johnson & Keeler	Henry Eiffert	Ck
4206	Tarpin James				
4207	" Betsy	order			
4208	" Patty	797.10	Johnson & Keeler	Henry Eiffert	Ck

Starr Roll 1894

We, the undersigned citizens of the Cherokee Nation, by right of Cherokee blood, do hereby acknowledge to have received of E. E. Starr, National Treasurer of the Cherokee Nation, the sums set opposite our names respectively, in full of our shares in the per capita distribution authorized by an Act of the National Council, dated ____MAY 3 1894____ 1894.

	Names of Head, and Members of Families	Amount	To Whom Paid	Witness to Payment	Remarks
4209	Trottingwolf Lincoln				
4210	" Susie	order			
4211	" Roy	797.10	Johnson & Keeler	Henry Eiffert	Ck
4212	Tyner Jefferson	265.70	Jefferson Tyner	L B Bell	
4213	Tyner Rubin B.				
4214	" Roxie A.				
4215	" Bessie				
4216	" George				
4217	" Sarah				
4218	Davis Draydon				
4219	Thomas Oscar	1859.90	R.B. Tyner	G W Benge	
4220	Tyner Annie	265.70	Annie Tyner	G W Benge	
4221	Taylor Perd				
4222	Gutie	order 531.40	C.W. Pool	G W Benge	on order
4223	Taylor Mack				
4224	Elbert	order 531.40	C.W. Pool	G.W. Benge	on order
4225	Taylor Laura				
4226	Robert	order			
4227	William				
4228	Lillie	1062.80	C W Pool	G W Benge	on order
4229	Taylor John F.				
4230	Maud	order 531.40	C.W. Pool	G W Benge	on order
4231	Thompson Eda J				
4232	" William C.				
4233	" George W.				
4234	" Stella L.				
4235	" Rhoda F.				
4236	" Ada I.	1594.20	E.J. Thompson	G.W. Benge	

Starr Roll 1894

We, the undersigned citizens of the Cherokee Nation, by right of Cherokee blood, do hereby acknowledge to have received of E. E. Starr, National Treasurer of the Cherokee Nation, the sums set opposite our names respectively, in full of our shares in the per capita distribution authorized by an Act of the National Council, dated ___MAY 3 1894___ 1894.

#	Names of Head, and Members of Families	Amount	To Whom Paid	Witness to Payment	Remarks
4237	Thompson James P.				
4238	" Yauless[sic]				
4239	" Earl	797.10	J.P. Thompson	G W Benge	
4240	Tiger Charles				
4241	" Lizzie				
4242	" George				
4243	" Mary				
4244	" Lillie	1328.50	Lizzie Tiger	L B Bell	
4245	Tacket Mary P.				A. Foyil
4246	Mirtle J.				
4247	Birt A	order			
4248	Maud E.				
4249	Levi A	Foyils order withdrawn 1328.50	A. Foyil M P Tacket	G W Benge L B Bell July 6 '94	on order
4250	Tague Nancy J	order 265.70	G.W. Eaton	Henry Eiffert	Eaton check
4251	Taylor David (Jr)				
4252	" Sallie				
4253	" Herbert	797.10	C W Pool	Henry Eiffert	
4254	Taylor Edward				
4255	" Cornelia	order			
4256	" Roy				
4257	" Mabelle				
4258	" Claud	1328.50	C.W. Pool	G W Benge	on order
4259	Taylor David (Sr)	265.70	David Taylor	G.W. Benge	
4260	Terrell Thomas J	~~order~~	Elizabeth Terrell	L B Bell	~~A. Foyil~~
4261	Elizabeth	531.40	~~A. Foyil~~	~~G W Benge~~	on order
4262	Taylor John M (Jr)	265.70	JM Taylor Jr	L B Bell	
4263	Twist Wm G.	order			Neilson
4264	" Oliver W.	531.40	F A Neilson	Henry Eiffert	order

Starr Roll 1894

We, the undersigned citizens of the Cherokee Nation, by right of Cherokee blood, do hereby acknowledge to have received of E. E. Starr, National Treasurer of the Cherokee Nation, the sums set opposite our names respectively, in full of our shares in the per capita distribution authorized by an Act of the National Council, dated ____MAY 3 1894____ 1894.

	Names of Head, and Members of Families	Amount	To Whom Paid	Witness to Payment	Remarks
4265	Tincup James				J.C.H.
4266	William				
4267	Dora	*order*			
4268	Henry				
4269	James (Jr)				
4270	May				
4271	Edward				
4272	Florence				
4273	Tincup Austin	2391.30	JC Hogan	Henry Eiffert	
4274	Randolph Joe	265.70	Lucinda Tincup	G.W. Benge	
4275	Terrell Edward M.	265.70	E.M. Terrell	G W Benge	
4276	Taylor Emma				
4277	" Mary E.				
4278	" Joseph	797.10	J.M. Taylor	G W Benge	
4279	Turner Tookah B.	*order*			R L Ba...
4280	" William D.				
4281	" Tookah				
4282	" Clarence W.	1062.80	R L Baugh	G.W. Benge	on orde...
4283	Talbert Mary				
4284	" Cora				
4285	" Ethel				
4286	" Rosa	1062.80	Jessie Talbert	G W Benge	
4287	Thomas Jennie				
4288	" Viola B.	531.40	Jennie Thomas	G W Benge	
4289	Tell Virdie	265.70	George Tell	J.C. Starr	
4290	Thomas Minnie				
4291	Jennie I.				
4292	Edward G	797.10	Minnie Thomas	J.C. Starr	
4293	Tadpole David				
4294	" Polly	531.40	David Tadpole	G W Benge	

Starr Roll 1894

We, the undersigned citizens of the Cherokee Nation, by right of Cherokee blood, do hereby acknowledge to have received of E. E. Starr, National Treasurer of the Cherokee Nation, the sums set opposite our names respectively, in full of our shares in the per capita distribution authorized by an Act of the National Council, dated ____MAY 3 1894____ 1894.

	Names of Head, and Members of Families	Amount	To Whom Paid	Witness to Payment	Remarks
4295	Tadpole Darkey	265.70	Johnson Fisher	G W Benge	
4296	Galkitten Wilson		D2644		David Tadpole
4297	Coffee Geo	531.40	David Tadpole	G W Benge	Guardian
	Tadpole Rosa	265.70	John Swimmer	G W Benge	
4298	Tadpole Lige				
4299	" Annie				
4300	" David (Jr)				
4301	" Sallie	1062.80	Lige Tadpole	G W Benge	
4302	Tucker Dave	7374			
4303	" Susan	7374			
4304	" Mary				
4305	" Katie	7374			
4306	" George	1328.50	Dave Tucker	G W Benge	
4307	Teehee[sic] Tilden	265.70	Tilden Tehee	J.C. Starr	
4308	Thompson Alison	D4			D4
4309	" Earnest W.	D4			D4
4310	" Mamie	~~R4~~ 797.10	F.B. Fite	G W Benge	D4
4311	Thompson Gilbert	D3			D3
4312	Cleo	~~D181~~	R848		
4313	Gilbert Jr	D3			D3
4314	Mathew	1062.80	F.B. Fite	G W Benge	D3
4315	Thompson Milton	265.70	F.B. Fite	G W Benge	D7
4316	Thompson James	~~D6~~ 265.70	17 F.B. Fite	G W Benge	~~D6~~ 17
4317	Taylor James L.	265.70	JC Hogan	Henry Eiffert	Chu 61364
4318	Teter Alice	order			J.C.H.
4319	Clara J				
4320	Mirtle	797.10	JC Hogan	Henry Eiffert	Ck
4321	Thornton Thomas J.	265.70	P. Bates	G.W. Benge	

Starr Roll 1894

We, the undersigned citizens of the Cherokee Nation, by right of Cherokee blood, do hereby acknowledge to have received of E. E. Starr, National Treasurer of the Cherokee Nation, the sums set opposite our names respectively, in full of our shares in the per capita distribution authorized by an Act of the National Council, dated ___MAY 3 1894___ 1894.

	Names of Head, and Members of Families	Amount	To Whom Paid	Witness to Payment	Remarks
4322	Towers William J.				J.C.H.
4323	Thomas B.				
4324	Minnie B.	order			
4325	Clem R.				
4326	Charlott J.				
4327	Maud				
4328	Gertrude	1859.90	JC Hogan	Henry Eiffert	Ck
4329	Teague Mary J.				
4330	Frances J.				
4331	Cora A	797.10	B.F. Teague	G.W. Benge	
4332	Terrell Thomas	order 265.70	A. Foyil	Henry Eiffert	A. Foyil
4333	Taylor John M (Jr)	265.70	John M Taylor Jr	L B Bell	
4334	Thompson Clarence	order			H. Longby
4335	Stella R	531.40	H. Longby	J.C. Starr	Paid on ord
4336	Thompson Thos L.	order 265.70	Howard Longby	J.C. Starr	H. Longby Paid on ord
4337	Thompson Eliza				
4338	" James W.				
4339	" Lewis				
4340	Martin Hernando				
4341	" Birdie				
4342	" John A.				
4343	" Dewit	1859.90	Eliza Thompson	G W Benge	
4344	Timpson Bear				E.N.R.
4345	Sallie				
4346	Susie				
4347	Sam	order			
4348	Nancy				
4349	Katie				
4350	Pigeon Charles	1859.90	E.N. Ratcliff	G W Benge	on order

Starr Roll 1894

We, the undersigned citizens of the Cherokee Nation, by right of Cherokee blood, do hereby acknowledge to have received of E. E. Starr, National Treasurer of the Cherokee Nation, the sums set opposite our names respectively, in full of our shares in the per capita distribution authorized by an Act of the National Council, dated ___MAY 3 1894___ 1894.

	Names of Head, and Members of Families	Amount	To Whom Paid	Witness to Payment	Remarks
4351	Taylor David	265.70	Dave Taylor	L B Bell	
4352	Tucker Caroline	order	order withdrawn		B.J.H. LWB
4353	" Mary	531.40	Caroline Tucker 9933	G W Benge	
4354	Torbitt Mary J.				J.S.T.
4355	" Willie J.		order withdrawn		
4356	" Walter T.	order			
4357	" Elmer H				
4358	" Arthur T.	1328.50	M.J. Torbitt	G W Benge	
4359	Timberlake Margaret L				
4360	Timberlake Jennie	531.40	Kate E Wolfe	G W Benge	
4361	Trott Wm L.				
4362	" William H.				
4363	" Dott F.	797.10	W^m L Trott	G W Benge	
4364	Trott John R.	265.70	J.R. Trott D389	G W Benge	
4365	Trott William O.	265.70	W^m O Trott D390 10386 R776	G W Benge	
4366	Tyner Ruth				
4367	" Clara				
4368	" Oliver				
4369	Nelson Charles	1062.80	Chas Tyner	G W Benge	
4370	Tittle James M.				
4371	" Annie				
4372	" Lee Daniel				
4373	" David				
4374	" Effie				
4375	" Jesse				
4376	" Earl	1859.90	J.M. Tittle	G W Benge	
4377	Dodge Orcona	265.70	Orcona Dodge	G W Benge	

Starr Roll 1894

We, the undersigned citizens of the Cherokee Nation, by right of Cherokee blood, do hereby acknowledge to have received of E. E. Starr, National Treasurer of the Cherokee Nation, the sums set opposite our names respectively, in full of our shares in the per capita distribution authorized by an Act of the National Council, dated ___MAY 3 1894___ 1894.

	Names of Head, and Members of Families	Amount	To Whom Paid	Witness to Payment	Remarks
4378	Thompson James A.				
4379	Sarah	531.40	J A Thompson	G W Benge	
4380	Trittheit[sic] Laura				
4381	West James				
4382	" Louisa	797.10	Henry Trittheat	G W Benge	
4383	Thompson Francis	265.70	Francis Thompson	G W Benge	
4384	Thompson Eugene				
4385	Duncan Claud E	531.40	E. Thompson	G W Benge	
4386	Thompson Earnest	DS			DS
4387	Allison G.	531.40 DS	F.B. Fite	G W Benge	DS
4388	Thomas John A.				
4389	" Isabella J.				
4390	" Thomas C.				
4391	" Henry R.				
4392	" Frank N.				
4393	" Jesse A.				
4394	" Lawrence				
4395	" Ellis				
4396	" Thuray				
4397	" Newton	2657.00	J.A. Thomas	G W Benge	
4398	Tucker Daniel	265.70	Betsy Smith	G.W. Benge	Now wife of Tu
4399	Tittle Susan J	265.70	S.J. Tittle	G W Benge	
4400	Tittle Rosa A	265.70	SJ Tittle	G W Benge	
4401	Trott Hardin H.				
4402	Eliza				
4403	May				
4404	Hardin				
4405	Belle	1328.50	Eliza Trott	G W Benge	

Starr Roll 1894

We, the undersigned citizens of the Cherokee Nation, by right of Cherokee blood, do hereby acknowledge to have received of E. E. Starr, National Treasurer of the Cherokee Nation, the sums set opposite our names respectively, in full of our shares in the per capita distribution authorized by an Act of the National Council, dated ___MAY 3 1894___ 1894.

#	Names of Head, and Members of Families	Amount	To Whom Paid	Witness to Payment	Remarks
4406	Cannon Annie				
4407	" Tommie	531.40	Eliza Trott	G W Benge	
4408	Thompson Thos F.				
4409	" Susan C.				
4410	Parks Susan	797.10	T.F. Thompson	G W Benge	
4411	Tovey Annie N.				
4412	" Thos W.				
4413	" Della M				
4414	" Laura A.				
4415	" Frank L				
4416	" Hooley B.	1594.20	A. N. Tovey	G W Benge	
4417	Thornton Geo. W.				
4418	" Orville E.				
4419	" Archie A				
4420	" Ora J.				
4421	" Nellie E				
4422	" Mary M.				
4423	" Nora V.	1859.90	G.W. Thornton	G.W. Benge	
4424	Thompson Dalton	265.70	Dalton Thompson	G W Benge	
4425	Talbert Eliza				
4426	Arua				
4427	Mary				
4428	Ellen				
4429	Carrie				
4430	Georgia	1594.20	Geo Talbert	L B Bell	
4431	Talbert Grover	265.70	GW Talbert	L B Bell	
4432	Taylor James	order P941 265.70	JC Hogan	Henry Eiffert	J.C.H. Ck
4433	Taylor William	order 265.70	F A Neilson	Henry Eiffert	Neilson order
4434	Taylor Clayborn	265.70	Clayborn Taylor	G W Benge	

Starr Roll 1894

We, the undersigned citizens of the Cherokee Nation, by right of Cherokee blood, do hereby acknowledge to have received of E. E. Starr, National Treasurer of the Cherokee Nation, the sums set opposite our names respectively, in full of our shares in the per capita distribution authorized by an Act of the National Council, dated ___MAY 3 1894___ 1894.

	Names of Head, and Members of Families	Amount	To Whom Paid	Witness to Payment	Remarks
4435	Taylor David	265.70	~~Clayborn~~ *David* Taylor	G W Benge	
4436	Tiger Sallie	265.70	*(Illegible)* Howie	G W Benge	
4437	Thompson Annie	265.70	Ben Hilderbrand	G W Benge	
4438	Tosser Charles	265.70 *4763*	G.W. Eaton	G.W. Benge	on order
4439	Trethart Sallie				
4440	Lowrey Wᵐ A				
4441	Randolph	*order*			
4442	Austin	1062.80	J S Thomason	Henry Eiffert	Ck
4443	Trout Lizzie	265.70	Lizzie Trout	L B Bell	P.105, B.3
4444	Underwood Mollie				
4446	" Charles	*order* 177			Geo W E
4446	" Henry	177			
4447	" Agnis	1062.80 *173*	Geo W Eaton	Henry Eiffert	Ck
4448	Vann Emitt				
4449	" Mary				
4450	" Quenie	797.10	Emitt Vann	G W Benge	
4451	Vann Jesse	265.70	Jesse Vann	G W Benge	
4452	Vann Clem I	265.70	Clem I Vann	G W Benge	
4453	Vann Daniel W.				
4454	Clarinda				
4455	Ada C				
4456	David W				
4457	Alice				
4458	Claud				
4459	Envina	1859.90	D.W. Vann	G W Benge	
4460	Vann Emma				
4461	Card Carrie	*order* 531.40	JC Hogan	Henry Eiffert	Ck

Starr Roll 1894

We, the undersigned citizens of the Cherokee Nation, by right of Cherokee blood, do hereby acknowledge to have received of E. E. Starr, National Treasurer of the Cherokee Nation, the sums set opposite our names respectively, in full of our shares in the per capita distribution authorized by an Act of the National Council, dated ____MAY 3 1894____ 1894.

	Names of Head, and Members of Families	Amount	To Whom Paid	Witness to Payment	Remarks
4462	Vann James T.				
4463	Nannie E				
4464	Martha P.	797.10	James T. Vann	G W Benge	
4465	Vann John				
4466	Reid				
4467	Joseph				
4468	Lila				
4469	Lula				
4470	John J.				
4471	Birt			L B Bell	
4472	Vann Charles	265.70	Sarah Vann	L B Bell	(Illegible)
4473	Vann Racheal				
4474	Starr Arch				
4475	" Susie	797.10	Caleb Starr	L B Bell	
4476	Vann Ruth				
4477	Joanna				
4478	Ralph				
4479	William W.				
4480	Cora				
4481	Callie				
4482	John H.	1859.90	Ruth Vann	L B Bell	
4483	Vann Sarah	265.70	W.C. Rogers	J.C. Starr (LBB)	
4484	Vann Joseph	order 265.70	F A Neilson	Henry Eiffert	Neilson
4485	Vann Sarah E	265.70	W.M. Gulliger	S.W. Mayfield	Pd on order July 2, 1895
4486	Vann Arch	265.70	Lee Mills	G W Benge	on order Mills
4487	Winton Edith				
4488	" Minerva				
4489	" May				
4490	" Moses	1062.80	K.L. Winton	G W Benge	

Starr Roll 1894

We, the undersigned citizens of the Cherokee Nation, by right of Cherokee blood, do hereby acknowledge to have received of E. E. Starr, National Treasurer of the Cherokee Nation, the sums set opposite our names respectively, in full of our shares in the per capita distribution authorized by an Act of the National Council, dated ___MAY 3 1894___ 1894.

	Names of Head, and Members of Families	Amount	To Whom Paid	Witness to Payment	Remarks
	~~Privit Geo~~				On the orp- Asylum R-
	~~" Dolly~~				
	~~Littlelou~~				
4491	Wasson Maggie				
4492	" Blain				
4493	" Florence	797.10	J C Wassam[sic]	G W Benge	
4494	Ward John F.	2381			
4495	" Ellola	2381			
4496	" Robert E	797.10	J.F. Ward	G W Benge	
4497	Winton Dan				
4498	" Ola P.				
4499	" Clarence	797.10	Dan Winton	G W Benge	
4500	Winton Loyd	265.70	Loyd Winton	G W Benge	
4501	Wilder Charlott				
4502	" Lydia				
4503	" Clem	797/10	Charlotte Wilder	G W Benge	
4504	Waybourne Roy				
4505	Addie (Ada)				
4506	Emma				
4507	Oma	1062.80	C.P. Waybourne	G W Benge	
4508	Walkingstick Peggie				
4509	" Sargent	5186			
4510	Walkingstick Chas	797.10	Peggie Walkingstick	G W Benge	
4511	Walkingstick Annie				
4512	" Dora				
4513	Keys Joanna				
4514	Brown Jennie	1062.80	Annie Walkingstick	G W Benge	

Starr Roll 1894

We, the undersigned citizens of the Cherokee Nation, by right of Cherokee blood, do hereby acknowledge to have received of E. E. Starr, National Treasurer of the Cherokee Nation, the sums set opposite our names respectively, in full of our shares in the per capita distribution authorized by an Act of the National Council, dated ____MAY 3 1894____ 1894.

	Names of Head, and Members of Families	Amount	To Whom Paid	Witness to Payment	Remarks
4515	Williams Lizzie				
4516	Charles				
4517	Pearl				
4518	Hattie M	1062.80	Lizzie Williams	G W Benge	
4519	Garret[sic] Margaret	265.70	Margaret Garrett	L B Bell	
4520	Walls Lizzie				
4521	Jack				
4522	Beaver				
4523	Backbone Polly	order 1062.80	C Hayden	Henry Eiffert	C. Hayden
4524	Walker Carrie				
4525	Ella				
4526	Willie	Del 332			
4527	Reid Martin	1062.80	Clem Hayden	G.W. Benge	
4528	Wells Emma E				
4529	Daisy				
4530	Jessie				
4531	Archie	1062.80	Emma E Wells	L B Bell	
4532	Wells Bessie				
4533	" Frank				
4534	" N.C.				
4535	Burl	1062.80	Emma E Wells	L B Bell	
4536	Wells Effie	265.70	Emma E Wells	L B Bell	
4537	Wright Wm W.	265.70	W^m W Wright	G.W. Benge	
4538	Whitaker James M	order 265.70	W T Whitaker	Henry Eiffert	W.T. Whitaker
4539	Wilson Rebecca V	185			
4540	" James R				
4541	" W^m H	797.10	R V Wilson	G W Benge	

Starr Roll 1894

We, the undersigned citizens of the Cherokee Nation, by right of Cherokee blood, do hereby acknowledge to have received of E. E. Starr, National Treasurer of the Cherokee Nation, the sums set opposite our names respectively, in full of our shares in the per capita distribution authorized by an Act of the National Council, dated ___MAY 3 1894___ 1894.

	Names of Head, and Members of Families	Amount	To Whom Paid	Witness to Payment	Remarks
4542	Ward John	order			J.C.H.
4543	" Lizzie	531.40	JC Hogan	Henry Eiffert	Ck
4544	Ward Alex G.				
4545	" Jesse				
4546	" Lucy F.				
4547	" Geo. W.				
4548	" Roxie M				
4549	" Wm M.	1594.20	A.G. Ward	J.C. Starr	
4550	Welch Birt	order			J.C.H.
4551	Rose Geo	531.40	JC Hogan	Henry Eiffert	Ck
4552	Wayborne[sic] Levi	265.70	Levi Waybourne	G W Benge	
4553	Wafford[sic] Ella	265.70	Ella Wofford	G W Benge	
4554	Whitaker Josh W.	~~D266~~ R745			
4555	" Bennie V				
4556	" Nola E.				
4557	" James S.	1062.80	Josh W Whitaker	G W Benge	
4558	Wright Ellis B.				
4559	" Elizabeth				
4560	" William E.				
4561	" Otto F.				
4562	" Mayes C.				
4563	" Bryant J.	1594.20	EB Wright	G W Benge	
4564	Meeks Annie	265.70	JC Hogan	L B Bell	Elizabeth W J.C. Hogan Gu
4565	Wright Lydia I.	265.70	EB Wright	G W Benge	
4566	Wood[sic] Geo G.	265.70	G.G. Woods	G W Benge	
4567	" Wyly			Minor	
4568	" Foister			"	
4569	" William	797.10	MR Wood	G W Benge	

Starr Roll 1894

We, the undersigned citizens of the Cherokee Nation, by right of Cherokee blood, do hereby acknowledge to have received of E. E. Starr, National Treasurer of the Cherokee Nation, the sums set opposite our names respectively, in full of our shares in the per capita distribution authorized by an Act of the National Council, dated ____MAY 3 1894____ 1894.

	Names of Head, and Members of Families	Amount	To Whom Paid	Witness to Payment	Remarks
4570	Ward Cornelius				
4571	" Katie				
4572	" William R				
4573	" Ellis B				
4574	" Chas R.	1328.50	Cornelious[sic] Ward	G W Benge	
4575	Waybourne Alice	265.70	M.E. Washam		
4576	Waybourne W^m				
4577	" Bula				
4578	" John T.				
4579	" Minnie				
4580	" Martha C	order			J.C.H.
4581	" Earl E	1594.20	JC Hogan	Henry Eiffert	Ck
4582	Whitaker Stephen D	D266 R745			W.T.W
4583	" Austin				
4584	" Victor	order			
4585	" Caroline				
4586	" Adeline	1328.50	W T Whitaker	Henry Eiffert	
4587	Warren Ida J.				
4588	" Annie V.				
4589	" Nelson G.				
4590	" Jesse M.	1062.80	J.F. Warren	G.W. Benge	
4591	Whitaker David	265.70	R.L. Baugh	J.C. Starr	Check on order
4592	" Martha	265.70	WT Whitaker	Henry Eiffert	
4593	Whitaker Sarah A	order 265.70	WT Whitaker	Henry Eiffert	W.T.W
4594	Wakefield Escobedo	265.70	W.T. Whitaker	Henry Eiffert	W T W
4595	Wakefield Lydia	order			W T W
4596	" Charles				
4597	" Edward				
4598	" Albert				

Starr Roll 1894

We, the undersigned citizens of the Cherokee Nation, by right of Cherokee blood, do hereby acknowledge to have received of E. E. Starr, National Treasurer of the Cherokee Nation, the sums set opposite our names respectively, in full of our shares in the per capita distribution authorized by an Act of the National Council, dated ___MAY 3 1894___ 1894.

#	Names of Head, and Members of Families	Amount	To Whom Paid	Witness to Payment	Remarks
4599	" Kergin				
4600	" Virgin	1594.20	Lydia Wakefield	G W Benge	
4601	Wakefield Bertie	265.70	W T Whitaker	Henry Eiffert	
4602	Wakefield Ollie	265.70	WT Whitaker	Henry Eiffert	
4603	Wakefield Thos	265.70	WT Whitaker	Henry Eiffert	
4604	Wilson Ellen	265.70	*(Illegible)* ~~P1560~~ Wilson	G W Benge	
4605	Wilson Ida				
4606	Hope				
4607	Bowman Earl				
4608	Lila				
4609	Clara	1328.50	Ida Wilson	G W Benge	
4610	Waybourne Ben				
4611	" Pearl	*order*			
4612	" William				
4613	" Otton	1062.80	J.C. Hogan	G W Benge	on order
4614	Waybourne Robert				J.C.H.
4615	Oscar	*order* 531.40	~~Geo Williams~~ ~~JC Hogan~~	Henry Eiffert	& I.L.B Ck
4616	Williams Geo	265.70	~~WT Whitaker~~	Henry Eiffert	W.T.W
4617	Whitaker Wᵐ T.				
4618	James E				
4619	William J				
4620	Emma				
4621	Maggie				
4622	Charles				
4623	Ora				
4624	Austin	2125.60	W.T. Whitaker	G W Benge	
4625	Ward Joel	*order* 265.70	WT Whitaker	Henry Eiffert	W.T.W

Starr Roll 1894

We, the undersigned citizens of the Cherokee Nation, by right of Cherokee blood, do hereby acknowledge to have received of E. E. Starr, National Treasurer of the Cherokee Nation, the sums set opposite our names respectively, in full of our shares in the per capita distribution authorized by an Act of the National Council, dated ___MAY 3 1894___ 1894.

	Names of Head, and Members of Families	Amount	To Whom Paid	Witness to Payment	Remarks
4626	Warren Arthur				
4627	" Mary	531.40	G H Warren	G W Benge	
4628	Williams Sarah				TJ Archer
4629	" Nellie				
4630	Williams Jesse	797.10	TJ Archer	J.C. Starr	
4631	Wever[sic] Jennie	265.70	GW Eaton	Henry Eiffert	GW Eaton Ck
4632	Watkins Nancy	order			
4633	" Minnie				
4634	" Thos				
4635	" Susie				
4636	" Charlott				
4637	" Fannie				
4638	" William	1859.90	C A Watkins	J.C. Starr	
4639	Williams Charlott[sic]	265.70	J.H. Akin	L B Bell	Octo 2, 1894
4640	Sixkiller Chas				JH Akin
4641	" John M.	531.40	Charlotte Williams	L B Bell	
4642	Writer Thomas			Henry Eiffert	Ck
4643	" Mary	531.40	WC Patton	L B Bell	
4644	Writer Abraham	265.70	Emeline Duck Guardian	G W Benge	
4645	Wafford[sic] Joseph	265.70	WC Patton	Henry Eiffert	
4646	Blueford				James Wofford Guardian
4647	Dora	531.40	James Wofford	J.C. Starr	
4648	Wafford Bettie	265.70	James Wofford	J.C. Starr	James Wofford Guardian
4649	Wafford Willie	265.70	James Wofford	J.C. Starr	James Wofford Guardian
4650	Wilkerson John				
4651	Lizzie				
4652	Lewis				
4653	Lucy				
4654	Racheal		Lizzie Wilkerson		

Starr Roll 1894

We, the undersigned citizens of the Cherokee Nation, by right of Cherokee blood, do hereby acknowledge to have received of E. E. Starr, National Treasurer of the Cherokee Nation, the sums set opposite our names respectively, in full of our shares in the per capita distribution authorized by an Act of the National Council, dated ___MAY 3 1894___ 1894.

	Names of Head, and Members of Families	Amount	To Whom Paid	Witness to Payment	Remarks
4655	Wilkerson Jack	1594.20	Lizzie Wilkerson	G W Benge	
4656	Wafford James	265.70	James Wofford	L B Bell	
4657	*(Illegible)* Emma	265.70	John Walker	L B Bell	Husband of childs mother
4658	Wolf Runing[sic]				
4659	" James Trolling	531.40	Johnson & Keeler	Henry Eiffert	Ck
4660	Williams Alice				
4661	" Maggolina	531.40	Alice Williams	L B Bell	
4662	Woody Ida	265.70	Ida Woody	G W Benge	
4663	Woodard John	*order* 265.70	C W Pool	G W Benge	on order
4664	Wallace Fannie F				
4665	" Wm B.	531.40	W. B. Wallace	L B Bell	
4666	Wiley Wooster				
4667	Aaron	531.40	Wooster Wiley	J.C. Starr	
4668	Williams Mattie				
4669	Belle				
4670	James (Jr)				
4671	Roy H.	1062.80	Mattie Williams	G W Benge	
4672	Williams Harrison				
4673	" Emma	531.40	L.M. Williams	G W Benge	
4674	Williams Geo				C.W.P
4675	Minnie B.	*order*			
4676	Andrew	797.10	C W Pool	G W Benge	on order
4677	Ward Joel				
4678	Florence				
4679	Minnie S				

Starr Roll 1894

We, the undersigned citizens of the Cherokee Nation, by right of Cherokee blood, do hereby acknowledge to have received of E. E. Starr, National Treasurer of the Cherokee Nation, the sums set opposite our names respectively, in full of our shares in the per capita distribution authorized by an Act of the National Council, dated ____MAY 3 1894____ 1894.

	Names of Head, and Members of Families	Amount	To Whom Paid	Witness to Payment	Remarks
4680	Clem				
4681	Lena E	1328.50	Joel Ward	G W Benge	
4682	Woodard Allen	*order*			
4683	Margaret				
4684	Oliver				
4685	Zak				
4686	John L				
4687	Nellie				
4688	Albert				
4689	Bert				
4690	Biddie		*Over paid C W Pool*		*on order*
4691	Alice	2657.00	C.W. Pool	G W Benge	*on order*
4692	Woodard W^m	*order*			
4693	*(Illegible)* Alfred				
4694	Woodard Plumy				
4695	Woodard Hannah	1062.80	C W Pool	G W Benge	*on order*
4696	Ward William	265.70	William Ward	G W Benge	
4697	Ward William W.				
4698	" Minnie				
4699	" Walter				
4700	" Manerva	1062.80	WW Ward	L B Bell	
4701	Williams Nervis	265.70	C.W. Pool	G W Benge	
4702	Wolf Foster	265.70	Foster Wolf	G W Benge	
4703	Whirlwind Lewis	265.70	C.W. Pool	G W Benge	*on order*
4704	Wolf Lewis				
4705	" Ellen C.				
4706	" Lettie J.				
4707	" Ruth E				
4708	" Lewis M				

Starr Roll 1894

We, the undersigned citizens of the Cherokee Nation, by right of Cherokee blood, do hereby acknowledge to have received of E. E. Starr, National Treasurer of the Cherokee Nation, the sums set opposite our names respectively, in full of our shares in the per capita distribution authorized by an Act of the National Council, dated ___MAY 3 1894___ 1894.

	Names of Head, and Members of Families	Amount	To Whom Paid	Witness to Payment	Remarks
4709	" Richard M				
4710	" Cogah	1859.90	Lewis Wolf	L B Bell	
4711	Walkley Henry	265.70	Allice *(Illegible)*	G W Benge	
4712	Ward Mack				
4713	" Bazzie W				
4714	" Thomas C				
4715	" Stella	1062.80	Mack Ward	G W Benge	
4716	" Bessie	265.70	A.M. Ward	J P Carter	Nov 13/94
4717	Williams Jackson	265.70	F A Neilson	Henry Eiffert	Neilson ord
4718	Warner Nannie				
4719	Warner Ivey L.	531.40	Nannie Warner	L B Bell	
4720	Werther Lucy				
4721	" Charles				
4722	" Minnie				
4723	" Oliver				
4724	" Alley				
4725	" Edward	1594.90	G.W. Werther	L B Bell	
4726	Walker Mary	265.70	Mary Walker	L B Bell	
4727	Wolfe Narcessa	265.70	A M Gott	L B Bell	
4728	White Hellen				
4729	Beunavista	531.40	J.C. White	J.C. Starr	
4730	Wafford[sic] Eli	265.70	Eli Wofford	Henry Eiffert	Sept 19/94
4731	Wanor Rosa L.				J.T.W.
4732	Opal	*order*			
4733	Willie				
4734	Jesse	1062.80	J. T. Wetlock	G W Benge	on order

Starr Roll 1894

We, the undersigned citizens of the Cherokee Nation, by right of Cherokee blood, do hereby acknowledge to have received of E. E. Starr, National Treasurer of the Cherokee Nation, the sums set opposite our names respectively, in full of our shares in the per capita distribution authorized by an Act of the National Council, dated ___MAY 3 1894___ 1894.

	Names of Head, and Members of Families	Amount	To Whom Paid	Witness to Payment	Remarks
4735	Woods William	order 265.70	J Warren Reed	G W Benge	
4736	Westoner Eliza				
4737	" Wm W.				
4738	" Thomas H.				
4739	" Lillie E				
4740	" Josephine				
4741	" Warren	1594.20	Eliza Westoner	L B Bell	
4742	Walker Wm J.				
4743	" Frank L.				
4744	" Lola B				
4745	" Watt				
4746	" Mary E.				
4747	" James A				
4748	" Mary V.	1859.90	W^m J Walker	G W Benge	
4749	Whitemare Chas	265.70	Thomas Carlisle	Henry Eiffert	Ck
4750	Weller Sarah L				
4751	Malinda A.	531.40	S.A. Wells	J.C. Starr	
4752	Washam Martha E				
4753	Meadow Leonard				
4754	Vann Mary J	797.10	M.E. Washam	G W Benge	
4755	Woods Roxie M	265.70	W.M. Gullager	S.W. Mayfield	
4756	Willison Mary J.	265.70	D1134 M J Willison	G W Benge	
4757	Wills Kate				
4758	" Ross	531.40	Kate Wills	G W Benge	
4759	Wolfe Katie				
4760	Paul				
4761	Ada				
4762	Brooks Samuel	1062.80	Kate Wolfe	G W Benge	
4763	Wassom[sic] Catharine				

Starr Roll 1894

We, the undersigned citizens of the Cherokee Nation, by right of Cherokee blood, do hereby acknowledge to have received of E. E. Starr, National Treasurer of the Cherokee Nation, the sums set opposite our names respectively, in full of our shares in the per capita distribution authorized by an Act of the National Council, dated ___MAY 3 1894___ 1894.

	Names of Head, and Members of Families	Amount	To Whom Paid	Witness to Payment	Remarks
4764	" Myrtle				
4765	" Nettie	797.10	Catharine Wasson	G W Benge	
4766	Williams Geo A.	265.70	1ˢ National Bank	Henry Eiffert	Fst Natl B
4767	Ward Jasper	265.70	Jasper Ward	G W Benge	
4768	Wright Maggie				
4769	Mabelle				
4770	Dora				
4771	Benge				
4772	Willie E.	1328.50	Maggie Wright	G W Benge	
4773	Williams Jennie				
4774	Alice				
4775	Claud				
4776	Williams Frank (Fred)	D3166 1062.80	Jennie Williams	G W Benge	
4777	Williams Joseph L.	265.70	J L Williams	G W Benge	
4778	Wolf John	265.70	John Wolfe	G W Benge	See Illinoi
4779	Walker Jane				
4780	" Blossom				
4781	" Susan	797.10	Janie Walker	G W Benge	
4782	Woodall Lucian				
4783	" Wᵐ B				
4784	" Eliza				
4785	" Anna				
4786	" Amanda				
4787	Armstrong James				
4788	" John				
4789	Rogers Maggie	2125.60	Lucian Woodall	G W Benge	
4790	Ward Wᵐ W.				
4791	" Henry H	531.40	Wᵐ W Ward	J.C. Starr	

Starr Roll 1894

We, the undersigned citizens of the Cherokee Nation, by right of Cherokee blood, do hereby acknowledge to have received of E. E. Starr, National Treasurer of the Cherokee Nation, the sums set opposite our names respectively, in full of our shares in the per capita distribution authorized by an Act of the National Council, dated ___MAY 3 1894___ 1894.

	Names of Head, and Members of Families	Amount	To Whom Paid	Witness to Payment	Remarks
4792	Wausett[sic] Chas				
4793	Eliza				
4794	Corntassel Ida	797.10	Chas Wauseatt	G W Benge	
4795	Williamson Maggie L	265.70	M.D. Williamson	G W Benge	
4796	Walker Daniel H				
4797	Mary A				
4798	John F.				
4799	Senora	1062.80	M.A. Walker	G W Benge	
4800	Walker Geo W				
4801	Mary				
4802	James		MV Walker	G W Benge	
4803	Etta				
4804	Trevis				
4805	Henry				
4806	David	1859.90	Mary V Walker	G W Benge	
4807	Walkley Geo				
4808	Mary A	531.40	George Walkley	J.C. Starr	
4809	Ward Caldeen				
4810	" James O				
4811	" Carl E	797.10	Caldeen Ward	J.C. Ward	
4812	Wilkerson Jane	265.70	Jane Wilkerson	G W Benge	
4813	Forster Thos	265.70	W.L. Moore	G W Benge	on order
4814	" Walter	265.70	Jane Wilkerson	G W Benge	
4815	Ward Thomas	265.70	Thomas Ward	L B Bell	
4816	Ward Geo				
4817	Aenus				
4818	Willie				
4819	Catharine				
4820	Nathaniel				

Starr Roll 1894

We, the undersigned citizens of the Cherokee Nation, by right of Cherokee blood, do hereby acknowledge to have received of E. E. Starr, National Treasurer of the Cherokee Nation, the sums set opposite our names respectively, in full of our shares in the per capita distribution authorized by an Act of the National Council, dated ___MAY 3 1894___ 1894.

	Names of Head, and Members of Families	Amount	To Whom Paid	Witness to Payment	Remarks
4821	Pearl	1594.20	Geo Ward	G W Benge	
4822	Woods Lizzie				
4823	Georgia A	531.40	Lizzie Woods	J.C. Starr	
4824	Ward Thos.				
4825	" Moses				
4826	" James				
4827	" Bertha				
4828	" John				
4829	" Ella	1594.20	Thos Ward	G W Benge	
4830	Williams Minnie				
4831	Dewit				
4832	Mattie				
4833	Susie	1062.80	Ed Williams	G W Benge	
4834	Walker Martha J.				
4835	Ollie				
4836	Nellie				
4837	Wm F.				
4838	Highsonger Itaska	1328.50	Martha J Walker	L B Bell	
4839	Ward Fannie				
4840	Henry	531.40	Augustus Ward	G W Benge	
4841	Warren Jas. F.	265.70	J F Warren	G W Benge	
4842	Williams Lucy	265.70	George Eaton	J.C. Starr	pd on order
4843	Wabourne Wilson L	265.70	G W Eaton	Henry Eiffert	Ck
4844	Young Nannie	order			Neilson
4845	" Ray V.				
4846	Webber Richard				
4847	" Calla	1062.80	F A Neilson	Henry Eiffert	order

Starr Roll 1894

We, the undersigned citizens of the Cherokee Nation, by right of Cherokee blood, do hereby acknowledge to have received of E. E. Starr, National Treasurer of the Cherokee Nation, the sums set opposite our names respectively, in full of our shares in the per capita distribution authorized by an Act of the National Council, dated ___MAY 3 1894___ 1894.

	Names of Head, and Members of Families	Amount	To Whom Paid	Witness to Payment	Remarks
4848	Young Mary L				
4849	" Cornelia B.				
4850	" Carrie E.	797.10	M. L. Young	G W Benge	
4851	Yokum May				
4852	" Johnie V.	531.40	C.V. Rogers	G W Benge	

Starr Roll 1894

Tahlequah, Ind. Ter., *June 2nd,* 189 4.

I, C. J. Harris, Principal Chief, and I, E. E. Starr, Treasurer, *of the Cherokee Nation, do hereby certify that the foregoing enrollment of Cherokees by blood, resident in Cooweescoowee District, is a correct transcript from the original census, authorized by the Act of the National Council, approved May 15th, 1893, and that the number ascertained to participate in the pre-capita distribution, provided for by the Act of the National Council, approved May 3rd, 1894, is 4855.*

Attest.
Seal of the Cherokee Nation.

C. J. Harris
Principal Chief.

E. E. Starr
Treasurer.

****

Delaware *(District)*

Starr Roll 1894

We, the undersigned citizens of the Cherokee Nation, by right of Cherokee blood, do hereby acknowledge to have received of E. E. Starr, National Treasurer of the Cherokee Nation, the sums set opposite our names respectively, in full of our shares in the per capita distribution authorized by an Act of the National Council, dated ____MAY 3 1894____ 1894.

#	Names of Head, and Members of Families	Amount	To Whom Paid	Witness to Payment	Remarks
1	Arrow, Will				Mills Bros
2	" J. Ann	order			
3	" Carrie				
4	" Liddia	1062.80	Will Arrow	L B Bell	by Mills own
5	Aleck, James	order			
6	" Nellie				
7	" U Sutt				
8	" Nannie				
9	" Coon				
10	" Nancy	1594.20	James Aleck	L B Bell	
11	Allborn, Becky				check
12	" Lydia	531.40	F M Crowell	L B Bell	on order
13	Aleck, Thomas				
14	" Ollie				
15	" Rebecca				
16	" Willie				check
17	" Celia	1328.50	Percy Wyly	J.C. Starr	on order
18	Alexander, Elmer	265.70	J.S. Thomason	J.C. Starr	check on order
19	Alexander, Elizabeth L.				
20	" Wilas L.				
21	" Effie L.				
22	" Una	1062.80	Elizabeth Alexander	L B Bell	check on order
23	Alexander, Joel B.	order			Percy Wyly
24	" Caroline				check
25	" Carrie	797.10	Percy Wyly	J.C. Starr	on order
26	Audrian, Winfield S.				
27	" Edna M.				
28	" Francis C.				
29	" Clyde W.				
30	" Richard O.	1328.00	W. S. Audrian	L B Bell	

Starr Roll 1894

We, the undersigned citizens of the Cherokee Nation, by right of Cherokee blood, do hereby acknowledge to have received of E. E. Starr, National Treasurer of the Cherokee Nation, the sums set opposite our names respectively, in full of our shares in the per capita distribution authorized by an Act of the National Council, dated ___MAY 3 1894___ 1894.

Names of Head, and Members of Families	Amount	To Whom Paid	Witness to Payment	Remarks
31 Audrain, Frank G.				
32 " Ralph R.				
33 " Anna C.				
34 " Mamie Irene	1062.80	*(Illegible)*	L B Bell	
35 Angel, Becky				
36 " Ida				
37 " Willie				
38 " Jessie				
39 " Laura				
40 " James H.	1574.20	Wm Angel	L B Bell	
41 Audrain, Mary J.	265.70	P L Walker	L B Bell	
42 Adams, Malinda	265.70	Malinda Adams	L B Bell	
43 Allen, Thomas				
44 " Myrtie				
45 " Pearl				
46 " Neoma				
47 " Plumie	1328.50	*(Illegible)* Allen	L B Bell	
48 Allen, Amarah				
49 " Olive I.	531.40	Mary Allen	L B Bell	
50 Alexander, Wallace	*order*			
51 " Cha's	531.40	L.B. Bell	J.C. Starr	*check on order*
52 Allen, Wm. B.				
53 " Callie				
54 " Ada B.				
55 " Ida				
56 " Eva O.	1328.50	Ann Allen	L B Bell	
57 Adair, John W	*order*			
58 " Nannie				
59 " John W. D.				*W C Patton*
60 " Joe F.				

Starr Roll 1894

We, the undersigned citizens of the Cherokee Nation, by right of Cherokee blood, do hereby acknowledge to have received of E. E. Starr, National Treasurer of the Cherokee Nation, the sums set opposite our names respectively, in full of our shares in the per capita distribution authorized by an Act of the National Council, dated ___MAY 3 1894___ 1894.

#	Names of Head, and Members of Families	Amount	To Whom Paid	Witness to Payment	Remarks
61	" Mack	1328.50	W.C. Patton	L B Bell	check on order
62	Ataway, Mary	265.70	Mary Atway[sic]	L B Bell	
63	Aleck, Nancy				
64	" Frank	531.40	Nancy Alleck	L B Bell	
65	Arwood, Cornelia				
66	" Oscie				
67	" Minnie				
68	" Alvin	1062.80	Cornelia Arwood	L B Bell	
69	Arwood, Hettie	265.70	Hettie Arwood	L B Bell	
70	Bearhead, Joe				F.M. Crowell
71	" Sallie				
72	" Peter	*order*			
73	" Sallie				Paid check
74	" Mike	1328.50	F.M. Crowell	J.C. Starr	on order
75	Bigacom, Redbird	265.70	Redbird Bigacom	L B Bell	(Illegible)
76	Budding, Lewis	265.70	J.S. Thomason	J.C. Starr	check on order
77	Beaver, Runabout	265.70	Dorcas Mouse	L B Bell	Son of Darby Mouse
78	Buzzard, Yellowbird				
79	" Betsy	531.40	Betsy Y Buzzard	L B Bell	
80	Mike Peggy	531.40	Peggy Mike	L B Bell	
81	Buzzard, Nate Yellow Bird				
82	Blackfox, John				
83	" Nancy				
84	" Oogusstah	797.10	John Blackfox	L B Bell	
85	Blackfox, Sam				
86	" Lucy				
87	" Joe				

Starr Roll 1894

We, the undersigned citizens of the Cherokee Nation, by right of Cherokee blood, do hereby acknowledge to have received of E. E. Starr, National Treasurer of the Cherokee Nation, the sums set opposite our names respectively, in full of our shares in the per capita distribution authorized by an Act of the National Council, dated _____MAY 3 1894_____ 1894.

#	Names of Head, and Members of Families	Amount	To Whom Paid	Witness to Payment	Remarks
88	" Susanne				
89	" Sally				
90	" Jonathin[sic]	1574.20	Sam Blackfox	L B Bell	
91	Bird, Lacey	265.70	Walsh & Shutt	Henry Eiffert	W & S
92	Beck, Oran				
93	" Leathy				
94	" Chavlet[sic]				
95	" Susie	1062.80	Oran Beck	L B Bell	
96	Beck, Dave	order			C.M. Mc
97	" Blanche				
98	" Vivia	797.10	Chas. M. McClellan & Son	J.C. Starr	check on order
99	Blagg, Thomas	265.70	Mary *(Illegible)*	L B Bell	
100	Buchanon, Joanne				
101	" Walter				
102	" Myrtle				
103	" Edgar				
104	" Ann				
	" Clyde	1594.20	Joseph Buchanon	L B Bell	
105	Bear Toter				
106	" Lizzie				
107	" Martha	797.10	Bear Toter	L B Bell	
108	Beaver, Nancy				
109	" Annie				
110	" Celia	797.10	Nancy Beaver	L B Bell	
111	Bryant, Ben F				W.J.G
112	" Alice	order			
113	" Leona				
114	" Roda	1062.80	W. J. Gilbreath	J.C. Starr	check on order

Starr Roll 1894

We, the undersigned citizens of the Cherokee Nation, by right of Cherokee blood, do hereby acknowledge to have received of E. E. Starr, National Treasurer of the Cherokee Nation, the sums set opposite our names respectively, in full of our shares in the per capita distribution authorized by an Act of the National Council, dated ___MAY 3 1894___ 1894.

	Names of Head, and Members of Families	Amount	To Whom Paid	Witness to Payment	Remarks
115	Beck, Zeke				
116	" Mary				
117	" Don				
118	" Jessie				
119	" Sallie				
120	" Tom				
121	" Irene				
122	" Jonus F				
123	" Sam	2391.30	Mary Beck	L B Bell	
124	Beck, Sabera	~~265.70~~ *no check*	A.R. Wilson & Bro	J.C. Starr	check ~~on order~~
125	" Johnie				
126	" Didd				
127	" Ula				
128	" Guy	1062.80	A.R. Wilson & Bro	J.C. Starr	check on order
129	Beck, Ludge	265.70	AR Wilson & Bro	E.W. Buffington	check on order
130	Beck, Joe	265.70 *order*	Chas. M. McClellan & Son	J.C. Starr	check on order
131	Beck, Sallie	265.70	Henry Beck	L B Bell	
132	Beck, Robert	265.70	Henry Beck	L B Bell	order
133	Brouddus, Augusta	*order*			J.C. Starr
134	" Corinthia				
135	" Dora	797.10	Augusta Brouddus	L B Bell	
136	Beck, Henry				
137	" Robert				
138	" Lora				
139	" Cornealius				
140	" Albert				
141	" Sinna				
142	" Ida	1859.90	Henry Beck	L B Bell	
143	Beck, Harlin	*order* 265.70	W.A. Gilbraith	J.C. Starr	check on order

Starr Roll 1894

We, the undersigned citizens of the Cherokee Nation, by right of Cherokee blood, do hereby acknowledge to have received of E. E. Starr, National Treasurer of the Cherokee Nation, the sums set opposite our names respectively, in full of our shares in the per capita distribution authorized by an Act of the National Council, dated ____MAY 3 1894____ 1894.

#	Names of Head, and Members of Families	Amount	To Whom Paid	Witness to Payment	Remarks
144	Bryant, John				
145	" Margaret				
146	" Sarah				
147	" Martha				
148	" Lula L.				
149	" Lottia S.				
150	" Bertha M				
151	" Benjamin F.	2125.60	John Bryant	L B Bell	
152	Beamer, John				AR Wilson & Bro
153	" Sarah	order			
154	" Pearlie				
155	" Oliver C.		AR Wilson & Bro	J.C. Starr	check on order
156	Beck, Jeff	265.70	Jeff Beck	L B Bell	
157	Beck, John	265.70	W.J. Gilbreath	J.C. Starr	check on order
158	Butler, Darcus	265.70	Jas F Crittenden	L B Bell	
159	Brown, Lucy	265.70	Lucy Brown	L B Bell	
160	Blevins, Sarah	order			J.C. Welch
161	" Joseph	265.70	J.C. Starr	J.C. Starr	check on order
162	" George				
163	" Josie	order			
164	" Gusta				check on order for 5
165	" Ollie	1328.50	J.C. Welch	J.C. Starr	
166	Blevins, Pleasant	265.70	J.C. Starr	J.C. Starr	check on order
167	Bucket, David				
168	" Aggie				
169	" Bettie				
170	" Jackie				
171	" Dawes				
172	" Sam				
173	" Lou				

Starr Roll 1894

We, the undersigned citizens of the Cherokee Nation, by right of Cherokee blood, do hereby acknowledge to have received of E. E. Starr, National Treasurer of the Cherokee Nation, the sums set opposite our names respectively, in full of our shares in the per capita distribution authorized by an Act of the National Council, dated ___MAY 3 1894___ 1894.

	Names of Head, and Members of Families	Amount	To Whom Paid	Witness to Payment	Remarks
174	Ketchum, Nancy	Carried to the letter K on copy roll Aug 13th 1897			
175	" John	2391.30	David Bucket	L B Bell	
176	Bushyhead, Jesse				
177	" Jenny				
178	" Willie				
179	" Annie				
180	" John				
181	" Maggie				
182	" Cornelia	1859.90	Jesse Bushyhead	L B Bell	
183	Butler, James P.				odr denied
184	" Nancy				GW Smith
185	" Homer	797.10	GW Smith	Henry Eiffert	on order check
186	Batt, Ned				
187	" Flora				
188	" Emma				
189	" Bennie				
190	" Adam	1328.50	Ned Batt	L B Bell	
191	Buzzard, Sam				
192	" J Hawker	order			
193	" Adam				
194	" Nellie				
195	" Bessie	1328.50	F.M. Crowell	J.C. Starr	Check on order
196	Bates, Pauline				
197	" Charles				
198	" Susie M.				
199	" Josephine				
200	Sheldon, Mary E.	1328.50	Pauline Bates	L B Bell	
	Carried to the letter S. on copy roll Aug 13, 1897				
201	Blackbird, James				Wyly
202	" Lucy	order			check
203	" Round	797.10	Percy Wyly	J.C. Starr	on order

Starr Roll 1894

We, the undersigned citizens of the Cherokee Nation, by right of Cherokee blood, do hereby acknowledge to have received of E. E. Starr, National Treasurer of the Cherokee Nation, the sums set opposite our names respectively, in full of our shares in the per capita distribution authorized by an Act of the National Council, dated ___MAY 3 1894___ 1894.

	Names of Head, and Members of Families	Amount	To Whom Paid	Witness to Payment	Remarks
204	Brown, Charley				*order carried*
205	" Frank				*by GW Smith*
206	" Pearl	797.10	G W Smith	Henry Eiffert	*check on order*
207	Blevins, Lee				
208	" Thomas				
209	" Walter L				
210	" William	*order*			
211	" Affsie[sic]				
212	" Francis				
213	" Mintie	1859.90	Lee Blevins	L B Bell	*L W Bush*
214	Ballard, Sarah	265.70	HC Ballard	L B Bell	*on order of*
215	" George	265.70	Geo Ballard	L B Bell	*Sarah Ballard*
216	Bird, Charley				
217	" Hester	531.40	Percy Wyly	Henry Eiffert	*Check*
218	Buffington, Wm	265.70	Wm W Buffington	L B Bell	
219	Ballard, Sam				
220	Ballard, Gaddie				
221	" Daubum	797.10	Sam Ballard	L B Bell	
222	Beatty, Alice B.	265.71	C L Washburn	L B Bell	
223	Ballard, Freeman				
224	" Edna				
225	" Nellie	797.10	Freeman Ballard	L B Bell	
226	Blaylock, Sarah				
227	" Mary E				
228	" Nellie J				
229	" Artelia C				
230	" Lotta A.				
231	" Julius T.				
232	" Alice E.	1859.90	Sarah Blalock[sic]	L B Bell	

Starr Roll 1894

We, the undersigned citizens of the Cherokee Nation, by right of Cherokee blood, do hereby acknowledge to have received of E. E. Starr, National Treasurer of the Cherokee Nation, the sums set opposite our names respectively, in full of our shares in the per capita distribution authorized by an Act of the National Council, dated ___MAY 3 1894___ 1894.

Names of Head, and Members of Families	Amount	To Whom Paid	Witness to Payment	Remarks
233 Berry, Amos				
234 " Etta M.	531.40	Amos Berry	L B Bell	
235 Berry, Charles	265.70	L.W. Buffington	J.C. Starr	check on order
236 Barnett Edward	265.70	Edward Bennett	L B Bell	
237 Barnett, Frank				
238 " Jessie L.	531.40	F.M. Barnett	L B Bell	
239 Breedlove, Walter W	265.70	Wm Howell	L B Bell	
240 Brown, Sarah	order			
241 " Addie	order			
242 " Lizzie				
243 " Jessie				
244 " Eugene	1328.50	F.M. Crowell	J.C. Starr	check on order
245 Brock, Charles	265.70	Sally Kufu	L B Bell	
246 Barger, Samuel				
247 " Edward				
248 " Isiac[sic] L.	797.10	Samuel Barger	J.C. Starr	
249 Blaylock, Gano.	265.70	J.S. Thomason	J.C. Starr	check on order
250 Bradley, Mary J	order			
251 " Henrietta	531.40	M J Bradley	L B Bell	
252 Barger, John	265.70	John Barger	L B Bell	
253 Breedlove, M. W.	265.70	Emely Breedlove		
254 Breedlove, Florence	265.70	Emely Breedlove		
255 Breedlove, Jennie	265.70	Emely Breedlove		
256 Blythe, Cora Dell				
257 " Napoleon	531.40	Solon James gardian[sic]		

280

Starr Roll 1894

We, the undersigned citizens of the Cherokee Nation, by right of Cherokee blood, do hereby acknowledge to have received of E. E. Starr, National Treasurer of the Cherokee Nation, the sums set opposite our names respectively, in full of our shares in the per capita distribution authorized by an Act of the National Council, dated ___MAY 3 1894___ 1894.

	Names of Head, and Members of Families	Amount	To Whom Paid	Witness to Payment	Remarks
258	Buzzard, Falling	*order*			F.M. Crowell
259	" Nancy				
260	" Sarah		D 1570		
261	" Rozen				
262	" John				
263	" Daniel				
264	" Joseph	1859.90	F.M. Crowell	J.C. Starr	*check on order*
265	Buzzard, Jackson	265.70	L.B. Bell	J.C. Starr	
266	Bulawsky, Josephine				
267	" Dora				
268	" Ida				
269	" Annie				
270	" Blanche	1328.50	August Bulawsky	L B Bell	
271	Buzzard, William	265.70	F.M. Crowell	J.C. Starr	*paid check on order*
272	Buzzard, Cornelius	265.70	F.M. Crowell	J.C. Starr	*check on order*
273	Blaingame[sic], Geo R.	265.70	Geo. R. Blosingome[sic]	J.C. Starr	
274	Ballard, Randolph				
275	" Miran				
276	" Arch				
277	" Robert				
278	" James				
279	" John				
280	" Claude	1859.90	Randolph Ballard	L B Bell	
281	Ballard, Wm				
282	" Charlotte				
283	" Annie				
284	" Lucinda				
285	" Sarah				
286	" Houston				
287	" Ruth M.				
288	" Ethel				

Starr Roll 1894

We, the undersigned citizens of the Cherokee Nation, by right of Cherokee blood, do hereby acknowledge to have received of E. E. Starr, National Treasurer of the Cherokee Nation, the sums set opposite our names respectively, in full of our shares in the per capita distribution authorized by an Act of the National Council, dated ____MAY 3 1894____ 1894.

	Names of Head, and Members of Families	Amount	To Whom Paid	Witness to Payment	Remarks
289	" Zoe	2391.30	Wm Ballard	L B Bell	
290	Ballard, Jane Anna	265.70	Wm Ballard	L B Bell	*order*
291	Ballard, Annie	265.70	Wm Ballard	L B Bell	
292	Burk, Martha J.				*G W Green*
293	" Maggie J.				
294	" Thos W.				
295	" William R.				
296	" John S.				
297	" Walter L.	1594.20	G.W. Green	J.C. Starr	*check on order*
298	Ballard, Sallie	*order* 265.70	F.M. Crowell	J.C. Starr	*check on order*
299	Beck, Susie				
300	" Arthur				
301	" Lula B.				
302	" Susie				
303	" Daniel				
304	" Scot	1594.20	Susie E. Beck	Henry Eiffert	*check*
	Bell, James M.				*Allotee*
305	Bell, Watie W.	265.70	Watie W Bell	Henry Eiffert	
306	Berry, Elisha	265.70	Elisha Berry	L B Bell	
307	Blackstone, Henry	265.70	Thomason Buffington	J.C. Starr	*check on order*
308	Barnett, Nancy	265.70	Riley Barnett	L B Bell	
309	Berry, William	265.70	J S Thomason	Aug 28 94 L B Bell	*No 68622 Check*
310	Brown, Mary				
311	Ferrell, Gertie				
312	Brown, Fintie	797.10	Mary Brown	L B Bell	

Starr Roll 1894

We, the undersigned citizens of the Cherokee Nation, by right of Cherokee blood, do hereby acknowledge to have received of E. E. Starr, National Treasurer of the Cherokee Nation, the sums set opposite our names respectively, in full of our shares in the per capita distribution authorized by an Act of the National Council, dated ____MAY 3 1894____ 1894.

	Names of Head, and Members of Families	Amount	To Whom Paid	Witness to Payment	Remarks
313	Black, Martha				
314	" Willie				
315	" Mae				
316	" Effie	1062.80	Martha Black	L B Bell	
317	Buffington, Lucien				
318	" Nannie	531.40	L W Buffington	L B Bell	
319	Blevins, Nancy				
320	" Augusta				
321	" Jack Jun.	797.10	Nancy Blevins	L B Bell	
322	Blevins, Ross	265.70	Nancy Blevins	L B Bell	
323	Black, Alice	265.70	Martha Black	L B Bell	
324	Buffington, James	265.70	F.F. Thompson	J.C. Starr	check 67534 J.F. Thomason
325	Buffington, Charles	265.70	Chas Buffington	L B Bell	J.F. Thomason
326	Butler, John E				
327	" Sallie				
328	" Lucian				
329	" Cora				
330	Johnson, Mamie Carried to letter J.	1328.50	Jno E Butler	L B Bell	
331	Buffington, Webster	265.70	D W Buffington	L B Bell	
332	Battles, Emily J.	265.70	Emily J Battles	L B Bell	
333	Balentine, Hamilton				
334	" Mary E.				
335	" Mary E, Jr.				
336	" Ellen S.	1062.80	Hamilton Ballentine	L B Bell	
337	Baker, Mollie A	order			JST
338	" Malissa E.	531.40	J.S. Thomason	J.C. Starr	check on order

Starr Roll 1894

We, the undersigned citizens of the Cherokee Nation, by right of Cherokee blood, do hereby acknowledge to have received of E. E. Starr, National Treasurer of the Cherokee Nation, the sums set opposite our names respectively, in full of our shares in the per capita distribution authorized by an Act of the National Council, dated __MAY 3 1894__ 1894.

#	Names of Head, and Members of Families	Amount	To Whom Paid	Witness to Payment	Remarks
339	Burton, Cynthia	265.70	Cynthia Barton[sic]	L B Bell	
340	Blevins, Jeff	265.70	Jeff Blevins	L B Bell	
341	Bell, Mary S				
342	" Lucien B				
343	Starr, Georgia A.	797.10	M.S. Bell	L B Bell	
	Carried to letter S. on copy roll				
344	Ballard, Thos				
345	" Jesse Lee	631.40	Thos. Ballard	J.C. Starr	
346	Burr, George				Geo. Burr in
347	" Geo Brittan	531.40	George Burr *Nov 14/96*	Robt B Ross, Idn by John Sevier	Detroit prison
348	Blevins, Nellie M.	265.70	F.M. Crowell	J.C. Starr	Minor
349	Buffington, Thos. M.	265.70	T M Buffington	L B Bell	
350	Blythe, Napoleon B.				
351	" William H.				
352	" John E.				
353	" Mary Jane				
354	" Fairy A.				
355	" Aubrey A.	1594.20	N B Blythe	L B Bell	
356	Bluejacket, Carrie	*order*			LBB
357	" Ida M.				
358	" Walter				
359	" Edward H.				
360	" Wm. T.	1328.50	L B Bell	L B Bell	Check 1062.80 Cash 265.70
361	Barger, Charles	265.70	Charles Barger	L B Bell	
362	Chopper, Daniel				
363	" Lucy	531.70	Lucy Chopper	L B Bell	

Starr Roll 1894

We, the undersigned citizens of the Cherokee Nation, by right of Cherokee blood, do hereby acknowledge to have received of E. E. Starr, National Treasurer of the Cherokee Nation, the sums set opposite our names respectively, in full of our shares in the per capita distribution authorized by an Act of the National Council, dated ___MAY 3 1894___ 1894.

#	Names of Head, and Members of Families	Amount	To Whom Paid	Witness to Payment	Remarks
364	Chopper, Su-gee				
365	" Emma				
366	" Liza				
367	" Henry				
368	" Joe	1328.50	Sugee Chopper	L B Bell	
369	Chopper, See-were	265.70	Percy Wyly	J.C. Starr	check on order P.W.
370	Chopper, Daylight				
371	" Jennie				
372	" Ester				
373	Tincup, Lucy	1062.80	Daylight Chopper	L B Bell	Mother in Law of Daylight Chopper
	Carried to letter T. on copy roll				
374	Creek Killer, Jurnarem	265.70	Jurnarem Creek Killer	L B Bell	
375	Creek Killer, Scott				
376	" Mary	order			Wyly
377	" Jay Gould				
378	" Rachel	1062.70	Mary Creek Killer	L B Bell	
379	Cheater, John	order			F.M. Crowell
380	" Casie	531.40	F.M. Crowell	J.C. Starr	check on order
381	Crittenden, Jas. F.				
382	" Lizzie				
383	" Lecta	797.10	J F Crittenden	L B Bell	
384	Cummins, Joe				P.W.
385	" Eliza	order			
386	" John				
387	" Dick				
388	" Sally	1328.50	Percy Wyly	Henry Eiffert	
389	Comingdeer, Joe				
390	" Polly				
391	" Celia	797.10	Joe Comingdeer	L B Bell	

Starr Roll 1894

We, the undersigned citizens of the Cherokee Nation, by right of Cherokee blood, do hereby acknowledge to have received of E. E. Starr, National Treasurer of the Cherokee Nation, the sums set opposite our names respectively, in full of our shares in the per capita distribution authorized by an Act of the National Council, dated ___MAY 3 1894___ 1894.

	Names of Head, and Members of Families	Amount	To Whom Paid	Witness to Payment	Remarks
392	Clark, Johnson				
393	" Leona E.	531.40	L.E. Clark	L B Bell	
394	Creek Killer, Jeff				
395	" Catahyah	*order*			
396	" Sally				
397	" Oolayah				
398	" Leonard				
	"				
399	" Sarah	1594.20	F.M. Crowell	J.C. Starr	*check on order*
400	Creek Killer, Charley	265.70	L B Bell	E E Starr	*check on order*
401	Creek Killer, Nancy	265.70	L B Bell	E E Starr	*check on order*
402	Crismon, Ida	265.70	L B Bell	E E Starr	*check on order*
403	Countryman, John Jr.	*order*			
404	" Leander	531.40	F.M. Crowell	J.C. Starr	*check on order*
405	Coody, John	3332 265.70	(Illegible)Bluejacket	L B Bell	
406	Carlisle, Eve S	265.70	Eve Carlile[sic]	L B Bell	
407	Comingdeer, Lee	*order*			
408	" Agie				*Wyly*
409	" Sevns[sic]	797.10	Agie Comingdeer	L B Bell	
410	Cunigan, George	265.70	J.L. Blevins	J.C. Starr	*check on order*
411	Cobb, Sam	*order*			*R. Wyly*
412	" Lizzie				
413	" Ella	797.10	Percy Wyly	J.C. Starr	*check on order*
414	Cobb, Joe Batt	265.70	Percy Wyly	Henry Eiffert	*Wyly*

Starr Roll 1894

We, the undersigned citizens of the Cherokee Nation, by right of Cherokee blood, do hereby acknowledge to have received of E. E. Starr, National Treasurer of the Cherokee Nation, the sums set opposite our names respectively, in full of our shares in the per capita distribution authorized by an Act of the National Council, dated ____MAY 3 1894____ 1894.

#	Names of Head, and Members of Families	Amount	To Whom Paid	Witness to Payment	Remarks
415	Cornshucker, Geo.				
416	" Sallie				
417	" Tom				
418	" Sam	order			
419	" Watie				Pd Check on order
420	" Arch	1594.20	Percy Wyly	J.C. Starr	
421	Chopper, Bird				
422	" Jennie				
423	" Mike				
424	" Darkey	1062.80	Bird Chopper	L B Bell	
425	Cawood, Matilda				
426	" Moses S.				
427	" Herbert				
428	" William F.				
429	" Sarah	1328.50	John T. Cawood	J.C. Starr	
430	Cawood, Andrew				
431	" Henderson	797.10			
432	" Jay L.	~~2125.60~~	John T. Cawood	J.C. Starr	
433	Cornshucker, Lizzie				
434	Cornshucker, TeeAnn				
435	Cornshucker, Laura	797.10	Lizzie Cornshucker	J.C. Starr	
436	Cornshucker, Heraham	265.70	Lizzie Cornshucker	J.C. Starr	
437	Cornshucker, Liza				
438	" Anna	order			Wyly check on order
439	" John	797.10	Percy Wyly	J.C. Starr	
440	Clark, Lizzy		3424		
441	" Mary				
442	" William				
443	" Franklin	1062.80	Lizzy Clark	L B Bell	
444	Camp, Mary	order			J.C. Starr Pd Check on order
445	" Claud F.	531.40	J.C. Starr	J.C. Starr	

Starr Roll 1894

We, the undersigned citizens of the Cherokee Nation, by right of Cherokee blood, do hereby acknowledge to have received of E. E. Starr, National Treasurer of the Cherokee Nation, the sums set opposite our names respectively, in full of our shares in the per capita distribution authorized by an Act of the National Council, dated ___MAY 3 1894___ 1894.

	Names of Head, and Members of Families	Amount	To Whom Paid	Witness to Payment	Remarks
446	Cary, David				
447	" Robert	531.40	David Cary	L B Bell	
448	Chatham, Mary A.	265.40	P.D Chatham	L B Bell	
449	Cheater, Stand	order			G W Smith
450	" Eva				
451	" Esuck	797.10	G W Smith	Henry Eiffert	
452	Cohee, Martha	265.70	J H Cohee	L B Bell	
453	Carey, Lee				
454	" Anna				
455	" Myrtle				
456	" Lillie	1062.80	Lee Carey	L B Bell	
457	Carey, Joseph				F.M. Crowell
458	" Ella	order			
459	" Effie				
460	" Ruth				
461	William Ross	1328.50	Joe Carey	L B Bell	F.M. Crowell
	carried to letter R. on Copy Roll				
462	Cushman, Jayson	265.70	L.W. Buffington	J.C. Starr	check on order
463	Cheater, Lacy				
464	" Katy				
465	" Bunnie				
466	" Josiah				
467	" Cornsilk				
468	" Timothy				
469	" Robin	1857.90	G W Smith	Henry Eiffert	check on order
470	Cheater, Enolia				
471	" Ga-hee-ga				
472	" John				
473	" Mariah				
474	" Flora	1528.80	Ga hee ga Cheater	L B Bell	

Starr Roll 1894

We, the undersigned citizens of the Cherokee Nation, by right of Cherokee blood, do hereby acknowledge to have received of E. E. Starr, National Treasurer of the Cherokee Nation, the sums set opposite our names respectively, in full of our shares in the per capita distribution authorized by an Act of the National Council, dated ___MAY 3 1894___ 1894.

#	Names of Head, and Members of Families	Amount	To Whom Paid	Witness to Payment	Remarks
475	Cheater, Charley	265.70	Charlie Cheater	L B Bell	
476	Cheater, Allsie	265.70	Gah he ga Cheater	L B Bell	
477	Cheater, Swimmer	265.70	Swimmer Cheater	L B Bell	
478	" Susie	265.70	Susie Swimmer	L B Bell	
479	Cowles, Martha A.				
480	" Charles E.				
481	" Maggie N.				
482	" Joseph W.				
483	" Will L.S.				
484	" James C.				
485	" Viola J.	1859.90	Martha A Cowles	L B Bell	
486	Cheek, Luly D.	★			Sarah Cheek is ★ mother of these children and guardian of this one.
487	" Phessant J.				
488	Sager, William	797.10	Sarah Cheek	L B Bell	
	Carried to letter S. on copy roll.				
489	Cheater, Jefferson				
490	" Qt-cle[sic]	531.40	Jefferson Cheater	L B Bell	
491	Cox, John S.				
492	" Martha				
493	" David	797.10	Martha Cox	L B Bell	
494	Cox, Marnie	265.79 *order*	E.N.Ratcliff	J.C. Starr	Pd Check on order
495	Christian, Susie	265.70	Benj Christy	L B Bell	
496	Cheater, George	*order*			
497	" Annie				
498	" Anna				
499	" Gunch ucha				
500	" Jimmie				
501	" Josine				Pd Check
502	" Che-lon-a-cha	1859.90	G.W. Smith	J.C. Starr	on order

Starr Roll 1894

We, the undersigned citizens of the Cherokee Nation, by right of Cherokee blood, do hereby acknowledge to have received of E. E. Starr, National Treasurer of the Cherokee Nation, the sums set opposite our names respectively, in full of our shares in the per capita distribution authorized by an Act of the National Council, dated ___MAY 3 1894___ 1894.

	Names of Head, and Members of Families	Amount	To Whom Paid	Witness to Payment	Remarks
503	Cox, Rebecca	*protest agent drawing*			
504	" Geo. A.		J.D.Cox *(illegible)*		
505	" Steve F				
506	" Lettie L				
507	" Marcus G				
508	" Flance[sic] D	1594.20	Rebecca Cox	L B Bell	
509	Carr, Susan				
510	" Frank				
511	" Fannie	797.10	Susan Carr	L B Bell	
512	Curey, Francis S.				
513	" Emma E.				
514	" Saphronia P				
515	" Cora N				
516	" Clarence E				
517	" Geo B				
518	" Chas T.				
519	" Albert W.				
520	" Florence				
521	" Ben. F.				
522	" Claud P.	2922.70	Sara Curey	L B Bell	
523	Coats, William				
524	" Bertha E				
525	" Jennie A				
526	" John H				
527	" Francis M				
528	" Geo. M^c				
529	" Wm P.				
530	" Chas J.	2125.60	William Coats	L B Bell	
531	Crockett, Mary A				
532	" Pearl				
533	" Inas	797.10	M.A. Crockett	L B Bell	

Starr Roll 1894

We, the undersigned citizens of the Cherokee Nation, by right of Cherokee blood, do hereby acknowledge to have received of E. E. Starr, National Treasurer of the Cherokee Nation, the sums set opposite our names respectively, in full of our shares in the per capita distribution authorized by an Act of the National Council, dated ___MAY 3 1894___ 1894.

	Names of Head, and Members of Families	Amount	To Whom Paid	Witness to Payment	Remarks
534	Copeland, Alexander				
535	" Nancy				
536	" Rabbit B				
537	" Bertha M				
538	" Geo W				
539	" Cordelia				
540	Cowels, Eddie				Step Children
541	" Cora B.	2125.60	Alex Copeland	L B Bell	
542	Chandler, Cornelia A.				
543	" Claud A				
544	" Felix C				
545	" Myrtle				
546	" Joh[sic] D				
547	" Ben H				
548	" Mariah				
549	" Homer E.	2125.60	Cornelia A Chandler	L B Bell	
550	Conner, Rebecca J.				
551	" O Lonzo				
552	" Crawford				
553	" Leela M				
554	" Leonard	1328.50	I M Conner	L B Bell	
555	Copeland, Riley				
556	" Delia	531.40	Rilm[sic] Copeland	L B Bell	
557	Crotzer, Emma				
558	" Rosa				
559	" Stella				
560	" Effie	1062.80	William Crotzer	L B Bell	
561	Covey, Susan				
562	" Bula				
563	" Preston	797.10	Susan Covey	L B Bell	
564	Countryman, Geo				
565	" Minerva				
566	" James				

Starr Roll 1894

We, the undersigned citizens of the Cherokee Nation, by right of Cherokee blood, do hereby acknowledge to have received of E. E. Starr, National Treasurer of the Cherokee Nation, the sums set opposite our names respectively, in full of our shares in the per capita distribution authorized by an Act of the National Council, dated ___MAY 3 1894___ 1894.

	Names of Head, and Members of Families	Amount	To Whom Paid	Witness to Payment	Remarks
567	" Sabra	1062.80	Geo Countryman	L B Bell	
568	Curtis, Mary A				
569	" Dulcie	531.40	W. E. Curtis	L B Bell	
570	Cunningham, Lulu				
571	" Mable				
572	" Nevah	797.10	J L Cunningham	L B Bell	
573	Curtis, Lula H.	265.70	Wm H. Curtis	L B Bell	
574	Countryman, Andy				
575	" Zimerhem				
	" [sic]				
576	" Rose Anna				
577	" Rebecca				
578	" John				
579	" Arthur E				
580	" Jackson	1859.90	Andrew Countryman	L B Bell	
581	Countryman, Geo	265.70	John Countryman	L B Bell	
582	Countryman, John	265.70	Andrew Countryman	L B Bell	
583	Courtney, Eliza				
584	" Edward				
585	" Minerva				
586	" Jessie				
587	" John W.	1328.50	Eliza Courtney	L B Bell	
588	Conner, Lucy J	*order*			
589	Cowell, Caleb W.	531.40	F M Crowell	Henry Eiffert	*(Illegible)* check
590	Clasby, Fanny				
591	" Anna	531.40	Randolph Bellew	L B Bell	Father
592	Chinochee, John	265.70	John Chinochee	L B Bell	

Starr Roll 1894

We, the undersigned citizens of the Cherokee Nation, by right of Cherokee blood, do hereby acknowledge to have received of E. E. Starr, National Treasurer of the Cherokee Nation, the sums set opposite our names respectively, in full of our shares in the per capita distribution authorized by an Act of the National Council, dated _____ MAY 3 1894 _____ 1894.

	Names of Head, and Members of Families	Amount	To Whom Paid	Witness to Payment	Remarks
593	Crowell, Lizzie				
594	" Erda				
595	" Allie				
596	" Frank				
597	" Hunter	1328.50	F M Crowell	L B Bell	
598	Chitwood, Lucy				
599	" Walter				
600	" Josie	797.10	Lucy Chitwood	L B Bell	
601	Cox, Rebecca				
602	" Jady D				
603	" Elva	797.10	Rebecca Cox	L B Bell	
604	Casey, Edward	*order*			J.C. Starr
605	" Lydia				
606	" Darkus	*order*			
607	" Susan				
608	" Edward Jr.				
609	" Charlotte				
610	" Geo. Benge Jr.	1859.90	J.C. Starr	J.C. Starr	*check on order*
611	Clarke, Eudotia				
612	" Eliza				
613	" Joel				
614	" Donia				
615	" Lola	1328.50	Eudotia Clark[sic]	L B Bell	
616	Carey, Jack				
617	" Freeman	531.40	GW Smith	Henry Eiffert	*check on order*
618	Chandler, Anna E.				
619	" Claude D				
620	" Vann S				
621	" Nancy L.				
622	" David	1328.50	*(Illegible)* Chandler	L B Bell	
623	Chandler, Tom A.	265.70 5220	T A Chandler	L B Bell	

293

Starr Roll 1894

We, the undersigned citizens of the Cherokee Nation, by right of Cherokee blood, do hereby acknowledge to have received of E. E. Starr, National Treasurer of the Cherokee Nation, the sums set opposite our names respectively, in full of our shares in the per capita distribution authorized by an Act of the National Council, dated ___MAY 3 1894___ 1894.

	Names of Head, and Members of Families	Amount	To Whom Paid	Witness to Payment	Remarks
624	Childers, Thos. J.	265.70		L B Bell	
625	Chu-na-wah	265.70	Chu nau wah	L B Bell	
626	Coatney, Mandy				*Children in care*
627	Kelley, Escal	531.40	John B. Landrum	L B Bell	*of John Landrum*
	carried to the letter K. on copy roll.				
628	Collins, John				
629	" Joe				
630	Collins, Sallie				
631	" Jesse				
632	" Bradley				
633	" Katy				
634	Beck, Lilly	1857.90	John Collins	L B Bell	*Living with the Collins family*
635	Collins, Henry	265.70	John Collins	L B Bell	
636	Carselowery[sic], James M				
637	" Katy E				
638	" Ellenor				
639	" Charles				
640	" Flossy				
641	" Pauline				
642	" Arthur				
643	" Stella	2125.60	K.E. Carselowey	L B Bell	
644	Carselowery[sic], Robert	265.70	K E Carselowey	L B Bell	
645	Cox, R. A.	265.70	J.S. Thomason	Henry Eiffert	
646	Charlie, Louisa	265.70	F.M. Crowell	J.C. Starr	*check on order*
647	Couch, Donnis M.				
648	" Geo. F.				
649	" Mentie L.				
650	" Lucy M.				
651	" Thos.	1328.50	L C Couch	L B Bell	

Starr Roll 1894

We, the undersigned citizens of the Cherokee Nation, by right of Cherokee blood, do hereby acknowledge to have received of E. E. Starr, National Treasurer of the Cherokee Nation, the sums set opposite our names respectively, in full of our shares in the per capita distribution authorized by an Act of the National Council, dated ___MAY 3 1894___ 1894.

	Names of Head, and Members of Families	Amount	To Whom Paid	Witness to Payment	Remarks
652	Charlesworth, Mary J.				
653	" Walter M.				
654	" Fred W.				
655	" Oliver I.				
656	" Henry A.				
657	" Susie B.	1594.20	Jas F Charlesworth	L B Bell	
658	Cook, Henry A.	265.70	Henry A Cook	Henry Eiffert	
659	Cook, Wm D	265.70	W D Cook	Henry Eiffert	
660	Cook, Isabella	265.70	Isabella Cook	Henry Eiffert	
661	Cook, Florence				
662	" Thomas	531.40	Herman Cook	Henry Eiffert	
663	Cobb, Mary E				
664	" Artie				
665	" Samuel A				
666	" Mary	1062.80	Sam S Cobb	L B Bell	
667	Chunstudy, Katy				
668	" Wally				
669	" Johnson	797.10	Wash England	L B Bell	on order
670	Chandler, Susan				
671	" Samuel				
672	" Lyda				
673	" David				
674	" Ella J.				
675	" Henry	1594.20	Pink Chandler	L B Bell	
676	Chandler, Wm		Pink Chandler	L B Bell	
677	Chandler, John		Pink Chandler	L B Bell	
678	Cave, Manora				
679	" Jas				

Starr Roll 1894

We, the undersigned citizens of the Cherokee Nation, by right of Cherokee blood, do hereby acknowledge to have received of E. E. Starr, National Treasurer of the Cherokee Nation, the sums set opposite our names respectively, in full of our shares in the per capita distribution authorized by an Act of the National Council, dated ___MAY 3 1894___ 1894.

	Names of Head, and Members of Families	Amount	To Whom Paid	Witness to Payment	Remarks
680	" Annie				
681	" Ona	1062.80	Menora Cave	L B Bell	
682	Dick Jeff				
683	" Thos				
684	" Jessie				
685	" Ira May				
686	" Mary E	1328.50	Jeff Dick	L B Bell	
687	Davis Dock				
688	" Becky				
689	" Geo				
690	" Awa-ie	1062.80	Becky Davis	L B Bell	
691	Doublehead Dick	*order*			J.S. Thomason
692	" Annie				
693	" Bird				
694	" Leaf				
695	" Jennie				
696	" Sallie	1594.20	J.S. Thomason	G W Benge	
697	Drywater Jess				
698	" Jennie				
699	" Good-money				
700	" Adam				
701	" Nancy				
702	" Synthia	1594.20	Jesse Drywater	L B Bell	
703	Dollar I-Ann				
704	" Aw-aie	531.40	Iann Dollar	Henry Eiffert	
705	Dirteater Nancy	265.70	Nancy Dirteater	L B Bell	
706	Dildun Rachel				
707	" John				
708	" James H				
709	" Nancy				
710	" Lethie				

Starr Roll 1894

We, the undersigned citizens of the Cherokee Nation, by right of Cherokee blood, do hereby acknowledge to have received of E. E. Starr, National Treasurer of the Cherokee Nation, the sums set opposite our names respectively, in full of our shares in the per capita distribution authorized by an Act of the National Council, dated _____MAY 3 1894_____ 1894.

	Names of Head, and Members of Families	Amount	To Whom Paid	Witness to Payment	Remarks
711	" Hester	1594.20 ~~1328.50~~		L B Bell	
712	Denton John	order ~~265~~.70	A.R. Wilson & Bro	G W Benge	check A.R. Wilson & Bro
713	Davis Katy				
714	" Nancy				
715	" Aleck				
716	" Nick				
717	" Sarah	1328.50	Katy Davis	L B Bell	
718	Davis Geo	265.70	S.N. Thomason	G W Benge	S.N. ~~Thomason~~ Check
719	Davis Jack	265.70	Katy Davis	L B Bell	
720	Dawes Jonathon	265.70	Jonathan Dawes	L B Bell	
721	Downing Houston				
722	" Lizzie				
723	" Nake				
724	" Oll-kin	1062.80	Lizzie Downing	L B Bell	
725	Doherty[sic] Will H				
726	" Josie				
727	" Claud				
728	" Charlie				
729	Jr. " William H.	1328.50	W H Dougherty	L B Bell	
730	Doherty Robt E	265.70	Rob E Dougherty	L B Bell	
731	Dale-da John				P.W.
732	" Jennie				
733	" Ross	order			
734	" Qua-lie-uke				
735	" Sallie				
736	" Oo-nas-ta				
737	" Shucker	1859.90	Percy Wyly	G W Benge	Check

Starr Roll 1894

We, the undersigned citizens of the Cherokee Nation, by right of Cherokee blood, do hereby acknowledge to have received of E. E. Starr, National Treasurer of the Cherokee Nation, the sums set opposite our names respectively, in full of our shares in the per capita distribution authorized by an Act of the National Council, dated ___MAY 3 1894___ 1894.

Names of Head, and Members of Families	Amount	To Whom Paid	Witness to Payment	Remarks
738 Dirtsheller[sic] Rider	265.70	Percy Wyly	G.W. Benge	
" ———— [sic]				P Wyly
739 " Akey	*order*			
740 " U-Sut				
741 " Sarah	1062.80	Rider Dirtseller	L B Bell	
742 Duncan Jas W	265.70	Jas W Duncan	L B Bell	
743 Duncan Narcisus				
744 " Nelly M				
745 " Forest F.				
746 " Allie V.				
747 " Carrie E				
748 " Luther L				
749 " Katy L				
750 " Louie E				
751 " Alvy R.	2391.30	Narcisus Duncan	L B Bell	
752 Duncan Fred B	265.70	Narcisus Duncan	L B Bell	
753 Daniels Ann	265.70	Ann Daniels	L B Bell	
754 Duncan Samantha				
755 " Ellen F.				
756 " James N				
757 " Oran A				
758 " Lee				
759 " Charles G	1594.20	Samantha Duncan	L B Bell	
760 Davis Artelia				
761 " Katy R	*order*			F.M. Crowell Check
762 " Nellie J	797.10	F.M. Crowell	G W Benge	
763 Duncan Sarah				
764 " Sally	531.40	Sarah Duncan	L B Bell	
765 Deems Clara	265.70	Clara Deems	L B Bell	
766 Dawson Wilburn A	265.70	W A Dawson	L B Bell	DEAD. 49 yrs old

Starr Roll 1894

We, the undersigned citizens of the Cherokee Nation, by right of Cherokee blood, do hereby acknowledge to have received of E. E. Starr, National Treasurer of the Cherokee Nation, the sums set opposite our names respectively, in full of our shares in the per capita distribution authorized by an Act of the National Council, dated ___MAY 3 1894___ 1894.

Names of Head, and Members of Families	Amount	To Whom Paid	Witness to Payment	Remarks
767 Duncan Layfayette[sic]				
768 " Charlotte				
769 " Rosetta				
770 " Chas.	1062.80 ~~10731~~ ~~D588~~	Lafayette Duncan	J.C. Starr	
771 Dawson Francis	1859.90	Katie Dawson	EW Buffington	
772 " Zona				
773 " Lula				
774 " Ray				
775 " Jessie				
776 " Jacob				
777 " Hugh				
778 Dawson John W.	265.70	JW Dawson	L B Bell	
779 Dawson W^m R	265.70	W^m R Dawson	L B Bell	
780 Daniels Phillip	*order*			*F M Crowell*
781 " Lucy				
782 " John				
783 " Alice	1062.80	F M Crowell	G W Benge	
784 Dawson Riley				
785 " Robert				
786 " Catherine				
787 " August				
788 " Matt	1328.50	Catherine Dawson	L B Bell	
789 Dawson Albert	265.70	Catherine Dawson	L B Bell	
790 Downing John	*order*			*F M Crowell*
791 " Jane				
792 " William				
793 " Mike	1062.80	John Downing	L B Bell	
794 Duncan James A.				
795 " Lucy A.				
796 " Dellen				
797 " Annie				
798 " Jimmie				

Starr Roll 1894

We, the undersigned citizens of the Cherokee Nation, by right of Cherokee blood, do hereby acknowledge to have received of E. E. Starr, National Treasurer of the Cherokee Nation, the sums set opposite our names respectively, in full of our shares in the per capita distribution authorized by an Act of the National Council, dated ___MAY 3 1894___ 1894.

	Names of Head, and Members of Families	Amount	To Whom Paid	Witness to Payment	Remarks
799	" Ludie				
800	" Charles	1859.90	James A Duncan	L B Bell	
801	Dawson Joseph				
802	" Florence				
803	" Clarence				
804	" Council	1062.80	Florence Dawson	L B Bell	
805	Dawson Elmer	265.70	Florence Dawson	L B Bell	This is a child two yea[rs] & son of Florence Daws[on]
806	Dawson John				
807	" Thos P				
808	" Robert B.				
809	" Iola B				
810	" Lenoma H				
811	" Rosa B				
812	" Chas B				
813	" Hattie J.	2125.60	John Dawson	L B Bell	
814	Dawson Orle H	265.70	Orle H Dawson	L B Bell	
815	Dennis Peter				
816	" Mary				
817	" Oscar				
818	" Nancy				
819	" Rachel				
820	" Susie				
821	" Wesley	1859.90	Peter Dennis	L B Bell	
822	Dawson James R				
823	" Vennie D				
824	" Ermine	797.10	James R Dawson	L B Bell	
825	Dawson Wilburn	265.70	Wilburn Dawson	L B Bell	26 yrs old
826	D~~oughty~~ oty Blanche	265.70	Blanche Dotty	L B Bell	

Starr Roll 1894

We, the undersigned citizens of the Cherokee Nation, by right of Cherokee blood, do hereby acknowledge to have received of E. E. Starr, National Treasurer of the Cherokee Nation, the sums set opposite our names respectively, in full of our shares in the per capita distribution authorized by an Act of the National Council, dated ___MAY 3 1894___ 1894.

	Names of Head, and Members of Families	Amount	To Whom Paid	Witness to Payment	Remarks
827	Donohoo Mattie				
828	" Lucelia	531.40	Phillip Donohoo	L B Bell	
829	Dawson Marion	265.70	Marion Dawson	L B Bell	
830	Daniels Robert	order 265.70	F M Crowell	G W Benge	check F M Crowell
831	Duncan Jas R				F.M. Conner
832	" Susan	order			
833	Kelley Alby				Jas R Duncan
834	" Cora	1062.80	F.M. Conner	G W Benge	their guardian
835	Daniel John M	order			Blevins
836	" Alice R				
837	" Mamie D				
838	" James				
839	" Robert				
840	" Lulu				
841	" Eliza				
842	" Mattie				
843	" Emma				
844	" William	2657.00	J.L. Blevins	G W Benge	
845	Davis John W				
846	" Minnie S	531.40	W T Davis	L B Bell	
847	Davis Geo W	265.70	W.T. Davis	L B Bell	
848	Downing William	order			
849	" Mandy				
850	" Thomas				
851	" Susie				
852	" Judy				
853	" Johnston				
854	" Arthur				
855	" Lucian	~~2125.60~~	William Downing	L B Bell	
856	" Cora	2391.30			
857	Downing Mary J	order 265.70	Mary J Downing	L B Bell	

301

Starr Roll 1894

We, the undersigned citizens of the Cherokee Nation, by right of Cherokee blood, do hereby acknowledge to have received of E. E. Starr, National Treasurer of the Cherokee Nation, the sums set opposite our names respectively, in full of our shares in the per capita distribution authorized by an Act of the National Council, dated ___MAY 3 1894___ 1894.

	Names of Head, and Members of Families	Amount	To Whom Paid	Witness to Payment	Remarks
858	Dameran John L				
859	" Mattie L				
860	" Henry A				
861	" Rex E				
862	" Eva N				
863	" Birdie A				
864	" Lee L				
865	" W^m O	2125.60	J L Dameran	L B Bell	
866	Dubois Mary A				
867	" Dora				
868	" Willie				
869	" Susie	1062.80	Mary Dubois		
870	Douthett Lulu P	265.70 ~~1062.80~~	Lulu Douthett ~~Mary Dubois~~	L B Bell	
871	Douthett Custus L	265.70	Emma Douthett	L B Bell	
872	Davis Lulu J				
873	" Asenah B	3790			
874	" Birtha L				
875	" Benjamin	1062.80	Dr. J T Davis	L B Bell	
876	Donaldson[sic] Rachel				
877	" Frank				
878	" W^m C				
879	" Ollie M				
880	" Annie				
881	" Artie	1594.20	Wm Donalson	L B Bell	
882	Duncan W^m	order			JST
883	" Martha				
884	" Jas Andrew	797.10	J S Thomason	Henry Eiffert	Ck
885	Duncan John E				
886	" Sue E				
887	" Ellis C				
888	" Robt S	1062.80	John E Duncan	L B Bell	

Starr Roll 1894

We, the undersigned citizens of the Cherokee Nation, by right of Cherokee blood, do hereby acknowledge to have received of E. E. Starr, National Treasurer of the Cherokee Nation, the sums set opposite our names respectively, in full of our shares in the per capita distribution authorized by an Act of the National Council, dated ___MAY 3 1894___ 1894.

Names of Head, and Members of Families	Amount	To Whom Paid	Witness to Payment	Remarks
889 Dick Oce	~~7521~~ 265.70	Oce Dick & Rbt Bay	L B Bell	See Cooweeskoowee Rolls
890 Darnell Sonora				
891 " Cora May	531.40	R D Darnell	L B Bell	
892 Dawes Jane	~~5594~~ 265.70	Alneda Kidd	L B Bell	
893 Dudley Ellen *order*	265.70	Percy Wyly	J.C. Starr	*on order* pd check no 68571 AUG 22 1894
894 Du-squ-an-nie				
895 " Rachel				
896 Cummingdeer Shucker	~~Carried to the letter C on copies~~			
897 " Becky	1062.80	Tee squant ni	L B Bell	
898 Dirtsheller Jess	*order* ~~265.70~~	Du squ au ni Percy Wyly	G W Benge	P Wyly
899 Dixon Henrietta	265.70	Henrietta Dixon	L B Bell	
900 Dee-caw-nas-ki				
901 " Jennie	*(No other information given.)*			
902 Dee-caw-nas-ki Nancy	797.10	L B Bell	Henry Eiffert	on order
903 Day W^m A				
904 " Ruth S	531.40	W^m A Day	L B Bell	
905 Dawson Texanna	10761 265.70	~~D406~~ Texanna Dawson	on letter L B ~~Bell~~	In custody of Mrs W.A. Dawson former wife of W.A. Dawson
906 England Sally				
907 " Fanny				
908 " Martin	797.10	Sally England	L B Bell	
909 England Joseph Sr	265.70	Viola Raines	L B Bell	order Age 73 yrs
910 Edmondson[sic] Lula				
911 " Stella				
912 " Hellen	797.10	Jeff Edmunson	L B Bell	

Starr Roll 1894

We, the undersigned citizens of the Cherokee Nation, by right of Cherokee blood, do hereby acknowledge to have received of E. E. Starr, National Treasurer of the Cherokee Nation, the sums set opposite our names respectively, in full of our shares in the per capita distribution authorized by an Act of the National Council, dated ___MAY 3 1894___ 1894.

Names of Head, and Members of Families	Amount	To Whom Paid	Witness to Payment	Remarks
913 England Wash	*order*			
914 " Pigeon				
915 " Wilson	797.10	DN *(Illegible)*	J.C. Starr	*Check on order*
916 England Joseph Jr	265.70	Saml Ward	L B Bell	*Age 68 yrs*
917 England Joseph	265.70	Joseph England	L B Bell	*Age 23 yrs*
918 Edmondson[sic] Florence				
919 " Cherry				
920 " Gonia B				
921 " Beula	1062.80	Florence Edmunson	L B Bell	
922 Edmondson Nancy				
923 " Turner J	531.40	Nancy Edmundson	L B Bell	
924 England Mollie				
925 " Johnie				
926 " Harmon				
927 " Maudie	1062.80	Becky England	L B Bell	
928 Evens Martha	265.70	B.F. Lamar	L B Bell	
929 England Ben C				
930 " Susan A.				
931 " Pett				
932 " Armergean				
933 " Ben Jr.	1328.50	Neal England	L B Bell	
934 England Lucy J	265.70	Charles S England	L B Bell	
935 England Eliza J.				
936 " Harry W.				
937 " Mary E.				
938 " W^m W				
939 " Joanna				
940 " Samuel	1859.90			
941 " Susie L.	~~2125.60~~ *order*	Eliza J England	L B Bell	
942 England Geo	265.70	J.S. Thomason	J.C. Starr	*Check on order*

Starr Roll 1894

We, the undersigned citizens of the Cherokee Nation, by right of Cherokee blood, do hereby acknowledge to have received of E. E. Starr, National Treasurer of the Cherokee Nation, the sums set opposite our names respectively, in full of our shares in the per capita distribution authorized by an Act of the National Council, dated ___MAY 3 1894___ 1894.

Names of Head, and Members of Families	Amount	To Whom Paid	Witness to Payment	Remarks
943 Elliott Hiram	order			JST
944 " " Jr.	531.40	J.S. Thomason	J.C. Starr	Check on order
945 Elliott Arch				
946 " Anna	531.40	Anna Elliott	L B Bell	
947 Elam Effie	3987 265.70	F.M. Crowell	J.C. Starr	Check on order FMC
948 Feeling Steve				In jail for
949 " Sally	531.40	Sally Feeling	L B Bell	three years
950 Frogg Noisy				F.M. Crowell
951 " Nancy	order			
952 " Lunnie				with Crowell's
953 " Mary	1062.80	Nancy Noisy Frog	L B Bell	consent
954 Fallen[sic] Blossom				
955 " Mary				
956 " Johnson	797.10	Falling Blossom	L B Bell	
957 Freeman Mary				should be
958 " Ben				Mary Freuman
959 " Sam				
960 Burchfield John				
961 " Anna	1328.50	Mary Treuman[sic]	L B Bell	suf Sept 12-94
962 Forkedtail Louis				
963 " Jennie				
964 " Oos kine				
965 " Ouia	1062.80	Louis Forkedtail	L B Bell	
966 Foreman Elam	order			A.R.W. & [sic]
967 " Laura				
968 " Nancy				
969 " Arch				
970 " Katy	1328.50	A.R.Wilson & Bro	J.C. Starr	Check on order
971 Fountain Nellie	265.70	Nellie Fountain	L B Bell	

Starr Roll 1894

We, the undersigned citizens of the Cherokee Nation, by right of Cherokee blood, do hereby acknowledge to have received of E. E. Starr, National Treasurer of the Cherokee Nation, the sums set opposite our names respectively, in full of our shares in the per capita distribution authorized by an Act of the National Council, dated ___ MAY 3 1894 ___ 1894.

	Names of Head, and Members of Families	Amount	To Whom Paid	Witness to Payment	Remarks
972	Featherhead Mose				
973	" Chickie				
974	" Susie				
975	" Sarah				
976	" Jeremiah	1328.50	Chickie Featherhead	L B Bell	
977	Fox Joe				*G.W. Smith*
978	" Annie				
979	" Walter	*order*			
980	" Lucy				
981	" Emma				
982	" Yuchie				
983	" Doctor				
984	" Wesley	2125.60	G.W. Smith	L B Bell	*Check on order*
985	Fluke[sic] Lou				
986	" Geo				
987	" Henry	797.10	Ford Flute	L B Bell	
988	Fields Ezekiel				
989	" Sabera				
990	" Annie				
991	" Cora	1062.80	Ezekiel Fields	L B Bell	
992	Fields Richard	265.70	Ezekiel Fields	L B Bell	*order*
993	Fields Linnie	265.70	Henry Eiffert	Henry Eiffert	
994	Fewerstine Rosa	265.70	Rosa Fewerstine	L B Bell	
995	Frick Nannie N	265.70	CL Washbourne	J.C. Starr	*Check on order July 24/94*
996	Fields Geo				
997	" Sarah				
998	" Tom				
999	" Mack				
1000	" Geo Jr				

Starr Roll 1894

We, the undersigned citizens of the Cherokee Nation, by right of Cherokee blood, do hereby acknowledge to have received of E. E. Starr, National Treasurer of the Cherokee Nation, the sums set opposite our names respectively, in full of our shares in the per capita distribution authorized by an Act of the National Council, dated ___MAY 3 1894___ 1894.

	Names of Head, and Members of Families	Amount	To Whom Paid	Witness to Payment	Remarks
1001	" Laura				
1002	" Sam				
1003	" Lizzie				
1004	" Jeff				
1005	" Minnie				
1006	" Adaline	2922.70	Geo Fields	L B Bell	
1007	Fields Feman	265.70	Geo Fields	L B Bell	
1008	Fields Betty				
1009	" Walker				
1010	" Carlotte				
1011	" Nancy				
1012	" Alica				
1013	" Ruphus				
1014	" Mary				
1015	" Henry				
1016	" Louisa	2310.30	Geo Fields	L B Bell	
1017	Fields Tim				
1018	" Sophronia				
1019	" Jimmie H				
1020	" Tim L Jr				
1021	" U Silas				
1022	" Ruth C.	1594.20	Tim Fields	L B Bell	
1023	Fields Bud				
1024	" Martha				
1025	" Lula				
1026	" Zekiel Jr				
1027	" Maggie				
1028	" Ella	1594.20	Bud Fields	L B Bell	
1029	Fields Wesley	265.70	Bud Fields	L B Bell	
1030	Fields Richard	265.70	Bud Fields	L B Bell	
1031	Fields Sam J.				

Starr Roll 1894

We, the undersigned citizens of the Cherokee Nation, by right of Cherokee blood, do hereby acknowledge to have received of E. E. Starr, National Treasurer of the Cherokee Nation, the sums set opposite our names respectively, in full of our shares in the per capita distribution authorized by an Act of the National Council, dated ___MAY 3 1894___ 1894.

	Names of Head, and Members of Families	Amount	To Whom Paid	Witness to Payment	Remarks
1032	" Myrtle				
1033	" Frasilla				
1034	" Thomas				
1035	" Cora				
1036	Phillips Bettie	1594.20	S J Fields	L B Bell	Sam Fields her Guardian
1037	Fields James S.				
1038	" Carlotte				
1039	" Robt				
1040	" Maude E.				
1041	" Laura	1328.50	Jas S Fields	L B Bell	
1042	Foreman Katy	order 265.70	Percy Wyly	J.C. Starr	P W Check on order
1043	Foreman John	order 265.70	Percy Wyly	J.C. Starr	P W Check on order
1044	Freeman Geo				
1045	" Ella				
1046	" Carrie B.				
1047	" Daniel				
1048	" Gerllie L.	1328.50	Geo Freeman	L B Bell	
1049	Fallenpots Geo	order	7958		E.W.
1050	" Martha				
1051	" Alex				
1052	" Tom	1062.80	Ed. Washbourne	J.C. Starr	Check on order
1053	Fields Moses				
1054	" James S. Jr.				
1055	" John T.	797.10	Moses Fields	J.C. Starr	
1056	Fields Albert				
1057	" Bessie E.				
1058	" Stella				
1059	" Wm H.	1062.80	Albert Fields	L B Bell	
1060	Fields Thomas	order 265.70	James W Duncan	J.C. Starr	Check on order check
1061	Fields Pleas	order 265.70	F.M. Crowell	Henry Eiffert	F.M. Crowell

Starr Roll 1894

We, the undersigned citizens of the Cherokee Nation, by right of Cherokee blood, do hereby acknowledge to have received of E. E. Starr, National Treasurer of the Cherokee Nation, the sums set opposite our names respectively, in full of our shares in the per capita distribution authorized by an Act of the National Council, dated ____MAY 3 1894____ 1894.

#	Names of Head, and Members of Families	Amount	To Whom Paid	Witness to Payment	Remarks
1062	Freeman Dan W				
1063	" Wm C.	531.40	Danl W Freeman	L B Bell	
1064	Fields Eliza J				F.M. Crowell
1065	" Lizzie				
1066	" Geo.				
1067	" Anna L.	1062.80	F.M. Crowell	J.C. Starr	Check on order
1068	Fields W^m	~~order~~ 265.70	F M Crowell	J.C. Starr	Check on order F.M. Crowell
1069	Ford Mollie W.				
1070	" Frank W.				
1071	" Reba E				
1072	" Mollie W	1062.80	Mollie W Ford	L B Bell	
1073	Frazier Polly	137			
1074	" Clowd W	137			
1075	" Maude	137			
1076	" Monte Clide	1062.80	J.E. Frazier	L B Bell	
1077	Frazier Annie				
1078	" Callie D.				
1079	" Jessie	79711,10	Saul Frazier	L B Bell	
1080	Flint Delila				
1081	" Dona				
1082	" Wm				
1083	" Cora				
1084	" Charles				
1085	" Nana				
1086	" Albert	1859.90	Dow Flint	L B Bell	
1087	Falling Johson[sic]	531.40			
1088	" Mary	~~1859.90~~	Johnson Falling	L B Bell	
1089	Frazier Ruth A				Check on order 7-13-1894 Ruth Frazier mother of this child

Starr Roll 1894

We, the undersigned citizens of the Cherokee Nation, by right of Cherokee blood, do hereby acknowledge to have received of E. E. Starr, National Treasurer of the Cherokee Nation, the sums set opposite our names respectively, in full of our shares in the per capita distribution authorized by an Act of the National Council, dated ___MAY 3 1894___ 1894.

	Names of Head, and Members of Families	Amount	To Whom Paid	Witness to Payment	Remarks
1090	Atchison Sarah	531.40	F.M. Crowell	J.C. Starr	
1091	Fields W^m A				
1092	" Geo A				
1093	" Lizzie				
1094	" W^m E	1062.80	W A Fields	L B Bell	
1095	Foreman W^m Y				
1096	" Sarah				
1097	" Nancy	797.10	W^m Y Foreman	J.C. Starr	
1098	Foreman Susan H.	265.70	Susan Foreman	L B Bell	
1099	Fields Callie	order			T.J. Monroe
1100	" Mathew	531.40	T.J. Monroe	J.C. Starr	Check on order
1101	Frazier Mary E	265.70	E B Fraser[sic]	L B Bell	
1102	Fields Johson[sic]	order			J.T. Gunter
1103	" Delila				
1104	" Victoria	797.10	J.T. Gunter	J.C. Starr	Check on order
1105	Flemming Mary	order	D1210		
1106	" Quilla	531.40	D1210 L B Bell	L B Bell	
1107	Foreman Arch				
1108	" Sabrina				
1109	" Hugh				
1110	" Lelia				
1111	Glass Charley	1328.50	Arch Foreman	L B Bell	Child of Arch Foreman
1112	Fox Adolphus	265.70	Wm Ballard D24	SW Mayfield	Check
1113	Fincannon Emma				
1114	" W^m A	531.40	Geo Fincannon	L B Bell	
1115	Glory Peter	order			

Starr Roll 1894

We, the undersigned citizens of the Cherokee Nation, by right of Cherokee blood, do hereby acknowledge to have received of E. E. Starr, National Treasurer of the Cherokee Nation, the sums set opposite our names respectively, in full of our shares in the per capita distribution authorized by an Act of the National Council, dated ___MAY 3 1894___ 1894.

#	Names of Head, and Members of Families	Amount	To Whom Paid	Witness to Payment	Remarks
1116	" Susie				
1117	Chuie Joe				
1118	Glory Wyly	1062.80	Peter Glory	L B Bell	W&B consent
1119	Goodmoney Rider				Wyly
1120	" Leecy	531.40 order	Percy Wyle	J.C. Starr	Check on order
1121	George Grant				
1122	" Jennie	order			
1123	" Oce				
1124	" Martha	1062.80	Geo Grant	L B Bell	
1125	Galcatcher Charlie				
1126	" Becky				
1127	" Frank				
1128	" Nancy				
1129	" Lallie				
1130	Wood Peckey				mother of Chas Galcatcher
1131	Galcather[sic] Snowmaker				
1132	Budding Jack	2125.60	Becky Galcatcher	L B Bell	Orphan
1133	George				
1134	" Katy	531.40	J.F. McClellan	J.C. Starr	J.F. McClellan Check on order
1135	George Parrell	265.70 order	J.F. McClellan	J.C. Starr	Check on order J.F. McClellan
1136	Glenn Annie				
1137	" Mattie				
1138	" Etta	797.10	Annie Glenn	L B Bell	
1139	Graham W^m	order			S M
1140	" Blueford	531.40	Simpson Miller	L B Bell	
1141	Gourd Dan R				
1142	" Lulu R	531.50	D R Gourd	L B Bell	

Starr Roll 1894

We, the undersigned citizens of the Cherokee Nation, by right of Cherokee blood, do hereby acknowledge to have received of E. E. Starr, National Treasurer of the Cherokee Nation, the sums set opposite our names respectively, in full of our shares in the per capita distribution authorized by an Act of the National Council, dated ___MAY 3 1894___ 1894.

Names of Head, and Members of Families	Amount	To Whom Paid	Witness to Payment	Remarks
1143 Garrison Mollie				
1144 " Nannie P				
1145 " Mollie V	797.10	L P Garrison	L B Bell	
1146 Goddard James				
1147 " Neva A				
1148 " Henry M				
1149 " James W	1062.80	Phoeba Goddard	L B Bell	
1150 Giboney Mitty A				Geo. Giboney father of these children
1151 " Ida L	531.40	Geo Giboney	L B Bell	
1152 Grass Alice G				FM Crowell
1153 Cowan Felix Jr	531.40	F.M. Crowell FM Crowell	J.C. Starr	Check on order
1154 Guess Martha	order			F.M. Crowell
1155 Miller Dora	531.40	F.M. Crowell	J.C. Starr	Check on order Minors
1156 Green Ralph S				
1157 " Evelyn V	531.40	G.W. Green	L B Bell	Father
1158 Grasshopper Jack	265.70	Jack Grasshopper	L B Bell	
1159 Gossett Demerias				
1160 " Geo.				
1161 " Arthur				
1162 " Steolin				
1163 " James	1328.50	J M Gossett	L B Bell	
1164 Guess Nelson				FM Crowell
1165 " Albert	order			
1166 " Liza	797.10	F.M. Crowell	J.C. Starr	Check on order
1167 Gray Susie	265.70	Susie Gray	L B Bell	
1168 Garbarino[sic] Mary E	265.70	Sarah Goberino	L B Bell	
1169 Garbarino Martha	265.70	Martha Goberino	L B Bell	

Starr Roll 1894

We, the undersigned citizens of the Cherokee Nation, by right of Cherokee blood, do hereby acknowledge to have received of E. E. Starr, National Treasurer of the Cherokee Nation, the sums set opposite our names respectively, in full of our shares in the per capita distribution authorized by an Act of the National Council, dated ___MAY 3 1894___ 1894.

Names of Head, and Members of Families	Amount	To Whom Paid	Witness to Payment	Remarks
1170 Garbarino Josephine	265.70	Josephine Goberino	L B Bell	
1171 Gunter Nancy A	265.70	C D Gunter	L B Bell	
1172 " Nancy	265.70	J S Alfrey	L B Bell	
1173 Gunter Calle D	265.70	C D Gunter	L B Bell	
1174 Gunter Sammie	265.70	Sammie Gunter ~~L B Bell~~	L B Bell	
1175 Guess Dave				
1176 " Nancy				
1177 " Sequoyah				
1178 " Polly	1062.80	Nancy Guess	L B Bell	
1179 Gibson John H				
1180 " Arrie T				
1181 " Quinton				
1182 " Mattie				
1183 " Mary				
1184 " Jennie	1594.20	John H Gibson	L B Bell	
1185 Galouch Nick				
1186 " Ailsie				
1187 " Nancy				
1188 " Lucy				
1189 " Jesse	1328.50	Ailsey Galouch	L B Bell	
1190 Grazier Martha				
1191 " Homer				
1192 " Elmer				
1193 " Luther	1062.80	M L Grazier	L B Bell	
1194 Gentry Maggie	265.70	R R Taylor	L B Bell	on order
1195 Gillum Ella	order			W W Miller
1196 " Myrtle	531.40	Ella Gillum	L B Bell	order of WW Miller

Starr Roll 1894

We, the undersigned citizens of the Cherokee Nation, by right of Cherokee blood, do hereby acknowledge to have received of E. E. Starr, National Treasurer of the Cherokee Nation, the sums set opposite our names respectively, in full of our shares in the per capita distribution authorized by an Act of the National Council, dated ___MAY 3 1894___ 1894.

	Names of Head, and Members of Families	Amount	To Whom Paid	Witness to Payment	Remarks
1197	Gooden[sic] Dock				
1198	" Betsy				
1199	" Lula				
1200	" Dave	1062.80	Betsy Gooding	L B Bell	
1201	Ghormley Ewing				
1202	" Ida				
1203	" Stella				
1204	" Carrie				
1205	" Bulah M	1328.50	E C Ghormley	L B Bell	
1206	Gray Jo Anna				
1207	" W^m	531.40	Joanna Gray	L B Bell	
1208	Hider Andy				
1209	" Polly				
1210	" Josiah	797.10	Percy Wyly	L B Bell	
1211	Hider Joe	265.70	Percy Wyly	L B Bell	
1212	Hogshooter Y Beaver	265.70	Y B Hogshooter	L B Bell	
1213	Hasten Emma				
1214	" Rosa				
1215	" Lydia	797.10	John Haston[sic]	L B Bell	
1216	Holland Josie				
1217	" Gordan S	531.40	Jim Holland	L B Bell	
1218	Handle Willie				F.M. Crowell
1219	" Lizzy				
1220	" Tom				
1221	" Dempson	order			
1222	" Rob Ross				
1223	" Bushyhead	1594.20	Lizzy Handle	L B Bell	
1224	Heldabrand John	order			G M Ewing
1225	" Anna				

Starr Roll 1894

We, the undersigned citizens of the Cherokee Nation, by right of Cherokee blood, do hereby acknowledge to have received of E. E. Starr, National Treasurer of the Cherokee Nation, the sums set opposite our names respectively, in full of our shares in the per capita distribution authorized by an Act of the National Council, dated ___MAY 3 1894___ 1894.

	Names of Head, and Members of Families	Amount	To Whom Paid	Witness to Payment	Remarks
1226	" Callie	797.10	John Heldebrand by Dr Crowell	L B Bell	
1227	Hider Jack	265.70	Andy Hyder	Henry Eiffert	Nov 12/94
1228	Halfbreed Webster	265.70	Webster Halfbreed	L B Bell	
1229	Harlin Oce				
1230	" Mary				
1231	" Iona				
1232	" Ruth				
1233	" Fannie				
1234	" Ada				
1235	" Mary	*order*			
1236	" Jesse				
1237	" Callie				
1238	" Charles	2657.00	Oce Harlin	J.C. Starr	
1239	Harlin John	265.70	Oce Harlin	J.C. Starr	
1240	Harlin Jas. E.				
1241	" Nancy A				
1242	" Lotty B				
1243	" Alniso V				
1244	" Sally K				
1245	" Jarett B	1594.20	Jas E Harlin	L B Bell	
1246	Harlin Ridge H	265.70	Jas E Harlin D2776	L B Bell	
1247	Harlin Ellis	265.70	Jas E Harlin	L B Bell	
1248	Hampton Elizabeth				
1249	" Mattie				
1250	" Non				
1251	" Pearl				
1252	" Mary				
1253	" Burton				
1254	" Gracie	1859.90	Elizabeth Hampton	L B Bell	

Starr Roll 1894

We, the undersigned citizens of the Cherokee Nation, by right of Cherokee blood, do hereby acknowledge to have received of E. E. Starr, National Treasurer of the Cherokee Nation, the sums set opposite our names respectively, in full of our shares in the per capita distribution authorized by an Act of the National Council, dated ___MAY 3 1894___ 1894.

Names of Head, and Members of Families	Amount	To Whom Paid	Witness to Payment	Remarks
1255 Hampton Geo	265.70	Elizabeth Hampton	L B Bell	
1256 Hardy Mollie				
1257 " John D				
1258 " Dudly R				
1259 " May				
1260 " Henry				
1261 " Mary	1594.20	J T Hardy	L B Bell	
1262 Hastings Lonisa	265.70	Lonisa Hastings	L B Bell	
1263 Hastings John R	265.70	Lonisa Hastings	L B Bell	*on order*
1264 Hatfield Nannie				
1265 " Winnie	531.40	J.S. Fields	L B Bell	
1266 Horsley Martha	265.70	Martha Horsly	L B Bell	
1267 Hill Eliza	265.70	Monna Daniel	L B Bell	
1268 " Minta	265.70	Minta Hill	L B Bell	
1269 Hill Oliver	265.70	Monna Daniel	L B Bell	
1270 Hill Raleigh	265.70	Monna Daniel	L B Bell	
1271 Howerton Elizabeth				
1272 " Ida M.				
1273 " Josie				
1274 " Dedd				
1275 " Levea				
1276 " Sara	1594.20	G W Howerton	L B Bell	
1277 Hiser Martha				
1278 " Lillie				
1279 " Mavery				
1280 " Lucy				
1281 " Dannie				
1282 " Oke				

Starr Roll 1894

We, the undersigned citizens of the Cherokee Nation, by right of Cherokee blood, do hereby acknowledge to have received of E. E. Starr, National Treasurer of the Cherokee Nation, the sums set opposite our names respectively, in full of our shares in the per capita distribution authorized by an Act of the National Council, dated ___MAY 3 1894___ 1894.

#	Names of Head, and Members of Families	Amount	To Whom Paid	Witness to Payment	Remarks
1283	" James				
1284	" Hugh				
1285	" Ollie	2391.30	Jacob M Hiser	L B Bell	
1286	Horsefly Watt	order 265.70	Percy Wyly	Henry Eiffert	Wyly Ck
1287	Horsefly John	order 265.70	Percy Wyly	Henry Eiffert	Wyly Ck
1288	Howard Emely C	265.70	Frank Howard	L B Bell	F.M. Crowell
1289	" Frank	265.70	Frank S Howard Jr	L B Bell	
1290	" Chanasah	265.70	Frank Howard	L B Bell	
1291	Howard Percy P	order 265.70	FM Crowell	Henry Eiffert	check Crowell
1292	Harlin Edgar			L B Bell	
1293	" Claude	531.40	Mary Harlin		
1294	Hearod Wm				
1295	" Chas				
1296	" Beula				
1297	" Jesse	1062.80	W M McCulloch	Henry Eiffert	Ck
1298	Herod Joseph	265.70	Joseph Herod	L B Bell	
1299	Harem L.B.	265.70	L B Harem	L B Bell	
1300	Hudson Sarah	265.70	Sarah Hudson	L B Bell	
1301	Hudson Sylbanus				F.M. Crowell
1302	" Mamie Z.				
1303	" Etta M	797.10	F.M. Conner	G W Benge	
1304	Harlin Samuel				
1305	" Bessie M.	531.40	Sam Harlin	L B Bell	
1306	Herod Belle	265.70	Belle Herod	L B Bell	

Starr Roll 1894

We, the undersigned citizens of the Cherokee Nation, by right of Cherokee blood, do hereby acknowledge to have received of E. E. Starr, National Treasurer of the Cherokee Nation, the sums set opposite our names respectively, in full of our shares in the per capita distribution authorized by an Act of the National Council, dated ____MAY 3 1894____ 1894.

Names of Head, and Members of Families	Amount	To Whom Paid	Witness to Payment	Remarks
1307 Herod Elzena	265.70	Elzena Herod	L B Bell	
1308 Harlin Albert				
1309 " Matilda J	531.40	J.C. Starr	L B Bell	
1310 Howell Eliza				
1311 " Martha			L B Bell	
1312 " Minnie	797.10	Wm Howell		
1313 Hickox Henry	~~265.70~~ order	FM Crowell	Henry Eiffert	Crowell
1314 Hollis Elzorah				
1315 " Effie E	531.40	Isacah Hollis	L B Bell	
1316 Hallum Mary				
1317 " Ora O.	531.40	Mary Hallum	L B Bell	
1318 Henderson James				mother &
1319 " Nellie	531.40	Susie B Henderson	L B Bell	wife - white
1320 Henderson Susie	265.70	Susie Henderson	L B Bell	
1321 Hawk Benjamin	~~265.70~~ order	FM Crowell	Henry Eiffert	F.M. Crowell
1322 Hill Rebecca				
1323 " Bessie				
1324 " Annie				
1325 " Isa	1328.50			
1326 " Henry W.	~~1062.80~~	H S Hill	L B Bell	
1327 Hawk Noah	~~265.70~~ order	F.M. Crowell	Henry Eiffert	Check Crowell
1328 Hudson James				
1329 " Stella E.	order			FM Conner
1330 " Ruphus D.	797.10	F M Crowell	Henry Eiffert	
1331 Hilderbrand Sam	~~265.70~~ order	L B Bell	3362 Henry Eiffert	check

318

Starr Roll 1894

We, the undersigned citizens of the Cherokee Nation, by right of Cherokee blood, do hereby acknowledge to have received of E. E. Starr, National Treasurer of the Cherokee Nation, the sums set opposite our names respectively, in full of our shares in the per capita distribution authorized by an Act of the National Council, dated ___MAY 3 1894___ 1894.

#	Names of Head, and Members of Families	Amount	To Whom Paid	Witness to Payment	Remarks
1332	Hilderbrand Chas	265.70 (8967)	Charles Hilderbrand	L B Bell	
1333	Hawkins George				
1334	" Robt	531.40	Jasper Hawkins	L B Bell	
1335	Hilderbrand Elijah				FM Crowell
1336	" Nan	order			
1337	" Jim	797.10	Elijah Hilderbrand	J.C. Starr	
1338	Hill John H				
1339	" Lou	531.40	Monna Daniel	L B Bell	
1340	Henderson Wᵐ P				
1341	" Bessie				
1342	Moore Elejah				Adopted children of Wᵐ P Henderson
1343	" John				
1344	" Lee	1328.50	WP Henderson	L B Bell	
1345	Houdeshell[sic] Wᵐ				
1346	" Wᵐ H	531.40	William Howdeshell	L B Bell	
1347	Henson Jack				Dead
1348	" Cherokee	43			
1349	" Bessie	43			
1350	" George	1062.80	Jack Henson	L B Bell	Dead
1351	Hopkins Johnie				
1352	" Maude S				
1353	" Thos A	797.10	L W Hopkins	L B Bell	
1354	Hairl[sic] Maude	265.70 (order)	J S Thomason	Henry Eiffert	CK
1355	Hitchcock Irenus	265.70	Irenus Hitchcock	L B Bell	
1356	Hall Jesse	265.70 (order)	LW Buffington	L B Bell	J S Thomason

Starr Roll 1894

We, the undersigned citizens of the Cherokee Nation, by right of Cherokee blood, do hereby acknowledge to have received of E. E. Starr, National Treasurer of the Cherokee Nation, the sums set opposite our names respectively, in full of our shares in the per capita distribution authorized by an Act of the National Council, dated ___MAY 3 1894___ 1894.

	Names of Head, and Members of Families	Amount	To Whom Paid	Witness to Payment	Remarks
1357	Horn W^m				
1358	" Liza J.				
1359	" Dora N				
1360	" Mary E				
1361	" Maggie				
1362	" Thomas				
1363	" Hooley	1859.90	Wm Horn	L B Bell	
1364	Harvey Victoria	order 265.70	J.T. Monna	L B Bell	
1365	Hawkins Ruth K				
1366	" Rhoda L				
1367	" Roswell D				
1368	" Charles G.	1062.80	M.G. Hawkins	L B Bell	
1369	Haynes Sarah				
1370	" Willie				
1371	" Oliver				
1372	" Winbell				
1373	" Thos E	1328.50	Sarah Haynes	L B Bell	
1374	Harry Sarah				
1375	" Walter				
1376	" Ellie				
1377	" Ollie				
1378	" Jake				
1379	" Lem	1594.20	Sarah Harry	L B Bell	
1380	Harry Lee	265.70	Percy Wyly	Henry Eiffert	
1381	Harry Elsie	265.70	Ed Washbrn[sic]	L B Bell	
1382	Hill Charley				
1383	" Mattie				
1384	" Johnie				
1385	" Awee	1062.80	Charley Hill	L B Bell	
1386	Hill Acie	order 265.70	Percy Wyly	Henry Eiffert	P.W.

320

Starr Roll 1894

We, the undersigned citizens of the Cherokee Nation, by right of Cherokee blood, do hereby acknowledge to have received of E. E. Starr, National Treasurer of the Cherokee Nation, the sums set opposite our names respectively, in full of our shares in the per capita distribution authorized by an Act of the National Council, dated ___MAY 3 1894___ 1894.

Names of Head, and Members of Families	Amount	To Whom Paid	Witness to Payment	Remarks
1387 Hummingbird Nancy	265.70	9957 Percy Wyly	Henry Eiffert	Ck order
1388 Hogshooter Shu-ta-kil	265.70	Hogshooter	L B Bell	79 yrs
1389 Hilderbrand Jas				F.M. Crowell
1390 " Ida	order			Consent of
1391 " Susan	797.10	Jas Hilderbrand	L B Bell	F.M. Crowell
1392 Harder Lizzie	order			Crowell
1393 " Willard	531.40	F M Crowell	L B Bell	
1394 Harris Mattie				
1395 " Richard L.				
1396 " Willie C.	797.10	Mattie Harris	L B Bell	
1397 Hawkins Lena				
1398 " Walter H				
1399 " Ralph				
1400 " Maude				
1401 " Ollie				
1402 " Edith	1594.20	Lena Hawkins	L B Bell	
1403 Homer Sol J	265.70	Mary Homer	L B Bell	
1404 Harlin David L.	order			Crowell
1405 " Lewis S				
1406 " Delbert				
1407 " Jas R.	contest			
1408 " Lillie M	1328.50	F.M. Crowell	J.C. Starr	Check on order
1409 Horseskin John	order 265.70	Percy Wyly	Henry Eiffert	P Wyly
1410 Inlow Henry				
1411 Grant Donle				
1412 " Geo	797.10	Henry Inlow	L B Bell	
1413 Inlow Thos				G.W.S.
1414 " Margarett	order			

Starr Roll 1894

We, the undersigned citizens of the Cherokee Nation, by right of Cherokee blood, do hereby acknowledge to have received of E. E. Starr, National Treasurer of the Cherokee Nation, the sums set opposite our names respectively, in full of our shares in the per capita distribution authorized by an Act of the National Council, dated ___MAY 3 1894___ 1894.

	Names of Head, and Members of Families	Amount	To Whom Paid	Witness to Payment	Remarks
1415	" Elmirah				
1416	" Susan	1062.80	G.W. Smith	G.W. Benge	Check
1417	Isabell Georgia A	DEAD.			
1418	" Bula C				
1419	" Morris	3717			
1420	" Jennie L.				
1421	" Olli M				
1422	" Josephine	1594.20	Geo A. Isbell	L B Bell	
1423	Isabell Thomas J	265.70	Geo A Isbell	L B Bell	
1424	Jones Josiah				
[sic]	" Nellie				
1425	" Jim				
1426	" Chick-a-lee-lee				order
1427	" Celia	1328.50	GW Smith	Henry Eiffert	Sept 15 1894
1428	James Silas	8920 order			Mills
1429	" Annie				
1430	" Mary ling	797.10	Mills and Washbourn	Henry Eiffert	Check
1431	Jordan Susie				
1432	" Ethel				
1433	" Lester	797.10	C F Jourdan	L B Bell	
1434	Johnson Sam				
1435	" Katy				
1436	" Maudie	797.10	Percy Wyly	Henry Eiffert	
1437	James Sabrina				
1438	" John				
1439	" Rex				
1440	" Ray B				
1441	" Ethel N	1328.50	Saml James	L B Bell	

Starr Roll 1894

We, the undersigned citizens of the Cherokee Nation, by right of Cherokee blood, do hereby acknowledge to have received of E. E. Starr, National Treasurer of the Cherokee Nation, the sums set opposite our names respectively, in full of our shares in the per capita distribution authorized by an Act of the National Council, dated ___MAY 3 1894___ 1894.

Names of Head, and Members of Families	Amount	To Whom Paid	Witness to Payment	Remarks
1442 Johnson Liza				
1443 " John W				
1444 " Emma				
1445 " Oscar				
1446 " Minnier	1328.50	E Johnson	J.C. Starr	
1447 James Peter	265.70	L W Buffington	L B Bell	Mills

****

(The information below was placed on the page containing #1447 Peter James' entry. The letters were originally handwritten and are typed as given.)

Vinita, I.T., June 23- 1894

on[sic] E. E. Starr
 Treasury C.N.
Dear Sir
 I hear by enter protest against the payment of order for Strip money to J.S. Thomason or any one else but Mills Bros. of Spavinaw as they are the only ones I have given an order to to draw and receipt for per capita money.

 Peter James

Attest (Illegible) Gore
 Jesse Cochran
 J.T. Henry

****

Vinita I.T.
May 29th 93

To the Treasure of the Cherokee Nation please pay to L.W. Buffington all of my money (one share) due me on account of the sale of the strip an in pursuance of the act of the National Council dated May 3" 94

Starr Roll 1894

We, the undersigned citizens of the Cherokee Nation, by right of Cherokee blood, do hereby acknowledge to have received of E. E. Starr, National Treasurer of the Cherokee Nation, the sums set opposite our names respectively, in full of our shares in the per capita distribution authorized by an Act of the National Council, dated ___MAY 3 1894___ 1894.

Names of Head, and Members of Families	Amount	To Whom Paid	Witness to Payment	Remarks
Witness JS Thomason LC Couch	1447	Peter James	his x mark	

****

Spavinaw IND. TER., June 19 1894

To THE
    HON. E. E. STARR, Treasurer Cherokee Nation:--
SIR:
    I **Peter James** citizen of the Cherokee Nation by blood and resident of **Delaware** district, for myself and family, consisting of my wife .... a Cherokee by blood and **Residence** .... children, do hereby authorize, appoint and empower and by these presents do constitute and appoint **Mills & Washborne** my true and lawful attorneys without revocation, and revoking all former power of attorney whatever, to collect, receive and receipt for the per capita distribution due myself and family, as provided in an act of the National Council, approved May 3rd, 1894, for the reason that my attendance at home is very necessary in order that I may protect and harvest my crop heretofore planted which is in great danger of waste in case I am not present, besides the expense of remaining at the place of payment until I can procure my money. This I deem of good and sufficient cause as contemplated in Section 6, of an Act approved May 3rd, 1894:

    ATTEST: SIGNED:
        Lee Mills   Peter James
        JS Henry

Subscribed to and sworn to before me, this .... day of .... 1894.

                                                .... Notary Public

                              June 20   1894

        RECEIVED OF   **Mills & Washborne**   265 $^{70}/_{100}$ Dollars, in full payment the per capita distribution for myself, wife and .... children, as per the foregoing Power of Attorney.

Starr Roll 1894

We, the undersigned citizens of the Cherokee Nation, by right of Cherokee blood, do hereby acknowledge to have received of E. E. Starr, National Treasurer of the Cherokee Nation, the sums set opposite our names respectively, in full of our shares in the per capita distribution authorized by an Act of the National Council, dated ___MAY 3 1894___ 1894.

Names of Head, and Members of Families	Amount	To Whom Paid	Witness to Payment	Remarks
IN THE PRESENCE OF			*Peter James*	
Lee Mills				
HC Cochran				
************				
1448 James Lorenzo				
1449 " Florrie	531.40	Ada James	L B Bell	
1450 James Mary E				
1451 " Ervin				
1452 " Houston				
1453 " Price				
1454 " Eva	1328.50	*(Illegible)* James	L B Bell	
1455 Jones Thos.				*F.M. Crowell*
1456 " Hattie				
1457 " Betsy E	*order*			
1458 " James H				
1459 " Joel				
1460 " Arvilla	1594.20	F.M. Crowell	J.C. Starr	*Check on order*
1461 Jones Leroy	~~265.70~~	F.M. Crowell	J.C. Starr	~~F.M. Crowell~~ *Check on order*
1462 Jones John				
1463 " Frank	*order*		*order to Conner*	F.M. ~~check~~ *Crowell*
1464 " Virginia	797.10	F.M. Crowell	Henry Eiffert	
1465 Jones W^m H				*G W Green*
1466 " Minnie E				
1467 " Martha A	797.10	GW Green	JC Starr	*Check on order*
1468 Jones Jas J.	265.70	Jas E ~~Whitman~~ *Julian*	L B Bell	*Minor*
1469 James Joseph	~~order~~70	Mills&Washborne	J.C. Starr	*Check on order*
1470 James Homer	265.70	W C James	L B Bell	

Starr Roll 1894

We, the undersigned citizens of the Cherokee Nation, by right of Cherokee blood, do hereby acknowledge to have received of E. E. Starr, National Treasurer of the Cherokee Nation, the sums set opposite our names respectively, in full of our shares in the per capita distribution authorized by an Act of the National Council, dated ___MAY 3 1894___ 1894.

	Names of Head, and Members of Families	Amount	To Whom Paid	Witness to Payment	Remarks
1471	Jordan Delia P				
1472	" Caroline				
1473	" James				
1474	" Madison				
1475	" John D				
1476	" Watie B				
1477	" Joseph L.	1859.90	DP Jourdan	L B Bell	
1478	James Tenessee[sic] E				
1479	" Clara D				
1480	" Albert B				
1481	" Lula B				
1482	" Cornelia				
1483	" Jesse L				
1484	" Claud F	1859.90	Solon James	L B Bell	
1485	James Calvin G	~~265~~.70	FM Crowell	Henry Eiffert	Crowell
1486	Jones Joanna				
1487	" Emma				
1488	" Myrtle				
1489	" James				
1490	Hammers Hannah				
1491	" Levi	1594.20	John Jones	L B Bell	
1492	Johnson Martha E	265.70	M E Johnson	L B Bell	
1493	Johnson Emma				GW Green
1494	" Thos.	1331.40 per order	G.W. Green	J.C. Starr	Check on order
1495	James Mattie				
1496	" Myrtle				
1497	" Zula	155			
1498	" Lola				
1499	" Buna				
1500	" Leland				
1501	" Lousa				

Starr Roll 1894

We, the undersigned citizens of the Cherokee Nation, by right of Cherokee blood, do hereby acknowledge to have received of E. E. Starr, National Treasurer of the Cherokee Nation, the sums set opposite our names respectively, in full of our shares in the per capita distribution authorized by an Act of the National Council, dated ___MAY 3 1894___ 1894.

	Names of Head, and Members of Families	Amount	To Whom Paid	Witness to Payment	Remarks
1502	" Frank	2125.60	Marston James	L B Bell	
1503	Johnson Charlotte				
1504	" Johnie				
1505	" Harvey				
1506	" Lottie	1062.80	Charlotte Johnson	L B Bell	
1507	Jackson W^m				
1508	" Ocie				
1509	" Lizzie				
1510	" Jessie				
1511	" Roy	1328.50	Wm Jackson	L B Bell	
1512	Jackson Alender[sic]	265.70	Ellender Jackson	L B Bell	
1513	Jackson Tosh	265.70	Ellen Jackson [mother]	L B Bell	
1514	Jun Stoody Will				
1515	" Lydia				
1516	" Susie				
1517	" Keywood				
1518	" Jaylum				
1519	" Sarah				
1520	" Sultus ti				
1521	" Fencer				
1522	" Andy	2128.60	Will Junstoody	L B Bell	
1523	Kaiser Catren [Catherine]				
1524	" Melton				
1525	" Henry				
1526	" Mary				
1527	" Catherine				
1528	" W^m	1594.20	Jack Kaiser	L B Bell	
1529	Ketcher Johnson				
1530	" Alice				
1531	" Susie				
1532	" Lee	1062.50	Sarah Johnson	L B Bell	

Starr Roll 1894

We, the undersigned citizens of the Cherokee Nation, by right of Cherokee blood, do hereby acknowledge to have received of E. E. Starr, National Treasurer of the Cherokee Nation, the sums set opposite our names respectively, in full of our shares in the per capita distribution authorized by an Act of the National Council, dated ___MAY 3 1894___ 1894.

Names of Head, and Members of Families	Amount	To Whom Paid	Witness to Payment	Remarks
1533 Ketcher Ross	265.70	Ross Ketcher	L B Bell	
1534 Keen Nancy				
1535 " Willie A				
1536 " Albert F.				
1537 " Arnold P				
1538 " James H				
1539 " Cora S				
1540 " John R	1859.90	Andrew Keen	L B Bell	
1541 Ketcher Charley				
1542 " Sarah				
1543 " Sager				
1544 " Henry	1062.80	Charley Ketcher	L B Bell	
1545 Kingfisher Jim	*order*			*Wyly*
1546 " Lizzie				
1547 " Charley				
1548 " Nancy	1062.80	Percy Wyly	Henry Eiffert	*Check*
1549 Ketcher Levi	265.70	G.W Smith	L B Bell	*Check 68584 GWS 8.25.1894*
1550 Ketchum Cornelius	265.70	Percy Wyly	Henry Eiffert	
1551 Kenney Chas D				
1552 " Mary C	531.40	Joe D Yeargin	L B Bell	
1553 Kelley[sic] Cordelia				
1554 " Eva May	DEAD.			
1555 " Myrta R				
1556 " Wm H.	1062.80	Wm Kelly	L B Bell	
1557 Keefer Sally				
1558 " Lizabeth				
1559 " Emma				

Starr Roll 1894

We, the undersigned citizens of the Cherokee Nation, by right of Cherokee blood, do hereby acknowledge to have received of E. E. Starr, National Treasurer of the Cherokee Nation, the sums set opposite our names respectively, in full of our shares in the per capita distribution authorized by an Act of the National Council, dated ___MAY 3 1894___ 1894.

Names of Head, and Members of Families	Amount	To Whom Paid	Witness to Payment	Remarks
1560 Brock Walter				
1561 " Geo.				Sally Keefer
1562 Hawkins Viola				mother of
1563 " Myrtle				these children
1564 " Lundy	2125.60	Sally Keefer	L B Bell	
1565 Kelley Margarett				
1566 " Ernest				
1567 " Fanny N	797.10	Morgan Kelly	L B Bell	
1568 Kelley Susan E				
1569 " Gracie				
1570 " Gertrue				
1571 " Effie				
1572 " Minnie M	1328.50	John D Kelly	L B Bell	
1573 Knight Thos R				
1574 " Rachel J				
1575 " Thom. M				
1576 " Henry S				
1577 " Fannie M				Tm Knight guardian
1578 Sixkiller Carrie B.	1594.20	Thos R Knight	L B Bell	of this child
1579 Knight Josiah S	265.70	TR Knight	L B Bell	
1580 Knight Morris F	265.70	TR Knight	L B Bell	
1581 Kelley Lucy G	order			J.S. Thomason
1582 " Claud C	531.40	J.S. Thomason	Henry Eiffert	
1583 Kidd Abrildia	order			LB Bell
1584 " Nancy				
1585 " Garfield				
1586 " Monroe				
1587 " Margarett				
1588 " Ida	1594.20	L B Bell	L B Bell	
1589 Kidd Felix	265.70	L B Bell	L B Bell	LB Bell

Starr Roll 1894

We, the undersigned citizens of the Cherokee Nation, by right of Cherokee blood, do hereby acknowledge to have received of E. E. Starr, National Treasurer of the Cherokee Nation, the sums set opposite our names respectively, in full of our shares in the per capita distribution authorized by an Act of the National Council, dated ___MAY 3 1894___ 1894.

	Names of Head, and Members of Families	Amount	To Whom Paid	Witness to Payment	Remarks
1590	Knight Robt. D				
1591	" Hermon				
1592	" Robt F				
1593	" Grover C				
1594	" W^m D	1328.50	R D Knight	L B Bell	
1595	Kingfisher Will	order			
1596	" Jennie				
1597	" Mary				
1598	" Joe				
1599	" Knocking about	1328.50	Jennie Kingfisher	L B Bell	
1600	Kingfisher Watie				
1601	" Susan				
1602	" Wallie				
1603	" Wa-di-ah	1062.80	Webb Kingfisher	L B Bell	
1604	Keen John				
1605	" Ann	order			Wyly
1606	" Soggy	797.10	John Keen	L B Bell	
1607	Krebs[sic] Theresa				
1608	" Edna				
1609	" Richard	797.10	Theresa Krebbs	L B Bell	
1610	Kell Chas L.	265.70	Chas L Kell	L B Bell	
1611	Kell Liza	265.70	Eliza Kell	L B Bell	
1612	Kell Mary	265.70	JW Gilbreath	Henry Eiffert	Alice Kell is the mo of this child
1613	Lacy James				
1614	" Lizzie				
1615	" Sally				
1616	" Scott				
1617	" Sam				
1618	" Walker				
1619	" Louisa				

Starr Roll 1894

We, the undersigned citizens of the Cherokee Nation, by right of Cherokee blood, do hereby acknowledge to have received of E. E. Starr, National Treasurer of the Cherokee Nation, the sums set opposite our names respectively, in full of our shares in the per capita distribution authorized by an Act of the National Council, dated ___MAY 3 1894___ 1894.

	Names of Head, and Members of Families	Amount	To Whom Paid	Witness to Payment	Remarks
1620	" Wallie				
1621	" Annie	2391.30	James Lacy	L B Bell	
1622	Lucas John	265.70	W.J. Gilbreath	J.C. Starr	Check on order
1623	Leaf Lydia				
1624	" Josiah *	order ~~withdrawn~~ order			Percy Wyly in Ft. Smith jail
1625	" Henry				
1626	" Fannie	1062.80	Lydia Leaf	L B Bell	
1627	Lee Laura				
1628	" Everett	531.40	L. Lee	L B Bell	
1629	Lane Rachel				
1630	" Alfred				
1631	" Delora	797.10	Rachel Lee	L B Bell	
1632	Lincoln Ada				
1633	" Florence K	531.40 (285)	Stephen Lincoln	L B Bell	
1634	Ladd Jenetta				
1635	" Percy H	531.40	Saml *(Illegible)*	L B Bell	on order
1636	Lamar Alex				* Minors
1637	" Mattie	531.40	James R ~~Lamar~~ Guardian	L B Bell	
1638	Lamar Jas R	265.70	James R Lamar	L B Bell	
1639	Lamar Thos B.F.				
1640	" Mariah				
1641	" Mable				
1642	" Jessie				
1643	" Lucas				
1644	" Maudie				
1645	" Nettie	1859.90	Thos BF Lamar	L B Bell	
1646	Lamar Chas E	265.70 order	F M Crowell	Henry Eiffert	F M ~~Chesitt~~ Crowell

Starr Roll 1894

We, the undersigned citizens of the Cherokee Nation, by right of Cherokee blood, do hereby acknowledge to have received of E. E. Starr, National Treasurer of the Cherokee Nation, the sums set opposite our names respectively, in full of our shares in the per capita distribution authorized by an Act of the National Council, dated ___MAY 3 1894___ 1894.

	Names of Head, and Members of Families	Amount	To Whom Paid	Witness to Payment	Remarks
1647	Lamar Ewing				F M Crowell
1648	" Annie E				
1649	" Frank	order			
1650	" Vande				
1651	" Maude				
1652	" Jas Riley	1594.20	F M Crowell	Henry Eiffert	Check
1653	Lamar Polly				
1654	" Jas L Jr	order 4125			Freeman
1655	" Edward	7503			
1656	" Susan	1062.80 3771	DW Freeman	Henry Eiffert	Check
1657	Lamar Biddie	265.70 order	DW Freeman	Henry Eiffert	Check Freeman
1658	Lamar Sally	265.70 order	DW Freeman	Henry Eiffert	Freeman *Check
1659	Large Ocie Q				
1660	" Mary V	531.40 order	J S Thomason	Henry Eiffert	
1661	Ladd Mary J				
1662	" Burris				
1663	" Maude				
1664	" Burnett				
1665	" Henry				
1666	" James				
1667	" Tula				
1668	" Clara F.	2125.60	J.B. Ladd	J.C. Starr	
1669	Lowe Sinnate[sic]	D2777			
1670	" Mamie				
1671	" Willie				
1672	" Flossy				
1673	" Ralph	1328.50	Sinnett W Lowe	L B Bell	
1674	Lowe James				
1675	" May				
1676	" Zelma				
1677	" Robert				

Starr Roll 1894

We, the undersigned citizens of the Cherokee Nation, by right of Cherokee blood, do hereby acknowledge to have received of E. E. Starr, National Treasurer of the Cherokee Nation, the sums set opposite our names respectively, in full of our shares in the per capita distribution authorized by an Act of the National Council, dated ___MAY 3 1894___ 1894.

	Names of Head, and Members of Families	Amount	To Whom Paid	Witness to Payment	Remarks
1678	" Rosa	1328.50	Jas Lowe	L B Bell	
1679	Lundy Josie				
1680	" Louie				
1681	" Rosa	797.10	Josie Lundy	L B Bell	
1682	Landrum Jonathon	265.70	H T Lawson	L.B. Bell	
1683	Landrum Hiram T.				
1684	" Arkansas				
1685	" Jas K	797.10	H T Landrum	L B Bell	
1686	Landrum Elizabeth				
1687	" Ada	531.40	Elizabeth Landrum	L B Bell	
1688	Landrum Cicero	265.70	Cicero Landrum	L B Bell	
1689	Landrum Chas.	265.70	Chas Landrum	L B Bell	
1690	Landrum John B.	order			Crowell
1691	" Charlotte				
1692	" Perry	order			
1693	" Lonzo				
1694	" Hiram				
1695	" Sally				
1696	" Mandy	1859.90	F M Crowell	Henry Eiffert	Check
1697	Lynch Syntha[sic]				
1698	" Andrew				
1699	" Mary				
1700	" Clark E				
1701	" Ruth E				
1702	" Emma O	1594.90	Cynthia Lynch	L B Bell	
1703	Lynch Eddie B	265.70	E B Lynch	L B Bell	
1704	Lynch Bert W	265.70	Bert W Lynch	L B Bell	

Starr Roll 1894

We, the undersigned citizens of the Cherokee Nation, by right of Cherokee blood, do hereby acknowledge to have received of E. E. Starr, National Treasurer of the Cherokee Nation, the sums set opposite our names respectively, in full of our shares in the per capita distribution authorized by an Act of the National Council, dated ___MAY 3 1894___ 1894.

	Names of Head, and Members of Families	Amount	To Whom Paid	Witness to Payment	Remarks
1705	Lynch Ruth	D487			
1706	" Lucian	D487			
1707	" Alex	D487			
1708	" John	D487			
1709	" Syntha	D487			
1710	" Claude	D487			J S T
1711	" Rose M	1859.90	J S Thomason	Henry Eiffert	Check
1712	Landrum Nellie	265.70	Nellie Landrum	L B Bell	
1713	Landrum Johnson				
1714	" Katy				
1715	" Nellie J.				
1716	" Clifton L	1062.80	Johnson Landrum	L B Bell	
1717	Large Frank				
1718	" Claude				
1719	" Bert	797.10	Fanny Large	L B Bell	
1720	Large Wm L.				
1721	" Sadie				
1722	" Effie	797.10	W.C. Large	L B Bell	
1723	Landrum Edward	265.70	Ed Landrum	L B Bell	
1724	Landrum Susie				
1725	Crutchfield Jimmie				These children living with Susie Landrum
1726	" Jo Alice	797.10	Susie Landrum	L B Bell	
1727	Landrum Ben S				
1728	" Sally				
1729	" Pansy				
1730	" Sareno M				
1731	" Lonie O.				
1732	" Margarette E				
1733	" Valerie	1859.90	B S Landrum	L B Bell	

Starr Roll 1894

We, the undersigned citizens of the Cherokee Nation, by right of Cherokee blood, do hereby acknowledge to have received of E. E. Starr, National Treasurer of the Cherokee Nation, the sums set opposite our names respectively, in full of our shares in the per capita distribution authorized by an Act of the National Council, dated ___MAY 3 1894___ 1894.

	Names of Head, and Members of Families	Amount	To Whom Paid	Witness to Payment	Remarks
1734	Leaf Dave				Percy Wyly
1735	" Dake	*order*			
1736	" Lizzie				
1737	" Felix				
1738	" Teacher				
1739	" Liza	1594.20	~~David~~ *Dake* Leaf	L B Bell	
1740	Landrum McLeod	265.70	McLeod Landrum	L B Bell	
1741	Landrum Samuel	265.70	Sam Landrum	L B Bell	
1742	Miller Martin				
1743	" David	531.40	Martin Miller	L B Bell	
1744	Mouse Deacon	*order*			Wyly
1745	" Sanannee				
1746	" Josie	797.10	Percy Wyly	Henry Eiffert	*Check*
1747	Mouse Jas				
1748	" Awaie				
1749	" Whip-poor-will				
1750	" Louie				
1751	" Akie				
1752	" John L				
1753	" Mattie	1859.90	Awaie Mouse	L B Bell	
1754	Mouse Lydia				
1755	" Beckie	531.40	Lydia Mouse	L B Bell	
1756	Mouse Nancy	265.70	Nancy Mouse	L B Bell	
1757	Mouse Beckie	265.70	Becky Mouse		
1758	" Sam M	265.70	Sam Mouse	L B Bell	
1759	Mouse Cornelius				
1760	" Darby				See Runabout Beaver
1761	Rider Sally	797.10	Dorcas Mouse	L B Bell	

Starr Roll 1894

We, the undersigned citizens of the Cherokee Nation, by right of Cherokee blood, do hereby acknowledge to have received of E. E. Starr, National Treasurer of the Cherokee Nation, the sums set opposite our names respectively, in full of our shares in the per capita distribution authorized by an Act of the National Council, dated ___MAY 3 1894___ 1894.

	Names of Head, and Members of Families	Amount	To Whom Paid	Witness to Payment	Remarks
1762	Martin John				
1763	" Lucinda	531.40	John Martin	L B Bell	
1764	" Mary				
1765	" Abraham				
1766	Lucas Newraney N	797.10	John Martin	L B Bell	Living with John Martin
1767	Martin W^m	265.70	John Martin	L B Bell	
1768	Martin Andrew				
1769	" Myrtle				
1770	" Hassie				
1771	" Idus	1062.80	Andrew J Martin	L B Bell	
1772	McGhee Susie	265.70	D.E. Haven	J.C. Starr	Check on order
1773	Muskrat Awaie[sic]	265.70	Awie Muskrat	L B Bell	
1774	Mitchell Walker				
1775	" Mary				
1776	" Myrtle	797.10	D A McGhee	L B Bell	on order
1777	Muskrat Thompson				
1778	" Wanenah				Thompson Muskrat guardian of this child
1779	Catlin Phenia	797.10	Thompson Muskrat	L B Bell	
1780	Muskrat Coffee	265.70	Wm Ballard	L B Bell	order
1781	Melton Simpson				
1782	" Lizabeth				
1783	" Narcissa				
1784	" Geo				
1785	" Rosa Bell				
1786	" Mandy M				
1787	Murphy Mandy				Mrs Melton her mother
1788	Carroll Nora	75			Simpson Melton guardian of these children
1789	" Toddie				
1790	" May	2657.00	S F Melton R276	L B Bell	

Starr Roll 1894

We, the undersigned citizens of the Cherokee Nation, by right of Cherokee blood, do hereby acknowledge to have received of E. E. Starr, National Treasurer of the Cherokee Nation, the sums set opposite our names respectively, in full of our shares in the per capita distribution authorized by an Act of the National Council, dated _____MAY 3 1894_____ 1894.

#	Names of Head, and Members of Families	Amount	To Whom Paid	Witness to Payment	Remarks
1791	Melton Wm F.				for Crowell J.S. Blevins
1792	" Louisa	*order*			
1793	" Cora				
1794	" Clara				
1795	" Annie	1328.50	W.F Melton	L B Bell	
1796	Miller Mary				
1797	" Robt.				
1798	" Jesse				
1799	" Daisy				
1800	" Felix				
1801	" Emma				
1802	" Jimmie				
1803	" Willie	2125.60	Mary Miller	L B Bell	
1804	Muskrat Dan	265.70	Daniel Muskrat	L B Bell	
1805	Melton Mary A	265.70	Mary Melton	L B Bell	
1806	Muskrat Jeff	265.70	Jeff Muskrat	L B Bell	
1807	Mitchell Don	265.70	Don Mitchell	L B Bell	
1808	Mitchell Sally A	265.70	D M Mitchell	L B Bell	order
1809	Muskrat James	~~order~~			
1810	" Maudie				
1811	" Claude				
1812	" Jacob	1062.80	James Muskrat	L B Bell	
1813	Muskrat W^m	265.70	Wm Muskrat	L B Bell	by permis of his guardian
1814	Mayes Wm P.				
1815	" Anna H				
1816	" Maggie M				
1817	" Maude N				
1818	" Claude J				
1819	" Joel B				

Starr Roll 1894

We, the undersigned citizens of the Cherokee Nation, by right of Cherokee blood, do hereby acknowledge to have received of E. E. Starr, National Treasurer of the Cherokee Nation, the sums set opposite our names respectively, in full of our shares in the per capita distribution authorized by an Act of the National Council, dated _____ MAY 3 1894 _____ 1894.

	Names of Head, and Members of Families	Amount	To Whom Paid	Witness to Payment	Remarks
1820	" Lizzie B				
1821	" Ridge				
1822	" Mary H.				
1823	Davis Sarah	2657.00	WP Mayes	L B Bell	Wm Mayes guardian of this child
1824	McGhee Dave				
1825	" Rosa				
1826	" David A.				
1827	" Dennis B.				
1828	" Eliza J				
1829	" John R				
1830	" Elizabeth				
1831	" Ester				
1832	" Florence	2391.30	D A McGhee	L B Bell	
1833	Messer John H	265.70	John A Mener	L B Bell	
1834	Muskrat James				
1835	" Joe	order			D E Haven
1836	" Lee				
1837	" Clide	1062.80	G.W. Smith	J.C. Starr	pd check on order 68570 AUG 22 1894
1838	McGhee T.J.	order			Crowell
1839	" Viola				
1840	" Clero				
1841	" Staten				
1842	" Joe F				
1843	" Quilikee	1594.20	F M Crowell	Henry Eiffert	check
1844	McGhee T.J. Jr	order 265.70	D E Haven	Henry Eiffert	D.E. Haven check
1845	Mouse Hummingbird	265.70	Katy Mouse	L B Bell	
1846	Mouse Katy	265.70	Katy Mouse	L B Bell	
1847	Miligan[sic] Sophronia	265.70	Saphronia Milligan	L B Bell	

Starr Roll 1894

We, the undersigned citizens of the Cherokee Nation, by right of Cherokee blood, do hereby acknowledge to have received of E. E. Starr, National Treasurer of the Cherokee Nation, the sums set opposite our names respectively, in full of our shares in the per capita distribution authorized by an Act of the National Council, dated ___MAY 3 1894___ 1894.

#	Names of Head, and Members of Families	Amount	To Whom Paid	Witness to Payment	Remarks
1848	Muskrat Mack				claimed by
1849	" Rachel				GW Smith
1850	" Jimmie	797.10	G W Smith	Henry Eiffert	on order check
1851	McGhee Jas M	order			Crowell
1852	" Martha				
1853	" Robt J.	797.10	F.M. Crowell	Henry Eiffert	
1854	McGhee Francis	265.70	D A McGhee	L B Bell	Father
1855	McGhee Sam B.				
1856	" Bell				
1857	" Birtie O.	797.10	Sam B McGhee	L B Bell	
1858	Moore Mary M	265.70	N B Weir	L B Bell	order to NB Weir
1859	Miller Ruphus				D.W.F.
1860	" Lucinda				
1861	" John H				
1862	" Mary E	order			
1863	" Joshua D				
1864	" Sally A				
1865	" Elizabeth	1859.90	D W Freeman	Henry Eiffert	Ck
1866	McGannon Maude O	265.70	W.S. Guardian (Illegible)	L B Bell	Minor
1867	Myers[sic] George				
1868	" Frank				
1869	" Edith	797.10	Geo Meyers	L B Bell	
1870	McCullough W^m	265.70	W^m P McCullough	L B Bell	
1871	McCullough John W				
1872	" Rachel J.				
1873	" Milton J.	797.10	M H McCullough	L B Bell	
1874	McCullough Jim F	265.70	M H McCullough	L B Bell	

Starr Roll 1894

We, the undersigned citizens of the Cherokee Nation, by right of Cherokee blood, do hereby acknowledge to have received of E. E. Starr, National Treasurer of the Cherokee Nation, the sums set opposite our names respectively, in full of our shares in the per capita distribution authorized by an Act of the National Council, dated ____MAY 3 1894____ 1894.

	Names of Head, and Members of Families	Amount	To Whom Paid	Witness to Payment	Remarks
1875	McCullough Pete	265.70	M H McCullough	L B Bell	
1876	McCullough Rachel J				
1877	" Geo E				
1878	" Joe H				
1879	" Nanny M.				
1880	" Chas H	1359.50	M H McCullough	L B Bell	
1881	Melton Wyly J				
1882	" Ella				
1883	" Homer				
1884	" Mollie				
1885	" Lucian				
1886	" Lizzie	1594.20	F.M. Crowell	Henry Eiffert	check
1887	Morrison Annie E				
1888	" Elsa Lee				
1889	" Ruth	797.10	W.H. Morrison	L B Bell	
1890	Moore Bettie				GW Green
1891	" Willie				
1892	" Sammie A.				
1893	" Annie	order			
1894	" Josephine				
1895	" Johnie				
1896	" Mary				
1897	" Louis Jr	2125.60	GW Green	Henry Eiffert	Ck
1898	McLaughlin Wm				
1899	" Annie	531.40	Wm McLaughlin	L B Bell	
1900	Downing Mattie	265.70	J H Akin	L B Bell	
1901	Mayes Susie				
1902	" Wm				
1903	" Joseph				
1904	" Josie				
1905	" Girtie				
1906	" Laura	1594.20	Susie Mayes	J.C. Starr	

Starr Roll 1894

We, the undersigned citizens of the Cherokee Nation, by right of Cherokee blood, do hereby acknowledge to have received of E. E. Starr, National Treasurer of the Cherokee Nation, the sums set opposite our names respectively, in full of our shares in the per capita distribution authorized by an Act of the National Council, dated ___MAY 3 1894___ 1894.

	Names of Head, and Members of Families	Amount	To Whom Paid	Witness to Payment	Remarks
1907	Monroe Thos				
1908	" Chas				
1909	" Maggie				
1910	" Nola				
1911	" Birtha	1328.50	T J Monroe	L B Bell	
1912	Maloney Ida L				
1913	" Scott C.				
1914	" Nellie G.	797.10	W.S. Maloney	L.B. Bell	
1915	Mathis Jane				
1916	" Eddie B				
1917	" Eliza	797.10	Jane Mathis	L B Bell	
1918	Muskrat Joseph D				
1919	" Nina P				
1920	" Ira D.				
1921	Thompson Lizzie	1062.80	JD Muskrat	L B Bell	*Joe Muskrat her guardian*
1922	Moore Mary				
1923	" Nora				
1924	" Walter				
1925	" Carrie	1062.80	Chas F Moore	L B Bell	
1926	Martin W^m				J.S.T.
1927	" John		*order*		
1928	" Caroline				
1929	" W^m Jr				
1930	" Lizzie	1328.50	J.S. Thomason	Henry Eiffert	*check*
1931	Miller Andrew				
1932	" Ida				
1933	" Lucinda				
1934	" Mahany				
1935	" Lee				
1936	" Mamie				
1937	" Sarah				
1938	" W^m	2125.60	Martha Miller	L B Bell	

Starr Roll 1894

We, the undersigned citizens of the Cherokee Nation, by right of Cherokee blood, do hereby acknowledge to have received of E. E. Starr, National Treasurer of the Cherokee Nation, the sums set opposite our names respectively, in full of our shares in the per capita distribution authorized by an Act of the National Council, dated ____MAY 3 1894____ 1894.

	Names of Head, and Members of Families	Amount	To Whom Paid	Witness to Payment	Remarks
1939	Miller John M				
1940	" Lucinda				
1941	" W^m				
1942	" Sarah				
1943	" Louisa				
1944	" Cornelius				
1945	" John Jr.				
1946	" Joseph	2125.60	John M Miller	L B Bell	
1947	Miller Avrey	265.70	John M Miller	L B Bell	
1948	Monroe Beulah				
1949	" Muta				Minors
1950	" Grover				Check
1951	" Theadore	1062.80	Thos J *Guard. (Illegible)*	L B Bell	
1952	Miller Nancy				
1953	Carey Lucy J	531.40	Nancy Miller	L B Bell	Child of Nancy Mill_
1954	Martin Florence				
1955	" Lycurgus C	*order*			
1956	" Allen J				JST
1957	" Frazier	1062.80	Florence Martin	L B Bell	
1958	Miller Stand				
1959	" Melvina				
1960	" Chas M.				
1961	" Dona E.				
1962	" John E.				
1963	" Minerva C.	1594.20	Stand Miller	L B Bell	
1964	Morgan Henry	*order*			JST
1965	" Austin				Ck
1966	" Ella	797.10	J S Thomason	Henry Eiffert	
1967	Melton Chas				
1968	" Narcissa	531.40	Bettie Melton	L B Bell	

Starr Roll 1894

We, the undersigned citizens of the Cherokee Nation, by right of Cherokee blood, do hereby acknowledge to have received of E. E. Starr, National Treasurer of the Cherokee Nation, the sums set opposite our names respectively, in full of our shares in the per capita distribution authorized by an Act of the National Council, dated ___MAY 3 1894___ 1894.

	Names of Head, and Members of Families	Amount	To Whom Paid	Witness to Payment	Remarks
1969	Mode Sarah				
1970	" Carlotta				
1971	" John R				
1972	" Francis M				
1973	" Martha J				
1974	" Maude M				
1975	" William E.				
1976	" Henry D.	2125.60	Isaac Mode	L B Bell	
1977	Martin Chas	order 265.70	L W Buffington D-2476	Henry Eiffert	Ck LW Buffington
1978	Maddex[sic] Lucinda				ENR
1979	Winfield Flora	order			
1980	" Manuel	797.10	E N Ratcliff	Henry Eiffert	check
1981	McGinnis W^m T				
1982	" Elizabeth				
1983	" Chas C	797.10	W.F. McGinnis	L B Bell	
1984	Martin John W				
1985	" Chas N				
1986	" Cora E				
1987	" Mamie				
1988	" Harry				
1989	" Walter	1594.20	JW Martin	L B Bell	
1990	Maddox Hooley				
1991	" Lucian E				
1992	" Eliza Bell	797.10	L B Bell	L B Bell	
1993	Marrs Olivia				
1994	" Hellena				
1995	" Edgar				
1996	" John				
1997	" Garland				
1998	" Olivia Jr.				
1999	" W^m				
2000	" Barney				

Starr Roll 1894

We, the undersigned citizens of the Cherokee Nation, by right of Cherokee blood, do hereby acknowledge to have received of E. E. Starr, National Treasurer of the Cherokee Nation, the sums set opposite our names respectively, in full of our shares in the per capita distribution authorized by an Act of the National Council, dated ___MAY 3 1894___ 1894.

	Names of Head, and Members of Families	Amount	To Whom Paid	Witness to Payment	Remarks
2001	" M L	2391.30	D M Marrs	L B Bell	
2002	Mayes Susie	265.70	Susie T. Mayes	L B Bell	
2003	Martin Richard L				
2004	" Nancy E				
2005	" Lee				
2006	" Joe E.				
2007	" Laura	1594.20	R L Martin	L B Bell	
2008	Martin Richard Jr	265.70	R L Martin	L B Bell	
2009	Mantooth Mary				
2010	" Edna	531.40	Mary E Mantooth	L B Bell	
2011	McLauthlin[sic] Geo	265.70	Geo McLaughlin	L B Bell	
2012	McLaughlin Frank	265.70	William McLaughlin	L B Bell	
2013	Matoy Wm	265.70 *order*	R.E. Vermillion	G W Benge	*check* R.E.V.
2014	" Nancy	265.70 *order*	D.E. Haven	G W Benge	*check* D.E.H.
2015	Mike Susie				F.M. Crowell
2016	" Bob	*order*			
2017	" Anna	797.10	Susie Mike	L B Bell	on order to Crowell
2018	Merrell Corintha	265.70	Corintha Merrell	L B Bell	
2019	" Gurthrue[sic]	265.70	Gertrude Merrell	L B Bell	
2020	McDowell Joe				
2021	" Jessie	531.40	Joe McDowell	L B Bell	
2022	McLauthlin[sic] Jas.				
2023	" Rachel F				
2024	" Ida M				
2025	" Annie				
2026	" Louisa E				

Starr Roll 1894

We, the undersigned citizens of the Cherokee Nation, by right of Cherokee blood, do hereby acknowledge to have received of E. E. Starr, National Treasurer of the Cherokee Nation, the sums set opposite our names respectively, in full of our shares in the per capita distribution authorized by an Act of the National Council, dated ___MAY 3 1894___ 1894.

	Names of Head, and Members of Families	Amount	To Whom Paid	Witness to Payment	Remarks
2027	" Susie	1594.20	Jas McLaughlin	L B Bell	
2028	McAffrey[sic] Fannie				
2029	" John				
2030	" Mollie				
2031	" Albert				
2032	" Hugh				
2033	" Logan				
2034	" Napoleon				
2035	" Walter				
2036	" Benjamin	2391.30	Hugh McCaffry	L B Bell	
2037	McAffrey Andrew	265.70	Hugh McCaffry	L B Bell	
2038	McLaughlin Josh				
2039	" Carrie				
2040	" Ile				
2041	" Maggie	1062.80	Carrie McLaughlin	L B Bell	
2042	McLaughlin Frank				
2043	" Carrie E				
2044	" Geo F	1062.80	Robt Ironsides	Henry Eiffert	
2045	Miller Nannie				
2046	" Joscine	531.40	Nannie Miller	L B Bell	
2047	McFall Eugene				
2048	" Raleigh L				
2049	" Vinnie N				
2050	" Frankie				
2051	" Eddie	1328.50	Eugenia McFall	L B Bell	
2052	Nellis Nancy				
2053	Davis Phillip	531.40	Wm Nellis	L B Bell	Nancy Nellis Guardian of this child
2054	Nidiffer Geo				
2055	" Minnie				
2056	" Jessie G.	797.10	Geo Nidiffer	L B Bell	

Starr Roll 1894

We, the undersigned citizens of the Cherokee Nation, by right of Cherokee blood, do hereby acknowledge to have received of E. E. Starr, National Treasurer of the Cherokee Nation, the sums set opposite our names respectively, in full of our shares in the per capita distribution authorized by an Act of the National Council, dated ___MAY 3 1894___ 1894.

	Names of Head, and Members of Families	Amount	To Whom Paid	Witness to Payment	Remarks
2057	Nicks Peter				
2058	" Rachel				
2059	" Teesin				
2060	" Occteeyer				
2061	" Claude	1328.50	Rachel Nicks	L B Bell	
2062	Nix Sabinia[sic]				
2063	" John				
2064	" James				
2065	" Frank				
2066	" Maudie				
2067	" W^m				
2068	" Geo				
2069	" Sarah	2125.50	Sabrina Nix	L B Bell	
2070	Nix Robt.	265.70	Sabrina Nix	L B Bell	
2071	Nance Sarah				
2072	" Minnie				
2073	" John				
2074	" Lula				
2075	" Claude				
2076	" James	1594.20	Sarah Nance	L B Bell	
2077	Nelson Sarah	265.70	James R. Lamar	S.W. Mayfield	Jas Lamar guardia of this child
2078	Nidiffer Sam				
2079	" Emma				
2080	" Isaac				
2081	" Sam Jr				
2082	" Zekiel				
2083	" John				
2084	" Henry	1859.90	Sam Nidiffer	L B Bell	
2085	Neighbors Lucy F				
2086	" Laurine L.				
2087	" Jas. W.	797.10	R B Neighbors	L B Bell	

Starr Roll 1894

We, the undersigned citizens of the Cherokee Nation, by right of Cherokee blood, do hereby acknowledge to have received of E. E. Starr, National Treasurer of the Cherokee Nation, the sums set opposite our names respectively, in full of our shares in the per capita distribution authorized by an Act of the National Council, dated ___MAY 3 1894___ 1894.

	Names of Head, and Members of Families	Amount	To Whom Paid	Witness to Payment	Remarks
2088	Nidiffer Freeman				
2089	" Edward O L				
2090	" Loisa S				
2091	" Lucy C				
2092	" Mary D				
2093	" Ella E				
2094	" Robt L H	1859.90	Freeman Nidiffer	L B Bell	
2095	Nidiffer Felix				
2096	" Joanna				
2097	" Josephine				
2098	" Anna				
2099	" Eveline				
2100	" Minnie				
2101	" Johnie				
2102	" Willie				
2103	" Bessie				
2104	" Freeman Jr	2657.00	Felix Nidiffer	L B Bell	
2105	Nivins Jessie B				
2106	" Hellen E				
2107	" Archie R	797.10	C L Washborn	L B Bell	
2108	Nall Joe Ella				
2109	" Dora	531.40	Joella Nall	L B Bell	
2110	Neff Geo W	265.70	F.M. Crowell	Henry Eiffert	check F.M. Crowell
2111	Nidiffer Chas	265.70	Chas Nidiffer	L B Bell	
2112	Nidiffer Nannie	265.70	HC Ballard	L B Bell	order of Nannie Nidiffer
2113	Norton Cora	265.70	Ashly Norton	L B Bell	Ashley Norton father of this child
2114	Owens Dave	order			P Wyly
2115	" Betsy				
2116	" Andy				
2117	" Jesse	1062.80	Percy Wyly	Henry Eiffert	

347

Starr Roll 1894

We, the undersigned citizens of the Cherokee Nation, by right of Cherokee blood, do hereby acknowledge to have received of E. E. Starr, National Treasurer of the Cherokee Nation, the sums set opposite our names respectively, in full of our shares in the per capita distribution authorized by an Act of the National Council, dated ____MAY 3 1894____ 1894.

	Names of Head, and Members of Families	Amount	To Whom Paid	Witness to Payment	Remarks
2118	Owens Charley				
2119	" Susie				
2120	" Jimmie				
2121	" Peggy				
2122	" Betsy	1328.50	Charley Owens	L B Bell	
2123	O'Fields Ben				
2124	" Annie				
2125	" Sam	*order*			*Wyly*
2126	" Bushy head				
2127	" Mindy				
2128	" Bettie	1594.20	Percy Wyly	J.C. Starr	*Check on order*
2129	O'Fields Mose				
2130	" Jennie				
2131	" Wallie				
2132	" James				
2133	" Phillip			L B Bell	
2134	O'Fields Dick				
2135	" Lizzie				
2136	" Ella	797.10	Ella O'Fields	J.C. Starr	
2137	Owens Slaten				*P.W.*
2138	" Thos	*order* 531.40	Percy Wyly	Henry Eiffert	
2139	O'Fields Austen				*F.M. Crowell*
2140	" Alcy	*order*			
2141	" Rosa F	797.10	F.M. Crowell	J.C. Starr	*Check on order*
2142	" Louetta	265.70	T.J. Monroe	L B Bell	*7-13-94*
2143	Olson Lydia				
2144	" Birtha				
2145	" Louis A				
2146	" Denis F				
2147	" Richard F				
2148	" Andrew B	1594.20	Ole Olson	L B Bell	

Starr Roll 1894

We, the undersigned citizens of the Cherokee Nation, by right of Cherokee blood, do hereby acknowledge to have received of E. E. Starr, National Treasurer of the Cherokee Nation, the sums set opposite our names respectively, in full of our shares in the per capita distribution authorized by an Act of the National Council, dated ___MAY 3 1894___ 1894.

#	Names of Head, and Members of Families	Amount	To Whom Paid	Witness to Payment	Remarks
2149	O'Fields Sam	265.70	J.S. Thomason	Henry Eiffert	
2150	Owens Lucy	265.70	Lucy Owens	L B Bell	JST P. Wyly
2151	Ownbey Viney				
2152	" Raymon S.				
2153	" Mary A	797.10	Viney Owenby	L B Bell	
2154	Perdue Jas. S.	265.70	Christen Johnson	L B Bell	Minor
2155	Pearch Josiah				F.M. Crowell
2156	" Sally				
2157	" Izia	order			
2158	" Alice				
2159	" Percy				child of
2160	Drywater Susie	1594.20	Sally Pearch	L B Bell	Sally Pearch
2161	Parchmeal John	order			Wilson
2162	" Jennie				
2163	" Annie				
2164	" Lucy				
2165	" Ben				
2166	" Fanny	1594.20	John Parchmeal	L B Bell	Wilson's order
2167	Parchmeal Price				P. Wyly
2168	" Nancy				
2169	" Ella	order			
2170	" Ga-we-yah				
2171	" Mean				
2172	" See-nas-tah	1594.20	Nancy Parchmeal	L B Bell	
2173	Parris Geo				
2174	" Nellie	531.40	Geo Parris	L B Bell	
2175	Patter[sic] Esta				
2176	" Geo				
2177	" Florence	797.10	Esta Potter	J.C. Starr	

Starr Roll 1894

We, the undersigned citizens of the Cherokee Nation, by right of Cherokee blood, do hereby acknowledge to have received of E. E. Starr, National Treasurer of the Cherokee Nation, the sums set opposite our names respectively, in full of our shares in the per capita distribution authorized by an Act of the National Council, dated ___MAY 3 1894___ 1894.

	Names of Head, and Members of Families	Amount	To Whom Paid	Witness to Payment	Remarks
2178	Polson Alice	265.70	J.T. Hardy	L B Bell	
2179	Patter[sic] Eliza				
2180	" Etty				
2181	" Joseph	797.10	Eliza Potter	J.C. Starr	
2182	Parris Bud				
2183	John Annie				
2184	" Rocsey				
2185	" Maggie	378			
2186	" Syntha				
2187	" Richard				
2188	Starr Willie				Annie Parris mother of these children
2189	" Martin	2125.60	John Anna Parris	L B Bell	
2190	Peak Catherine				
2191	" Ed W	order			DE Haven
2192	" Thos. S.				
2193	" Spencer R	1062.80	D E Haven	Henry Eiffert	Chk
2194	Proctor Luella	order			D E H
2195	" Lillie May	531.40	DE Haven	Henry Eiffert	
2196	Powell Robert				
2197	Powell Iva Ann				
2198	" Vick				
2199	" Jennie				
2200	" Richard				
2201	" Lee				
2202	" Dora				
2203	" Lavinnie	2125.60	Robt Powell	L B Bell	
2204	Polson Henry	265.70	Henry Polson	L B Bell	
2205	Prather Richard				
2206	" Georgie A				
2207	" Jesse				
2208	" Effie				

Starr Roll 1894

We, the undersigned citizens of the Cherokee Nation, by right of Cherokee blood, do hereby acknowledge to have received of E. E. Starr, National Treasurer of the Cherokee Nation, the sums set opposite our names respectively, in full of our shares in the per capita distribution authorized by an Act of the National Council, dated ___MAY 3 1894___ 1894.

	Names of Head, and Members of Families	Amount	To Whom Paid	Witness to Payment	Remarks
2209	" Callie				
2210	" Richard L Jr				
2211	" Samuel H	1859.90	Richard Prather	L B Bell	
2212	Plank Mersiller	*order*			
2213	" Lavadie				
2214	" Russell	797.10	T.J. Monroe	L B Bell	*order*
2215	Powell Richard W				
2216	" Mary	531.40	R W Powell	L B Bell	
2217	Prather Lee B				
2218	" Fannie				
2219	" Lee Bell				
2220	" Annie O				
2221	" Minnie O				
2222	" Florence K				
2223	" W^m D	1859.90	Lee B Prather	L B Bell	
2224	Perry Nat M				
2225	" Elizabeth	531.40	N M Perry	L B Bell	
2226	Perry Zekiel				
2227	" Sylvesta				
2228	" Stella	797.10	Ezekiel Perry	L B Bell	
2229	Perry Oliver V				
2230	" Artemos				
2231	" Earnest				
2232	" Effie				
2233	" Myrtle				
2234	" Oliver H				
2235	" Claude	1859.90	N M Perry	L B Bell	*order*
2236	Perry Columbus	265.70	J.C. Starr	J.C. Starr	*pd on order Nov. 27 1894*

Starr Roll 1894

We, the undersigned citizens of the Cherokee Nation, by right of Cherokee blood, do hereby acknowledge to have received of E. E. Starr, National Treasurer of the Cherokee Nation, the sums set opposite our names respectively, in full of our shares in the per capita distribution authorized by an Act of the National Council, dated ___MAY 3 1894___ 1894.

	Names of Head, and Members of Families	Amount	To Whom Paid	Witness to Payment	Remarks
2237	Parks Johnson				
2238	" Melvine				
2239	" Arhena				
2240	" James				
2241	" Missouri	1328.50	Johnson Parks	L B Bell	
2242	Polson Freddie				
2243	" Jasper L	531.40	W^m A Polson	L B Bell	
2244	Prather Hattie	265.70	Hattie Prather	L B Bell	
2245	Phillips Josephine				
2246	" Julia				
2247	" Bassie				
2248	" Susie				
2249	" Gracie				
2250	" Spencer				
2251	" Budd				
2252	" Joe	2125.60	*(Illegible)* Phillips	L B Bell	
2253	Pauppa Jumper				E.W.
2254	" Chelouncha				
2255	" Phesant				
2256	" James				
2257	" Sauchjin	1328.50	*(Illegible)* Jumper	L B Bell	
2258	Past Jas M	265.70	William Mayes	Emmet Starr	Check By order
2259	Perry Sion M				
2260	" Floid L	531.40	S M Perry	L B Bell	
2261	Preston Mattie				
2262	" Clara				
2263	" Zack	order			DW Freeman
2264	" Maley	1062.80	DW Freeman	Henry Eiffert	Check

Starr Roll 1894

We, the undersigned citizens of the Cherokee Nation, by right of Cherokee blood, do hereby acknowledge to have received of E. E. Starr, National Treasurer of the Cherokee Nation, the sums set opposite our names respectively, in full of our shares in the per capita distribution authorized by an Act of the National Council, dated _____MAY 3 1894_____ 1894.

#	Names of Head, and Members of Families	Amount	To Whom Paid	Witness to Payment	Remarks
2265	Paden James				
2266	" Lucy				
2267	" Howard				
2268	" Maggie				
2269	" Homer				
2270	" Jim Jr.				Five yr's old
2271	" Coffee				
2272	" Jim	2125.60	Jas Paden	L B Bell	One Mo. old
2273	Paden Benj.	DEAD.			
2274	" Lena				
2275	" Tom				
2276	" Taylor				
2277	" W^m				
2278	" Maude				
2279	" Russell				
2280	" Kitty				
2281	" Martha	2391.30	Ben Paden	L B Bell	
2282	Pierce Robt.	265.70	F.M. Crowell	G W Benge	F M Crowell
2283	" Naoma				
2284	" Chas. E.				
2285	" Thos. E.	797.10	John Dawson Guardian	L B Bell	
2286	Pierce William	265.70 order	F.M. Crowell	G W Benge	F M Crowell
2287	Pierce Nancy J	265.70	N J Pierce	L B Bell	
2288	Patterson Zona				
2289	" Sarah A				
2290	" Alice	797.10	Zona Patterson	L B Bell	
2291	Painter Lavernia				
2292	" Ada				
2293	" Evy				
2294	" John	1062.80	Mathew A Painter	L B Bell	

Starr Roll 1894

We, the undersigned citizens of the Cherokee Nation, by right of Cherokee blood, do hereby acknowledge to have received of E. E. Starr, National Treasurer of the Cherokee Nation, the sums set opposite our names respectively, in full of our shares in the per capita distribution authorized by an Act of the National Council, dated ___MAY 3 1894___ 1894.

	Names of Head, and Members of Families	Amount	To Whom Paid	Witness to Payment	Remarks
2295	Poplin Catherine				
2296	" Annie J				
2297	" Ora A	797.10	Catherine Poplin	L B Bell	
2298	Paden Hassie				
2299	" Laura	531.40	Laura Paden	L B Bell	
2300	Parks Richard B	265.70	R B Parks	L B Bell	
2301	Parks Mary J				
2302	" Eva				
2303	" Chas				
2304	" Johnie				
2305	" Ora				
2306	" Owen B	1594.20	Mary J Parks	L B Bell	
2307	Parks John	265.70	John Parks	J.C. Starr	
2308	Parker Geo	265.70	R. T. Parks	L B Bell	
2309	Prather Thos W				
2310	" Chas. D.	531.40	Thos W Prather	L B Bell	
2311	Parks Richard T				
2312	" Ruth				
2313	" Tadius				
2314	" Wain B				
2315	" Elizabeth	1328.50	R.T. Parks	L B Bell	
2316	Parks Maggie	265.70	Maggie Parks	L B Bell	
2317	Payne Julius	265.70	Flora Payne	L B Bell	
2318	Parks Jas. G.	265.70	Jas G Parks	L B Bell	
2319	Parks Minnie	265.70	Minnie Parks	L B Bell	
2320	Prather Daniel	265.70	Caroline Prather	L B Bell	

Starr Roll 1894

We, the undersigned citizens of the Cherokee Nation, by right of Cherokee blood, do hereby acknowledge to have received of E. E. Starr, National Treasurer of the Cherokee Nation, the sums set opposite our names respectively, in full of our shares in the per capita distribution authorized by an Act of the National Council, dated _____MAY 3 1894_____ 1894.

	Names of Head, and Members of Families	Amount	To Whom Paid	Witness to Payment	Remarks
2321	Prather Caroline	265.70	Caroline Prather	L B Bell	
2322	" Ella	~~265.70~~ by order	Henry Eiffert	J.C. Starr	Henry ~~Eiffert~~
2323	Prather Georgia E	265.70	Henry Eiffert	S.W. Mayfield	
2324	Payne Elizabeth	265.70	Elizabeth Payne R854	L B Bell	
2325	Porter Lizzie	265.70	N.D. Porter	L B Bell	husband
2326	Parks Isaac D	265.70 D101	Isaac D Parks	L B Bell	
2327	Qualate Nannie				⎱ Nannie Qualate mother
2328	" Johnie				⎰ of this child
2329	" Houston				and the guardian of
2330	Sevens Ruphus				this child
2331	Silversmith Dlphus[sic]	1328.50	Nancy Qualate	L B Bell	
2332	Qualate Celia	~~1328.50~~ 265.70 order	~~Mary Qualate~~ GW Smith	~~L B Bell~~ Henry Eiffert	check. GW Smith
2333	Rogers Wilson				
2334	" Susie				
2335	" Betsie				
2336	" Akie				
2337	" Jennie	3654			Ten yr's old
2338	" Jennie Jr.	1594.20	Susie Wilson	L B Bell	Three Mo's old
2339	Rabbit Thos.	265.70 order	JC Welch	Henry Eiffert	JC Welch check
2340	Ridge Beaver				
2341	" Sally				
2342	" James	797.10	Beaver Ridge	L B Bell	
2343	Ridge Adam	3654			
2344	" Jennie	~~3654~~ Dead			
2345	Cloud Lydia ⎫				⎧ Jennie Ridge mother
2346	" Ola ⎬				⎨ of these children
2347	" Watt ⎭				⎩ Adam Ridge in
2348	Ridge Young	1594.20	Adam Ridge	L B Bell	Ft Smith jail

Starr Roll 1894

We, the undersigned citizens of the Cherokee Nation, by right of Cherokee blood, do hereby acknowledge to have received of E. E. Starr, National Treasurer of the Cherokee Nation, the sums set opposite our names respectively, in full of our shares in the per capita distribution authorized by an Act of the National Council, dated ___MAY 3 1894___ 1894.

	Names of Head, and Members of Families	Amount	To Whom Paid	Witness to Payment	Remarks
2349	Raven Boney[sic]				
2350	" Ocine				
2351	" Jeremiah	797.10	Bony Raven	L B Bell	
2352	Russell Sam W.				
2353	" Susie				
2354	" Mary				
2355	" Jack				
2356	" Jesse				
2357	" Dave	1594.90	Susie Russell	L B Bell	
2358	Rounds Jack	*order*			J.S. Alfrey
2359	" Annie				
2360	" Annie Jr.	797.10	J S Alfry[sic]	Henry Eiffert	Check
2361	Redbird Sally				
2362	" Lethie				
2363	" Charlotte				
2364	" Sam	1062.80	W.J. Gilbreath	J.C. Starr	Check on order
2365	Runabout Jas.				
2366	" Sa-ki-(?)				
2367	" Ja-hake	*order*			Washborn
2368	" Sa-u-gee-s-ki				
2369	" Che-Woan				
2370	" I-hak-lan				
2371	" Cummins	1859.90	Geo Runabout	L B Bell	Washborn
2372	Ridge Nellie				
2373	" Susie				
2374	" Annie	797.10	Nellie Ridge	L B Bell	
2375	Raines Viola				
2376	" Geo M.				
2377	" Wm H.				
2378	" Gordon B.				
2379	" Hitta E.	1328.50	Viola Raines	L B Bell	

Starr Roll 1894

We, the undersigned citizens of the Cherokee Nation, by right of Cherokee blood, do hereby acknowledge to have received of E. E. Starr, National Treasurer of the Cherokee Nation, the sums set opposite our names respectively, in full of our shares in the per capita distribution authorized by an Act of the National Council, dated ___MAY 3 1894___ 1894.

Names of Head, and Members of Families	Amount	To Whom Paid	Witness to Payment	Remarks
2380 Rogers Samuel				
2381 " Lelia M	531.40	Saml Rogers	L B Bell	
2382 Reed Nancy				
2383 " Luna				
2384 " Lulu				
2385 " Lou Etta				
2386 " John				
2387 " Pearl	1594.20	DN Fink	Henry Eiffert	check DN Fink
2388 Rogers Thos T.				
2389 " Laura A				
2390 " Thos. J				
2391 " Rolla A				
2392 " Zilpha P				
2393 " Wm E.	1594.20	Thos T. Rogers	L B Bell	
2394 Ridge Sally	265.70	(Illegible)	L B Bell	
2395 Ridge Darsie J.				
2396 " Sarah B.	531.40	C L Washbourne	L B Bell	
2397 Riley Joseph L	265.70	Ren[sic] Lee	Henry Eiffert	Ran Lee check
2398 Rogers Berilla				
2399 " George	531.40	Berilla Rogers	L B Bell	
2400 Rogers Robt	265.70	Mrs Berilla Rogers	L B Bell	JSH
2401 Rogers Otto	265.70	Mrs Berilla [sic]	L B Bell	
2402 Ratlingourd Jim	265.70	Oran Beck	L B Bell	
2403 Riley Thos. J.				
2404 " Bertha A				
2405 " Frank				
2406 " Willis	1062.80	Thomas J Riley	L B Bell	

Starr Roll 1894

We, the undersigned citizens of the Cherokee Nation, by right of Cherokee blood, do hereby acknowledge to have received of E. E. Starr, National Treasurer of the Cherokee Nation, the sums set opposite our names respectively, in full of our shares in the per capita distribution authorized by an Act of the National Council, dated ___ MAY 3 1894 ___ 1894.

Names of Head, and Members of Families	Amount	To Whom Paid	Witness to Payment	Remarks
2407 Richardson Delia F.	265.70	H.T. Richardson	L B Bell	
2408 Risingfawn Joseph	265.70	Joseph Risingfawn	L B Bell	
2409 Rolston Zacheriah	265.70	Z Rolston	L B Bell	J.S.T.
2410 Remsen Julia E				
2411 " Josephine R				
2412 " Alvi M	797.10	Julia E Remsen	L B Bell	
2413 Raper Geo	order			W.W. Miller
2414 " Chick		D1585		
2415 " Joe	797.10	W.W. Miller	Henry Eiffert	Check
2416 Raper John H				
2417 " Sarah E				
2418 " Mary E				
2419 " Sarah J				
2420 " Willie	1328.50	John H Raper	L B Bell	
2421 Rogers James	265.70	Jas Rogers	L B Bell	
2422 Roach Mattie				
2423 " Drucilla N				
2424 " Chas				
2425 " Thos J.	1062.80	Mattie Roach	L B Bell	
2426 Ridge John R				
2427 " Noble J.				
2428 " Geo M				
2429 " Hellen F.	1062.80	C.L. Washbourne	J.C. Starr	pd check No AUG 22 1894
2430 Rattlingourd W^{m}				
2431 " Lizzie				
2432 " Lizzie[sic]	797.10	William R. Gourd	L B Bell	

Starr Roll 1894

We, the undersigned citizens of the Cherokee Nation, by right of Cherokee blood, do hereby acknowledge to have received of E. E. Starr, National Treasurer of the Cherokee Nation, the sums set opposite our names respectively, in full of our shares in the per capita distribution authorized by an Act of the National Council, dated ___MAY 3 1894___ 1894.

#	Names of Head, and Members of Families	Amount	To Whom Paid	Witness to Payment	Remarks
2433	Ritter Ditha	D525			
2434	" Howell	order D525			F. Camen
2435	" Ada E	D525			
2436	" Willie W	1062.80	F.M. Camen	G W Benge	check
2437	Roseborough Lucy				
2438	" Lena				
2439	" Jessie				
2440	" Claude	1062.80	William M Roseborough	L B Bell	
2441	Risingfawn Jennie	order			F M Crowell
2442	Hilderbrand John	531.40	Jenny Risingfawn	L B Bell	on order of Crowell
2443	Ralston Lewis				
2444	" Francis				
2445	" Ida				
2446	" Lulu				
2447	" Johnie	1328.50	Eliza Ralston	L B Bell	
2448	Ralston Fannie	265.70	Fannie Ralston	L B Bell	
2449	Ridge Moses				
2450	" Elijah	531.40	Moses Ridge	L B Bell	
2451	Ridge Jeremiah	265.70	F M Crowell	Henry Eiffert	FM Crowell check
2452	Ridge John	265.70	John Ridge	L B Bell	
2453	Sapsucker John				Mills Bros
2454	" Susie	order			
2455	" Price				
2456	" Nancy				
2457	" Geo				
2458	Sutawagie Annie ⎫				Susie Sapsucker
2459	" Susie Ann ⎭	1859.90	Susie Sapsucker	L B Bell	mother of these children
2460	Sapsucker Luke	order			Mills Bros
2461	" Sally	531.40	Mills Bros	J.C. Starr	Check on order

Starr Roll 1894

We, the undersigned citizens of the Cherokee Nation, by right of Cherokee blood, do hereby acknowledge to have received of E. E. Starr, National Treasurer of the Cherokee Nation, the sums set opposite our names respectively, in full of our shares in the per capita distribution authorized by an Act of the National Council, dated ____MAY 3 1894____ 1894.

	Names of Head, and Members of Families	Amount	To Whom Paid	Witness to Payment	Remarks
2462	Starr Jesse				
2463	" Jennie	531.40	Jess Starr	L B Bell	
2464	Stick Emily	8923			F.M. Crowell
2465	" Eli	order.40	Emily Stick	L B Bell	on order of Crowell
2466	Sixkiller Sally				
2467	" Linnie	531.40	Sally Six	L B Bell	
2468	Stick Joe				
2469	" Polly	531.40	D.N. Fink	J.C. Starr	Check on order 7-13-1894
2470	Starr Sally				
2471	" Lydia				
2472	" Turner				
2473	" Tee Ann	1062.80	Sally Starr	L B Bell	
2474	Summerfields[sic] Jack	265.70	Jack Summerfield	L B Bell	
2475	Summerfield Isaac				
2476	" Ava				
2477	" Jess				
2478	" Swimmer				
2479	" Beckie				
2480	" Maryling				
2481	" Aggie	1859.90	Isaac Summerfield	L B Bell	
2482	Six Lander				
2483	" Jennie				
2484	" Ground-hog				
2485	" Umphrey	1062.80	Lander Six	L B Bell	
2486	Shotpouch Frank				F M Crowell
2487	" Betsy	order			
2488	" Lilla				
2489	" Drager	1062.80	F.M. Crowell	J.C. Starr	Check on order

Starr Roll 1894

We, the undersigned citizens of the Cherokee Nation, by right of Cherokee blood, do hereby acknowledge to have received of E. E. Starr, National Treasurer of the Cherokee Nation, the sums set opposite our names respectively, in full of our shares in the per capita distribution authorized by an Act of the National Council, dated ____MAY 3 1894____ 1894.

	Names of Head, and Members of Families	Amount	To Whom Paid	Witness to Payment	Remarks
2490	Starr Zeke				F M Crowell
2491	" Nancy	order			
2492	" Sally				
2493	" Lilla				
2494	" Jesse				
2495	" Canuke	1594.20	F.M. Crowell	J.C. Starr	Check on order
2496	Starr Nancy	order 265.70	Nancy Starr & Crowell	L B Bell	Crowell 1st order
2497	Starr Geo	order			FM Crowell
2498	" Nake				
2499	" Rachel	797.10	F.M. Crowell	J.C. Starr	Check on order
2500	Snail Nellie				McClellan &Son
2501	" John				
2502	" Sally	order			
2503	" Sarah				
2504	" Charlie				
2505	" Sam				
2506	" Nancy	1859.90	J F McClellan	Henry Eiffert	Ck
2507	Snail Ned	265.70	J F McClellan	Henry Eiffert	Ck
2508	Snail Eli	order			Wilson & Bro
2509	" Sarah				
2510	" John	797.10	A.R. Wilson & Bro	J.C. Starr	Check on order
2511	Snail Joe	order 265.70	J.F. McClellan	J.C. Starr	Check on order
2512	Squirrel Peter				
2513	" Betsy	531.40	Ed Washborn	L B Bell	
2514	Snail Jennie				
2515	" Cora				
2516	" Peggie				
2517	" George	1062.80	A.R. Wilson & Bro	J.C. Starr	Check on order
2518	Snail Gilbert	265.70	AR Wilson & Bro	Henry Eiffert	order Sept 13 94

Starr Roll 1894

We, the undersigned citizens of the Cherokee Nation, by right of Cherokee blood, do hereby acknowledge to have received of E. E. Starr, National Treasurer of the Cherokee Nation, the sums set opposite our names respectively, in full of our shares in the per capita distribution authorized by an Act of the National Council, dated ____MAY 3 1894____ 1894.

	Names of Head, and Members of Families	Amount	To Whom Paid	Witness to Payment	Remarks
2519	Sanders Susie				
2520	" Della M				
2521	" Edith I	797.10	John Martin	L B Bell	order

****

(The information below was inserted in the logbook before the page containing #2525 Arthur Sumers[sic] and #2526 Calvin Sumers, and is typed as given.)

Protest
To whom this May Consene

Hon E. E. Starr

Treasurer Cherokee Nation. Sir

the undersigned would most respectfully beg leave to file this as a protest against the right of George C. Summers to draw the per-capita shares of her own minor children viz:- Arthur and Calvin Summers for the following reasons to- wit:

first, That her children are not orphans and are in her charge, her own by issue, as well as by decree of a Court of Competent Jurisdiction. That aside from parentage by issue, she obtained a decree from the Circuit Court for Deleware District for Divorce, Allimony & Custody of the said children. Consequently there could exist no cause for the pointing of a guardian, unless she was in capacitated by Law.

second That any paper purporting to Guardian papers is, and can only be illegal or fraudulent, and for the reason of the above she claims that she can be the only one having the legal right to draw for her children who had been enroled to her family by the Census Takers of Deleware Dist. but through strategy & misrepresentation made to the recent reviseing Committee, the names of said minors was taken from her family and enroled seperately, with George C Summers as purporting to be their guardean.

Starr Roll 1894

We, the undersigned citizens of the Cherokee Nation, by right of Cherokee blood, do hereby acknowledge to have received of E. E. Starr, National Treasurer of the Cherokee Nation, the sums set opposite our names respectively, in full of our shares in the per capita distribution authorized by an Act of the National Council, dated _____MAY 3 1894_____ 1894.

	Names of Head, and Members of Families	Amount	To Whom Paid	Witness to Payment	Remarks

Now for the reasons above given, the undersigned would most respectfully ask that you make the proper and necessary investigation as to their purported Guardean should papers held by said G.C. Summers and pray that if my grounds are found to be well taken that I be allowed to draw the share of said minor children.

Very Respectfully
Lizzie Summers

****

2522	Sumers[sic] Lizzie	265.70	Lizzie Sumers	L.B. Bell	
2523	" Freddie	order			
2524	Hall Nute	~~531.40~~	C.M. Ball	J.C. Starr	Check on order
2525	Sumers Arthur				Geo C. Sumers guardian of these children
2526	" Calvin	531.40	Geo C. Summers	L B Bell	
2527	Still Geo	order			W.J.G.
2528	" Mary				
2529	" Acie				
2530	" Geo W	1062.80	W.J. Gilbreath	J.C. Starr	Check on order
2531	Still Louis				W.J.G.
2532	" Callie	order		J.C. Starr	ord to J.G. for Nos 2531-32 & 33
2533	" Linnie	797.10			
2534	Gamble Pearlie	265.70	Callie Still	L B Bell	Callie Still mother of this child
2535	Squirrel Carley	~~265.70~~	Cherokee Squirrel	L B Bell	on order Percy Wyly
2536	Scales Martha				
2537	" Ethel				
2538	" Grover				
2539	" Joseph				
2540	" Lillie	1328.50	GW Scales	L B Bell	

363

Starr Roll 1894

We, the undersigned citizens of the Cherokee Nation, by right of Cherokee blood, do hereby acknowledge to have received of E. E. Starr, National Treasurer of the Cherokee Nation, the sums set opposite our names respectively, in full of our shares in the per capita distribution authorized by an Act of the National Council, dated ___MAY 3 1894___ 1894.

	Names of Head, and Members of Families	Amount	To Whom Paid	Witness to Payment	Remarks
2541	Still Johnie				W.J.G.
2542	" Jimmie	order			
2543	" Mary E	797.10	W.J. Gilbreath	J.C. Starr	Check on order
2544	Seaborn Sadie	265.70	W.I. Thornton	L B Bell	
2545	Stanley Annie				
2546	" Bessie	531.40	Ed Stanley	L B Bell	
2547	Sturdivant John	order			Wilson
2548	" Lizabeth	531.40	A.R. Wilson & Bro	J.C. Starr	Check on order
2549	Shackleford Martha				
2550	" Ollie				
2551	" Effie				
2552	" Charley	1062.80	Martha Shackleford	L B Bell	
2553	Smith John				
2554	" Lida				
2555	" Lucy				
2556	" Emma				
2557	" Jennie				
2558	" Rachel				
2559	" Sam				
2560	Wolfe Nellie				Lyda Smith mother of these children
2561	" Nancy	2391.30	John Smith	L B Bell	
2562	Selvege[sic] John B				
2563	" Sabra	531.40	John B Selvidge	L B Bell	
2564	Strong Augusta				
2565	" Phillip	531.40	John Strong	L B Bell	
2566	Six Enoch				
2567	" Ida				
2568	Mitchel Sabina	797.10	Ida Six	L B Bell	Ida Six mother of this child

Starr Roll 1894

We, the undersigned citizens of the Cherokee Nation, by right of Cherokee blood, do hereby acknowledge to have received of E. E. Starr, National Treasurer of the Cherokee Nation, the sums set opposite our names respectively, in full of our shares in the per capita distribution authorized by an Act of the National Council, dated ___MAY 3 1894___ 1894.

#	Names of Head, and Members of Families	Amount	To Whom Paid	Witness to Payment	Remarks
2569	Sager Melia				
2570	" Debra				
2571	" Callie				
2572	" Liens				
2573	" James				
2574	" Ollie M.	1594.20	Melia Sager	L B Bell	
2575	Scrapper Thos				
2576	" Sally				
2577	" Palinia				
2578	" Malinda				
2579	" Nancy				
2580	" Louie	1594.20	Sally Scrapper	L B Bell	
2581	Snell Jonica				
2582	" Katy				
2583	" Coonie				
2584	" Charley				
2585	" Ella				
2586	" Onia				
2587	" Nannie	1859.90	Jonica Snell	L B Bell	
2588	Starr John	265.70	D.N. Fink	J.C. Starr	on order
2589	Starr Jas				
2590	" Linnie				
2591	" Geo				
2592	" Mack				
2593	" Young W.				
2594	" Maggie	1594.20	Jas Starr	L B Bell	
2595	Snell Annie	265.70	Annie Snell	L B Bell	
2596	Snell Charey[sic] E.	265.70	C.E. Snell	L B Bell	
2597	Raven Joe				Annie Snell mother of these children
2598	" John	531.40	Annie Snell	L B Bell	

Starr Roll 1894

We, the undersigned citizens of the Cherokee Nation, by right of Cherokee blood, do hereby acknowledge to have received of E. E. Starr, National Treasurer of the Cherokee Nation, the sums set opposite our names respectively, in full of our shares in the per capita distribution authorized by an Act of the National Council, dated ___MAY 3 1894___ 1894.

	Names of Head, and Members of Families	Amount	To Whom Paid	Witness to Payment	Remarks
2599	Sulsar Sparrow				
2600	" Lucinda				
2601	" Annie				
2602	" Willie	1062.80	Lucinda Sulsar	J.C. Starr	
2603	Suagee Sam	265.70	Eva White	L B Bell	
2604	Snell Nellie				
2605	" Peter				
2606	" Ed				
2607	" Jennie				
2608	" Carlotte				
2609	" Syntha	1594.20	Nellie Snell	J.C. Starr	
2610	Sharp Frogg				
2611	" Caw-ta-ya				
2612	" Carrie				
2613	" Will				
2614	" Chenasie F	1328.50	Frog Sharp	L B Bell	
2615	Starr Geo				
2616	" Aggie	531.40	Aggie Starr	J.C. Starr	
2617	Starr John	265.70	W.P. Mayes	J.C. Starr	sent check
2618	Starr Will				
2619	" Mary	531.40	William Starr	L B Bell	
2620	Sevens Joe	265.70 order	F.M. Crowell	G W Benge	FM Crowell
2621	Snell Jas.				
2622	" Liza				
2623	" Squirrel				
2624	" Susie	1062.80	Jas Snell	L B Bell	
2625	Sutton Alex	265.70 4471	GW Green	J.C. Starr	check GW Green

Starr Roll 1894

We, the undersigned citizens of the Cherokee Nation, by right of Cherokee blood, do hereby acknowledge to have received of E. E. Starr, National Treasurer of the Cherokee Nation, the sums set opposite our names respectively, in full of our shares in the per capita distribution authorized by an Act of the National Council, dated ___MAY 3 1894___ 1894.

	Names of Head, and Members of Families	Amount	To Whom Paid	Witness to Payment	Remarks
2626	Suagee Stand				Walsh & Shutt
2627	" Nora				
2628	" Robert	order			
2629	" Dennis B				
2630	" Thos J				
2631	" Stand W Jr				
2632	" Bessie m				
2633	" Margie E				
2634	" Roy Lee	2391.30	Walsh & Shutt	J.C. Starr	Check on order
2635	Suagee Peter	order 265.70	J.S. Thomason	J.C. Starr	Check on order
2636	Shoemaker Rebecca				
2637	" Rachel	order			
2638	" Nora A				
2639	" John W	1062.80	William J Shoemaker	L B Bell	
2640	Still Green	265.70	John Martin	L B Bell	order
2641	Starr Hickory				
2642	" Emona J				
2643	" Lulu				
2644	" Jessie B				
2645	" Emma				
2646	" Ezekiel				
2647	" Susan E	#150			
2648	Webster Riley	2125.60	Lulu Starr	Henry Eiffert	
2649	Starr Cale John	265.70	J C Starr	L B Bell	check
2650	Smith Ossie				
2651	" Mary				
2652	" Rusk	797.10	J. Warren Reed	C.W. Starr	order
2653	Shamblin Geo				
2654	" Sarah	order			
2655	" Bessie				
2656	" Pleasant				Z.F. Melton

Starr Roll 1894

We, the undersigned citizens of the Cherokee Nation, by right of Cherokee blood, do hereby acknowledge to have received of E. E. Starr, National Treasurer of the Cherokee Nation, the sums set opposite our names respectively, in full of our shares in the per capita distribution authorized by an Act of the National Council, dated ___MAY 3 1894___ 1894.

#	Names of Head, and Members of Families	Amount	To Whom Paid	Witness to Payment	Remarks
2657	" Charles	1328.50	L B Bell	L B Bell	L B Bell
2658	Stoody Geo	order			Mills Bros
2659	" Betsy	order			
2660	" Louie				
2661	" Mary				
2662	" Willie	1328.50	Geo Stoody	L B Bell	
2663	Sixkiller James	order			Marie A Milton
2664	" Claude Lee	531.40	Mary A Melton	J.C. Starr	Check on order
2665	Scrapper Henry				
2666	" Lettie				
2667	" Sallie				
2668	" Elige				
2669	" Fannie				
2670	" Earnest	1594.20	Henry Scrapper	L B Bell	
2671	Snell Eli				
2672	" Katie				
2673	" Lucy				
2674	" Louie				
2675	" Alice	1328.50	Katie Snell	L B Bell	
2676	Silversmith John				
2677	" Katie				
2678	" Rachel				
2679	" Bettie				
2680	" Mandy				
2681	" Mary	1594.20	John Silversmith	L B Bell	
2682	Silversmith Aggie				
2683	Fox Joe	531.40	S. N. Fink	J.C. Starr	Check on order
2684	Sloan Edward				
2685	" Jennie				
2686	" Willie				
2687	" Mary				

Starr Roll 1894

We, the undersigned citizens of the Cherokee Nation, by right of Cherokee blood, do hereby acknowledge to have received of E. E. Starr, National Treasurer of the Cherokee Nation, the sums set opposite our names respectively, in full of our shares in the per capita distribution authorized by an Act of the National Council, dated ___MAY 3 1894___ 1894.

	Names of Head, and Members of Families	Amount	To Whom Paid	Witness to Payment	Remarks
2688	" Minnie				
2689	" May				
2690	" Sam				one of this family was not numbered and was not paid Jas. E Sloan
2691	" Eva Jos. E.	2125.60	Ed Sloan	L B Bell	
2692	Swatt Steen				
2693	" Easter				
2694	" Louisa				
2695	" Thomas				
2696	" Oliver				
2697	" Wesley	1594.20	Easter Swatt	L B Bell	
2698	Swatt Willie	265.70	Will Swatt	L B Bell	
2699	Swatt Scott	265.70	T.J. Muskrat	J.C. Starr	Check on order
2700	Snell Betsy				
2701	" Joe	531.40	Betsy Snell	L B Bell	
2702	Snell Dave	265.70	J.C. Starr	J.C. Starr	
2703	Stevenson W^m F				
2704	" Maggie				
2705	" Chunnie				
2706	" Mary T				
2707	Polson Dudley	1328.50	J.W. Stephenson	L B Bell	John Stevenson guardian of this child.
2708	Smith Emma				
2709	" Wilbert				
2710	" Iva N	order			DE Haven
2711	" Oscar	1062.80	D.E. Havens	J.C. Starr	Check on order
2712	Squirrel Sam				
2713	" Betsy	531.40	Sam Squirrel	L B Bell	
2714	Snider Dora				
2715	" Laura				
2716	" Minnie				

Starr Roll 1894

We, the undersigned citizens of the Cherokee Nation, by right of Cherokee blood, do hereby acknowledge to have received of E. E. Starr, National Treasurer of the Cherokee Nation, the sums set opposite our names respectively, in full of our shares in the per capita distribution authorized by an Act of the National Council, dated ___MAY 3 1894___ 1894.

	Names of Head, and Members of Families	Amount	To Whom Paid	Witness to Payment	Remarks
2717	" Dora Jr	1062.80	Dora Snider	L B Bell	
2718	Snider Syntha				
2719	" Elbert				
2720	" Flid				
2721	" Roy	1062.70	Andrew Snider	L B Bell	
2722	Stilly Ora D				Lucy Stilly mother of these children
2723	" Cora B				
2724	Daniels John				
2725	Stilly Lucy	1062.80	Lucy Stilly	L B Bell	
2726	Smith Florence C	265.70	Florence C Smith	J.C. Starr	
2727	Smith Walter E.	265.70	Walter E Smith	L B Bell	
2728	Smith E Bird	265.70	Bird E Smith	L B Bell	
2729	Stover W^m				
2730	" Edith				
2731	" Rogers[sic]				
2732	" W^m A	1062.80	Wm Stover	L B Bell	
2733	Smith W^m L	265.70	W^m L Smith	L B Bell	
2734	Smith Walter F	265.70	WF Smith	L B Bell	
2735	Smith Henry				
2736	" Myrtle				
2737	" Willie M				
2738	" Percy W	1062.80	Margaret Smith	L B Bell	
2739	Smith Margaret	265.70	Margaret Smith	L B Bell	
2740	Smith Sarah P				
2741	" Gnat				
2742	" Homer	797.19	Sarah P Smith	L B Bell	
2743	" Willie L				order

Starr Roll 1894

We, the undersigned citizens of the Cherokee Nation, by right of Cherokee blood, do hereby acknowledge to have received of E. E. Starr, National Treasurer of the Cherokee Nation, the sums set opposite our names respectively, in full of our shares in the per capita distribution authorized by an Act of the National Council, dated ___MAY 3 1894___ 1894.

#	Names of Head, and Members of Families	Amount	To Whom Paid	Witness to Payment	Remarks
2744	" Pearl H.	531.40	R F Wyly	JP Carter	on Letters of Guardianship
2745	Stop Sally				P.W.
2746	" Tom	531.40	Percy Wyly	Henry Eiffert	
2747	Sunday Henry	order			Washbourne
2748	" Nancy				
2749	" Lee				
2750	Bird Sinnie	1062.80	Nancy Henry	L B Bell	
2751	Sanders Watt	265.70	Percy Wyly	J.C. Starr	Check on order
2752	Scott Sabrina				
2753	" W^m T				
2754	" Susie D				
2755	" Mattie E	1062.80	Bart Scott	L B Bell	
2756	Smith Robt L	265.70	Henry Eiffert	Robt B Ross	pd Sept 15/96
2757	Shouse Lee				
2758	" Lotta				
2759	" Clarence	797.10	Lee Chouse[sic]	L B Bell	
2760	Shouse Louisa				
2761	" Ada				
2762	" Harry	797.10	Louisa Shouse	L B Bell	
2763	Shouse Nimma	265.70	Louisa Shouse	L B Bell	
2764	Smith Catharine				
2765	" John N				
2766	" Eliza L				
2767	" Montazuma	1062.80	Catherine Smith	L B Bell	
2768	Samuels Emma J				
2769	" Robbie	531.40	Jas Woodall	L B Bell	order to Jas Woodall
2770	Smith Athie A	265.70	Athie A Smith	J.C. Starr	

Starr Roll 1894

We, the undersigned citizens of the Cherokee Nation, by right of Cherokee blood, do hereby acknowledge to have received of E. E. Starr, National Treasurer of the Cherokee Nation, the sums set opposite our names respectively, in full of our shares in the per capita distribution authorized by an Act of the National Council, dated ___MAY 3 1894___ 1894.

	Names of Head, and Members of Families	Amount	To Whom Paid	Witness to Payment	Remarks
2771	Smith Maggie	265.70	Solon James	L B Bell	
2772	Smith Elizabeth				
2773	" Bell				
2774	" Ollie				
2775	" Cora				
2776	" Walter				
2777	" Mude S	1594.80	James M Smith	L B Bell	
2778	Squirrel Daniel	order 265.70	F.M. Crowell	J.C. Starr	Check on order
2779	Smith Walter				
2780	" Darcus				
2781	" Susie				
2782	" Dater				
2783	" Lizzie				
2784	" Maudie				
2785	" Rachel				
2786	" Culeyah	2125.60	Walter Smith	L B Bell	
2787	Sixkiller Luke				
2788	" Emma				
2789	" Myrta	797.10	Emma Sixkiller	L B Bell	
2790	Summers Caroline				
2791	Barger Franklin				
2792	" W^m E	797.10	Caroline Summers	L B Bell	
2793	Suagee David	order			F.M. Crowell
2794	" Lucinda				
2795	" Laura	order 265.70	Laura Suagee F M Crowell	L B Bell	F.M. Crowell
2796	" Sarah				
2797	" Nellie				
2798	" Jo Ella				
2799	" Mark	order			
2800	" Wilson				
2801	" Mandy				
2802	" Maude	2391.30	David Suagee	L B Bell	

Starr Roll 1894

We, the undersigned citizens of the Cherokee Nation, by right of Cherokee blood, do hereby acknowledge to have received of E. E. Starr, National Treasurer of the Cherokee Nation, the sums set opposite our names respectively, in full of our shares in the per capita distribution authorized by an Act of the National Council, dated ___MAY 3 1894___ 1894.

Names of Head, and Members of Families	Amount	To Whom Paid	Witness to Payment	Remarks
2803 Stokes Mattie B	265.70	Mattie B Stokes	L B Bell	
2804 Stewart Celina				
2805 " Geo. W				
2806 " Mary J.	797.10	W N Stewart	L B Bell	
2807 Stewart John H	265.70	Jon H Stewart	L B Bell	
2808 Stewart W^m N Jr	265.70	W N Stewart	L B Bell	
2809 Smith Minnie J	order			F.M. Crowell
2810 " Hugh E.				
2811 " Minnie A				
2812 " Wm E.	1062.80	F.M. Crowell	J.C. Starr	Check on order
2813 Suagee Joel B	265.70	F.M. Crowell	J.C. Starr	Check on order F M Crowell
2814 Sixkiller Chas				F M Crowell
2815 " Linnie	order			
2816 " Young W.	797.10	F.M. Crowell	J.C. Starr	Check on order
2817 Squirrel Jack	265.70	Jack Squirrel	L B Bell	
2818 Six John W	order 265.70	J.C. Starr	J.C. Starr	Check on order Minor
2819 Sutton W^m H				
2820 " Wm D. Jr				
2821 " Katie				
2822 " Lizzie				
2823 " David				
2824 " Edward				
2825 " Alexander	1859.90	W^m H Sutton	L B Bell	
2826 Smith John	265.70	John Smith	L B Bell	
2827 Sager Nancy R	265.70	Nancy R Sager	L B Bell	
2828 Sutton John	4746 265.70	John Sutton	L B Bell	

Starr Roll 1894

We, the undersigned citizens of the Cherokee Nation, by right of Cherokee blood, do hereby acknowledge to have received of E. E. Starr, National Treasurer of the Cherokee Nation, the sums set opposite our names respectively, in full of our shares in the per capita distribution authorized by an Act of the National Council, dated _____MAY 3 1894_____ 1894.

	Names of Head, and Members of Families	Amount	To Whom Paid	Witness to Payment	Remarks
2829	Smith W^m A				
2830	" Rosa				
2831	" Mary				
2832	" Jesse				
2833	" Alma				
2834	" Della				
2835	" Carrie R	1859.90	John T Gunter	L B Bell	*on order*
2836	Sutton Mary	265.70	Mary Sutton	L B Bell	
2837	Simerson Lourina				
2838	Queen Joe	531.40	Lonnie Simerson	L B Bell	
2839	Simerson Cora				ENR
2840	" Blanche	*order* 531.40	Cora Simerson	L B Bell	
2841	Spraddling[sic] Okla	265.70	Okla Spradling	L B Bell	
2842	Smith Clearcy				
2843	" Cora P				
2844	" Ruth L				
2845	" Birtha	1062.80	Clarissa Smith	L B Bell	
2846	Six Sam	265.70	G W Ward	L B Bell	
2847	Sayers Henry				
2848	" W^m F	531.40	Henry Sayers	L B Bell	
2849	Sayers W^m	265.40[sic]	Wm Sayers	L B Bell	
2850	Scott Chewkee				
2851	" Jesse	531.40	Cherokee Scott	L B Bell	*wife of Marion Scott*
2852	Scott Annie				
2853	" Cornelius	531.40	James Scott	L B Bell	
2854	Strout Liza A	265.70	Eliza A Strout	L B Bell	

Starr Roll 1894

We, the undersigned citizens of the Cherokee Nation, by right of Cherokee blood, do hereby acknowledge to have received of E. E. Starr, National Treasurer of the Cherokee Nation, the sums set opposite our names respectively, in full of our shares in the per capita distribution authorized by an Act of the National Council, dated ____MAY 3 1894____ 1894.

	Names of Head, and Members of Families	Amount	To Whom Paid	Witness to Payment	Remarks
	~~Stephens Spencer S~~.				Allotte[sic]
2855	" Sarah				
2856	" Jessie	531.40	S S Stephens	L.B. Bell	
2857	Stephens Flossie I	265.70	Flossie I. Stephens	L B Bell	
2858	Stephens Earnest L	265.70 *order*	E.N. Ratcliff	J C Starr	pd check ENR
2859	Shelton Norman B	265.70	E.M. Thompson	L B Bell	on order
2860	Scott Cherokee				
2861	" Lillie M				
2862	" Birtha A				
2863	" Geo. W				
2864	" Jas. W				
2865	" Chas. D	1594.20	Cherokee Scott	L B Bell	
2866	Scott John B	265.70	John B Scott	L B Bell	
2867	Scott Cherokee B				E.N. Ratcliff
2868	" Price	*order*			
2869	" Nola				
2870	" Geo.	1062.80	Cherokee Scott	L B Bell	with EN Ratcliff consent
2871	Stephens Bell				
2872	" Marshal C				
2873	" Laura				
2874	" Carrie L				
2875	" Mary E	1328.50	WE Halsell	Henry Eiffert	W E H check
2876	Swain Rebecca M	265.70	Henry Eiffert	L B Bell	order
2877	Scott Polly Ann				
2878	" Minnie				
2879	" Geo	797.10	Polly Ann Scott	L B Bell	
2880	Shelton Annie B	265.70	A.B. Shelton	L B Bell	

Starr Roll 1894

We, the undersigned citizens of the Cherokee Nation, by right of Cherokee blood, do hereby acknowledge to have received of E. E. Starr, National Treasurer of the Cherokee Nation, the sums set opposite our names respectively, in full of our shares in the per capita distribution authorized by an Act of the National Council, dated ___MAY 3 1894___ 1894.

	Names of Head, and Members of Families	Amount	To Whom Paid	Witness to Payment	Remarks
2881	Sixkiller Carlotte	265.70	J R Knight	L B Bell	order to J R Knight
2882	Secrest Ollie	265.70	Ollie Secrest	Henry Eiffert	on order by check No - 72727 Sept 17 94
2883	Stollcup[sic] Sally	~~D1002~~ 9808			
2884	" Francis	531.40 ~~D1002~~ 9808	Sally Stallcup	J.C. Starr	
2885	Sweetwater W^m	order 265.70	F.M. Crowell	J.C. Starr	F.M. ~~Crowell~~ check
2886	Smith Dennis				
2887	" Deborah		*(No other information given.)*		
2888	" Emma				
2889	Summerfield Will				
2890	" Wallie				
2891	" Sam				
2892	" Charley				
2893	" Katy				
2894	" Lucy				
2895	" Lee				
2896	" Leach				
2897	" Celia				
2898	" Willie	2657.00	Will Summerfield	L B Bell	
2899	Smith Jay				
2900	" Maude				
2901	" Zella J	797.10	Jay Smith	L B Bell	
2902	Sarahos Polly				
2903	" Elmer				
2904	" Alberta S				
2905	" Franklin	1062.80	Polly Sarahos	L B Bell	
2906	Snake Wolf	order			Percy Wyly
2907	" Peter				
2908	" Jackson				
2909	" Margarett				
2910	" Chas	1328.50	Percy Wyly	J.C. Starr	Check on order

Starr Roll 1894

We, the undersigned citizens of the Cherokee Nation, by right of Cherokee blood, do hereby acknowledge to have received of E. E. Starr, National Treasurer of the Cherokee Nation, the sums set opposite our names respectively, in full of our shares in the per capita distribution authorized by an Act of the National Council, dated ___MAY 3 1894___ 1894.

#	Names of Head, and Members of Families	Amount	To Whom Paid	Witness to Payment	Remarks
2911	Sheldon Wᵐ F	265.70	Mrs Pauline Bates	L B Bell	
2912	Thompson Rachel	265.70	Rachel Thompson	L B Bell	
2913	Tehee Stalk	265.70	Percy Wyly	J.C. Starr	*Check on order*
2914	Tehee[sic] Charley				
2915	" Nancy				
2916	" Susie				
2917	" Alex				
2918	" Young Bird				
2919	" Jimmie	1594.20	Charley Teehee Sr	L B Bell	
2920	Tehee Charley Jr				
2921	" Lizzie				
2922	" Mary				
2923	" Cloud				
2924	" Carrie	1328.50	Charley Teehee Jr	L B Bell	
2925	Tehee Eli				
2926	" Olsie				
2927	" Dave				
2928	" Gun-ga-nal-a				
2929	" Geo.	1328.50	Eli Teehee	L B Bell	
2930	Talbot Syntha				
2931	" John				
2932	" Thornton				
2933	" Florence				
2934	" James				
2935	Hannea Cleveland	1594.20	D A McGhee	L B Bell	
2936	Mitchel Lula	~~1857.90~~ ~~D A McGhee~~ 265.70	W. J. Gilbreath	J.C. Starr	*Syntha Talbot Check on order mother of these children*
2937	McLauthlin Willie	265.70 [118]	W. J. Gilbreath	J.C. Starr	

377

Starr Roll 1894

We, the undersigned citizens of the Cherokee Nation, by right of Cherokee blood, do hereby acknowledge to have received of E. E. Starr, National Treasurer of the Cherokee Nation, the sums set opposite our names respectively, in full of our shares in the per capita distribution authorized by an Act of the National Council, dated ___MAY 3 1894___ 1894.

	Names of Head, and Members of Families	Amount	To Whom Paid	Witness to Payment	Remarks
2938	Taylor Nannie				
2939	" Geo.	*order*			
2940	" Francis				
2941	" Flora				
2942	" Effie				
2943	" Henry				
2944	" Delora				
2945	" Betty C	2125.60	W.J. Gilbreath	J C Starr	Check on order
2946	Thomas Arch				
2947	" Fred				
2948	" Laura				
2949	" Lillie Bell				
2950	" Elizabeth	1328.50	Arch Thompson	L B Bell	
2951	Taffelmire Elizabeth	265.70	GW Smith	Henry Eiffert	check order G W Smith
2952	Tassel John	*order*			P W
2953	" Jesse	531.40	Percy Wyly	J.C. Starr	Check on order
2954	Thompson John	*order*			Wyly
2955	" Aggie	531.40	Percy Wyly	Henry Eiffert	
2956	Tau-u-nea-cie Edward				
2957	" Jane				
2958	" Susie	797.10	Jane *(Illegible)*	L B Bell	
2959	Tau-u-nea-cie Daniel	265.70	GW Smith	Henry Eiffert	check on order
2960	Tau-u-nea cie Louis	*order* 265.70	D.N. Fink	J.C. Starr	check on order
2961	Tabler Leathie	265.70	J C Starr	L B Bell	order
2962	Turner Minnie E	3684			
2963	" Rubie	531.40	Minnie Turner	L B Bell	

Starr Roll 1894

We, the undersigned citizens of the Cherokee Nation, by right of Cherokee blood, do hereby acknowledge to have received of E. E. Starr, National Treasurer of the Cherokee Nation, the sums set opposite our names respectively, in full of our shares in the per capita distribution authorized by an Act of the National Council, dated ___MAY 3 1894___ 1894.

	Names of Head, and Members of Families	Amount	To Whom Paid	Witness to Payment	Remarks
2964	Thornton Will I.				
2965	" Emanda				
2966	" Minnie				
2967	" Eva				
2968	" Alice	1328.50	W. I. Thornton	L B Bell	
2969	Trout Geo				
2970	" Martha				
2971	" Logan				
2972	" James				
2973	" Henry				
2974	" Isaac				
2975	" Georgie				
2976	" Creed				
2977	" Ruphus C.	2391.30	Geo Trout	L B Bell	
2978	Tanner Pheasant				
2979	" Betsy				
2980	" Josie				
2981	" Tooker				
2982	" Joe				
2983	" Jackson				
2984	" Allsie				
2985	" Minnie	2125.60	Betsy Tanner	L B Bell	
2986	Tanner Tom	265.70	Percy Wyly	J.C. Starr	check on order Percy Wyly
2987	Timbrook[sic] Mattie				
2988	" Earling				
2989	" Jananita	797.10	Mattie Tenbrook	L B Bell	
2990	Tanner John	order 265.70	J.S. Thomason	J.C. Starr	check on order J.S. Thomason
2991	Tanner Charley				Percy Wyly
2992	" Betsy	order 531.40	Percy Wyly	J.C. Starr	check on order

Starr Roll 1894

We, the undersigned citizens of the Cherokee Nation, by right of Cherokee blood, do hereby acknowledge to have received of E. E. Starr, National Treasurer of the Cherokee Nation, the sums set opposite our names respectively, in full of our shares in the per capita distribution authorized by an Act of the National Council, dated ___MAY 3 1894___ 1894.

	Names of Head, and Members of Families	Amount	To Whom Paid	Witness to Payment	Remarks
2993	Turner Will				
2994	" Nellie				
2995	" Lillie				
2996	" Taylor				
2997	" Sam				
2998	" Daniel	1594.20	Nellie Turner	L B Bell	
2999	Thomas Tom				
3000	" Chas.				
3001	" Henry				
3002	" Myrtle				
3003	" Jefferson				
3004	" Daisy				
3005	" Marth[sic]				
3006	" Jas Albert	2125.60	Thm Thomas	L.B. Bell	
~~3007~~					
3008	Tiley Polina				
3009	" Minnie O				
3010	" Mary G	797.10	Wm Tyly	L B Bell	
3011	Tittle Fred	~~265.70~~ order	F.M. Crowell	J.C. Starr	check on order
3012	Trott Lillie O.	265.70	Susan Payne	L B Bell	Minor
3013	Toolate John				
3014	" Annie				
3015	" Kah-na-lu-st				
3016	" Ah-cher-nuste				
3017	" Alice				
3018	" Davis				
3019	" Buck	1859.90	John Toolate	L B Bell	
3020	Tiger W^m	~~265.70~~ order	L W Buffington	L B Bell	Tom Bluejacket guardian of these children
3021	" Tom				
3022	" Eugene	531.40	Thomas Bluejacket [guardian]	L Bell	

Starr Roll 1894

We, the undersigned citizens of the Cherokee Nation, by right of Cherokee blood, do hereby acknowledge to have received of E. E. Starr, National Treasurer of the Cherokee Nation, the sums set opposite our names respectively, in full of our shares in the per capita distribution authorized by an Act of the National Council, dated ___MAY 3 1894___ 1894.

	Names of Head, and Members of Families	Amount	To Whom Paid	Witness to Payment	Remarks
3023	Trott Jas C				
3024	" Dora		Dora Trott		
3025	" Willie	797.10	~~Martha Black~~	L B Bell	
3026	Trott Homer	265.70	Dora Trott	L B Bell	
3027	Trott Birdie	265.70	Birdie Trott	L B Bell	
3028	Thomason Rachel F				
3029	" Birtha				
3030	" George L				
3031	" Grover C.	1062.80	J S Thomason	L B Bell	
3032	Thompson Louis[sic] K	265.70	Lewis K Thompson	L B Bell	
3033	Tittle Robt W.	265.70	Robt Tittle	L B Bell	
3034	" Dora A	265.70	Dora Tittle	L B Bell	
3035	Tittle Dan L.				
3036	" Henry C.				
3037	" Otis W				
3038	" Gracie P				
3039	" Heigh T				
3040	" Mary J				
3041	" Robt J Jr	1859.90	Robt Tittle	L B Bell	
3042	Taylor John M				
3043	" Roy S	531.40	J M Taylor	L B Bell	
3044	Taylor Syntha J				
3045	" Chester				
3046	" Vinnie				
3047	" Thos				
3048	" Lee				
3049	" Girtie				
3050	" Birtie				
3051	" Searse				
3052	" Hubert				

Starr Roll 1894

We, the undersigned citizens of the Cherokee Nation, by right of Cherokee blood, do hereby acknowledge to have received of E. E. Starr, National Treasurer of the Cherokee Nation, the sums set opposite our names respectively, in full of our shares in the per capita distribution authorized by an Act of the National Council, dated ___MAY 3 1894___ 1894.

	Names of Head, and Members of Families	Amount	To Whom Paid	Witness to Payment	Remarks
3053	" Winnie D	2657.00	R R Taylor	L B Bell	
3054	Thomas Nicholas	265.70	Nicholas Thomas	L B Bell	
3055	Tyley Abe				
3056	" Etta	531.40	Abe Tyley	L B Bell	
3057	Tanner Jas				
3058	" Annie				
3059	" Joe				
3060	" Mary	1062.80	Jas Tanner	L B Bell	
3061	Tee-sa-da-skey Annie				
3062	" Mouse				
3063	" Nancy				
3064	" Peggie	1062.80	Betsy Gooding	L B Bell	
3065	Taylor Martha	2974			
3066	" Robt J	2974			
3067	" Geo M	2974			
3068	" Frank R	2974			
3069	" W^m H	~~2974~~ 1328.50	Geo W Taylor	L B Bell	
3070	Tynon Arie				
3071	" W^m				
3072	" Henry				
3073	" John				
3074	" Thomas				
3075	" Ruphus				
3076	" Joe	1859.90	Andrew Tynon	L B Bell	
3077	Tucker Martha	order			*F.M. Crowell*
3078	" Cornelia	531.40	F.M. Crowell	J.C. Starr	*check on order*
3079	Thompson Joe L				
3080	" Alice				
3081	" Ada	797.10	J L Thompson	L B Bell	

Starr Roll 1894

We, the undersigned citizens of the Cherokee Nation, by right of Cherokee blood, do hereby acknowledge to have received of E. E. Starr, National Treasurer of the Cherokee Nation, the sums set opposite our names respectively, in full of our shares in the per capita distribution authorized by an Act of the National Council, dated ___MAY 3 1894___ 1894.

	Names of Head, and Members of Families	Amount	To Whom Paid	Witness to Payment	Remarks
3082	Theurer Alta				
3083	" Mary E				
3084	" Lena				
3085	Johnson Lee	1062.80	Alta Theurer	L B Bell	
3086	Umphrey David				
3087	" James				
3088	" W^m				
3089	" John				
3090	" Fannie				
3091	" Andrew				
3092	" Graden	1859.90	David Umphrey	L B Bell	
3093	Vann Chick-alee-la				
3094	" Gee-woan				
3095	" Leach	797.10	Chickalely Vann	L B Bell	
3096	Vann Dick	*order*			
3097	" Lizzie				
3098	" John	797.10	Dick Vann	L B Bell	
3099	Vann Dick				
3100	" E Anna				
3101	" Celia	265.70	Celia Vann	L B Bell	
3102	" Nancy				
3103	" Beaver				
3104	" Jennie				
3105	" Lydia				
3106	" Rusk	1859.90	Dave Vann	L B Bell	*Dora Vann draws for seven*
3107	" Geo	265.70	Celia Vann	L B Bell	
3108	Vann Dave W				
3109	" Pearl				
3110	" John H				
3111	" Fanny M				
3112	" Flora E	1328.50	D W Vann	L B Bell	

Starr Roll 1894

We, the undersigned citizens of the Cherokee Nation, by right of Cherokee blood, do hereby acknowledge to have received of E. E. Starr, National Treasurer of the Cherokee Nation, the sums set opposite our names respectively, in full of our shares in the per capita distribution authorized by an Act of the National Council, dated ____MAY 3 1894____ 1894.

	Names of Head, and Members of Families	Amount	To Whom Paid	Witness to Payment	Remarks
3113	Vann Jim G	265.70	Jim G Vann	J.C. Starr	
3114	" Nancy	265.70	Nancy Vann	J.C. Starr	
3115	Vann Nakie[sic]	265.70	Nokie Vann	J.C. Starr	
3116	Victor Dee				
3117	" Octa				
3118	" Fred	797.10	S.G. Victor	L B Bell	
3119	Wright Nelson	order			Mills Bros
3120	" Lucy	531.40	Mills Bros	Henry Eiffert	J.S.T. Ck
3121	Wright Lunnie	order 265.70	L W Buffington	L B Bell	L W Buffington
3122	Williams[sic] Toney				
3123	" Charlotte				
3124	" Price				
3125	" Rowe				
3126	" Olkin				
3127	" Sarah				
3128	" Haven	1859.90	Toney William	L B Bell	
3129	Weir Sam	order			J S Thomason
3130	" Early	531.40	Sam Weir by J. S. Thomason	Henry Eiffert	Ck
3131	Wilson Young P				
3132	" Katy	order			Wyly
3133	" Ridge				
3134	" Oo-ki-lie				
3135	" Jennie				
3136	" Nannie	1594.20	Percy Wyly	Henry Eiffert	Ck
3137	Washbourne Claude L				
3138	" Joy L				
3139	" Rollin R				
3140	Thompson Hattie				Claude Washbourn
3141	" Ethel	1328.50	C R Washbourne	L B Bell	guardian of these children

Starr Roll 1894

We, the undersigned citizens of the Cherokee Nation, by right of Cherokee blood, do hereby acknowledge to have received of E. E. Starr, National Treasurer of the Cherokee Nation, the sums set opposite our names respectively, in full of our shares in the per capita distribution authorized by an Act of the National Council, dated ___MAY 3 1894___ 1894.

	Names of Head, and Members of Families	Amount	To Whom Paid	Witness to Payment	Remarks
3142	Washbourne Ed N				
3143	" Carrie L				
3144	" Lula	797.10	EN Washburn	L B Bell	
3145	Washbourne Percy H				
3146	" Wood W				
3147	" Claude L Jr				
3148	" Myra M				
3149	" Rosco C				
3150	" Noble				
3151	" Percy H Jr.				
3152	" Lula R	2125.60	C L Washbourne	L B Bell	
3153	Washbourne Walter	265.70	C L Washbourne	L B Bell	
3154	Washbourne Bert	265.70	C L Washbourne	L B Bell	
3155	Welch John				J.F. McClelland
3156	" Eve				
3157	" Mary				
3158	" Ne-nu-we				
3159	" Nancy	1328.50	JF McClelland	Henry Eiffert	check
3160	West Sally	265.70	Sally West	L B Bell	
3161	Woffard[sic] Will				
3162	" Onia				
3163	" Arch				
3164	" Ned				
3165	" John				
3166	" Ridge				
3167	" Bennie	2125.60	Will Wofford	L B Bell	
3168	Woffard Charlie	265.70	W.M. Gullager	S.W. Mayfield	
3169	Witt William F				
3170	" Elmer L				
3171	" Della J	797.10	David Witt	L B Bell	order

Starr Roll 1894

We, the undersigned citizens of the Cherokee Nation, by right of Cherokee blood, do hereby acknowledge to have received of E. E. Starr, National Treasurer of the Cherokee Nation, the sums set opposite our names respectively, in full of our shares in the per capita distribution authorized by an Act of the National Council, dated ___MAY 3 1894___ 1894.

	Names of Head, and Members of Families	Amount	To Whom Paid	Witness to Payment	Remarks
3172	Witt Isabell				
3173	" Bell				
3174	" Allie				
3175	" Abe				
3176	" Dee				
3177	" Tip	1594.20	Felix Witt	L B Bell	
3178	Witt Orlando	265.70	Felix Witt	L B Bell	on order
3179	Witt John W	265.70	David Witt (John W Witt struck through)	L B Bell	
3180	" Nannie	265.70	Felix Witt	L B Bell	
3181	Witt David	265.70	David Witt	L B Bell	
3182	Wilson Bird	265.70	Ida Hicks Admr	L B Bell	
3183	Wolfe Daniel	265.70	Arch Foreman	L B Bell	on order
3184	Wetzel Martha				
3185	" Minnie				
3186	" Lulu	797.10	DK Wetzel	L B Bell	
3187	Wyly Geo		8965		
3188	" Nannie				
3189	" Annie				
3190	" John				
3191	" Eliza				
3192	" Sam				
3193	" Sally	1859.90	Geo Wyly	L B Bell	
3194	Wilson Mary				
3195	" Bertha	531.40	Wm Wilson	L B Bell	
3196	Watson Mary A				
3197	" Chas				
3198	" John C	797.10	Wm Watson	L B Bell	

Starr Roll 1894

We, the undersigned citizens of the Cherokee Nation, by right of Cherokee blood, do hereby acknowledge to have received of E. E. Starr, National Treasurer of the Cherokee Nation, the sums set opposite our names respectively, in full of our shares in the per capita distribution authorized by an Act of the National Council, dated ___MAY 3 1894___ 1894.

	Names of Head, and Members of Families	Amount	To Whom Paid	Witness to Payment	Remarks
3199	Wicked[sic] Webb				J.C. Welch
3200	" Sarah	order			
3201	" Richard				
3202	" Lottie				
3203	" Edith				
3204	" Lurhenia	1594.20	Sarah Wicket	L B Bell	
3205	Welch Cobb				
3206	" Ailsie				
3207	" Mollie				
3208	" Cora				
3209	" Oslie	1328.50	Cobb Welch	L B Bell	
3210	White Hill	order 265.70	D.N. Fink	J.C. Starr	check on order 7-13-1894
3211	Woods Will H				
3212	" Martin C	6436			
3213	" Mary A.				
3214	" Lewis E				
3215	" Lucy B.				
3216	" Harriett E				
3217	" Willie O				
3218	" Maudie M	2125.60	Will H Woods	L B Bell	
3219	Woods Chas W.				
3220	" Jas. M				
3221	" Lewis				
3222	" Will P				
3223	" Mamie E.	1328.50	Charley Wood[sic]	L B Bell	
3224	Wright Jas				
3225	" Ailsie				
3226	" Jackson				
3227	" Elmira				
3228	" Sarah				
3229	" Thomas				
3230	" Josie	1859.90	Jas Wright	Henry Eiffert	

Starr Roll 1894

We, the undersigned citizens of the Cherokee Nation, by right of Cherokee blood, do hereby acknowledge to have received of E. E. Starr, National Treasurer of the Cherokee Nation, the sums set opposite our names respectively, in full of our shares in the per capita distribution authorized by an Act of the National Council, dated ___MAY 3 1894___ 1894.

	Names of Head, and Members of Families	Amount	To Whom Paid	Witness to Payment	Remarks
3231	Woods Frank				
3232	" W^m H				
3233	" Lavinnie				
3234	" James M				
3235	" Columbus				
3236	" Bennie V	1594.20	Frank Woods	L B Bell	
3237	Woods Henry				
3238	" Samantha				
3239	" Houston				
3240	" Viella				
3241	" Tympy				
3242	" Marion	1594.20	Henry Woods	L B Bell	
3243	Woods Mandy	265.70	Henry Woods	L B Bell	on order
3244	Woodall Wash				
3245	" Susan				
3246	" Annie				
3247	" Louisa				
3248	" John				
3249	" Nancy	1594.20	Wash Woodall	L B Bell	
3250	Wolfe Ella				
3251	" Ethel				
3252	" Jennie May	797.10	Ella Wolf[sic]	L B Bell	
3253	Ward Geo M				
3254	" Martha J				
3255	" Nancy l[sic]	797.10	GM Ward	L B Bell	
3256	Ward John M	265.70	JM Ward	L B Bell	
3257	Welch James	265.70 order	WF Smith	Henry Eiffert	check W.F.S.
3258	Welch Dave				
3259	" Ester				
3260	" Nancy				

Starr Roll 1894

We, the undersigned citizens of the Cherokee Nation, by right of Cherokee blood, do hereby acknowledge to have received of E. E. Starr, National Treasurer of the Cherokee Nation, the sums set opposite our names respectively, in full of our shares in the per capita distribution authorized by an Act of the National Council, dated ____MAY 3 1894____ 1894.

	Names of Head, and Members of Families	Amount	To Whom Paid	Witness to Payment	Remarks
3261	" Celia				
3262	" Dave Jr.	1328.50	Dave Welch	L B Bell	
3263	Welch Ed	265.70 R.E. Snell (265.70 Dave Welch struck)		L B Bell (L B Bell struck)	cash 83.20 Check 182.50
3264	Walker Sophronia				
3265	" Albert W				
3266	" Martha J	797.10	Susan *(Illegible)*	L B Bell	on order
3267	Walker Adda	3777			
3268	" Bertha	531.40	Adda Walker	L B Bell	
3269	Ward Vann	265.70	R E Vermillion	L B Bell	R E Vermillion
3270	Ward Sam				
3271	" Louisa				
3272	" Minnie				
3273	" Mimie				
3274	" Joe				
3275	" Zona				
3276	" Hugh				
3277	" Rosa				
3278	" Lillie				
3279	" Beula				
3280	" Dalena	2922.70	Saml Ward	L B Bell	
3281	Wyly Percy				
3282	" Jas R.				
3283	" Lee				
3284	" Thurman	1062.80	Percy Wyly	L B Bell	
3285	Wyly John				P.W
3286	" Saggie				
3287	" Joe				
3288	" Littie				
3289	" Annie				
3290	" Jane Ann				
3291	" Akie				

Starr Roll 1894

We, the undersigned citizens of the Cherokee Nation, by right of Cherokee blood, do hereby acknowledge to have received of E. E. Starr, National Treasurer of the Cherokee Nation, the sums set opposite our names respectively, in full of our shares in the per capita distribution authorized by an Act of the National Council, dated ___MAY 3 1894___ 1894.

	Names of Head, and Members of Families	Amount	To Whom Paid	Witness to Payment	Remarks
3292	" Linnie	2125.60	Percy Wyly	Henry Eiffert	Ck
3293	Wallaskey Willie				
3294	" Wallie	531.40	Wallie Wallesky	L B Bell	
3295	Ward Louisa				
3296	" Lola				
3297	" Elva				
3298	" Alta	1062.80	W W Ward	L B Bell	
3299	Ward Will W	265.70	W W Ward	L B Bell	
3300	Wetzel Chas				
3301	" Ida May				
3302	" Claude				
3303	" Oliver				
3304	" Earl	1328.50	Wm Stover	L B Bell	
3305	Ward John				
3306	" Dora				
3307	" Laura				
3308	" Leolla				
3309	" Cornelia				
3310	" Winnie	1594.20	John Ward	L B Bell	
3311	Watermelon Chas	order			Percy Wyly
3312	" Akie				
3313	" Jennie				
3314	" Oon-junst				
3315	" Lucy				
3316	" Thompson	1594.20	Percy Wyly	Henry Eiffert	Check
3317	Wilson Jess				
3318	" Beckie				
3319	" Charley				
3320	" Annie				
3321	" Rachel				
3322	" Round				

Starr Roll 1894

We, the undersigned citizens of the Cherokee Nation, by right of Cherokee blood, do hereby acknowledge to have received of E. E. Starr, National Treasurer of the Cherokee Nation, the sums set opposite our names respectively, in full of our shares in the per capita distribution authorized by an Act of the National Council, dated _____ MAY 3 1894 _____ 1894.

	Names of Head, and Members of Families	Amount	To Whom Paid	Witness to Payment	Remarks
3323	" Polly	1859.90	Jess Wilson	L B Bell	
3324	Wilson Joe				P.W
3325	" Rachel				
3326	" Charlotte	*order*			
3327	" Taakee				
3328	" Unack				
3329	" Eli				
3330	" Sarah				
3331	" Mary	2125.60	Percy Wyly	Henry Eiffert	
3332	Wolfe Will				
3333	" Susanna[sic]				
3334	" Mouse				
3335	" Ben				
3336	" Tincup				
3337	" Akie	1594.20	Susanah Wolf	L B Bell	
3338	Wyly Rachel	265.70	Rachel Wyly	J.C. Starr	
3339	Ward Joe L				
3340	" Alma				
3341	" Stella				
3342	" May				
3343	" Mattie L	1328.50	Joe L Ward	L B Bell	
3344	Wilson Oliver E				
3345	" Mary Bell				*Minors*
3346	" Arthur U	797.10	Sarah Wilson	L B Bell	
3347	Williams Mary A				*Notice*
3348	" Elgin M	531.40	Mary A Williams	L B Bell	
3349	Williams Vennie M	265.70	Vinnie M *(Illegible)*	L B Bell	*J.S. Thomason*
3350	Willis Ollie S	265.70	C W Starr	L B Bell	*order*

Starr Roll 1894

We, the undersigned citizens of the Cherokee Nation, by right of Cherokee blood, do hereby acknowledge to have received of E. E. Starr, National Treasurer of the Cherokee Nation, the sums set opposite our names respectively, in full of our shares in the per capita distribution authorized by an Act of the National Council, dated ___MAY 3 1894___ 1894.

	Names of Head, and Members of Families	Amount	To Whom Paid	Witness to Payment	Remarks
3351	Weir Nathan B	125			
3352	" May E	125			
3353	" Renie J	125			
3354	" Chas S	125			
3355	" Ruth A	1328.50	N.B. Weir 125	L B Bell	
3356	Woodard Ann E	265.70	F M Conner 7582	Henry Eiffert	F M *check Conner*
3357	White Jas E				
3358	" W^m H				
3359	" Joe S				
3360	" Hooley C	1062.80	Jas E White	L B Bell	
3361	Walker Mary M				
3362	" Jas A				
3363	" Narcissa O				
3364	" Earl P	1062.80	P L Walker	L B Bell	
3365	Walker M Rex	265.70	P L Walker	L B Bell	
3366	Williams Malinda				
3367	" Laura		*order*		
3368	" W^m				
3369	" Mattie				
3370	" Allie				
3371	" Mayes				
3372	" Carlotta		*(Illegible)* 1		
3373	" Riley	2125.20	Geo Williams 7	L B Bell	
3374	Williams Columbus	265.70	Geo Williams	L B Bell	
3375	Walker Little				F.M. *Crowell*
3376	" Nellie		*order*		
3377	Hunter Sookie				*consent of* F M *Crowell*
3378	Pigeon Lizzie	1062.80	Little Walker	L B Bell	

Starr Roll 1894

We, the undersigned citizens of the Cherokee Nation, by right of Cherokee blood, do hereby acknowledge to have received of E. E. Starr, National Treasurer of the Cherokee Nation, the sums set opposite our names respectively, in full of our shares in the per capita distribution authorized by an Act of the National Council, dated ___ MAY 3 1894 ___ 1894.

	Names of Head, and Members of Families	Amount	To Whom Paid	Witness to Payment	Remarks
3379	Wolk Chas.				F M Crowell
3380	" Alcy				
3381	" Nellie	order			
3382	" Polly				
3383	" John				
3384	" Jesse				
3385	" Lucy				
3386	" W^m	2391.30	F M Crowell	Henry Eiffert	Ck
3387	Wolk Eliza	265.70	Henry Eiffert	Henry Eiffert	
3388	Ward Isabell				
3389	" John D				
3390	" Minnie O				
3391	" Lelia M				
3392	" Genovia A				
3393	" Aletha				
3394	" Carrie M				
3395	" Lena N	2125.60	T.J. Ward	L B Bell	
3396	Wilson Martha E				
3397	" Elgin D				
3398	Wall Lula B				
3399	" John M	1062.80	~~Jonathan~~ B.A. Wilson	L B Bell	
3400	Welch Nannie B				
3401	" Veda E	531.40	Joseph E Welch	L B Bell	
3402	Watermelon Suake				
3403	" Nancy				
3404	" Lucy	797.10	Suake Watermelon	L B Bell	
3405	Ward Geo D.				
3406	" John E.				
3407	" Ethlynn	797.10	Eliza Ward	L B Bell	
3408	Ward Jas. O.	265.70	J O Ward	L B Bell	

Starr Roll 1894

We, the undersigned citizens of the Cherokee Nation, by right of Cherokee blood, do hereby acknowledge to have received of E. E. Starr, National Treasurer of the Cherokee Nation, the sums set opposite our names respectively, in full of our shares in the per capita distribution authorized by an Act of the National Council, dated ___MAY 3 1894___ 1894.

	Names of Head, and Members of Families	Amount	To Whom Paid	Witness to Payment	Remarks
3409	Woodall Stand G	265.70	S.G. Woodall	L B Bell	
3410	Woodall Jas.				
3411	" Anna N				
3412	" Margarett A		D2787		
3413	" Frank F.				
3414	" Jeff A				
3415	" Benj J				
3416	" Mary	1859.90	Jas Woodall	L B Bell	
3417	Walker Nannie				
3418	" Jennie				
3419	" Jimmie				
3420	" John E	1062.80	Jas Walker	L B Bell	
3421	Ward Jas H				
3422	" Mary A				
3423	" Jas. L.				
3424	" Sarah E				
3425	" Geo V	1328.50	Mary A Ward	L B Bell	
3426	Winfield Henry	265.70	JS Thomason	Henry Eiffert	J.S.T.
3427	Welch Ned	265.70	Dave Welch	L B Bell	
3428	Woodall Peter				
3429	" Nana				
3430	" Mavel	797.10	Peter Woodall	L B Bell	
3431	Woodall Nolen	265.70	Peter Woodall	L B Bell	
3432	Woodall W^m C				
3433	" Margarette E				
3434	" Susan E	797.10	W.C. Woodall	L B Bell	
3435	Woodall Stand W.	265.70	W C Woodall	L B Bell	

Starr Roll 1894

We, the undersigned citizens of the Cherokee Nation, by right of Cherokee blood, do hereby acknowledge to have received of E. E. Starr, National Treasurer of the Cherokee Nation, the sums set opposite our names respectively, in full of our shares in the per capita distribution authorized by an Act of the National Council, dated ___MAY 3 1894___ 1894.

	Names of Head, and Members of Families	Amount	To Whom Paid	Witness to Payment	Remarks
3436	Woodall Jas T. Sr				
3437	" Bettie				
3438	" Leander				
3439	" Lewis				
3440	" Ira				
3441	" Isaac				
3442	" Jas.				
3443	" Ocie	2125.60	James T. Woodall	L B Bell	
3444	Woodall Walter	265.70	James T. Woodall	L B Bell	
3445	Woodall Lizzie L	265.70	I.E. Parker	L B Bell	
3446	Winberger Rachel	265.70	Rachel Winberger	L B Bell	
3447	Woodall W^m				
3448	" Jas M	531.40	James T. Woodall	L B Bell	on order
3449	Wingfield Robt	order			JST
3450	" Lucinda	531.40	J S Thomason	Henry Eiffert	Ck
3451	Wofford Annie				
3452	" Alta				
3453	" Lizzie	order			JST
3454	" Jack				
3455	" Pearl	1328.50 ~~1067.80~~	Annie Wofford	L B Bell	
3456	Whitney Louella E				
3457	" Mack W				
3458	" Fred C				
3459	" Mary E	1062.80	Louella Whitney	L B Bell	
3460	White Josiah	265.70	Josiah White	L B Bell	
3461	Wilson Eliza	265.70	P L Walker	L B Bell	

Starr Roll 1894

We, the undersigned citizens of the Cherokee Nation, by right of Cherokee blood, do hereby acknowledge to have received of E. E. Starr, National Treasurer of the Cherokee Nation, the sums set opposite our names respectively, in full of our shares in the per capita distribution authorized by an Act of the National Council, dated ___MAY 3 1894___ 1894.

Names of Head, and Members of Families	Amount	To Whom Paid	Witness to Payment	Remarks
3462 Walley[sic] Still				
3463 " Nancy				
3464 " Jennie	797.10	Nancy Wally	L B Bell	
3465 White Henry				
3466 " Evie				
3467 " Samantha				
3468 " Mary				
3469 " Nancy				
3470 Cornsilk Charley	1594.20	Eva White	L B Bell	
3471 Ward Thos J. Jr	265.70	T J Ward	L B Bell	One day old
3472 Wright Lizzie				
3473 " Bessy				
3474 " Ethel	797.10	Lizzie Wright	L B Bell	
3475 Yeargain[sic] Mary J				
3476 " May				
3477 " Kate				
3478 " Tumer A				
3479 " Robt. P.	1328.50	Mary J Yeargin	L B Bell	
3480 Yeargain Joe	265.70	Joe Yeargin	L B Bell	
3481 Yeargain Scott A	265.70	May J Yeargin	L B Bell	order
3482 Yeager Laura				
3483 " Ninie				
3484 " Claude	797.10	Laura Yeager	L B Bell	
3485 Yarbrough Minerva	~~D875~~ 10333			
3486 " Ceals L	531.40	Geo S Yarbrough	L B Bell	
3487 Yong[sic] Robt A	265.70			
3488 Nannie	265.70	Malinda Adams	L B Bell	
3489 Yong Jas	265.70	Jas Young	L B Bell	

Starr Roll 1894

We, the undersigned citizens of the Cherokee Nation, by right of Cherokee blood, do hereby acknowledge to have received of E. E. Starr, National Treasurer of the Cherokee Nation, the sums set opposite our names respectively, in full of our shares in the per capita distribution authorized by an Act of the National Council, dated ___MAY 3 1894___ 1894.

Names of Head, and Members of Families	Amount	To Whom Paid	Witness to Payment	Remarks
3490 Yong John W	265.70	J W Young	L B Bell	
3491 Youngbeaver Will	265.70	Mills Bros	Henry Eiffert	Mills Bros

Starr Roll 1894

Tahlequah, Ind. Ter., *June 1st,* 189 4.

I, C. J. Harris, Principal Chief, and I, E. E. Starr, Treasurer, of the Cherokee Nation, Do hereby certify that the foregoing enrollment of Cherokees by blood, resident in Delaware District, is a correct transcript from the original census authorized by the Act of the National Ciuncil[sic], approved May 15th, 1893, and that the Number ascertained to participate in the pre-capita distribution provided for by the Act of the National Council, approved May 3rd, 1894, is 3493.

Attest.
Seal of the Cherokee Nation.

C. J. Harris
Principal Chief.

E. E. Starr
Treasurer.

****

Index

1" NATNS BANK 122
1ST NAT BANK VINITA 191
1ST NATIONAL BANK 267
1ST NATIONAL BANK - VINITA ... 94
A R WILSON & BRO 59
ABERCRUMBIE, Ruth 2
ABERCRUMBY, John 2
ADAIR
    Charles B 93
    David J 90
    David W 93
    Donnie 91
    Dora S 94
    E A 91,134
    Edward A 91
    Fannie 90
    Ida L 94
    J F 90
    Joe F 273
    John W 273
    John W D 273
    Joseph F 90
    Lola D 90
    Mack 274
    Maggie 90
    Minnie 92
    Nannie 273
    Patton A 91
    R K 93,123
    R S 92
    Rachel T 93
    Robert N 93
    Robt E 94
    Robt L 92
    Rollan K 93
    Sadie K 93
    Susan T 93
    V H 91
    Viola 91
    Virgil H 91
    Walter T 90
    Walter T, Jr 90
    W^m P 90
ADAMS
    Carrie F 92
    Leo D 92
    Malinda 273,396

W^m H 92
ADINGTON
    Alice 1
    Annie 1
    Joel 1
    Liddia 1
    Oscar 1
    Trumon 1
    William 1
ADKINS, Mary 1
AGNES
    Ella 1
    John L 1
    Josephus 2
    Mary E 1
    Robert M 1
    Walter 2
    Walter S 1
AHSHUTZ, Mary 91
AKIN
    Fannie C 93
    J H 127,217,262,340
    Reuby L 93
    Ulrich R 93
    Vinita J 93
    Walter S 93
    Willie M 93
AKINS, J H 93
ALBERTY
    Cyntha 221
    Cynthia 94,200
    David 91
    E C 206
    Eli 91
    Elnora 91
    Emma 91
    Frank 91
    Geo W 91
    George 94
    Lizzie 94
    Mary 91
    William 91
    W^m 91,203
ALECK
    Celia 272
    Coon 272
    Frank 274

Index

James 272
Nancy 272,274
Nannie 272
Nellie 272
Ollie 272
Rebecca 272
Thomas 272
U Sutt 272
Willie 272
ALEXANDER
  Aggie 1
  Andy 1
  Caroline 272
  Carrie 272
  Cha's 273
  Effie L 272
  Elizabeth 272
  Elizabeth L 272
  Elmer 272
  James 1
  Joel B 272
  John 1
  Una 272
  Wallace 273
  Wilas L 272
ALFRED
  Fannie 2
  Maggie 2
  Sue 2
ALFREY, J S 313,356
ALLBORN
  Becky 272
  Lydia 272
ALLECK, Nancy 274
ALLEN
  Ada B 273
  Amarah 273
  Ann 273
  Callie 273
  D N 94
  Eliza 2
  Eva O 273
  Henry 94
  Ida 273
  Jennie 94
  Joe C 94
  John 94

Lula 94
Mary 94,273
Minnie W 44
Myrah 94
Myrtie 273
Neoma 273
Noah 90
Olive I 273
Pearl 273
Plumie 273
Rebecca 94
Susan 90
Susan E 94
Thomas 273
William 90
W^m B 273
ALLIN, Elliza 2
ALLISON
  Elmer R 90
  James 90
  John 90
  Mary 90
  Una 90
  Willie 90
ALLOWAY
  Belle 91
  C C 91
  Delilah 91
  Katie 91
  Leroy 91
  Salina 91
  William 91
ALLTON
  David C 94
  Eliza B 94
  Joseph 94
  Percy 94
  Susie 94
ALSTON
  Sarah C 95
  William 95
AMOS
  A A 1
  Amand A 1
  Edwin R 1
  Ethel M 1
  James E 1

Index

William A 1
ANDERSON
  Addie 94
  Austin 90
  Bettie 1
  George 1
  Gladys 93
  J C 93
  James 1
  Mabel W 93
  Mandy 21
  Nannie E 90
  Nellie 90
  Rachel C 94
  Rebecca 93
  Rena 90
  Susan 1
  W^m 94
ANDREW, Mary 2
ANDREWS
  Callie D 93
  Mary E 93
ANGEL
  Becky 273
  Ida 273
  James H 273
  Jessie 273
  Laura 273
  Willie 273
  W^m 273
ANSHUTZ, Mary 91
ARCHER
  Charlotte 90
  F J 202
  Florence 94
  John E 94
  Mary F 90
  Mattie 94
  T J 262
ARLEDGE
  Addie 91
  Clarie 91
  John 91
  Maggie 91
  Maud 91
  Sarah 91
AR-LOO-LEE
  Eliza 93
  John 93
  Susie 93
ARMOR
  Annie 93
  Daisy 93
  George 93
  Myrtle 93
  Norma 93
ARMSTRONG
  Albert 92,138
  Frank 92,93,138
  James 267
  John 267
ARNOLD
  Cecil 92
  Georgia 92
  Halbert 92
  Herbert 92
  Jennie 119
  Jennie O 91
  Joseph 92
  Mary 92
  Myrtle 92
  Victoria 92
ARROW
  Carrie 272
  J Ann 272
  Liddia 272
  Will 272
ARWOOD
  Alvin 274
  Cornelia 274
  Hettie 274
  Minnie 274
  Oscie 274
ASHBARK, Annie 20
ASHBROOK
  Clarence 93,209
  Sadie 93,209
ASHES
  Jake 1
  John 2
ASHLEY, Walter A 54
ASKINS
  Alice 1
  Lucinda 1

Index

Lucretia ... 1
ATAWAY, Mary ... 274
ATCHISON, Sarah ... 310
ATKINS
    Authur ... 95
    Lizzie ... 95
    Martha ... 91
    Martha J ... 91
ATWAY, Mary ... 274
AUDD
    Clare ... 90
    Clyde ... 90
    Coody ... 90
    Flora ... 90
    Mary ... 90
AUDRIAN
    Anna C ... 273
    Clyde W ... 272
    Edna M ... 272
    Francis C ... 272
    Frank G ... 273
    Mamie Irene ... 273
    Mary J ... 273
    Ralph R ... 273
    Richard O ... 272
    W S ... 272
    Winfield S ... 272
AUTRY, Mary ... 8
BACHTEL
    Daniel ... 99
    Elzy ... 99
    Mary ... 99,162
    Mary J ... 241
    Odus ... 99
BACKBONE
    Calvin ... 7
    Polly ... 258
BACKMAN, William ... 79
BACON
    Bernice M ... 8
    Binia ... 9
    C H ... 8
    Charles B ... 8
    Dana B ... 8
    Harnage ... 9
    Harvey ... 110
    Henry ... 47
    Irine ... 9
    J D ... 9
    Jeanie ... 9
    John L ... 8
    Lucy B ... 8
    Sarah ... 8
    Willie ... 9
BADGETT
    Mamie ... 109
    Mary ... 109
    Ross ... 109
    W R ... 109
BAILY
    Amanda W ... 10
    Benjamin L ... 10
    Francis ... 10
    John C ... 10
    John S ... 10
    Malinda ... 10
    Mary J ... 10
BAKER
    Earl ... 107
    Eliza ... 107
    Elizabeth ... 101
    Jno H ... 101
    John O ... 97
    Joseph F ... 97
    M L ... 107
    Maggie ... 97
    Malissa E ... 283
    Millie E ... 107
    Minnie M ... 107
    Mollie A ... 283
    Polly J ... 97
    Sallie E ... 107
    Sarah A ... 101
    Susan E ... 101
    Webster C ... 101
    W^m R ... 107
BALDRIDGE, James ... 6
BALENTINE
    Ellen S ... 283
    Hamilton ... 283
    Mary E ... 283
    Mary E, Jr ... 283
BALL
    Alfred C ... 105

Index

C M 105,122,363
J S 105
James T 105
John C 105
Julia C 105
Lydia J 105
Mary J 105
Missouri A 105
Rachel 105
W^m E 105

BALLARD
   Alma M 96
   Annie 281,282
   Arch 281
   Charlotte 281
   Claude 281
   Daubum 279
   Edna 279
   Ethel 281
   Freeman 279
   Gaddie 279
   Geo 279
   George 279
   H C 96,279,347
   Henry C 96
   Henry T 96
   Houston 281
   James 96,281
   Jane Anna 282
   Jesse Lee 284
   John 281
   Lucinda 281
   Miran 281
   Nellie 279
   Randolph 281
   Robert 281
   Ruth M 281
   Sallie 282
   Sam 279
   Sarah 279,281
   Thos 284
   W^m 281,282,310,336
   W^m R 105
   Zoe 282

BALLINGER
   Bird B 99
   Ethel 99
   Julia A 99
   Thos B 99

BANE
   B F 10
   Cordie 10
   Duff 10
   Fanny 10
   Josie 10
   Leanord 10
   Madge 10
   Vina 10

BANKHEAD
   Charles 102
   Elizabeth 102
   Eva 102
   Frader 102
   Frank G 102
   G W 102
   Geo W 102
   Jno H 102
   Joel T 102
   John 102
   John H 102
   John L 102
   Lottie 102
   Mary 102
   Susie 102
   Unise A 102

BANTY
   Alice 85
   John 85

BARBER
   Charlotte 5
   Dannie 57
   Dutch 5
   Gropes 5
   Jane 5
   Johnson 1,5
   Johnston 5
   Man 5

BARD
   Daniel 96
   E H 102
   Elizabeth H 102
   Emily L 102
   James R 102
   L M 102

Laura M 102
Robt B Ross 102
S B 102
Sarah B 102
Thos D 102
BARGARINO, Martha 312
BARGER
   Charles 284
   Edward 280
   Franklin 372
   Isiac L 280
   John 280
   Samuel 280
   W^m E 372
BARKER
   Artemus B 111
   Charlie 3
   Elvia C 9
   Emma 3
   Ethel G 111
   Eva 111
   Ida L 3
   Joseph 3
   Josie G 111
   Kate 3
   M A 111
   Mary A 111
   Mrs W H 56
   Sallie B 9
   Sequoyah 111
   Susan 3
   William H 9
   W^m H 9
BARNDOLLAR, J J 106,167,225
BARNES
   Alexander 3,10
   Ancy Bell 3
   Antonie W 3
   Bashe 10
   Charles 5
   Cornelius 5
   Elba 10
   Ellis 10
   Flora L 110
   Hiram 5
   Jane 5
   John 10
Lelia 5
Mandy L 110
Martha 3
Winona 5
BARNETT
   Annie F 98
   Dora S 98
   Edward 280
   F M 280
   Frank 280
   Ida 6
   J N 6
   Jessie L 280
   Joel 60
   Mary B 98
   Nancy 282
   Riley 282
BARNEY, Felix 95
BARNS, Louiza 11
BARNWELL
   Carlton 97
   E C 97
   Elizabeth C 97
   Middleton 97
   Steven 97
BARRETT
   Bessie 110
   John 110
   Lee 110,113
   Sophronia 110
BARTHELL
   Annie 98
   Frank 98
   Mollie 98
BARTON, Cynthia 284
BATES
   Charles 278
   Josephine 278
   Mrs Pauline 377
   P 250
   Pauline 278
   Susie M 278
BATT
   Adam 278
   Bennie 278
   Emma 278
   Flora 278

Index

Ned 278
BATTLES
  Addie 97
  Bruce 97
  Daisy...97
  Emily J......................................283
  Fannie 97
  Foster 97
  Fox..97
  Stephen 97
  William..97
  Zedie...97
BAUGH
  Dollie..96
  J L 190
  Joel L 96
  Joel L, Jr 96
  Lotta 96
  Monna J.......................................97
  R L 16,35,40,42,43,97,249,260
  Robt L...97
BAY, Rbt.......................................303
BEAMER
  John 277
  Oliver C 277
  Pearlie.......................................277
  Sarah...277
BEAMS, Susan F.............................108
BEAN
  Annie 104
  Deverre 104
  Dot..111
  Edward 111
  Eliza..111
  Ellen 6
  Estah 104
  Eveline......................................104
  Henry..104
  Joe 112
  Laura...111
  Lucy..104
  Mamie.......................................104
  Nannie 6
  Russel 6
  Susan 6
  Ton-yah 108
  Tot..111

Ward 104
Watt..98
BEAR
  W D 112
  W^{m} D 112
BEAR TOTER.................................275
  Lizzie..275
  Martha 275
BEARD
  Annie 112
  Beulah.......................................112
  Henry..112
  John M......................................112
BEARGREESE
  Ellen 9
  Nelly 6
  Runaway...................................... 9
  Sarah... 9
BEARHEAD
  Joe 274
  Mike 274
  Peter..274
  Sallie...274
BEARPAW, Cynda 6
BEATTY
  Alice B......................................279
  Emaline....................................... 9
  Mamie... 9
BEATY, Emaline 9
BEAVER
  Annie 275
  Celia 275
  Charles.. 3
  Cherry 3
  Geo 99
  George 99
  James 3
  Lucy.. 3
  Martha 3,12,68
  Mary 3
  Nancy 275
  Rabbit 3
  Runabout 274,335
  Sarah M 3
  Thomas 3
  Willie 3
BECK

Index

Albert	276
Arthur	282
Ausborn	104
Blanche	275
Carroll	6
Chas	113
Chavlett	275
Cloud	6
Cornealius	276
Cyntha	7
Daniel	282
Dave	275
Dave Jr	104
David	104
Didd	276
Don	276
E J	113
Eliza	6
Ellis	104
Emma J	113
George	104
Gertrude B	105
Guy	276
H B	6
Harlin	276
Harvey M	105
Henry	276
Henry G	6
Ida	276
Irene	276
J W	15
Jeff	277
Jessie	276
Jessie B	7
Joe	276
John	277
John H	105
John W	7,15
Johnie	276
Jonus F	276
Leathy	275
Leoger	10
Lilly	294
Lora	276
Ludge	276
Lula B	282
Malinda	6
Martha	104
Mary	276
Nannie	10
Oran	275,357
Rachel	110
Robert	276
Sabera	276
Sallie	276
Sam	276
Samuel	95
Sarah	110
Scot	282
Sinna	276
Susie	275,282
Susie E	282
Thomas	6,110
Thos	6
Tom	276
Ula	276
Vianna	10
Vivia	275
W B	14
W M	9
Walter	104
Walter Ray	105
Wesley	104
William A	105
William P	10
Zeke	276

BEESON

Edward	151
Perry	113

BELL

Andrew L	102
Dannel H	108
Emma W	102
Etta	102
Ida L	102
James M	282
John M	102
L B	1,2,3,5,6,7,8,9,10,11,12,13, 14,15,16,17,18,19,20,21,22,23,24,25, 26,27,28,29,30,31,32,33,34,35,36,37, 38,39,40,41,42,43,44,45,46,47,48,49, 50,51,52,53,54,55,56,57,58,59,60,61, 62,63,64,65,66,67,68,69,70,71,72,73, 74,75,76,77,78,79,80,81,82,83,84,86,

87,88,91,93,94,95,96,97,99,100,101,
102,104,105,106,107,108,109,112,113
,114,116,117,119,120,121,122,123,
124,125,130,132,134,135,136,137,138
,140,142,143,144,146,147,149,150,
152,153,154,155,157,163,164,165,166
,167,168,169,172,174,175,176,177,
178,180,181,183,184,185,187,188,189
,191,193,194,196,197,199,200,201,
202,206,207,208,209,211,213,214,215
,217,218,221,222,223,224,225,226,
228,229,231,233,234,236,237,238,239
,241,242,245,246,247,248,251,252,
254,255,256,258,259,262,263,264,265
,266,268,269,272,273,274,275,276,
277,278,279,280,281,282,283,284,285
,286,287,288,289,290,291,292,293,
294,295,296,297,298,299,300,301,302
,303,304,305,306,307,308,309,310,
311,312,313,314,315,316,317,318,319
,320,321,322,323,325,326,327,328,
329,330,331,332,333,334,335,336,337
,338,339,340,341,342,343,344,345,
346,347,348,349,350,351,352,353,354
,355,356,357,358,359,360,361,362,
363,364,365,366,367,368,369,370,371
,372,373,374,375,376,377,378,379,
380,381,382,383,384,385,386,387,388
,389,390,391,392,393,394,395,396,
397
  Lucien B 284
  M S 284
  Mary S 284
  Mattie 108
  Mattie M 108
  Nannie C 102
  Sallie 61
  Watie W 282
BELLEW, Randolph 292
BENDER, E B 181,185,225
BENDURA
  Charley 181
  Eddie 95
  John 95
BENGE
  C W 102
  Charles O 108

  Elizabeth 259
  G E 163
  G W 90,91,92,93,94,95,96,97,98,
99,100,101,102,104,105,106,107,108,
  109,110,111,112,113,114,115,116,
  117,118,119,120,121,122,123,124,125
,126,127,128,129,130,131,132,133,
134,135,137,138,139,140,141,142,144
,145,146,147,148,149,150,151,152,
153,154,155,156,157,158,159,160,161
,162,163,164,165,166,167,168,169,
170,171,172,173,174,175,176,177,178
,179,180,181,182,183,184,185,186,
187,188,189,190,191,193,194,195,196
,197,198,199,201,202,203,204,205,
206,207,208,209,210,211,212,213,214
,215,216,217,218,219,220,221,222,
223,224,225,226,227,228,229,230,231
,232,233,234,235,236,237,238,239,
240,241,242,243,244,246,247,248,249
,250,251,252,253,254,255,256,257,
258,259,260,261,262,263,264,265,266
,267,268,269,270,296,297,298,299,
301,303,317,322,344,353,359,366
  Geo W 188,236
  Rot 180
  W^m H 180
BENNETT
  Emily 8
  Glenn 102
  J H 102
  Joseph 102
  Marion 102
  Mary 109
  Mary E 102
  Roxie 102
  Simpson 8
BERRY
  Amos 280
  Annie Marie 108
  Charles 280
  Elisha 282
  Etta M 280
  Fannie L 108
  William 282
BERTHOLF
  Alice C 7

Amanda J ... 7
Betty ... 7
Claud ... 6
Dewit T ... 7
Electa ... 8
Emma H ... 7
Grover ... 6
Isaac ... 7
Isaac W ... 7
Jessie M ... 7
John ... 55,88
John R ... 8
Lelia ... 5
Minnie ... 5
Myrtle M ... 7
Nonnie ... 6
Octavia ... 5,6
Percy E ... 8
Richard ... 5,6
Thomas ... 5,7
Thomas E ... 8
William ... 5
William H ... 7
Willie ... 7
BIBB, George ... 208
BIBLES
  Arthur ... 104
  Bessie Ann ... 107
  Clem ... 107
  Cora B ... 104
  Cris R ... 104
  Delila ... 107
  Edward ... 102
  Eva M ... 107
  Geo ... 106
  Geo B ... 106
  George B ... 107
  Henry ... 102
  J T ... 107
  James ... 102
  James P ... 104
  James T ... 107
  Jess ... 102
  Jno A ... 107
  John ... 106
  Josephine ... 107
  Lewis ... 102,104
  Lewis A ... 104
  Lizzie J ... 107
  Margaret ... 102
  Mary ... 107
  Rebecca ... 106
  Sallie ... 102
  Wiley ... 102
  W^m C ... 107
  W^m G ... 104
  W^m H ... 107
  W^m T ... 107
BIGACOM, Redbird ... 274
BIGBY
  Betsy ... 6
  John ... 6
BIGELOW
  Emma ... 106
  W^m ... 106
BIGHEART, Alice ... 108
BIGWOOD
  Arlena ... 108
  J H ... 109
  James ... 108
  James H ... 109
  L J ... 108
  Laura ... 109
  Lidy Jane ... 108
  Myrtle ... 108
BILLINGSIE, Frank ... 159
BILLINGSLEA
  Frank ... 110
  Helen ... 110
  Jennette ... 110
  Joe ... 110
  Mack ... 110
  Willie ... 110
BIRD
  Charles ... 3
  Charley ... 279
  Emily ... 95
  Hester ... 279
  Lacey ... 275
  Lillie ... 3
  Lily ... 3
  Marion ... 3
  Pearl ... 95
  Sinnie ... 371

Index

BIVIN, Sophronia............................109
BIVINS
   Catherine G................................101
   David T..101
   S 109
   Walter M......................................101
BLACK
   Alice 283
   Effie 283
   Mae 283
   Martha 283,381
   Willie 283
BLACKBIRD
   James 278
   Katie 100
   Lizzie 100
   Lucy 278
   Round 278
BLACKFOX
   Joe 274
   John 274
   Jonathin 275
   Lucy 274
   Nancy 274
   Oogusstah 274
   Sally 275
   Sam..274,275
   Susanne..275
BLACKHAW, Sarah 11
BLACKMAN
   O 87
   William 3
BLACKMON
   O 40
   Sarah... 7
BLACKSTONE
   Dewit 9
   Edward 2
   Frank.. 2
   George 2
   George W 3
   Gypsie... 2
   Henry 282
   Jennie... 9
   Jossie 2
   Katy 2
   Louise 9
   Mollie 2
   Nannie 9
   Nip.. 2
   P N 9,60
   Peachie 2
   Pleasant.. 9
   R 3,14,21,23,27,30,38,49,50,
   55,62,66,71,75,78,86
   R E 2,3,7,11,13,14,15,17,21,23,
   27,30,35,38,39,41,49,50,55,62,66,71,
   72,75,78,87
   Robert 9
   Robert E....................................... 2
   Robert N 3
   Robt 17,30
BLACKWELL
   King David 99
   Rosa..99
   Soloman..99
BLAGG, Thomas 275
BLAINGAME, Geo R 281
BLAIR
   Emma 102
   John 99
   Maude 102
   Min 102
BLAKE
   Georgia 97
   Jennie A 97
   Nita E...97
   Samuel C 97
BLALOCK, Sarah 279
BLAYLOCK
   Alice E...279
   Artelia C 279
   Charles...111
   Gano 280
   John 111
   Julius T..279
   Lotta A...279
   Mary E...279
   Nellie J...279
   Sarah..279
   Susan 111
BLEDSOE
   Bell 96
   Belle 96

Index

Henry W	96
Sallie M	96

BLEVINS
- Affsie 279
- Augusta 283
- Francis 279
- George 277
- Gusta 277
- J L 286, 301
- J S 337
- Jack Jun 283
- Jeff 284
- Joseph 277
- Josie 277
- Lee 279
- Mintie 279
- Nancy 283
- Nellie M 284
- Ollie 277
- Pleasant 277
- Ross 283
- Sarah 277
- Thomas 279
- Walter L 279
- William 279

BLOSINGOME, Geo R 281
BLOSSER, Joseph D 109

BLUEJACKET
- (Illegible) 286
- Carrie 284
- Edward H 284
- Ida M 284
- Thomas 380
- Tom 380
- Walter 284
- W^m T 284

BLYTHE
- Aubrey A 284
- Cora Dell 280
- Eliza 6
- Fairy A 284
- J S 109
- Jackson 6
- James 98
- Jemima S 109
- John E 284
- Mary 106

- Mary Jane 284
- N B 284
- Napoleon 280
- Napoleon B 284
- William H 284

BOGGS
- (Illegible) 99
- Blue 4,5
- Canzada 4,5
- Polly 4,5
- Purly 10
- William T 10
- W^m T 10

BOLES
- Cherokee 2
- Frank 2
- Fred 2
- Holland 2
- Jennie 2
- Perl 2

BOLIN
- Annie 5
- Eliza 5
- John 5
- Kate 5
- Moza 5
- Ross 5

BOLING
- J M 108, 112, 158
- Julia M 112

BOND
- Ed S 109
- Francis L 109
- S W 109
- W^m P 109

BONE
- Ida 106
- Ruth Jane 106

BONNY, Samuel 100

BOOT
- Mary 154
- Nellie 110
- William 110

BOOTH
- Alice 95
- F M 95
- Grover G 95

410

Index

Liddie 95
BOUDINOT
  Nannie 97
  Sallie 97
  Samson 97
  Susan 97
BOUGHER
  Charles 100
  Florence 100
  William R 100
BOWLING, J M 238
BOWLS
  Richard 7
  Thomas 6
BOW^{M}AN
  Clara 261
  Earl 261
  Lila 261
BOYD
  J D 188
  Jane 100
  S Samuel E 100
BOYNTON, Nancy E 105
BOZEMAN
  Lizzie 102
  W E 102
BRACKEN
  Alton 8
  Bessie 8
  Cornelia 8
  Harry 8
  Hubbard 8
  Tracy P 8
BRACKETT
  Bessie S 110
  Margaret 110
BRADLEY
  Henrietta 280
  M J 280
  Mary J 280
BRADSHAW
  A C 43
  Albert H 108
  Charley 96
  Ellen 96
  Emma F 108
  Ethel T 108
  Eva L 108
  J B 112
  J W 96
  James 43
  Jessie P 108
  Lizzie 43
  Nora 112
  Oscar 108
  Rose E 112
  Sophia 96
  Susan S 108
BRADY
  Ed 108
  Edeth 101
  Frank 101
  Geo W 101
  Hettie 108
  Lizzie 101
  Mary 101
BRANHAM, Charles 28
BRANNAN & HAYES 31,50
BRANSON
  Attie 105
  Emma 105
BRASSFIELD, John 113
BRAY
  Geo 7
  George 7
  John 102
  Richard 10
  William 10
BREAD, Samuel 111
BREEDLOVE
  Emely 280
  Florence 280
  Jennie 280
  M W 280
  W W 174
  Walter W 280
BREEDON
  Martha 104
  Sarah 104
BREWER
  Charles D 11
  Cherry 11
  D 11
  Delila 11

Oliver P 11
William 111
BRICE
   Alexina T 7
   Annie L 7
   Charles M 7
   Czrina V 7
   Georgia C 7
   Walter 7
   Walter J 7
BRIDGES
   Augustus 8
   Charles 8
   Joe 8
   Nannie J 8
   Thomas H 8
BRIGHT, Nay 3
BRIMAGE
   Frederick 5
   Rachel 5
   Susan 5
   Thomas 46
BRINK
   Albert 102
   Charles 102
   Georgia 102
   Lidia 102
   M J 102
   Mary 102
BROADWELL, G R 138
BROCK
   Charles 280
   Geo 329
   Lewis C 110
   Ollie 110
   P G 110
   Walter 329
BROOKS
   Mary W 6
   Samuel 109,266
BROUDDUS
   Augusta 276
   Corinthia 276
   Dora 276
BROWN
   Ada 98,111
   Addie 280
   Albert B 99
   Amos 98
   Anna H 105
   Annie 97
   Beatrice 99
   Benjamin 8
   Bessie May 101
   Bill 95
   Carrie 95
   Celia 98
   Charles 113
   Charley 279
   Docie 8
   Ebbin 98
   Eddie 109
   Edner M 99
   Effie M 99
   Ellis P 99
   Emily 109
   Emmet V 95
   Ethel H 105
   Eugene 280
   F E 99
   Fintie 282
   Florence R 98
   Frances E 99
   Frank 111,279
   Geo H 105
   Geo Hammer 105
   George 106,113
   George A 8
   Gertie 8
   Herman 109
   Hiram C 99
   Ida 111
   James 9,21
   James H 109
   James M 98,99
   Jas 9
   Jennie 257
   Jessie 280
   Joana 106
   John B 98
   John G 95
   John L 112
   Johnnie A 112
   Josephine 101

Index

Kiowa 95
Larkin 111
Laura E 112
Lillie 101
Lizzie 113,280
Lizzie H 105
Lou 113
Loui F 113
Louisa 101
Lucy 277
Luther 96
Lydia 101
Manchie 8
Margaret C 98
Martha A 97,111
Mary 111,282
Mary E 99
Mary H 106
Minnie L 101
Mollie V 99
N L 99
Nancy L 99
Nannie 95,111
Nathie 98
Nora H 99
Ollie Belle 108
Patrie Ellen 108
Patsey M 99
Pearl 279
Pearl H 105
Quinn 8
Rachel 8
Rachel H 106
Rebecca 102
Richard 109
Robt L 102
Rufus 101
Ruth E 106
S L 98
Sallie E 99
Sarah 111,280
Sarah E 106
Sarah Ellen 106
Sarnia E 112
Sila H 106
Susan F 98
Susan L 98
Thomas 96
Thos 111
Thos W 101
Tillie 101
Troy 8
W H 111
W P 111
Wade H 9
Walter P 95
William 8,106
W^m 98,109
W^m P 111
Zenie 108
BROWNING
   Fannie M 109
   M J 109
   Mary J 109
   May 206
   Robert E 109
BRYAN
   Ella P 95
   Rachel M 112
   Roy V 95
   S A 95,188
BRYANT
   Alice 275
   Ben F 275
   Benjamin F 277
   Bertha M 277
   J V 96
   James A 96
   Jessie 96
   John 277
   Joseph V 96
   Leona 275
   Leonidas 96
   Lottia S 277
   Lula L 277
   Margaret 277
   Martha 277
   Roda 275
   Sarah 277
   Vinnie 96
BUCHANAN, W^m 101
BUCHANNAN
   Bertha 3
   J A 43

Index

Mary 101
BUCHANNON, J C 3
BUCHANON
   Ann 275
   Clyde 275
   Edgar 275
   Joanne 275
   Joseph 275
   Myrtle 275
   Walter 275
BUCKET
   Aggie 277
   Bettie 277
   David 277, 278
   Dawes 277
   Jackie 277
   Lou 277
   Sam 277
BUCKMASTER
   Lillie 113
   Mary L 113
BUDDING
   Jack 311
   Lewis 274
BUFFING, Susie 112
BUFFINGTON
   Carrie R 95
   Charles 283
   Chas 283
   Cooie 160
   Coo-ie 95
   D W 283
   E W 155, 191, 200, 201, 209, 212, 217, 218, 276, 299
   F F 283
   James 283
   L W 171, 218, 280, 283, 288, 319, 323, 343, 380, 384
   Lucien 283
   Nannie 95, 283
   Susie 112
   T M 284
   Thomason 282
   Thos M 284
   Webster 283
   W^m 279
   W^m W 279

BULAWSKY
   Annie 281
   August 281
   Blanche 281
   Dora 281
   Ida 281
   Josephine 281
BUMGARNER
   John W 7
   Samuel 7
BURCHFIELD
   Anna 305
   John 305
BURDETT, J 27
BURGESS
   Alena 100
   Bean 112
   Benjamin 112
   Cora 100
   Daniel 100
   Hettie 100
   Jack 100
   John 100
   Mattie 100
   Sarah 158
   W^m 100
BURK
   Amy 2
   Eva 2
   Fannie 2
   Fannie W 2
   Florence L 2
   Hellen E 2
   John S 282
   Maggie J 282
   Martha J 282
   Thos W 282
   Walter L 282
   William R 282
BURNES, Sam 106, 109
BURNS
   Bernie D 106
   Etta H 109
   Lillie D 109
BURR
   Aaron 6
   Alice 98

Index

Andy 22
Blanche 98
Etta 98
Frank 7
Geo 284
Geo Brittan 284
George 284
Harris 98
James W 98
Jessie E 98
John W 98
Samuel 98
BURROWS
  Chas C 10
  Christopher 10
  Edward N 10
  James 9
  James Edward 10
  Jas 9
  John H 10
  Thomas C 10
  Tobe 9
  Whit 9
BURTON, Cynthia 284
BUSH, L W 279
BUSHYHEAD
  Annie 278
  Charley 108
  Charlotte 107
  Cornelia 278
  Delila 107
  Ellen 107
  Emma 107
  Isaac 107
  Jenny 278
  Jesse 278
  John 278
  Maggie 278
  Martha 107
  Nancy 107
  Sarah 107
  Smith 112
  Willie 278
  Wilson 107
  W^m 107
BUSSEY
  Dava 100

Dottie 100
Emma 100
Frankie 100
Freddie 100
Johnnie 100
Maud F 100
BUSTER
  Charles 112
  Ellen 112
  James 112
  John 112
  John, Jr 112
  Watie 112
  William 112
  W^m 112
BUTLER
  Bear 11
  Carrie L 96
  Cora 283
  Darcus 277
  Fount G 96
  Frank 110
  Homer 278
  James P 278
  Jno E 283
  John E 283
  Lizzie D 96
  Lucian 283
  M G 96
  M J 115
  Mannie G 96
  Mary G 96
  Mattie 110
  Nancy 278
  Richard 9
  Robt E 96
  Ruth 9
  Sallie 283
  Samuel 9
  Sokinna 11
  Susie 11,26
  W^m S 115
BUZZARD
  Adam 278
  Bessie 278
  Betsey 110
  Betsy 274

Betsy Y 274
Cornelius 281
Daniel 281
Falling 281
J Hawker 278
Jackson 281
John 281
Joseph 281
Nancy 281
Nate Yellow Bird 274
Nellie 278
Rozen 281
Sam 278
Sarah 281
William 281
Yellowbird 274
BYNUM, R N 233
BYRD
   Daisy 101
   Edward 101
   Elizabeth 104
   Henry 101
   Henry A 104
   Jane 101
   Leroy A 104
   Mary E 104
   Prince E 104
   Randolph S 104
C M LONDON & CO 92
CALDWELL
   Ben M 118
   Callie 118
   Fannie 118
   J J 118
   John L 118
   Lula 118
   Mary 118
CALVERT
   Amanda A 128
   Charles 115
   Charles E 128
   Cynthia 115
   Maude 115
   S E 128
   Sarah E 128
   William 115
CAMEN

F 359
   F M 359
CAMP
   Claud F 287
   James M 235
   Mary 287
   Ora M 235
CAMPBELL
   Alex C 11
   Bean 13
   Betsy 122
   Betty 11
   Carrie 123
   Charlotte 11
   Delora 99
   Flora 123
   J E 105,106,125,138,145,148, 155,196,215,218,223,225
   J W 185
   James 12
   James A 11
   John 13
   Lizzie 12
   May 11
   Minnie 11
   Minnie Rosa 126
   Rope 122
   Saml 13
   Samuel 12
   W^m R 123
CANADA
   Fannie E 125
   Henry Lee 125
   Ida 125
CANARY
   Anola 12
   Emma P 12
   J D 12
   Simon C 12
CANDY
   George 119
   Sam 130
CANNON
   Annie 254
   S P 14
   Sterling P 14
   Tommie 254

Index

CAPPS, Mary 16,38
CARD, Carrie 255
CAREY
   Anna 288
   Effie 288
   Ella 288
   Freeman 293
   Gabriel 123
   Jack 293
   Jessie 131
   Joe 288
   Joseph 288
   Lee 288
   Lelia M 123
   Lillie 288
   Myrtle 288
   Ruth 288
   W V 193,214,215,225
   W^m V 95,123,138,196,214,225
CAREYT, Lucy J 342
CARLILE
   Charles 11
   Eve 286
   Henrietta 119
   Lena 11
   Robert 11
   Stephen 11
   Stephen, Jr 11
CARLISLE
   Eve S 286
   Thomas 266
CARMAN
   Hugh 113
   Katie 113
CARMEN, Joshua 113
CARMICLE
   Annie B 122
   Clarence 121
   Lewis 121
   Mary 121,122
   Mary E 122
   Ora J 121
   Thomas 122
   Walter 122
   William C 121
CARMON
   Addie N 193
   Annie B 193
   Geo L 193
   Robt L 193
   Spencer W 193
CARPENTER, Claud 15
CARR
   Beulah M 120
   Clidy 132
   Edward 132
   Fannie 290
   Frank 290
   Frank N 120
   Ivsie 91
   John 126
   Josie M 120
   Minnie 132
   N F 120,176
   Quinn 132
   Sarah A 120
   Sarah L 120
   Susan 290
   Tessie 132
   Waller W 122
   W^m A 121
CARRELL, J M 126
CARRINGTON
   Annie D 115
   R E 115
   Wyly V 115
CARROLL
   Mary C 126
   May 336
   Myrtle J 126
   Nora 336
   Toddie 336
CARSELOWERY
   Arthur 294
   Charles 294
   Ellenor 294
   Flossy 294
   James M 294
   Katy E 294
   Pauline 294
   Robert 294
   Stella 294
CARSELOWEY, K E 294
CARTER

Alma A 127
Annie 121
Candis J 115
Deloria 115
Flossie E 127
Indianola M 127
J P 3,126,265,371
John R 120
May M 127
Minnie 130
Sarah 120
Walter 121
William S 127
CARTSINGER, F L 116
CARTWRIGHT
   Essie 114
   J H 114
   John H 114
   Letitia 114
   Wm Thos 114
CARVER
   Frank 15
   James 15
   Lizzie 15
   Nannie 15
   Walter 15
   Willie 15
CARY
   David 288
   Robert 288
CASEY
   Arch 128
   Charlotte 293
   Darkus 293
   Edward 293
   Edward, Jr 293
   Geo Benge, Jr 293
   Lydia 293
   Susaj 293
CASH
   John A 16
   Samuel 16
CASS
   Alonzo B 119
   Josie E 119
CATES
   Edmond 115

Emma 115
Levena 115
T A 115
CATLIN, Phenia 336
CAVE
   Annie 296
   Jas 295
   Manora 295
   Menora 296
   Ona 296
CAVENDER
   S F 121
   Sarah F 121
CAWOOD
   Andrew 287
   Henderson 287
   Herbert 287
   Jay L 287
   John T 287
   Matilda 287
   Moses S 287
   Sarah 287
   William F 287
CESSNA, Sallie 124
CHAMBERLAIN
   Abbie E 127
   Abbie O 128
   Amery P 129
   Arthur F 128
   Catharine D 128
   Clara E 128
   Dollie E 128
   Emma G 128
   Eunice 127,128
   Evastus D 128
   Flora H 128
   Maggie L 128
   Mary 128
   N B 128
   Nelson B 128
   Pearl L 129
   Robt L 129
   William N 128
   Winfred C 128
   W^m C 128
CHAMBERLIN
   A F 127,128,179

E W	118
Ed W	118
Edward R	118
John R	118
Laura H	118

CHAMBERS

Bettie	141
Clara	129
Claude	123
Clementine	119
Cora	129
David	130
Eliza D	131
Evans	123
Ezekiel	131
Geo S	126
Halla	135
Henry C	119
J P	126
James	119, 130
Jefferson P	126
Jennie	129
Jessie S	131
Joe H	131
John	241
Johnny	119
Joseph	122, 130
Joseph W	131
Juliette	129
Katie	130
Leo	131
Lewis	129
Lizzie	129
M	132
Mack	135
Manda B	126
Mary	119, 233
Mattie	241
Maxwell	132
Minnie	122
Nancy J	122, 130
Nannie E	131
Pearl I	131
Pickens	130
Robert	13
Robt	131
Sanders	129

Tee-see	123
Tee-sey	122
Torchee chu	241
Tuxie	131
Vann	129
White	129
William D	131
William L	131
Willie E	131
W^m A	131
W^m W	131

CHANDLER

Anna E	293
Ben H	291
Claud A	291
Claude D	293
Cornelia A	291
David	293, 295
Ella J	295
Felix C	291
Henry	295
Homer E	291
Joh D	291
John	295
Lyda	295
Mariah	291
Myrtle	291
Nancy L	293
Pink	295
Samuel	295
Susan	295
Susie	132
T A	293
Tom A	293
Vann S	293
W^m	295

CHANEY

Ada	177
Addie	177
Chas P	124
Della	124
Eliza	124
Ethel	124
Florence E	113
Ida B	113
J M	124
Julia	124

Louella	124
Mamie	124
Sadie	124
Susan	124
Willie	177

CHAPMAN
Cynthia	117
Don L	117
Mary E	117

CHARLESWORTH
Fred W	295
Henry A	295
Jas F	295
Mary J	295
Oliver I	295
Susie B	295
Walter M	295

CHARLEY
Frank	120
Jennie	126
Lelia	120
Lillie	120
Mary	120
Ross	120
Samuel	120
Sarah J	120

CHARLIE
Jennie	126
Louisa	294
Ruth	126

CHATHAM
Mary A	288
P D	288

CHE GO NELEN 183

CHEATER
Allsie	289
Anna	289
Annie	289
Bunnie	288
Casie	285
Charley	289
Charlie	289
Che-lon-a-cha	289
Cornsilk	288
Enolia	288
Esuck	288
Eva	288
Flora	288
Ga hee ga	288
Gah he ga	289
Ga-hee-ga	288
George	289
Gunch ucha	289
Jefferson	289
Jimmie	289
John	285,288
Josiah	288
Josine	289
Katy	288
Lacy	288
Mariah	288
Qt-cle	289
Robin	288
Stand	288
Susie	289
Swimmer	289
Timothy	288

CHECOTAH
Aggy	13
Jeff	13
Martin	13

CHEEK
Luly D	289
Phessant J	289
Sarah	289

CHESNUT
Alex	117
Amanda	117
Hallie	117
Mary	117

CHILDERS
Levi	113
Thos J	294

CHILDES
Lucre Kia N	129
Thomas B	129

CHILOLM, Ingue 122
CHINOCHEE, John 292

CHISHOLM
Arley	13
Bettie	13
Eliza	13
Emely	13
George	13

Index

Grover C 13
Ida...13
Jackson 13
James 13
Jas 13
Kate 13
Lena 13
Lizzie 13
Stanly 13
Thomas 13
Thos 13
CHISM
   Dannel 188
   Jim 188
   Teder 188
CHISOLM
   Arle 130
   Ezekiel 130
   Ingue 122
   Jackson 130
   Lizzie 130
   Lucy 119
   Nancy L 130
   Nancy S 130
   Oo-li-chey 130
   Rose 130
   Tuxie 130
CHITWOOD
   Josie 293
   Lucy 293
   Walter 293
CHOATE
   E L 126
   J B 116
   John B 116
   Robt M 116
   Rufus Mark 126
   W S 115
   William P 126
   W^m S 115
CHOPPER
   Bird 287
   Daniel 284
   Darkey 287
   Daylight 285
   Emma 285
   Ester 285

Henry 285
Jennie 285,287
Joe 285
Liza 285
Lucy 284
Mike 287
See-were 285
Sugee 285
Su-gee 285
CHOUSE, Lee 371
CHRISTIAN, Susie 289
CHRISTY, Benj 289
CHU NA WAH 294
CHUIE, Joe 311
CHU-NA-WAH 294
CHUNSTUDY
   Johnson 295
   Katy 295
   Wally 295
CLARK
   Addie C 125
   C P 69
   Effie M 118
   Emily L 125
   Emily Lee, Jr 125
   Eudotia 293
   Franklin 287
   Geo W 118
   Geo W, Jr 118
   Henry 118
   Hermon 12
   Johnson 286
   Josie 117
   L E 286
   Leona E 286
   Lizzie M 118
   Lizzy 287
   Lucy C 125
   Lydia 118
   Lydia A 118
   Mary 287
   Mary E 125
   Richard 12
   Ross 118
   Sarah E R 125
   Sequoyah D 125
   Sophia 12

Index

Susie 118
W C 118
W H 221
William 287
W^m A 117
W^m C 118
CLARKE
  Donia 293
  Eliza 293
  Eudotia 293
  Joel 293
  Lola 293
  Mattie 114
CLASBY
  Anna 292
  Fanny 292
CLAY
  Annie 14
  Columbus 14
  Lizzie 45
  Lula 14
  Minnie 14
  Willie 14
CLAYWELL, Kate 132
CLEGHORN
  Fannie 120
  Rosa 164, 120
  Thomas 120
CLELAND
  Amelia 113
  E S 115
  Emmet S 115
  Emmet S, Jr 115
  G W 95
  Geo W 113
  Geo W, Jr 113
  J B 114
  Jas B 114
CLINE
  Benjamin 15
  Eli 15
  Ezeikiel 15
  Ezekiel 15
  John 15
  May 15
  Ross 15
CLINGAN

Claude 121
Cora M 114
J K 121
Judge K 121
Mary J 114
Mattie E 114
Samuel D 114
Therman A 114
W D 114
W^m D 114
CLINKSCALES
  A M 128
  Annie E 128
  Louis D 128
  Lucille 128
CLOUD
  Henry 122
  John 12
  Joseph 15
  Josuah 14
  Lydia 355
  Ola 355
  Watt 355
  Zamuel B 122
COATNEY, Mandy 294
COATS
  Annie L 127
  Bertha E 290
  Charles 115
  Charles F 127
  Charles J 115
  Chas J 290
  Clara H 115
  Ellen L 115
  Ethel N 118
  Francis M 290
  Geo M^c 290
  J E 127
  James 117
  James B 117
  James E 127
  Jennie A 290
  Jennie B 117
  John 113, 115
  John H 290
  John W 127
  L J 127

Louisa J 127
Samuel 118
William 115,290
W^m P 290
COBB
  A C 114
  Albert B 114
  Alex C 114
  Alice 17
  Artie 295
  Belle 114
  Bent 16,59
  Bernie 16
  Charles 17
  Edos 16
  Edward 17
  Ella 286
  Eula 16
  Evaline 114
  Grover C 16
  J B 113,114
  J B, Jr 108
  Jack 17
  James 17,45
  Jeff 45
  Joe Batt 286
  Joel B 113
  John 120
  Lizzie 286
  Mack 120
  Mary 295
  Mary E 16,295
  Mary J 114
  S S 113,183
  Sam 286
  Sam S 295
  Sam'l S 113
  Samuel A 295
  Simpson 16
  Susan 16,17
  William 17
COBBSTILL
  Jacob 13
  Mark 13
  Martha J 13
COCHRAN
  Alex 123,218

Annie 123
Clarence 122
Clinton 122
Clue 131
George 119,158
H C 325
Jennie 123
Jenny 123
Jesse 323
Jessie 122,131
Jessie, Jr 122
John 122
Julia 119
Lettie 123
Return 123
Ruthie 123
Susie 122
Victoria 119
Zeddie 123
CODRY, William 125
COEHN, H C 113
COFFEE
  Geo 250
  George 130
COHEE
  J H 288
  Martha 288
COKER
  Arthur L 123
  Benjamin F 123
  Calvin 124
  Calvin E 124
  Calvin F 123
  Charley 125
  David N 122
  Eliz J 124
  Elizabeth 122
  Frenklin R 124
  Ida Mary 124
  John 132
  John R 124
  Joseph C 123,124
  Josie 122
  Lewis 123
  Lillie C 125
  Lizzie 124
  Mary 122

Mary E	125
Mary L	123
Mattie T	123
Miller	123
Myers Willie	124
Ora	122
William P	124
W^m W	123

COLBARD
Annie	117
Gudger	117
Myrtle	117
Odin	117

COLE
Bertie	116
Bonney M	114
Boon	116
Clem	116
Dora	116
Drewsy	116
Effie	116
Felix	116
Jack H	116
Jennie E	116
John	116
L B	114
Laura R	114
Lucy	116
Mart E	116
Mary	116
Mary A	116
Maude	116
Sissie	116
Vinnie	116

COLEMAN
John	11,12
Nancy	11
Newton	12
Samuel	12

COLESTONE
Clementine	11
Taxie	11

COLLIER
Charlotte	116
Chas A	132
Flora	116
James	116

Katie	116
Lettie	116
Mack	116
S M	116

COLLINS
Albert H	126
Annie	116,126
Aurora	14
Bradley	294
Cora	14
Eliza	116
Emma	14
George	131
Henry	294
Ida M	131
Jesse	294
Joe	294
John	294
Katy	294
Mary F	126
Mary J	12
Oerid	14
Roseol	14
Sallie	294
Thomas E	12
William L	12
Wynonna	14

COLSTON
Bettie	127
Charles	121
Cynthia	127
Kynes	127
Lizzie	127
W C	119
Wilson	127

COMINGDEER
Agie	286
Celia	285
Joe	285
Lee	286
Polly	285
Sevns	286

COMPTON
Chillia	17
Clark	15
Ernest	17
Larrance	15

Index

Thomas 17
COMWELL, James 125
CONDRY
   Mary A 165
   Savanah 210
   Sterling H 165
CONEY
   E J 127
   Eliza J 127
   George 127
CONKLIN
   Annie 117
   Bertha 117
CONNALLY
   Bettie 15
   Emily J 15
   Jas 15
   Maggie M 15
CONNER
   Crawford 291
   F M 301, 317, 392
   I M 291
   Leela M 291
   Leonard 291
   Lucy J 292
   O Lonzo 291
   Rebecca J 291
COODY
   Amanda 115
   Belinda 125
   Daniel R 14
   Eula 115
   John 286
   John H 124
   Lewis 14
   Lewis W 14
   Mary A 124
   Minnie 115
   Myrtletopie 14
   Richard H 124
   Sarah J 115
   William E 124
COOK
   Florence 243, 295
   Henry A 126, 295
   Herman 295
   Isabella 295
   Isabelle 126
   Thomas 295
   Thomas M 243
   W D 295
   W^m D 126, 295
COON
   Bernard L 240
   Ellen 132
COOPER
   Alice 128
   Glen 128
   Laura 128
   Onida 128
COPELAND
   Alex 291
   Alexander 291
   Bertha M 291
   Cordelia 291
   Delia 291
   Geo W 291
   Nancy 291
   Rabbit B 291
   Riley 291
   Rilm 291
CORBAN
   Frank 120
   Sarah 120
CORDRY
   Andy 16
   Bessie 16
   Hugh 16
   John 16
   Lula 16
   Percy 16
   Thomas 16
   Wilson 16
CORLINE, Thomas 46
CORNSHUCKER
   Anna 287
   Arch 287
   Geo 287
   Heraham 287
   John 287
   Laura 287
   Liza 287
   Lizzie 287
   Sallie 287

Index

Sam 287
TeeAnn 287
Tom 287
Watie 287
CORNSILK
   Charley 396
   Stephen 15
CORNTASSEL, Ida 268
COSSTEPHENS
   Nancy 14
   William 14
COUCH
   Cherokee 121
   Clara 121
   Cynthia 124
   Donnis M 294
   Geo F 294
   James C 121
   Jessie F 121
   Jno F 121
   L C 294,324
   Lucy M 294
   M M 124
   M W 121
   Mae 121
   Marion W 121
   Mentie L 294
   Mitchell M 124
   Nannie 124
   Nannie E 121
   Robt L 121
   Thos 294
   Victoria E 121
   William 121
COUGHRAN
   Eliza 14
   Franzell 14
   Jasper 14
   Jesse 14
   Johnson 14
   Lyda 14
   Mary 14
   William 14
COUNTRYMAN
   Andrew 292
   Andy 292
   Arthur E 292

Eva 125
Geo 291,292
George 125
Hoolie 125
Jackson 292
James 291
John 292
John, Jr 286
Leander 286
Minerva 291
Nora 125
Rebecca 292
Riley 125
Rose Anna 292
Sabra 125,292
Zimerhem 292
COURTNEY
   Edward 292
   Eliza 292
   Jessie 292
   John W 292
   Minerva 292
COVEY
   Bula 291
   Preston 291
   Susan 291
COWAN
   A C 114
   Alex C 114
   Cherrie 114
   Felix 127
   Felix, Jr 312
   Stella 114
   Terry 114
COWAND
   Annie C 14
   Thomas W 14
COWART
   Alie 17
   Joanna 17
   John 17
   Slater 17
COWELL, Caleb W 292
COWELS
   Cora B 291
   Eddie 291
COWLES

Charles E 289
James C 289
Joseph W 289
Maggie N 289
Martha A 289
Viola J 289
Will L S 289
COX
  Annie.....................................180
  David 289
  Elva..293
  Flance D 290
  Freddie...................................180
  Geo A 290
  J D 290
  Jady D....................................293
  John S 289
  Lettie L 290
  Marcus G 290
  Marnie 289
  Martha 289
  R A 294
  Rebecca 290,293
  Steve F 290
COYNE
  Maggie...................................118
  Mary Ellen 118
CRAIG
  Carl..127
  Edna E 129
  Elgy C....................................129
  Eva S 129
  Frank W 129
  George 127
  Granvil...................................127
  Granville................................127
  Katie 129
  Laura......................................129
  Robt Q 129
  W L..129
  Wᵐ L......................................129
CRAMP, Sallie............................68
CRAMPS, Tildon 12
CRANE
  Bettie 12
  Bolivar.....................................15
  Dony..13

Ella 12
Francis 12
George 13
Henry.......................................13
Lacy...12
Louisa............................15,39,59
Maud..15
Nannie 13
Nora...12
Susie 132
CRAPO
  Charles....................................23
  Collins 27
  James 27
CRAWLER
  Dutch 12
  Elsey 12
  Elsie 12
CREECH
  Alice 130
  Jefferson 131
  Lulu 130
  Nettie 131
  Rebecca 130
  Ruth 130
  Willie....................................130
CREEK
  Belle M 132
  Mary 132
CREEK KILLER
  Catahyah 286
  Jay Gould..............................285
  Jeff..286
  Jurnarem 285
  Leonard................................286
  Mary 285
  Nancy 286
  Oolayah 286
  Rachel 285
  Sally......................................286
  Sarah.....................................286
  Scott.....................................285
CRIDDENTON, John...............42
CRISMON, Ida.......................286
CRITTENDEN
  Abraham 130
  Andy.......................................16

Index

Charles 15,16
Charles W 15
Ellen 16
George W 16
J F 285
James 15,16
Jas F 277,285
John H 129
Katie 15
Lecta 285
Lizzie 285
Mary J 15
Robert 16
Sam 129
Thomas 16
W S 117
Watt S 117
CRITTENDON
   Abraham 130
   Andrew F 120
   Barbara 129
   Cordia 130
   Ira 130
   John H 129
   Killie 129
   Riley 130
CROCKETT
   Inas 290
   M A 290
   Mary A 290
   Pearl 290
CROMWELL
   Campbell 117
   Cornelius 196
   Lewis R 119
   Margaret 117
CROSLAND
   Ida 12
   Richard, Jr 12
   William 12
   Willie 12
CROSSLAND
   Cephas 11
   Kate 11
   Lizzie 11
   Lottie 11
   Richard 11

William 12
CROTER, William 291
CROTZER
   Effie 291
   Emma 291
   Rosa 291
   Stella 291
CROW
   Claude 114
   H C 114
   Johnson 114
   L E 131
   Laura E 131
   Lucinda 114
CROWDER
   Ethel Lee 121
   Geo A 121
   Jerry M 121
   Rosa 119
   Sarah 121
   Sarah A 121
CROWELL
   (F M) 337
   Allie 293
   Dr. 315
   Erda 293
   F M 156,272,274,278,280,281,
282,284,285,286,288,292,293,294,298
,299,301,305,309,310,312,314,317,
318,319,321,325,326,331,332,333,338
,339,340,347,348,353,359,360,361,
366,372,373,376,380,382,392,393
   Frank 293
   Hunter 293
   Lizzie 293
CRUTCHFIELD
   Alice 93,123
   Claude 120
   Cuba 126
   Dolphus 119
   Eli 17
   Ewing H 126
   Graqdy 120
   Ida 126
   J K 120,126
   James 131
   Jennie 119

Index

Jennie M 123
Jimmie 93, 334
Jo Alice 334
John A 17
John H 127
John K 126
Kate 122
L L 127
Leroy A 126
Leroy C 126
Leroy T 127
Lewis 17
Maggie O 126
Mary 17, 120
Roy 120
Sabrina J 127
Sarah 17
Susie 122
Taylor F 128
Thomas 17
Thos 122
Vinita 131
CUMIFORD
  Bennie F 117
  Henry S 117
  Julia 117
  Julia A 117
  Pleasant 117
  Robt 117
  Rosie A 117
CUMMINGDEER
  Becky 303
  Shucker 303
CUMMINGS
  Cora 119
  David 119
  Edna 119
  Grace 119
  Mary 119
  Penny 119
  Ruby 119
CUMMINS
  Dick 285
  Eliza 285
  Flora B 118
  Joe 285
  John 285

  Maggie E 118
  Sally 285
CUNIGAN, George 286
CUNNINGHAM
  Alf 129
  J L 292
  Lulu 292
  Mable 292
  Nevah 292
CURBY
  Charles 162
  Chas 162
CUREY
  Albert W 290
  Ben F 290
  Chas T 290
  Clarence E 290
  Claud P 290
  Cora N 290
  Emma E 290
  Florence 290
  Francis S 290
  Geo B 290
  Saphronia P 290
  Sara 290
CURRY
  Anna May 125
  Charles J 125
  Jay 14
  Jennie O 15
  Jesse 14
  Laura 14
  Lenora 14
  M E 125
  Mamie Viola 125
  Margaret E 125
  Sabrina L 125
  Susie Lee 125
  W V 176
  W^m V 176
CURTIS
  Dulcie 292
  Lula H 292
  Mary A 292
  W E 292
  W^m H 292
CURTSINGER

Index

Etta 116
Fannie L 116
Fred 116
CUSHMAN, Jayson 288
DAILY
Joseph Crossland 12
Thomas 12
DALE
James 138
Joseph 176
DALE-DA
Jennie 297
John 297
Oo-nas-ta 297
Qua-lie-uke 297
Ross 297
Sallie 297
Shucker 297
DAMERAN
Birdie A 302
Eva N 302
Henry A 302
J L 302
John L 302
Lee L 302
Mattie L 302
Rex E 302
W^m O 302
DAMERON
Luella 139
Samuel D 139
DANDERSON
John Otis 141
Lizzie 141
DANIEL
Alice R 301
Eliza 301
Emma 301
James 301
John 18
John M 301
Joseph 18
Joseph M 125
Ludie 20
Lulu 301
M 139
Malcre 20

Mamie D 301
Mary 18
Mattie 301
Monna 316,319
Richard 20
Robert 301
William 301
DANIELS
Alice 299
Ann 298
Annie 136
Eddie 136
Gar-ker-les-top 136
George 136
Jesse J 139
John 299,370
Kay-hor-key 136
Lucinda 136
Lucy 299
M 140
Marmaduke 139
Osa 136
Phillip 299
Richards 136
Robert 301
Stafford 139
Susie 136
Thomas 136
William D 139
DANNELS, Rebecca A 138
DANNENBERG
Alice 133
Elizabeth 133
Grady 133
J C 83,135,226,233,242
N W 133
Nath B 133
Oby 133
Truxie 133
DARNELL
Cora May 303
R D 303
Sonora 303
DAUGHERTY
Agnes 139
Charles 133
Clem H 133

430

Index

Dave 110
Dora..110
Ethel 139
Ett 133
Jennie...139
John 134,139
DAVENPORT
  GuAlma 142
  J S 142,164,172
  Willard 142
DAVID, Draydon 247
DAVIDSON
  Mary M...138
  William 138
DAVIS
  Ace 20
  Aleck 297
  Alice V 136
  Ammon...18
  Artelia...298
  Arthur 136
  Asa..20
  Asenah B 302
  Awa-ie 296
  Barney 135
  Becky..296
  Benjamin 302
  Betha..18
  Bettie 17
  Bird...135
  Birtha L 302
  Brilla...19
  Burwell 141
  Charles.....................................17,135
  Cicero 19
  Ciscera 19
  Claude..137
  Cora..137
  Daisie..20
  Daniel 19
  Dawson..137
  Dock 296
  Dr J T...302
  Earl 18
  Edna E 137
  Ella 18,28,135,137
  Frog 141

  Geo 296,297
  Geo W 301
  Hanna 20
  Hattie...141
  Henry...18
  Isaac...20
  Jack..18,297
  James...20
  Jane S...19
  Jeder...18
  Jeff..20
  Jefferson 18
  Jennie......................................27,135
  Jng 56
  Joe D..18
  Joel M..20
  John 20,133,135,141
  John B..136
  John D 135
  John W....................................20,301
  Jug 17
  Katy 297
  Katy R 298
  Kim..135,141
  Leonie..17
  Letha N 20
  Lizzie...20
  Lonzo D 18
  Loranza D 18
  Loyd 137
  Lucinda..19
  Lucy...20
  Lugy 17
  Lulu 135
  Lulu J...302
  Lyta..136
  Mable...136
  Mack...141
  Mary 80,141
  Maud..66
  Minnie S 301
  Minta..17,26
  Mollie 17
  Monroe D 141
  Nancy 17,297
  Nanie 17
  Nannie 17,19

Napoleon C	135
Nellie	135
Nellie J	298
Neppie	141
Newton	136
Nick	297
Olivia	137
Phillip	345
Pollie	18
Rachael	19
Rachel	141
Rila	19
Robert L	20
Ros	17
Ruth	20
Sam T	19
Samuel L	18,19
Sarah	297,338
Stand	28
Stanu	18
Susan	139
Susan J	18
Susie	17,135,141
Sydny	19
Theadore	20
Thomas	135
Thompson	18
W T	301
William	20,135

DAWES

Jane	303
Jonathan	297
Jonathon	297

DAWSON

Albert	299
Allice	138
August	299
Burton	138
Catherine	299
Chas B	300
Clarence	300
Council	300
Dick W	138
Elbert	138
Ella	138
Elmer	300
Ermine	300
Florence	300
Francis	299
Frank	138
Hattie J	300
Hugh	299
Iola B	300
J W	299
Jacob	299
James	138
James R	300
Jessie	299
John	138,300,353
John W	299
Joseph	300
Katie	299
Laura	138
Lenoma H	300
Lula	299
Marion	301
Matt	299
Mrs W A	303
Orle H	300
Ray	299
Riley	299
Robert	142,299
Robert B	300
Rosa B	300
Texanna	303
Thos P	300
Vennie D	300
W A	298,303
Wilburn	300
Wilburn A	298
W^m C	138
W^m R	299
Zona	299

DAY

Ruth S	303
W^m A	303

DEAL

Mack	138
William	138
W^m	138

DEE-CAW-NAS-KI 303

Jennie	303
Nancy	303

DEEMS

Index

Clara 298
Edna 140
Johny 140
DEGE
   C F 133
   Charles F 133
   James T 133
   John J 133
   Laura 133
   Laura A 133
   Mary E 133
   Phillip 133
   Walter T 133
   William 133
DELONA, Charles 18
DELOZIER
   Fontain G 134
   Georgie V 134
   John E 134
   Manford V 134
DENBO
   Belle 135
   Jno L 135
   Lettie V 135
   Minnie M 135
   N V 135
   Nettie V 135
   Oce 135
   Robt L 135
DENBOO, M M 135
DENNIS
   Mary 300
   Nancy 300
   Oscar 300
   Peter 300
   Rachel 300
   Susie 300
   Wesley 300
DENNY, D L 187
DENTON
   Frank 141
   Hettie 141
   John 297
   Mattie 141
   Randolph 139
   Rufus 141
   Susie 141

Unce 141
DENVER, George 135
DERRICK
   Eddie 137
   Henrietta 137
   Jennie A 137
   Josie 137,204
   Jossie 137
   Katie 137
   Nellie 137
DIAL
   Bettie E 132
   Daniel F 132
   Hugh H 132
   Lelia A 132
   M E 134
   Mary E 134
   Mary T 134
   N H 132
   Nancy 133
   Nathaniel H 132
   Nola M 132
DICK
   Alsie 136
   Arthur 138
   Belle 141
   Bertha 138
   Cassie 136
   Cherokee 139
   Christie 134
   Ellen 136
   Ellis 139
   George 134,139
   Ira May 296
   Jacob 136
   Jeff 296
   Jessie 296
   Joseph 136
   Lorenzo 134
   Mary 139
   Mary E 296
   Myrtle 134
   Oce 303
   Oce C 140
   Rosie 139
   Thomas 139
   Thos 296

Index

Walter 134
Washington 138
Willie 141
DICKSON
   Claude 137
   Cynthia 137
   G B 137
   Serena 137
DILDUN
   Hester 297
   James H 296
   John 296
   Lethie 296
   Nancy 296
   Rachel 296
DIMOND
   James 135
   Polly 135
DINTPOT
   Conner 178
   Nellie 178
DIRTEATER, Nancy 296
DIRTSELLER, Rider 298
DIRTSHELLER
   Akey 298
   Jess 303
   Ricer 298
   Sarah 298
   U-Sut 298
DIXON, Henrietta 303
DOBKINS
   Ben 140
   Hugh 140
   Ida 140
   Nora 140
DODGE, Orcona 252
DODSON
   Nancy 141
   W J 141
DOHERTY
   Charlie 297
   Claur 297
   Josie 297
   Robt E 297
   Will H 297
   William H, Jr 297
DOLLAR
   Aw-aie 296
   Iann 296
   I-Ann 296
DON CARLOS
   Annie B 149
   Frank L 149
   Lewis A 149
   Susan M 149
DONALDSON
   Annie 302
   Artie 302
   Frank 302
   Ollie M 302
   Rachel 302
   W^m C 302
DONALSON, W^m 302
DONNELLY
   Ada 140
   Emma 140
   Emma J 140
   Henry 140
   James 140
   Mattie 140
   Paul 140
   Thomas 140
   Willie 140
DONOHOO
   Mattie 301
   Phillip 301
DOOLY
   Earth 134
   Margaret J 134
   Mirth 134
   N 134
DOTTY, Blanche 300
DOTY, Blanche 300
DOUBLEHEAD
   Annie 296
   Bird 18,296
   Dick 296
   Filie 18
   Jennie 296
   Leaf 296
   Sallie 296
DOUGHERTY
   Rob E 297
   W H 297

DOUGHTY, Blanche 300
DOUGLAS
   Ella 138
   John A 138
   Nancy 138
   Walter C 138
DOUTHETT
   Custus L 302
   Emma 302
   Lulu P 302
DOWELL
   Claude 141
   Lee J 141
   Morgan 141
   Virdia A 141
   William E 141
DOWNEY, Joe 33
DOWNING
   Alex 189
   Arthur 301
   Benjamin 20,137
   Clem 189
   Cora 301
   Cornelia 189
   Daria 19
   Dave 18
   David 18,136
   Edward 19
   Ellis 137
   Enorley 136
   Felix 134
   Geo 19
   George 19,20,137
   Houston 297
   Jacob 137
   James 137
   Jane 19,299
   Jesse 19
   Jo 20
   John 299
   Johnston 301
   Joseph 19
   Judy 301
   Kate 19
   Leroy 138
   Lizzie 134,297
   Lucian 301
   Lucie 19
   Lucy 19
   Mandy 301
   Mano 20
   Mantie 204
   Mariah 19
   Mary 136
   Mary J 301
   Mattie 340
   Mike 299
   Nake 297
   Nancy 134,189
   Nannie 19
   Nellie 137
   Oll-kin 297
   Peggie 140
   Peggy 140
   Polly 160
   Richard 138
   Sallie 136
   Samuel 19
   Sarah 20,136
   Susie 301
   Thomas 19,301
   Walter 142
   William 35,204,229,299,301
   Wooster 137
DRAKE
   Bessie W 137
   Emily J 137
   Emma L 137
   J P 137
   John E 137
   Mary B 137
   N S 88
   Nannie E 137
DREW
   Ellen E 140
   George 133
   Jennie 140
   Jessie B 140
   Nana 140
   Pearl 140
   Ruby 140
   Willie R 140
   W^m H 140
DRYDEN

Flora	132
H R	132
Laura	132
Lucy A	132
Mary E	132
Mattie B	132
Rose E	132
William	132

DRYWATER

Adam	296
Good-money	296
Jennie	296
Jess	296
Jesse	296
Nancy	296
Susie	349
Synthia	296

DU SQU AN NI 303

DUBOIS

Dora	302
Mary	302
Mary A	302
Susie	302
Willie	302

DUCK

Emaline	134
Emeline	262
George	134
Jack	21
John	134
Linda	21
Rachael	21
Richard	134
Tahnie	21
Wolf	20

DUDLEY, Ellen 303
DUGLASS, Nancy 92

DUNAGAN

Georgia	19
James B	19
Lula	19
Mary A	19
Summer C	19

DUNCAN

Allie V	298
Alvy R	298
Annie	299
Carrie E	298
Charles	300
Charles G	298
Charlotte	299
Chas	299
Claud E	253
Dellen	299
Elizabeth	18
Ellen F	298
Ellis C	302
Ethel	140
Forest F	298
Fred B	298
Henry	138
J 205	
James	19
James A	299, 300
James N	298
James W	308
Jas Andrew	302
Jas R	301
Jas W	298
Jimmie	299
Joana C	133
John C	133
John E	302
Katy L	298
Lafayette	299
Layfayette	299
Lee	298
Lizzie	138
Louie E	298
Lucy A	299
Ludie	300
Ludlen	19
Luther L	298
Maggie	19
Martha	302
N M	134
Nannie	18
Narcisus	298
Nelly M	298
Nettie M	134
Oran A	298
Robt S	302
Rosetta	299
Sally	298

Index

Samantha ...298
Saml ...19
Samuel ...18
Sarah ...298
Sue E ...302
Susan ...301
Thomas ...18
W T ...140
Walter T ...140
William ...19
W^m ...302

DUNN
  Phebie ...18
  Pheby ...18

DUPREE
  Bessie ...139
  C B ...139
  Charlotte B ...139
  Elmer ...139
  Emma ...139
  Herbert ...139
  J J ...133
  M E ...139
  Maud E ...139
  W E ...139
  W^m E ...139
  Wright ...139

DU-SQU-AN-NIE ...303
  Rachel ...303

DYER
  Eliza ...20
  Sarah ...20

DYKES
  Ara Bella ...21
  Arabella ...21
  Bunk ...21
  Mary S ...21
  Nable H ...21
  Nettie C ...21

EARBOB, Lily ...65

EARLY
  S A ...21,28
  Susan A ...21

EARNEST
  Albert ...21
  Ellen ...21
  J E ...21

  Leroy ...21
EATEN, G M ...132
EATIN, G M ...132
EATON
  Callie ...144
  Calvin ...144
  Elizabeth ...145
  Ellis M ...144
  G W ... 51,119,141,144,157,159,218, 228,238,248,255,262,269
  Geo ... 125,139,144,158,228
  Geo W ...242,255
  George ...269
  Lelia ...144
  Mattie ...144
  Merritt ...144
  Mollie ...144
  Nancy ...144
  Richard ...144
  Taylor ...142
  Walter ...144
  Willie ...144

ECKERT
  Adie ...21
  Ammanda ...21
  Lizzie ...21
  Louiza ...21
  Richard ...21

ECKSTEIN
  Melvina ...21
  Melvira ...21

EDMONDSON
  Beula ...304
  Cherry ...304
  Florence ...304
  Gonia B ...304
  Hellen ...303
  Lula ...303
  Nancy ...304
  Stella ...303
  Turner J ...304

EDMONS
  Susie ...143
  William ...143

EDMUNSON
  Florence ...304
  Jeff ...303

Index

EDWARDS
   Bell 22
   Kate 22
   Mary 22
   Rose 22
   Susan 142
   W S 142
   William 22
EIFFERT
   H 46,157
   Henry 1,2,3,5,6,7,8,9,10,11,12,13,14,
15,16,17,18,19,20,21,22,23,24,25,26,
27,28,29,30,31,32,33,34,35,36,37,38,
39,40,41,42,43,44,45,46,47,48,49,50,
51,52,53,54,55,56,57,58,59,60,61,62,
63,64,65,66,67,68,69,70,71,72,73,74,
75,76,77,78,79,80,81,82,83,86,87,88,
90,92,95,97,98,100,102,105,106,108,
110,112,113,116,117,119,120,121,122
,125,128,129,130,132,133,134,135,
136,137,138,139,141,142,143,144,145
,146,148,150,151,152,153,154,155,
157,158,159,161,162,163,164,167,170
,175,176,177,179,181,182,183,184,
185,187,188,190,191,193,194,195,196
,197,198,201,202,203,206,207,209,
210,211,212,213,214,215,216,217,218
,219,220,221,222,223,224,225,226,
227,228,230,231,232,233,234,235,236
,237,238,239,240,241,242,243,244,
245,246,247,248,249,250,251,254,255
,256,258,259,261,262,263,265,266,
267,269,275,278,279,282,285,286,288
,292,293,294,295,296,302,303,306,
309,315,317,318,319,320,321,322,325
,326,328,329,330,331,332,333,334,
335,338,339,340,341,342,343,345,347
,349,350,352,355,356,357,358,359,
361,367,371,375,376,378,384,385,387
,388,390,391,392,393,394,395,397
   M A 22
EIFRFERT, Henry 57
EIGGERT, Henry 260
ELAM, Effie 305
ELARIDGE, Jesse 238
ELDRIDGE, Jeff 200
ELIOTT

James 22
Jane 22
Robert 21
ELLIOTT
   A E 142
   Anna 305
   Annie E 142
   Arch 305
   Archie 144
   Delia 144
   Elizabeth 142
   George 142
   Georgie 142
   Hiram 305
   Hiram, Jr 305
   Jack 143
   James 22,142
   Jessie 144
   Lizzie 142
   Mamie 142
   Mary 144
   Maude 142
   Riley A 142
   Robert 21
   Sarah 142
   Watt 144
   W^m H 142
   W^m T 142
ELLIS
   Annie 143
   Colbert 168
   E 111
   E S 6,22,53,57,71,77,85,
86,111,137
   Eaby 142
   Edward 168
   Eli 143
   Isaac M 142
   Jessie 168
   July 143
   Lizzie 168
   Mary 144
   May 144
   Minnie 168
   Nancy 143
   Nellie 168
   Ollie 144

Otto	144
Robert	143
Rosey	142
Thomas	142
Webster	142
William	142

ELLISON

C E	144
Charlotte E	144
Robert S	144

EMERSON

Emma	143
G E	143
George	143,144
Georgia	143

ENGLAND

Armergean	304
Becky	304
Belle	143
Ben C	304
Ben, Jr.	304
Benjamin	143
Beulah	143
Charles S	304
Eliza J	304
Elvie	143
Fanny	303
Frances	143
Geo	304,305
Harmon	304
Harry W	304
Joanna	304
John	143
Johnie	304
Joseph	143,304
Joseph, Jr	303,304
Lucy	143
Lucy J	304
Martin	303
Mary E	304
Maudie	304
Mollie	304
Neal	304
Pett	304
Pigeon	304
Sally	303
Samuel	304
Susan A	304
Susie L	304
Wash	295,304
Wilson	304
W^m W	304

ENLOE, Willie 141

EPLE

Annie	21
Bessue	21
Ella	21

ERWIN, Charles 144

ESSEX

Addie	143
C B	143
Cae C	143

ETTER

Bertie	142
E A	142

EVANS

Alice	21
Catherine	21
Effie	143
Eliza	143,144,242
James P	143
Kate	22
Minnie	22
Robt H	143
Ruler	21,35
Sue	22
Walter	21
Walter N, Jr	144
William	21

EVENS, Martha 304

EWERS

Chas E	193
Eloise M	193
John Y	193
William A	193

EWING, G M 314
EXSTEIN, Melvina 59

EZELL

Eva	143
Ola	143

FAGAN, Joseph 152

FAIR

Bettie	145
Dora	145

Index

Ella 145
Rena 145
Ross 145
FALLEN
  Blossom 305
  Charles 147
  Ida 148
  Jess 147
  John 147
  Johnson 305
  Lucinda 147
  Mary 305
  S J 148
  Sarah J 148
FALLENPOTS
  Alex 308
  Geo 308
  Martha 308
  Tom 308
FALLING
  Henry 25
  Johnson 309
  Johson 309
  Maggie 25
  Mary 309
FALLING BLOSSOM 305
FARMER
  Alice 24
  Belle 24
  Gracie 24
  Isabella 24
  Leaty 24
  Lewis 24
  May 24
FARNAR
  Leo V 151
  Salcie 151
FAY
  Alfred J 145
  Linne A 145
FEATHERHEAD
  Chickie 306
  Jeremiah 306
  Mose 306
  Sarah 306
  Susie 306
FEELING

Sally 305
Steve 305
FEILSON, F A 131,132,144
FERRELL, Gertie 282
FEWERSTINE, Rosa 306
FIELD
  Emaline 149
  Nellie 151
FIELD EATER 145
  Nancy 145
FIELDS
  Abie 25
  Adaline 307
  Albert 308
  Alexander 25
  Alica 307
  Amanda J 146
  Anna L 309
  Annie 306
  Bessie E 308
  Betsy 23
  Bettie 23
  Betty 307
  Bird 151
  Bud 307
  Bushyhead 24
  Calie L 24
  Callie 310
  Carlotte 307
  Carrie R 146
  Charles 25
  Charley 149
  Charlie 147
  Charlott 26
  Claud 25
  Cora 147,306,308
  Coreline B 24
  Cyrintha 147
  Delila 310
  Della 151
  Dick O 146
  Dora 151
  Edward 151
  Eliza J 309
  Elizabeth J 146
  Ella 24,151,307
  Elmer 232

Emaline	149
Ethel	151
Ezekiel	306
Fannie	147
Feman	307
Frank	25
Frasilla	308
Frederick	25
Geo	306, 307, 309
Geo A	310
Geo, Jr	307
George	147
Henry	307
Henry F	146
J S	316
James	26, 145
James S, Jr	308
Jeff	307
Jeff J	147
Jeffie	147
Jesse	25
Jessie	151
Jimmie H	307
Joel M	25
John	26
John T	308
Johson	310
Joseph	147
Joseph A	24
Kate	24
Lafayette	147
Laura	307
Levi O	146
Lewis	147
Linnie	147, 306
Lizzie	307, 309, 310
Lou	151
Louisa	307
Louvenia	24
Lucy O	146
Lula	307
Mack	306
Maggie	307
Martha	307
Mary	307
Mary W	24
Mathew	310
May	147
Mike	185
Minnie	307
Mollie	26, 151
Moses	308
Myrtle	308
Nancy	307
Pat	185
Pearl	147
Pleas	309
Rachael E	24
Richard	25, 306, 307
Roy	151
Ruphus	307
Ruth C	307
Sabera	306
Sam	307, 308
Sam J	308
Sarah	24, 306
Sophronia	307
Squirl	23
Stella	308
Susan E	150
T R	150
Texanna	25
Thomas	151, 308
Thomas F	24
Thomas R	150
Thos F	24
Tim	307
Tim L, Jr	307
Tom	306
U Silas	307
Vicie	25
Victoria	310
W A	310
Walker	307
Walter G	24
Walter L	150
Wert	25
Wesley	307
William	151
William L	146
William S	24
W^m	151, 309
W^m A	310
W^m E	310

Index

W^m H 308
Zekiel, Jr 307
FILMO
   Cherry 23
   Della 23
   Ella 23
   Emma 23
   George 23
   Hattie 23
   Millard 23
   Neppie 23
FINCANNON
   Emma 310
   Geo 310
   W^m A 310
FINK
   D N 357,360,365,378,387
   S N 368
FIRST NAT'L BANK OF VINITA .133
FISHER
   Aggie 145
   Annie 145
   Ben 145
   Betsey 145
   Carrie 25
   Charlotte 145
   Eliza 145
   Ella 146
   Elouisa 25
   George 26
   Henry 25
   Isaac 146
   Jake 145
   Jessie 145
   Johnson 145,250
   Josie 145
   Lucy 145
   Lucy B 25
   Maggie 145
   Moses 146
   Ollie 25
   Richard 146
   Rufus 145
   Sarah 145,146
   Susie 146
   William 26
FISK

Cora 24
Harry 24
Menerva 24
Mrs 56
W^m 56
FITE
   B F 88
   Bartow 88
   F B 146,250,253
   Frances 146
   Julia P 146
   William P 146
FITZGERALD
   Catherine 150
   Elnora 150
   Mamie 150
   Martha J 151
   Nora 151
   Polly 150
   Richard 151
   William R 150
FITZSIMMONS
   Ida J 149
   John A 149
   M E 149
   Mary E 149
   Mary J 149
   Susan J 149
FIZGERALD, E H 150
FLANNAGAN
   Charlie A 149
   Frank J 149
   Jessie B 149
   Mary 149
   Mary E 149
   Mike 149
   Truda H 149
   William W 149
FLEMINGS, Maria 151
FLEMMING
   Mariah 113
   Mary 310
   Quilla 310
FLETCHER
   J L 25
   Mary A 25
   Mattie 218

Index

    Rachael M..........25
    Thomas..........150
FLINT
    Albert..........309
    Amos V..........149
    Caroline W..........149
    Charles..........309
    Cora..........309
    Delila..........309
    Dona..........309
    Dow..........309
    Essie..........152
    Eva..........152
    Florence..........152
    James E..........152
    L D..........149
    M T..........152
    Nana..........309
    Sabra..........152
    Victoria..........149
    Willie..........152
    W^m..........309
FLOURNOY
    Annie..........147
    Clara..........147
    D H..........147
    Lilla..........147
    Rolly..........147
    Walter..........147
FLOWERS, Minty..........25
FLOYD
    Annie L..........150
    Carrie..........150
    Donie May..........150
    George R..........150
    James D..........150
    Miller B..........150
FLUKE
    Geo..........306
    Henry..........306
    Lou..........306
FLUTE, Ford..........306
FLYING
    Crawford..........25
    J P..........25
    Jons P..........25
    Leonard..........25
    Nepie..........25
FOIL, A..........152
FOLLEY
    Adelina..........23
    Clarance..........23
    Kate..........23
    Laura..........23
    Lawrance..........23
    Lizzie..........23
    Margaret..........23
    Mary..........23
    Nellie..........23
    Patrick..........23
    Sarah..........23
FOOL
    Ceily..........75
    Celey..........23
    Jack..........23
    John T..........23
    Thomas..........23,75
    William..........23,76
FOOY, Samuel..........25
FORD
    Frank W..........309
    Mollie W..........309
    Reba E..........309
FOREMAN
    A W..........151
    Ada..........152
    Ada L..........152
    Amanda..........152
    Amelia G..........148
    Andy..........146
    Arch..........305,310,386
    Charles..........148
    Charles H..........24
    David W..........150
    Dock..........148
    Doss..........148
    E G..........148
    Elam..........305
    Ellis..........148
    Eminta..........151
    Emma..........23
    Emma E..........151
    Essie..........148
    Everett G..........148

Flora E	151
H L	150
Henry	148
Herman L	150
Hugh	310
Ina	23
Isabell	148
J G	152
Jack	19
James	148
James L	148
Jennie M	152
Jeremiah	148
Jesse E	24
Jno A	152
Jno E	152
John	308
John T	24
Johnson	24
Johny F H L	152
Joseph	148
Josie G	152
Katy	305,308
Laura	148,305
Lelia	310
Leonard W	152
Lulu S	152
Maggie B	148
Mary	51
Maude	148
Nancy	305,310
Nancy E	24
Nannie	148
Nellie	148
Nelson	148
Perry A	152
Sabrina	310
Samuel	24
Sarah	310
Sarah C	148
Susan	25
Susan H	310
Taylor W	152
Victoria E	152
Victory	24
William	24
William J	24
W^m	24
W^m Y	310
FORKEDTAIL	
Jennie	305
Louis	305
Oos kine	305
Ouia	305
FORSTER	
Jane	152
John	152
Lulu	151
Susie	152
Thos	268
Walter	268
FORSYTHE	
Jane	148
Lulu L	148
Sarah E	148
FORTNER	
Annie W	146
B F	151
Frank B	146
Grace	151
Lucille	151
Lucy J	151
Ralph H	146
Samuel H	146
W R	146
FOSTER	
Artemim	150
Artemus	150
Baby	150
Belle	149
Benjamin	5
Bluford	25
Dora	149
Jane	149
Jefferson	25
Joseph	202
Lucy	25
Martha	153
Mattie	153
Samuel	153
Sarah	25
Sylva E	153
FOUNTAIN, Nellie	305,306
FOUST	

Bertha	150
J W	150
Rosie E	150
Thos J	150

FOX
Adolphus	310
Annie	306
Doctor	306
Emma	306
Joe	306,368
Lucy	306
Walter	306
Wesley	306
Yuchie	306

FOYIL
A	122,137,148,179,207,248,251
Charlott	152
Milo	152

FRANCE, Sallie 153

FRANCIS
Carrie E	148
Nancy	148,176

FRANKS
Caraal	146
Edgar	147
Ida	146
Joel	147
Josephine	146,147
Lillie	146
Lulu	147
Mary	146
Myrtle	147
William	146

FRASER, E B 310

FRAZIER
Annie	309
Bettie	22
Callie D	309
Clowd W	309
Daniel	22
Daniel, Jr	22
Ella	22
Emma	22
Ethel	149
Ivie	23
J E	309
Jessie	309
John	23
John Sen	22
John, Jr	22
Lelia	149
Lewis	23
Lizzie	22
M C	149
Mary	22
Mary E	310
Maude	309
Monte Clide	309
Polly	309
Robert	22
Ruth	310
Ruth A	310
Sallie	22
Saul	309
Serena	22
Undeen	22
Walter	22

FREEMAN
Ben	305
Carrie B	308
D W	332,339,352
Dan W	309
Daniel	308
Danl W	309
Ella	308
Geo	308
Gerllie L	308
Mary	305
Sam	305
W^m C	309

FREENEY
Charlotte	26
Ella	26
John E	26
Martha	26
Mary	26
R C	26
Robert	26
Susie	26
Walter	26

FRENCH
Maud	206
Thomas	146

FREUMAN, Mary 305

Index

FRICK, Nannie N 306
FRITZ
    Edward 150
    Elizabeth 150
    Fannie 150
    Frances 150
    Katie 150
FROGG
    Lunnie 305
    Mary 305
    Nancy 305
    Noisy 305
FRY, Lovely 22
FRYE
    Amelia 152
    Annie 152
    Culla 152
    Jennie 152
    Katie 152
    Kittie 152
    Mack 152
    William 152
FRYER
    Edward B 148
    Paul W 148
    W^m H 148
GALAGHER
    Birdie 151
    Tom 170
GALCATCHER
    Becky 311
    Charlie 311
    Chas 311
    Ellen 158
    Frank 311
    Henry 158
    Joseph 158
    Lallie 311
    Lee 158
    Lou 158
    Mary 158
    Mattie 158
    Nancy 158,311
    Thomas 158
GALCATHER, Snowmaker 311
GALKILLER, Wilson 153
GALKITTEN, Wilson 250

GALLOWAY, Dollie E 159
GALOUCH
    Ailsey 313
    Ailsie 313
    Jesse 313
    Lucy 313
    Nancy 313
    Nick 313
GAMBLE, Pearlie 363
GANT
    John 157
    Katie 157
    Maggie 157
    Mattie 157
    William 157
GARBARINO
    Josephine 313
    Mary E 312
GARLAND
    Agnis 159
    Boxta 159
    David 29
    Dollie 159
    Dorie 159
    Elizabeth 159
    Florie 159
    Francis 159
    John 29,159
    Lewis 29
    Libbie 29
    Lillie 159
    Lizzie 29
    Sim 29,57,58
    Tookah 29
GARLIN
    S L 155
    Sallie 155
GARRET, Margaret 258
GARRETT, Margaret 258
GARRISON
    L P 312
    Mollie 312
    Mollie V 312
    Nannie P 312
GARVIN
    Earnest 27
    Henry 27

Index

Laura ... 27
GASS
  Louisa ... 154
  Lucy A ... 154
  Martha ... 154
GASSOWAY
  Henry W ... 154
  Lulu B ... 154
  Mary E ... 154
  May ... 154
  Noma ... 154
GAYLOR
  Bettie ... 153
  Grover ... 153
  Hogan ... 153
  Lena ... 153
  Perry ... 153
  Thomas ... 153
GEAR
  Rosa ... 153
  Sam ... 153
GEARHEART, Rachel ... 155
GENTRY
  Maggie ... 313
  W E ... 18,19,73
  W E & Co ... 63,79
GEORGE ... 311
  Grant ... 311
  Jennie ... 311
  Katy ... 311
  Martha ... 311
  Oce ... 311
  Parrell ... 311
GERTZ
  James ... 83
  Wilson ... 60
GHORMLEY
  Bulah M ... 314
  Carrie ... 314
  E C ... 314
  Ewing ... 314
  Ida ... 314
  Stella ... 314
GIBBS
  Charles ... 155
  Charlotte ... 155
  Eliza ... 155
  J L, Jr ... 155
GIBONEY
  Geo ... 312
  Ida L ... 312
  Mitty A ... 312
GIBSON
  Arrie T ... 313
  James E ... 26
  Jennie ... 313
  John H ... 313
  Mary ... 313
  Mary N W ... 26
  Mattie ... 313
  Minnie L ... 26
  Nannie ... 28
  Nettie ... 26
  Quinton ... 313
  W M ... 12,22,33,38,50,75
  W N ... 54,78
  William M ... 26
  W^m ... 26,33,56,74,76
  W^m N ... 44
GILBERT
  Allen ... 155
  Dennis ... 155
  George ... 155
  Kiamitia C ... 155
GILBRAITH, W A ... 276
GILBREATH
  J W ... 330
  W J ... 275,277,331,356,363,364,377,378
GILLIS, Ellen ... 154
GILLSTRAP
  Demsey ... 155
  Jennie M ... 155
GILLUM
  Ella ... 313
  Myrtle ... 313
GILMORE
  Cherokee ... 30
  Cyrus M ... 30
  Harry W ... 30
GILSTRAP, Levi ... 159
GIRTY
  Alexander ... 27
  Daniel ... 26
  Daniel, Jr ... 26

Index

Dan'l 26
Ester 26,27
James 27
Jennie 27
Martha 27
Mary 26,27,30
Ned 27
Oscar 26
Peggie 26
Snake 27
Susie 26
Thomas 27
Uh-k hu-ster 27
William 30
Wilson 27
GIRTZ
  James 11
  Wilson 74
GLASS
  Annie 155
  Betsey 155
  Buck 155
  Charles 29
  Charley 310
  Cornelius 27
  Eliza 155
  Ellen 155
  Geo W 155
  George 27,154
  James 155
  Jennie 155
  John 155
  Johnson 155
  Lizzie 27
  Louis 154
  Mary 154
  Mattie 27
  Mollie 155
  Nellie 154
  Oma 154
GLENN
  Annie 311
  Etta 311
  Mattie 311
GLORY
  Peter 311
  Susie 311

Wyly 311
GOARD
  Franklin 27
  James 27
  Jessie 27
  Lizzie 27
GOBERINO
  Josephine 313
  Martha 312
  Sarah 312
GODDARD
  Henry 157
  Henry M 312
  James 312
  James W 312
  K L 155
  Katie L 155
  Lidia Thomas 155
  Neva A 312
  Phoeba 312
  W^m 156
GOOBYKOONTZ, Amanda 156
GOODALL
  Caroline 157
  Elizabeth 157
  Ida 157
  Lee 157
  Lila 157
  William E 157
GOODEN
  Betsy 314
  Dave 314
  Dock 314
  Lula 314
GOODHUE, Jennie 159
GOODIN, John 166
GOODING, Betsy 314,382
GOODMAN
  Albert A 156
  Catherine B 156
  Eddie J 156
  Joseph W 156
  Ora M 156
  Robert F 156
  Susan 156
  W S 156
GOODMONEY

Leecy...311
Rider...311
GOODWIN, W^m.............................157
GOODYKOONTZ
   Amanda..156
   Ethel P..156
   Frank A..156
GORE, *(Illegible)*...............................323
GOSS
   Alice...153
   Amy...159,216
   Ben F..153
   Lelia...159
   Wash..153
GOSSETT
   Arthur..312
   Demerias..312
   Geo...312
   J M..312
   James..312
   Steolin..312
GOTT
   A M...265
   Ale..156
   Susan..156
GOURD
   A R...159
   Alex R..159
   Artemissie R.....................................159
   Artemus...159
   Augusta..157
   Calvin...158
   Charles R...159
   D R...311
   Dan...158
   Dan R..311
   Dorothee R..157
   Edward..158
   George...158
   Gertie R...159
   Grass R..159
   Henry R...157
   Jack..158
   James R..157
   Jeeter R..157
   John R...159
   L R..227

Looney R...157
Lulu R..311
Nora R...159
Paralee..158
Paralee R...158
Sarah R..157
Susie...159
Taylor...158
Tecumseh R..157
Thos R..158
GRACE
   A C...159
   Alcie C...159
GRAHAM
   Alsey..28
   Blueford...311
   Eddie..29
   Elcy..28
   Florance P...28
   J W...29
   James...29
   John F..29
   Joseph W...29
   Marion...29
   Moissouri..28
   Nancy..28
   Robert L..29
   Sarah...28
   Temp V...29
   W^m..311
GRANT
   Donle...321
   Geo..311,321
GRASON, Watt......................................26
GRASS
   Alice G..312
   Benjamin...158
   Josie...40
   Minnie..158
   Vinil...158
GRASSHOPPER, Jack........................312
GRAVES
   Bettie...26
   Thomas..26
GRAVETT, J M....................................154
GRAVIT, James....................................154
GRAVITT

Index

Addie 154
Alice 154
C F 154
Columbus F 154
Earl 154
James M 154
Jefferson M 154
Lillie P 154
Luther O 154
Ora B 154
Ular 154
GRAY
 Annie L 153
 Birt 159
 Desota 28
 Electa V 28
 Emmit E 28
 Frances E 157
 Frank E 220
 J C 157
 Jo Anna 314
 Joanna 314
 M 153
 Mary A 153
 Mary E 157
 Nancy M 28
 S W 20,28,30,33,34,35,41,49,58
 Susie 312
 Walter 157
 W^m 314
GRAYSON
 Claude R 156
 Della E 156
 Jennie M 156
 Kate R 156
 Myrtle 156
 Nancy 30
 S W 26
 Sam 13,27,32,41,57,156
 Samuel 13
 Sarah 44
 Vinie 156
GRAZIER
 Elmer 313
 Homer 313
 Luther 313
 M L 313

Martha 313
GREEN
 Emeline 155
 Ernest 157
 Ethel 157
 Evelyn V 312
 G W 282,312,325,326,340,366
 Herbert Lee 157
 J R 159
 Maggie 157
 Melvina 159
 Ralph S 312
 Sallie 56
GREENWAY, Alonzo G 155
GREER
 E O 155
 Eugenia O 155
 Kirmie L 155
GRIFFIN
 Addie 28
 Bettie 28
 Camodole 29
 Carolina 29
 Commodoe 30
 Enoch 28
 George 28
 Jack 48
 James Sen 28
 James, Jr 28
 Joseph 28
 Kate 28,30
 Looney 29
 Lucinda 54
 Luggie 29
 Mary 28,29
 Nannie 28,77
 Ned 29
 Olie 11
GRIGGS
 Abert 29
 Alice 156
 Charles 29
 Colonel 153
 Elizabeth 30
 Frank 153
 Henry 30
 J R 156

Index

Jessie..................................156
Jno R..................................156
Johnny................................156
Mary E.................................29
Patty....................................29
Volie....................................30
W H................................29,30
W J....................................153
GRIPENKERL, Mary.............27
GRITTS
   Dora...................................27
   Franklin 27
   Susie..................................29
GROVE
   Bettie..................................27
   Suiate.................................28
GROVES
   Annie..................................27
   Bettie..................................27
   Chas E 28
   Eliza...................................28
   Eveen.................................28
   Eward 28
   Fannie................................28
   Isaac..............................18,28
   James.................................28
   Johnson..............................28
   Poram 28
   Susan 28
GUEN, Mary........................225
GUESS
   Albert................................312
   Dave 313
   George..............................156
   Liza...................................312
   Martha..............................312
   Nancy 313
   Nelson...............................312
   Polly 313
   Sequoyah 313
GULAGER
   Christian 13,20,32
   W M...............67,74,131,135,221
   W^m...........................226,242
   W^m M 55,159
GULLAGER
   W H..................................135
W M.............. 9,15,150,217,266,385
GULLIGER, W M.................256
GUNTER
   C D...................................313
   Calle D..............................313
   George..............................173
   Henry................................154
   J E....................................158
   J T.....................144,156,170,310
   Jno T.................................156
   John E...............................158
   John T...............................374
   Luman...............................173
   Mabel................................156
   Nancy 313
   Nancy A............................313
   Sammie.............................313
   Sammie E 158
GUSTER
   Charles E 29
   Elizabeth............................29
   Henry.................................29
   Melvina..............................29
GUSTINE, Melvina................29
GWARTNEY
   Carrie J 154
   Dollie................................154
   Mary A 154
   Stella E 154
   Susan 154
HABICH
   George E...........................162
   Lula....................................99
HADDOCK
   Charles..............................172
   John..................................172
   Rettie................................172
HADEN, C 133
HAIR
   Annie................................174
   Eddie................................174
   Eliza.................................175
   Jane..................................174
   Joseph................................37
   Lillie.................................163
   Martha 37
   Nellie 37

Index

Sarah 174
William M 164
HAIRL, Maude 319
HALFBREED
Lucinda 33
Webster 315
HALL
Annie 171
Benjamin 165
Bessie 169
Blanche 169
Catherine 165
David C 169
Dora 171
Ed 169
Eugen 169
Eugene 164
F 165
Frank 165
Frederick 165
Ibbie 165
J M 100,142,143,159,168,183,
202,216,245,246
Janie P 169
Jesse 319
Jesse Swan 168
John 171
John R 171
Joseph Ann 168,169
Josephine 171
Lizie 106
Ludy S 169
M E 169
Martha 165
Mary E 169
Mary J 171
Maude 171
May E 164
Nute 363
Rhoda 165
S R 171
Sewel W 169
W H 165
William 171
W^m O 168
HALLEY, John 243
HALLUM

Mary 318
Ora O 318
HALSELL
Alice 170
Clarence 170
E L 170,217
Eva 170
Ewing 170
Mary 170
Pauline 170
W E .. 100,119,141,143,152,161,163,
184,202,212,213,218,224,244,375
HAMMER
Annie 160
Jennie 35
Josephine 35
Lizzie 167
Looney 35
Ned 160
HAMMERS
Hannah 326
Levi 326
HAMNER, Peggy 35
HAMPTON
Andy 162
Burton 315
Clara 162
Dora 162
Elizabeth 163,315,316
Floretta M 163
Geo 316
Grcie 315
Lulu 162
Mary 315
Mattie 315
Non 315
Pearl 315
W^m 163
HANCOCK
Viola S 168
W A 168
HANDLE
Bushyhead 314
Dempson 314
Lizzy 314
Rob Ross 314
Tom 314

Index

Willie..................314
HANDLES
  Frona..................30
  John..................30
  Sallie..................30
  Susie..................30
HANES
  Ama V..................174
  Charles E..................174
  Delilah..................174
  Gertrude..................174
  Henny C..................174
  Lee R..................174
  Nathaniel..................174
  Sonore..................174
  Thomas..................174
HANKS
  Calvin..................30
  Calvin J..................31
  Daisie..................31
  Emma..................31
  Emma, Jr..................31
  Emma, Sr..................31
  Ora M..................30
  Otto..................30
HANNEA, Cleveland..................377
HARDER
  Lizzie..................321
  Willard..................321
HARDGE, Sarah..................173
HARDY
  Dudly R..................316
  Henry..................316
  J T..................316,350
  John D..................316
  Mary..................316
  May..................316
  Mollie..................316
HARDYSHELL, Clint..................36
HAREM, L B..................317
HARGROVE
  Andrusha..................61
  G S..................61
  Magnora..................61
HARLAN
  F B..................170
  George..................169

James..................169
Jessie..................102
Minnie B..................169
N L..................170
Nathan L..................170
W L..................169
Wm L..................169
HARLAS, Eliza..................30
HARLIN
  Ada..................315
  Albert..................318
  Alniso V..................315
  Bessie M..................317
  Callie..................315
  Charles..................315
  Claude..................317
  David L..................321
  Delbert..................321
  Edgar..................317
  Ellis..................315
  Fannie..................315
  Iona..................315
  Jarett B..................315
  Jas E..................315
  Jas R..................321
  Jese..................315
  John..................315
  Levi..................164
  Lewis S..................321
  Lillie M..................321
  Lotty B..................315
  Mary..................315,317
  Matilda J..................318
  Nancy..................315
  Oce..................315
  Ridge H..................315
  Ruth..................315
  Sally K..................315
  Sam..................317
  Samuel..................317
  Zeke..................164
HARLOW
  Alabama..................164
  Alexander..................174
  Alice..................174
  Bertha..................174
  Bessie..................164

Clifford L	170	Charles J	167
James	174	Cheasquah	37
Jno H	170	Chester	36
John	164	Christopher	36
Joseph	174	Claud	32
Laura	164	Colonel P	36
Nellie	164	Cora B	172
Ola	170	David	32
P A	174	Denis V	34
Peggie A	174	E E	398
Samuel	164	Effie	34
Walter	174	Ellen	37
William	164	Emily	36

HARMON

Benjamin	31	Emma	167
Claude	162	Filo	38
Cyntha	31	Flora M	163
Daniel	31	Fred W	167
Elizabeth	31	Gertie N	163
Flora A	162	H W	167
Henrietta	31	Hanna	36
Henryeta	31	Hannah	36,38
John	33	I J	163
Laura	31	Ida J	163
Lena	31	James	37
Lillie	162	James H	173
Mary	33	James S	36
McGilbrie	31	Janett	33
		Janey	167

HARNAGE

C L	169	Janine	36
Charles D	35	Jas S	35
Custus L	169	Joe B	35
Ezekiel	165	Johana	167
Jennie	35	John	36,37
Richard	35	John P	37
William W	35	Joseph	36
HARPPER, Emma	34	Katie L	167

HARRIS

Amelia	172	Lottie	166
Baxter	166	Lucinda	156
Beacher	36	Lucy	33,36
Bettie	33	Mack	166
Bird	37	Marlin	33
C B	36	Martha	34,167
C J	89,207,271,398	Mary J	172
Cal J	37	Mary S	37
Charles	33,38,167	Mattie	321
		Minnie	167
		Nancy D	172

Parker 37
Parker C 36
Philo 38
Richard L 321
Robert 36
Robert P 167
Roy S 163
Sallie 36
Sue T 167
Suella 37
Susan 63,172
Thomas 32,34,36,37
Ula-lah S 163
William 32
William R 37
Willie 36
Willie C 321

HARRISON
  A P 163
  Andrew P 163
  Clifford 160
  D W 163
  Dolly M 160
  Floyd 160
  Irene 160
  L M 160
  Mary A 163
  Nathan 163
  Nevada 163

HARRY
  Ellie 320
  Elsie 320
  Jake 320
  Lee 320
  Lem 320
  Ollie 320
  Sarah 320
  Walter 320

HARTGROVE, William 145
HARVEY, Victoria 320

HASTEN
  Emma 314
  Lydia 314
  Rosa 314

HASTINGS
  John R 316
  Lonisa 316

HASTON, John 314

HATCHET
  Nancy 160
  Thomas 160

HATFIELD
  Nannie 316
  Winnie 316

HAUSE
  Caleb 173
  Che nah sah 168
  Che-nah-sah 168
  D M 173
  Daniel M 173
  George W 173
  Joseph 173
  Lillie V 173
  Ruth E 173
  Sarah 173

HAVEN, D E 336,338,344,350,369
HAVENS, D E 369

HAWK
  Benjamin 318
  John 168
  Mary 168
  Noah 318
  Peter 168
  Wily 168

HAWKINS
  C H 165
  Charles G 320
  Edith 321
  George 319
  Glendyn E 165
  Jasper 319
  Katie E 165
  Lena 321
  Lundy 329
  M G 320
  Mary L 165
  Maude 321
  Myrtle 329
  Ollie 321
  Ralph 321
  Rhoda L 320
  Robt 319
  Roswell D 320
  Ruth K 320

Rutha 165
Viola 329
Walter H 321
HAWORTH
   Ida 174
   Lucille S 174
   Pearsie E 174
HAYDEN
   C 258
   Carrie 160
   Charley 160
   Chas 142
   Cl;Em 182
   Clara 160
   Clarence 160
   Clem 161,189,258
   Essie 161
   Ida M 160
   Lela 161
   Lona 160
   Minnie 160
HAYES
   Cora 31
   Eliza 32
   Elvira 34
   Emma 32
   Estela 31
   Jennie 164
   O L 30,40,48,51,66,75
   Pearl 31
   Ric^d 32
   Richard 32
   Vicie 31
   William 34
HAYNES
   Oliver 320
   Sarah 320
   Thos E 320
   Willie 320
   Winbell 320
HAYWORTH, O H 174
HEADRICK
   John 37
   Rebecca 34
   Saml 37
HEADRICKS
   Mary J 37

Samuel 37
William 32,37
HEAPS
   Sarena 166
   Serena 166
   Walter 166
HEAROD
   Beula 317
   Chas 317
   Jesse 317
   W^m 317
HEATH, Olive 35
HEATON, Ester 31
HEDDY
   Ella M 170
   Ethel 170
HEDRICK
   Rebecca 34
   Saml 37
HEFERMON
   Annie 36
   Joanna 36
   Pearl 36
HEFFERMAN, Joanna 36
HEFFLEFINGER
   Elizabeth 163
   Erasmus 163
   Fannie B 163
HEFNER
   L M 167
   Lula M 167
   Roy 167
HELDABRAND
   Anna 314
   Callie 315
   John 314
HELDEBRAND, John 315
HELDERBRAND
   Ben 168
   John 170
HELTERBRAND
   Annie J 161
   Benj 168,169
   Dennis 161
   Eliza 168
   Ezra 168
   James F 161

John	170
John T	161
John W	161
Joseph	164
Joseph J	161
Laura	169
Lucinda	168
Richard	170
Rosie	168
Sampson	168
Samuel	170
Separa	168
Susan	170
Thomas A	161

HELVENSTON
Addie	32
Charles	32
Claud	32
John	32
Mary E	32
Ruth	32

HENCHOZ
Jennie	35
Luellen	35

HENDERSON
Bessie	319
James	318
Lena	165
Lewis B	165
Maud	165
Nellie	318
Samuel	165
Susie	318
Susie B	318
W P	140,243,319
W^m P	319

HENDRICK, William	1

HENDRICKS
Joseph	37
Mack	172
Rob't L	172

HENDRIX
Caroline	35
Cassie	172
Chancy	36
Haretta	35
Mack	172

Manerva	36
Milo D	35
Minerva	36
Robert	167,172
Robt	173
Tee-see	172
Theodosia	35
White	167
Willis	167,173
Willis, Jr	167,173

HENLY
Clarie	164
Edward	164
Lillie M	164
Walter	164

HENRY
Ada A	167
Addie	162
Agnes	168
Albert G	164
Alice	162
Amelia D	167,168
Archie B	167
Archie Lee	165
Ben	162
Besie L	164
Clarence	164
Dewitt	164
Elsie	167
Eva May	167
Gibb	164
Ione	171
J S	324
J T	323
Jerry	166
Jessie	162
John	161
Josiah	162,243
Levi J	173
Mabel	167
Marie	164
Mark	168
Murriel	166
Myrtle	164
Nancy	371
Odney	165
Patric	164,165

Index

Patrick 137,164,165
Polly 168
Rachel 162
Rose 162
W A 167
Walter 166
William 162
HENSON
   Alice 173
   Andrew 163
   Bessie 319
   Cherokee 319
   Chilla 163
   George 319
   Jack 319
   Joseph 173
   Lorena 173,183
   Luvena 163
   Maggie 173
   Martha 163
   Richard 173
HERBERGER
   Annie 166
   Polly 166
   William M 166
HEREFORD
   Burk 34
   James, Jr 34
   Jess 34
   Joseph L 34
   Lennie B 34
   Robert 34
   Sabra 34
HEROD
   Belle 317
   Ely 168
   Elzena 318
   Joseph 317
HERVEY, Agnes 38
HEWITT, Susan R 167
HHEATON
   Benjamin 31
   Charles 31
   David 31
   Ester 31
HIBBS
   Carl C 35

David A 35
Emma M 35
John A 35
Mary E 35
Mary M 35
Sylvester 35
HICK, Robt L 172
HICKOX, Henry 318
HICKS
   Aaron 33
   Amelia 166
   Andrew 166
   Annie 166
   Cora 175
   Ed D 99
   Eddie 166
   Elvia 166
   Frank 166
   Geo 33
   George 33
   Henry 172
   Ida 172,386
   J R 172
   John R 172
   Joseph 30
   Lona 166
   Mary 33
   Ross 172
   Willie 166
HIDER
   Andy 314,315
   Jack 315
   Joe 314
   Josiah 314
   Polly 314
HIGH
   Albert 171
   Eddie 171
   Sarah 171
   William J 171
HIGHLAND
   James 169
   Maggie 169
   Nettie 169
   Patrick 169
   Sarah 169
   William 169

HIGHSMITH
- Cora E 169
- M F 169
- Mary F 169
- Myrtle A 169
- Roy B L 169

HIGHSONGER, Itaska 269

HIGHTMAN
- Bee 160
- Henry 160
- Maude 160
- Mollie 160

HILDERBRAND
- Ben 255
- Charles 319
- Chas 319
- Cherokee 175
- David 170
- Elijah 319
- Elmira J 36
- George 30
- Ida 321
- Jack 72
- Janus 175
- Jas 321
- Jessie 30
- Jim 319
- Joe 92, 170
- John 359
- Joseph 36, 162
- Mary 32, 72
- Minnie 32
- Mose 30
- Nan 319
- Nannie 32
- Peggie 32
- Sallie 30
- Sam 318
- Stephen 32
- Susan 321
- Tookah 36

HILL
- Acie 320
- Annie 318
- Awee 320
- Bessie 318
- Charley 320
- Davis 170, 171
- Eliza 316
- Fannie E 171
- George R 171
- H S 318
- Henry W 318
- Isa 318
- James J 171
- John H 319
- Johnie 320
- Lou 319
- Mattie 320
- Minta 316
- Oliver 316
- Rachel 170
- Raleigh 316
- Rebecca 318
- Robt L 172
- Rob't L 172

HILTERBRAND, Minnie 32

HINDS
- Claud 68
- Franklin 68
- Henry 68
- Ida 68

HINDSELMAN
- Ada E 165
- S E 165
- Sarah E 165

HISER
- Dannie 316
- Hugh 317
- Jacob M 317
- James 317
- Lillie 316
- Lucy 316
- Martha 316
- Mavery 316
- Oke 316
- Ollie 317

HITCHCOCK, Irenus 319
HOCKET, Francis 173
HODGES, Sarah 173
HOFFMAN
- Allen 166
- Ella 170
- James 166

Minnie 166
Ruth 166
HOGAN
  Ellen 167
  Emma 194
  Georgan 166
  Georgian 166
  Graham 162
  J C 90,96,97,98,105,117,133,153,
  154,161,162,168,175,181,182,191,212
  ,217,225,231,232,249,250,251,254,
  255,259,260,261
  John Z 162
  Mable 162
  Margaret M 162
  Tynie 166
HOGSHOOTER 321
  Shu-ta-kil 321
  Y B 314
  Y Beaver 314
HOLDER
  Amanda 32
  J H 32
HOLDERMAN
  Bertie J 172
  C E 172
  Curtis E 172
  Henry C 172
  Mary 172
HOLLAND
  Gordan S 314
  Jim 314
  Josie 314
HOLLEMAN
  Beulah 161
  Charley 161
  Fred 161
  Harvey 161
  Henry 161
  J J 161
  Martha 161
HOLLINGSWORTH, J F 74
HOLLIS
  Effie E 318
  Elzorah 318
  Isacah 318
HOLLY

Ada 163
Ethel A 163
HOLT
  Charles W 160
  John W 160
  Melvia 161
  Nora 160
  Sabra R 160
  Sarah 160
  Victoria 161
  Walter L 161
HOMER, Sol J 321
HOMMER
  Jennie 35
  Peggie 35
HOOD
  Charles 31
  Daisie 33
  David 33
  Hannah 75
  Harrison 163
  Henry 33
  Jackson 33
  James 30
  Jane 31
  John 31,75
  Lena 75
  Lizzie 31
  Mary 31
  Maud 31
  Nettie 163
  Nora 31
  Radford 163
  Sallie 33
  Sterling 33
  Susan 163
  Vanda 75
  William 30
HOOPING, John Cely 32
HOPKINS
  Johnie 319
  L W 319
  Maude S 319
  Thos A 319
HOPPER, Jennie 29
HORN
  Charles W 161

Cynthia	161
Dora N	320
Fannie	21
Florence	161
Geo W	34
George W	34
Hooley	320
James A	34
Jno W	162
Liza J	320
Maggie	320
Margaret	161
Mary E	320
Pearl	162
Robt L	161
Ruby	162
Thomas	320
Thomas L	161
William	21
William J	161
W^m	320
W^m G C	161

HORNSTINE, Samuel 213

HORSEFLY
Arey	170
James	170
John	317
Nannie	170
Watt	317
Willie	170

HORSEKIN, John 321

HORSLEY
Martha	316
Mary	245

HORSLY, Martha 316
HOSLEY, Mary 166

HOSMER
John	36
Solomon P	37

HOUDESHELL
W^m	319
W^m H	319

HOUSE, Martha 165

HOUSELY
Elizabeth	171
Louisa R	171
Mary E	171

HOWARD
Chanasah	317
Charles	37
Emely C	317
Frank	317
Frank S, Jr	317
Hellen	37
Percy P	317
Russell	32

HOWDESHELL, William 319
HOWEL, W^m 164, 188

HOWELL
Becky	33
Eliza	318
Emmit L	33
Isaac	33
Martha	318
Minnie	318
Mose	37
W^m	280, 318

HOWERTON
Dedd	316
Elizabeth	316
G W	316
Ida M	316
Josie	316
Levea	316
Sara	316

HOWIE
(Illegible)	255
Mary	162
Thomas	162

HOWLAND
John	34
Mary	34
Suanna	34
Susan	34
Susanna	34
William	34

HOYT
Emma	34
Florance	35
Hemnan L	35
Milo A	35
Susan	35

HUDSON
Etta M	317

Index

Harrison A 165
James 318
L B 165
Lewis B 165
Mamie Z 317
Ruphus D 318
Sarah 317
Stella E 318
Sylbanus 317
HUGHES
  Eliza 160
  Ella 160
  George 160
  Margaret 160
  Martha E 36
  W^m 160
HUGHS
  George 31
  Jane 31
HULL, J M 120
HULSEY
  Charles 33
  Earl 33
  Ella V 33
  Honzo 34
  Josephine 174
  Laurinda 33
  M J 177
  Rosalee 33
  Roscoe 33
  Sarah M 33
  Susan 33
HUMMINGBIRD, Nancy 321
HUMPHRY, John 170
HUNT
  Charles 171
  Fannie 171
  Janey 171
  Joseph, Jr 171
  Lucille 171
  Nancy 171
  Nathaniel 171
  Ruth 171
HUNTER
  Charles 171
  Lucretia 174
  Maude 168

Sookie 392
Willie 174
HUNTON
  Julia A 32
  Lovena 32
  W A 32
HURD, George 167
HURST
  Albert J 173
  Annie M 172
  Christopher C 173
  Ella 173
  Gracie A 172
  John 173
  John W 172
  Maggie E 172
  Rachel 173
  S R 172
  Sylvester 172
  Walter E 172
HUTCHENS, Lydia 33
HUTCHESON, K B 17
HUTCHINS
  Bluford R 174
  Charles 201
  Low W 174
  Nettie 174
  R B 55
HUTCHINSON, R B 56
HUTTON, Thomas 164
HYSON, Thomas 20
INLOW
  Elmirah 322
  Henry 321
  Margarett 321
  Susan 322
  Thos 321
IRONSIDES, Robt 345
ISABELL
  Bula C 322
  Geo A 322
  Georgia A 322
  Jennie L 322
  Josephine 322
  Morris 322
  Olli M 322
  Thomas J 322

Index

ISERAL
   Peggie 38
   Walter 38
ISREAL, Susie 38
ITCHEL, Sabina 364
IVEY
   Ada 38
   Belle 38
   Della 38
JACKSON
   Alender 327
   Andrew 175
   Annie 40
   Bryant B 176
   Carnelius 38
   Caroline 176
   Cuffs 38
   E A 177
   Eliza 176
   Ellen 327
   Ellender 327
   Henryetta 40
   Honnar 38
   Hugh E 175
   J A 175
   Jennie 177
   Jessie 327
   Jno A 175
   Josephine 40
   Jules L 148
   Lidie 175
   Lizzie 327
   Lucy A 39
   Lular 38
   Lydia 175
   Mack 176
   Maggie 175
   Martha E 175
   Mary 38
   Mary E 176
   Mary O 176
   Minnie 175
   Ocie 327
   Roy 327
   Sarah 175
   Susan 40,177
   Tosh 327
   Willie 40
   W^m 175,327
JAMES
   Ada 325
   Albert B 326
   Annie 322
   Buna 326
   Calvin G 326
   Clara D 326
   Claud F 326
   Cornelia 326
   Ervin 325
   Ethel N 322
   Eva 325
   Florrie 325
   Frank 327
   Homer 325
   Houston 325
   Jesse L 326
   John 322
   Joseph 325
   Leland 326
   Lola 326
   Lorenzo 325
   Lousa 326
   Lula B 326
   Marston 327
   Mary E 325
   Mary ling 322
   Mattie 326
   Myrtle 326
   Peter 323,324,325
   Price 325
   Ray B 322
   Rex 322
   Sabrina 322
   Saml 322
   Silas 322
   Solon 280,326,372
   Tenessee E 326
   W C 325
   Zula 326
JENKINS
   Amanda 177
   Annie 177
   Elias H 177
   Fannie 177

    H M 177
    Henry W 177
    Jno H 177
    Mandy M 177
    Maude M 177
    Walter L 177
JENNINGS
    Artemer 49
    Eloise 49
    George, Jr 38
    George, Sr 38
    Lizzie 38
    Nellie 38
    Sallie 38
JOHN
    Annie 350
    Cydney 39
    Effie 39
    Lafeyette Bros 39
    Maggie 350
    Richard 350
    Rocsey 350
    Syntha 350
    Thomas L 39
JOHNS, Frances 229
JOHNSON
    A F 176
    Ada L 176
    Alexander 40
    Annie 39
    Arthur T 176
    Bettie 40
    Charles 176
    Christen 349
    Charlotte 327
    Claude 175
    Claude M 176
    Dora 178
    E323
    Eddie 176
    Ella 175,176
    Ellie 233
    Ellsee 233
    Emma 323,326
    Flonnce E 176
    Frank 176
    Fredrick W O 176

    Harvey 327
    Howard B 176
    Jennie 176
    Jessie 176
    Joe 176
    John 177
    John W 176,323
    Johnie 327
    Josephine B 176
    Katy 322
    Lee 383
    Lillyetta 176
    Liza 323
    Lottie 327
    M E 326
    Maggie 40
    Mamie 283
    Mamie L 178
    Martha E 326
    Martin 40
    Mary E 176
    Maudie 322
    Mina M 176
    Minnier 323
    Morris S 176
    Mr 215
    Oscar 323
    Riley 65
    Robert H 176
    Sam 322
    Sarah 176,327
    Thos 326
    Willie 176
JOHNSON & KEELER 136,159,213,
215,222,234,235,245,246,247,263
JOHNSON AND KEELER 112,121,
135,162,176,216
JOHNSTON, Mamie L 178
JOLLY, Lucy D 176
JONES
    Ada 175
    Agnes 177
    Ara 175
    Arvilla 325
    Betsy E 325
    Carrie 177,178
    Celia 322

Index

Chaney 177
Charles 38,61
Chas 83
Chick-a-lee-lee 322
Cleavland 39
Coowie 38
D V 175
Ella 39
Emma 326
Frank 325
Hattie 325
James 326
James H 325
Jas J 325
Jeans 175
Jennie 175
Jess 38
Jim 322
Joanna 326
Joel 325
John 325,326
John E 175
Josiah 322
Leroy 325
Levi 175
Magnola 178
Magnolia 178
Margaret 38
Martha A 325
Mary 38,175
Mary Allice 129
Minnie E 325
Myrtle 326
Nancy A 177
Nellie 322
Oliver 175
Oscar 38
Pearl 197
Perry 175
Pierce 38
Rufus 38
Theodora 177
Thos 325
Vera 175
Virginia 325
W^m H 325
JORDAN

Alex 40
Alex V 40
Alexander 22
Alix V, Jr 40
Belle 22
Caroline 326
Charles 40
Delia P 326
Ethel 322
Fannie 22
Frost 39
Irene 40
J L 39
James 326
James A 39
John C 39
John D 10,39,326
John V 39
Jos M 39
Joseph H 39
Joseph L 326
Joseph M 39
Kate 38
Lester 322
Madison 326
Mason 39
Mirtle 22
N E 177
Perry 38
Robert 40
Sarah E 39
Susie 322
Watie B 326
William S 39
JORDON
 Daisey 177
 Lucy 177
 Nancy E 177
 Victoria M 177
JOURDAN
 C F 322
 D P 326
JOURNEYCAKE
 Eliza A 177
 Jessie B 177
 Okie 177
 Robert J 177

JULIAN
- Ed C 39
- Ed P 39
- Etta P 39
- Evan 39
- R W 39
- Robert W 39
- Susan 39
- Susan J 39
- William B 39

JUN STOODY
- Andy 327
- Fencer 327
- Jaylum 327
- Keywood 327
- Lydia 327
- Sarah 327
- Sultus ti 327
- Susie 327
- Will 327

KAISER
- Catherine 327
- Catren 327
- Henry 327
- Jacj 327
- Mary 327
- Melton 327
- W^m 327

KASH
- Ella 42
- J A 42
- James M 42
- Perry 42

KAY
- Angie 180
- J B 180
- Ora L 180
- William E 180

KEEFER
- Emma 328
- Lizabeth 328
- Sally 328,329

KEELER
- Albert 178
- Chas R 178
- Frank 178
- Frederick 178
- G B 121,178
- Josephine 178
- Lillie 178
- Maude 178
- Minnie 178
- Pearl 178
- Willard 178

KEELER & JOHNSON 136
KEELER AND JOHNSON 108

KEEN
- Albert F 328
- Andrew 328
- Ann 330
- Arnold P 328
- Cora S 328
- James H 328
- John 330
- John R 328
- Nancy 328
- Soggy 330
- Willie A 328

KEENER
- Aggie 180
- Thomas 180

KEITH
- Albert 40
- Freeman 40
- Gordan 42
- Hampton 42
- J N 42
- J R 42
- Mathew 41
- Matthew 41
- Mirtice 42

KELL
- Alice 330
- Bud T 42
- Chas L 330
- Eliza 330
- James 132,178
- Liza 330
- Mary 330

KELLEY
- A A 179
- Alby 301
- Claud C 329
- Cora 301

Index

Cordelia 328	Blancha 41
Effie 329	Frederick A 41
Elijah 42	George 41
Ellen 42	Ida 41
Ernest 329	Jessie 41
Escal 294	John 41
Eva May 328	John L 41
Fanny N 329	Lucindy 41
Fred L 179	Nannie 41
Fred L, Jr 179	Neville C 41
Gertrue 329	Sarelda 41
Gracie 329	William W 41
Jack 42	**KETCHER**
Lucy G 329	Alice 327
Lulu N 179	Charley 328
Margarett 329	Henry 328
Minnie M 329	Johnson 327
Myrta R 328	Lee 327
Pauline G 179	Levi 328
Riddle A 42	Ross 328
Sabrina E 179	Sager 328
Susan E 329	Sarah 328
William 181	Susie 327
Willie 42	**KETCHUM**
W^m 328	Cornelius 328
W^m H 328	John 278
KELLY	Nancy 278
Dee B 42	**KETTLE**
Elijah 42	Jane 41
Fannie 181	Jennie 5
John 16,42	John 41
John D 329	Nacy 40
Morgan 329	**KEYES**
William 181	Albert L 178
KENDELL	Bettie 179
Frankie 181	Blue 178
Frostie 181	Campbell 179
KENNEDY, Edward 85	Carrie 179
KENNEY	Dennis 178
Chas D 328	G B 178
Mary C 328	James M 178
KEP-HEART	Jane E 181
R E 180	Jessie 178
Ruth E 180	John L 181
KERR	Katie 179
Adda 41	Leroy 178,181
Albert 41	Lillie 179,181

Index

Lizie 179
Lizzie 178,179
Lucy 179
Lucy L 179
Lulu 179
Lydia E 179
Minnie 179
Monroe 179
Myrtle 178
Nan J 178
Nellie 178,179
Nettie 179
Osie 181
Pearl 178
Richard 181
Samuel H 179
Shellie 179
Tishie 181
Victoria 179
KEYS
   Addie 41
   Ed 41
   Ellen 41
   George 42
   J M 178,228
   James 41
   James M 144
   James N 181
   Jess 41
   Joanna 257
   L E 179
   L L 179
   Leroy 41
   Mattie 178
   Nippy 16
   Richard 41,181
   S H 179
   Samuel 41
   Samuel, Jr 41
   Susan F 181
   Thomas L 181
   William 42
   Willie 41
KIDD
   Abrildia 329
   Alneda 303
   Felix 329

   Garfield 329
   Ida 329
   Margarett 329
   Monroe 329
   Nancy 329
KIMBROUGH, John 181
KINDRED
   Ellen 41
   Mary 41
   William A 41
KING
   Carrie 180
   Etta 180
   Jennie 180
   Jesse 180
   Joel B 180
KINGFISHER
   Charley 328
   Jennie 330
   Jim 328
   Joe 330
   Knocking about 330
   Lizzie 328
   Mary 330
   Nancy 328
   Susan 330
   Wa-di-ah 330
   Wallie 330
   Watie 330
   Webb 330
   Will 330
KINGKILLER, Betsy 181
KINNISON
   Addie R 180
   Austraphine 180
   John A 180
   Joseph D 180
   Lenora A 180
   Lizzie V 180
   Oma E 180
   Paschal B 180
KINNISSON, P B 180
KIRK
   Amanda 42,180
   Cyrus R 42
   Francis M 42
   Geo 25,42

    George J................................42
    John 180
    Quinn D................................42
    Samantha E..........................42
    Viola......................................42
    Walter F................................42
KLAUS
    Alice A 180
    Annie M................................180
    Robt......................................180
    Robt, Jr 180
KNIGHT
    Fannie M 329
    Grover C 330
    Henry S.................................329
    Hermon.................................330
    J R...376
    Josiah S.................................329
    Morris F................................329
    R D...................................216,330
    Rachel J 329
    Robt D..................................330
    Robt F...................................330
    T R...329
    Thom M................................329
    Thos R 329
    Tm 329
    W^m D 330
KNIGHTKILLER
    Alley.....................................180
    Betsy.....................................181
    Zeke......................................180
KOEHLER
    Alice 43
    Annie 43
    Charles...................................43
    George 43
    John 43
    Lizzie.....................................43
    Margrett.................................43
    Mary E...................................43
    William B..............................43
KREBBS, Theresa.........................330
KREBS
    Edna......................................330
    Richard 330
    Theresa 330

KUFU, Sally.................................280
KUHN
    Jane.......................................181
    W J 144
KYLE
    Adda......................................40
    Charles...................................40
    Daisie.....................................40
    James 40
    Maggie...................................40
    Pollie......................................40
    Robert 40
LA BARGE, Daniel........................47
LA BOYTAUX
    Mollie 188
    Willis 188
LA HAY, Joe M 4
LACEY
    Henry.....................................45
    James 45
    Jane..45
    Susan 45
LACY
    Annie 331
    James 330,331
    Jane..45
    John D 184
    Lizzie...............................45,330
    Lizzy......................................45
    Louisa 330
    Miles L 184
    Myrtle 184
    Sally......................................330
    Sam.......................................330
    Scott......................................330
    Shellie M 184
    Walker 330
    Wallie 331
    William D 184
LADD
    Burnett..................................332
    Burris....................................332
    Clara F..................................332
    Henry....................................332
    J B...332
    James 332
    Jenetta...................................331

Mary J	332
Maude	332
Percy H	331
Tula	332
LAFAN, Sarah	186
LAFAYETTE BRO	83
LAFAYETTE BROS	71

LAFEYETTE
Mose W	14
Moses W	2,5

LAFEYETTE BROS 1,14,33,34,41

LAFON
Amos	186
Claude	186
Essie	186
Flossie	186
Sarah	186

LAGLEY, Lucinda ... 185

LAHAY
Joe M	4
John F	187
Joseph M	187
Maggie	187

LAHOY, J M ... 187

LAMAR
Alex	331
Annie E	332
B F	304
Biddie	332
Chas E	331
Edward	332
Ewing	332
Frank	332
James R	331,346
Jas	346
Jas L, Jr	332
Jas R	331
Jas Riley	332
Jessie	184,331
Lucas	331
Mable	331
Mariah	331
Mattie	331
Maude	332
Maudie	331
Nettie	331
Paden	184
Polly	332
Sally	332
Susan	332
Thos B F	331
Ursula	184
Vande	332

LAMB
Jesse B	183
Jessie B	183
Lawrence E	183
Mary J	183

LAMBERT, Jno E ... 224

LAND
Annie A	186
De Loyd	186
Houston E	186
J C	186
Joseph C	186
Joseph G	186
Roxie M	186
Susan E	186
William H	186

LANDRUM
Ada	333
Arkansas	333
B S	334
Ben M^c	188
Ben S	334
Benjamin M^c	188
Charlotte	333
Chas	333
Cicero	333
Clifton L	334
E M	204,205
Ed	183,334
Edward	334
Elizabeth	333
H T	165,183,333
Hiram	333
Hiram T	333
Jas K	333
John	294
John B	294,333
Johnson	334
Jonathon	333
Katy	334
Lewis	182

Index

Lonie O 334
Lonzo 333
Lulu 182
Mandy 333
Margarette E 334
McLeod 335
Mony 182
Nannie 182
Nellie 334
Nellie J 334
Pansy 334
Perry 333
Sally 333,334
Sam 335
Samuel 335
Sareno M 334
Susie 334
Thomas 182
Valerie 334
LANE
   Alfred 331
   Delora 331
   Estelle 184
   Maude 184
   Queen 45,47
   Rachel 331
LANG, Eliza 109
LANGLEY
   Alexandria 184
   Bathanie 184
   Charles 187
   Fannie 184
   H 98,213
   James 45
   Johnnie 184
   Lucinda 187
   Maggie 185
   Margarite L 184
   Noah 185
   Sallie 45
   Susie 45
   Thomas 185
LANGLY
   Howard 213
   James 45
LARGE
   Bert 334

Claude 334
Effie 334
Fanny 334
Frank 334
Mary V 332
Ocie Q 332
Sadie 334
W C 334
W^m L 334
LARRY
   Billy 153
   Cora 153
   James 188
   Martha A 153
   Nellie 153
   Willis 153
LASLEY
   George 184
   James 44
   Joseph 183,184
   Minnie 44
   Nancy 183
   Robert 44
   Samuel 183
LASLY, Joseph 184
LATTA
   Cintha 43
   Felix 43,47
   Henry 43
   Lavena 46
   Mary 43
LATTIE, Emily 47
LATTY
   Luvenna 46
   Mary 46
   Maud 46
   Rachael 46
LAWRENCE, E H 52
LAWRY
   Anderson 46
   Clarinda 46
   Earrie 46
   Ellen 44
   Ellis 46
   Elliza 46
   Emma 46
   George 46

Index

Geter B 44
Henry 46
James 46
James M, Sr 46
James, Jr 46
Jennie 46
John 46
Laura 44
Mary 46
Minnie 46
Mose 46
Omma 44
Pickens 44
Raphael 46
Susan, Jr 46
Susan, Sr 46
William 47
LAWSON, H T 333
LAWTHER
  Grover C 187
  Josie 187
  Madenia 187
  Willie A 187
LEACH
  Annie E 188
  Burton 44
  Franklin 44
  George C 188
  J W 188
  John W 188
  Kate 44
  Mima 44
LEADER
  Andrew 47
  Charles 47
  Duncan 47
  Ellen 47
  Edward 47
  James 47
  Peggie 47
  Pollie 47
  Reaner 47
  Ruth 47
  Thomas F 47
  Thos 33
  Thos F 47
LEAF

Dake 335
Dave 335
David 335
Fannie 331
Felix 335
Henry 331
Josiah 331
Liza 335
Lizzie 335
Lydia 331
Teacher 335
LEBARGE
  Ida 47
  Jane 47
  Juliette 47
  Martha 47
  Maud 47
LEE
  Annie 27
  Betsie 46
  Everett 331
  John 46
  John, Jr 46
  L331
  Lafaett 46
  Laura 331
  Lilly 47
  Lizzie 46
  Rachael 46
  Ran 357
  Ren 357
  Robert 46
  Walter 46
  Walter, Jr 47
  Walter, Sr 47
LEFORCE
  F M 186
  Fannie M 186
  Flossie M 186
  Sallie 183
LENARD, James 101
LENDER, Poly 11
LENOIR
  Annie C 183
  M O 183
  Mary O 183
LENOX

Birtie	188	Riley D	182
F L	188	Virgie Lee	182
Fanny L	188	W R	182
Mirtle	188	William	185

LEPHEW, Henry 43
LESSENBEE, Jack 183
LESTER, Lular P. 87
LEWIS
   Alice 188
   Bird 183
   C E. 182
   Caroline E 182
   Charles 183
   Che-go-neler 183
   Che-wan 183
   David 183
   Dena 43
   Francis 44
   Geo W 182
   Ida 43
   Jane 44
   Jeff 183
   Jennie 183
   John 183
   Joseph 183
   Lydia 183
   Nannie 183
   Runabout 183
   Sallie 183
   Samuel 188
   Silba 43
   William 183
LINCOLN
   Ada 331
   Florence K 331
   Stephen 331
LINDSAY
   Annie R 182
   Carrie R 182
   Clyde 182
   Edna 182
   Flora 182
   Goodon 182
   Hattie 182
   Joseph 182
   Maria 182
   North 182

LINDSEY
   Bettie 47
   Bettie J 47
   Douglas 44
   Edward 44
   Francis 44
   Grady 44
   Hattie 182
   Ida 44
   Lewis 44
   Mary 44
   Robert 44
   W R 182
   William 44
   W^m D 182
LINDSY, H 63
LININGTON, G W 106
LIPE
   Beulah 185
   C C 185,239
   Caspar 185
   Clarence 185
   Clark C 185
   Clinton 185
   D W 187
   Herman V 185
   J G 187
   Jake, Jr 185
   Jno G 187
   Lola 187
   Maggie E 185
   Mary E 187
   Nannie E 187
   Victoria S 187
LIPSEY
   Lizzie 185
   Stella 185
LITTLE
   Boog 186
   Claude J 186
   Elizabeth 186
   Frank 186
   George 106

Joseph C	186
Lulu Belle	106
Martha Ella	106
Mary L	186
William	186

LITTON
A P	188
Cecil	188
Jamitu	188
Nellie W	188

LIVINGSTON
Alfred	181
Loonie	181
Robert	181
Sarah	95,181

LLOID
Albert L	187
Clarence	187
G C	187
Jennie	187
Laura	187
Maggie E	187
Nannie R	187
Rachel	187
Robt L	187
Thomas	187
William	187

LOCKER
Nellie	185
Richard M	185

LOFLIN
Addie A	182
Chas M	182
Chester C	182
Clarence R	182
H A	133,182
Harris A	182
Rebecca J	182
Stella	182
Vaul D	182

LONG
Eliza	186
J E	48
Mattie	79

LONGBY, H	251

LOOKING
Arch	183
Maggie	183

LOONEY, William	45
LOUTHER, Eugene	187

LOVETT
John	185
Louisa	196

LOWE
Flossy	332
James	332
Jas	333
Mamie	332
May	332
Ralph	332
Robert	332
Rosa	333
Sinnate	332
Sinnett W	332
Willie	332
Zelma	332

LOWERRY
Annie	45
Ellis	45
Elsie	45
Henry C	45
Jefferson	45
John, Jr	45
John, Sr	45
Johnson	45
Kate	45
Murtle	45
William	45

LOWERY
H C	9,11,15,29,45,52,53, 54,56,66,88
Henry	184
John	45
N C	46

LOWEY, H C	2

LOWREY
Austin	255
Randolph	255
W^m A	255

LOWRY
Alice	44
H C	9,11,15
James	46
Return	44

LOWTERS
- Jessie..............181
- Katie L............181
- Lee.................181
- Mathew............181
- Millard F..........181
- Watson B..........181

LOWTHER, Jane..........188

LUCAS
- John................331
- Newraney N........336

LUCKY
- G W.................186
- Martin..............186
- Myrtle..............186
- Sabrina.............186
- Sarah F.............186

LUCY, Sevorrover..........47

LUNDY
- Josie................333
- Louie................333
- Rosa.................333

LUTON
- Dempsey............184
- Joseph M...........184
- Lewis................184
- Rebecca............184
- Ruthie...............184
- Samuel..............184
- Willie................184

LYMAN
- Callie................186
- Evaline..............185
- James...............185
- Johnson............170,185,186
- Joseph..............185
- Martha..............185

LYNAM, Mary..........185

LYNCH
- Alex..................334
- Andrew..............333
- Bert W...............333
- Clark E...............333
- Claude...............334
- Clausene.............43
- Cynthia..............333
- E B....................333
- Eddie B...............333
- Emma O..............333
- Getter.................43
- Jack....................43
- John..................334
- Joseph................43
- Lizzie..................43
- Lucian................334
- Lucy....................45
- Mary..................333
- Nellie..................43
- Rachel................184
- Rose M...............334
- Ruth..................334
- Ruth E................333
- Susan...............43,60
- Susan T...............43
- Syntha...........333,334

MABRY
- Charley..............196
- Clarance..............51
- Ethel M................51
- John....................51
- Robert...............196
- Sallie...................51

MACKEY
- Laura..................49
- Y J......................24

MADDEN
- Lelitia..................55
- Minnie................106
- Ora....................106

MADDEX, Lucinda..........343

MADDISON
- D M...................203
- Nannie...............203
- Virgie.................203

MADDOX
- Eliza Bell............343
- Hooley...............343
- Lucian E.............343

MALONEY
- Ida L.................341
- Nellie G..............341
- Scott C...............341
- W S...................341

MANAHAN

475

Emma	194
Frank	195
Frank, Jr	195
Henry A	194
Mary E	195
Samuel C	194
Susan	194
MANES, Olif V	209

MANNAN
Johnson	202
Lucy	202
Peggie	202
Wooster	202

MANTOOTH
Edna	344
Mary	344
Mary E	344

MANUEL
Elgie	189
Elizie	189
Wilson	189
MARCUM, Sallie	49

MARKER
Laura	193
William R	193

MARKHAM
Allen	49
Burk	49
C D	230
Cissaro	49
Doc	55
John	49
Nancy	206
Sallie	189

MARKS
Albert B	198
Fannie	198
Marjore M	198
Walter R	198
MARKUM, C D	190
MARKUS, Mattie	54

MARONEY
Bailey B	196
Elizabeth W	196
William H	196
MARROW, Nancy	55

MARRS
Barney	343
D M	344
Edgar	343
Garland	343
Hellena	343
John	343
M L	344
Olivia	343
Olivia, Jr	343
W^m	343
MARSH, Fred W	188

MARSHALL
Charly	56
Cornelia	56
Ether	50
Fannie	50
Matte J	50
Mirtle	50
Paul	50
William B	50

MARTIN
Abraham	336
Allen J	342
Amanda	194,200
Andrew	336
Andrew J	336
Annie	51,185,196
Annie L	195
Arcena	193
Augusta	194
Avis R	195
Birdie	251
Bunch	52
Caroline	341
Carrie	195
Charlotte	197
Chas	343
Chas N	343
Clara	195
Claude D	197
Cora	51,194
Cora E	343
Cunnie A	221
David	197
David E	200
Dewit	251
Eunice	198

Flora L	195
Florence	342
Frank B	195
Frazier	342
G A	195,206
G W	195
Geo A	195
Geo W	191,195
George D	51
George M	195
George N	200
Harry	343
Harvey	198
Hassie	336
Hernando	251
Idus	336
J A	51
J M	195
J W	343
James	51,52,195
James A	195
Jane	52
Jennie	197
Jno E	198
Jno W	198
Joe E	344
Joel	195
John	51,336,341,362,367
John A	51,251
John M	195
John W	343
Joseph K	195
Josie J	195
Laura	344
Lee	344
Lelia E	195
Levi T	200
Lizzie	20,197,341
Lucinda	336
Lucy	199
Lycurgus C	342
M H	199
Mabel E	200
Mamie	343
Mandy	195
Martha T	191
Mary	336
Mary C	191
Myrtle	336
Nancy	198
Nancy E	344
Ola	195
Patsy M	206
Pearl	195
Polly	194
R L	344
Richard L	344
Richard, Jr	344
Robert	195
Robert C	191
Robt L	195
Rudolph	197
Ruth E	191
Sallie	52
Sarah	194,195
Susan	194
Susie	197
Susie J	200
Thomas A	191
Tom	195,206
Viola	197
W	45
W N	16,21,28,29,34,41,42,45, 54,59,65,71,83,87,88
Walter	343
William H	195
William P	195
Willie A	221
Willie V	193
W^m	106,195,336,341
W^m J	191
W^m P	195
W^m, Jr	341
MATHEWS, Ada	206
MATHIS	
Eddie B	341
Eliza	341
Jane	341
MATOY	
Nancy	344
Wm	344
MATTHEW	
Ada	206
Mary L	206

William L L	206

MAUCK
Emily	189
Jacob	189
Maggie	189
Nora	189
Ora	189
W P	189

MAXFIELD, Steven 202

MAYES
Anna H	337
Carrie M	191
Claude J	337
Edwin	191
F W	90
Fred	65
G W	191
Geo W	191
George	191
Girtie	340
Hall	191
Jessie	191
Jno T	191
Joel B	337
Joel B, Jr	190
Joseph	340
Joseph F	191
Josie	340
Laura	340
Lilia	191
Lizzie B	338
Maggie M	337
Martha E	191
Mary	190
Mary D	191
Mary H	338
Maude N	337
Mina V	191
Nannie R	191
Pixie	191
Richard	191
Ridge	338
S H	191
Sallie	153
Sam H	191
Simon	191
Susan	190
Susie	191,340,344
Susie T	344
Thomas	191
Tip C	190
W A	191
W H	129,185
W P	338,366
Wash, Jr	191
Watt A	191
Wiley B	191
William	352
W^m	338,340
W^m H	190
W^m L	191
W^m P	337

MAYFIELD
Alena	199
Annie	48
Clarence	199
Elijah	196
Elijah, Jr	196
Elizabeth	196
Ella	48
Frances M	196
Frederick	196
I M	196
John	48
John T	196
Julia	196
Lena E	199
Logan	199
Luther	199
Nora	48
Roy	48
S W	9,15,74,97,135,150,217,221, 256,266,310,346,355,385
Sarah	56,206

MAYOR
Fred	191
Ida	191
Lee	191
Paralee	191
William	191

MAYS
S H	191
Thomas	191

M^{C}AFFREY

Index

Albert 345
Andrew 345
Benjamin 345
Fannie 345
Hugh 345
John 345
Logan 345
Mollie 345
Napoleon 345
Walter 345
M^CBAIN, Thomas 190
M^CCALEB
   Addison F 194
   Flossie 194
   Lulu 194
M^CCARTER
   Frances 205
   Frank 205
   Fred 205
   J H 205
   John 205
   Liddie 205
   Moses 205
   Nannie 205
   Ruby 205
   Thomas 205
M^CCAULLEY, C B 21
M^CCAULLY, C B 21
M^CCAY
   Alfred 190
   Elbrina D 190
   James J 190
   John B 190
   Rebecca 190
   William, Jr 190
M^CCLAIN
   Annie 200
   Jess 49
   Josie 49
   Kalley 49
   Lelila 49
   Maria 200
   Martha 200
   Minnie 200
   Thomas 34
   William 49,202
   William F 49

M^CCLANAHAN, Willie 11
M^CCLELLAN
   Chas M & Son 275,276
   J F 88,311,361
M^CCLELLAND, J F 385
M^CCLELLEN, Margaret 22
M^CCLURE
   Charles 51
   Dellie 51
   Edwin 51
   Fannie 197
   Francis 51
   Hattie 51
   Henry 50
   Hugh 197
   James 50
   John 52
   Kate 26,50,77
   Lucy 50
   Margaret 197
   Mattie 50
   Robert 50
   Roy 197
   Slater 197
   Thomas 50
   William 52,197
   W^m 52
M^CCOBB
   A F 108
   Addison F 194
   J F 181
M^CCOMIE
   Bonnie C 206
   Isabella C 206
M^CCONNELL
   Lizzie 196
   W F 196
M^CCORKLE
   D W 49
   David W 49
   Emma 49
M^CCOY
   Arch 206
   Arch C 206
   Augustine B 206
   C F 193
   Charley 189

Index

Chester F	193
Frank	189
Hoolie	200
Jno A	200
Margaret	200
Margarette	200
Mary A	200
Mary E	158

M^CCRACKEN, Dora 189
M^CCRACKEN
  J W 203
  James 202
  James T 202
  Jno 202
M^CCRACKEN, Joe 189
M^CCRACKEN
  John W 203
  Katie 202
  Russell 202
  Willie 202
M^CCRARY
  James R 198
  Jno R 198
  Mary E 198
  N P 198
  Napoleon P 198
  Sterling P 198
  William C 198
M^CCULLOCH, W M 317
M^CCULLOUGH
  Chas H 340
  Geo E 340
  Jim F 339
  Joe H 340
  John W 339
  M H 339,340
  Milton J 339
  Nanny M 340
  Pete 340
  Rachel J 339,340
  W^m 339
  W^m P 339
M^CDANIEL, A L 201
M^CDANIEL, Alex L 119
M^CDANIEL
  Alex L 201
  Charles R 196
  Cinderella 48
  Claude I 196
  Eliza 50
  Ella 59
  Estella 49
  Fanny 49
  George 57
  Ida 48
  Jessie R 196
  Jno M 196
  John 52
  John A 196
  Johnson 48
  Katie 201
  Lewie 48
  Mamie 201
  Mary 59
  Nancy 57
  Robert 48,201
  Rose 52
  Stephen 48,50
  Susie 201
  Thomas 36,57,78
M^CDANNIEL
  Martin 202
  Willie 202
M^CDONALD
  C C 206,209
  I N 197
  Isaac N 197
  J O 197
  John O 197
  Newton O 197
  Ray 197
  Roy 197
  V T 193
  Velma E 197
  Virgil T 193
M^CDONOLD
  Edward 54
  Emmily 54
  George 54
  Narcenah 54
  Ora B 54
  Texas A 54
  William C 54
M^CDOWELL

Index

Jessie 344
Joe 344
M^CEACHIN, Maggie 48
M^CELHANEY, Mary 199
M^CELHANY, Mary 199
M^CELMEEL
   Elizabeth 56
   Ora 56
   Peter 56
   William H 56
M^CFALL
   Eddie 345
   Edward L 203
   Eugene 345
   Eugenia 345
   Frankie 345
   John 203
   John V 203
   Lizzie M 203
   Louisa M 203
   Raleigh L 345
   Vinnie N 345
M^CGANNON, Maude O 339
M^CGEE
   Albert 199
   Nellie J 199
   Sarah A 199
M^CGHEE
   Ambrose H 199
   Bell 339
   Berley 199
   Birtie O 339
   Clero 338
   D A 336,338,339,377
   Dave 338
   David A 338
   Dennis B 338
   Eliza J 338
   Elizabeth 199,338
   Ester 338
   Florence 338
   Francis 339
   Jas M 339
   Jno H 199
   Joe F 338
   John R 338
   Joseph H 199
   Martha 339
   Mary A 199
   Quilikee 338
   Rhodee 199
   Robt J 339
   Rosa 338
   Sam B 339
   Staten 338
   Susie 336
   T J 338
   T J, Jr 338
   Viola 338
M^CGINNIS
   Chas C 343
   Elizabeth 343
   W F 343
   W^m T 343
M^CGLAMOR, Rosa 50
M^CGLOOMOR
   Felix 50
   Rosa 50
M^CINGTUSH
   Chesie 55
   Daniel N 55
   Freland 55
   Luellen 81
   Thomas 49
   Vann A 55
   Woldo E 55
M^CINTOSH
   Cheesie 55
   Ellen 201
   J R 203
   Lou 191
   Lucille 191
M^CINTUSH
   Beatrice 203
   Bell 203
   Jno R 203
   John 203
   Maria L 203
   Myrtle 203
M^CKAY
   Jno S 198
   Mary J 197
   W^m 197,198
M^CKENZIE, James 202

Index

M^CKENZIE, Jefferson 189
M^CKENZIE, Liddie 202
M^CKENZIE
   Mary 189
   Nancy 189
M^CKENZY
   Frances 189
   John S 189
   Simon 189
M^CKNIGHT
   Addie L 191
   Louisa Z 191
   Martha E 191
   Ruth 191
M^CLAIN
   James 57
   Loyd 191
   Martha 191
   R L 191
   W^m 43, 49
M^CLAUGHLIN
   Annie 340
   Carrie 345
   Carrie E 345
   David C 51
   Francis 51
   Frank 344, 345
   Geo 344
   Geo F 345
   Ile 345
   Jas 345
   Josh 345
   Leo B 51
   Maggie 345
   William 344
   W^m 340
M^CLAUTHLIN
   Annie 344
   Geo 344
   Ida M 344
   Jas 344
   Louisa E 344
   Rachel F 344
   Susie 345
   Willie 377
M^CMAKINS
   Andrew 55
   Charles 55
   Jennie 55
   Kennie 55
   Parker 55
   Savana 55
M^CNAIR
   Clem 191
   Henrietta 191
   Kinney 191
   Oscar 191
   R L 194
   Robert L 194
M^CNEAL, Elizabeth 55
M^CNULTY
   Annie 52
   Cherokee 52
   George W 52
   Jeff 52
   Lena 52
   Leona E 52
   Maud A 52
   Thomas 52
M^CNUTTY, Ruth 9
M^CPHEARSON
   Ben F 191
   Harriet 56
   Jack 56
   Lewis 191
   Veneere 191
M^CPHERSON
   Ben F 191
   Harriett 56
M^CSPADDEN
   Clem 203
   Ella B 205
   Florence E 205
   Floyd 203
   Forest K 205
   Herbert T 203
   Lizzie P 205
   Maude 205
   May 203
   Oscar L 205
   Roscoe C 203
   Sallie 203
   Serena 203
   Theodore R 205

Thomas B	205
Zoe	203

MEADOW, Leonard 266

MEASELS
- Emily 53, 77
- Jeff 53

MEASLES
- Algie 53
- Barnie 53
- Ellis 53
- Emily B 53
- Minner 53
- Vannie 53

MEEK
- Lizzie T 199
- Mary F 199
- Mary J 199
- Walter G A 199

MEEKS
- Abrum 197
- Annie 259
- Annie B 197
- Charles 33
- James B 197
- Lillie 197
- M J 199
- Myrtle 197
- Sabina E 197
- William A 197

MEHER
- Charles 53
- David 53
- Elvira 53
- Frank 53
- Henry 53
- Jess 53
- William 53

MEHLIN
- Chas H 204
- Elizabeth 204
- J G 204

MELTON
- Annie 337
- Bettie 342
- Carrie 145
- Chas 342
- Clara 337
- Cora 337
- Ella 340
- Geo 336
- Homer 340
- James 145
- Landy M 336
- Lee 145
- Lizabeth 336
- Lizzie 340
- Louisa 337
- Lucian 340
- Mary 337
- Mary A 337, 368
- Mollie 340
- Narcissa 342
- Narcissa 336
- Rosa Bell 336
- S F 336
- Simpson 336
- W F 337
- W^m F 337
- Wyly J 340
- Z F 367

MENER, John A 338

MERONEY
- Dillard 193
- Jno L 193
- Lou 193
- Mabel 193

MERRELL
- Corintha 344
- Gertrude 344
- Gurthrue 344
- J C 196
- Josie C 196

MERREN, J F 190

MESSER, John H 338

MEYERS, Geo 339

MICHELS, Mollie 194

MICKELS, Mollie 194

MIKE
- Anna 344
- Bob 344
- Peggy 274
- Susie 344

MILAN
- Alice 205

Index

Charles 205
Jennie 205
Jessie 205
Nula 205
Sarah 205
Viola 205
MILES
   Eliza 206
   Louisa 200
   Rosie L 200
   W E 206
MILIGAN, Sophronia 338
MILLER
   Andrew 341
   Annie 55,189
   Avrey 342
   Berl 203
   Caladonia 50
   Caroline 56
   Charles 50
   Charles W 201
   Chas M 342
   Cornelius 342
   Cornna 201
   Critt 188
   Daisy 337
   David 335
   David A 201
   Dona E 342
   Dora 312
   E H 119,198
   Eliza M 52
   Elizabeth 339
   Ellen H 198
   Emma 337
   Etha 50
   Etta R 198
   Eva M 188
   Felix 337
   Francis E 50
   George 50,51
   Guy 198
   Henry 50
   Henry Mayes 201
   Homer 203
   Ida 341
   Jake 58
   James J 50
   Jane 201
   Janetta 54
   Jess T 49
   Jesse 337
   Jesse V 55
   Jimmie 337
   Jno L 55
   John 51
   John E 342
   John H 49,188,339
   John L 55
   John M 342
   John, Jr 342
   Joscine 345
   Joseph 200,201,342
   Joseph G 201
   Joshua D 339
   Lee 341
   Lenora 49
   Leo W 52
   Lou O 201
   Louisa 342
   Lucinda 339,341,342
   Mahany 341
   Mamie 52,341
   Martha 341
   Martin 335
   Mary 51,198,337
   Mary E 54,188,339
   Mattie 50,54,188,198
   Melvina 342
   Minerva C 342
   Mormie 203
   Nancy 56,342
   Nannie 201,345
   Nellie 203
   Neppa 203
   Noah 54
   Pearl 198
   Ray 198
   Robt 337
   Rosa 203
   Ruphus 339
   Sally A 339
   Samuel 58
   Sarah 341,342

Simpson 311
Stand 342
Thomas 203
Toney 56
W A 121,204
W W 313,358
Warren H 204
Will B 188
William 201
Willie 201,337
W^m 341,342
MILLHOLLAN
  Daisey B 201
  John D 201
  Sarah F 201
MILLHULLAND, J T 201
MILLIGAN
  Caleb 48
  Frank 48
  Gracie 48
  Saphronia 338
  Susie 48
MILLINER
  Florence 199
  John 199
  Josephine 200
  Mary 199
  William 199
MILLNER, Mary 200
MILLS
  Annie L 190
  George 202
  James E 190
  James L 191
  L 256
  Lee 256,324,325
  Lewis 202
  Looney 202
  M W 190
  W R 95
  W^m R 190
MILLS & WASHBORNE 324,325
MILLS AND WASHBOURN 322
MILLS BROS 272,323,359,368, 384,397
MILTON
  Annie 190

David 190
Elizabeth J 190
Julia 190
Mary A 368
Mary H 190
William H 190
MINKS, Nelly 56
MITCHEL, Lula 377
MITCHELL
  Bertine 200
  Bruce 200
  D M 337
  Don 337
  Franklin 200
  Isaac G 56
  Mary 336
  Myrtle 336
  Nancy W 56
  R M 56
  Sally A 337
  W M 200
  Walker 336
  W^m D 200
MIZER
  Carsalowie 206
  John W 206
  Lillie 206
  Susie 206
MODE
  Carlotta 343
  Francis M 343
  Henry D 343
  Isaac 343
  John R 343
  Martha J 343
  Maude M 343
  Sarah 343
  William E 343
MOKUM
  John V 244
  Mary 244
MONKS, Peggie 55
MONNA, J T 320
MONROE
  Beulah 342
  Birtha 341
  Chas 341

Dora	56
Grover	342
Maggie	341
Mirtle	56
Muta	342
Nannie	56
Nola	341
T J	310,341,348,351
Theadore	342
Thos	341

MOON
Daniel	196
Donnie	196
Eliza	196
John	189
Lulu	196
Nora	196
Swusie	189
William	189
W^m	189

MOORE
Addie	190
Annie	340
Bettie	340
Carrie	341
Charlotte	198
Chas F	341
Elejah	319
Ellis	193
Fannie L	193
Frank P	193
Jessie J	193
John	319
Johnie	340
Josephine	193,340
Lee	319
Lizzie	193
Louis, Jr	340
Mary	340,341
Mary M	339
Noah	193
Nora	341
Sammie A	340
Thomas	201
W L	132,151,181,188,209,228
Walter	341
Willie	340

W^m L	141,157,173,184

MORGAN
Austin	342
Bettie	54
Eli	54
Ella	342
Florance	54
Hannah E	54
Henry	342
J J	7,56
Josephine	54
Katie	203
Lizzie	54
Lone	54
Lou E	143
Malinda J	56
Malinda J, Jr	56
Mark	54
Martha J	54
Maud M	56
Minnie	143
Sophrona	54

MORRELL
Delila	194
James	194
Lillie	194
Mary	194
Minerva	194
Rachel	194
Senora	194
William P	194

MORRIS
Albert	198,199
Bessie	198
Carry	53
Charles	33,55
Dee	206
Della	55
Ella	53
Frances	173
Harry	53
Henry	206
Jno H	199
John W	55
Jordan	199
Jumbo	173
Lila	206

Lula...181
　　Lydia..53
　　Mary...55
　　Mertie..173
　　N J..190
　　Nancy J......................................55,190
　　Rosie...199
　　Sarah C...55
　　Stand W...53
　　Thad..206
　　William O..199
MORRISON
　　Annie E..340
　　Claude..194
　　Delia L...194
　　Ellen..194
　　Elsa Lee...340
　　Maggie V..194
　　Mollie M...194
　　Robert T...194
　　Ruth...340
　　Susan K..194
　　W H...340
MORROW, J T...55
MORSE, Ida H......................................193
MORTEN, W N..9
MORTZ, Clara S...................................206
MOTTE
　　Emily..56
　　Joseph..56
　　William...56
MOUSE
　　Akie...335
　　Awaie..335
　　Beckie..335
　　Becky...335
　　Cornelius...335
　　Darby..274,335
　　Deacon...335
　　Dorcas..274
　　Hummingbird..................................338
　　Jas...335
　　John L..335
　　Josie...335
　　Katy...338
　　Louie..335
　　Lydia..335

　　Mattie..335
　　Nancy...335
　　Sam..335
　　Sam M...335
　　Sanannee...335
　　Whip-poor-will.................................335
MULKEY
　　Charles A...53
　　Earnest..52
　　Eliza J...53
　　Elizabeth...53
　　Honzo S...53
　　Jack A...52
　　James..52
　　James D..53
　　James E, Jr..52
　　James J...52
　　John R...51
　　Johnathan D......................................53
　　Julia..52
　　L A...1,52
　　Lewis A...52
　　Lewis W..53
　　Richard J...51
　　Rose E C...53
　　Vida..52
　　W R..51
　　Warren O..53
　　Watt..52
　　William R..51
　　Wyly A..53
MULLIGAN, Susie..................................48
MUNSON, Henry.................................204
MURPHY
　　Annie...201
　　Augustine..54
　　Bettie..49
　　Bunnie..54
　　Corny..55
　　Edney..49
　　Emma...49
　　Iris..54
　　James..49
　　Jessie C...54
　　Leila..54
　　Mandy...336
　　Minnie M..49

Oliver	54
Pearlla A	49
Sarah	55
Wyche	54

MURRAY
Elmo	202
Frank	202
Jack	202
Mark	202
Robt L	202
Ross	202
Susie	202

MURRY
James	52
Malcolm	53
Mary E	52
Nannie	52

MUSGROVE
Andrew L	201
Clara E	201
Clem R	201
Cora A	201
Ellen	94,200
F M	201,202
Frank F	201
Frank M	201
J T	221
Jas T	94,202,221,245
Maggie M	201
Willie	94,200
Willie A	202

MUSKRAT
Awaie	336
Awie	336
Calhoun	50
Claude	337
Clide	338
Coffee	336
Dan	337
Daniel	337
Eliza	50
Ira D	341
J C	341
Jack	50
Jacob	337
James	337,338
Jeff	337
Jimmie	339
Joe	338,341
Joseph	51
Joseph D	341
Lee	338
Mack	339
Maudie	337
Nina P	341
Rachel	339
Susan	51
T J	369
Thompson	336
Wanenah	336
W^m	337

MUSRAT
Annie	48
Arch	48
Beckey	48
James	48
Katie	48
Lewis	48
Lyda	48
Malinda	48
Mary	48
Nicy	48
Sallie	48
Thomas	48
Wilson	48

MYERS
Deely	190
Edith	339
Eunice	191
Frank	339
George	339
Hiram	191
John S	190
Marion A	190
Olena F	191
Orlena F	190
Walter P	190

NALL
Dora	347
Joe Ella	347
Joella	347

NANCE
Claude	346
James	346

Index

John 346
Lula 346
Minnie 346
Sarah 346
NARCOMIE, Farney 57
NARE, Walter 209
NASH
   E B 207
   Edgar F 207
   Fairy F 207
   Lewis R 207
NAVE
   Alice 209
   Francis 106
   Ida 209
   Joseph 209
   Joseph, Jr 209
   Lila 209
NEAL
   James 46,47,57
   Martha 57
   Nannie 57
   Pollie 57
   Richard, Jr 57
   Richard, Sr 57
   Samuel 57
NEFF
   Ezra 57
   Geo W 347
   Hooly 57
   Mattie 57
   William 57
NEIGHBORS
   Jas W 346
   Laurine L 346
   Lucy F 346
   R B 346
NEILSON 172
   F A 97,99,100,101,105,108,112,
   119,122,129,130,135,138,139,141,144
   ,145,147,152,154,155,157,158,164,
   166,167,168,173,174,176,184,187,196
   ,200,201,202,206,209,212,214,217,
   218,221,228,230,232,233,236,237,238
   ,239,241,242,248,254,256,265,269
NELLIS
   Nancy 345

W^m 345
NELMS
   Abbie 207
   Allen 207
   Arch 207
   Felix 207
   James 207
   John 207
   John, Jr 207
   Luke 207
   Mary 207
   Sarah P 208,209
   Victoria 207
NELSON
   Baby Ann 208
   Charles 252
   Chas 252
   Effie 57,208
   Ella 208
   J C 208
   Jess W 57
   Mary 71
   Polly A 208
   Sarah 346
   Sarah P 93
NICHOLS
   A B 208
   Augustus B 208
   Claude 208
   Clifford 208
   Lucy 208
   Maude 208
   Octava 207
   T O 208
   Willie 208
NICHOLSON
   Daniel G 208
   E V 207
   Ed V 207
   Eva M 207
   Henry 208
   Henry F 57
   J E 208
   James E 208
   James P 207
   Lettie M 208
   Lizzie 57

Mary H 57
Ora C 207
R H 208
R R 208
Richard E 208
Richard H 208
Richard R 208
Sim 208
T K 208
Thos K 208
NICKLES
   Frank 207
   John 207
   Josephine 207
NICKOLS, Taylor O 208
NICKS
   Claude 346
   Occteeyer 346
   Peter 346
   Rachel 346
   Teesin 346
NIDIFFER
   Anna 347
   Bessie 347
   Chas 347
   Edward O L 347
   Ella E 347
   Emma 346
   Eveline 347
   Felix 347
   Freeman 347
   Freeman, Jr 347
   Geo 345
   Henry 346
   Isaac 346
   Jessie G 345
   Joanna 347
   John 346
   Johnie 347
   Josephine 347
   Loisa S 347
   Lucy C 347
   Mary D 347
   Minnie 345,347
   Nannie 347
   Robt L H 347
   Sam 346

Sam, Jr 346
Willie 347
Zekiel 346
NIPPERS
   Aallice 209
   Alice T 209
   Robert 209
NITTS
   Ice 57
   Nagy 57
NIVENS
   Delila 57
   Floyd 57
   Jeff C 57
   Jessie 58
   Josephine 58
   Julia 57
   William 58
NIVINS
   Archie R 347
   Hellen E 347
   Jessie B 347
NIX
   Frank 346
   Geo 346
   James 346
   John 346
   Maudie 346
   Robt 346
   Sabinia 346
   Sabrina 346
   Sarah 346
   W^m 346
NIXON, C T 102
NOBLE, Ellen 208
NOBLES
   Cleveland 208
   Ellen 208
   Joel M 208
   Roscoe 208
NOISY FROG, Nancy 305
NOLEN
   Clara N 209
   J A 209
   Janus 209
   Newton 209
   Saphronia 209

Index

NORMAN
- Albert C ... 207
- Clyde C ... 207
- Cynes W ... 207
- J A ... 207
- James A ... 207
- M J ... 207
- Martha J ... 207

NORTON
- Ashley ... 347
- Ashly ... 347
- Cora ... 347

NORWOOD, A H ... 119,120,141, 161,163,164,238

OAKLEY, William T ... 39

ODELL
- Margaret ... 209
- Margeret ... 209
- Martha ... 209
- Mary ... 209

O'FIELDS
- Alcy ... 348
- Annie ... 348
- Austen ... 348
- Ben ... 348
- Bettie ... 348
- Bushy head ... 348

OFIELDS, Chick ... 210

O'FIELDS
- Dick ... 146,348
- Ella ... 348

OFIELDS, Fannie ... 210

O'FIELDS
- James ... 348
- Jennie ... 348
- Levi ... 146
- Lizzie ... 348
- Louetta ... 348
- Lucy ... 146
- Mindy ... 348
- Mose ... 348
- Phillip ... 348
- Rosa F ... 348
- Sam ... 348,349
- Wallie ... 348

OFIELDS
- William ... 210
- W^m ... 210

OLIVER
- James M ... 210
- Jamie ... 210
- Maude ... 210
- Rexie ... 210
- Sarah ... 210
- Savanah ... 210
- William F ... 210

OLSON
- Andrew B ... 348
- Birtha ... 348
- Denis F ... 348
- Louis A ... 348
- Lydia ... 348
- Ole ... 348
- Richard F ... 348

ONEAL, Lou ... 209

OSKEESON, W^m ... 211

OSKISON
- John ... 210,211
- Richard ... 210

OWEN
- Alice ... 210
- Alice, Jr ... 210
- Cherokee I ... 209
- Cora S ... 209
- Janey ... 210
- Narcissa ... 210
- Owen ... 210
- Robt L ... 210
- Robt O ... 210
- William ... 210
- William O ... 210
- William O C ... 210
- William Otway ... 210
- W^m ... 210

OWENBEY
- Mary A ... 349
- Raymon S ... 349
- Viney ... 349

OWENS
- Andy ... 347
- Betsy ... 347,348
- Charley ... 348
- Dave ... 347
- Henry ... 58

Jesse.................................347
Jimmie..............................348
Lucy..................................349
Martin................................58
Peggy................................348
Samuel................................ 8
Slaten................................348
Susie.................................348
Thos..................................348

PACE
Lora..................................213
Minnie..............................213
Nellie................................213

PADEN
Ben...................................353
Benj..................................353
Coffee...............................353
Hassie...............................354
Homer..............................353
Howard.............................353
James...............................353
Jas....................................353
Jim....................................353
Jim, Jr...............................353
Kitty..................................353
Laura.................................354
Lena..................................353
Lucy..................................353
Maggie..............................353
Martha..............................353
Maude..............................353
Russell..............................353
Taylor...............................353
Tom..................................353
W^m................................353

PAINTER
Ada...................................353
Evy....................................353
John..................................353
Lavernia............................353
Mathew A.........................353

PALMORE
Acie..................................213
C F....................................214
Chas F..............................213
Evaline.............................214
Eveline.............................214

Ina....................................213
J A....................................214
James A............................214
Newton D.........................213
Paul A...............................214

PALMOUR
Alaska..............................215
B F....................................216
Ben F................................216
Bessie..............................216
D S...................................216
David S............................216
Emily E.............................216
Emma G...........................216
Emma L............................216
Fannie A...........................216
Fronie B K........................216
Hugh................................216
J D....................................215
Jno D................................215
John D, Jr.........................216
John R..............................216
Keziah..............................215
Lelia.................................216
Lila...................................216
Mary.................................216
Mollie...............................215
Robert..............................216
Roxie M............................216
Sallie................................216
Virginia............................216

PALONE, Wilson..............212

PANTHER
Collins..............................216
Eliza.................................216
Lillie.................................216

PARCHMEAL
Annie................................349
Ben...................................349
Ella...................................349
Fanny...............................349
Ga-we-yah.......................349
Jennie...............................349
John..................................349
Lucy..................................349
Mean.................................349
Nancy...............................349

Price	349
See-nas-tah	349

PARHAM, Emma 214

PARKER
- Albertus 85
- Edna 215
- Emma 215
- Geo 354
- I E 395
- Jess 59
- Job 215
- Josephine 215
- Laura 215
- Lizzie 59

PARKINSON
- Addie M 211
- Rachel M 211
- Ruth 211

PARKS
- Ada 213
- Alexander B 211
- Annie 213
- Arhena 352
- Bernie 211
- Chas 354
- Elizabeth 354
- Eva 354
- Isaac D 355
- James 352
- Jas G 354
- Jno R B 211
- John 354
- Johnie 354
- Johnson 352
- Maggie 354
- Mary E 211
- Mary J 354
- Maude 213
- Melvine 352
- Milton B 211
- Minnie 354
- Missouri 352
- Or 354
- Owen B 354
- R B 354
- R T 354
- Richard 213
- Richard B 354
- Richard T 354
- Robert 213
- Robt C 211
- Robt C, Jr 211
- Robt G 211
- Rosie 213
- Ruth 354
- Sterling 213
- Susan 254
- Susan A 211
- Tadius 354
- Wain B 354

PARNOSKEY, Sarah 59
PARRIE, Bud 350

PARRIS
- Andrew 59
- Anna 218
- Annie 59, 350
- Annie E 213
- Arch 214
- Charles 59
- Cora 214
- Delbert C 213
- F W 214
- Fannie 59
- Frank 213
- Frank W 214
- Geo 349
- Henry 214
- John 59, 213
- John Anna 350
- Katie 214
- Lemuel 214
- Levi 213
- Marion 213
- Mattie 214
- Mose 59
- Nellie 349
- Rachel 218
- Susie 214
- William 217
- Willie 218

PARRISH
- Alvin H 214
- Bertha 215
- George Lee 215

James L	215
John M	215
Joseph D	215
Walter S	215
William T	215

PARSLEY
Nannie	214
Pauline	214

PARSONS
Cora I	215
E W	215
Henry F	215
Rosetha A	215
William O	215

PAST, Jas M 352

PATE
Albert N	217
Althea	217
Althea F	217
J B	217
Joseph B	217
Laura R	217
Mary A	217

PATHKILLER, Charles 213

PATRICK
Cleavland N	60
John A	60

PATTEN, W C 134

PATTER
Eliza	350
Esta	349
Etty	350
Florence	349
Geo	349
Joseph	350

PATTERSON
Alice	353
Sarah A	353
Zona	353

PATTERSON MERCTL CO 15
PATTERSON MERITL CO 37

PATTON
Arminty	218
Chas H	215
Duckie	185
Earl	185
Elizabeth M	218
Emmie	218
Eva	217
Jane	217
John H	218
W C	100,134,135,163,212,221, 242,262,274
William W	218

PAUPPA
Chelouncha	352
James	352
Jumper	352
Phesant	352
Sauchjin	352

PAYNE
A M	216
Alice	221
Amsey M	216
Andrew L	217
Chas H	217
Claude	214
Dflora	354
Elizabeth	355
Floyd B	217
George A	214
Henry	214
J J	214
John	216
Joseph Earl	216
Julius	354
Laura	216
Lewis L	216
Rosie E	217
Ruth A	217
Susan	380
Wesley	214
Winona	217
W^m P	214

PEAK
Catherine	350
Ed W	350
Spencer R	350
Thos S	350

PEARCH
Alice	349
Izia	349
Josiah	349
Percy	349

Index

Sally..349
PEEK
  Dollie M 211
  Gracie O 211
  Henry H 211
PEIRSON, Mary..............................121
PENNYTON, B D....................136,207
PEPPIN, Mary..................................216
PERDUE, Jas S.................................349
PERRY
  Amanda 212
  Artemos 351
  Claude...351
  Columbus......................................351
  Earnest....................................212,351
  Effie...351
  Elizabeth.......................................351
  Ezekiel...351
  Floid L 352
  Marion S..212
  Mary G 212
  Myrtle 351
  N M 351
  Nat M..351
  Oliver H...351
  Oliver V...351
  S A..212
  S M 352
  Silas A 212
  Sion M 352
  Stella..351
  Sylvesta 351
  Zekiel...351
PETEE
  Eddie..217
  Hiram...217
  Myrtle 217
PETTEE, Myrtle..............................217
PETTIT
  Aggy..58
  Tim..58
  Timothy 58
PETTY, John T..................................59
PETTYJOHN
  Alice 58
  Geo 58
  Georgie A 58

Thomas A 58
PEVEHOUSE
  Arthur W 211
  Sarah E 211
  Sonora...211
  W F...211
PEVIHOUSE, Lizzie.......................217
PFAMEKUCH
  A...218
  Agnes...218
  Charles...218
PHARRIS
  Alena 211
  J L...212
  John 211,212
PHARRISS
  Agnes...212
  Allen 212
  Farley W 212
  Jackson L.......................................212
  Minnie 212
  P H..212
  Pleasant H......................................212
PHEASANT
  Geo 58
  George 58
  Jane...58
PHILIPS
  Ettie...142
  Myrtle 142
PHILLIPS
  Alice 87
  Andrew 59
  Bassie 352
  Bettie 308
  Budd 352
  Caroline 59
  Charles..87
  Elizabeth...58
  Elma 58
  Fannie 58
  Frank...................................58,59,216
  Gracie 352
  H P, Sr 58
  Harvey 58
  Henry..59,87
  Henry P, Sr 58

Henry, Jr 58
  Ida 58
  Jess 58
  Joe 352
  Joscine 352
  Josephine 352
  Julia 352
  Julias 87
  Laura 58
  Mary 59
  Nancy 58
  Roxie 58
  S J 308
  Spencer 352
  Susie 352
  W M 59
  Walter 58
  William M 59
  Willie 87
PICKAMAN
  Augustus 218
  Clara 217
  Clarence 217
  Jennie 218
  Martha 217
PICKARD
  Mary E 59
  Narcis J 59
  William 59
PIERCE
  Augustus 213
  Chas E 353
  Hazel M 213
  J R 6,7,33,37,40,56,81
  M T 213
  N J 353
  Nancy J 353
  Naoma 353
  Raymond O 213
  Robt 353
  Thos E 353
  William 353
PIGEON
  Charles 251
  John 227
  Lizzie 392
  Looney 214

  William 214
PINNER
  Elizabeth 212
  John 212
  Pearley 212
PLANK
  Lavadie 351
  Mersiller 351
  Russell 351
POLSON
  Alice 350
  Dudley 369
  Freddie 352
  Henry 350
  Jasper L 352
  W^m A 352
POOL
  C W 92,95,98,102,143,196,
  203,209,214,247,248,263,264
POOLE
  C W 113,154,155,184,
  213,222,236
  Chas W 213
  Claude 213
  Walton 213
POORBOY, George 213
POORWOLF, Charlotte 60
POPE
  Andy 60
  Benjamin 60
  Charles 60
  James 60
  James, Jr 60
  James, Sr 60
  Jennie 60
  Sarah E 60
  Sydney 60
POPLIN
  Annie J 354
  Catherine 354
  Ora A 354
PORTER
  Carey 215
  Florence 214
  Iris 215
  James D W 215
  Lenora 60

Index

    Lizzie 355
    Mamy 59
    Mary J 58
    N D 355
    Pleasant S 59
    William A 59
POTATO, Edward 212
POTTER
    Eliza 350
    Esta 349
POTTS
    Henry 211
    Mary B 212
    Susan 211
POWELL
    Arthur 214
    Dora 350
    Iva Ann 350
    Jennie 350
    Lavinnie 350
    Lee 350
    Mary 351
    R W 351
    Richard 350
    Richard W 351
    Robert 350
    Robt 350
    Vick 350
PRATER
    Geo D 212
    Hattie 212
    Jane 43
    Watt 212
    William 212
PRATHER
    Annie O 351
    Callie 351
    Caroline 354,355
    Chas D 354
    Cherokee E 217
    Daniel 354
    Eddie 217
    Effie 350
    Ella 355
    Fannie 351
    Florence K 351
    George E 217

    Georgia E 355
    Georgie A 350
    Hattie 352
    Jesse 350
    Josie M 217
    Lee B 351
    Lee Bell 351
    Lizzie 217
    Minnie O 351
    R L 175
    Richard 350,351
    Richard L, Jr 351
    Samuel H 351
    Thos W 354
    W^m D 351
PRESTON
    Clara 352
    Dora 60
    Maley 352
    Mattie 352
    Zack 352
PRICE
    Addie 59
    Annie Bell 215
    Charles 218
    Dan C 215
    Don C 215
    George 218
    J M 215
    James 212
    Jane 59
    Joseph M^c D 215
    Leonard 59
    Looney 215
    Monte 215
    Monti 215
    Thomas 59
PRIVIT
    Dolly 257
    Geo 257
    Littlelou 257
PROCTOR
    Lillie May 350
    Luella 350
PROPP, Mary E 212
PRUETT, Mary A 211
PUCKETT

Ellen	212
Fannie	212
Peche	212
PUGH, Mary J	59
PUMPKIN	
George	211
Peggy	211
PURYEAR, Florida	60
PUTNAM, Josie	211
PUYOR	
Florida	60
Francis M	60
Hamilton Z	60
PYATT	
Bessie L	211
Fannie C	211
Marchie	211
QUALATE	
Celia	355
Houston	355
Johnie	355
Mary	355
Nannie	355
QUEEN	
George	218
Joe	374
QUINTIN, John A	1
QUINTON	
Bell	120
Ethel	60
Felix	218
Isaac	60
Jack	218
Jess	218
John	60
Nancy	60
Nellie	218
Roxie	60
RABBIT	
Alsie	219
Andy	219
Ida	219
Mattie	219
Ross	219
Sallie	219
Thos	355
RAGSDALE	

Thomas	65
Thos	65
RAILEY	
George	228
Martha	228
Oliver W	228
Oscar C	228
William H	228
RAIN	
Artie M	64
Nannie	64
RAINES	
Geo M	356
Gordon B	356
Hitta E	356
Viola	303,356
W^m H	356
RALEY	
Bertha Pearl	225
Nancy J	225
William L	225
RALSTON	
Eliza	359
Eva R	226
Fannie	359
Francis	359
Ida	359
Johnie	359
Lewis	359
Lillie D	226
Lulu	359
Mary C	227
R D	227
Robt D	226
Robt L	227
Ruby	227
Viole	227
RAME, Fred	227
RANDOLPH, Joe	249
RAPER	
Alvin	219
Charles	227
Chick	358
Claude	219
Elizabeth	219
Ella	227
Geo	358

Index

Henry M 219
Jack 219
Jno A 219
Joe 358
John H 358
Leonard 228
Louis 219
Mary E 358
Nancy 219
Sarah E 358
Sarah J 358
Thomas 228
William P 219
Willie 358
RATCLIFF
   E N 170,227,251,343,375
   E R 289
   Eva E 227
   Eva M 227
   Finnis R 227
   Fred F 227
   James W 227
   Norville 227
RATLEY
   Levina 61
   Lizzie 61
   Lydia 61
   Rider 61
RATLIFF
   Jefferson 65
   Lorence 65
RATLINGOARD, John 65
RATLINGOURD
   Jim 357
   Liddie 227
RATLY, Jeff 65
RATTLINGOARD, John 65
RATTLINGOURD
   Lizzie 358
   William R 358
   W^m 358
RAVEN
   Boney 356
   Bony 356
   Jeremiah 356
   Joe 365
   John 365

Ocine 356
Willie 64
RAVIN, Albert 20
RAY
   Acy 60
   Pearl 60
   Sallie 61
RAYMOND
   Amanda 227
   Jess 60
REASE, Richard 221
REAVES
   C D 65
   Charles 65
   D W 65
   Dimor W 65
   Effie M 65
   John 65
   Mollie 65
   Mollie E 65
   Willie T 65
   W^m T 65
REDBIRD
   Charlotte 356
   Lethie 356
   Sally 356
   Sam 356
REDDING
   Amanda L 61
   Eliza C 61,62
   Isaacesco 62
   Jessie M 62
   Lula M 61
   Samuel 61
REDDINGTON, Isabell 221
REDMOND, Malinda 222
REED
   Almira 225
   Andy 222
   Claude 229
   Cyntha A 229
   Elmira 225
   J W 167
   J Warren 266,367
   John 357
   Lenora 222
   Lou Etta 357

Index

Lucy 225
Lulu 357
Luna 357
Nancy 222, 357
Pearl 357
Thomas L 229

REESE
   Charles 64
   Cleaveland 64
   Felix 64
   Nancy 64
   Nellie 64
   Rachael 64
   Tukie 64

REEVES
   Angerona 63
   Arlie 60
   Bailey 63
   Bertha 60
   Lettie 63
   Nannie 63
   Nettie 60
   Ollietta 63

REID
   Alice 64
   Bertha 64
   Clarance A 64
   Earnest 64
   Francis R 64
   Gracie 64
   Josephine 64
   Leola 64
   Martin 258
   Mary R 64

REINHARDT
   Ada 224
   Cassie 224
   Chas 224
   Henry H 224
   Kinney 224
   Nancy 224
   Sarah 224
   Walter 224

REMSEN
   Alvi M 358
   Josephine R 358
   Julia E 358

REYNOLDS
   Bessie 225
   William A 42
   W^m G 225

RHOMER
   Maggie B 65
   May 65
   May F 65
   Nora 65

RICE
   Annie 221
   Ida 221
   James A 221
   James A, Jr 221
   Ruby 221
   Violet E 221

RICHARDS, Eliza 226

RICHARDSON
   Delia F 358
   H T 358

RICHEY
   Mary 63
   Mary A 63

RIDDLE
   F J 226
   Fannie J 226
   Fred F 226
   Ida J 226
   James H 63
   Louisa 227
   W^m 63

RIDER
   Austin 224
   B W 224
   Bluford W 224
   Charles R 228
   James 224
   John 224
   Josephine 65
   Liddie 224
   Maude 224
   May 224
   Nannie 65
   Percivall 224
   Sally 335
   Sam 224
   Thomas 221

William P 224
RIDGE
  Adam 355
  Annie 356
  Beaver 355
  Darsie J 357
  Elijah 359
  Geo M 358
  Hellen F 358
  James 355
  Jennie 355
  Jeremiah 359
  John 229,359
  John R 358
  Moses 359
  Nellie 356
  Noble J 358
  Sally 355,357
  Sarah B 357
  Susie 356
  Young 355
RIGGS
  Eliza 229
  Frank 223
  H O 223
  Joseph 228
  Josie 229
  Laura 223
  Nadia 223
  Rosie E 228
RILEY
  Allwood 224
  Belle 228
  Bertha A 357
  Bettie 224
  Clnora 225
  Cora 219,225
  Elizabeth 225
  Frank 357
  Geo W 223
  Grover C 220
  J S 225
  James S 225
  John 228
  John M 219,220
  John W 225
  Johnson 20,47,65

Joseph L 357
Lewis 225
Lucy 219
Mattie 219
Minnie 225
Minnie V 116
Nannie 219
Nannie E 219
Owens 220
R R 224
Rebecca H 116
Richard 174,219
Rufus R 224
S R 224
Sallie L 225
Samuel R 224
Thomas J 357
Thos J 357
Wilder 219
Willis 357
RINGO
  Charles 226
  George G 226
  L A 226
  Libbie 226
  Lucy A 226
  Nona F 226
  William P 226
RIPPETOE
  Arthur B 223
  Bessie M 223
  Cora E 223
  Isaac 223
  Rebecca 223
RISINGFAWN
  Jennie 359
  Jenny 359
  Joseph 358
RISMAN
  Dannie 226
  John 226
  Martha 226,227
RITTER
  Ada E 359
  Ditha 359
  Howell 359
  Willie W 359

ROACH
- Chas 358
- Drucilla N 358
- Mattie 358
- Thos J 358

ROBBINS, Mahala 62

ROBBS
- *(Illegible)* 32
- Mary 37,62
- Mina 62

ROBERSON
- Albert 62
- Arthur 105
- Charles 62
- Cyntha E 225
- Dora 106
- Emma 49
- Freddie 105
- George 105
- Hank 225
- Jack 223
- John 25
- John, Jr 62
- Laura 66
- Lizzie 62,66
- Lola 105
- Lucy 62
- Lulu 105
- Maggie 62
- Mary 49
- Mary J 225
- Miltoh 49
- Nancy 62
- Nora 105
- Richard 66
- Samuel 62
- Sarah F 223
- William 62
- William H 223

ROBERTS
- Annie 221
- Arthur 63,221
- Callie 219
- Charles A 223
- Commodore 63
- Earl L 221
- Eliza 6
- James T 223
- Jno H 221
- Joseph 6
- Lena 221
- Leroy 63
- M E 223
- Marion 221
- Mary 221
- Mary E 223
- Maurice 63
- Mury 63
- Nancy 63
- Vennie 63
- William 63
- William E 223

ROBINS
- Benj 62
- Benjamin 62
- Charles 62
- Claud 62
- Henry 62
- James 62
- Josie V 223
- Mahala 62
- W L 223

ROBINSON
- Ella 62,63
- John C 62
- Mary E 63
- P P 218

ROBISON
- Chas W 223
- Clara 223
- De Witt 223
- Effie 218
- Esta 223
- Henrietta 218
- Jessie 218
- Joseph C 223
- Josie 218
- Katie 223
- Mary E 223
- Minerva 223
- Minnie E 223
- Rosie E 223
- Samuel L 223

ROCK

Index

Daniel 63
Jane..63
John 63
Lee...63
(ROGERS), Mrs Berilla 357
ROGERS
   Akie 355
   Allie B 228
   Alva M...227
   Arthur L 221
   Athelstan..227
   Berilla...357
   Betsie..355
   C V 184,203,205,226,270
   Catherine 220
   Charles..144
   Charles H 228
   Chicken..201
   Claud 220
   Claude...220
   Clem V 226
   Coone 65
   Cora L...220
   Dave 64
   David M..220
   Delila 228
   Ed 218
   Edgar 227
   Emma 61
   Eva..220
   Frank...219
   Frank W..218
   George 65,226,357
   Granville..221
   Guy R 220
   H C 222
   Henry...227
   Henry C 222
   Homer...227
   Ida..222
   J R 193,220
   Jack...226
   Jackie..226
   Jackson 222
   James..358
   Jane...228
   Jas..358
   Jennie..355
   Jennie H 221
   Jennie, Jr 355
   Jinnie H 221
   Jno M..221
   John 219
   John M..114
   Joseph...220
   Joseph R 220
   Josie..227
   Julia 222
   Knox 220
   L M...220
   L P 222
   La Vega 65
   Laura A.............................159,220,357
   Lavega 65
   Lelia M 357
   Lena M 220
   Lewis 209,227
   Louisa P 222
   Love..220
   Lulu N 222
   M E...220
   M K 222
   Maggie..267
   Martin G 220
   Mary 5,61,77,226
   Mary E..220,221
   Mary K 222
   Maude...224
   Nancy E 220
   Nora M 218
   Oscar L 220
   Otto...357
   Paul...220
   Pearl..219
   R W 222
   Ried 61
   Robt..226,357
   Robt L...226
   Robt R 220
   Rodge W 222
   Rolla A 357
   Rosie...226
   Roy..227
   Ruth 224

Index

Sallie ... 219
Saml ... 357
Samuel ... 357
Sarah ... 220,222
Sue M ... 228
Susie ... 222,355
T J ... 227
Thomas J ... 227
Thomas L ... 221
Thos J ... 357
Thos L ... 225
Thos T ... 357
Vickie R ... 220
W C ... 101,135,176,183,222, 226,244,256
W R ... 222
Wellington ... 222
Willie P ... 226
William C ... 222
William E ... 222
William G ... 222
William H ... 222
Willington ... 222
Wilson ... 355
W^m E ... 357
Zilpha P ... 357
ROLAND, Emily ... 63
ROLLINGS
  Pastey ... 221
  Patsy ... 4
ROLLINS
  Cora ... 228
  Mina ... 228
ROLSTON
  J D ... 223
  James D ... 223
  Z ... 358
  Zacheriah ... 358
ROME
  Andrew ... 43
  James ... 43
  Thomas ... 43
ROSE, Geo ... 259
ROSEBOROUGH
  Claude ... 359
  Jessie ... 359
  Lena ... 359
  Lucy ... 359
  William M ... 359
ROSENTHAL
  E ... 224
  Elizabeth ... 224
  Nancy H ... 224
ROSS
  Arra ... 61
  Carry ... 61
  Charles F ... 61
  Charles R ... 225
  Clarence S ... 225
  Comodore ... 220
  Cora ... 61
  Daniel ... 65
  Eddie ... 228
  Geo S ... 228
  George ... 220
  Jack ... 228
  James ... 65
  Jennie ... 65
  Jennie P ... 64
  Jess ... 61
  Jess T ... 61
  Jesse T ... 61
  Jessie ... 225
  John Y ... 64
  Johnson ... 61
  Joshua ... 64
  Joshua, Jr ... 64
  Leonard ... 227
  Lizzie ... 61
  Lora L ... 61
  Mary E ... 225
  Melissa ... 228
  Minnie ... 225
  Nannie ... 65
  Nellie ... 228
  Nora ... 61
  Ola F ... 178
  Ozy ... 61
  Pearl E ... 61
  Perry ... 225
  Robert F ... 61
  Robert, Jr ... 61
  Robt B ... 3,55,74,131,284,371
  Robt F ... 61

Index

Roy V 228
Susan 64
Susan E 225
Tim 61
Walter Lee 225
Waska L 61
Wasker L 61
Wayne M^{c}V 228
William 61,288
W^m P 65
ROUNDS
   Annie 356
   Annie, Jr 356
   Jack 356
ROWDEN
   Amona 224
   Luvana 224
ROWE, Nita 191
RUCKER
   Dora 219
   Ernest 219
   F M 219
   Mabel 219
   Ola Ave 219
RUDDLE
   Jene 221
   Norris 221
RUDDLES
   Charles 226
   Clara 226
   Jessie 226
   Jessie, Jr 226
RUNABOUT
   Che-Woan 356
   Cummins 356
   Geo 356
   I-hak-lan 356
   Ja-hake 356
   Jas 356
   Sa-ki-*(?)* 356
   Sa-u-gee-s-ki 356
RUNNELS
   Ella 63
   George 63
   Jess 63
   Minnie 63
   William 63

RUNYAN
   C C 222
   Elma 222
   Katie 222
   Sammie 222
RUSSELL
   Campbell 64,71,72
   Carlisle 64
   Christopher 64
   Connie 64
   Dave 356
   Edward 62
   Fannie 62
   Gus 62
   Jack 356
   Jesse 356
   Martha A 64
   Mary 356
   Maud M 62
   Robert L 62
   Sam W 356
   Susie 356
   W R 62
   Walter R 62
   William H 62
   W^m H 62
RYNE, John 227
SAGE, Nancy 164,234
SAGER
   Callie 365
   Debra 365
   James 365
   Liens 365
   Melia 365
   Nancy R 373
   Ollie M 365
   William 289
SALLEY, S B 168
SALLIE, Sarah B 168
SALSBERRY, Catharine 240
SAMPSON, Austin 239,243
SAMSON
   Austin 243
   Jim 242
SAMUEL, Myra 235
SAMUELS
   Emma J 371

Index

Robbie	371

SANDERS
- Annie 230
- Berry 229
- Charles 241
- Clara 241
- Clem 239
- Clyde 67
- Della M 362
- Dora 71
- Edith I 362
- Edward 237
- Etta 241
- Etta J 237
- Eva 241
- Frances 230
- Frank 239,241
- Geo M 238
- Gunter 237
- Henry 171
- Irene 232
- James 232
- Jesse 230
- John 72,241
- Joseph 230
- Katie 241
- Leler 71
- Martha 241
- Martha J 241
- Maud 67
- Nancy 66
- Nealy 67
- Nellie 230
- Nicholas 232
- Oce 232
- Rat 230
- Sallie 71
- Susan 126,243
- Susie 362
- W E 108,157
- Watt 371

SANFORD
- Lacy Nellie 243
- Mattie Lacy 243
- Minnie Lacy 243

SAPSUCKER
- Geo 359

- John 359
- Luke 359
- Nancy 359
- Price 359
- Sally 359
- Susie 359

SARAHOS
- Alberta S 376
- Elmer 376
- Franklin 376
- Polly 376

SARVER
- Ivan E 238
- Winona 238

SAYERS
- Henry 374
- W^m 374
- Wm F 374

SCALES
- A P 68
- Amanda 68
- Callie 68
- Ethel 363
- G W 363
- Grover 363
- J A 68
- Joseph 363
- Lillie 363
- Martha 363
- P H 6,86
- P J 1,17,18,31,32,58,61,80,86
- Pete 18,31
- Pete J 72
- Peter J 72
- Rose 72
- Sophie 72

SCHRIMSHER
- Eddie 233
- J G 226
- John G 242
- Laura 233

SCOONOVER
- Annie 71
- Grover C 71
- Henry 71
- Henry F 71
- Mary A 71

Rebecca A	71
Stonewall W	71
Thomas J	71

SCOTT
Alfort	40
Annetta	40
Annie	71,374
Bart	371
Birtha A	375
Buck	73
Chas D	240
Chas E	375
Cherokee	374,375
Cherokee B	375
Chester	73
Chewkee	374
Corinne	73
Cornelius	374
D L	242
Dave	73
Elmira	225
Geo	375
Geo W	375
George	73
Gurtrude	73
Ida L	73
James	73,374
Jas W	375
Jeff	40
Jesse	374
John B	375
Kiah	73
L L	240
Lee	73
Lena L	240
Lillie M	375
Lucy A	73
Lulu	240
Mattie E	371
Minnie	375
Nola	375
Patterson	73
Polly Ann	204,375
Price	375
Sabrina	371
Sanford	67
Sue	242
Susie D	371
Vivian	73
William A	40
W^m T	371

SCRAPPER
Earnest	368
Elige	368
Fannie	368
Henry	368
Lettie	368
Louie	365
Malinda	365
Nancy	365
Palinia	365
Sallie	368
Sally	365
Thos	365

SCRIMPSHER
Bessie B	242
Earnest	242
John G	242
Juliette	242
Juliette, Jr.	242

SCRIMSHER, John G 242

SCROGGINS
Effie	232
Jess E	232
Lola	232
Lucy	231
Maude	231
Oma	232

SCUDDER
Aimie C	235
Alford B	71
Bessie	71
Cherokee G	71
Gordon H	235
Ida J	235
Julia I	235
L B	71
L K	235
Laura K	235
Lewis B	71
M E	235
Maggie L	235
Mary E	235
Narcisus J	71

Nellie V 235
Newton G 235
William H 235
W^m H 235

SCUDER
   J M 71
   Jacob M 71

SEABORN, Sadie 364

SEARS
   Calvin 239
   Charlott 231,239
   Charlotte 231
   David 231
   Ida 231
   Joel 231
   Mary 231
   Sam 231
   Steven 231

SECREST, Ollie 376

SELVEGE
   John B 364
   Sabra 364

SELVIDGE, John B 364

SEQUITCHIE
   Archie 236
   Joe 242
   Martha 235

SEQUOYAH
   Dave 229
   Dick 229
   Lucy 229
   Maud 229
   Maude 229

SETTLE
   Arthur 234
   Eugene 234
   Lee 234
   Lore Ann 234
   Martha 234
   Randolph 234

SEVENS
   Joe 366
   Ruphus 355

SEVERE, Jack 34

SEVERS
   Barton 73
   Bessie M 72
   Charles J 73
   Ellen 73
   Emma M 73
   F B 3,20
   Florance E 72
   Sam 30
   Samuel B 73
   Samuel B, Jr 73
   Samuel B, Sr 72

SEVIER
   Alice 66
   Anna E 66
   Callie 66
   Charlie F 66
   George 67
   J A 66
   J J 66
   James 67
   James C, Jr 66
   James J 66
   Jerry 66
   Jess 66
   Joe 67
   John 66,284
   John A 69
   John C 69
   Leo 66
   May 69
   Susan 66

SEVORROVER, Lucy 47

SHACKLEFORD
   Charley 364
   Charlotta 230
   Cora 230
   Effie 364
   Martha 364
   Ollie 364
   W R 230

SHAMBLIN
   Bessie 367
   Charles 368
   Geo 367
   Pleasant 367
   Sarah 367

SHANAHAN
   Charlotte 233
   Ella 233

Jennie	240
Kittie	233
Maggie	240
Mary	233
P	233
Pat	233
William	233
Winnie	233

SHARP
Carrie	366
Caw-ta-ya	366
Chenasie F	366
Frog	366
Frogg	366
Mary E	237
N A	237
Nancy A	237
Will	366
W^m C	237

SHEEHAN, Annie 240

SHELDON
Mary E	278
W^m F	377

SHELTON
A B	375
Annie B	375
Norman B	375

SHEPARD
Boon	66
Charles	67
Charles, Jr	66
Edward	66
Eliza	74
Gus	66
Mollie	74
Richard	68
Rick	68
Watie	66

SHEPERD
Elizabeth	74
Mollie	74

SHEPHERD
Bessie	79
Boon	66
William E	79

SHEPPARD, Eliza 74
SHERIFF, John 69

SHIMP
John	239
Louisa	239
Thos Ray	239

SHINN
Alexander	71
Columbus	72
Jane E	71
John	72
Joseph	71

SHOEMAKE
Ada	74
Calvin B	68
Charles	68
Charles F	68
Claud	68
Effie	12
Frederick M	74
Gergie	66
Harmon	69
Harmon A	69
Hugh	68,72
J H	74
J W	12
James	74,120
James H	74
James W	69
Jennie	120
Jess S	72
John W	68,74
Lula B	67
Lula G	68
Maggie M	68
Mary E	67
Mattie B	68
Maud	68,72
Minnie N	68
Oscar	72
R W	74
Richard W	74
Rody	67
Rose A	69
Thomas H	67
W H	67
William H	67
William H, Jr	66
William, Sr	66

Index

SHOEMAKER
- Atta M 243
- John W 367
- Nora A 367
- Rachel 367
- Rebecca 367
- William J 367

SHOTPOUCH
- Betsy 360
- Drager 360
- Frank 360
- Lilla 360

SHOUSE
- Ada 371
- Clarence 371
- Harry 371
- Lee 371
- Lotta 371
- Louisa 371
- Nimma 371

SHUETZ
- Phillip 73
- Susana 73

SHUMAKE
- H J 68
- J S 72

SHUTT
- Bessie 232
- C W 232
- Clem W 232
- J W 232
- Jno W 232

SILK
- Alice 241
- Levi 241
- Melvina 241
- Nancy J 241
- William 241

SILVERSMITH
- Aggie 368
- Bettie 368
- Dlphus 355
- John 368
- Katie 368
- Mandy 368
- Mary 368
- Rachel 368

SIMERSON
- Blanche 374
- Cora 374
- Lonnie 374
- Lourina 374

SIMMONS
- Alexander 69
- Columbus 69
- Maggie 69
- Sarah 69

SIMMS, H L 68
SIMON, Sarah 235
SIMONS, Benty 69
SIMPSON, Eliz 71

SIMS
- Jess C 68
- Tennessee 68

SIX
- Enoch 364
- Ground-hog 360
- Ida 364
- Jennie 360
- John W 373
- Lander 360
- Sally 360
- Sam 374
- Umphrey 360

SIXKILLER
- Carlotte 376
- Carrie B 329
- Chas 262,373
- Claude Lee 368
- Cora 143
- Eliza 231
- Emma 372
- Emma T 242
- Fannie 144
- Hooley 230
- James 242,368
- Jas 242
- Joel H 238
- John M 262
- Joseph 232
- Linnie 360,373
- Lola 230
- Luke 372
- Martin 230

Index

Mary 230
Maude 230
Myrta 372
Rachel 230
Sally 360
Samuel 143
Young W 373
SKA-LANE
   Aggie 234
   Bear 234
   Danniel 235
   Dick 235
   James 234
   Jennie 234
   John 234
   Joseph 235
   Lizzie 235
   Mary 235
   William 233, 235
SKIDMORE
   A F 238
   Annie E 238
   Annie F 238
   Ben F 238
   Clarence H 238
   Eugene O 238
   Letitia F 238
   Ottis T 238
SKILLMAN
   Bessie 240
   Sarah 240
SKIMMERHORN, James 37
SKINNER
   Betsey A 232
   Dora 243
   Gallagher 232
   James W, Jr 232
   Johnie 240
   L C 232
   Louie 240
   Lucy C 232
   Mary 232
   Morgan D 232
   Nat 240
   Ray 240
   Rosie L 232
   Tom F 232

   Willie 232
SLOAN
   Cora 229
   Ed 369
   Edward 368
   Ellec G 229
   Ellic G 229
   Eva 369
   Hattie 230
   Jas E 369
   Jennie 368
   Lizzie 229
   Mary 368
   May 369
   Minnie 369
   Nora 229
   Robert 229
   Sam 369
   T A 229
   Thomas A 229
   Willie 368
SMALLWOOD, Samuel 68
SMART
   Athalie 233
   Dasy P 233
   Hellin 67
   Henry 67
   L R 233
   Susie P 233
SMEDLY
   J L 69
   Jackson 69
   John L 69
   Richard 69
   William 69
   W^{m} 69
SMITH
   Alice 236
   Allice 236
   Alma 374
   Athie A 371
   Bell 372
   Betsey 239
   Betsy 253
   Beulah 237
   Bird E 370
   Birtha 374

Index

Carrie R 374
Carty......................................66
Catharine 371
Catherine 371
Cherry....................................72
Clarence................................235
Clarissa.................................374
Clearcy 374
Cora.......................................372
Cora P...................................374
Culeyah.................................372
Darcus...................................372
Dater 372
David......................................72
Deborah 376
Delia 70
Della 374
Dennis...................................376
E Bird 370
Edward 67
Eliza..................................72,240
Eliza L 371
Elizabeth.....................239,240,372
Elizabeth R 239
Emma 73,364,369,376
Famous 66,72
Floid 79
Florance 72
Florence C 370
Frank..........................72,73,237
Freeman................................235
G W 278,279,288,289,293,
306,322,328,338,339,355,378
Georgia A 235
Gnat 370
Harrison................................239
Henry....................................370
Hiram R 237
Homer...................................370
Hugh E..................................373
Iva N 369
James 240
James M................................372
James O 238
Jay 376
Jennie...............................67,364
Jesse.....................................374

Jno H 238
John 70,364,373
John N 371
Joseph 72,233
Juletta 67
Juliaetta T 73
Juni 67
Junie 67
Kiahna 66
Kittie E 237
Kittie J 233
Laura.....................................240
Lida.......................................364
Lizzie 66,372
Logan....................................239
Louiza 72
Lucy......................................364
Lulitin 67
Lutie 72
Lyda......................................364
Mabel....................................239
Maggie..................................372
Mammie 67
Margaret 370
Martha 66
Martha M..............................233
Mary 367,374
Mary J...................................238
Maud......................................72
Maude...................................376
Maude A 235
Maudie..................................372
May 67
McCoy 67
Mike 238
Minnie 70
Minnie A 373
Minnie J 373
Mittie 72
Montazuma 371
Mude S 372
Myrtle...................................370
Nancy 73
Nancy J.................................242
Nannie 72
Newton 240
O J 233

Ollie	372
Oscar	369
Ossie	367
Pearl H	371
Percy W	370
Rachel	364,372
Roach	73
Robt E	239
Robt L	371
Rosa	374
Rusk	367
Ruth L	374
S S	239
Sallie	73
Sallie A	239
Sam	364
Samuel	73,74
Sarah P	370
Simmy	70
Susie	72,73,236,372
Sylvester S	239
Thomas	73
Tressie	239
Vernon	79
Viola	240
W F	370,388
W L	242
W M	235
Walter	67,372
Walter E	370
Walter F	370
Wilbert	369
William	240
Willie	67
Willie L	370
Willie M	370
Wilson	67
Winnie	239
W^m A	374
W^m E	373
W^m L	370
Zella	151
Zella J	376
SMOKE, Sallie	136
SNAIL	
Charlie	361
Cora	361
Eli	361
George	361
Gilbert	361
Jennie	361
Joe	361
John	361
Nancy	361
Ned	361
Nellie	361
Peggie	361
Sally	361
Sam	361
Sarah	361
SNAKE	
Chas	376
Jackson	376
Margarett	376
Peter	376
Wolf	376
SNELL	
Alice	368
Annie	365
Betsy	369
C E	365
Carlotte	366
Charey E	365
Charley	365
Coonie	365
Dave	369
Ed	366
Eli	368
Ella	365
Jas	366
Jennie	366
Joe	369
Jonica	365
Katie	368
Katy	365
Liza	366
Louie	368
Lucy	368
Nannie	365
Nellie	366
Onia	365
Peter	366
R E	389
Squirrel	366

Susie 366
Syntha 366
SNIDER
   Andrew 370
   Dora 369,370
   Dora, Jr 370
   Elbert 370
   Flid 370
   Laura 369
   Minnie 369
   Roy 370
   Syntha 370
SNOW
   Mary A 236
   Rachel 236
SNYDER
   Annie 236
   Perry E 236
   Thomas B 236
SOAP, Thomas 70
SONEGOOYAH 243
SOUNEGOOYAH 243
   Lizzie 243
SOUTH
   Charles C 233
   Ellen 233
   J C 233
   Kate 233
   Wilson C 233
SOUTHERLAND
   A 240
   Arabella 240
   Pollie 237
SOWER, Winona 238
SPANIARD, Lucy 47
SPENCER
   Allen 179
   Lillie 179
   Samuel F 237
SPLITNOSE
   Betsey 74
   Charles 71
   Nannie 74
   Thomas 71
SPRADDLING, Okla 374
SPRADLING, Okla 374
SPRIGGS

   Alexander 230
   Annie B 230
   Henry A 230
   John B 230
   M A 145,229
   Marnie P 230
   Mary A 229
SPURLOCK
   Hannah 240
   Hardin H 240
   Lone B 240
SQUIRREL
   Betsy 361,369
   Carley 363
   Cherokee 363
   Daniel 372
   Jack 373
   Peter 361
   Sam 369
STALLEY
   James 231
   Jessie 231
   Nannie 231
   Noley 231
STANLEY
   Annie 364
   Bessie 364
STAQRR
   J C 310
   Martin 350
   Will 366
   William 366
   Willie 350
STARKS
   Charles 73
   Lucy 73
   Mattie 73
STARR
   Aggie 366
   Arch 256
   Bean 71
   Blue W 231
   Bluford 231
   Bunch 70
   C C 44
   C W 367,391
   Cale John 367

Index

Cale W 173
Caleb 44,256
Calvin 74
Canuke 361
Charles 129
Charley C 231
Cherokee 70
Cooie 44
E E ... 85,89,92,271,286,323,324,362
Eliza 70
Ella 241
Ellis 70
Emma 367
Emmet 207,352
Emmit 241
Emona J 367
Ezekiel 367
Fannie 70
Fredrick 69
Frost 70
Geo 361,365,366
George C 241
Georgia A 284
Glenn 231
Henry 70,237
Hickory 367
Ida 242
J C 2,5,7,14,25,26,35,38,50,
53,56,62,65,67,77,78,79,91,94,95,97,
98,100,101,105,106,108,112,119,120,
122,123,124,125,126,129,130,131,
132,133,134,135,138,139,140,141,144
,147,148,149,151,152,154,155,157,
158,159,161,162,164,166,167,168,169
,172,173,174,176,177,179,181,184,
185,187,194,196,199,200,201,202,203
,204,206,212,213,215,217,219,221,
222,223,228,230,233,235,238,239,241
,242,243,244,245,249,250,251,256,
259,260,262,263,265,266,267,268,269
,272,273,274,275,276,277,278,280,
281,282,283,284,285,286,287,288,289
,293,294,299,303,304,305,306,308,
309,310,311,312,315,318,319,321,323
,325,326,331,332,336,338,340,348,
349,350,351,354,355,356,358,359,360
,361,363,364,365,366,367,368,369,
370,371,372,373,375,376,377,378,379
,380,382,384,387,391
J X 325
James 70
Jas 365
Jennie 360
Jess 360
Jess M 231
Jesse 360,361
Jessie B 367
John 71,365,366
Joseph 241
Kate 70
Leesie 70
Lettie B 241
Lilla 361
Linnie 365
Lucy 70
Lulu 367
Lydia 360
Mack 365
Maggie 365
Mary 73,366
Mary B 241
Milo 69
Mollie 69
Moss 70
Nake 361
Nancy 361
Nelly 70
Orange W 231
Peggie 233
Peggy 233
Rachel 361
Richard 69
Ruth 69
Sally 360,361
Samuel 70
Sis 69
Sophia 70
Spihechee 70
Squirrel 69
Susan 69
Susan E 367
Susie 256
Tee Ann 360
Teesa 70

Index

Thomas 69,70
Thos 69,70
Tucksie 44
Turner 360
Tuxie 69
Watt 241
William 70,71
Young W 365
Zeke 361
STEALER
  David 242
  Jennie 242
  Lewis 242
  Mariah 242
  Sarah 242
  Thomas 242
STEELE, R V 74
STEELER
  George 234
  Johnson 234
  Lydia 231
  Nancy 234
  Willie 234
STEENS
  Annie 231
  Sarah 230
  Susan 230
STEPHENS
  Bell 375
  Carrie L 375
  Earnest L 375
  Flossie I 375
  Jessie 375
  Laura 375
  Marshal C 375
  Mary E 375
  S A 236
  S S 375
  Sarah 375
  Spencer A 236
  Spencer S 375
STEPHENSON
  Alice 74
  James 74
  Samantha 74
  Thomas 74
STERLING
  Ella 232
  Lillie E 232
STEVENSON
  Chunnie 369
  J W 369
  John 369
  Maggie 369
  Mary T 369
  W^m F 369
STEWARD
  John J 238
  Mina 238
  W C 238
STEWART
  Annie 71
  Celina 373
  Geo W 373
  John H 373
  Jon H 373
  Mary J 373
  W N 373
  William H 71
  W^m N, Jr 373
STICK
  Eli 360
  Emily 360
  Joe 360
  Polly 360
STILES, Lizzie 231
STILL
  Acie 363
  Beula 74
  Callie 363
  Clarance 74
  Geo 363
  Geo W 363
  Green 367
  Jimmie 364
  Johnie 364
  Linnie 363
  Louis 363
  Mary 363
  Mary E 364
  Samuel 230
  William H 74
STILLY
  Cora B 370

Lucy	370
Ora D	370

STINGER
Albert	241
Cora	241
Louisa	241
Noble D	241

STOKES
Ewing	236
Floyd M	234
Georgia A	234
Grreta	234
Hershel	236
Mary	236
Mattie B	373
Maude	236
Oliver M	234
Robert	236
William	236

STOLLCUP
Francis	376
Sally	376

STONE
Foster	108
Lelia	108

STOODY
Betsy	368
Geo	368
Louie	368
Mary	368
Willie	368

STOP
Sally	371
Tom	371

STORN, Chas W 190

STOUT
Abram	229
Annie B	229
Ellen	229
Jaeb	229
James	229
Louisa	229
Mary A	229
Nancy E	229
Susan	229

STOVALL
Lucille	238
Susie	238

STOVER
Edith	370
Rogers	370
W^m	370,390
W^m A	370

STRANGE
M R	235
Mary R	235

STRICKLAND
Elizabeth L	239
Katie C	239
Roger	239
S C	239
Sarah C	239

STRONG
Augusta	364
John	364
Phillip	364

STROUP
Clara	230
Earl	230
Jessie	230
Pearl	230
Royal	230

STROUT
Eliza A	374
Liza A	374

STUBBS, Jno S 198

STUCKER
Lewis	237
Minerva	236
Myrtle	237
Pearl	237

STUPP
George C	242
Laura	242

STURDIVANT
John	364
Lizabeth	364

SUAGEE
Bessie M	367
David	372
Dennis B	367
Jo Ella	372
Joel B	373
Laura	372

Lucinda	372
Mandy	372
Margie E	367
Mark	372
Maude	372
Nellie	372
Nora	367
Peter	367
Robert	367
Roy Lee	367
Sam	366
Sarah	372
Stand	367
Stand W, Jr	367
Thos J	367
Wilson	372

SUDDERTH
Hallie B	237
Linnie	237
Luise	237

SUDDETH, J P 237

SULLIVAN
Annie	237
Arthur I	238
Conrad D	238
Eliza	237
Frank	232
Geo L	242
George	237
George T	238
Georgia	237
James	232
Jeff D	238
Jefferson D	242
Jno L	237
John W	242
Mary	237
Maude E	238
Nancy	232
Oral Lee	238
W S	238
William	237
Willie S	238
W^m H	238

SULSAR
Annie	366
Lucinda	366

Sparrow	366
Willie	366

SUMERS
Arthur	362,363
Calvin	362,363
Freddie	363
Geo C	363
Lizzie	363

SUMMERFIELD
Aggie	360
Ava	360
Beckie	360
Celia	376
Charley	376
Isaac	360
Jack	360
James	72
Jess	360
Katy	376
Leach	376
Lee	376
Lucy	376
Maryling	360
Sam	376
Swimmer	360
Wallie	376
Will	376
Willie	376

SUMMERFIELDS, Jack 360

SUMMERS
Arthur	362
Calvin	362
Caroline	372
G C	363
Geo C	363
George C	362
Joseph	231
Lizzie	363

SUNDAY
Alex	233
Annason	233
Avy	68
Betsey	231
Edward	239
Edward, Jr	239
Ellen	233,239
Emily	231

Index

- Ezekiel 231
- George 68
- Henry 371
- Izra 68
- James 68
- Jane 239
- Lee 371
- Lena 68
- Lou 239
- Maggie 239
- Nancy 100,371
- Peggie 68
- Susie 231
- Thomas 68
- W E 101
- William 233,239

SUTAWAGIE
- Annie 359
- Susie Ann 359

SUTHERLIN
- Allie B 237
- Herbert F 237
- Leroy 237
- Pollie 237
- Sam A 237

SUTTON
- Alex 366
- Alexander 373
- David 373
- Edward 373
- John 373
- Katie 373
- Lizzie 373
- Mary 374
- W^m D, Jr 373
- W^m H 373

SWAIN
- Nancy 78
- R M 167
- Rebecca M 375

SWAN
- Boudinot 236
- Paul 236
- Susie 236

SWARM, Nellie 236

SWATT
- Easter 369
- Louisa 369
- Oliver 369
- Scott 369
- Steen 369
- Thomas 369
- Wesley 369
- Will 369
- Willie 369

SWEATMAN, Mattie 233

SWEETEN
- Clein 234
- Cora 234
- Emoria 234
- Eva 234
- Philip 234
- Phillip 234
- Rebecca 234
- Samuel 234

SWEETWATER, W^m 376

SWIM
- John 236
- Mary E 236
- R W 236
- Sarah E 236

SWIMMER
- John 230,250
- Nannie 38
- Susie 289

SYKES
- Alex 67
- Marion 67

TABLER, Leathie 378

TACKET
- Birt A 248
- Levi A 248
- M P 248
- Mary P 248
- Maud E 248
- Mirtle J 248

TADPOLE
- Annie 250
- Darkey 250
- Dave 153
- David 249,250
- David, Jr 250
- Lige 250
- Polly 249

Index

Rosa..............................250
Sallie.............................250
TAFFELMIRE, Elizabeth...............378
TAGUE, Nancy J......................248
TAKUN
   John V...........................244
   Mary.............................244
TALBERT
   Arua.............................254
   Carrie...........................254
   Cora.............................249
   Eliza............................254
   Ellen............................254
   Ethel............................249
   G W..............................254
   Geo..............................254
   Georgia..........................254
   Grover...........................254
   Jessie...........................249
   Mary.........................249,254
   Rosa.............................249
TALBOT
   Florence.........................377
   James............................377
   John.............................377
   Syntha...........................377
   Thornton.........................377
TALLY
   Andrew............................76
   Bettie............................76
   Sibert............................76
   Sirbert...........................76
TANNER
   Allsie...........................379
   Annie............................382
   Betsy............................379
   Charley..........................379
   Jackson..........................379
   Jas..............................382
   Joe..........................379,382
   John.............................379
   Josie............................379
   Mary.............................382
   Minnie...........................379
   Pheasant.........................379
   Tom..............................379
   Tooker...........................379

TARPIN
   Betsy............................246
   James............................246
   Patty............................246
TASSEL
   Jesse............................378
   John.............................378
TASSELL, Whitewater.................244
TASSLE, WhiteWater..................244
TAU-U-NEA CIE, Louis................378
TAU-U-NEA-CIE
   Daniel...........................378
   Edward...........................378
   Jane.............................378
   Susie............................378
TAYLOR
   Adda.............................244
   Andrew J.........................243
   Annie............................244
   Betty C..........................378
   Brtie............................381
   C C..............................244
   C H..............................243
   C H, Jr..........................243
   Caldonia C.......................244
   Campbell.........................243
   Chester..........................381
   Claud............................248
   Clayborn.....................254,255
   Cornelia.........................248
   Dave.............................252
   David....................248,252,255
   David, Jr........................248
   David, Sr........................248
   Delora...........................378
   Delta L..........................244
   Edward...........................248
   Effie............................378
   Elibert..........................247
   Emma.............................249
   Flora............................378
   Francis..........................378
   Frank R..........................382
   Geo..............................378
   Geo M............................382
   Geo W............................382
   Georgie L........................158

Index

Girtie..........381
Gussie B..........244
Gutie..........247
Henry..........244,378
Herbert..........248
Hubert..........381
Icum..........75
J M..........128,131,249,381
Jackson..........244
James..........254
James L..........250
John..........76
John F..........247
John M..........381
John M, Jr..........248,251
Joseph..........249
Juletta..........75
Kate..........132
Laura..........247
Lee..........381
Lillie..........247
Looney..........54
Mabelle..........248
Mack..........247
Martha..........382
Mary E..........249
Mattie..........244
Maud..........247
Nannie..........378
Perd..........247
R R..........246,313,382
Robert..........247
Robt J..........382
Roy..........248
Roy S..........381
Sallie..........248
Searse..........381
Stacy B..........243
Syntha J..........381
Thos..........381
Vinnie..........381
Waliam..........101
William..........247,254
Winnie D..........382
Wm H..........382
Wm T..........244
TEAGUE

B F..........251
Cora A..........251
Frances J..........251
Mary J..........251
TEE SQUAT NI..........303
TEEHEE
   Charley, Sr..........377
   Kate..........77
   Tilden..........250
TEE-SA-DA-SKEY
   Annie..........382
   Mouse..........382
   Nancy..........382
   Peggie..........382
TEHEE
   Alex..........377
   Carrie..........377
   Charley..........377
   Charley, Jr..........377
   Cloud..........377
   Dave..........377
   Eli..........377
   Geo..........377
   Gun-ga-nal-a..........377
   Jimmie..........377
   Lizzie..........377
   Mary..........377
   Nancy..........377
   Olsie..........377
   Stalk..........377
   Susie..........377
   Young Bird..........377
TELL
   George..........249
   Virdie..........249
TENBROOK, Mattie..........379
TERLEY, Alsie..........244
TERRELL
   Albert..........76
   E M..........249
   Ed M..........76
   Edward M..........249
   Elizabeth..........248
   Lula M..........76
   May..........76
   Oliver C..........76
   Pearl..........76

Thomas	251
Thomas J	248
Una	76
Willie E	76

TETER
Alice	250
Clara J	250
Mirtle	250

THEURER
Alta	383
Lena	383
Mary E	383

THOMAS
Arch	378
Chas	380
Daisy	380
Edward G	249
Elizabeth	378
Ellis	253
Frank N	253
Fred	378
Henry	380
Henry R	253
Isabella J	253
J A	253
Jas Albert	380
Jefferson	380
Jennie	249
Jennie I	249
Jese A	253
John A	253
Laura	378
Lawrence	253
Lillie Bell	378
Marth	380
Minnie	249
Myrtle	380
Newton	253
Nicholas	382
Oscar	247
Thom	380
Thomas C	253
Thuray	253
Tom	380
Viola B	249

THOMASON
Birtha	381
George L	381
Grover C	381
J S	92,93,95,99,102,109,110, 111,128,138,142,150,163,164,169,171,193,198,217,226,235,240,242,243, 255,272,274,280,282,283,294,296,302 ,304,305,319,323,324,329,332,334, 341,342,349,367,379,381,384,391,394 ,395
Rachel F	381
S N	297

THOMPSON
Ada	382
Ada I	247
Aggie	378
Alice	382
Alison	250
Allison G	253
Annie	255
Arch	378
C A	6,59,76,77,78,80,81, 83,86,87,88
Charles	75
Clarence	251
Cleo	250
Dalton	254
Daniel	246
E	253
E C	214
E J	247
E M	375
Earl	248
Earnest	253
Earnest W	250
Eda J	247
Eliza	251
Ethel	384
Ethel May	243
Eugene	253
Eula L	243
Exa	243
Florance E	77
Francis	253
George L	243
George W	247
Gilbert	250
Gilbert, Jr	250

Index

Gracie 75
H D 243
Hattie 384
Hicks E 243
Hooley D 243
J A 253
J L 382
J P 248
Jack 3,24,75
James 227,250
James A 253
James P 248
James W 251
Jennie 75,246
Jessie 246
Jim 227
Joe L 382
John 378
John M 243
Kate 75
Lettie 244
Lewis 251
Lewis K 381
Lizzie 246,341
Louis K 381
Malinda 77
Malinda L 77
Mamie 250
Mary 244
Mary E 244
Mathew 250
Milton 244,250
Narcisa 75
Nellie F 77
Newton 246
Nora B 77
Rachel 377
Rhoda F 247
Sarah 253
Stella L 247
Stella R 251
Susan C 254
T F 243,254
Thos F 243,254
Thos L 251
W D 243
William 75
William C 247
William D 243
Yauless 248
THORNBERRY
   Annie 76
   John 76
   Lena 76
   Rachel 76
   Willie 76
THORNBOROUGH, Hortensia 243
THORNTON
   Alice 379
   Archie A 254
   Emanda 379
   Eva 379
   G W 254
   Geo W 254
   Henry J 245
   James 244
   Josie M 168
   Lizzie 245
   Marion 245
   Mary 245
   Mary M 254
   Minnie 379
   Nellie E 254
   Nora V 254
   Ora J 254
   Orville E 254
   Smith 245
   Thomas J 250
   W I 364,379
   Will I 379
TIBLOW, Wesley 120
TIGER
   Charles 248
   Eugene 380
   George 248
   Lillie 248
   Lizzie 248
   Mary 45,248
   Robert 45
   Sallie 255
   Tom 380
   W^m 380
TILEY
   Mary G 380

Index

Minnie O 380
Polina 380
TIMBERLAKE
   Jennie 252
   John A 77
   Margaret L 252
   William 77
TIMBROOK
   Earling 379
   Jananita 379
   Mattie 379
TIMPSON
   Bear 251
   John 77
   Katie 251
   Nancy 251
   Sallie 251
   Sam 251
   Susie 251
TINCUP
   Austin 249
   Dora 249
   Edward 249
   Florence 249
   Henry 249
   James 249
   James, Jr 249
   Lucinda 249
   Lucy 285
   May 249
   William 249
TITTLE
   Annie 252
   Clyda L 75
   Dan L 381
   Daniel 252
   David 252
   Dora 381
   Dora A 381
   Earl 252
   Effie 252
   Fred 380
   Gola 75
   Gracie P 381
   Heigh T 381
   Henry C 381
   J M 252

James M 252
Jesse 252
Lee 252
Lizzie 75
Mary J 381
Otis W 381
Robt 381
Robt J, Jr 381
Robt W 381
Rosa A 253
S J 253
Susan J 253
TOLBERT, Rufus 77
TONEY
   Betty 76
   Calvin 76
   George 75
   Isaac 136
   Jennie 75
   John 75
   Levi 76
   Looney 76
   Mary 75
   Nancy 75
   Sequah 5
   Susan 76
   Thomas 5
TOOLATE
   Ah-cher-nuste 380
   Alice 380
   Annie 380
   Buck 380
   Davis 380
   John 380
   Kah-na-lu-st 380
TORBITT
   Arthur T 252
   Elmer H 252
   M J 252
   Mary J 252
   Walter T 252
   Willie J 252
TOSSER, Charles 255
TOVEY
   A N 254
   Annie N 254
   Della M 254

Index

Frank L 254
Hooley B 254
Laura A 254
Thos W 254
TOWERS
   Charlott J 251
   Clem R 251
   Gertrude 251
   Maud 251
   Minnie B 251
   Thomas B 251
   William J 251
TRAINOR
   T J 244
   Thomas J 244
TRAP, Joe 244
TRENT
   Edward 77
   Ella 77
   Jeff 185
TRETHART, Sallie 255
TREUMAN, Mary 305
TRIPLET
   Edward 76
   M A 77
   Mary A 77
TRIPLETT, Ed 76
TRITTHEAT, Henry 253
TRITTHEIT, Laura 253
TROTT
   Belle 253
   Birdie 381
   Dora 381
   Dott F 252
   Eliza 253,254
   Hardin 253
   Hardin H 253
   Homer 381
   J R 252
   Jas C 381
   John R 252
   Lillie O 380
   May 253
   William H 252
   William L 75
   William O 252
   Willie 381
   W^m L 75,252
   W^m O 252
TROTTINGWOLF
   Lincoln 247
   Roy 247
   Susie 247
TROUT
   Creed 379
   Geo 379
   Georgie 379
   Henry 379
   Isaac 379
   James 379
   Lizzie 255
   Logan 379
   Martha 379
   Ruphus C 379
TUCKER
   Andrew 245
   Annie 246
   Calvin 245
   Caroline 252
   Cornelia 382
   Daniel 253
   Dave 250
   Eva 246
   Florence 246
   George 250
   Guy 246
   John 246
   Katie 250
   Martha 382
   Mary 250,252
   May 245
   Munroe 245
   Nellie 245
   Susan 250
   Thomas 245
   Viola 245
   Wesly 245
TULLY
   John 76
   John D 76
TURNER
   C Q 94
   C W 64,228
   Clarence W 249

Index

    Daniel 380
    Edith 244
    John W 244
    Lillie 380
    Minnie E 378
    Nellie 380
    Racheal 244
    Rachel 244
    Rubie 378
    Sam 380
    Stella 244
    Taylor 380
    Tennessee 244
    Tookah 249
    Tookah B 249
    Will 380
    William D 249
TURNOVER, Margaret 75
TURQUETT
    Jasper 75
    Nannie 75
TWIST
    Oliver W 248
    W^m G 248
TYLEY
    Abe 382
    Etta 382
TYLY, W^m 380
TYNER
    Aaron 245
    Annie 247
    Austin 246
    Bessie 247
    Bushyhead 245
    Carter 245
    Clara 252
    Cleve 246
    Clinton 246
    Davis 245
    Delila 245
    Ella 222
    Emitt 246
    Emma 246
    Fannie 245
    Fannie A 246
    Frayzer 222
    George 246,247

    James 245
    James, Jr 245
    Jefferson 247
    John 245,246
    John A 246
    Laura 246
    Lenard 246
    Lewis 245
    Lewis C 245
    Lou W 246
    Lulu 222
    Lydia 74
    Lydia J 245
    Lydia, Jr 74
    Maggie 74
    Mary 74
    Maud 246
    May 246
    Oliver 252
    Quatie 245
    R B 247
    R J 74
    R R 246
    Racheal 245
    Ralph 245
    Redbird 245
    Roxie A 247
    Rubin B 247
    Rubin R 246
    Ruth 252
    Sarah 247
    Susie 245
    Thomas J 245
    Wever 246
TYNON
    Andrew 382
    Arie 382
    Henry 382
    Joe 382
    John 382
    Ruphus 382
    Thomas 382
    W^m 382
UMPHREY
    Andrew 383
    David 383
    Fannie 383

Graden	383
James	383
John	383
W^m	383

UNDERWOOD
Agnis	255
Charles	255
Henry	255
Mollie	255

VANN
Ada	78
Ada C	255
Alice	255
Arch	256
Beaver	383
Birt	256
C E	3,78,84
Callie	256
Celia	383
Charles	256
Charles E	78
Chick-alee-la	383
Chickalely	383
Clarinda	255
Claud	255
Clem	79
Clem I	255
Cooie	78
Cora	256
D W	255,383
Daniel W	255
Dave	383
Dave W	383
David	65,77
David W	255
Dick	383
Dora	383
E Anna	383
Edward	78
Elizabeth	78
Ellen	77
Elnora	79
Emitt	255
Emma	255
Envina	255
Fanny M	383
Flora E	383
Frank	78
Frederix	78
Gee-woan	383
Geo	383
George	78
Georgia A	77
H J	1,6,12,23,25,32,50,57,61, 68,70,75,76,80,84,86
Hampton	79
Herman J	79
Holmes	78
James T	256
James W	77,78
Jennie	383
Jesse	255
Jim G	384
Joanna	256
John	256,383
John H	256,383
John J	256
John S	78
Joseph	78,79,256
Leach	383
Lila	256
Lizzie	78,79,383
Lola	79
Lula	256
Lular	77
Lydia	383
Martha P	256
Mary	255
Mary J	266
Maud	78
Mittie	78
Nakie	384
Nancy	79,383,384
Nannie E	256
Ninnie	78
Nokie	384
Pearl	383
Perry	78
Quenie	255
Racheal	256
Ralph	256
Reid	256
Robert, Jr	78
Robert, Sr	78

Rusk	383
Ruth	256
Sarah	256
Sarah E	256
Sophia	79
William	77,78,79
William W	256
William, Jr	77

VAUGHT
General	78
Jennie	78
Joanna	78
John	78
Joseph	78
Lucinda	78
Lucy	78

VERMILLION, R E 344,389

VICKERY
Andrew	79
Bettie	79
Charles	79
Henry	79
John	79
Nancy	79
Samuel	79
Susan	79
Timsey	79

VICTOR
Dee	384
Fred	384
Octa	384
S G	384

VINITA
Albert	124
Da-ro-ta-ro	124
Dora	124
Johnny	124

VORE
Charles F	77
Frank	77
Frank, Jr	77
Hellen	77
Irvin	30,79
Irving	79

W & SHUTT 133
WABOURNE, Wilson L 269
WAFFORD
Bettie	262
Blueford	262
Dora	262
Eli	265
Ella	259
James	263
Joseph	262
Willie	262

WAKEFIELD
Albert	260
Bertie	261
Charles	260
Edward	260
Escobedo	260
Kergin	261
Lydia	260,261
Ollie	261
Thos	261
Virgin	261

WALES, Julia....................................163

WALKER
Adda	389
Albert W	389
Bertha	389
Blossom	267
Carey	83
Carrie	258
Daniel H	268
David	268
Earl P	392
Ella	258
Etta	268
Frank L	266
Geo W	268
Henry	268
James	268
James V	266
Jane	267
Janie	267
Jas	394
Jas A	392
Jennie	394
Jimmie	394
John	263
John E	394
John F	268
Little	392

Lola B	266
M A	268
M Rex	392
M V	268
Martha J	269,389
Mary	265,268
Mary A	268
Mary E	237,266
Mary M	392
Mary V	266,268
Nannie	394
Narcissa O	392
Nellie	269,392
Ollie	269
P L	273,392,395
Senora	268
Sophronia	389
Susan	267
Trevis	268
Watt	266
Willie	258
W^m F	269
W^m J	266

WALKINGSTICK

Annie	257
Chas	257
Dora	257
Peggie	257
S R	244
Sargent	257

WALKLEY

Geo	268
George	268
Henry	265
Maggie	209
Mary A	268
Sallie	209

WALL

John M	393
Lula B	393

WALLACE

Cid	83
Clora	83
Fannie F	263
Jennie	83
John T	83
Lilly	83
Lindsey	83
Nannie	83
W B	263
W^m B	263

WALLASKEY

Wallie	390
Willie	390

WALLEY

Jennie	396
Nancy	396
Still	396

WALLS

Beaver	258
Jack	258
Julia	119
Lizzie	258

WALLY, Nancy 396
WALSH & SHUTT 30,52,53,71, 77,102,211,275,367
WALSH AND SHUTT 16,17
WALSH AND SHUTT 28,30,60,69, 125,130,133,150,175,176,185,212,218, 231

WANOR

Jesse	265
Opal	265
Rosa L	265
Willie	265

WARD

A G	259
A M	265
Aenus	268
Aletha	393
Alex G	259
Alma	391
Alta	390
Augustus	269
Bazzie W	265
Bertha	269
Bessie	265
Beula	389
Caldeen	268
Carl E	268
Carrie M	393
Catherine	268
Chas R	260
Clem	264

Cornelia	390	Lelia M	393
Cornelious	260	Lena E	264
Cornelius	260	Lena N	393
Dalena	389	Lillie	389
Dora	390	Lizzie	259
Eliza	393	Loella	390
Ella	269	Lola	390
Ellis B	260	Louisa	389,390
Ellola	257	Lucy F	259
Elva	390	Mack	265
Ethlynn	393	Manerva	264
Fannie	269	Martha J	388
Florence	263	Mary A	394
G M	388	Mattie L	391
G W	374	May	391
Genovia A	393	Mimie	389
Geo	268,269	Minnie	264,389
Geo D	393	Minnie O	393
Geo M	388	Minnie S	263
Geo V	394	Moses	269
Geo W	259	Nancy	388
Henry	269	Nathaniel	268
Henry H	267	Pearl	269
Hugh	389	Robert E	257
Ida L	3	Rosa	389
Isabell	393	Roxie M	259
J C	268	Sam	389
J F	257	Saml	304,389
J M	388	Sarah E	394
J O	393	Stella	265,391
James	269	T J	393,396
James O	268	Thomas	268
Jas H	394	Thomas C	265
Jas L	394	Thos	269
Jas O	393	Thos J, Jr	396
Jasper	267	Vann	389
Jesse	259	W W	264,390
Joe	389	Walter	264
Joe L	391	Will W	390
Joel	261,263,264	William	264
John	259,269,390	William R	260
John D	393	William W	264
John E	393	Willie	268
John F	257	Winnie	390
John M	388	W^m M	259
Katie	260	W^m W	267
Laura	390	Zona	389

Index

WARNER
- Ivey L 265
- Nannie 265

WARREN
- Annie V 260
- Arthur 262
- G H 262
- Ida J 260
- J F 260,269
- Jas F 269
- Jesse M 260
- Mary 262
- Nelson G 260

WARSPEAKER, Lavena 81
WARTUCK, Nancy 86

WARWICK
- Albert S 81
- Alice C 81
- Francis M 82
- George F 81
- J M 82
- Jack 84
- Jacob M 81
- Jacob N 84
- Lena 84
- Thomas A 84
- William L 81

WASHAM
- M E 260,266
- Martha E 266

WASHBORN 356
- C L 347
- Ed 361

WASHBOURNE
- Bert 385
- C L 306,357,358,385
- C R 384
- Carrie L 385
- Claude 384
- Claude L 384
- Claude L, Jr 385
- Ed 308
- Ed N 385
- Joh L 384
- Lula 385
- Lula R 385
- Myra M 385

- Noble 385
- Percy H 385
- Percy H, Jr 385
- Rollin R 384
- Rosco C 385
- Walter 385
- Wood W 385

WASHBRN, Ed 320

WASHBURN
- C L 279
- E N 385

WASSAM, J C 257

WASSOM
- Catharine 266
- Myrtle 267
- Nettie 267

WASSON
- Blain 257
- Catharine 267
- Florence 257
- Maggie 257

WATERMELON
- Akie 390
- Chas 390
- Jennie 390
- Lucy 390,393
- Nancy 393
- Oon-junst 390
- Suake 393
- Thompson 390

WATKINS
- C A 262
- Charlott 262
- Della 55
- Fannie 262
- Joel M 88
- John 88
- Kate 55
- Lucy 88
- Minnie 262
- Nancy 262
- Susie 262
- Thos 262
- William 262

WATSON
- Adda C 87
- Adda, Jr 87

Annie	83
Chas	386
Drucilla	87
Ellen	83
George	83
John	83
John C	386
Lucy	87
Luda	83
Mary A	386
Nathaniel	87
Nellie	83
Robert	83
W^m	386

WATTS
Eddie	95
Henryetta	81
Jacob	88
John	81,88
Lavenia	81
Lucy	95
Mary	88
Nannie	88
Thomas	81
William	81

WATUCK
Alcy	84
Alice	85
Alsie	86
Alsy	85
Cornelius	85,86
Dora	85
Fannie	84,85,86
Ice	84,85,86
John	84,85
John W	86
Lila	85
Liley	84
Lilly	86
Lily	85
Luna	85
Lunie	84,85
Nancy	86
Pollie	86
Polly	84,85

WAUSEATT, Chas..........268
WAUSETT
Chas	268
Eliza	268

WAYBORNE, Levi..........259
WAYBOURNE
Ada	257
Addie	257
Alice	260
Ben	261
Bula	260
C P	257
Earl E	260
Emma	257
John T	260
Levi	259
Martha C	260
Minnie	260
Oma	257
Oscar	261
Otton	261
Pearl	261
Robert	261
Roy	257
William	261
W^m	260

WEAVER
Alice	80
Fannie	80
Felix	80
Florance D	80
Florence D	80
Hermon	80
Laura B	80
Maud	80
Nancy	80

WEBBER
Calla	269
Richard	269

WEBSTER, Riley..........367
WEIR
Chas S	392
Early	384
May E	392
N B	339,392
Nathan B	392
Renie J	392
Ruth A	392
Sam	384

Index

WELCH
  Ailsie 387
  Birt......................................259
  Celia 389
  Cobb 387
  Cora 387
  Dave 388,389,394
  Dave, Jr............................389
  Ed 389
  Ester....................................388
  Eve......................................385
  J C................................277,355,387
  James 388
  John 385
  Joseph E.............................393
  Mary 385
  Mollie 387
  Nancy 385,388
  Nannie B............................393
  Ned 394
  Ne-nu-we 385
  Oslie 387
  Veda E................................393

WELLER
  Malinda A...........................266
  Sarah L 266

WELLS
  Archie 258
  Besey 82
  Bessie 258
  Burl......................................258
  Charles H.............................88
  Daisy...................................258
  Effie 258
  Elizabeth M 82
  Emma E..............................258
  Frank...................................258
  James M................................88
  Jessie...................................258
  Joseph J 82
  L C..82
  Lutilia 82
  Mary 82
  N C......................................258
  S A.......................................266

WERTHER
  Alley 265

  Charles................................265
  Edward 265
  G W 265
  Lucy....................................265
  Minnie 265
  Oliver..................................265

WEST
  Calvin 82
  Ellis 80
  Frank....................................80
  J C..44
  James 253
  James K P 82
  Jane......................................82
  Jeff.......................................82
  John 42,79,80,82,87
  John H, Jr.............................80
  Laura....................................79
  Louisa.................................253
  Luellen 79
  M E.......................................82
  Margaret 79
  Mary 80
  Nannie 80
  Rich 80
  Richard 42
  Richrd..................................80
  Robert E...............................81
  Robt E..................................81
  Sally...................................385
  T C.......................................80
  Thomas C 80
  William................................82
  William C 81

WESTONER
  Eliza....................................266
  Josephine 266
  Lillie E................................266
  Thomas H 266
  Warren 266
  W^m W 266

WETLOCK, J T......................265
WETTACK, J T......................218

WETZEL
  Chas 390
  Claude.................................390
  D K 386

Earl	390
Ida May	390
Lulu	386
Martha	386
Minnie	386
Oliver	390
WEVER, Jennie	262
WHIPPLE, Andrew	157
WHIRLWIND, Lewis	264

WHISENHUNT
- Jas 82
- Jeff 82
- John E 37
- Noah 81
- William 81

WHITAKER
- Adeline 260
- Austin 260,261
- Bennie V 259
- Caroline 260
- Charles 261
- David 260
- Emma 261
- James E 261
- James M 258
- James S 259
- Josh W 259
- Maggie 261
- Martha 260
- Nola E 259
- Ora 261
- Sarah A 260
- Stephen D 260
- Victor 260
- W T 95,108,113,116,117,142, 161,177,181,188,206,211,219,220,231, 235,236,258,260,261
- William J 261
- W^m T 261

WHITE
- Beunavista 265
- Eva 366,396
- Evie 396
- Hellen 265
- Henry 396
- Hill 387
- Hooley C 392
- J C 265
- Jas E 325,392
- Joe S 392
- Josiah 395
- Mary 396
- Nancy 396
- Rosie 160
- Samantha 396
- W^m H 392

WHITEMARE, Chas 266

WHITEWATER
- Arch 83
- David 83
- Lee 163
- Lizzie 83
- Sallie 83
- Thomas 83
- Tobin 83

WHITFIELD
- Mary 82
- William 82

WHITINGTON
- George 9
- Lilla 9

WHITNEY
- Fred C 395
- Louella 395
- Louella E 395
- Mack W 395
- Mary E 395

WHITZENHUNT
- Andrew B 81
- Charles E 81
- Fred 81
- Henryetta 81
- Jane H 81
- Jeff W 82
- Joanna 81
- John E 81
- Lily O 82
- Mary A 81
- Mattie 82
- Nancy 81
- Noah 81
- Robert L 81
- Ruth 82
- Wyly 81

Index

Young E............81
WICKED
   Edith............387
   Lottie............387
   Lurhenia............387
   Richard............387
   Sarah............387
   Webb............387
WICKET
   Abert............83
   Alice............82
   Alpha............79
   Bettie M............83
   Jessie............31,83
   John............82,83
   John, Jr............83
   Lem............79
   Mammie............83
   Nannie............83
   Newt............88
   Ophelia............88
   Ruth............79
   Sarah............387
   Vaden............82
WICKETT, Ruth............79
WILDER
   Charlott............257
   Charlotte............189,257
   Clem............257
   Lydia............257
WILEY
   Aaron............263
   Wooster............263
WILKERSON
   Ace............86
   Annie............87
   Arley............80
   Carnelius............87
   Cordelia............86
   Daniel............86
   Eli............80
   Eliza............80
   Ellen............80,86
   Estellar............86
   Frost............86
   Jack............263
   James............83

   Jane............268
   John............86,262
   John H............87
   Katie............86
   Lewis............262
   Lizzie............80,262,263
   Lona............86
   Lucy............262
   Luster............87
   Margaret............86
   Margaret, Jr............87
   Mary............86
   Mattie............80
   Nancy............80
   Osa............86
   Racheal............262
   Robert............86
   Ruth............80
   Sarah............80
   Spencer............86
   Susan............80
   Walter............86
   Whilby............86
WILKINSON, Louia J............241
WILLIAM, Toney............384
WILLIAMS
   Alice............263,267
   Allie............392
   Andrew............263
   Belle............263
   Carlotta............392
   Charles............258
   Charlott............262
   Charlotte............262,384
   Claud............267
   Columbus............392
   Dewit............269
   Ed............269
   Elgin M............391
   Emma............263
   Frank............267
   Fred............267
   G W............77,87
   Geo............261,263,392
   Geo A............267
   Harrison............263
   Hattie M............258

Haven	384
J L	267
Jackson	265
James, Jr	263
Jennie	197,267
Jesse	262
Joseph L	267
L M	263
Laura	392
Lizzie	258
Lucy	269
Maggolina	263
Malinda	392
Mary A	391
Mattie	263,269,392
Mayes	392
Minnie	269
Minnie B	263
Nancy D	87
Nellie	262
Nervis	264
Olkin	384
Pearl	258
Price	384
Riley	392
Rowe	384
Roy H	263
Sarah	262,384
Susie	269
Toney	384
Vennie M	391
W^m	392

WILLIAMSON
M D	268
Maggie L	268

WILLIS
Armer	6
Bessie E	6
Claud M	6
Ollie S	391
P E	84
Prestly E	84
W L	36
Walter	6

WILLISON
M J	266
Mary J	266

WILLS
Kate	266
Ross	266

WILSON 349
A R & Bro	276,277,297,305, 361,364
Ada L	81
Annie	20,390
Arthur U	391
Beckie	390
Bertha	386
Bird	386
Charley	390
Charlotte	391
D A	393
Elgin D	393
Eli	391
Eliza	395
Ella	86
Ellen	261
Finny	86
George	71
Hope	261
Ida	261
James R	258
Jennie	384
Jess	390,391
Joe	391
Jonathan	393
Katy	384
Martha E	393
Mary	386,391
Mary Bell	391
Melvina	81
Nannie	384
Oliver E	391
Oo-ki-lie	384
Polly	391
R V	258
Rachel	390,391
Rebeca V	258
Ridge	384
Round	390
Sarah	391
Taakee	391
Unack	391
William	86

Index

Wᵐ 386
Wᵐ H 258
Young P 384
WILSON & BRO 361
WINBERGER, Rachel 395
WINFIELD
   Flora 343
   Henry 394
   Manuel 343
WING
   Dora 209
   Otis 209
   Vick 209
   Victoria 209
WINGFIELD
   Lucinda 395
   Robt 395
WINPIGLE, Bessie 86
WINTON
   Clarence 257
   Dan 257
   Edith 256
   K L 256
   Loyd 257
   May 256
   Minerva 256
   Moses 256
   Ola P 257
WITT
   Abe 386
   Allie 386
   Bell 386
   David 385,386
   Dee 386
   Della J 385
   Elmer L 385
   Felix 386
   Isabell 386
   John W 386
   Nannie 386
   Orlando 386
   Tip 386
   William F 385
WOFFARD
   Arch 385
   Bennie 385
   Charlie 385

John 385
Ned 385
Onia 385
Ridge 385
Will 385
WOFFORD
   Alta 395
   Annie 395
   Eli 265
   Ella 259
   Jack 395
   James 262,263
   Laura 222
   Lizzie 395
   Pearl 395
   Will 385
WOLF
   Cogah 265
   Ella 388
   Ellen C 264
   Foster 264
   John 267
   Katur 109
   Lettie J 264
   Lewis 264,265
   Lewis M 264
   Richard M 265
   Ruth E 264
   Susanah 391
WOLF RUNING 263
   James Trolling 263
WOLFE
   Ada 266
   Akie 391
   Ben 391
   Daniel 386
   Ella 388
   Ethel 388
   Jennie May 388
   John 267
   Kate E 252
   Katie 266
   Mouse 391
   Nancy 364
   Narcessa 265
   Nellie 364
   Paul 266

Index

Susanna 391
Tincup 391
Will 391

WOLK
  Alcy 393
  Chas 393
  Eliza 393
  Jesse 393
  John 393
  Lucy 393
  Nellie 393
  Polly 393
  W^m 393

WOOD
  Charley 387
  Foister 259
  Geo G 259
  M R 259
  Pecky 311
  William 259
  Wyly 259

WOODALL
  Amanda 267
  Anna 267
  Anna N 394
  Annie 388
  Benj J 394
  Bettie 395
  Eliza 267
  Emma 82
  Emma V 82
  Frank F 394
  Ira 395
  Isaac 395
  James T 395
  Jas 371,394,395
  Jas M 395
  Jas T, Sr 395
  Jeff A 394
  John 388
  Leander 395
  Lewis 395
  Lizzie L 395
  Louisa 388
  Lucian 267
  Margarett A 394
  Margarette E 394

Mary 394
Mavel 394
Nana 394
Nancy 388
Nannie 82
Nolen 394
Ocie 395
Peter 394
S G 394
Stand G 394
Stand W 394
Susan 388
Susan E 394
Susie 82
Thomas F 82
W C 394
Walter 395
Wash 388
W^m 395
W^m B 267
W^m C 394

WOODARD
  Albert 264
  Alice 264
  Allen 264
  Ann E 392
  Annie 87
  Arlie 87
  Bert 264
  Biddie 264
  George 87
  Hannah 264
  John 87,263
  John L 264
  Lizzie 87
  Margaret 264
  Martha 87
  Mary 87
  Nannie 87
  Nellie 264
  Oliver 264
  Plumy 264
  Sarah 87
  Susan 87
  William 82
  W^m 264
  Zak 264

Index

WOODS
- Bennie V 388
- Chas W 387
- Columbus 388
- Frank 388
- G G 259
- Georgia A 269
- Harriett E 387
- Henry 83,388
- Houston 388
- James M 388
- Jas M 387
- John 87
- Laura 87
- Lavinnie 388
- Lewis 387
- Lewis E 387
- Lizzie 269
- Lucy B 387
- Mamie E 387
- Mandy 388
- Marion 388
- Martin C 387
- Mary A 387
- Mattie 87
- Maudie M 387
- Roxie M 266
- Samantha 388
- Tympy 388
- Viella 388
- Will H 387
- Will P 387
- William 266
- Willie O 387
- W^m H 388

WOODSON, M D 187

WOODY, Ida 263

WRIGHT
- Ailsie 387
- Benge 267
- Bessy 396
- Bryant J 259
- Dora 267
- E B 259
- E V 259
- Elizabeth 259
- Ellis B 259
- Elmira 387
- Ethel 396
- Jackson 387
- Jas 387
- Josie 387
- Lizzie 396
- Lucy 384
- Lunnie 384
- Lydia I 259
- Mabelle 267
- Maggie 267
- Mayes C 259
- Nelson 384
- Otto F 259
- Sarah 387
- Thomas 387
- William E 259
- Willie E 267
- W^m W 258

WRITER
- Abraham 262
- Annie 134
- Jennie 4,134
- Mary 262
- Thomas 262

WYCHE
- Robert D 82
- Robt D 82

WYLEY, Josephine 87

WYLY
- Akie 389
- Annie 386,389
- Eliza 386
- Geo 386
- Jane Ann 389
- Jas R 389
- Joe 389
- John 386,389
- Josephine 87
- Lee 389
- Linnie 390
- Littie 389
- Nannie 386
- P 298,303,321,347,349
- Percy .... 272,278,279,285,286,287, 297,298,303,308,311,314,317,320,321 ,322,328,331,335,347,348,363,371,

Index

376,377,378,379,384,389,390,391
- R F 371
- Rachel 391
- Saggie 389
- Sally 386
- Sam 386
- Thurman 389

WYNCHE, John W 88

YARBROUGH
- Ceals L 396
- Geo S 396
- Minerva 396

YEAGER
- Claude 396
- Laura 396
- Ninie 396

YEARGAIN
- Joe 396
- Kate 396
- Mary J 396
- May 396
- Robt P 396
- Scott A 396
- Turner A 396

YEARGIN
- Joe 396
- Joe D 328
- Mary J 396
- May J 396

YOKUM
- Johnie V 270
- May 270

YONG
- Jas 396
- John W 397
- Nannie 396
- Robert A 396

YOUNG
- Carrie E 270
- Cornelia B 270
- J W 397
- Jas 396
- M L 270
- Mary L 270
- Nannie 269
- Ray V 269

YOUNGBEAVER, Will 397

YOUNT
- Mary 88
- Sarah 88

ZIEGLER, Mary 106

ZUFALL
- Benjamin 88
- George, Jr 88
- Grace 88
- Herbert 88
- Irenna 88
- John 88
- Lewis 88
- Maggie 88
- Maggie, Jr 88
- Maggie, Sr 88
- Mattie 88
- Nannie 88
- Otto 88
- Pearl 88
- Roy 88

www.ingramcontent.com/pod-product-compliance
Lightning Source LLC
Chambersburg PA
CBHW020237030426
42336CB00010B/517